Features That Reinforce Key Concepts and Engage Students

GLOBAL RETAILING BOXES

Highlight both U.S.- and foreign-based companies that have adjusted or tailored their retailing practices to the culture and environment in which they do business.

Chapter

1 International Expansion at Disney
2 Disney Faces Illness Aboard Cruise Ships
3 Bottle Bills and the Beverage Industry
4 South Africa Uses the Web to Increase Franchise Activity
5 Hispanic Consumers and the Do-It-Yourself Paint Segment
6 Focus on Technology: Island Pacific, Inc.
7 La Ciudad de Los Niños (Kids City International)
8 International Accounting Standards
9 Armani Sets Up Shop in Moscow
10 The Retail Council of Canada's National Retail Certification Program
11 Wal-Mart and Mexican Retailers
13 IKEA Under Fire for Poor Service
14 The Foreign Corrupt Practices Act

INTERNET IN ACTION BOXES

Focus on how retailers and e-tailers are using the Internet and other forms of technology to increase sales and productivity and to encourage customer satisfaction. These boxes illustrate how the advent of the Internet and the rise of technology have changed the face of retailing, both in advantageous and, in some cases, disadvantageous ways.

Chapter

1 eBay: Successful Niche E-tailing
2 A Brief History of E-commerce and E-tailing
3 E-commerce: Sounds Good, But How Do We Measure Performance?
4 New E-grocer Succeeds Where Others Have Failed
5 VALS Online Survey
6 Focus on Technology: Island Pacific, Inc.
7 A Company Specializing in GIS
8 More Companies Placing Financial Information on Websites
9 Armani Sets Up Shop in Moscow
10 Surfers Beware: Employers May Be Monitoring Your Computer Use
11 BLS Releases Key Data Too Early
12 Malls Begin Using the Internet for Communications to Customers
13 The Golden Rules of Online Customer Service
14 Internet Brand and Trademark Abuse on the Web
15 Retail Sector Outperforms Others in Respect Survey of Online Companies

BLUNDERS OR BEST PRACTICES BOXES

Present real-life retailing scenarios, along with the details and circumstances of a decision that was made. The student can then assess whether he or she thinks that the retailer performed a "best practice" or a "blunder."

Chapter

- **1** Language Blunder Changes Meaning of Message
- **2** What's in a Name? The Toy Wars
- **3** Failure to Scan Environment Results in Logistics Problems
- **4** Initial Marketing of Products
- **5** McDonald's Matches Strategy to Consumer Wants Abroad
- **6** Database Marketing Tips from an Expert
- **7** The Biggest Mall in the World
- **8** Playing with the Books: An Unwise Strategy
- **9** Dell and the Cash Conversion Cycle
- **10** Supervisor Portals Use Technology to Help Manage HR Functions
- **11** Kohl's Pricing Policies Under Fire
- **12** McDonald's IMC Blunders
- **13** Lands' End: Best Practices in Customer Service
- **14** Giant Food Inc.: An Example of Professional Ethics
- **15** Online Grocers Benefit from Niche Retailing

SHERWIN-WILLIAMS COMPANY CONTINUING CASES

Appear at the conclusion of every chapter. These cases take students behind the scenes of a large national paint manufacturer, with numerous company-operated retail locations as well as many independent retailers, to gain a greater understanding of the day-to-day challenges this retailer faces.

ADDITIONAL END-OF-CHAPTER CASES

Challenge students to apply chapter concepts to a specific issue while presenting a big-picture view, allowing students to see a tie-in to all subject areas. Cases range in length and focus on small, medium, and large retailers.

Chapter

- **1** The Retail Environment: Niche Retailing
- **2** Best Buy Ensures Customer Value Through Technology
- **3** Guilford Home Furnishings Faces Competition
- **4** Target Enters the Super Center Competition
- **5** eCraft Furniture and the Internet Marketing Dilemma
- **6** Circuit City, Multichannel Retailing, and Online RIS
- **7** Retailer on the Go: Homier Mobile Merchants
- **8** Cal Corporation's Ratio Analysis
- **9** Veterinarians and Merchandising Decisions
- **10** The Container Store: Consistently One of the Best Places to Work
- **11** Online Auctions Pose Competitive Threat to Retailers
- **12** Auntie Anne's Pretzels: From Small-Town Girl to Global Pretzel Entrepreneur
- **13** Customer Service at AutoZone Stores
- **14** MCI and the Legal Environment
- **15** Office Depot Seeks to Diversify Its Pool of Workers

Integrated Retail Management

(Indian Adaptation)

Integrated Retail Management

(Indian Adaptation)

James R. Ogden, Ph.D.
Kutztown University of Pennsylvania

Denise T. Ogden, Ph.D.
Penn State Berks—Lehigh Valley

In this adaptation, materials have been changed, altered and/or deleted to suit the Indian environment.

Published by:

HOUGHTON
MIFFLIN

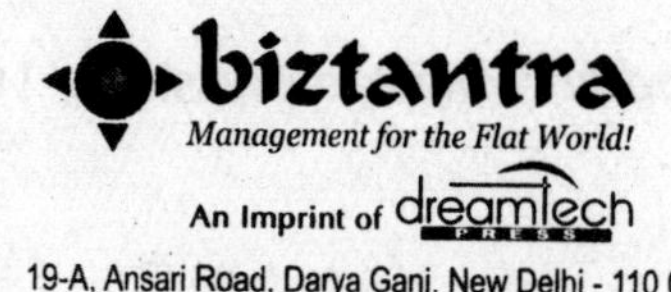

19-A, Ansari Road, Darya Ganj, New Delhi - 110 002
Website: www.biztantra.in

This edition has been published by arrangement with the **Houghton Mifflin Co., USA** and published in India by **Biztantra, An Imprint of Dreamtech Press, 19-A, Ansari Road, Daryaganj, New Delhi-110002.**

Reprint Edition: 2008

Printed at : Himal Impressions, 168, Raja Garden, New Delhi.

Brief Contents

Contents

Chapter 13 CUSTOMER SERVICE IN RETAILING 380

PART 5 INDIAN SUPPLEMENT

Preface

In this special Indian adaptation of *Retailing: Integrated Retail Management* the original edition has been changed with additional text, alterations to chapter sequence and deletions of some content in order to make it more suitable to the target audience in the Indian subcontinent. Additionally, a number of specific Indian case studies have also been incorporated into the text in order to make it more relevant to Indian students. As such the book will not be of use to students outside of the Indian subcontinent

There has been an explosion in the organized retailing formats in India. These include departmental stores, shopping malls, hypermarkets and franchise retail chains. Organized retailing exposing shoppers to a comfortable ambience and good service is beginning to evolve and gather momentum. Well-lit and elegant stores have sprung up in different parts of India—not just metros but other cities and suburbs also. To take into account rapid changes brewing up in Indian subcontinent, an Indian supplement is being included in this special Indian Adaptation prepared by Prof. Mukesh Pandey who teaches marketing at the FORE School of Management in New Delhi and has also had firsthand experience of working in industry.

There is a Chapter on Retailing in India providing the overview of the organized retailing activity in India taken as a whole. while coffee retailing is another Chapter in the supplement spotlighting new trends in coffee drinking at coffee bars such as Barista, Café Coffee Day and Qwiky's. The case study on food retailing focuses on the changes coming to pass in retailing of processed foods. Case studies on large format rural retail stores and supply chain dynamics for McDonald's and Domino's further bring up other issues in fast organizing retailing industry in India. In order to provide a comprehensive coverage of organized retailing in key segments, major retailers in food and grocery, apparels, books & music, watches, jewellery and greeting cards have been covered as 8 short cases.

WHY STUDY RETAILING

All of us have experienced retailing at close quarters. As consumers, we interact with retailers of different hues and colors every day of the week We visit retail outlets, shop online with our favorite e-tailers, and see ads for retailers on television and in newspapers. The fact is, retailing is ingrained into everyone's activities. Given the importance of retailing to world economies, it is essential that we understand the processes involved in retailing and their implications for those students who study about this important business activity.

Although it appears that retailing is a relatively simple activity, the fact of the matter is, it isn't. The study of retailing encompasses all areas of business study. To be a successful retail manager, one must understand accounting, finance, management, information technology, marketing, and other business activities involved in the effective planning and execution of retail plans. The more you understand these processes, the better retail professional you will be.

Because retailing encompasses all areas of business, it is sometimes difficult to see the "big picture" as it relates to retailing. Most retail texts present students with a series of chapters that provide useful information but fail to explain how the various activities involved in retailing affect each other. The approach of Retailing: Integrated Retail Management is to offer the student an overview of the retail process through the use of an integrated retail management (IRM) plan. The steps involved in retailing as presented in the text are tied together through the IRM plan. The flow chart depicting the IRM plan appears on every chapter opener, so that students can retain the big picture of the flow of operations at a typical retail establishment. Additionally, the concept of e-tailing is included throughout the text, and not treated as a stand-alone chapter. This helps emphasize that e-tailing is a form of retailing that uses many of the same models as other forms.

Of the many retailing texts to choose from, we hope that you will prefer Retailing: Integrated Retail Management, with its integrated approach, clear organization, and comprehensive, up-to-date coverage. The Instructor's Resource Manual serves to highlight concepts being taught in the text. We are confident that after browsing through this text, you will find that the organization and topic coverage is current, easy-to-follow, and accessible to students.

STRUCTURE AND ORGANIZATION OF CONTENT

As mentioned earlier, this retailing text relies on an integrative approach to help the reader see the big picture regarding the retailing process. Through the integrated retail management (IRM) flow chart provided at the onset of each chapter, the reader will be able to see where each of the various concepts fit in to the overall retail management process. In other words, instead of teaching students chapter material, this text reinforces the teaching of "subject" areas. This approach allows students to utilize critical thinking instead of chapter memorization. As one of the book's reviewers commented, "The organization of the textbook is logical and student-friendly in approach, which enhances the user's learning and the emphasis on the role and importance of strategy in retailing."

Part 1 of the text, which includes Chapters 1 and 2, offers the reader an overall, macro view of the world of retailing. Each of the environments that have an impact on retail decision making is presented. Retail decision makers rely on their understanding of the macro environment to make the best possible decisions with regard to their operations.

Chapter 1, "The World of Retailing," presents a definition of retailing and takes an in-depth look at the macro environment surrounding the retail decision maker. The IRM flow chart is presented, and a brief overview of each step in the process is given, providing an outline of the text's framework. Careers in retailing are discussed, to give the student a quick picture of what jobs typically exist within a retailing operation.

Chapter 2, "Customer Value, Services, and Retailing Technologies," continues to explore the external retail environment by providing an in-depth look at three environments that are important to the retail decision maker. Chapter 2 covers important concepts such as quality, service, price, and equity development for retailers. The area of services retailing is presented and systems used for creating retail relationships are explored. The chapter ends with full coverage of technology in retailing and e-tailing; e-tailing and e-commerce; and finally laws, ethics, and corporate social responsibility.

Part 2, consisting of Chapters 3 through 5, deals with the creation of effective retail strategies. The coverage of each chapter relates back to the importance of an effective retail strategy and how this strategy provides a guide for the development of retail tactics. Chapter 3, " An Overview of the Retail Planning and Management Process," gives an overview of the retail planning and management process. Each of the steps in the management process is intro- duced in this chapter and expanded upon later within the text. Chapter 4, "The Retail Environment: A Situational and Competitive

Analysis," explains the process of creating a situational and competitive analysis and explains retail institutions. Chapter 5, "Evaluation and Identification of Retail Customer," concludes the part with extensive coverage on evaluating and identifying retail customers. This coverage includes the application of demographic, psychographic, geographic, geodemographic, and behavioristic data in retail problem solving.

Part 3 of the text, encompassing Chapters 6 through 10, is concerned with internal planning and management. It includes information about research, retail information systems, market and location selection, operations manage- ment, merchandise buying and selling, and human resource management. Chapter 6, "Retail Information Systems and Research," provides an in-depth look at changes in retail information systems - systems such as radio frequency identification (RFID), POS terminals, and self-checkout. In addition, a method of gathering marketing and market research is provided and reinforced at the end of the chapter. This chapter provides the reader with tools and skills that are easily transferable to other classes. A particular area of emphasis is on resources useful in undertaking the research process. One of the text's reviewers commented: "Three cheers for the excellent coverage of secondary data and Internet research." Chapter 7, "Selecting the Appropriate Market and Location," provides coverage of the processes used in selecting a market and a physical- or cyber-location for a retailer. Chapter 8, "Financial Aspects of Operations Management," presents the different methods of managing retail operations, with a focus on financial analysis. Merchandise buying and handling is covered in Chapter 9, "Merchandise Buying and Handling," and finally, in Chapter 10, "Human Resource Management," discussion centers on the human resource management function.

Part 4 of the text, covering Chapters 11 through I5, deals with the issues of retail tactical executions and ends with coverage of laws, ethics, diversity, and trends in retailing. Chapter 11, "Pricing in Retailing," is an introduction to , retail tactics, focusing on pricing in retailing-namely pricing objectives and policies. The student is provided information about both setting a price and adjusting the price once it is set. Chapter 12, "Developing an Effective Integrated Marketing Communications Mix," presents an integrated marketing communications process, including the use of various media to assist the retailer in communicating with stakeholders. This chapter also integrates the concepts of store layout and design with customer communications. Because it has been proven that it is cheaper to keep a current customer than to get a new one, Chapter 13, "Customer Service in Retailing," offers suggestions on creating superior customer service. Chapter 14, "Laws and Ethics," provides information on laws and ethics specifically related to retail management. Chapter 15, "Services Retailing, Diversity, and Trends," ends the text with a discussion of diversity and trends in the retail environment. Coverage of diversity includes such important areas as equal opportunity and recruitment, whereas the section on trends focuses on the areas of economy, environment, and society.

As an integrating element for the text, a continuing case study is provided at the end of each chapter. The integration is further developed with an in-depth case study, found in Appendix B, of an entrepreneurial organization involved in trying to expand its market through the use of retail dealers.

USEFUL FEATURES

Throughout our careers teaching at the collegiate level, we have always sought to improve upon our instruction. We encourage students to tell us how and why they learn and which activities they enjoy and find beneficial-and they do give us their opinions! They also indicate which textbooks they like and why they like them. Based on our experience and student feedback, we have created a text incorporating the following very useful features:

INTEGRATED APPROACH

Students like to see the big picture of the subject they're studying. They also like to know how each element of the subject area relates to their career choices. We have developed a one-page integrated retail management (IRM) flow chart that allows the student to see where each element in the study of retailing fits into the whole. The flow chart appears at the beginning of every chapter for easy reference.

OPENING VIGNETTE

Every chapter begins with an attention-grabbing example of retailing in action. The vignettes lead the reader into the core subject areas in each chapter. The vignettes are classic retail stores or current, cutting-edge examples that help to excite the student.

BOXED INSERTS

Three types of boxed inserts-Internet in Action, Global Retailing, and Blunders or Best Practices-appear interspersed in each chapter. The boxes bring cutting-edge ideas and best practice topics to the forefront of the chapters.

The information provided in each of the inserts was developed through extensive research of current topics of interest for retail practitioners. Many of our associates and colleagues suggested relevant subjects that they would like to see in a text. We took their suggestions and integrated them with our data to provide boxes on e-tailing, global retailing, and blunders or best practices in some of the largest and smallest retailers. Topics were carefully chosen to support chapter concepts.

BOLDFACED KEY TERMS

Key terms are boldfaced in the running text and defined in the margin, to provide the student a better understanding of the material he or she is reading. The highlighted terms and their definitions are intended to facilitate the flow of information. We don't want students to stop reading because they don't understand a word. Instead of interrupting the reading and studying process to look up a word, students have the definition right at hand.

END-OF-CHAPTER SUMMARIES

A summary is provided at the end of each chapter. The summary is a quick reference of all the key topics covered in the chapter. It is not a substitute for reading the chapter material.

QUESTIONS FOR DISCUSSION

A Questions for Discussion section appears at the end of each chapter. The questions can be used as homework assignments or to generate in-class discussion. Students can also use these questions to help them study for exams. Pedagogically, the questions reinforce what students have read and force them to use critical reasoning skills to answer them.

E- TAILING EXERCISES

E-tailing exercises can be found at the end of each chapter. These exercises require students to go online, perform a given task, and then answer a series of questions. The purpose of these exercises is to show students the intercon- nectivity of online retailers and traditional retailers. Instructors can utilize each of the exercises or pick and choose those that are most appropriate to the material being presented in class.

CASES

Each chapter ends with two cases that allow students to process the material that was presented to them in the text and apply their new retail knowledge. The first case in each chapter focuses on the Sherwin-Williams Company (SW). SW was chosen because of its large number of retail units. In addition, SW distributes through retailers other than its own and offers products on a business-to-business level. The second case at the end of each chapter is a standalone case, involving large, medium, and small retailers or e-tailers. The cases focus on chapter coverage, providing yet another tie-in to the reading material.

APPENDIXES

Appendix A, "Careers in Retailing: Nine Dimensions for Job Acquisition," contains in-depth information on what retailers look for in potential employees. Appendix B, " An In-Depth Case Study: Z-Tech, Inc. (dba Z-Coil)," is a comprehensive, standalone case. The student, to solve the case, must have a basic understanding of the concepts provided within the text. This appendix can be utilized either as chapters are covered or at the end of the course, thus giving the instructor another option for facilitating students' learning.

INSTRUCTOR'S RESOURCE MANUAL (Available on CD)

To create full integration and comprehensive coverage, the text authors have developed the Instructor's Resource Manual. Included in the Instructor's Resource Manual are many helpful tools to help the instructor create a complete, integrated course: chapter objectives, a lecture outline, suggested answers to the questions for discussion, as well as suggested case solutions. Additional classroom exercises and follow-up questions are also provided to stimulate in-class discussion and to help students apply what they've learned throughout the text.

ACKNOWLEDGMENTS

We are very excited to be part of an outstanding team at Houghton Mifflin. We are grateful to our former book rep, now senior marketing manager at Houghton Mifflin, Steve Mikels, for generating the project. In addition, we are grateful for the guidance and leadership of editor-in-chief George Hoffman.. Julia. Perez was an understanding taskmaster who kept us informed, on track, and excited about completing the project. Paula Knetz did a fantastic job of "cleaning up" the project and helped us complete the project on time and with focus. Linda Blundell pursued excellent photos and ads to fit the content. The energy and dedication of the whole Houghton Mifflin team was wonderful, and their friendship and understanding through trying times was noticed and appreciated.

We would be remiss if we did not mention our fantastic families, who have been supportive of our work throughout our lives. We would like to thank our children, David, Anne, and Kari Ogden, for their understanding throughout the development of the project. Our college-student children, David and Anne, helped us create the text with student users in mind and increased our empathy for students taking collegiate course work. Finally, our parents were, and continue to be, our great inspiration. Thanks to our moms, Ninfa Alarid and Marianne Ogden, and our dads, Diego Alarid and Dr. Russell L. Ogden (deceased), for their inspiration.

The quality of this book and its Instructor has been enhanced through the insights and helpful comments of all our reviewers. We are grateful for all the time and energy they put into the project to help make it great! Specifically, we would like to thank:

Chad W. Autry, Bradley University

Anne L. Balazs, Mississippi University for Women

Gayle Brown-Litwin, Hofstra University

James W. Camerius, Northern Michigan University

Judith Grenkowicz, Kirtland Community College

Kathleen Gruben, Georgia Southern University

Mary A. Higby, University of Detroit Mercy

Dexter Hinton, New York University-Stern

Patricia Holman, Montana State University-Billings

Terence L. Holmes, Murray State University

Rhea Ingram, Columbus State University

Ruth Krieger, Oklahoma State University

Cathy Martin, University of Akron

Carolyn Predmore, Manhattan College

James Rakowski, University of Memphis

Jill Slomski, Mercyhurst College

Robert. L. Stephens. Macon State College

Retailing

An Introduction to

Part 1

Retailing

Part 1 examines the external, or macro, environment that affects all retail decision making. Because decisions aren't made in a vacuum, retail decision makers must have a clear understanding of their environments. Chapter 1, "The World of Retailing," provides a definition of retailing and describes the world in which retailers operate. Chapter 2, "Customer Value, Services, and Retailing Technologies," introduces the reader to three external environments: customers, customer value, and technology.

The World of Retailing

Chapter
1

It was always my endeavor to do everything I could to establish a good reputation by giving good measure and quality, to avoid every trick that would save a penny at the expense of the other fellow.

Henry A. Sherwin

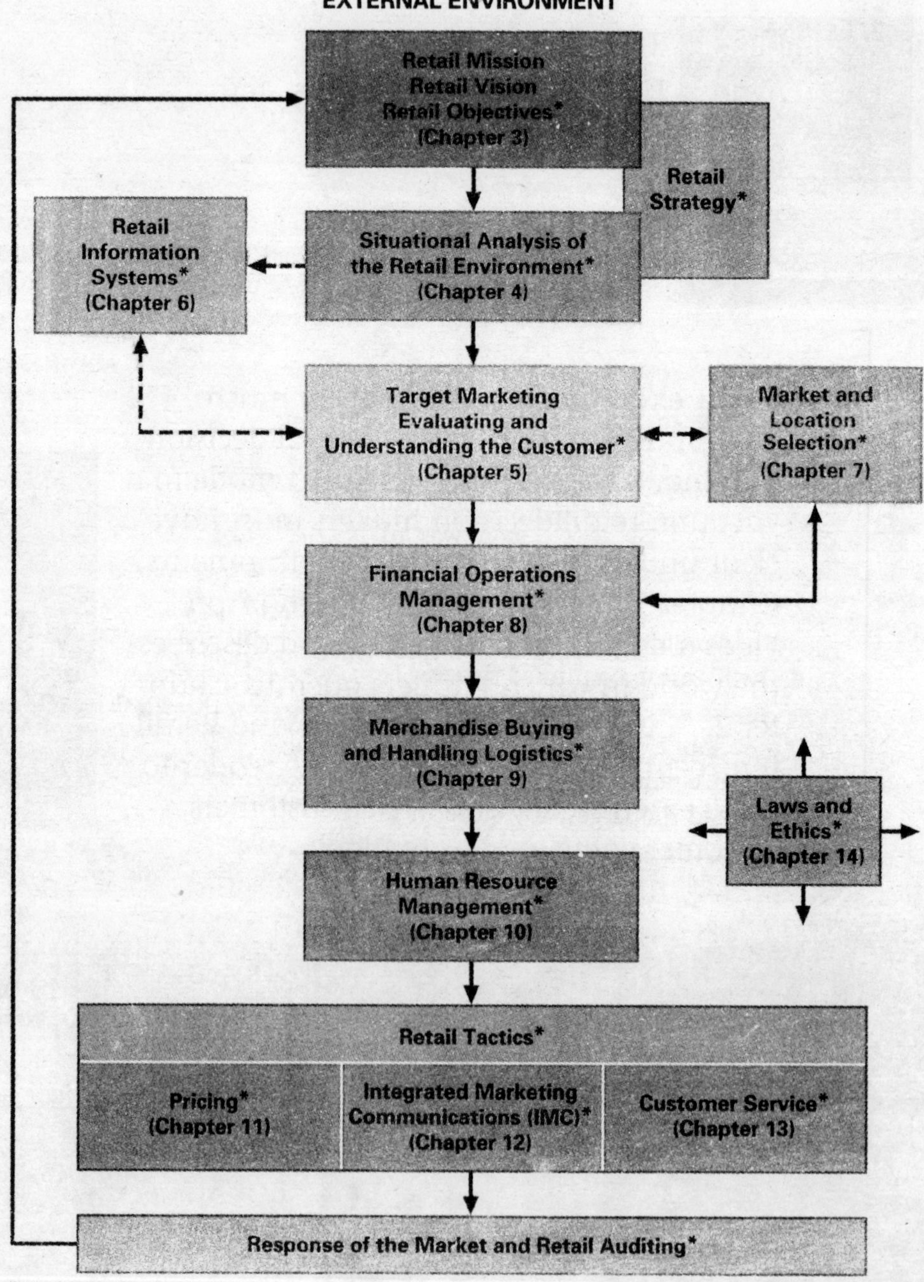

*Evaluation and control occurs at all these stages.

CHAPTER OBJECTIVES

After completing this chapter, you will be able to:

1. Describe activities involved in retail management and explain how retailing fits into the overall marketing program.
2. Explore the difference between e-tailing and retailing, and describe how e-tailing can be integrated into the overall retailing function.
3. Provide an overview of career opportunities available in the retailing field.
4. Identify the text organization and understand the importance of integrated retail management for retailing success.

Toys "R" Us: Adapting to Change

When Toys "R" Us started business in 1948, the company's mission was to be the "worldwide authority on kids, families and fun."[1] Toys "R" Us is living up to its mission and expanding its retail operations in ways that will ensure continued success. For example, Toys "R" Us partnered with Amazon.com to develop a better and more convenient logistical e-tailing system. In 2002, Toys "R" Us opened the largest toy store in the world in New York City's Times Square, complete with an indoor 60-foot ferris wheel.[2]

In addition to its Toys "R" Us USA division, the company has six other divisions: Toys "R" Us International, Kids "R" Us, Babies "R" Us, Imaginarium, Toysrus.com, and Babiesrus.com. Combined, the company boasts more than 1,400 stores worldwide. The Toys "R" Us businesses are a good illustration of the evolution of a small retailer into an $11 billion worldwide retailer and e-tailer.[3] Since the company's inception in 1948, Toys "R" Us has reacted successfully to the volatile retail environment and continues to evolve.

INTRODUCTION

Today is a great yet challenging time to be studying retail management. The retail environment is extremely dynamic and is demanding increasing skills and education. In the early 2000s, events such as the attack on New York's World Trade Center and the downturn of the U.S. economy after eight years of growth posed, and continue to pose, challenging times for retail professionals.

To succeed in retailing, current and future retailers must be able to adapt to a constantly changing environment. This book will give you a basic understanding of the functions of retailing, along with a framework you can use to help you become a more knowledgeable and effective member of a retail organization. Successful retailers are able to anticipate and adapt to change. They also have theoretical and pragmatic training that provides them with the tools that help make businesses and organizations successful.

macro retail environment The external environments that affect retailers.

To effectively adapt to environmental change, it is imperative that the retail manager have a good grasp of the **macro retail environment** prior to developing a retail plan. An understanding of retailing's external environments, aided by collection of appropriate data on those environments, provides useful information for the retailer and is the starting point for the development of effective integrated retail management (IRM) plans.

WHAT IS RETAILING?

integrated retail management (IRM) flow chart A chart that provides a framework to guide retail decision making.

retail The sale of goods and services in small quantities directly to consumers.

commodity Something useful that can be traded; can refer to physical objects or services.

retailer A company or an organization that purchases products from individuals or companies with the intent to resell those goods and services to the ultimate, or final, consumer.

ultimate consumers Families, individuals, and/or households that plan to consume the products or services themselves.

To effectively manage and integrate all of the many retailing functions, it is necessary to develop an overall plan for the retail organization. Although planning is essential to success in retailing, the first two chapters focus on acquiring the requisite knowledge of retailing and of the environments that affect the retailer and the many retail institutions. Figure 1.1 represents the **integrated retail management (IRM) flow chart.** This chart can be used as a guide for retail decision making. In addition, it will serve as a framework for the future retailer. Each chapter discusses one or more of the elements that make up the flow chart. This chapter is dedicated to the macro retail environment.

The retail environment is represented at the top of the flow chart to highlight the importance of the macro environment for all areas of retail management. The following topical areas relate to the external environment.

The term **retail** refers to "the sale of goods or **commodities** in small quantities directly to consumers."[4] Thus, a **retailer** is a company or an organization that purchases products from individuals or companies with the intent to resell those goods and services to the ultimate, or final, consumer. The U.S. federal government considers a retailer a business that sells more than 50 percent of its products to the ultimate consumer. **Ultimate consumers,** or *end users,* are families, individuals, and/or households that plan to consume the products or services themselves. The toothpaste you used this morning, the shampoo you used last night, and the gasoline that powers your vehicle are all products that were purchased for personal consumption from a retailer.

business sales Sales from one business organization to another business organization; also called *business to business* or *B2B*.

In addition to selling to end users, some retailers sell products to other intermediaries, such as other businesses, universities, hospitals, and so on. These transactions are considered nonretail transactions. Nonretail transactions, or **business sales** (or *business to business*, also referred to as *b-to-b* or *B2B*), are sales in which the purchasers plan to use the products or services in their business operations or to resell them. The vast majority of retailing

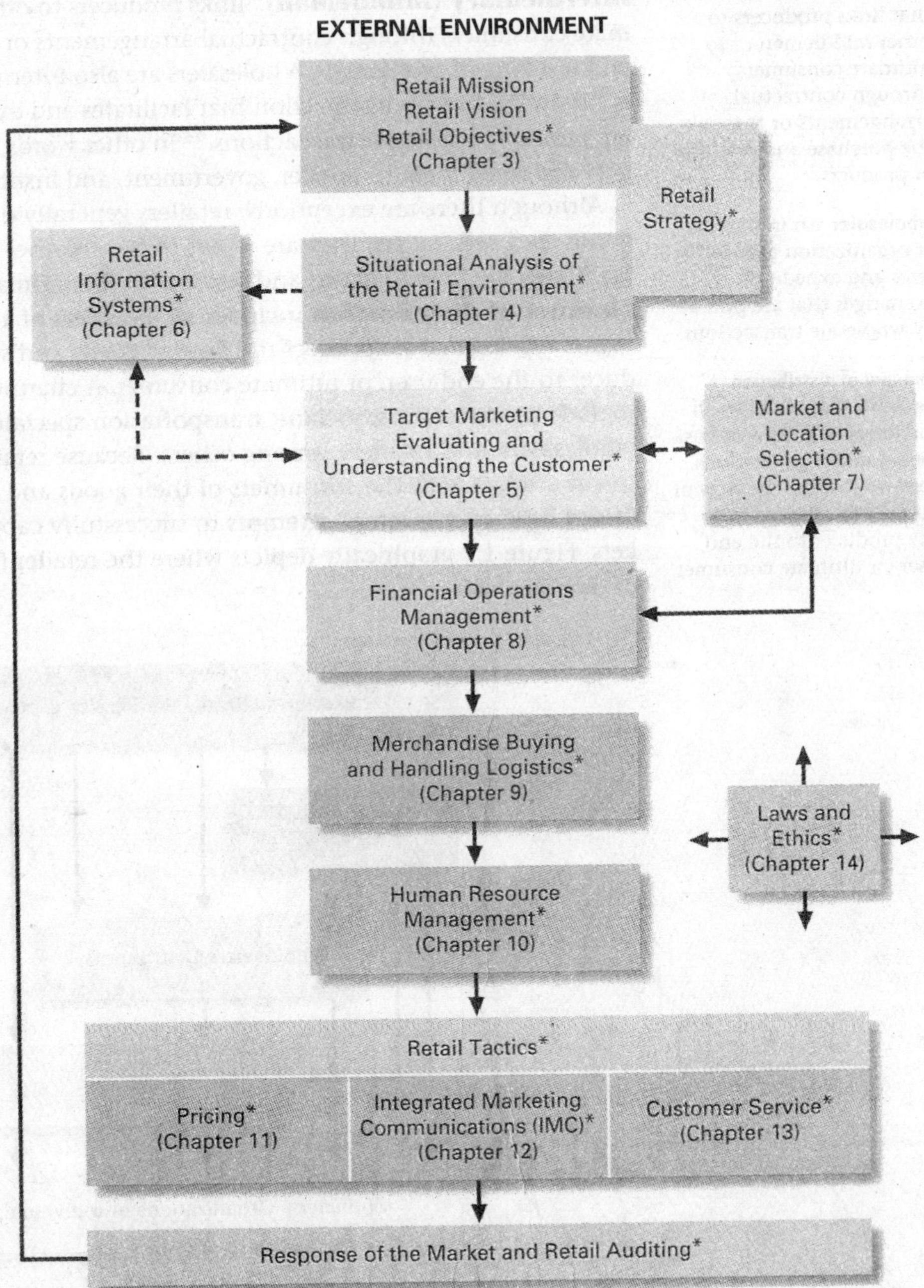

FIGURE 1.1 Integrated Retail Management (IRM) Flow Chart

occurs in stores throughout the world. Other venues for retailing include vending machines, door-to-door sales, cybersales (or e-tailing), cart sales (such as hot dog or pretzel stands), "party sales" (such as Tupperware parties), point-of-consumption sales (such as purchasing drinks on an airplane), telephone sales, infomercial sales, and other creative methods.

Retailers are often referred to as *intermediaries, middlemen,* or *in-betweens* because of the positions they hold in the marketing process. A **marketing intermediary (middleman)** "links producers to other middlemen or to ultimate consumers through contractual arrangements or through the purchase and reselling of products."[5] Wholesalers are also intermediaries. A **wholesaler** is "an individual or organization that facilitates and expedites exchanges that are primarily wholesale transactions."[6] In other words, wholesalers buy products and resell them to reseller, government, and institutional users.

marketing intermediary (middleman) A business that links producers to other middlemen or to ultimate consumers through contractual arrangements or through the purchase and reselling of products.

wholesaler An individual or organization that facilitates and expedites exchanges that are primarily wholesale transactions.

channel of distribution A network that includes all members of a team of businesses and organizations that help direct the flow of goods and services from the producer to the end user, or ultimate consumer.

Although there are exceptions, retailers generally do not produce the goods they sell; rather, they are a part of the channel of distribution that facilitates the flow of goods and services to the ultimate consumer. A **channel of distribution** includes all members of a team of businesses and organizations that help direct the flow of goods and services from the producer to the end user, or ultimate consumer. A channel of distribution may include producers, logisticians, transportation specialists, warehousers, wholesalers, and retailers, among others. Because retailers have the most frequent contact with the consumers of their goods and services, they are the "front line" in marketers' attempts to successfully capture and develop markets. Figure 1.2 graphically depicts where the retailer falls within the channel of distribution.

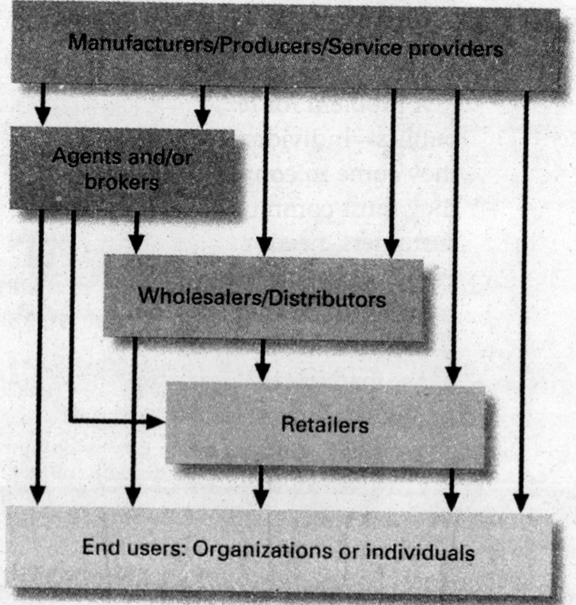

FIGURE 1.2 **Channel of Distribution** (Source: *Marketing's Powerful Weapon, "Point of Purchase Advertising"* [Washington, DC: POPAI, 2001]. Reprinted by permission.)

American Express is an example of a facilitator, because it helps consumers purchase retail products by providing them with credit.

A problem for retailers is communicating with the large number of publics—individuals, groups, organizations, and institutions—with which they come in contact. Because retailers interact with the ultimate consumer, they must communicate with their customers to ensure that they know their customers' needs and wants. Because retailers purchase products from producers, wholesalers, and other groups or individuals, they must also develop good communications systems for those groups.

To provide customers with the products they need and want and to effectively manage all of the retail functions, retailers must also deal with additional "facilitators." **Facilitators** are external individuals or groups that help the retailer make a sale. American Express, Visa, Diners Club, and MasterCard are all facilitators because they help consumers purchase retail products by providing them with credit, or payment systems. Store-based retail credit cards, owned and managed by organizations external to the retailer (such as Tower Records or JCPenney), are also facilitators. Shipping companies and installers are facilitators because they help ensure that products get to retailers and consumers. Banks are facilitators because they allow the retailer to borrow money to help its operations run smoothly. Advertising

facilitators External individuals or groups that help the retailer make a sale.

agencies facilitate sales of products by communicating with the consumer via some medium such as television, radio, newspapers, or the Internet. Retailers must develop effective communications channels for all of their facilitators.

product line A group of related products that satisfy a class of need, serve a particular market, have similar methods of distribution, or fall within a specific range of prices.

Finally, retailers must have a good working relationship with other businesses and producers because they need to select product lines to place in their stores for sale to the ultimate consumer. A **product line** is a group of related products that satisfy a class of need, serve a particular market, have similar methods of distribution, or fall within a specific range of prices.

THE RETAIL MANAGEMENT FUNCTION

As mentioned earlier, an essential element in becoming an effective and successful retailer is planning. Each major function of retailing must strive for the same goals. It is important that all retail functions become integrated so that there is little overlap in work to be performed by retail employees. Although external environmental factors will have an impact on the end-of-year bottom line for retailers, those who plan can overcome many external problems.

Take a look at the largest retailers in the United States, listed in Table 1.1. What have they done well? What areas could they improve on?

During the recession in 1990, Wal-Mart surpassed all other retailers to become the retail leader in the United States.[7] Since "winning" that title, Wal-

TABLE 1.1

LARGEST U.S. RETAILERS BY SALES

2001	2002
1. Wal-Mart	1. Wal-Mart
2. Kroger	2. Home Depot
3. Home Depot	3. Kroger
4. Sears	4. Sears
5. Kmart	5. Target
6. Albertson's	6. Albertson's
7. Target	7. Kmart
8. JCPenney	8. Costco
9. Costco	9. Safeway
10. Safeway	10. JCPenney

Sources: Christian Millman, "Stores Still Sell in Downturn," *The Morning Call,* July 22, 2001, pp. D1, D4; Thelma Snuggs, "Retailing: The Quest to Keep Up with Market Forces," *Black Collegian,* 23:2 (February 2003), pp. 68–74.

Wal-Mart, Inc., is the world's largest retailer. Other companies use Wal-Mart as a model when planning retail strategies. Shown here is the interior of one of the stores.

Mart has continued to maintain its retail dominance. Despite a sluggish economy in the United States and a recession during the holiday season of 2001, Wal-Mart's same-store sales grew more than 4.5 percent. In 2002, Wal-Mart posted sales of $219.8 billion and earnings of $6.6 billion.[8] What is the key to Wal-Mart's success? A thorough understanding of its customers and superior strategic planning. Wal-Mart's sales have continued to grow in all economic climates, even when the retailer faced bad press, such as coverage of the sex discrimination in pay and promotions lawsuit filed in 2001 by six women, which by 2003 grew to a class-action suit on behalf of 1.5 million women.[9] Successful retail management begins and ends with an outstanding retailing mission that engenders superior retail strategies.

INTEGRATED RETAIL MANAGEMENT

seamless Functioning as one cohesive unit, with no "seams," or vulnerabilities, in the strategy that may weaken the company.

It is the job of retail owners and managers to make sure the entire retail operation is running under a "seamless" integrated effort. **Seamless** means the business functions as one cohesive unit, with no "seams," or vulnerabilities, in the strategy that may weaken the company. The concept of striving toward a seamless organization refers back to early manufacturers. When placing two units together, such as drywall in building a house, the consumer does not want to see the spot where the two units are joined; rather, he or she wants the wall to appear as one unit. The same principle applies to retailing: the consumer does not want to "see" the individual units such as accounting, selling, and finance. Consequently, the retailer must strive to appear as one unit to its customers.

integration The condition wherein all parts of the retail organization have the information necessary to carry out their functions and the strategic philosophies are incorporated consistently throughout the plan.

In a retail organization that has achieved **integration,** all parts of the organization have the information necessary to carry out their function, and the strategic philosophies are incorporated consistently throughout the plan. The integrated retail management (IRM) flow chart on page 7 offers an overview of the required retail functions and where and how they fit together. The remainder of this section briefly introduces the elements of the IRM flow chart—an overview of what will be covered in more depth later in the text.

Imagine that you are in the process of researching graduate programs for your continued study of retailing or marketing. As the following sections illustrate, you will need to complete many steps before you reach your final decision.

RETAIL MISSION, VISION, AND OBJECTIVES. First, you must address the necessity for planning. You need to be prepared and think things through to create a plan. You want to make the best decision possible in your selection of the perfect graduate school for you. This is your *mission statement.* You want to be able to look back after graduation and know that the school you picked helped you in both your career advancement and your personal life. Retailers such as Crate and Barrel or Toys "R" Us also have a mission and/or corporate objectives that serve as their mission (although theirs will not be the same as yours!).

As you go through graduate school, you will likely develop a mental picture of what life will be like in your new career. This image will be your vision. A *vision* lets you see the results that you hope to obtain. Likewise, retailers have a vision of how they would like others to perceive them. Once you know why you want to attend graduate school (those needs and wants satisfiers), the rest of your planning should emanate from your mission and vision.

You will need a plan that helps you achieve your goals. In addition to a mission and a vision, a list of required information and short-term goals and objectives will help keep you on target. The items on this list are known as the *objectives.* Objectives need to be clear, measurable, and realistic. Retailers use objectives to create a clear vision of what they need to accomplish to be successful. You will use your objectives to evaluate the effectiveness of your graduate school plan. Similarly, retailers need to determine the success of their IRM plans. By evaluating the outcome of the plan in light of the company's objectives, the retail manager knows whether the company is "on track"and is able to identify what is working and what isn't.

SITUATIONAL ANALYSIS. You will need to access all possible information on various colleges and universities that offer advanced degrees in retailing and marketing. In other words, you will need to perform a *situational analysis.* The information you want for each college or university may include type of institution, degree requirements, location, faculty quality, overall indications of quality programs from sources outside the institution, and admissions requirements. You may also want to find information about the placement rates and salaries of former students, job opportunities in the field, and quality of work life. Knowledge of all of these factors will help you make the best-informed decision.

In making a decision about which graduate school to attend, it is important to know what makes a graduate school successful and how success is defined. Similarly, retailers need to know what products and services have been successful for their business and for those of their competitors. You may want to generate your situational analysis from talks with former students, peers, and friends. Retailers use *retail information systems* to generate data and information that will help them make decisions.

STRATEGY. Once the situation is effectively analyzed, a strategy for achieving the mission or vision is required. You may decide that you want to work part time at finding your school and studying for graduate admissions tests, or perhaps your strategy is to work full time. Whichever strategy you choose, it will determine how you proceed in finding the school of your choice. Similarly, retailers pursue strategies. A **strategy** provides the total directional thrust of the retail plan. It should be communicated to all of those involved in the retail management process. The strategy should guide the retail management plan and should influence all the tactical executions that the retailer decides to use. In addition, the strategy helps identify those environments under which the retailer operates (*i.e.,* social, technological, physical, legal, political, and economical).

strategy Planning that provides the total directional thrust of the retail plan.

TARGET MARKET. The next step in your graduate school planning would be determining which schools "fit" your stated mission or vision. Likewise, retailers need to discover who their current and potential customers may be. Because many schools will not meet your needs, you don't want to waste time contacting and applying to all schools that offer graduate degrees; rather, you should focus only on those that will provide you with a return on your investment. In the same way, retailers cannot, and should not, try to appeal to every single individual in the world, nation, region, or market. Retailers cannot be all things to all people. They need to understand their customers just as you need to understand the schools to which you are applying.

LOCATION SELECTION. One objective you may have set for your higher education quest involves the school's location. Perhaps you want to attend graduate school in the West. The University of Montana or Colorado State University may be among the choices available to you.

Other options are to take courses via distance learning or to use other technology to help you obtain your degree. In this step, you will be deciding where you want to study. You may choose to use the Internet to help with your information quest. An excellent resource for this is All Business Schools (allbusinessschools.com), a searchable site on business education programs. Retailers participate in the same type of decision-making process. They decide where they should locate their retail outlet(s). The decision centers on the best market and the best physical location within that market to place the retail outlet. Would it be better to have a "brick-and-mortar" store? Would a "cyberstore" be preferable? Or would it be best to have both a brick-and-mortar store and a cyberstore (often referred to as "brick-and-click")? Location is yet another decision that will determine the effectiveness and profitability of a retail organization.

FINANCIAL CONSIDERATIONS. If you discover many options for graduate school, you should assess your financial obligations before making any decisions. When choosing people to help you, you must be willing to compensate them. For example, if you enroll in a preparatory class for your graduate admissions exams, you will need to pay the instructor a flat fee or an hourly fee. In addition, once enrolled in graduate school, you will be burdened with many more financial obligations. Where will the cash flow come from? Will you charge your education on your Visa or American Express card, or will you pay cash? When is the tuition due? Retailers also worry about financial matters. They need to have clear management systems for all operations, including the financial aspects of running the business.

LOGISTICS. As you begin to check that everything is in place, your next set of decisions will involve the actual process of getting to and graduating from your educational program. How will you get to school? Where will you get your books and supplemental course material? Where can you get additional material required for successfully completing your degree? How will you ensure you have the finances you need to finish your degree? Like you, retailers are also concerned with **logistics,** which for the retailer is the process of getting products to customers. Retailers must have products and services that customers need and want, and they must make sure these items are in the stores when the customers want them. It is bad business to run out of products, but it is also bad business to purchase too many products and have to "eat" the costs associated with those that don't sell. Imagine taking four semesters of marketing courses only to find out that the requirements for your major have changed and you are ineligible for degree completion or graduation. Perhaps you were advised incorrectly, or perhaps you didn't pay attention to changes in the college curriculum. You will have wasted a lot of time and money.

logistics The process of getting products to customers.

You may have to use many sources of financing to help pay for your advanced degree, such as assistantships, scholarships, and/or loans from a bank, your parents, or your spouse. Who is going to make sure the college is paid when required? Who will see to it that you have the material requirements for the course, such as paper, writing implements, books, academic journals, and a computer? Where will these items be stored? Similarly, retailers must consider who is going to buy and handle their merchandise. They have to decide from whom to buy and how the products will be inventoried.

HUMAN RESOURCES. Because many people will be involved in your graduate school preparation, someone has to be in charge of your human resources as well as your physical resources. Certain people perform specific functions more effectively than others and thus are of greater value. For an organization, the **human resources** function "ensures that the company has

human resources A function that ensures that a company has the right mix of skilled people to perform its value creation activities effectively.

the right mix of skilled people to perform its value creation activities effectively," thus creating more value.[10] How can a retailer utilize the best people to ensure that its customers have a pleasant shopping experience? This is the problem for human resource management.

RETAIL TACTICS. Tactics are the last steps on your journey to graduate school. **Tactics** are the actual executions of the overall plan. Your tactics will provide for short-term (less than one year) executions that will make your education a success. Tactics must be specific. They should indicate who is undertaking what task and when that task is to be accomplished. Usually each task has a specific quantitative or qualitative objective that can be measured to ensure all of the objectives have been met.

tactics The actual executions of the overall plan; provide for short-term (less than one year) actions.

Tactics might include methods to manage your finances. For example, if other people will be kicking in money to help reduce your costs, when will you "charge" these financiers? Will you bill them prior to your entry into the graduate program so that you have an accurate accounting of expenses and sufficient liquidity to pay the charges when they come due? Retailers also make decisions regarding paying bills and receiving monies owed to them. They decide how much customers pay for a product or service. They also research how much customers expect to pay. Retailers have to decide whether to provide discounts to entice people to buy. Finally, the costs associated with running a business have to be assessed to ensure a sufficient profit margin.

INTEGRATED MARKETING COMMUNICATIONS. Communication will play a large role in your graduate school search. Do you want to advertise

Blunders or Best Practices?

Language Blunder Changes Meaning of Message

The following retailing story has been passed around from person to person and via the Internet. In 1987, a retail entrepreneur wanted to create and sell T-shirts to commemorate the Pope's visit to Miami. Because his target market was primarily Catholic and Hispanic, the entrepreneur decided to use the Spanish language on the shirts. On the backs of the shirts he placed the phrase "I Saw the Pope." This phrase was translated into Spanish but for some reason, no matter how hard he tried, he couldn't sell any. What was the cause for this lack of sales? He soon learned that instead of writing "I Saw the Pope" (*El Papa*), he had mistranslated and written "I Saw the Potato" (*la papa*).

This example serves as a lesson on the importance of understanding the retail markets in which one operates.

Source: "Marketing Blunders," retrieved December 2002 from www.home.hawaii.rr.com/kingcharles/humor/market.htm.

your need for funding for graduate school by sending letters to people who may be interested in helping you achieve your goals, or would you prefer to meet with them in person? Do you want to use the Internet to communicate with government agencies or colleges that have special financial aid programs? When applying to graduate programs, do you prefer to apply online, in person, or through the mail? What information do you need to get into the graduate program of your choice? Perhaps you will need to use facilitators such as the Educational Testing Service (ETS), which offers the Graduate Management Admissions Test (GMAT) that is required for admission. Retailers use **integrated marketing communications (IMC)** to integrate and coordinate all of their marketing communications efforts.[11] Retailers use IMC to determine the best ways to communicate to consumers and to make many other important communication decisions.

integrated marketing communications (IMC) The process of integrating and coordinating all of a firm's marketing communication activities.

CUSTOMER SERVICE. When choosing a graduate school, you want to be sure you will feel comfortable in your surroundings and with the courses and offerings available to you. In effect, you are a consumer of the school's services. Likewise, retailers need to ensure that their customers have an adequate level of service. Customers should feel comfortable in the store, be able to navigate the store easily, and be able to make purchases in a convenient manner. Thus, retailers are very concerned about the level of customer service they offer.

LAWS AND ETHICS. Everything you do when applying to graduate school must be in line with national, state, and local laws. For example, if you are an out-of-state student, you must pay out-of-state tuition. Retailers must also obey the laws of the country in which they do business. In the United States, retailers fall under federal, state, and local laws.

Ethics also play an important role in your school search. You will be asked to provide information on applications and must take care that the information is truthful. Retailers should also strive to do business in an ethical manner in all markets in which they operate.

EVALUATION AND CONTROL. Finally, you will want to assess how successful your graduate program was. Of course, you can't do this until after you graduate, but you can set objectives for each step you take in the graduate program. An example would be the objective of grade point average (GPA). Perhaps you want to achieve at least a 3.75 GPA on a 4.0 scale. In this case, at the end of each semester you can compare your GPA to that of your objective. If you are at or above your objective, you know things are working. If you are below the expected GPA, you know you need to control for this problem by making changes in your plan to raise the GPA to a minimum of 3.75. Although evaluation and control is often one of the last steps undertaken, it is vital to all aspects of planning.

Retailers evaluate and control for problems they encounter. Formal evaluations are important because they help the retailer assess accomplishments and gauge whether the plan was efficiently executed. When things go wrong, actions should be taken to control and fix the problem. For example, when retailers buy the wrong products for consumers, they need to be aware of this mistake so that it doesn't happen again.

RETAILING VERSUS E-TAILING

e-tailing A form of retailing utilizing the Internet, the World Wide Web (WWW), and other electronic forms of commerce to take the place of or supplement a physical retail location.

e-commerce The conduct of selling, buying, logistics, or other organization management activities via the Web.

E-tailing is a form of retailing utilizing the Internet, the World Wide Web (WWW), and other electronic forms of commerce to take the place of or supplement a physical retail location. E-tailing is a specialized form of e-commerce. **E-commerce** is "the conduct of selling, buying, logistics, or other organization-management activities via the Web."[12] Examples of e-tailers, both service and product, include eBay.com and Amazon.com. Although e-tailers conduct business in cyberspace, they require the same planning processes that brick-and-mortar retailers use.

In the early 1990s, when e-tailing gained wide acceptance, all one needed to be successful, in theory, was an idea. E-tailing promised the potential for high sales with reduced capital expenditures. Early e-tailers believed millions of computer users would surf the Web to find great deals on cars, electronics, books, toys, and thousands of different products. E-tailers saw the potential for making millions of dollars, but gave little thought to the requirements of a successful business venture. Consequently, many e-tail businesses were started with insufficient marketing and retailing expertise. Marketing plans were put together to secure funding for the businesses, but many of those plans didn't work. Early e-tailers failed because of poor business execution.

Founded in 1995, eBay has become one of the most popular Internet destinations. There are tens of millions of registered eBay users from all over the world. (Reproduced with the permission of eBay Inc. Copyright © eBay Inc. All rights reserved.)

gross margin The revenue remaining from the sales of products once the production costs have been subtracted.

One key to successful e-tailing is to achieve high gross margins for products. Simply stated, a **gross margin** is the revenue remaining from the sales of products after subtracting production costs. The larger the margin, the more money there is to spend on advertising and brand development. Successful e-tailers, such as eBay, have high gross margins. One partner of Rosewood Capital, a venture capital fund, stated, "If gross margins are 40% to 50%, the company has a shot of surviving."[13]

Although the concept of e-tailing seemed almost revolutionary at first, e-tailing has since become a mainstream method of reaching customers, and it is still growing. The overall objective of e-tailing is to create sales, manage additional retail functions such as buying and logistics, and find and identify new retail markets and opportunities using electronic technologies. E-tailers have discovered that the original method of selling products on the Web didn't work because many firms failed to integrate all aspects of retailing into their web strategies.

With advances in Web servers and browsers, e-tailing and e-commerce grew at amazing rates from their beginnings in the last decade. Organizations have discovered that the Web is indeed a powerful tool for managing the retail function of providing customers with products that satisfy their needs. However, successful e-tailers use the Web in a seamlessly integrated fashion rather than as a stand-alone vehicle for doing business. Retailers have begun to utilize the Web as an integrated marketing communication (IMC) vehicle to provide information to customers about products and services. In addition, many financial retailers have begun to use the Web to deliver customer response management (CRM) products. Many companies have invested in Internet-based supply chain management software. Still other firms have utilized the Web to provide product tracking for product and service orders.

Many retailers have found that by combining their retail operations with e-tail operations, they can exceed customer needs and wants and return a profit to the company. They can create their own Web stores and enter into partnerships, or strategic alliances, to leverage their human and capital resources. To understand the distinctions between e-tailing and retailing, one must understand that the two concepts are not mutually exclusive. In other words, a business may need both e-tailing and retailing to create an effective integrated retail management plan.

The main distinction between e-tailing and retailing is the venue used to create effective marketing. In the planning phase, the retailer needs to decide which types of distribution will best reach its targeted market. With e-tailing, the retail manager uses cyberspace to create a retail business relationship with customers; with traditional retailing, most transactions occur in a physical (brick-and-mortar) location.

Numerous types of retailers have found that e-tailing provides a venue for better serving their target markets. For example, companies involved in mail-order businesses such as catalogs, flyers, or magalogs (catalogs that have the look of a magazine) have found that the Web offers their customers the advantage of being able to track orders, inquire about delivery dates, and

INTERNET IN ACTION

eBay: Successful Niche E-tailing

Founded in September 1995, eBay was the first online auction. eBay paved the way for individuals and businesses to sell goods through auction or fixed price to a worldwide audience. Pierre Omidyar, a software developer from California, started eBay when he ran into a dead end after trying to help his girlfriend connect with other Pez candy dispenser collectors. His girlfriend, who later became his wife, was frustrated because, like other collectors, she was bound by geographical constraints. Omidyar's interest in the Internet, coupled with his desire to help his girlfriend, pushed him to develop a software program that allowed people from all parts of the globe to post information about items for sale in one location. Other people could then visit the website and bid for the goods listed. Living up to its mission—"to help practically anyone trade practically anything on earth"—eBay has become one of the Internet's largest success stories.

eBay's services include an online bill payment service, a marketplace designed especially for automotive items, connections to international buyers and sellers, connections to other stores from eBay's Internet site, live auctions, and a means to find professionals for any business needs, such as accounting and Web design. The search for a Pez dispenser ballooned to a way for geographically diverse people to come together, share goods, and trade stories. Thus, a small idea sparked a great enterprise. eBay had forged into new territory and, despite some growing pains, is today a highly successful enterprise.

Sources: eBay homepage at www.ebay.com; Matthew W. Beale, "E-commerce Success Story: eBay," *E-Commerce Times* (2000), retrieved May 2003 from www.ecommercetimes.com; eBay Company Overview, retrieved July 2002 from www.pages.ebay.com/community/aboutebay/overview/index.html; "1st Person—Pierre Omidyar", retrieved September 2002 from www.tbwt.com/interation/1pomid/html/1a.htm.

check for items on back order. E-tailers as well as customers have benefited from these added advantages. For the e-tailer, payments for goods and services are immediate, thus creating an increase in cash flow and providing an efficient way to reorder inventory. Because only credit or debit cards are used for purchases, paperwork is minimal or nonexistent. Having customers print out receipts from their own printers also reduces the costs of paper receipts for the retailer.

Although the beginning of the e-commerce era promised much success, people and businesses hoping to strike it rich on the "e" bandwagon often overlooked numerous obstacles. Many fledgling e-tailers lacked clear direction. Some major pitfalls were lack of customer service, hard-to-navigate websites, lack of (or limited) product information, unclear systems of payment, ineffective logistics, and too many out-of-stock situations. In general, many e-businesses failed because of poor planning, execution, and integration. The majority of those e-tailers failed to take into account the integrated nature of retailing. Since January 2000, an estimated 500 e-tailers, or dot-coms, have gone out of business and countless others have downsized (see Figure 1.3).[14] In contrast, a significant number of large brick-and-mortar retailers, by utilizing the process of *environmental scanning* during their situational analysis, have entered

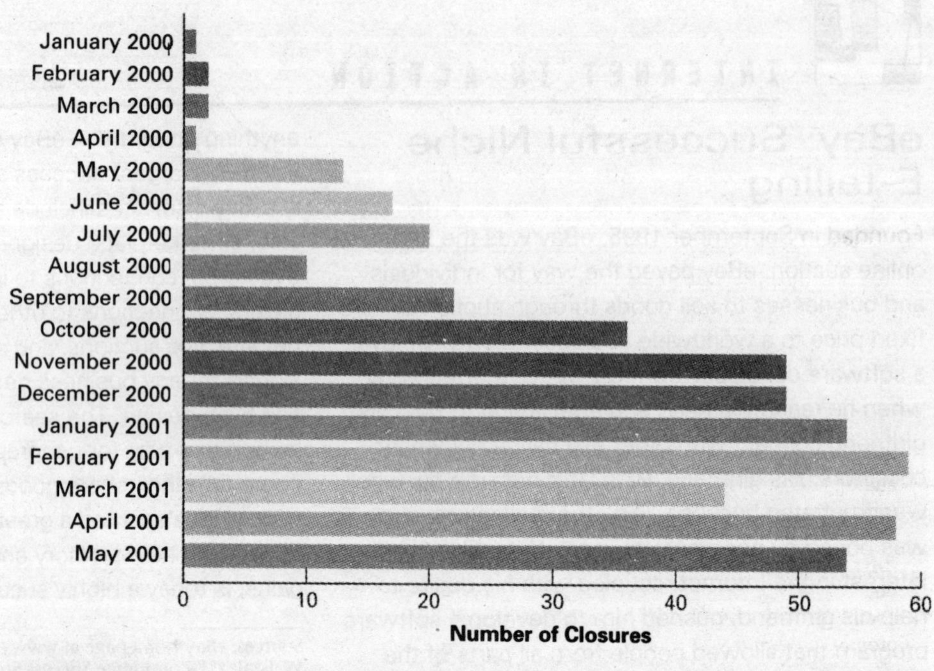

FIGURE 1.3 **Dot-Com Closures** (Source: Jon Swartz, "Dot-Com Decline Sees No End Soon," *USA Today*, June 7, 2002.)

the e-tail market with better results. The key to successful retailing and e-tailing is the total integration of all the controllable elements of the retail management mix, along with an effective retail plan and strategy.

CAREERS IN RETAILING

In the United States and around the world, retailers make up a significant portion of all employers. According to the U.S. Bureau of the Census, *Census of Retail Trade,* traditional retailers in the United States provide around 25 million jobs. If you add in all retailers, including e-tailers and service retailers (such as banks), the number comes closer to 50 million jobs. Any way you look at the numbers, more people are employed in retailing than in any other industry. If you want to work with customers, there is not a better field of study. Retail graduates work for large companies such as Sears, Target, Disney, or The Gap. They also work for smaller retailers such as regional airlines (Southwest, Southeast, Mesaba) or small mom-and-pop retailers. Some even prefer to take a chance and open their own businesses.

Because retailing is labor intensive, there will always be open positions within the industry. With thousands of retailers opening every year and with many retailers becoming international, the number of employment opportunities is growing rapidly.

Appendix A offers hints on securing positions within the retail industry. Figure 1.4 outlines selected retail positions.

Depending on the areas you wish to work in, salaries in retailing are competitive. Entry-level management trainee positions can pay in the upper $30,000 range, with liberal benefits. It is not uncommon for managers of large stores to make more than $100,000 a year, with generous benefits.

Retail careers offer all individuals the chance to succeed. Great opportunities abound for women and men of all races. Retailing also offers a good deal

Accountant Responsibilities include auditing, recording, and summarizing transactional information.

***

Advertising Specialist Works with outside advertising agencies to develop communication methods and promotional strategies.

***

Buyer (Assistant Buyer or Senior Buyer) Responsibilities include acquisition of merchandise, controlling sales, forecasting profits, and optimizing the product mix. Opportunity to specialize in specific product lines (such as women s sportswear). Also works with suppliers through product acquisition, negotiation, and evaluation. May be asked to assist in development of point-of-purchase displays, in conjunction with corporate merchandisers.

***

Catalog Manager Responsibilities include managing the operations for the catalog, including merchandise acquisition and customer fulfillment.

***

Commercial Artist/Visual Director Duties include creating the illustration of advertisements and handling the package design. May also be asked to communicate divisional merchandising directives to stores and to partner with the Merchandise Team Manager in organizing and executing selling-floor fixture/merchandise moves.

Collections and Credit Specialist Assists with the develoment of credit terms, types of credit accepted, credit eligibility, and collections of delinquent accounts.

***

Department Manager/Assistant Manager Responsibilities include ensuring that displays are effective and illustrate the retailer s mission. Must train, lead, control, and evaluate departmental sales staff. Also assists buyers in merchandising purchase decisions.

***

District Manager Responsible for maximizing sales volume and profits for assigned stores through effective management; development of field and store staff; and execution of company programs, policies, and procedures.

***

Line Manager Works with other line managers. Responsible for either the hard lines or the soft lines of the store, to provide leadership on all sales-floor processes, ensuring that merchandising and floor events conform to high standards of quality. Plans and directs all sales events for maximum profits, sales, guest service, team spirit, and team development.

***

Merchandise Manager Assists buyers and departmental managers with merchandise buying to ensure that all departments are offering an integrated product mix. Works closely with a team of associates to ensure accuracy and timeliness of the markdown process. May be asked to act as a liason between buyers and store managers.

***

Operations Manager Ensures that all store operations are running smoothly and profitably by inspecting, marking, and distributing merchandise.

***

Personnel Manager Recruits and helps retain employees. Performs various training functions and outlines benefits and compensation for employees. Must provide all human resource needs and engage in personnel forecasting.

***

Store Manager Oversees all operations of a specific store. Develops creative plans to increase store sales and decrease losses. Provides training and development for Assistant Store Manager and Associates. Ensures consistency of store presentation with company standards. Maintains communication with district/regional management to stay abreast of company initiatives.

***

Miscellaneous Positions Positions available for e-tail managers, warehouser/warehouse specialists, salespersons, site location specialists, or merchandise analysts.

FIGURE 1.4 **Help Wanted: Retail Positions**

GLOBAL RETAILING

International Expansion at Disney

When Disney Corporation decided to create a retail outlet in Europe, the company spent a lot of time and money on its new project, Euro Disney, located in Paris. Disney was inspired by the success of its Tokyo Disneyland, which had generated, for Disney, 10 percent of the gate receipts and rides and 5 percent of all sales of food, drink, and souvenirs without investing any money. Disney created essentially the same agreement with Euro Disney regarding percentages. However, it also invested $4.4 billion to retain a 49 percent interest in the project, hoping to realize the large return that Tokyo Disney was generating at the time. But after Euro Disney's opening in April 1992, the company realized that its latest investment may have been unwise.

During the first year of opening Euro Disney, a recession hit Europe. Profits from all properties (especially the hotels) were nonexistent and, because of falling property values, the equity that was invested in the physical real estate fell in value. In addition, Disney failed to realize that European customers were price conscious. It also didn't count on the great demand for breakfast at its park restaurants and on Europeans' desire for wine with meals. To compound these problems, Disney had a harder time training some of its French employees in efficiency and customer satisfaction.

Disney had created an empire based on the needs and wants of its U.S. and Japanese consumers, and ignored the wants and needs of the European market. The result was disappointing

sales at Euro Disney. Although tourists loved to frequent Euro Disney, they failed to spend as much money as did customers at other Disney parks. In 1998, Euro Disney was the most popular tourist attraction in France, with around 12.5 million visitors. Although Disney corrected many of its errors, only time will tell if these changes will be enough to generate visitors who are willing to spend money. Keeping in mind its mistakes in Europe, Disney plans to open a park in Hong Kong in 2006 and one in Shanghai sometime after 2010.

Sources: James Sterngold, "Cinderella Hits Her Stride in Tokyo," *New York Times*, February 17, 1991, p. 6; Peter Gumbel and Richard Turner, "Fans Like Euro Disney but Its Parent's Goofs Weigh the Park Down," *Wall Street Journal*, March 10, 1994, p. A12; Bruce Orwall, "Disney Net Fell 71% in Fiscal 4th Quarter," *Wall Street Journal*, November 5, 1999, p. A3; "Hong Kong Betting $3 Billion on Success of New Disneyland," *Cleveland Plain Dealer*, November 3, 1999, p. 2-C; Charles Fleming, "Euro Disney to Build Movie Theme Park Outside Paris," *Wall Street Journal*, September 30, 1999, pp. A18, A21; Jasmine Yap, "Its Eyes on China, Disney Steps into Hong Kong," *International Herald Tribune* (online), January 9, 2003.

of geographic mobility: retail outlets exist in every city of every state in the United States and worldwide.

A retailing career also poses many challenges. Workweeks can be long, particularly during holiday seasons. Retail professionals may have to manage temporary employees as well as perform many different activities in a day. Therefore, a strong work ethic is essential for success in retail management. In addition, retail employees must be flexible and creative in their positions, and they must have analytical skills. The universal functions of management—planning, organizing, leading, and controlling—are imperative for success in a retail career.

In summary, retailing is a very dynamic field and needs dynamic individuals to implement programs that will generate a significant return to store owners. Individuals who desire success, both personal and financial, are in high demand. If you have the enthusiasm necessary for success, integrated retail management will offer you a satisfying career and quality of life.

TEXT ORGANIZATION

As you read through the textbook, you will notice that the major focus is on the integration of the retail management functions necessary for successful retailing. You need to understand the flows and processes that go into the retailing function and how these flows and processes fit into the big picture of retailing.

As a student of integrated retail management, you will encounter each process or variable needed for effective retailing and see the strategy that goes into the use of all tactical areas. Retailers must be aware of the environments in which they do business. They must understand what environments will affect their retail operations and have plans that take those environments into account. In other words, retailers must be *proactive* rather than *reactive* in their retail operations.

This text follows the integrated retail management plan presented earlier in this chapter. By following this outline, you will understand the importance of each step in the plan.

This chapter began by looking at the retail macro environment. It provided an outline and a general understanding of retailing and e-tailing. The chapter outlined a flow, or system, for retail planning. Chapter 2 also concentrates on the external, or macro, environment by looking at the all-important environment of customers. The chapter discusses the importance of developing an understanding of customers, customer value, and retailing technology. It provides hints on how to create relationships with customers to encourage loyalty.

Chapter 3 provides a detailed overview of the retail management flow chart. In this chapter, the book begins to take a more micro approach to retail management. The chapter provides an in-depth insight into each element of the IRM plan. Chapters 4 through 13 look at each of these elements in detail and offer suggestions for implementation.

In Chapter 14, the book returns to a more macro view of the retail environment. This chapter discusses laws that affect retailers and explores principles of ethics in retailing. Chapter 15 covers trends in retailing, diversity, and an example of the IRM process.

Appendix A offers guidelines for breaking into and succeeding in the field of retailing. Appendix B is an in-depth case study of Z-Coil, a manufacturer and retailer of specialty footwear.

To further engage the student in analytical thinking, each chapter concludes with one continuing case featuring Sherwin-Williams Company and one case featuring selected companies, including Best Buy, Target, Circuit City, Cal Corporation, and the Container Store.

Hopefully this text will serve both as a point of reference and a pragmatic manual. Keep it for future use in other classes and as an on-the-job resource.

SUMMARY

The field of retailing is dynamic, challenging, and exciting! The retail environment has seen many changes and will continue to do so. Retailing encompasses all business activities that provide customers with goods and/or services that satisfy or exceed their needs. Successful retailers today are integrating all of their functions to return an investment to their owners and at the same time provide wanted goods and services to their customers.

Retailers serve two groups of customers: the ultimate consumer, or end user, of products and the companies that produce products and services to sell to end users (business-to-business, or B2B). Retailers provide a critical function in the distribution channel. E-tailing is a specialized combination of e-commerce and retailing using the World Wide Web.

Retailing offers numerous employment opportunities, including managers, accountants, merchandisers, and buyers. The world of retailing entails much hard work, but it also offers many rewards.

KEY TERMS

macro retail environment (6)
integrated retail management (IRM) flow chart (6)
retail (6)
commodity (6)
retailer (6)
ultimate consumers, (6)
business sales (7)
marketing intermediary (middleman) (8)
wholesaler (8)
channel of distribution (8)
facilitators (9)
product line (10)
seamless (11)
integration (12)
strategy (13)
logistics (14)
human resources (14)
tactics (15)
integrated marketing communications (IMC) (16)
e-tailing (17)
e-commerce (17)
gross margin (18)

QUESTIONS FOR DISCUSSION

1. In your own words, explain the term *retailing*. Is your definition the same as the definition that the U.S. Census Bureau uses? If not, what are the differences?
2. What aspects of a retailing career appeal to you? What aspects might you find less desirable?
3. What challenges do you think chief executive officers of retailing companies face?
4. How does retailing on the Web (e-tailing) differ from traditional brick-and-mortar retailing? How are they similar?
5. Describe how you think retailers will use technology and marketing during the next decade.

E-TAILING EXERCISE

Identify four different retailers for which you would consider working. Look up their websites, and answer the following questions.

1. Based on the information on the websites, rank the retailers in order of their attractiveness as a potential employer.
2. What characteristics helped you rank your choices in question 1?
3. In what ways could each retailer make its website more user friendly for potential employees?

Continuing Case 1.1

Sherwin-Williams Company: Early Beginnings

In 1866, a person who needed to buy paint had to purchase the ingredients separately and, just as with a food recipe, measure the amounts needed, mix them, and adjust the mix until the desired combination was reached. This was quite a tedious process until two young men from Ohio formed the Sherwin-Williams Company.

The company started in 1866 by Henry A. Sherwin, a paint salesman from Cleveland in his early 20s. Sherwin invested his life savings of $2,000 to help form the company. The company started out by painting carriages and buggies, the most popular form of transportation at that time. Early on, Sherwin planned to sell paint to other companies. In addition, he planned on aggressively pursuing the homeowner market, a relatively new market at the time. In the late 1860s, Sherwin partnered with Edward P. Williams.

From the beginning, Sherwin-Williams was a market leader. In 1880, it became the first company in the paint industry to offer a money-back guarantee on its ready-mixed paint. Sherwin-Williams' entrepreneurial spirit and dedication to product quality persist today.

The legacy of Sherwin-Williams Company is rich with information on how to run a retail business. With more than 135 years of operation, the company has survived many obstacles and enjoyed many successes. The information on Sherwin-Williams is used to integrate the information from this textbook to help you gain an in-depth understanding of retailing and how the different functions fit together. Sherwin-Williams Company was chosen because it is a stable and successful manufacturer and retailer that displays strong integrated retailing management. One continuing Sherwin-Williams Company case appears at the end of each chapter.

In this advertisement, Sherwin-Williams appeals to women and their desire to obtain the perfect paint color.

Questions

1. What types of careers do you think would be available today at Sherwin-Williams Company?
2. Would e-tailing be an effective retailing medium for Sherwin-Williams? Why or why not?
3. If you were a manager at Sherwin-Williams, what would you do to attract quality employees to the company?

4. Create a hypothetical integrated retail management flow chart for Sherwin-Williams Company.

Sources: Information from the following websites retrieved May 2003: www.newstarproductions.com/Sherwin-Williams.htm; www.topoftheline.com/paintouchbumr.html; www.csuchico.edu/plc/pwe00007.html; www.sherwinwilliams.com.

Case 1.2

The Retail Environment: Niche Retailing

Many retailers are trying to capture niche markets by capitalizing on their names and brand successes. The strategy is to broaden the retailers' customer bases by developing special retail outlets that allow them to capture new markets or expand their current market base.

Limited Brands, owners of The Limited Stores, has created a joint venture with partner Shiseido Company to create a new group of stores that specialize in beauty care. The name of the venture is Aura Science. In addition, Victoria's Secret has created a spinoff company called Beauty. Aimed toward Victoria's Secret customers, Beauty sells cosmetics and skin care products. The products will complement the Victoria's Secret line of clothing and lingerie.

Another example of niche marketing is Hot Topic, a marketer of trendy clothing for teens and young adults. Hot Topic has created a trendy, upscale retail outlet called Torrid that concentrates on marketing to plus-size teen customers.

Retailers are discovering that the path to success in a very competitive environment is through product differentiation and appealing to a well-defined group of consumers.

Questions

1. Based on your knowledge of the retailing environment, do you think niche marketing is a successful strategy? Why or why not?
2. Do you believe these retail formats are just a fad, or will they endure for some time?
3. What are the advantages of creating a niche strategy for retailers? What might be some major disadvantages?
4. What suggestions would you give to a retailer that decides to undertake a niche strategy in terms of its tactical executions?

Sources: Robin Garrison Leach, "Plus-Size Teens Find More Fashion, Better Fit in St. Louis—Area Stores: Retailers Wake Up to Eager Market for Contemporary Chic That Flatters Figures," *St. Louis Post-Dispatch,* December 7, 2002, p. L32; Kathy Showalter, "Limited, IBI Takes Wraps off Plans for Stores, Goods," *Business First,* October 12, 2001, p. A13; Dina El Boghdady, "An Industry-Wide Makeover; Specialty Stores Attract a Growing Share of Customers," *Washington Post,* July 23, 2002, p. E1.

Customer Value, Services, and Retailing Technologies

Chapter

2

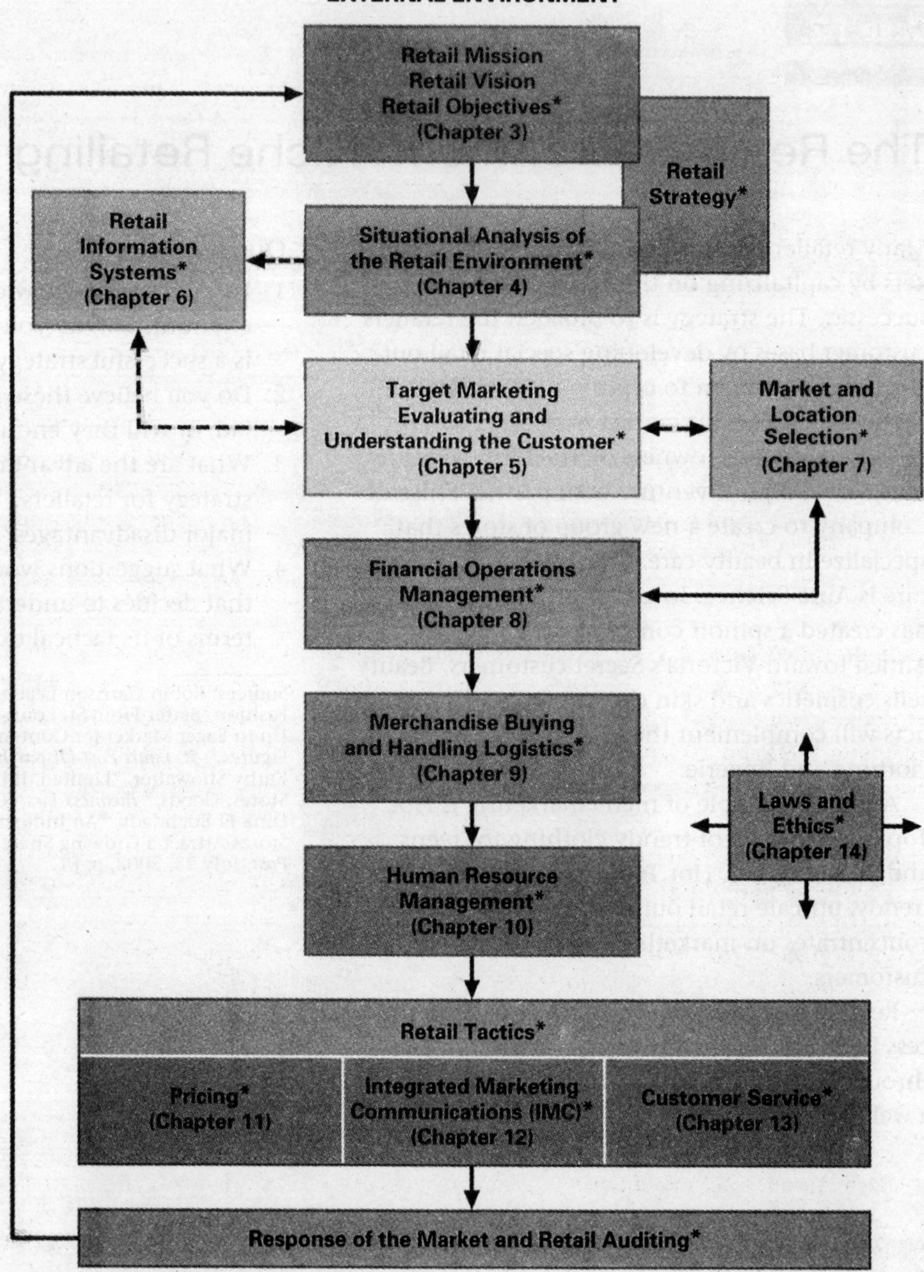

An organization that is strong and stable and is ready to commit time, money, and patience will be more apt to reap rewards than the quick-hitting opportunist.

Richard Miller, Market Response International

CHAPTER OBJECTIVES

After completing this chapter, you will be able to:

1. Explain how retail decisions are affected by the marketing concept and the extended marketing concept to create customer value.
2. Define *value* and explain its importance to the retailer.
3. Compare and contrast customer service and services retailing.
4. Identify the dimensions that are important to the customer in building a relationship.
5. Differentiate between e-commerce and e-tailing and explain the advantages and disadvantages of each.
6. Define and explain the importance of ethics and corporate social responsibility in building strong relationships with customers.

Dillard's Focus on the Customer

Dillard's Incorporated was started by William T. Dillard in 1949. Dillard's philosophy was to focus on giving customers value. In 1964, Dillard realized that malls offered a great deal of potential to reach a large number of the rapidly growing suburban populations. As a result, he opened a Dillard's department store in a mall in Austin, Texas.[1] As the mall format grew, so did Dillard's department stores. In 2002 there were 350 stores in 29 states, and the company earned about $8.5 billion in sales.[2]

Dillard's sells brand-name and private-label merchandise with a focus on apparel and home furnishings.[3] Some of the ways in which the company has built value are based on William Dillard's philosophies. He placed service and quality as top priorities. His department stores were among the first to use technology to improve their efficiency. The company used computerized checkout systems and inventory tracking systems and sought innovation to improve value.

William Dillard passed away in February 2002,[4] but he remains one of the visionaries in retailing who early on realized that customers add value and equity to retail operations. His son, William Dillard II, has succeeded him and continues to employ his father's retail philosophies.

INTRODUCTION

This chapter continues our focus on the external environment as it relates to retailing. Chapter 1 dealt with the overall nature of retailing. This chapter examines who retail customers are and how their buying decisions and purchase behaviors affect the retailer. In addition, it covers important aspects of the technological environment and that environment's relationship to retail management. The chapter concludes with a discussion of ethics and social responsibility in retailing. This topic is covered at length later in the text but is touched on in this chapter as it relates to customer value, services, and retailing technologies.

marketing concept The philosophy that an organization should try to satisfy customers' needs through a coordinated set of activities that also allows the organization to achieve its goals.

extended marketing concept The concept of exceeding customer wants and needs at a profit.

In retailing, the customer is the king or queen. All of a retailer's marketing and retailing efforts should be directed toward pleasing the customer. The **marketing concept** is "a philosophy that an organization should try to satisfy customers' needs through a coordinated set of activities that also allows the organization to achieve its goals."[5] In other words, the marketing concept is the attempt to satisfy customer wants and needs at a profit. In retailing, there is an extension of the marketing concept. The **extended marketing concept** is to take "satisfying" a step further and try to "wow" customers by exceeding their expectations, needs, and wants so that they will want to return to the store to make future purchases.

To exceed customer wants, the retailer must understand its customers and what they offer the retailer. An excellent way to gain an understanding of the customer is to develop an understanding of the "value" of a customer. Thus, the first part of this chapter focuses on the development of customer value. What economic value does the customer provide for the retailer?

relationship marketing A type of marketing that focuses on building long-lasting relationships with customers.

Understanding customer value is not the only important issue in dealing with customers. A retailer must also engage in **relationship marketing**—that is, build long-lasting relationships with customers. The next section of the chapter discusses the many ways to develop this relationship, whether for a brick-and-mortar business, an e-tailing business, or a combination of each (bricks-and-clicks). Next, the chapter explores services retailing and the differences between customer service and services retailing. Advances in technology assist retailers and e-tailers in the relationship-building process. These are discussed in detail later in the chapter and in Chapter 13.

Think of your relationships with retailers. Are they positive or negative? What makes them good or bad? To gain insight into these questions, you first need to understand what value the customer brings to the retail organization.

CUSTOMER VALUE

Excellent retailers understand that their job is not to merely satisfy their customers but to *excite* them and induce them to return to the store. To exceed customers' expectations and excite them, the retailer must have flexibility and the ability to continually force change within the store environment. New shopping experiences should be created to stimulate the customer's return to

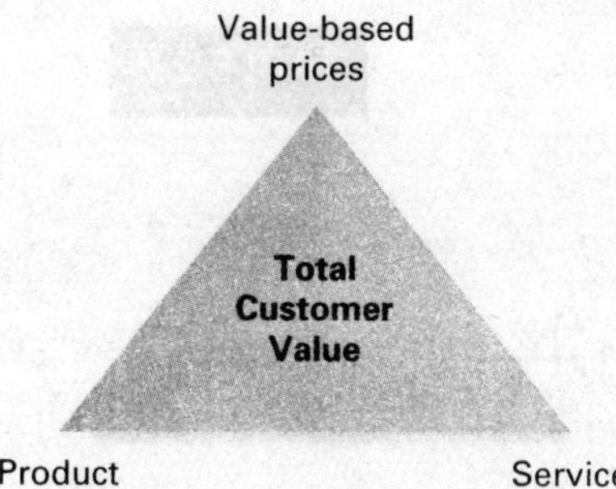

FIGURE 2.1 The Customer Value Triad (Source: Adapted from Earl Naumann, *Customer Value Toolkit* [Cincinnati, Ohio: Thompson Executive Press, 1995], p. 17.)

value An amount, as of goods, services, or money, considered to be a fair and suitable equivalent for something else; monetary worth of something; relative worth, utility, or importance.

the store or online site to make additional purchases. Thus, value becomes the basis for the customer's differentiation between one retailer and another.

Think about your experiences with service retailers such as banks. What makes one bank different from another? They all offer the same basic products (checking accounts, savings accounts, CDs, money market funds, and so on), but you prefer to do business with a specific bank or branch. Telephone companies offer the same services, yet you choose one over another. What entices you to make those selections? The answer is your perception of the value that the company provides to you, the customer. Value is a concept that the customer defines. What one customer considers valuable, another may not.

So how can retailers create value in customers' minds? First, the retailer must understand the variables that make up the concept of value. **Value** is defined as "an amount, as of goods, services, or money, considered to be a fair and suitable equivalent for something else."[6] The retailer must decide not only on the value of products and services but also on the value of customers. The premise for overall customer value is elementary; however, the executions needed to create this value are not. To keep these related concepts clear, see Table 2.1, which lists four important areas related to value.

What makes a customer "valuable"? Earl Naumann, who has written extensively on customer service, suggests that the concept of value can be seen within a "customer value triad."[7] The triad consists of three separate variables: value-based prices, product quality, and service quality (see Figure 2.1). Product and service quality provide the "pillars" of the triad and are the bases for value-based pricing. When retailers provide poor service or have products of poor quality, value-based pricing fails. If the price line is set in an inconsistent manner, sales will decline. High product quality is important, but not enough to ensure total customer value. The quality of the products or services, additional services provided, and the pricing strategy all influence value perceptions. All three variables must be in place to achieve true integration in customer value.

To achieve true value within the organization, the retailer should integrate value into the overall strategy. Integrating value into the strategy results in 10 essential retailing outputs (see Table 2.2).

TABLE 2.1

CUSTOMER VALUE

The following four areas are important concepts related to customer value

1. The customer's perception of the value provided by the retailer
2. The equity, both financial and informational, that the customer provides to the retailer
3. The importance of developing strong relationships with customers
4. The integration and utilization of technology to support customer relationships and increase customer equity

TABLE 2.2

RETAILING VALUE OUTPUTS

1. Understanding customer choices
2. Identifying customer segments
3. Increased competitive options (e.g., increased product lines or products)
4. Avoidance of price wars
5. Improved service quality
6. Strengthened retail communications
7. A focus on what is meaningful to customers
8. Customer loyalty
9. Improved brand success
10. Stronger customer relationships

Source: S. MacStravic, "Questions of Value in Health Care," *Marketing Health Services,* Winter 1997, pp. 50–53. Reprinted by permission of the American Marketing Association.

QUALITY, SERVICE, AND PRICE (QSP)

QSP Categorization of customer value by quality, service, and/or price.

The outputs shown in Table 2.1 help create additional differentiation for the retailer. An understanding of the outputs helps the retailer integrate overall customer value into the IRM plan. It is often difficult to represent, or express, customer value because it is hard to measure. One suggestion for expressing customer value is to categorize the value by quality, service, and/or price (**QSP**). Customer value can be expressed in terms of a combination of the retailer's overall service, quality, and price.[8] As such, a retailer needs to understand that a combination of these three variables will affect how much value customers believe they have gained by shopping at a particular retail outlet. Because of the high costs associated with trying to be a leader in all three areas, retailers often concentrate on one or two manageable areas to create value differentiation.

It would be very expensive, and strategically unwise, for example, for Saks Fifth Avenue to try to compete on price when the basis for its strategy and differentiation is quality products and service. Likewise, for a discount retailer such as Kmart or Wal-Mart to try to offer high-end services would mean a price increase to cover their costs. Since the strategy of both of these retailers is to provide quality, low-cost goods, an increase in customer service to a level equivalent to Saks would be inconsistent with their strategy and could possibly have a negative impact on sales. This is not to say that these retailers should not try to maintain a minimal level of QSP; rather, they should concentrate on the areas in which they have the greatest competitive advantage (price for Wal-Mart or Kmart; quality products and services for Saks).

EQUITY

An understanding of customer value helps develop a long-term, loyal customer base. The underlying theme is to create equity in the retail operation by

equity The marketing and financial value that the customer provides for the retailer.

name equity The value of the organization's name.

customer equity The value of the complete set of resources, tangible and intangible, that customers invest in a firm.

brand equity The consumer's perceived level of quality for the retailer's product lines.

brand associations Attributes or personality that the owners of a brand wish to convey to their current or potential customers.

making customers want to return to the store or online site. **Equity** is simply the marketing and financial value that the customer provides for the retailer. Retailers attempt to develop **name equity**—that is, the value of the organization's name as well as equity for the brands they sell (brand equity). **Customer equity** is "the value of the complete set of resources, tangible and intangible, that customers invest in a firm."[9] Retailers must seamlessly incorporate equity in all of the activities they perform.

BRAND EQUITY. Brand equity refers to the consumer's perceived level of quality for the retailer's product lines. Often consumers cannot make a quantitative judgment on the actual quality of the retail organization and the products it carries, so they use the brand as an indicator of the organization's overall quality.[10] That is, if the consumer has a positive perception of the brand, this may translate into a highly positive perception of the store. Four elements, or variables, are essential in the development of brand equity: brand-name awareness, brand loyalty, perceived brand quality, and brand associations.[11]

BRAND ASSOCIATIONS. The concepts of brand-name awareness, brand loyalty, and perceived brand quality are self-explanatory. **Brand associations** refer to the attributes or personality that the owners of the brand wish

Saks Fifth Avenue is an upscale retailer that competes on quality and service instead of price.

Although Hallmark started with a line of greeting cards, its product offerings have expanded to include stationery, gifts, ornaments, and partyware.

to convey to their current or potential customers. In other words, marketers often connect some type of lifestyle, or personality, to a brand. Hallmark suggests that you will send a Hallmark card "When you care enough to send the very best."

APPLYING THE CONCEPTS OF VALUE AND EQUITY

Let's look at the value and equity a customer may represent to the retailer by examining buying habits. Think of a retailer you visit at least once a week on average. This might be a gas station, a convenience store, a local "watering hole," your school's bookstore, or a fast-food restaurant. Write down the average amount of money you spend at that retail outlet for each week. Then multiply that amount by the number of weeks in a year, or 52. Next, multiply that figure by 5 (years), then by 10 (years). Finally, multiply that figure by 20 years. That final number is your value to the retailer. For example, by purchasing just an average of $20 worth of gasoline a week, you generate a value to that gas station of $1,040 per year, $5,200 for 5 years, $10,400 for 10 years, and $20,800 over a 20-year period. In this example, if you multiply $1,040, the amount generated to the gas station by one person in one year, by 10,000 happy customers, you will see that this retailer earns more than $10 million a year in sales. Imagine keeping these customers over their lifetimes! Indeed, customers are valuable.

Customer value must be integrated into all retail operations. Retailers provide value when they adopt a customer-oriented approach. Value must be present when creating customer service. The retailer must create value when communicating price to customers. In addition, value must be communicated to customers through effective integrated marketing communication (IMC). Perhaps the greatest need for the concept of value is through the use of customer retention marketing. Finally, remember that value must be communicated to *all* members of the retailer's channel of distribution.

SERVICES RETAILING

The services industry comprises a diverse range of retail businesses. Banks, credit unions, airlines, hotels and motels, many transportation companies, lawn care companies, restaurants, and even your university are services retailers. Although these retailers do not sell products in the typical sense, most are heavily involved in logistics systems and transport, distribute, and utilize various types of physical goods. Governments and charities often describe themselves as being in the services industry. Organizations set up as not for profit, as well as those set up for profit, are involved in the acquisition and distribution of services to end users.

The services sector showed huge growth during the 1990s and early 2000s, and by 2001 it employed more than 41 million people. In the United States, employment in the services sector increased 44.4 percent between 1991 and 2001, whereas the rest of the economy grew only 22.1 percent. Services sector employment is projected to grow 2.9 percent per year through the year 2010.[12] In addition, the average hourly wage of workers in the services sector ($14.67 in 2001) is above the average for all workers ($14.32 in 2001), and the average workweek is 32.7 hours.[13] In the year 2000, around 38 million people were employed in the services sector, making it the largest of the nine industry classifications for the U.S. government.[14]

SERVICES RETAILING DEFINED

Because of the large numbers of individuals and businesses involved in services retailing, it is beneficial to operationally define what we would consider a service business. An abridged definition would deal with the actual ownership of the outputs from service retailers. In **services retailing,** customers rarely take permanent ownership of anything tangible; rather, needs satisfiers are generated from the performance of the retailer.

services retailing A type of retailing in which the "product" being sold is actually a service; the customer derives value from the "service product" that is provided.

Suppose you are in Manhattan (New York City) and want to get from Greenwich Village to midtown. You have several options, but a taxi seems like the quickest way. The taxi company that owns the taxi you hire is a service retailer allowing you to have temporary ownership in the length of the ride. You don't want to buy the cab just to travel 25 to 30 blocks; rather, you want to use the taxi temporarily. The value you receive is the relatively fast trip down Broadway into midtown and the fact that you don't have to expend your energy by walking. Thus, services offer customers value that usually perishes once the service is completed.

Services retailing should not be confused with customer service that is provided to customers. The difference is that in the case of services retailing, the "product" being sold is actually a service. Thus, the customer derives value from the "service product" that was provided. As an example, consider gift wrapping. Although the physical act of gift wrapping is a service, what the consumer is really buying is the physical gift enclosed in the wrapping, not the wrapping itself. Another example is the installation of an air-conditioning unit. The consumer is actually buying the unit, not the installation. The installation is a value-added (or profit-generating) service that complements the physical good. On the other hand, if a consumer goes to Holiday Hair for a haircut, the primary motive for the trip is the haircut itself; thus, the "product" is the service performed.

TANGIBILITY VERSUS INTANGIBILITY

To observe the differences between products and services, it is useful to utilize a continuum, or spectrum, based on the degree of tangibility. G. Lynn Shostack[15] proposed such a model, presented in Figure 2.2.

The products and services are positioned on the spectrum based on their level of tangibility. The more tangible the products and services are, the

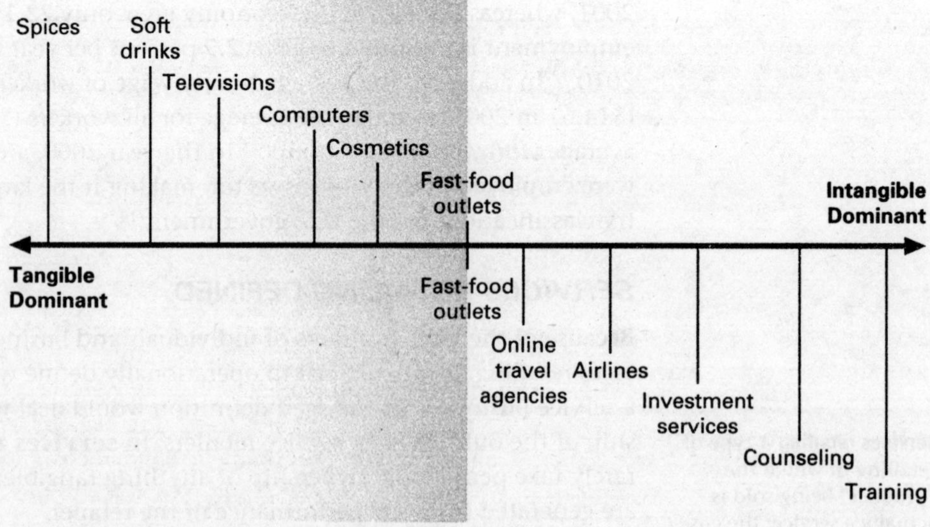

FIGURE 2.2 **Continuum of Tangible and Intangible Elements in Goods and Services** (Source: Adapted from G. Lynn Shostack, "Breaking Free from Product Marketing," *Journal of Marketing*, 41 [April 1977], p. 77. Reprinted by permission of the American Marketing Association.)

Service retailers may not sell tangible products; therefore, the performance of the retailer is extremely important. FTD is a service retailer that uses independent florists that adhere to the highest quality and service standards to provide same-day delivery of floral orders to people in nearly every area of the United States.

NO TIME TO THINK ABOUT VALENTINE'S DAY?

MAKE IT EASY. PLAY IT SMART.

February 14th may be circled in red on your calendar but somehow it always seems to arrive out of the blue. This year, don't sweat it. With flowers from FTD, you'll be her hero without the hassle.

Play her suave romantic lead or just play it smart. FTD has hundreds of floral bouquets to choose from, as well as other unique gift ideas like chocolate, teddy bears and sure-to-please spa gifts. And if Valentine's Day takes you by surprise—relax. FTD has same-day flower delivery. FTD florists will take good care of your flowers and deliver just what you ordered. No surprises. Except a special one for her.

Visit an FTD florist, dial 1-800-SEND-FTD, or shop online at FTD.COM. Come on guys, don't get blindsided by Friday, February 14th. Visit, call or click FTD. You'll be glad you did. And so will she.

VISIT AN FTD FLORIST — FTD.COM — 1-800-SEND-FTD

higher they are placed on the tangible, dominant end of the spectrum. The lower the tangibility, the closer the products and services fall toward the intangible dominant area. Thus, very tangible products, such as soft drinks and spices, would be perceived as highly tangible dominant, whereas teaching and investment management would be seen as highly intangible dominant.

Although services are not new to consumers, the academic study of services retailing is relatively young. Early researchers in services marketing created four main differences between service and product marketing. The researchers focused on the *intangibility of services*, the *heterogeneity of services*, the *perishability of output*, and the *simultaneity of production and consumption* of the service.[16] In this regard, one could look back at the Shostack model for intangibility of the product (or service) offering. The more intangible the offering, the more likely that it is a service. Similarly, with the heterogeneity of the service, the more variable (or heterogeneous) the offering, the more likely that it is a service.

Perishability refers to how long the offering lasts. In services retailing, the product begins to perish almost immediately.

Finally, services are produced and consumed at (relatively) the same time. Once a plane takes off and begins to make its way to its final destination, the consumption of that service has started. Thus, services provide for production and consumption of the offering almost simultaneously.

DIFFERENCES BETWEEN GOODS AND SERVICES

Recent work in this area has increased the number of variables that help differentiate between services and physical goods. Christopher Lovelock proposes eight areas of differentiation between physical goods and services (see Table 2.3).[17]

The *nature of the product* refers to a product being a physical object, whereas a service is seen more as a "performance."[18] With services, there is often more *interaction between the retailer and the customer* because the *customer is involved in the actual production of the service.* In services retailing, the customer becomes *part of the product.* For example, it is the customer's money that is actually loaned to a bank; the bank provides a secure place for the deposit of the money. The customer, in turn, states preferences as to where to place the money, such as in a certificate of deposit (CD) account, a checking with savings account, a money market account, or a savings account. The customer thus develops the product in conjunction with the bank's personnel.

Because the customer is involved and often is part of the service offering, and because the service is created at the time of delivery, there are many *quality control problems* for the retailer. The service cannot be checked or regulated prior to being sold. On the airline flight discussed earlier, the customer may have one or more unpleasant experiences, such as air turbulence, surly flight attendants, a cold meal, or delay or even cancellation of the flight. However, the customer does not know how the flight will turn out prior to boarding and actually consuming the service.

TABLE 2.3

LOVELOCK'S DIFFERENTIATION BETWEEN PHYSICAL GOODS AND SERVICES

1. The nature of the product
2. Customer/Retailer interaction and involvement in the production process
3. People as part of the product
4. Greater difficulties in maintaining quality control standards
5. Harder for customers to evaluate
6. Absence of inventories
7. Relative importance of the time factor
8. Structure and nature of distribution channels

Source: Services Marketing 3e by Lovelock, ©1996. Reprinted by permission of Pearson Education, Upper Saddle River, NJ.

It is often *hard for the consumer to evaluate the service* received from a service retailer. Think of the last time you used a repairperson. The only way you could evaluate the service provided was by operating the unit to verify that it worked after the repair. You probably knew little about the replacement parts you paid for. You also had no way of knowing if someone else could have done a better job (and perhaps charged a lower price). Because of such factors, services involve some risk to the customer.

In services retailing, the retailer *keeps no inventory* since the service is intangible. The problem this creates in the retailing of services is the possibility of stockouts. For example, customers in Buffalo, New York, may have a hard time finding someone to shovel their driveways after a heavy snowfall because all snow removal personnel are tied up with other customers. In this case, the snow removal service experiences a temporary stockout, resulting in a displeased or even angry customer.

Conversely, there are times when the services retailer may have too many employees "on the clock" with nothing to do. Suppose a drought in Indiana has slowed down growth of people's lawns. In this situation, providers of lawn-cutting services are likely to find themselves with too many employees, because the lawns need to be cut less often than normal.

Today's customers are demanding and do not like to wait to receive a service. Therefore, the *time factor* becomes extremely important. Because services are performed in "real time," the retailer must understand that there are limits to the customer's patience and willingness to wait. For example, when people go out to eat, they are typically willing to wait only about 10 minutes for a table. If many restaurants with similar offerings are available, the need to wait is lessened. Thus, service retailers must provide the service expeditiously to retain their customers.

Finally, services use *different channels of distribution*. Often services can be distributed electronically, such as e-tickets at an airport kiosk or hotel reservations via a personal computer.

THE SERVICESCAPE

With this in mind, retailers need to create unique strategies and tactics to ensure that they are meeting customers' needs and wants. Although services retailing follows the same basic flow that product retailing does, some modifications are necessary in the actual execution of the IRM plan.

Mary Jo Bitner suggests that the design of the services retailer's physical environment will play a major role in differentiating that retailer from competitors. This physical environment design is called a *servicescape*.[19] Much like a landscape, a **servicescape** encompasses all the variables of the service operation that are visible to consumers, including facilities, personnel, equipment, and the service's customers.

servicescape All the variables of the service operation that are visible to consumers, including facilities, personnel, equipment, and the service's customers.

SERVICES RETAILING ADJUSTMENTS

Due to the differences between retailing a physical good and retailing a service, some adjustments to operations are suggested in the areas of human resource supervision, customer involvement, pricing, and control and evaluation.

GLOBAL RETAILING

Disney Faces Illness Aboard Cruise Ships

Many of the differences between goods and services as described by Christopher Lovelock became apparent when The Walt Disney Company experienced problems with its cruise ships. Disney, a global corporation, faced a service provider's nightmare when an outbreak of the Norwalk virus sickened more than 200 passengers on the *Disney Magic* cruise ship. The virus causes nausea, vomiting, diarrhea, and abdominal pain. Disney offered to fly sick passengers home, but only one couple accepted. This was the second outbreak in a month on the *Disney Magic*. Although federal health officials declared the ship safe, Disney chose to cancel the following cruise so that the ship could be thoroughly disinfected. This marked the first time that Disney had to cancel a voyage since the company began offering cruises in 1998.

The disinfection process includes cleaning surfaces with bleach or other chemicals and steaming or discarding things that cannot be disinfected. In this case, Disney discarded all mattresses and pillows. The sheets, towels, and pillowcases were washed in 160-degree water. Stuffed animals, available in gift shops, were washed, then stored in warehouses for thirty days before going back on shelves. In an effort to keep customer satisfaction high, Disney offered sick passengers a free future cruise. Those people affected by the cancellation received refunds and half-price offers for a future cruise.

In the case of a cruise, the customer takes part in developing the final product, so when a customer becomes sick during the experience, the satisfaction level can drop. In addition, the perishability of services and quality of the experience present control challenges for services retailers, whose "products" are more intangible than tangible.

Sources: Denise Grady, "U.S. Health Officials Call Cruise Ships Safe, in Spite of Outbreaks," *New York Times*, November 28, 2002 (East Coast edition), p. 32; Jim Buynak, "Disney Ships' Illness Grows; 40 More Passengers, One Crewmember Report Sick," *Knight Ridder Tribune Business News*, November 29, 2002, p. 1; Sandra Pedicini, "Disney Magic Returns After More Passengers Become Ill," *Knight Ridder Tribune Business News*, November 30, 2002, p. 1.

HUMAN RESOURCES. Services retailing requires a greater emphasis on human resources than does product retailing. Closer supervision of sales and service personnel is necessary. Because of the specialized nature of performing services (think of airline pilots), minimizing employee turnover is more important. Although not always practiced, the salary of service personnel usually should be higher. To maintain control and ensure quality, the service retailer needs to conduct employee performance reviews more frequently. Finally, employee scheduling needs to be flexible; thus, more time needs to be spent on this function in services retailing than in product retailing.

CUSTOMER INVOLVEMENT IN THE PRODUCTION OF SERVICES. One of the differentiating aspects of services retailing is that at times the customer is part of the service output. Think of an amusement park. Part of the fun is the hustle and bustle of the park. Participating with other patrons in the rides, games, and other attractions heightens one's experience. In this way, customers become part of the service experience. Because of this, there must be more involvement by customers in the production of the service.

Customers must be continually evaluated for their level of satisfaction with the offered service. Frequent customer feedback helps ensure that the quality of the service is acceptable.

PRICING OF SERVICES. The pricing of services is somewhat harder than the pricing of physical goods. Many service retailers provide estimates of what the service will cost. A related concern is that services generally are based not on price but on one of the other controllable marketing variables, such as the channel of distribution, location, and service value. It is difficult to calculate the value of a service (quality of the service relative to the price). Therefore, value is often defined by the customer: the customer establishes the real value by choosing to patronize or not patronize a particular retailer.

Closely tied to pricing is the retailer's integrated marketing communication (IMC). Because services are intangible, customers have a hard time identifying service value. In that regard, it may be important to link the service with physical goods. This is a good argument for cross-selling services and products. Many service providers, such as portrait photographers, house painters, and hair salons, offer "before" and "after" pictures to help create value in their customers' minds. An additional determinant of value in services retailing is the prestige associated with the service itself or the service domain.

SERVICE PRICE ADJUSTMENTS. Complaints about services need special attention. Customers cannot return a service once it has been performed. Because of this, many service retailers offer fairly liberal price adjustments for unsatisfactory service performance. The service retailer must have *specific,* written information about these types of service price adjustments. Many offer to redo the service if it is not satisfactory. For example, when a plumber comes to the house to fix a leaking faucet and gets the dripping to stop, the customer is satisfied. But what if the faucet starts leaking again a few months later? Should the plumber provide a second repair job at no charge to the customer? Should the plumber offer to make a follow-up visit to make sure the faucet is still working properly? The solution is up to the plumber service. Services retailers must keep in mind that an unhappy customer is likely to talk to others about the unsatisfactory service experience, and the retailer's reputation could be jeopardized if the problem is not addressed and fixed.

CONTROL AND EVALUATION OF SERVICES. Control and evaluation is difficult for services retailers. Because employees represent the services retailer, the service provider has a greater chance of losing good employees to its competitors. Likewise, in services retailing it is easier to steal customers than in product retailing. For example, a new airline may exploit the weaknesses of other airlines in an attempt to lure leisure travelers. Therefore, services retailers would be wise to develop both employee and customer loyalty programs. An example of a customer loyalty program is the Blockbuster Rewards Gold Program, in which members get points for renting videos and can redeem the points for free movies. Examples of employee loyalty programs include gifts based on service anniversaries and trips awarded for outstanding performance.

The overall IRM program set up by the services retailer must be evaluated. Although the services retailer can use some of the same evaluative tools that product retailers use, certain problems are unique to services retailing. For example, there are no (or limited) inventories; thus, inventory turn cannot be measured. In addition, services are labor intensive; thus, personnel costs are generally higher. Services retailers should use cost accounting, which allows them to assign costs for services performed. Using a costing system along with a return on net worth ratio provides the services retailer with better information than do many of the other techniques used for product retailing.

A services retailer's profit should be generated after the costs of labor are factored in (thus replacing the gross margin for products). Recordkeeping for each job performed is essential. It allows the retailer to see how much profit was generated from each job and makes estimations of costs quoted to customers more accurate. Finally, records for sales support personnel, a non-revenue generating function, should be kept separate from records used to record revenue production.

As we have seen, although services retailers can use a generic IRM flow chart to develop their retail plans, they must be aware of the differences in the ways they execute their tactics, manage, and evaluate and control.

CREATING RELATIONSHIPS

According to Earl Naumann, a consultant specializing in customer satisfaction:

> Customers are not targets! Customers are probably a firm's most valuable asset, and they should be nurtured, developed, and treated accordingly. Each and every customer should be the objective of proactive, bonding relationships. And customers, in person, should be integrated into the firm's decision-making processes.[20]

To develop and keep a loyal customer base, retailers must build relationships with their customers. When developing a relationship strategy, the customer must be integrated into the retailer's overall strategic direction. Thus, objectives and strategies must be customer focused.

Solid customer relationships provide long-term, loyal customers. "[T]he longer a customer stays with a company, the more that customer is worth. Long-term customers buy more, take less of a company's time, are less sensitive to price, and bring in new shoppers. Best of all, they have no acquisition or start-up cost."[21] A major concern to retailers should be customer retention. According to Lois Geller, partner and president of Mason & Geller LLC/Direct Marketing in New York City, some large companies report that 95 percent of profits come from long-term customers.

Customer retention is important to retailers because when a customer leaves, it costs the retailer three to seven times more money to get a new customer than to retain the current customer.[22] Table 2.4 lists the fifteen elements that should be incorporated into customer retention strategies according to Lois Geller.

TABLE 2.4

FIFTEEN ELEMENTS TO INCREASE CUSTOMER RETENTION

1. *Deliver a high-quality, high-value product.* Because a product represents a particular company, retailers must make sure that the product or service fulfills and exceeds expectations.
2. *Make every single contact count.* Every contact with the customer is important. Retailers must make sure that all points of contact with the customer make positive impressions.
3. *Know your customers.* Successful retailers use marketing database resources to build a customer file so they know which customers are buying, what they are buying, and how much they are spending.
4. *Know when customers defect.* Retailers should have some type of flag in their system that goes off when a long-standing customer stops buying from them. A method to woo back customers is to send these customers a note reminding them of how much their business is appreciated. Retailers should try to find out the reasons customers leave so that these areas can be improved.
5. *Keep the company at the top of customer's minds.* Successful retailers develop an integrated marketing communication program that keeps them in touch with customers and customers thinking of their business.
6. *Modify your product/service mix.* Retailers should make the product/service mix exciting for customers. A business could try different arrangements that will catch customers' attention.
7. *Always close the loop in marketing programs.* Retailers must continuously improve tracking of results and implement changes that will improve effectiveness.
8. *Deliver excellent customer service.* Customers want to be treated with respect. If there are problems, it's important for retailers to listen and respond quickly.
9. *Keep customer retention programs human.* Customer retention programs should be made more personable to show customers that the retailer is empathetic to customer desires.
10. *Use partnerships to build customer retention.* By partnering with other companies to provide benefits for customers, retailers can increase loyalty.
11. *Do the unexpected.* Many times customers do not expect to be treated well. Retailers can take customers by surprise with excellent service after the sale. One example is a retailer who sends thank you notes or telephones customers to find out how they liked their purchase.
12. *Use databases to maximize the personalization of offers.* When retailers learn about their customers' buying habits, they can use direct-mailing efforts to personalize their appeals.
13. *Identify the timing and frequency of customer promotions.* Customer databases can be used to help deliver timely information to customers.
14. *Utilize retail and catalog synergies.* Multiple distribution strategies can be used to improve customer retention.
15. *Incorporate online marketing into the strategy.* A retailer can keep the store open 24/7 by integrating Internet selling into its strategy.

Source: Lois Geller, "Customer Retention Begins with the Basics," *Direct Marketing,* September 1997, pp. 58–62. Reprinted by permission of Hoke Communications, Inc.

Retailers must also strive to create positive working relationships with suppliers. Effective management of the supply chain translates into increased retailer productivity and greater profitability. Supply chain management is discussed in more detail in Chapter 9 when the concept of logistics is explored.

Many other methods can be utilized to create long-term relationships with customers; we will discuss some of these methods in Chapter 13 when we integrate customer retention and customer service. For now, bear in mind that long-term relationships are essential in developing and adding value to the retail organization.

TECHNOLOGY IN RETAILING AND E-TAILING

retail technology Any tool that helps retailers succeed in carrying out strategy.

Technology is any tool that helps one succeed in a given endeavor. **Retail technology** is any tool that helps a retailer succeed in carrying out strategy. Advances in the technological environment are important to retailers for many reasons, one of which is customer value. Retail technology can be used to create customer relationships and to integrate and develop effective retailing operations. Although technology is covered throughout the textbook, there are some general concepts of technology that we should address at this time.

Technology in retailing can manifest itself in many areas. For example, integrated marketing communications (IMC) benefit by allowing for, among other things, digital photography, direct marketing, database use, videoconferencing, and in-store telecommunications. In addition, technologies can help develop and monitor the retailer's customer value and retention strategies and executions.

Technology is used for forecasting and the development of financial and accounting systems. In addition, technology can be used for service retailing, e-tailing, franchising, and market segmentation. Other uses of technology include electronic data interchange (EDI), electronic fund transfers, point-of-sale information, and perpetual inventory systems.

Technology has been developed for many areas of logistics, including inventory replenishment, inventory management, customer relationships, and geographic information systems. Optimal store atmospheres as well as retail audits can be managed with the assistance of technology. In short, technology offers the retailer new and exciting ways to expand on existing or future market opportunities.

E-TAILING AND E-COMMERCE

Today very few successful retailers fail to use some form of technology in their day-to-day business operations. More than 100,000 companies have Internet addresses, and more than 20,000 companies have homepages on the Internet.[23]

Many retailers now adopt strategies of e-tailing along with traditional retailing. E-commerce, on the other hand, utilizes the Internet and cyberspace to assist in the operation of a business (not retailing specifically, but any business). To most casual Internet surfers, e-commerce means shopping online. To a workaholic, it may mean accessing Amazon.com to buy a birthday or anniversary present, saving the time it would take to "physically" shop.[24] Businesses may view the Internet as an advanced communications medium

INTERNET IN ACTION

A Brief History of E-commerce and E-tailing

The Internet started out in 1969 as a private communications system created for the U.S. Department of Defense. Since its initial development, the Internet has evolved into a communications medium used by individuals and companies for research and to convey company and product information as well as to sell products and services. During the 1970s and 1980s, the system increased in power, convenience, and speed. The latter half of the 1990s saw the Internet erupt into an economic platform that began to alter business strategies and business development. The Internet gave a platform to e-commerce that had never existed before.

Electronic commerce, or e-commerce, allegedly started about 125 to 130 years ago with the use of Western Union's money transfer system. It expanded with the development of credit cards during the late 1900s. In the early to mid-1980s, the ATM (automated teller machine) was developed and gave e-commerce another large push.

On the supply side, e-commerce evolved from two movements facilitated by the Internet. The first was the decrease in costs of long-distance calling. The second was the increased use of database management software and corporate intranets that streamlined the purchasing process for many large, progressive companies. On the demand side, the development of e-mail increased access to business and e-tailer networks. Because most customer service contact activities had become routine, e-tailers found this service could be provided effectively with a computerized process, saving time and money for both consumer and e-tailer. Thus, electronic systems have changed the way we do business in the twenty-first century.

that reduces transaction costs. In reality, all of these may be reasons to use e-commerce, but by no means are they all-inclusive.

Technology has changed the way the world operates. E-commerce gives users/customers online capabilities that they have never enjoyed. It also provides retailers with more capabilities than ever before. Retailers can develop computerized functions that allow them to eliminate some service workers, thus reducing costs and potential errors. Technology can help reduce risk and capital tie-ups. It can help create and keep customers, and increase the value of the entire retail operation. E-commerce has seen rapid development and execution.

Some examples of successful exploitation of e-tailing and e-commerce would include electronic filing of income taxes, online billing for services and products, and financing and delivery of goods and services with follow-up services necessary to create customer loyalty. Customers can track the movement of their orders for goods and services using the Internet.

E-tailing includes buying and selling items over the Internet, using credit and debit cards, and facilitating the integration of all retail functions. The Internet provides an easy way to bring buyers and sellers together at a reasonable cost. Even "resellers" have availed themselves of the Internet. eBay, the company that hosts the "world's largest garage sale," allows its customers the luxury of shopping at any time of the day at an economical cost (depending on who is buying and what their definition of *economical* is).

E-tailers can instantaneously create pages of data on price elasticity for their customers while looking at marginal costs and product availability. Technology has played, and will continue to play, a large role in the development of better retail practices.

ECONOMIC IMPACT OF E-TAILING AND E-COMMERCE

E-tailing and e-commerce contribute to perceived value by consumers. Retailers and consumers thousands of miles away from each other can complete business transactions in a matter of seconds. Information can be exchanged within retail organizations or between retailers and consumers. Although technology is accessible worldwide, the U.S. economy has generated larger increases from the use of technology than most other countries have. Perhaps this is due to policies that encourage the free market system and the exchange of communications. When allowed to compete in a cyberworld, retailers can generate savings through economies of scale. The more buyers there are, the cheaper the product or service per unit.

Computer prices have rapidly declined, allowing retailers to replace labor with capital resources. Because the prices of computers are significantly lower than just a few years ago, many more people have access to cyberspace through their PCs. Retailers can develop retention and customer value tactics that take advantage of the increasing numbers of PC users. Due in part to falling prices, the U.S. inflation rate declined from 1994 to 1998. In addition, in the early 2000s the United States suffered an economic slowdown. However, because technology investments are driven not by product competition but by competition to advance sales and reduce expenses, revenues increase. Technological processes allow for a reduction in inventories due to forecasting and faster production and distribution that increase efficiency. Thus, there will be fewer inventories on hand during recessionary periods.

When all of these benefits are summed, the U.S. economy will most likely continue to move to higher levels of creative economic expansion.

We have seen that e-tailing and e-commerce are good for the economy. What are their major advantages for retailers?

ADVANTAGES OF E-TAILING AND E-COMMERCE

The greatest advantage that e-tailing provides to retailers is speed. Think about the last time you did research for a term paper. Chances are you used the Internet to help you gather information for your paper. Why didn't you just walk over to the library and physically go through the shelves? Most likely because of the time-consuming nature of that process compared to conducting research online. Similarly, the World Wide Web (WWW) and the Internet allow retailers to exchange messages and complete business transactions almost instantaneously. Even slow connections are faster than the old method of "call and talk." In addition, customers can find almost any product they want via e-tailers. Information can be updated immediately, thus reducing the communications problems common when relying on outdated information. Marketing executions and promotions can be changed frequently if needed. Customer relationships can be solidified using cybermarketing.

Another advantage of e-tailing is cost savings. Electronic commerce reduces costs for business expenses such as printing, postage, marketing, distribution, personnel, phones, and packaging. Many of the physical plant costs associated with operating a brick-and-mortar retail outlet can be reduced or eliminated through e-tailing, allowing the e-tailer to reinvest in other business operations such as additional marketing and pricing. E-commerce has also lowered many of the entrance barriers for potential retailers.

To customers, the most important advantage of these technologies may be pricing. Prospective buyers simply surf the Net to find the lowest-cost product available. In addition to realizing a cost savings, customers don't have to spend their time physically looking for the product.

The cost benefits for consumers may put the e-tailer in a disadvantageous position, however. Competing on price drives prices down, thus potentially reducing profit margins. A solid tactical execution would be to make sure the e-tail sales systems downplay price and are not used as a competitive advantage by competitors (unless the e-tailer really does have the lowest prices available). The effect of price competition could actually mean a loss of sales and a reduction in the e-tailer's profit margins. E-tailers must utilize tactics other than price to drive sales. These tactics might include convenience, customer service, and promotions, among others. All of these functions need to be integrated in e-tailing just as in a typical brick-and-mortar business.

Doing business in cyberspace helps eliminate national boundaries. Drawing power can be increased, as well as market size. E-tailers conduct business all over the world, not just in their own backyards. Distance as a barrier to international retailing is almost eliminated in e-tailing, except for shipping costs. The international retailer must pay attention to the systems used by other global retailers. Ethics and laws become important restraints in e-tailing. National customs and buying behavior are also important areas of awareness for the international e-tailer. Finally, e-tailers need to create separate customer retention and customer value executions for each of their international markets.

Conducting business in cyberspace breaks down international boundaries. The Coca-Cola Company has over eighty websites that cater to the language and customs of different areas of the world. (Coca-Cola, the Dynamic Ribbon, and the Contour Bottle are registered trademarks of The Coca-Cola Company.)

DISADVANTAGES OF E-TAILING/E-COMMERCE

E-tailing and e-commerce also have many disadvantages. The largest disadvantages involve consumer privacy and security. Consumers are very concerned about their privacy and about how retailer information is used. In addition, they are concerned about the security of shopping online. Anything sent over the Internet passes through many different computers before it reaches its final destination. Because of this, the entire channel of communication needs to have security measures in place.

Consumers are concerned that hackers may access their credit card or bank account information, resulting in potential damaged credit ratings and financial loss. To minimize this problem, retailers should develop encryption systems where needed. An **encryption system** codes data so that the data can be understood only by the intended user. Many encryption systems have been developed for e-tailing. This security measure is crucial for an e-tailer's success.

encryption system A system that codes data so that the data can be understood only by the intended user.

Another disadvantage in e-commerce is the pitfalls in establishing and maintaining a website. Although it may seem that setting up a "simple" website would be inexpensive, the opposite may in fact be true. Experts are needed to help develop and create the site, as well as to make the site workable. If the developer lacks expertise in HTML, CGI scripting, ODBC, JAVA, and other Web development features, the website may actually drive away customers instead of increasing the customer base—and sales. An informational website must be evaluated and updated frequently. A transaction management website is even more complex and needs continuous evaluation and control.

For e-tailing efforts to succeed, top management must make e-tailing a priority. Because of rapidly changing technologies, websites and other methods of e-tailing must continuously be monitored and changed. Retail managers must adapt and be willing to change with the times.

As technology advances, retailers need to develop new uses to increase sales while reducing costs. An emphasis should be placed on customers and customer value to create and maintain the all-important retailer-customer relationship.

LAWS, ETHICS, AND CORPORATE SOCIAL RESPONSIBILITY

In developing an understanding of customer value and retention, the retailer must be aware that ethics and corporate social responsibility have an impact on the customer–retailer relationship. It is very hard to repair the bond between customer and retailer once that trust is broken. Because retailers are always in the public eye, ensuring that they operate in an ethically and socially responsible manner is a challenge.

Ethical behavior helps develop relationships and trust, and increases profits and sales. In addition, by operating ethically, managers and employees feel positive about themselves and about their companies. Think about people you know who treat you fairly and with respect and those whom you feel you can't trust. With whom would you more likely want to do business? The same principles hold for retailing. Customer trust means long-term, loyal customers, which means greater sales and stability.

LAWS AND ETHICS

Although laws and ethics are covered in detail in Chapter 14, the topic has great importance for customer value. The many corporate scandals that dominated the news during the early 2000s caused business ethics to come under public scrutiny, perhaps more than at any other time in recent history. Add to this the pressure retailers face in generating same-store sales and increased profit reports, and an environment is created that lends itself to questionable retail practices. Although very few retailers are known to engage in unethical practices, the actions of just a few affect many employees, consumers, and other companies. To make it through tough financial times, a company can opt to file for bankruptcy, a form of which provides a retailer protection from its creditors.

Blunders or Best Practices?

What's in a Name? The Toy Wars

Seven young Austrians who wanted to use the Web as a vehicle to display art and their view of corporate America created etoy (singular, not plural) in 1994. In 1999, eToys, the online toy retailer, sued the founders of etoy because they believed the etoy name and online site confused their customers.

Many in the online community were upset and consequently launched "virtual" attacks on the eToys website. These denial of service (DOS) attacks locked out customers during the holiday retail season, dropping availability by 2 percent. As a result, eToys dropped the lawsuit. According to Sean M. Dugan of *InfoWorld*, the eToys lawsuit was a blunder because it "smacks of a big-money corporation using its muscle to push around the little guy." eToys filed for bankruptcy protection in 2002, but the etoy website is still active. Perhaps this blunder turned out to be a best practice for a site that no one had ever heard of before the lawsuit.

Here is the etoy disclaimer taken from the company's website:

> From the moment of market introduction in 1994, etoy has been fully dedicated to the Internet. The dot.com brand (etoy.com) amounts to much more than a common website: over the past years etoy established its own experimental universe in and around the famous domain www.etoy.com and developed hundreds of insane digital tools, its own terminology and value system to research and extend the limits of the digital through the excessive use of technology and human resources.
>
> While every precaution has been taken in the preparation of this venture, the etoy.CORPORATION assumes no responsibility for misunderstandings, confusion and dangerous mutations, or for any kind of damages resulting from the perception of experimental etoy.CODE and related media viruses.

Sources: Archie Cotterell, "Web-warfare in Cyberspace," *The Spectator* (London), June 29, 2002, pp. 41–42; Sean M. Dugan, "The War over a Single Letter—eToys vs. etoy and Civil Disobedience Protests via the Web," *InfoWorld* (online edition), retrieved September 2002 from www.infoworld.com.

Retail organizations must ensure they follow sound ethical standards. Retailers should stick to their codes of ethics and do what is right for the consumer and society. In the long run, ethical retail practices pay off both financially and in the creation of customer value. A strong example of ethics in retailing is JCPenney Company, founded on James Cash Penney's work ethic and social philosophy of taking good care of the customers and the community.[25] The stores' employees still follow this work ethic. Ethics may be even more important to e-tailers and those engaged in e-commerce activities that do not involve sales. Conducting business over the Web creates many opportunities to engage in questionable business practices or even fraud.

CORPORATE SOCIAL RESPONSIBILITY (CSR)

corporate social responsibility (CSR) The commitment of business to contribute to sustainable economic development, working with employees, their families, the local community, and society at large to improve their quality of life.

The World Business Council for Sustainable Development defines **corporate social responsibility (CSR)** as "the commitment of business to contribute to sustainable economic development, working with employees, their families, the local community and society at large to improve their quality of life."[26] In essence, corporate social responsibility makes business a partner with the community to improve society. This in turn strengthens the relationship between the retailer and its customers and increases the value of the firm.

Figure 2.3 illustrates the relationship of businesses in society. The figure shows that businesses must answer to two primary aspects of their operations: (1) the quality of their management and (2) their impact on society in the marketplace, workplace, environment, and community.

More and more companies are realizing that they improve their company image when they work to improve their communities. By recognizing the interdependence of businesses and society, retailers can make a positive

More and more companies are realizing the importance of corporate social responsibility. This photo shows Habitat for Humanity volunteers helping to build a home.

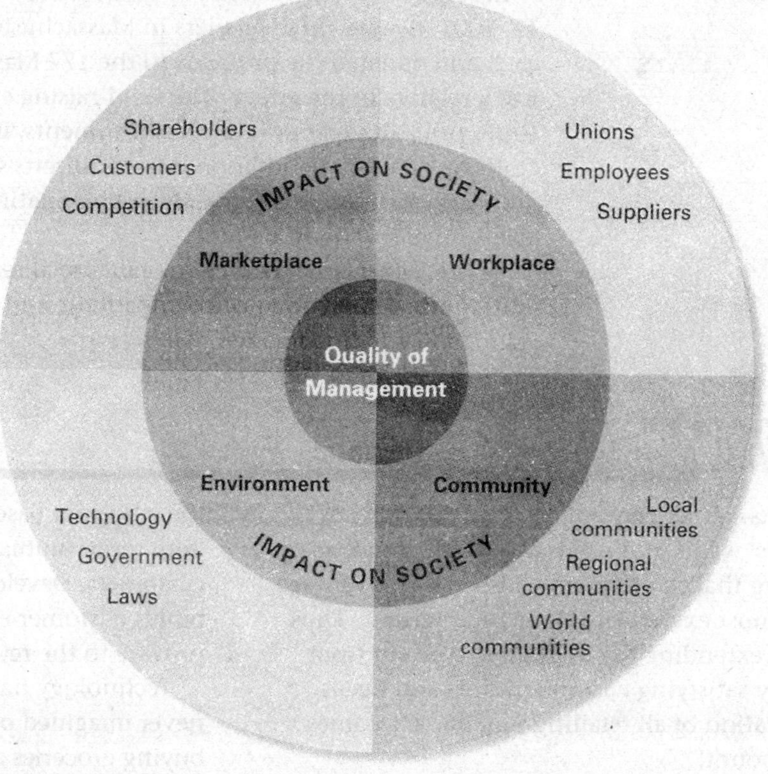

FIGURE 2.3 **Business in Society** (Source: Mallen Baker, "Corporate Social Responsibility—What Does It Mean?" retrieved January 2003 from www.mallenbaker.net. Reprinted by permission.)

impact. For example, in July 2002, Citibank, the global financial services company, announced that the Citigroup Foundation awarded a $1 million grant to Habitat for Humanity International (HFHI), a nonprofit organization dedicated to building homes for people who cannot otherwise afford a home. Citibank had also awarded two previous grants to HFHI, for a total of $3 million. More than 6,000 employees in 20 states volunteered 64,000 hours to build 63 homes homes for HFHI. Citibank believes that a stronger commitment to the community is good for the company because it increases employer, customer, and shareholder loyalty.[27]

Cy's Work Clothes of Troy, Michigan, provides another example of CSR. Cyril Feldman, president of Cy's Work Clothes, wanted to do something about the tight budgets that many schools were experiencing. The company developed a program that allows schools in need of lab, shop, and specialty work wear to buy the clothing for below-wholesale prices. The cost-savings programs help schools get the clothing necessary to ensure safety in the labs and classrooms.[28]

In response to the terrorist attacks on the World Trade Center on September 11, 2001, twenty-three retailers in Massachusetts sold American flags for $1 each and donated the proceeds to the 177 Massachusetts families who had lost a relative in the attack. The fund-raising effort involved more than 900 stores from all types of retail establishments, including grocery, furniture, and clothing retailers. In addition, Massachusetts's newspapers, television stations, and radio stations joined the effort by donating free air time to publicize the event.[29]

As these examples show, corporate social responsibility can help ensure that customers view companies as empathetic and understanding of societal needs.

SUMMARY

The marketing concept means satisfying customers' wants and needs at a profit. Retailers are finding that to maintain competitive advantage, they must exceed customer expectations. Thus, when extending the marketing concept from merely satisfying customer wants and needs, integration of all retailing functions becomes paramount.

Because the world of retailing is constantly changing, retail professionals must be up to date on the latest techniques and theories that affect (both positively and negatively) the retail firm. Understanding customer value allows retailers to incorporate consumers' wants and needs into their integrated retail management plans. Without this understanding, a retailer is at a competitive disadvantage.

It is important to distinguish between providing services and being a service retailer. In services retailing, the product being sold is a service. Most retailers provide some type of service beyond their core offerings, but they are not services retailers if their core offerings are tangible as opposed to intangible.

Because customers are demanding more and more service from retailers, an understanding of the customer base can help the retailer create long-term, mutually beneficial relationships with customers. Developing customer relationships builds customer equity, the value that customers provide to the retailer.

Technology has created capabilities that were never imagined possible. From online banking to buying groceries and other products online, e-tailing is becoming an increasingly important channel of distribution. It is important for retailing professionals to stay current with all the changing technologies and to understand the difference between selling tangible products versus intangible services (services retailing) as well as the impact of technology on their retail businesses.

As we move forward into the twenty-first century, ethics and social responsibility will play an increasing role in retailers' visions and missions. The development and implementation of a sound work ethic for employees and stakeholders will become paramount for success. Ethics and social responsibility build stronger communities, increase profits and sales, and develop positive, long-term relationships. They also make retail employees feel positive about themselves and the firms they work for.

KEY TERMS

marketing concept (30)
extended marketing concept (30)
relationship marketing (30)
value (31)
QSP (32)
equity (33)
name equity (33)
customer equity (33)
brand equity (33)
brand associations (33)
services retailing (35)
servicescape (39)
retail technology (44)
encryption system (48)
corporate social responsibility (CSR) (50)

QUESTIONS FOR DISCUSSION

1. What are some ways retailers can exceed customer expectations?
2. What is your definition of *customer value*? Compare your definition with a classmate's. How are the two definitions similar? How are they different?
3. Name a business that values you as a customer. How long have you patronized this business? What makes you continue to shop there?
4. Is it easier for a retailer that has a physical location to provide good customer service than it is for a retailer with a Web-based location? Explain your answer.

E-TAILING EXERCISE

Go to the following websites:

www.jcpenney.com (JCPenney)
www.dell.com (Dell Computers)
www.ikea.com (IKEA)
www.tiffanys.com (Tiffany's)

Navigate through the sites to answer the following questions:

1. What evidence can you find that shows the retailer values its customers?
2. If you found evidence, explain how the retailer makes customers feel appreciated.
3. If you found no evidence, explain how the retailer could implement the value concept online.

Continuing Case 2.1

Sherwin-Williams Company: Corporate Social Responsibility

Sherwin-Williams Company has created many initiatives to maintain its commitment to corporate and social responsibility. In May 2002, Sherwin-Williams was honored by Renovation Program officials for a donation of 10,000 gallons of paint used in the restoration of the Pentagon after the terrorist attacks of September 11, 2001.

In June 2002, Sherwin-Williams participated in a project sponsored by the Kempsville, Virginia, Covenant Division of Habitat for Humanity. The company contributed paint for a project that asked homeowners to donate at least $15 to have volunteers paint the curbs in front of their homes. The money raised was used to build a home for a local single mother and her children.

In each instance, Sherwin-Williams received positive publicity. In addition, federal employees, members of Congress, consumers, and other community, regional, and national groups recognized Sherwin-Williams through various public relations channels. One of the awards the company received was a "Piece of the Pentagon Award." "The contribution made by Sherwin-Williams is representative of the American Spirit to see the Pentagon made whole again," said Lee Evey, Pentagon Renovation Program manager.

Questions

1. Why did Sherwin-Williams undertake these particular projects?
2. What benefits did Sherwin-Williams gain through its corporate social responsibility efforts?
3. How has Sherwin-Williams developed customer relationships through its CSR efforts?
4. What customer value do you perceive Sherwin-Williams developed from its CSR activities?
5. What ethical considerations should companies look at in supporting community projects?
6. Why should Sherwin-Williams be involved in projects of these types?

Sources: Sandra Jill Pennecke, "Volunteers Begin Painting Before the House Is Built," *The Virginian-Pilot*, June 30, 2002; "Nation's Largest Paint Company Joins Forces with Nation's Armed Forces in Pentagon Repair Efforts," Sherwin-Williams Company press release, retrieved May 23, 2002, from www.sherwinwilliams.com/InvestorRelations/Press_Releases/2002/PR_05232002.

Case 2.2

Best Buy Ensures Customer Value Through Technology

Best Buy Company, Inc., of Minneapolis is a specialty retailer of consumer electronics, personal computers, entertainment software, and appliances. The company operates under several trade names, including Best Buy, Future Shop, Magnolia Hi-Fi, Media Play, On Cue, Sam Goody, and Suncoast. Best Buy has more than 1,900 retail stores in the United States, Canada, Puerto Rico, and the

U.S. Virgin Islands. In 2002, Best Buy was ranked 15th in the Top 100 Retailers by Stores Online. Best Buy is also ranked by *Fortune* as one of "America's Most Admired Companies." According to Best Buy's strategic planning philosophy, "It is the objective of the Board and senior management to continually create shareholder value, while at the same time upholding highly ethical business practices and promoting corporate responsibility."

An important part of customer value is allowing customers a mechanism by which to provide feedback to the retailer. Best Buy utilizes a call center to handle customer concerns. One problem with the call center was that managers could not listen to both sides of the conversation, so often monitoring consisted of managers sitting beside a customer service employee (agent) and listening to the employee's side of the story. Of course, any time a manager sat with an employee, the employee was on his or her best behavior. Sometimes managers were able to connect to both conversations by using a headphone and jack system, but the employee was also aware when this took place.

In early 2000, Best Buy installed Equality Balance, a product that digitally records calls and allows managers to evaluate how agents are responding to customers without the agents knowing they are being monitored. The product also monitors e-mails to record the types of messages received and how agents respond to them. Best Buy management installed the system because they wanted to witness customer interactions as they occurred, without the knowledge of the customer service agent. When the agents cannot predict when they will be monitored, they are most likely on their best behavior at all times instead of just when they see a manager observing them.

Future technological innovations include a process to score agents on how well they deal with customers. This procedure will attempt to further quantify customer relationship skills. Management also plans to install Equality Balance at other Best Buy call centers and to outsource work to call centers that handle Best Buy's customer calls on a contractual basis.

Questions

1. How does the Equality Balance product enable managers to deliver value to customers?
2. What are the pros and cons of the Equality Balance system?
3. What types of problems may Best Buy experience when it outsources the customer service center function?
4. What do you think of the agent scoring system Best Buy plans to use?
5. If you were a customer service agent at a Best Buy call center, what would you think of the system?
6. How could Best Buy measure the return on investment for the Equality Balance product?

Sources: Best Buy Investor Relations, retrieved September 2002 from www.bestbuy.com/About/InvestorRelations/index, "2002 America's Most Admired Companies," retrieved September 2002 from http://www.fortune.com/lists/mostadmired/snap_196.html; "The Strategic Planning Process," retrieved September 2002 from http://media.corporate-ir.net/mediafiles/nys/bby/reports/bby.spp.pdf; Michael Cohn, "Best Buy Beefs Up Customer Value at the Call Center," *Internet World*, June 2002, pp. 42–43.

Effective Retail

Part 2

Strategies

Part 1 dealt with many important external, or macro, environments that affect retailers. Armed with a good understanding of these environments, retail managers can make better, more informed decisions. Part 2 takes a more micro approach, looking at the retail management functions.

Chapter 3 provides expanded coverage of the IRM flow chart. Each major step in the IRM is discussed in more detail. Chapters 4 and 5 look at the information necessary to build a solid situational analysis for the retail organization. Specifically, Chapter 4 addresses retail institutions involved in the situational analysis, and Chapter 5 focuses on identifying and evaluating potential retail customers.

An Overview of the Retail Planning and Management Process

Chapter
3

The only constant in the universe is change!
Dr. J.R. (Doc) Ogden

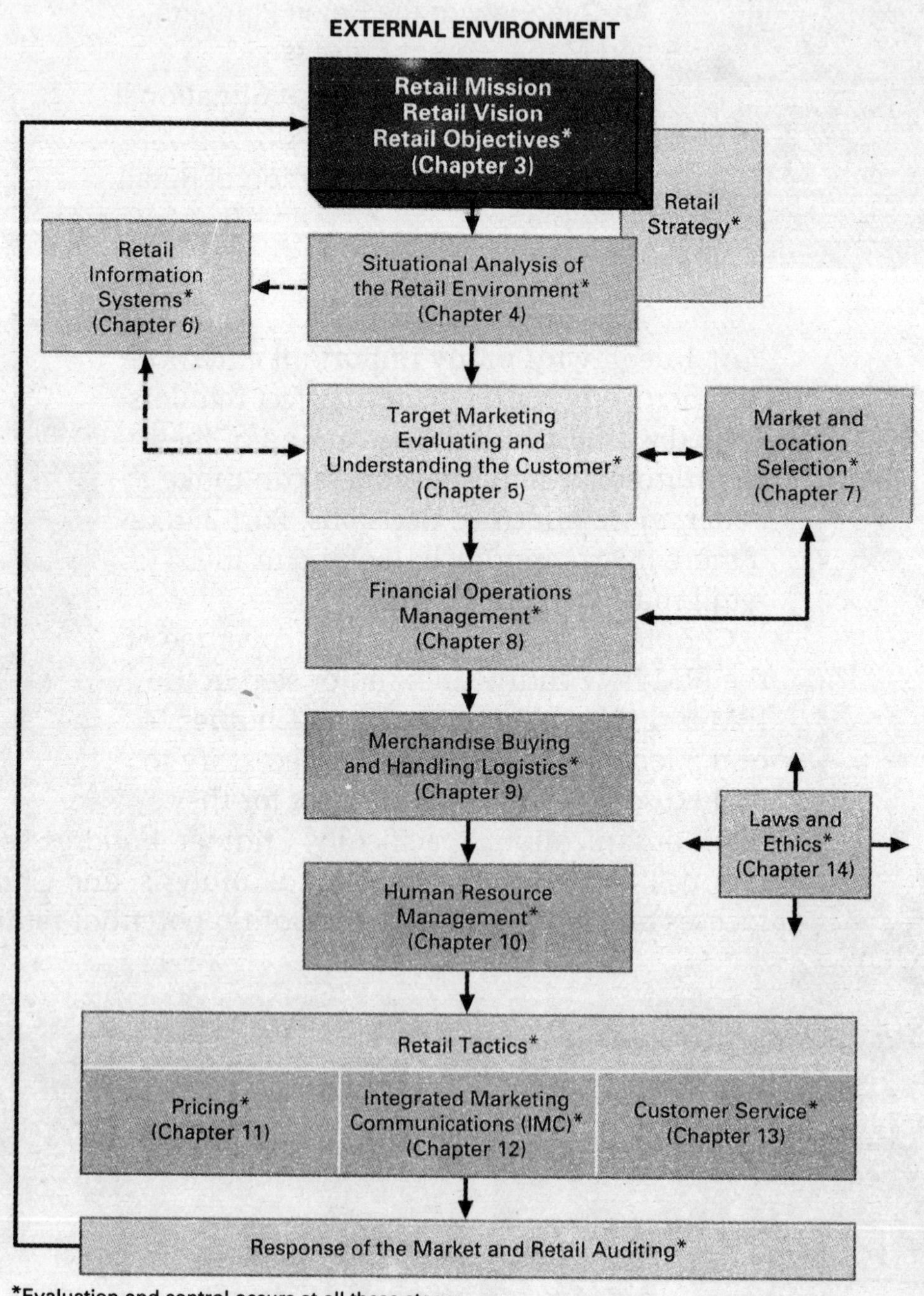

*Evaluation and control occurs at all these stages.

CHAPTER OBJECTIVES

After completing this chapter, you will be able to:

1. Discuss the importance of a retailer's mission and vision.
2. Describe the activities that take place when conducting a situational analysis.
3. Define *strategy* and describe how retailers develop strategic plans.
4. Explain the importance of target marketing and understanding the behavior of a market segment.
5. Describe how retailers determine markets and select retail locations.
6. Discuss the following areas in relation to retail operations: financial operations management, merchandise buying and handling, human resource management, retail tactics, laws and ethics, and evaluation and control.

Neighborhood Markets

Wal-Mart is the world's largest retailer, known for its discount stores and supercenters. One of the company's strengths is its strategic planning and innovative marketing. Because the discount store format is in the maturity phase of the retail life cycle, Wal-Mart has recently moved into a new type of retail format. These new stores are called *neighborhood markets*.

The neighborhood market concept focuses on convenience-oriented customers who want a smaller, easy-to-navigate store. These neighborhood markets provide a grocery store format in which typical Wal-Mart shoppers can shop during the week. First opened in 1998, the markets range from 42,000 to 55,000 square feet.[1] The format complements the supercenter stores, which are frequented more often on weekends.

Each neighborhood market caters to the community in which it is located. For example, if the residents of a particular area are from a certain ethnic background, the neighborhood market carries more products targeted toward that demographic segment.

Wal-Mart plans to expand from 49 markets in 2003 to 240 markets by 2005.[2] Although estimated sales are lower than those of a typical Wal-Mart supercenter, the lower revenues are offset by lower real estate costs because of the smaller locations. Watch out, supermarkets—the neighborhood market is coming your way![3]

INTRODUCTION

This chapter centers on the processes involved in the development and execution of an integrated retail management plan. The chapter moves from a macro view of retailing to a more micro approach. It provides an overview of the retail planning process by utilizing an integrated retail management (IRM) flow chart. Some of these topics have entire chapters devoted to them later in the text; this chapter provides more concise coverage.

planning The establishment of objectives, policies, and procedures to carry out goals.

Planning is defined as the establishment of objectives, policies, and procedures to carry out goals. Planning is very important because it gives direction for capital and human resource expenditures. It allows for the development of logistical systems that are fully integrated into the retailer's way of doing business, as well as for the most effective methods of communicating with customers through integrated marketing communications. In addition, the plan provides data to be used by decision makers when developing effective plans for their specialized areas.

THE RETAILER'S MISSION AND VISION

The heart of any plan is clear knowledge of exactly why the business or organization exists. The old saying, "If you don't know where you're going, you won't get there"—or better yet, "If you don't know where you're going, you're already there"—is humorous, but it exemplifies the need for careful planning. The first question the successful retailer needs to ask is: Why are we in business? The intelligent retailer will spend a lot of time and resources to answer that question, because without an answer retail executions will be ineffective. Thus, the first step in overall retail planning is to create a mission statement for the retail organization. All steps in the integrated retail management plan will then follow logically from that one guiding principle.

Although the steps illustrated in the IRM flow chart are sequential, in reality the successful retail manager may work at different levels within the flow chart simultaneously. While the mission statement is being updated, for example, the retailer also may be working on a strong merchandise buying and handling plan. The ultimate goal is to create sales and profits in the most efficient and cost-effective manner possible. Also note that although the arrows in the flow chart show a downward flow, in practice the flows can go in both directions. For example, if the situational analysis shows a change in consumers' needs, and as a result the retailer adds another line to their products, the mission statement may be updated to reflect the change in the operation.

MISSION

mission statement A statement that explains why the firm is in business, what it does, and what it stands for.

The first step in the flow chart is the retail mission. A *mission statement* is, simply put, the reason the organization is in business. Originally mission statements were also called *corporate objectives, retail objectives,* or *value statements.* However, the mission statement is much more. The **mission statement** pro-

"Our old mission statement was more eloquent, and dignified, but not nearly as effective."

vides information that answers the following questions about the retailer: Why are we in business? What do we do? What do we stand for? A good mission statement speaks of commitment to the customer, employees, shareholders, and society.[4]

Think about questions you may encounter during your next job interview. The interviewer may ask you to tell "a little bit about you and your background." You need to summarize more than 20 years of your life in a few statements. You don't want to provide too much information, which would give the interviewer information overload; rather, you should give enough information to allow the interviewer to make a positive decision about your skills and background. The mission statement does the same thing for potential or current stakeholders of the retail organization.

The key to a successful mission statement is to turn it into a value held by the organization's employees. The mission statement, because it guides the retailer through good times and bad, should be the starting point for any retail business. All plans and processes emanate from the mission statement. Thus, an effective mission has employee and stakeholder buy-in.

Figure 3.1 provides examples of actual mission statements from some better-known retailers. Although these mission statements are simple, they reflect what the retailers actually do within their business empires. Note that most of the missions focus on customer satisfaction (the marketing concept) while providing a return to stockholders and other stakeholders.

VISION

vision statement A statement that focuses on the firm's future goals.

Closely related to the mission statement is the retailer's vision. While the mission statement deals with why the retailer is in business, it is grounded in the present. A **vision statement,** on the other hand, evolves from the mission but focuses on future goals. A good vision statement contains (1) a statement of a desired future for the retailer, (2) a reminder to the retailer of "why we do

PROCTER & GAMBLE

P&G people are committed to serving consumers and achieving leadership results through principle-based decisions and actions.

We will provide products and services of superior quality and value that improve the lives of the world s consumers.

As a result, consumers will reward us with leadership sales, profits, and value creation, allowing our people, our shareholders, and the communities in which we live and work to prosper.

Ben & Jerry's

Our Mission Consists of Three Interrelated Parts:

PRODUCT MISSION: To make, distribute, and sell the finest quality, all-natural ice cream and euphoric concoctions with a continued commitment to incorporating wholesome, natural ingredients and promoting business practices that respect the Earth and the environment.

ECONOMIC MISSION: To operate the company on a sustainable financial basis of profitable growth, increasing value for our stakeholders, and expanding opportunities for development and career growth for our employees.

SOCIAL MISSION: To operate the company in a way that actively recognizes the central role that business plays in society by initiating innovative ways to improve the quality of life locally, nationally, and internationally.

STARBUCKS

Establish Starbucks as the premier purveyor of the finest coffee in the world while maintaining our uncompromising principles while we grow.

- Provide a great work environment and treat each other with respect and dignity.
- Embrace diversity as an essential component in the way we do business.
- Apply the highest standards of excellence to the purchasing, roasting, and fresh delivery of our coffee.
- Develop enthusiastically satisfied customers all of the time.
- Contribute positively to our communities and our environment.
- Recognize that profitability is essential to our future success.

FIGURE 3.1 **Examples of Actual Mission Statements** (Sources: Courtesy of the Procter & Gamble Company; Courtesy of Ben & Jerry's; Courtesy of Starbucks.)

what we do," (3) values for the retailer to live by, and (4) enough information to serve as a touchstone for making the hard decisions on retail policy.

A vision provides many benefits for the retailer, including:

- Alignment of everyone on the team, so that they work for the same thing and move in the same direction
- Inspiration for employees
- An articulation of retailer values
- Motivation for all employees and stakeholders

ChevronTexaco

The ChevronTexaco Way

At the heart of the ChevronTexaco Way is our vision to be the global energy company most admired for its people, partnership, and performance.

Trammell Crow Company

To be the acknowledged leader in commercial real estate services, known for:

- Superior customer service
- Operational excellence
- Rewarding work environment
- Value creation for all stakeholders

GEICO

GEICO provides its customers a peace-of-mind guarantee that their assets and income are protected from financial loss, up to their policy limits, in the event of an accident. We will be recognized as a leader in providing quality insurance products and services by all who deal with GEICO in any manner.

FIGURE 3.2 **Examples of Vision Statements (abridged)** (Sources: Reprinted with permission of ChevronTexaco Corporation; courtesy of Trammell Crow Company; Courtesy of GEICO.)

When creating vision statements, retailers should answer the following questions:

- What values do we, and should we, have as retailers?
- What are we working toward?
- How should we set up our retail climate?
- Who are we as people?
- What image do we want to present to our customers?
- What image do we want to present to our employees?
- What image do we want to present to shareholders?

Vision statements should be updated regularly and should be distributed to everyone affected by them.[5] Figure 3.2 provides abridged versions of vision statements by some of today's retailers.

RETAIL OBJECTIVES

Mission statements speak to the present, whereas vision statements point toward an ideal future for the retail manager. Mission and vision statements usually are used to create a series of *retail objectives,* which, for the larger chains, are often referred to as *corporate objectives*. Much like vision statements, retail objectives are goals. The main difference is that whereas vision statements tend to be long term, **retail objectives** are for a medium-length term and provide measurable goals.

retail (corporate) objectives Goals that are for a medium-length term and provide measurable statements.

Retail objectives should (1) have a time line, or deadline, (2) be measurable and quantifiable, and (3) be realistic. Each objective needs a deadline so that management can evaluate whether the objective was met in a timely fashion. In addition, each objective must be measurable. "To increase sales" is a poorly worded objective. How much of an increase should be achieved? By when should it be achieved? A better objective would read, "to increase sales in the Health and Beauty Aids department by 15 percent prior to November 13." The second version allows the retail manager to ascertain whether or not the objective has been met. If, when November 13 arrives, sales are up 9 percent, the manager will know the objective has not been met and will move to investigate the reasons why.

Retail objectives must also have a realistic degree of attainability. If an objective is set too high, the result may be the opposite of what the retailer desired. If no one reaches the objective, it is probably impossible to attain. When it comes to objectives, the old adage, "If you can't measure it, you can't manage it" holds true.

ANALYZING THE RETAIL ENVIRONMENT: THE SITUATIONAL ANALYSIS

Once the mission, vision, and objectives are in place, the retail manager can begin an assessment of the overall retail environment. Because the only constant in the universe is change, retail professionals must prepare for change to occur. Chapter 4 explores situational analysis processes in depth.

A situational analysis gives the basic history of the retailer: What is the retailer's current position in the marketplace, and how did it get there? What is the retailer's growth pattern? What is the sales history, including sales volume? What product offerings has the retailer had in the past, and what are the current product offerings? What markets has the retailer served? What markets have the greatest competitive advantage? What markets are available that the retailer currently does not serve?

environmental scanning A systematic process whereby the retailer acquires and uses information to assist in the management and planning of future actions.

One of the more important functions of the situational analysis is the concept and implementation of environmental scanning. **Environmental**

scanning is the acquisition and use of information to assist in the management and planning of future actions.[6] The retailer needs to pay particular attention to any environment that could potentially affect operations. These environments may include social, legal, physical, economic, competitive, political, or technological environments, to name a few. Many retailers pay particular attention to the competitive environment, because competition is a driving force behind environmental change.

Figure 3.3 illustrates the environments that need to be considered in the process of environmental scanning. The forces affecting the environment come from within the organization (intraorganizational environment), the task being completed (task/mediating environment), and outside the organization (macro environment).

To scan these important environments, the retailer needs to develop a system. The following five-step process is useful in developing a system for environmental scanning:

1. Identify all relevant environments.
2. Look for relevant changes in these environments.
3. Understand and evaluate these changes in terms of their nature, direction, and magnitude.
4. Analyze and forecast the impact and timing of the changes; assess the potential consequences of the changes.
5. Create responses to the environmental changes through changes in strategy.

The retailer can look for environmental changes in newspapers, magazines, the business press, the trade press, trade associations, conferences, trade shows, the Internet, and other types of secondary sources.

The overall idea governing environmental scanning is to identify any environment that may affect the retailer and then forecast the impact of that environmental change. Armed with this information, the successful retail manager

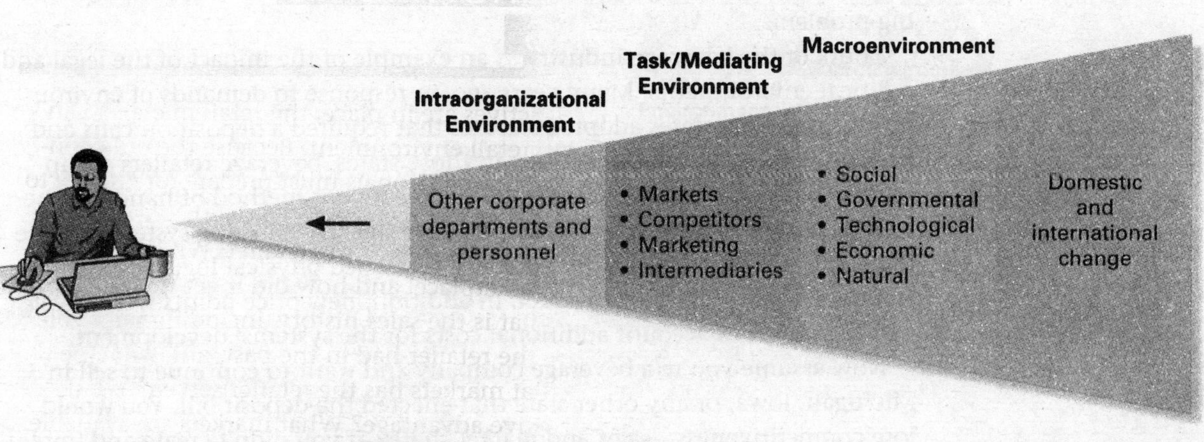

FIGURE 3.3 Environmental Scanning

GLOBAL RETAILING

Bottle Bills and the Beverage Industry

Prior to World War II, the beverage industry required deposits on beverage containers so that glass bottles would be returned. The bottles were then washed, refilled, and resold. After World War II, cans replaced bottles, first in the beer industry. With the advent of the 1960s, the soft-drink industry followed with "no-deposit, no-return" bottles and cans. Because beverage companies were no longer reusing cans and bottles, a marked increase in litter resulted. Consequently, environmentalists proposed bottle bills in their state legislatures. Bottle bills placed a mandatory refundable deposit on beer and soft-drink containers.

In 1970, British Columbia enacted the first beverage container recovery system in North America. In 1971, Oregon was the first state in the United States to pass a bottle bill requiring deposits on beer and soft-drink containers. As of 2002, ten states and eight Canadian provinces have some type of bottle law.

Some benefits of bottle bills include reduced litter and conservation of natural resources by reducing the amount of solid waste that gets sent to landfills. Another benefit, according to the Container Recycling Institute, is the creation of jobs in the retail, distribution, and recycling sectors. The recycling industry that has resulted from bottle bills has revenues in excess of $200 million per year.

Sources: "What Is a Bottle Bill?" *Bottle Bill Resource Guide,* retrieved July 2002 from www.bottlebill.org/what_are_b-bills.htm; "The Ten Cent Incentive to Recycle," Container Recycling Institute, 1997, retrieved July 2002 from www.container-recycling.org/publications/tencent/tencentintro.html.

can integrate these changes into any plans being developed and create responses to the changes. Thus, the retailer takes a proactive approach to solving problems.

Think of the beverage industry as an example of the impact of the legal and political environments. Many years ago, in response to demands of environmentalists, some states adopted statutes that required a deposit on cans and bottles. To continue to do business in those states, beverage retailers set up systems that would allow for the most cost-efficient method of handling the returned bottles and cans. The retailers developed accounting systems for the cans and bottles. Suppliers and retailers developed physical logistical systems for handling the returned product. In addition, new price points were developed to take into account additional costs for the systems' development.

Now assume you're a beverage company and want to continue to sell in Michigan, Iowa, or any other state that enacted the deposit bill. You would lose competitiveness—sales and market share—if you didn't create and implement the systems prior to the bill's passage in the states' congressional bodies.

If, however, you had an environmental scanning system in place, you could decide whether to do business in that state, and if the answer was yes, you would develop the systems necessary to manage all the additional problems. Finally, you might be able to stall the legislation (through lobbying or other methods) until you have your systems in place. As you can see, analyzing the situation is important.

The retail manager must continually look to the retailer's mission and vision statements to identify those environments that have the greatest potential impact on the overall retail operation. The environmental data must be accessible by all of the retailer's decision makers and must be integrated throughout the retail organization.

RETAIL STRATEGY

retail strategy A plan that provides the retail decision maker with a framework for current and future actions and dictates how objectives will be achieved.

Strategy refers to how a given objective will be achieved.[7] Overall, a **retail strategy** provides the retail decision maker with a framework for current and future actions and dictates how objectives will be achieved. The strategy is a logical deduction from the retailer's mission and vision statements. Although there are many different levels of strategy, the retail strategy represents the retail organization's big picture of how to address and satisfy the marketplace. To stay in business, it is essential to have an integrated retail strategy.

Strategies must be dynamic. In essence, "strategies can form as well as be formulated."[8] Thus, it is important for a retailer to develop a system of strategic thinking. Strategic thinking is "a way of thinking about customers, competitors, and competitive advantage."[9] The overall concept of **strategic thinking** is to utilize the retail mission statement, the vision statement, the environmental scanning analysis, and the situational analysis to understand the environmental forces that affect a retail business. The idea is to be able to create or control the future environment, not just react to it.[10] According to Michael Porter, "Strategy is about making choices, trade-offs; it's about deliberately choosing to be different."[11]

strategic thinking Utilization of the retail mission statement, the vision statement, the environmental scanning results, and the situational analysis to understand the environmental forces that affect a retail business.

In developing a retail strategy, the retail professional needs to keep in mind the customers, the competitors, the capital resources, and the human resources available to execute the strategy. Strategic plans tend to be about a year in length but often can be prepared for longer time periods, such as five or ten years. Long-term plans help the retailer get a better picture of the retail future. The plan may be extended, modified, or terminated depending on its perceived effectiveness.

controllable variables Those areas of the retail operation that can be effectively controlled and changed by retail managers.

uncontrollable variables Those areas of the retail operation that cannot be controlled by retail managers.

Overall, a guiding retail strategy is generally made up of two types of variables: controllable and uncontrollable. **Controllable variables** are those areas of the retail operation that can be effectively controlled and changed by retail managers. These may include all management functions, logistics, store locations, product offerings, integrated marketing communication, and to some extent, price. **Uncontrollable variables** may include those environments mentioned in the section on environmental scanning, including the legal, technological, and competitive environments. Other uncontrollable variables include product or service seasonality, product or service obsolescence, and consumers' changing needs and wants.

RETAIL INFORMATION SYSTEMS

retail information system (RIS) A system in which data are gathered and stored, turned into useful information, and disseminated to employees and managers to assist in making retail decisions.

Data needed to develop an effective retail strategy can, in part, be generated from the situational analysis, mission statement, and vision statement. In addition, the integration of a **retail information system (RIS),** in which all data are gathered, stored, turned into useful information, and disseminated to employees and managers, can be a powerful tool in the development of the retail strategy.

Retail information systems are created and used to generate data and information for retail decision makers such as retail strategists and tactical specialists. For example, in 2003, 7-Eleven, Inc. added touch screen and signature terminals in 5,300 of its U.S. convenience stores. These devices reduce checkout times and improve the handling of credit card information.[12]

In this information age, retail information is critical to survival for retailers. The RIS can be manual or electronic. Most large retailers prefer to generate and disseminate their data electronically, although manual systems are still in use, primarily by smaller retailers.

To develop effective retail strategy, data are needed. Shown here is a retail researcher collecting data from a mall patron.

A good RIS provides data based on marketing research undertaken by the retailer. The data can be primary or secondary. **Primary data** are generated specifically to solve some problem. **Secondary data** have already been collected and analyzed in another context. Secondary data are *not* gathered to solve a particular problem. Consider television advertising. To create advertising prices, advertising agencies rely on secondary data collected by Nielsen Media Research, Inc.[13] Nielsen gathers viewership patterns and demographic data about viewers to help television stations and networks set a price for the air space they sell to agencies and ultimately to the retailer.

primary data Data that have been generated specifically to solve a problem.

secondary data Data that have already been collected and analyzed.

TARGET MARKETING

Earlier we saw that it is very important for the retailer to have an understanding of its customer. This information is used in virtually every step of the integrated retail management plan. Customer information is placed into the RIS so that all employees, from service providers to CEOs, have access to the data and can gain a clear understanding of what the store's customers need and want.

IDENTIFYING MARKET SEGMENTS OF THE TARGET MARKET

Stated simply, the **target market** represents all of those individuals to whom the retailer plans to aim its marketing efforts. After deciding on the target market, the retailer must decide whether to segment the market or go after the entire market with a mass marketing strategy. **Segmentation** is the process of breaking up the target market into more controllable subgroups. With a **mass marketing approach,** the retailer utilizes one unique marketing mix to try to capture the entire market. With a **segmented approach,** the retailer breaks up the mass market into submarkets (called *segments*) and then develops a unique marketing mix for each segment.

target market All of those individuals toward whom the retailer plans to aim its marketing efforts.

segmentation The process of breaking up the target market into more controllable subgroups.

mass marketing approach An approach in which the retailer utilizes one unique marketing mix to try to capture the market.

segmented approach An approach in which the retailer breaks up the mass market into submarkets (called *segments*) and then develops a unique marketing mix for each segment.

To assess how large or small the market may be, the retail professional should count the number of potential end users. The best way to do this may be to count repeat customers. Utilizing superior marketing and retailing techniques, the retailer can usually get the consumer to try a product or service for the first time. Only after the consumer has used the product does the retailer know if she or he will continue to purchase or decide not to repurchase. Ways to capture this information are discussed further in Chapter 6.

Certain qualifications exist for a useful target market, including (1) the *ability* to purchase the product or service from the retailer, (2) the *willingness* to buy the product or service, and (3) a *sufficient number of people* in the market to generate profits. Determining the projected number of end users is important during the forecasting and location decision processes. Many retailers have made errors in judgment about inventory levels by looking at initial sales of products. In addition, the retailer needs to know where customers are located geographically. To do this effectively, the retailer can utilize geographic information systems, which provide population statistics for a given area.

The *ability* to buy means the consumer must have adequate cash or credit to make the purchase. Most people wouldn't qualify as a member of the Rolls-

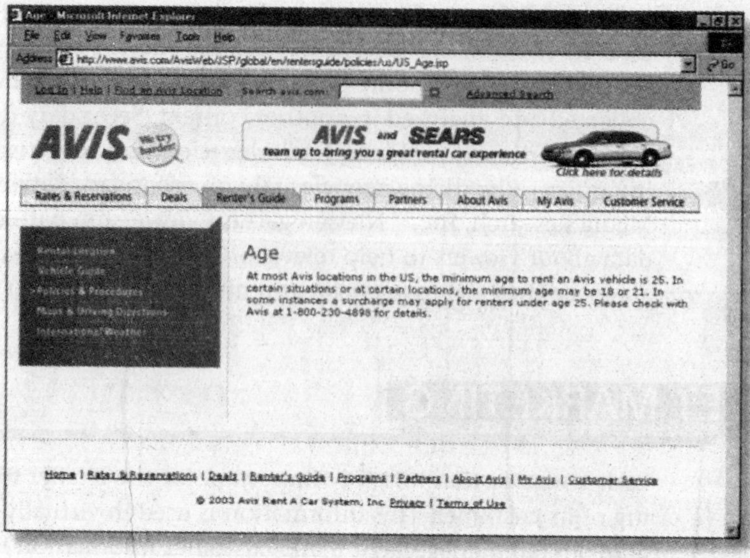

To have a useful target market, consumers must have the ability to purchase the product or service. For example, Avis has rental requirements such as a minimum age qualification. These requirements typically vary by state and country.
(Courtesy of Avis Rent A Car System, Inc.)

Royce target market, simply because they do not have enough discretionary income during their lifetime to pay for a vehicle in this price range. Adequate money or credit to make a purchase is an important factor in assessing the market's ability to purchase, but the retailer may also want to look for other things that may hamper a consumer's ability to buy. For instance, rental-car firms set a minimum age for the car renter. If the person is under the minimum age—say, 25—he or she will be unable to purchase the service.

Similarly, many insurance providers will not offer certain customers car insurance, based on their driving records. The more accidents and moving-traffic citations a person has, the less likely the person will be able to purchase insurance from a preferred carrier. Many life insurance companies may refuse to sell life insurance to someone who has a short potential lifespan due to a catastrophic disease.

Willingness to buy refers to the consumer's perception of the retailer or in some cases, lack of a perception. A consumer who has had an unpleasant experience with a retailer may choose not to shop at that establishment again. In addition, the disgruntled consumer may pass on the story to others, thus discouraging other potential customers from shopping at the store. This is why superior customer service is important for all retailers. The integration of excellent customer service into the overall retail management plan, and particularly into the development of a target market and market segments, is essential. Customers who have no experience with the retailer and thus no prior perceptions about the firm may be excellent prospects for part of the retailer's target market. Only those customers who are unwilling to shop at the retailer's store should be excluded from the target market.

UNDERSTANDING THE BEHAVIOR OF THE TARGET MARKET

After retail professionals have determined the composition of the target market(s), they need to obtain an overall understanding of the market. Retailers should study the behaviors of consumers in their target market(s) (or market segments) so they can develop an effective and cost-efficient retail marketing mix (tactical executions).

typical customer profile A description of a retailer's most frequent customers.

For the most part, a retailer should develop a **typical customer profile** for the target market or market segment. This profile should contain the information that will enable the retailer to create effective tactical executions. For example, the retailer may want to know the usage patterns of its customers. By researching the buying habits of heavy users versus light users, it is easier to formulate budget allocations and target those customers most valuable to the retailer.

Generally, when studying the overall market and trying to understand the market's behavior, a retailer looks at the four *ICs*: demographi*cs*, geographi*cs*, psychographi*cs*, and behavioristi*cs*. These concepts are covered in Chapter 5. For now, note that these data are necessary to allow the retailer to tailor its tactics toward the target market and market segments. Think of a product you have seen advertised that interests you. Using the same spokesperson in all advertising for this product may not be effective. Your parents may respond better to the Rolling Stones, whereas you may respond better to Kid Rock or Eminem. The more the retailer knows about the customer, the more successful it will be.

MARKET AND LOCATION SELECTION

The next task in developing a good understanding of the market is to generate research for decisions about location of the retail business. The market and location selection information is generally found within the section on target markets in the retailer's integrated retail management plan. This decision is based on information from the situational analysis, the mission and vision statements, and the RIS. A retailer must decide how many stores or facilities are needed and whether their locations will be bricks-and-mortar only, on the Internet only, or a combination of both (bricks-and-clicks). These decisions are vital for the retailer in generating competitive advantage and in making sound investments when it comes to purchasing expensive physical property. Chapter 7 covers store location in greater depth.

FINANCIAL OPERATIONS MANAGEMENT

operations management The ability of the retailer to efficiently manage all of the functions necessary in running the retail business.

Operations management refers to the ability of the retailer to efficiently manage all of the functions necessary in running a retail business. Financial operations management is difficult because the task of turning ideas and concepts into numbers and then turning numbers back into useful information is quite challenging. In reality, there is no significance in the number 6, for example. The vital information lies in what that number 6 represents and what it implicates for the big picture. To effectively control financial operations, the retailer must understand both accounting and finance concepts.

Financial operations concepts range from asset management to budgeting. By thoroughly understanding and managing financial operations, the retail manager can then undertake resource allocation to make the integrated retail plan highly efficient and effective. Keep in mind that the financial operations plan *must* be integrated into all other areas of the retail plan. Because resources are often limited, the retailer must use every last resource effectively and efficiently.

The financial operations plan includes many statements that are important to the retail business. The retailer may use these statements to show the major stakeholders how well the business is doing at any point in time. The retailer must at a minimum satisfy the wants and needs of its stakeholders (or the owners), including the retail management hierarchy, the employees, the Internal Revenue Service, and the customers. Financial operations management entails complex decision making. Based on these decisions, the retailer must implement an overall integrated retail management plan. Typical decision-making issues may pertain to the format of a retail outlet; the size and physical layout of a store; and the allocation of sales space, warehouse space, and office space. These important decisions are at least in some part based on the overall financial operations plan.

Inventories are managed through the use of inventory planning. Thus, the financial operations management plan is directly tied to the additional logistical decisions that retail managers must make. Through a logical and well-integrated flow, the retailer will be able to develop effective merchandise buying and handling strategies centered around the financial operation of the retail business.

MERCHANDISE BUYING AND HANDLING: LOGISTICS

Although merchandise management may include financial operations, because of its importance it is treated as a special topic within the textbook. **Merchandise buying and handling** includes the physical purchase of products and services and how those products and services are brought to the retail outlet, handled, and finally placed ready for sale. The price of a product or service has an impact on the retailer's ability to "move" its inventory and should be integrated into merchandise buying and selling.

merchandise buying and handling The physical purchase of products and services and how those products and services are brought to the retail outlet, handled, and finally placed ready for sale.

Within the scope of merchandise buying and selling is the concept of logistics. *Logistics* is defined by the Council of Logistics Management as "that part of the supply chain process that plans, implements, and controls the efficient, effective flow and storage of goods, services, and related information between the point of origin and the point of consumption in order to meet customers' requirements."[14] Simply stated, **logistics** is every action taken to ensure that products and services get from the point of origin to the final consumer.

logistics Every action taken to ensure that products and services get from the point of origin to the final customer.

Supply chain management is "the systemic, strategic coordination of the traditional business functions and tactics across these business functions within a particular company and across businesses within the supply chain for

Blunders or Best Practices?

Failure to Scan Environment Results in Logistics Problems

Although there are many examples of poor and good supply chain management, companies still make mistakes in these areas. In the 1970s, the Chilean government imposed high taxes on imported vehicles. In the late 1970s, the government drastically dropped the tariffs, and as a result the demand for vehicles was much greater than the supply. By 1981, vehicles that were once a luxury became affordable by many Chileans, and waiting times of five months for a vehicle were not uncommon.

In 1982, car dealerships ordered up to 10 times more than the typical amount, even though there were signs of recession in the economy. Of course, by this time many Chileans already owned vehicles and were unwilling to spend more due to the higher prices and the risky economy. Car dealers found themselves in a terrible situation: they had an enormous amount of excess inventory and nowhere to store it. Some dealers were forced to store more than a year's supply of vehicles.

The lesson to be learned is that companies must incorporate environmental analysis into their strategic planning. Had the car dealerships taken into account the various environments affecting consumer demand for products, they may have avoided the inventory buildup.

Source: David A. Ricks, *Big Business Blunders* (Homewood, IL: Dow Jones-Irwin, 1983), pp. 97–98.

supply chain management The coordination of the traditional business functions and tactics across business functions within a particular company and across businesses within the supply chain for the purposes of improving the long-term performance of the individual companies and the supply chain as a whole

the purposes of improving the long-term performance of the individual companies and the supply chain as a whole."[15] Thus, supply chain management is a strategic process, whereas logistics is more of a tactical process.

In conjunction with executing an excellent logistical plan and having an effective management system for the supply chain, the retailer needs to pay particular attention to inventory, order processing, and fulfillments. Finally, decisions about transportation, storage, and additional warehousing issues must be made in this section of the integrated retail management plan.

Merchandise buying and handling also refers to the decisions the retailer makes about the companies from which it will purchase. What kind of system would allow for purchasing products in the most convenient yet most economical manner? In addition, the retailer must determine where to buy inventory and how to evaluate the sources of supply for the retail outlet. Good negotiation skills are important when trying to get the best deal possible for products.

Think about the purchase of a car. How do you get the best deal for the car you want? Through up-front negotiation. In the majority of cases, by paying the least amount of money possible during the purchase phase, you save a lot of future money (*i.e.,* less interest, lower fees, a shorter financing period). The result is the same when the retailer buys inventory: the less that is paid up front, the greater the savings that are realized. These savings can be passed on to the customer or reinvested into the retail operations.

As the supplies come in, the retailer has to make sure they are all accounted for and in good working condition. The retailer must also mark the products to verify how much product is on hand and must stock the products to make them available to customers.

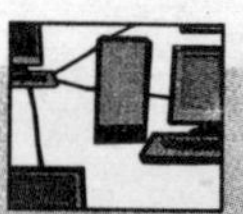

INTERNET IN ACTION

E-commerce: Sounds Good, But How Do We Measure Performance?

Although evaluation and control are important at each step of strategy development, in the e-commerce environment it is often difficult to determine how to measure business performance. *Performance* is defined as a company's ability to generate expected value. In traditional retailing, three primary categories are used to assess performance: asset productivity indicators, shareholder value, and growth and survival indicators. According to researcher Esmeralda Garbi, these traditional categories pose limitations for online vendors. The biggest obstacle is the difficulty in capturing real and long-term firm performance in an e-commerce environment. The traditional retail plan measurements, such as sales per square foot of retail space, are meaningless in an e-tailing environment. Other difficulties include large expenses incurred by new Internet companies, the speculative nature of Internet investments, and the negative profitability characteristic of new Internet ventures—all of which make it difficult to use the traditional measurements of firm performance.

Some performance indicators that may be more reliable are number of unique visitors, number of recurring visits, and development of a large customer base. In general, because companies operating online behave differently than traditional retailers, the performance measures must reflect those differences.

Source: Esmeralda Garbi, "Alternative Measures of Performance for E-companies: A Comparison of Approaches," *Journal of Business Strategies*, 19:1 (2002), pp. 1–17.

HUMAN RESOURCE MANAGEMENT

After the logistical plan has been developed, the human resource element of the retail operation must be planned and managed. The overall job of the retail professional when it comes to human resource management is to make sure all employees are working toward the same goals, are working as a team, and are experiencing job satisfaction. The retailer must reward those employees who are contributing the most to the organization and eliminate or retrain employees who are performing below expectations. Because of the many tasks involved in retailing (see Table 3.1), human resource management is integrated throughout all operations. Additional coverage of human resource management appears in Chapter 10.

The key to human resource management is to ensure that the retailer's objectives are met. The best way to achieve objectives is by ensuring customer satisfaction (or, better yet, exceeding expectations), employee satisfaction, and stakeholder satisfaction.

RETAIL TACTICS

tactical executions The day-to-day operational activities that implement the strategic plan.

Included in the final sections of an effective integrated retail management plan is the plan's execution, or tactical executions. **Tactical executions** are the day-to-day tasks that implement the strategic plan. The planning process

TABLE 3.1

SELECTED TYPICAL RETAILING TASKS

- Selling merchandise
- Selling services
- Demand analysis and forecasting
- Research
- Shipping
- Receiving and handling merchandise
- Delivery
- Credit operations
- Reverse logistics (merchandise returns)
- Supply chain management
- Inventory control
- Theft control
- Supplier contacts
- Negotiation
- Cash receipts
- Customer service
- Merchandise marking
- Integrated marketing communications management
- Pricing

moves systematically toward the overall execution of the IRM plan. In retailing, there are three main tactical areas: pricing, integrated marketing communications (IMC), and customer service. This is where "the rubber meets the road" and where the retailer directly reaches the consumer.

The tactical executions must be integrated, or they will lose their effectiveness. Many of the tactical areas can also be used for retail differentiation, thus becoming a strategic element. For example, pricing tactics really are a reflection of the retailer's strategic decision regarding the level of retailing in which to become involved; that is, discount retailers offer low prices, and upscale retailers charge higher prices. Thus, the executions must be carefully planned and must follow the various retail strategies that have been developed. It is imperative that seamless integration be achieved during these executions. The following sections cover the three tactical areas in more detail.

PRICING

In each of the tactical execution phases, planning is undertaken just as in the overall IRM plan. Each tactical plan should include the same three areas used in the overall retail management plan: objectives, strategy, and tactics. Retail pricing includes the development of a pricing policy. A *pricing policy* refers to the direction all pricing in the retail firm will take. Each decision about price must be integrated and synergistic with the rest of the retail plan and retail variables.

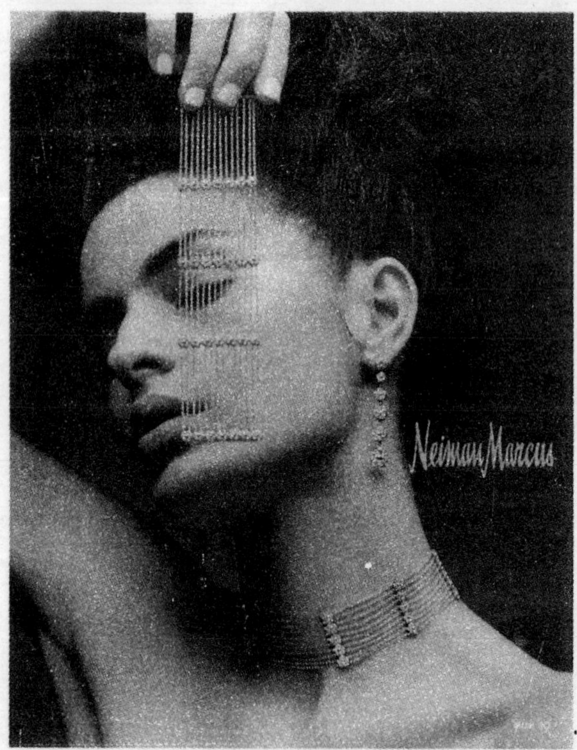

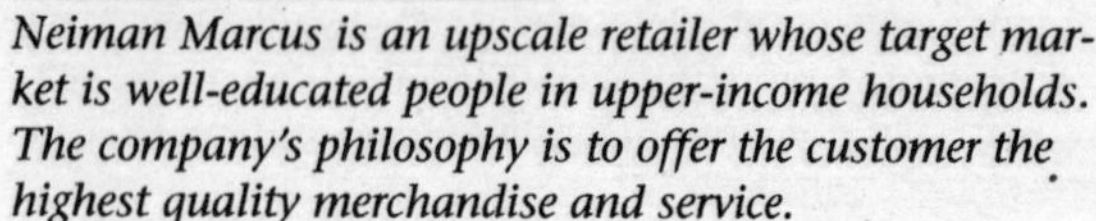
Neiman Marcus is an upscale retailer whose target market is well-educated people in upper-income households. The company's philosophy is to offer the customer the highest quality merchandise and service.

A discount retailer, Target aims its efforts toward a more upscale clientele than its competition does. This advertisement depicts the quality and prices typical of the retailer.

Decisions regarding pricing objectives generally are based on sales, profits, return on investment (ROI), or cash flow. The objectives should be outlined and a price policy developed based on all of the objectives.

Once the objectives and policies are in place, an overall pricing strategy can be developed. That strategy should give direction to all decisions made regarding the pricing variable. The strategy should help the retailer determine which types of tactics are appropriate.

The tactics accomplish the actual execution of price. The tactics are developed based on the objectives, policies, and strategy for the pricing variable. A section should be included in the IRM plan that covers any necessary price adjustments (markups, markdowns, discounts, and so on) that will be made periodically during the duration of the retail plan.

INTEGRATED MARKETING COMMUNICATIONS (IMC)

Integrated marketing communications (IMC), often referred to as *marketing communications* or *MARCOM*, comprise all the tactics utilized to reach the retailer's targeted audience. The IMC mix is generally made up of any communication variables, including public relations, publicity, direct marketing, cybermarketing, personal selling, sales promotion, and advertising. To ensure continuity, the IMC plan must be integrated within itself and with the other retail management variables. Objectives, strategy, and tactics are necessary to create the synergy and integration needed to carry out all of these functions.

CUSTOMER SERVICE

customer services Anything a retailer provides in addition to the core product or service that adds value.

Customer services are anything a retailer provides in addition to the core product or service that adds value.[16] Customer service concepts will be discussed in detail in Chapter 13. For now, it is important to know that customer service tactics are crucial to the retailer's success. In e-tailing, customer service is essential to keep customers happy with their orders and to maintain a high level of customer response management (CRM).

As with the other tactical executions (IMC and price), the retailer must develop a plan for the execution of customer service, and this plan should follow the objectives, strategy, and tactics of the business.

LAWS AND ETHICS

law A rule established by authority, society, or custom.

ethics Concepts of right and wrong behavior.

A **law** is "a rule established by authority, society, or custom."[17] **Ethics** involves "systematizing, defending, and recommending concepts of right and wrong behavior."[18] The laws and ethics governing the retailer's markets should guide all retail plans and actions. International retailing poses special issues; the retailer must be familiar with the laws, ethics, and customs of the places it does business. The retailer involved in e-tailing must be familiar with the numerous laws governing online business practices. Because the advent of e-tailing is relatively recent, laws relating to e-commerce are still being developed.

Any retailer conducting interstate commerce is bound not only by local and state laws but by many national laws as well. The federal government has restrictions on how firms may conduct business, as do regional, state, and local authorities. Retailers involved only in intrastate commerce are not subject to most federal regulations, but they must still operate under regional, local, and state laws.

Finally, many trade associations impose a code of ethics on their members. Members of these groups must follow the codes of ethics to maintain their memberships in good standing. Figure 3.4 shows a typical code of ethics for retailers. In-depth coverage of laws and ethics as they pertain to retailing appears in Chapter 14.

EVALUATION AND CONTROL

Perhaps the most important part of the integrated retail management plan is planning for effective evaluation and control. *Evaluation* refers to continuous monitoring of the retail plan to make sure it is performing up to expectations. Perhaps the easiest way to assess the plan's effectiveness is by examining the objectives. If the objectives were not achieved, something may be wrong with the plan. Perhaps the objectives were set too high, or perhaps the environment changed and wasn't effectively monitored.

— Forward —

In a Society which not only permits but encourages the private ownership of productive property and one which also engages in large and multitudinous public works, there appears, on every hand, a necessity for the appraisal of property. In fact, property appraisals are used throughout the economic, governmental, legal, and social activities of such a society.

As the vocation of property appraisal has developed during past decades from a business occupation into a profession, certain concepts have emerged and become clear. The word property is now given to physical things and also to the legal rights of ownership of tangible or intangible entities. Appraising is now considered to encompass three classes of operations, namely,

1. The estimation of the cost of producing or replacing physical property,
2. The forecasting of the monetary earning power of certain classes of property,
3. The valuation or determination of the worth of property.

Because of the specialized knowledge and abilities required of the appraiser which are not possessed by the layman, there has now come to be established a fiduciary relationship between him and those who rely upon his findings.

The American Society of Appraisers occupies a unique position among professional appraisal societies in that it recognizes and is concerned with all classes of property: real, personal, tangible, and intangible, including real estate, machinery and equipment, buildings and other structures, furnishings, works of art, natural resources, public utilites, gems and jewelry, investment securities, and so forth. It is also unique in that it recognizes the threefold character of the appraisal function.

In recognizing the need for the highest professional competence among appraisers, the American Society of Appraisers actively supports recognized institutions of higher learning in their scholastic programs that are designed to provide the necessary academic background to both appraiser aspirants and to the qualified professionals who desire to update and broaden their professional skills.

The Society has established an Educational Foundation to assist those institutions of higher learning that actively provide scholastic training and research in the various appraisal disciplines.

The necessity for a set of authoritative principles and a code of professional ethics, broad enough to cover all classes of property as well as the complexities of the various appraisal procedures, is a pressing one. Previous statements of principles have dealt almost exclusively with real estate. Existing codes of ethics are, in large measure, couched in such general moralistic terms that they are impractical for specific application.

Violation of any provision or rule of the Code should not give rise to a civil cause of action and should not create any presumption or evidence that a legal duty has been breached nor should it create any special relationship between the appraiser or any other person. This code is designed to provide guidance to appraisers and to provide a structure for regulating conduct of members of the ASA through disciplinary actions. Violations of the Code are not designed or intended to be the basis of any civil liability. (January 1990)

To meet the need for a comprehensive set of guideposts and for a specific code of ethics, the Society has prepared and presents herewith *The Principles of Appraisal Practice and Code of Ethics of the American Society of Appraisers.*

FIGURE 3.4 **Excerpt from the Code of Ethics of the American Society of Appraisers** (Source: American Society of Appraisers, "Principle of Appraisal Practice and Code of Ethics." Reprinted by permission of the American Society of Appraisers.)

As a student, you can measure your classroom objectives by looking at your grades throughout the semester. If you created an objective of getting an A in your retail management class, it would be wise to see if you are achieving that objective by referring to the grades you received on exams, papers, and presentations. Did you ace that all-important semester project? At the end of the semester, if you find that you didn't get an A, you need to evaluate why. Was it because you didn't study enough? Or did you study the wrong material? Maybe you didn't attend classes regularly. Whatever the reason, you need to evaluate the outcome.

After evaluating your success or failure and figuring out the reasons for any unmet objectives, you need to modify your plan to make sure you will succeed in the future. The control in the class situation would be either to increase your study time and attendance or to lower your objective to a more reasonable and achievable level—such as setting the goal of getting a B or C.

Retailers must do the same thing: they must evaluate whether their objectives were too high or whether they failed in the execution of their integrated retail management plan.

Another method of control for retailers is the development of a contingency plan. A *contingency plan* consists of alternative strategies or tactics to achieve the stated objectives. Contingency plans are used if the preferred strategies or tactics are hampered by uncontrollable environmental changes. The retailer must be able to respond to events such as power outages, changes in the economy, supplier bankruptcies, price wars, natural disasters, and so on.

It is essential to include all elements of the integrated retail management plan when assessing the performance of the business. For example, the forecasts should be rechecked. The IMC tactics should be scrutinized. The environmental scanning undertaken during the planning period should be examined in case any environmental changes have occurred.

Many formal tools are available to help retailers evaluate and control. Many of the methods are quantitative techniques, but several qualitative techniques exist as well. For example, focus groups can be used to check for mistakes in execution and to gain valuable insights into how the retailer is perceived. Information gathered for the RIS is important, as are data generated from the execution of the customer service variable. Certainly the financial statements would be helpful in assessing the success of the retail establishment.

Because of the tremendous costs associated with the development of the integrated retail management plan, evaluation and control are not options—they are requirements. Proactive plans help keep the retailer competitive in today's retail environment.

SUMMARY

Planning is crucial in today's retail environment. A comprehensive integrated retail management plan (IRM) is necessary to contain costs and generate the highest revenues possible.

The IRM plan starts with the mission and vision statements. The mission statement describes what the company does and the vision statement states future goals. The situational analysis provides a historical and current picture of the business, its competitors, and its potential growth. A retail strategy is developed based on the mission, vision, and situational analysis. The strategy provides guidance on how the objectives will be achieved. Retail information systems (RIS) are used to collect and disseminate data and information to employees and managers.

The customers to whom a retailer aims its marketing efforts are collectively called the *target market*. Along with determining the target market, a retailer must decide where to locate the business and whether to have an online presence. Merchandise buying and handling involve decisions related to the purchase of the products and how the products (or services) will be delivered to the final customer. Human resource management decisions establish who will run the day-to-day activities of the retailer. Retail tactics are comprised of three areas: pricing, the determination of the prices of products and services; integrated marketing communications (IMC), the coordination of all communication regarding the retailer and its products and services; and customer service, the decisions about which value-added services geared toward meeting and exceeding expectations are offered.

Decisions regarding laws and ethics occur at all phases of the IRM process. Local, state, national, and in some cases international regulations may dictate present and future action. To monitor the IRM plan, retailers need to set up an effective evaluation and control system. A good evaluation and control system, when applied to the plan step by step, will save the successful retailer additional costs in both time and money.

KEY TERMS

planning (60)
mission statement (60)
vision statement (61)
retail (corporate) objectives (64)
environmental scanning (64)
retail strategy (67)
strategic thinking (67)
controllable variables (67)
uncontrollable variables (67)
retail information system (RIS) (68)
primary data (69)
secondary data (69)
target market (69)
segmentation (69)
mass marketing approach (69)
segmented approach (69)
typical customer profile (71)
operations management (71)
merchandise buying and handling (72)
logistics (72)
supply chain management (72)
tactical executions (74)
customer services (77)
law (77)
ethics (77)

QUESTIONS FOR DISCUSSION

1. Explain the purpose of a mission statement and a vision statement. Why it is important for a company to have a mission? Why must it have a vision?
2. What is the difference between strategy and tactics? Is one more important than the other?
3. When would a retailer engage in environmental scanning? What types of information might a retailer of women's accessories gather?
4. Why is it important for retailers to have an integrated retail management plan? What are characteristics of a good IRM plan?
5. What information is included in an effective definition of a retailer's target market?
6. Why is the evaluation and control function important in the implementation of a retail plan?

E-TAILING EXERCISE

Choose a retailer that has a website, and using the IRM flow chart as a guide, answer the following questions:

1. How does the retailer approach each area in the IRM flow chart?
2. How do you think the company performs evaluation and control of its strategy?
3. In what areas could the company improve?

Continuing Case 3.1

Sherwin-Williams Company: Mission and Operations

Sherwin-Williams Company has been in business for more than 135 years. The founders were involved in paint sales and the glass business. Almost immediately, Sherwin-Williams became a market leader and today is the number one paint company in the United States and number two worldwide. The company's mission is as follows:

Being the world leader in the world of paint

In maintaining all this we are committed to remaining ahead in the marketplace, providing quality products and service. We are therefore committed to the pursuit of excellence and to the achievement of the highest standards in the industry.

Customer Satisfaction is therefore our pledge, our duty. Being so driven we are committed to providing what is complementary to this goal . . . a highly trained and motivated management staff and workforce, focused on accomplishing these objectives and rewarded for achieving them. Satisfying the needs of our customers is seen as our purpose. Sherwin-Williams will be providing cutting edge technology, a wide range of products and building our relationships and service to achieve these goals.

In being the market leader, we intend to be the most profitable company on returns on investments.

We are committed to our customers . . . and the community.

Sherwin-Williams is a vertically integrated corporation, meaning the company manufactures and retails its products. A multichannel distributor, Sherwin-Williams utilizes its extensive retail network to market its products. Sherwin-Williams's main competitors in the manufacturing area include The Valspar Corporation; RPM, Inc.; E.I. DuPont de Nemours & Company; Imperial Chemical Industries PLC; and Akzo. Glidden, Benjamin Moore, K-Moore, Duron, and Pittsburgh Paints are the largest brands competing with Sherwin-Williams, along with many local and regional brands. Major paint retailers that compete with Sherwin-Williams include Benjamin Moore Paint Stores and other home centers that sell paint, such as Home Depot and Lowe's. A Fortune 500 company, Sherwin-Williams has increased dividends annually since 1979, which reflects its strong financial position.

Sherwin-Williams operates more than 2,500 stores in the United States, Canada, and Puerto Rico. In addition, its products are sold at many small and large independent and chain retail outlets. One of Sherwin-Williams's divisions caters to the do-it-yourself (DIY) market. Sherwin-Williams identifies its DIY market products as "home decorating ideas" rather than as "paint and accessories." Within that market, the company sells wall coverings (paint and wallpaper) and paint accessories. It also provides individualized customer services, such as offering home decorating ideas.

Questions

1. What are the strengths and weaknesses of Sherwin-Williams's mission statement?
2. Create a two- to three-page IRM outline for Sherwin-Williams. You may use any outside resources that you need.
3. Which of the IRM flow chart sections were the most difficult to develop for the company?
4. To which IRM areas do you think Sherwin-Williams should pay particular attention?

Sources: The APMP Superior Fund, Michigan Technological University, School of Business and Economics, retrieved July 2002 from www.newstarproductions.com/Sherwin-Williams.htm.; Sherwin-Williams's homepage at www.sherwin.com. Mission statement courtesy of Sherwin-Williams Company.

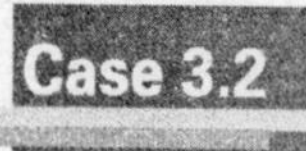

Guilford Home Furnishings Faces Competition

"We're very sorry that the back seam opened on your new sofa," said Lisa Guilford. "As a small token of our appreciation for you as our valued customer, we've not only fixed the seam, but want you to accept this pair of matching throw pillows with our compliments."

Background

Guilford Home Furnishings (GHF) was founded in 1961 as a manufacturer of upholstered furniture. Originally its business model was a traditional one: a manufacturer that sold to retailers through a group of self-employed manufacturers' representatives. In the late 1970s, when credit was very tight, the firm went through a cash flow crisis as retailers stretched payments out beyond 120 days. This was when Lisa and Scott Guilford's father, Karl, who was the primary stockholder and president at the time, made the momentous decision to open a factory outlet. Though damaging to his trade relations, the gambit paid off with an immediate improvement in GHF's cash position.

At this time, Karl Guilford also added private-label bedding to the line and several years later further complemented it with bedroom suites and kitchen sets manufactured in South Carolina. GHF's price points were set for the budget-conscious consumer and were considered the most competitive in the five-county area. On occasion, customers came from out of state to buy GHF furniture.

Recently GHF had seen many large retailers move into the market. They built huge showrooms, carried multiple lines hitting several price points, and hired aggressive salespeople who derived most of their income from commissions rather than salary. Some of these operations had after-sale service that took care of repairs. Most of their advertising took the form of inserts in the Sunday newspapers as well as innovative, if not occasionally downright quirky, television spots. The outlet also had sales that correlated with major holidays.

Customer Relationships

GHF didn't have many customer complaints, but when it did, the company would turn itself inside out to rectify the problem. There were two reasons for this. First, Karl Guilford always told all his employees that he wanted to treat people the same way he expected other merchants to treat him. Second, because GHF's most effective advertising was word of mouth, it couldn't afford to have ill will among anyone.

The furniture industry is widely known for working on thin margins. Craig Edmunds, the accounting manager, worked hard finding little ways to keep the company profitable. Instead of using commercial distributors for industrial and office supplies, he would often stop by a Wal-Mart or a Staples on the way home from work. The savings he realized were substantial.

One day, while walking through the showroom, Craig overheard the conversation between Lisa Guilford and a former unhappy customer. The woman was now beaming with delight: not only had her furniture been repaired promptly, but she was getting a pair of throw pillows at no cost. "Does anyone know what that costs us?" Craig asked himself. "I'll have to check that out."

Back in his office, Craig looked up the price of fabric. On average it was $12 per yard, which meant GHF's wholesale cost was about $10 for just giving away. How hard did he have to look for $13 in cost savings?

Later in the day, Craig stopped by Lisa's desk to tell her what he had found. The throw pillows that GHF was giving away cost the company about $13 out of pocket. If GHF sold throw pillows with the furniture when ordered, it would charge $28 per pair. "We're not only forgoing $15 of profit but costing GHF another $13 whenever we give these things away. To me, it looks like a waste of money," explained Craig.

Lisa replied, "My father started the practice years ago. It was a good idea back then and probably still is!"

"Back then it might have been," replied Craig. "But today we have all the large retailers moving into town, cutting prices, and running all sorts of sales. If we keep on giving stuff like those pillows away, I'm afraid that we're not going to stay in business for very much longer. I think we should put a stop to the practice—the sooner, the better!"

"Maybe so, but we have to look beyond the cost," said Lisa. "What's the value of a satisfied customer to GHF? Many of our customers are now third generation, meaning their grandparents bought from Dad."

Craig insisted, "I think you need to look at your customers again. The customer in the new millennium is driven by price and price alone!"

Questions

1. Does GHF still have a viable approach to customer relations?
2. Support or refute the points that Craig is trying to make to Lisa.
3. How might you go about segmenting the home furnishings market to accommodate the business models represented by GHF as well as the large furniture merchandisers that have moved into town?
4. Prepare a recommended a course of action for Lisa, and explain your reasoning.

Source: This case was prepared from actual business situations by Richard R. Young, Ph.D., associate professor of business logistics, Penn State Berks–Lehigh Valley. It is intended to foster class discussion and not to suggest either appropriate or inappropriate administrative behavior.

The Retail Environment: A Situational and Competitive Analysis

Chapter

4

The one who adapts his policy to the times prospers, and likewise that the one whose policy clashes with the demands of the times does not.

Niccolo Machiavelli

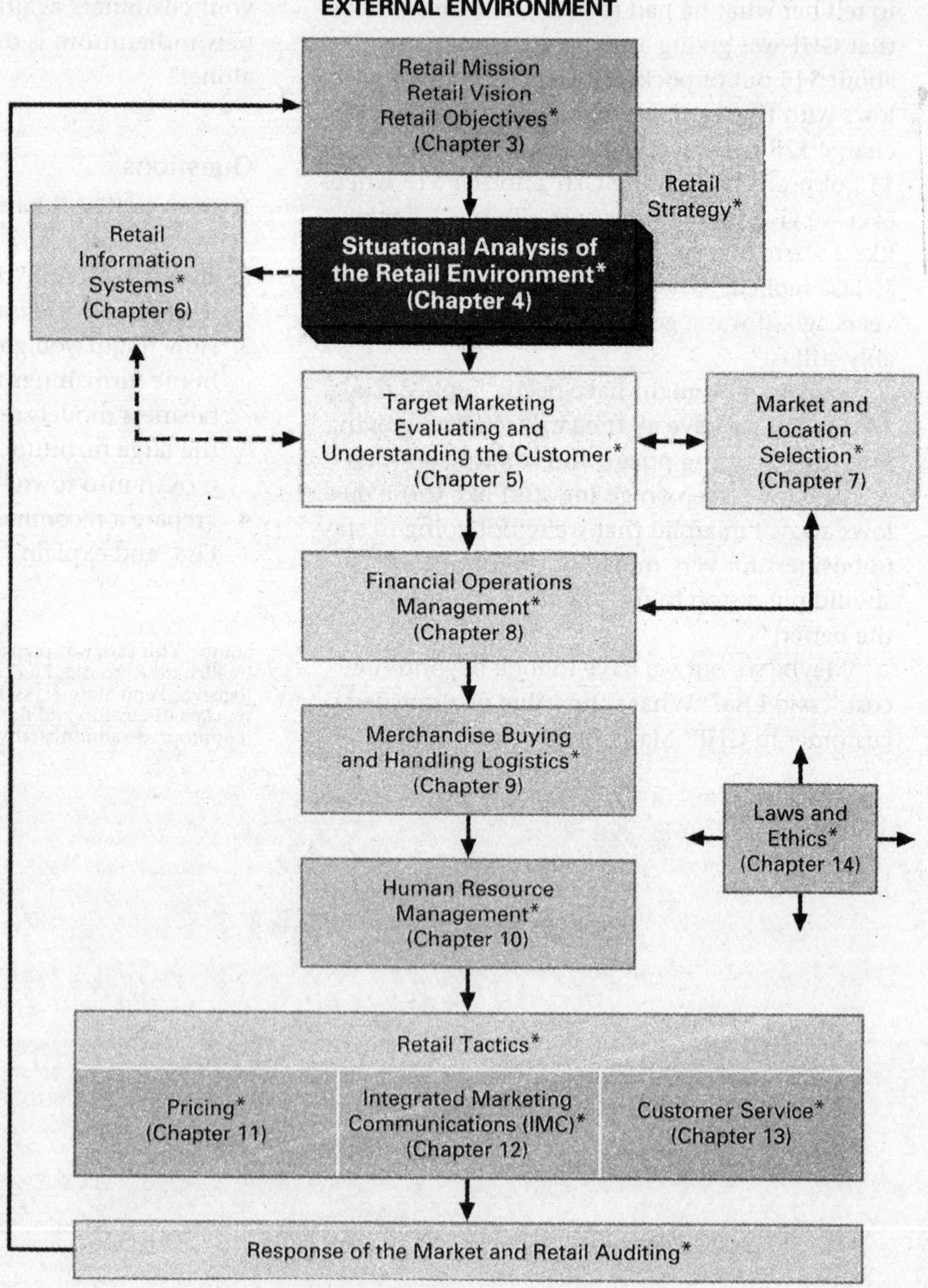

*Evaluation and control occurs at all these stages.

CHAPTER OBJECTIVES

After completing this chapter, you will be able to:

1. Describe the information that comprises a situational analysis.
2. Define the various types of retail establishments by ownership, strategy, and census classifications.
3. Explain the purpose of methods such as NAICS and classification of retailers by ownership and strategy.
4. Describe the elements that comprise a competitive analysis.

Young Entrepreneurs Find Niche

By conducting a situational analysis, companies can get a big picture of what is occurring in the environment. A savvy person can find a niche and become a retailer very easily. Take Sneakerpimp.com, an online retailer of rare styles of Nike tennis shoes. The website states, "Our goal is to offer nothing but the most exclusive kicks on the Internet."[1] Eric Eways, 16 years old, and Joe Guerro, 27 years old, are the founders of Sneakerpimp.com. They decided to target a market of fanatics for Nike shoes. They are subverting Nike's marketing strategy by obtaining limited-run models of Nike shoes. Often Nike produces a special issue of shoes to celebrate a particular occasion. For example, Nike's Greeks shoes are embroidered on each heel with the Greek letters alpha phi alpha. Nike produced about 2,000 Greeks in honor of Alpha Phi Alpha's sponsorship of Philadelphia's Greek Picnic, an annual gathering of African American fraternities. Other examples include the sneaker with a Puerto Rican flag on the heel to celebrate Puerto Rican Day and Nike Year of the Horse shoes, released in Taiwan.

Eways and Guerro purchase the shoes from retailers and then resell the shoes online for twice or more what they paid for them. Often they sell the shoes to retailers in Japan that are willing to pay more than $500 a pair for bulk orders. Although Nike audits retailers to look for bulk purchases, Eways and Guerro have established a network that avoids detection.[2]

INTRODUCTION

To effectively manage the retail business, the professional retailer must be aware of the environment in which the business operates. As stated in the previous chapter, it is essential that the retailer understand the current business situation as well as the environment that will affect that particular retail business. This chapter focuses on these issues. The chapter begins with an overview of a situational analysis, then discusses classification systems for retail businesses, and concludes with a look at some methods for undertaking a competitive analysis. Achieving a clear understanding of the overall retail operation enables the retailer to make better decisions regarding the executions of the integrated retail management (IRM) plan.

THE SITUATIONAL ANALYSIS

The situational analysis of a retail organization provides the big picture: an overview of the company as a whole. Several things must be considered as inputs into the situational analysis. The analysis should include a product/service history and evaluation. It should analyze the competition and assess the geographical aspects of retail locations. Finally, the situational analysis should examine current consumers (evaluating customers is discussed in detail in the next chapter). A listing of the strengths and weaknesses of the retailer's product(s) or service(s) can be added to help strengthen the analysis. Specifically, a SWOT (**s**trengths/**w**eaknesses/**o**pportunities/**t**hreats) analysis might be performed, resulting in a "problems and opportunities graph."[3]

COMPANY ANALYSIS

company analysis An analysis that includes data on sales and profit figures, company mission/vision, company's risk or conservative orientation, corporate resources, level of aggressiveness, market share, sales trends, etc.

The **company analysis** should include as much of the following data as possible:

- Sales and profit figures
- Company mission and vision
- Risk position (risk oriented or more conservative)
- Corporate (or organizational) resources, including, but not limited to, financial, technological, and human
- Aggressiveness
- Market share
- Sales trends

In addition, the following information is very useful in developing an effective retailing plan:

- What are the various environments (social, political, technological, cultural, economic, legal, natural, etc.) that may affect the company and the retailing plan execution?

- Within the industry, what have been the overall trends in sales?
- Within the industry, what have been the overall trends in market share?
- What business practices are used in the industry?
- Will major upcoming events have an effect on the product or service?

This analysis should be in-depth but concise.

PRODUCT HISTORY AND ANALYSIS

product history and analysis An analysis that addresses the question "What do customers want and/or need?"

A **product history and analysis** should address the question "What do customers want and/or need?" Much of the necessary data may be found within the company itself. The retail manager or planner should understand how and why all the retailing mix variables fit together. Often these variables have been developed over time. No decisions should be made in a vacuum. Retail strategy and tactics (product, price, channels of distribution, and integrated marketing communications [IMC]) should be integrated and should match the firm's character. The following pieces of information are necessary to develop an effective product analysis:

- Product/service background
- Current problems facing the product, brand, or service
- Past retail successes or failures
- Past years' budgets and financial statements
- Past to present media spending

In addition, there should be a product evaluation that includes (but is not limited to) the following information:

- What is the quality of the product or service?
- How is the product or service differentiated?
- What aspects comprise the "total product"? (The total product concept includes the physical product or service, the benefits offered by the retailer, the needs/wants satisfiers that the company fulfills, and the retail brand and image.)
- What has been added or deleted from the product or service line over the past five years? What will be added or deleted in the future?
- How do intermediaries (wholesalers and other suppliers) feel about the retailer and its products?
- Is distribution effective? What type of distribution system is utilized? Is distribution intensive, selective, or exclusive?
- What problems have consumers experienced? How can these problems be addressed and/or corrected?
- What are the features and benefits that are unique to the retailer? Are there features that differ sufficiently from those of the competition to allow for adequate differentiation? Specifically, how is differentiation achieved (if at all)?

- How do consumers perceive the retailer (*e.g.*, high tech, old fashioned, modern, trendy)?
- Are customers satisfied?
- What are the company's return policies?
- Are warranties or guarantees offered?
- How wide is the product selection?

Each individual situational analysis dictates a need for either more or less information. This information is found by conducting primary research; thus, a large amount of consumer testing is used to generate data necessary to answer certain questions. The ultimate goal is to develop a clear picture of the current retail environment using the data gathered in the situational analysis.

TYPES OF RETAIL INSTITUTIONS

The decade of the 2000s will witness many dramatic changes in retailing. Many of these changes will affect the types and classifications of existing retail institutions. These institutions are generally based on some type of classification system that mirrors the retailer's business operations. For example, a retailer that specializes in getting the consumer a product or service in the most convenient way possible could be classified as a convenience retailer. Think of how many different retailers you know that specialize in convenience products. You have probably thought of 7-Eleven, Stop-and-Go, or perhaps even Sheetz or Loaf-and-Jug. What would you call retailers that specialize in the sale of food products? If you say "supermarkets," you are correct. There is some overlap among the types of retailers that exist and also some differences in the way they are classified. For example, a convenience store and a supermarket may both be classified as food retailers. The classification systems discussed next will help you better understand the various types of retail institutions.

It is important to understand the types of retail institutions because they have a competitive impact on business. With this knowledge, managers are better prepared to develop comprehensive competitive analyses for use in their retail businesses. Retail professionals must strive to stay current with the numerous changes in their environments that may affect their businesses as well as their professional lives. Remember the Wal-Mart neighborhood market concept (see Chapter 3).

SIC TO NAICS

Standard Industrial Classification (SIC) A government classification system that uses numbers or codes to identify business types.

Traditionally, retailers used a system of retail classification that was developed for the U.S. Census Bureau in 1930, called the **Standard Industrial Classification,** or **SIC.** Within this system, each type of retailer (and, for that matter, all U.S. businesses) is given a special set of numbers, or code. The SIC code identifies businesses and classifies them together to better collect and analyze business data.

Although it sounds somewhat complicated, the SIC is not hard to understand. The broad categories of business are first separated by two-digit codes. For retailing, the first two digits are in the 50s. For example, a grocery store falls under the 54 SIC code, which covers all food retailers. An additional number is given to indicate the type of food retailer. Thus, a grocery store is assigned the 541 SIC code. Finally, a fourth number is assigned to further identify exactly what type(s) of products the store sells. As a retailer, you can access those retail data by SIC code. To do this, go to the U.S. Census Bureau website (*www.census.gov/mrts/www/mrts.html*).

The internationalization of retailing has created some problems in attempting to identify businesses by SIC codes. Many nations use classification systems other than SIC. In response to this change in the retail environment, the United States is converting to a new system of classification, called the **North American Industrial Classification System,** or **NAICS** (pronounced "nakes"). The NAICS system will allow "apples and apples" comparisons in terms of economic statistics reported by many countries. Our neighbors, Mexico and Canada, helped develop the system and will also use it to make international North American comparisons for their retail categories. The conversion to NAICS from SIC started in 1997 and is scheduled to be completed in 2004. It is still possible to access NAICS information with SIC information on the website *www.census.gov/epcd/www/naics.html*. This conversion is crucial to the expanded North American retail trade industry.

North American Industrial Classification System (NAICS) A business coding system that will replace the SIC system. NAICS provides better accuracy and improved comparability with other countries.

According the NAICS Association,[5] the six-digit NAICS codes provide for newer industries and reorganize the categories on a production- or process-oriented basis. The codes accommodate more types of businesses and allow for more detail than do the four-digit SIC codes. Table 4.1 shows the NAICS hierarchical structure and the sectors identified by the codes.

The international NAICS agreement specifies only the first five digits of the code. An optional sixth digit identifies subdivisions of NAICS industries that accommodate user needs in individual countries. Thus, at the five-digit level country codes are standardized, but the use of the six-digit code can differ among U.S., Canadian, and Mexican counterparts. If you are curious about the codes for other types of businesses, the NAICS Association website (*www.naics.com*) has a search engine that looks up specific codes from key words. Table 4.2 shows some examples of NAICS codes.

Using these data makes it easier to generate retail classification systems that provide insights into the various retail institutions. Following are additional classification methods that will help you understand the different types of retailers.

CLASSIFICATION BY OWNERSHIP

Besides using the SIC or NAICS government systems for retail classification, a number of other methods help clarify how retailers are classified. Although most retailers are small (the majority of all retailers have only one outlet for their goods and services),[6] the majority of sales and employment in retailing

TABLE 4.1

NAICS HIERARCHY AND SECTORS

Hierarchy Structure	
XX	Industry Sector (20 broad sectors up from 10 SIC)
XXX	Industry Subsector
XXXX	Industry Group
XXXXX	Industry
XXXXXX	U.S., Canadian, or Mexican National specific

NAICS Sectors

Code	
11	Agriculture, Forestry, Fishing, and Hunting
21	Mining
22	Utilities
23	Construction
31–33	Manufacturing
42	Wholesale Trade
44–45	Retail Trade
48–49	Transportation and Warehousing
51	Information
52	Finance and Insurance
53	Real Estate and Rental and Leasing
54	Professional, Scientific, and Technical Services
55	Management of Companies and Enterprises
56	Administrative and Support and Waste Management and Remediation Services
61	Education Services
62	Health Care and Social Assistance
71	Arts, Entertainment, and Recreation
72	Accommodation and Food Services
81	Other Services (except Public Administration)
92	Public Administration

comes from large retailers. Based on these ownership differences, the top three classifications for retail ownership are (1) independents, (2) chains, and (3) franchises. In addition, many people also classify by (4) leased departments and (5) cooperatives.

independent retailer A type of retailer that operates a single establishment.

INDEPENDENTS. An **independent retailer** operates only one retail establishment. The majority of these stores are owner or family managed. The ease of entry into this type of retailing makes the independent retail store attractive to those with few capital resources. Although independent retailers make up 80 percent of all retailers, their sales represent only 40 percent of retail sales.[7]

TABLE 4.2

EXAMPLES OF NAICS CODES

Code	Retail Establishment
452110	Department stores
451120	Toy stores
448120	Apparel stores, women's and girls' clothing

Independent retailers have the advantage of being able to respond quickly to their customers' needs and wants. In addition, the owners of independent retail operations usually have many community contacts and are active in local chambers of commerce. They rely on these connections to generate business within the community. Because many independents are located in neighborhoods and rural locations, rental expenses tend to be less than for stores located in major shopping districts. Due to the smaller size and location, independent retailers have greater opportunities than other types of retailers to build customer relationships.[8]

A downside to being an independent retailer is the inability to capitalize on economies of scale; therefore, the independent's prices are usually higher than those of larger corporate chain stores. Another disadvantage is a lower level of expertise among personnel. Because independents are traditionally smaller than corporate chains, they have a smaller personnel base. They have fewer resources for hiring and training qualified experts in each of the functional retail areas—IMC, buying, management, and accounting.

In his book *Competing with the Retail Giants,*[9] Kenneth Stone offers independent retailers the following suggestions for competing with large chain stores.

Independent retailers represent the majority of retailers. Shown here is a small, independent retailer on a main street of Anytown, USA.

1. Improve merchandising.
2. Revive marketing practices.
3. Provide outstanding service to customers.
4. Treat the customer right.
5. Improve the efficiency of business.
6. Implement changes.
7. Build teams.

Stone suggests that by paying attention to these critical areas, the small retailer can effectively compete for the consumer dollar against the larger, corporate-owned retail chains.

strategic clarity The commitment to achieve an in-depth understanding of the retailer's strengths and weaknesses, including the strengths and weaknesses of its integrated retail management plan and marketing program.

One of the most important variables for success as a small, independent retailer is to develop strategic clarity. **Strategic clarity** is the commitment to achieve an in-depth understanding of the retailer's strengths and weaknesses, including the strengths and weaknesses of its integrated retail management and marketing programs. One key outcome of strategic clarity is the ability to acquire knowledge of markets and to develop an effective marketing program.[10] To compete in the retail environment, independent retailers often band together to form cooperative agreements. Co-ops are covered in detail later in this chapter.

chain store A retailer that operates multiple (more than one) retail stores.

CHAINS. Corporate **chain stores** operate multiple (more than one) retail stores. Although the majority of chain operations are small, the bulk of sales in retailing come from the larger chain stores such as Wal-Mart, Sears, and Home Depot. Many chain stores are divisions of larger companies. Intimate Brands Company, for example, owns a number of chain stores, including Victoria's Secret and Bath & Body Works. J.C. Penney Corporation owns 1,049 domestic and international JCPenney department stores in the United States, Puerto Rico, and Mexico; 54 Renner department stores in Brazil; and the Eckerd chain of more than 2,600 drugstores in the United States.[11]

economies of scale Achieving lower costs per unit through higher-quantity purchases.

The biggest advantage of operating a chain store is the ability to reduce costs through **economies of scale.** By purchasing in large quantities, the big chains can purchase products at reduced costs, thereby gaining the ability to pass on the lower costs to their customers. The large-volume purchases also allow these retailers to negotiate with suppliers for a lower per-product cost. In addition to lower costs for purchases, the large chains generally use computerized systems for inventory control, ordering, and theft control. By reducing the costs associated with these functions, the chains can, once again, pass the savings on to their customers in the form of lower product and service prices.

Due to their size, chains have the advantage of using information technology more efficiently than smaller retailers. Many large chains, such as Office Depot and Target, can monitor instantly what is currently selling and what remains in inventory. Technology also allows chains to link directly with suppliers and have merchandise shipped when it falls below a given level.[12]

Finally, chains are able to hire and train the "best and brightest" minds in the retail business and have specialists for each functional area within the

By purchasing in large quantities, big chains such as Wal-Mart can purchase products at reduced costs and pass on the lower costs to their customers.

business. For example, chains can have specialists assigned to the buying function as well as the selling function.

Chain store operations also have some disadvantages. The biggest drawback is the cost associated with running a large operation. As the chain's size increases, so do its financial commitments. Furthermore, many chain operations are slower to respond to environmental problems due to bureaucracies typical in larger businesses. Another disadvantage is the difficulty in tailoring the product assortment to different geographic areas. To take advantage of economies of scale, chains often purchase the same products for all their stores.

As we have seen, independents and chain operations come with unique sets of advantages and disadvantages. The disadvantages, when understood, can be minimized or eliminated by good management, however.

franchise A contractual agreement between a franchisor and a franchisee that allows the franchisee to operate a retail establishment using the name and (usually) the franchisor's operating methods.

franchisor A business that grants the franchisee the privilege to use the franchisor's name and (usually) operating practices.

franchisee The owner of a retail establishment who has a contract with the franchisor to use the franchise's name and (usually) methods of operation.

FRANCHISES. A **franchise** is a contractual agreement between a franchisor and a franchisee. This agreement allows the franchisee to operate a retail establishment using the name and (usually) the franchisor's operating methods. Simply stated, a **franchisor** is the owner of a franchise and can be a wholesaler, manufacturer, or service provider. McDonald's, for example, is a franchisor. McDonald's creates contracts with individual owners of restaurants and allows the owners to use the McDonald's name. The **franchisee** is the owner of the restaurant who has a contract with McDonald's to operate the

GLOBAL RETAILING

South Africa Uses the Web to Increase Franchise Activity

The mission of the Franchise Advice and Information Network (FRAIN) is "to supply high quality information and support services to individuals and small, medium, and micro enterprises (SMMEs) to ensure growth and improvement of new and existing franchising business."

FRAIN's vision is to utilize franchises to grow market activity in South Africa. According to FRAIN's website (*www.frain.org*), franchising is "a relatively safe way to enter into business, but most South Africans do not have access to opportunities to support, to enable them to utilise [*sic*] it."

FRAIN's website offers information on every aspect of franchising, including the legal aspect, financial considerations, training programs, and franchise opportunities. This website is a great example of how organizations are using the Internet to increase and encourage market activity.

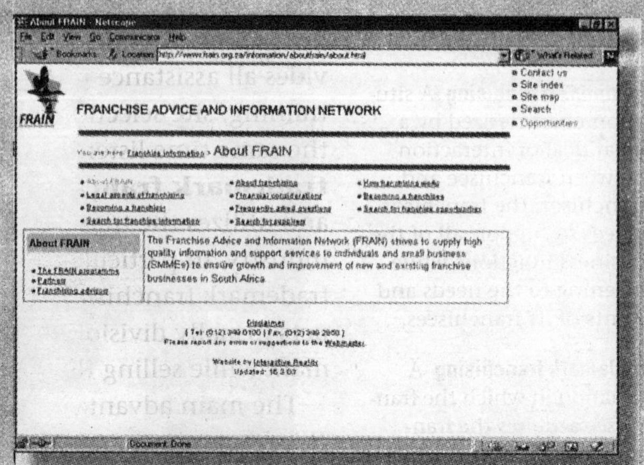

(Reprinted by permission of FRAIN.)

FRAIN partners include the Department of Trade and Industry of South Africa, the Franchise Association of Southern Africa, and the CSIR, an African technology and research organization.

Source: Franchise Advice and Information Network homepage, retrieved July 2003 from www.frain.org.za.

establishment under the McDonald's name and (usually) follow McDonald's operating practices.

Depending on the contract, the franchisee pays the franchisor a fee plus royalties, typically based on sales, for the right to own and operate the business in a particular location (generally geographical). In return, the franchisor offers the franchisee expert assistance in site selection, building requirements, IMC, employee or managerial training, and advice or requirements for product or service offerings.

The franchisee receives all profits from the operation of the retail business after paying the royalty and thus is motivated to try to increase sales as much as possible. Because franchisors have more expertise in their areas and have greater resources, they generally design the systems for the operation of the franchised business. In a franchise program, the parties gain from the increased size of the organization and are able to share resources while dividing costs associated with running a retail operation. In comparison to other types of retailers, franchisors' networks grow rapidly with few capital and managerial resources, while franchisees gain "instant" expertise as well as a large market presence.

product franchising A situation in which the franchisee agrees to sell the franchisor's products or services.

business franchising A situation characterized by a great deal of interaction between franchisee and franchisor; the franchisor agrees to support all of the business functions while listening to the needs and wants of its franchisees.

trademark franchising A situation in which the franchisee acquires the franchisor's identity and utilizes the trademarks developed by the franchisor.

During the past two decades, franchising has been split among product, business, and trademark franchising. In **product franchising,** the franchisee agrees to sell the franchisor's products and services. In **business franchising,** the franchisee follows the McDonald's model, wherein a lot of interaction goes on between franchisor and franchisee. The franchisor provides all assistance necessary to carry out the business functions (advertising, training, site selection, accounting, planning, and other executions) while at the same time listening to the needs and wants of its franchise holders. In **trademark franchising,** the franchisee acquires the franchisor's identity and utilizes the trademarks developed by the franchisor. The transportation industry, in particular the automobile industry, exemplifies both product and trademark franchising. General Motors allows its dealers to sell certain products (usually divisional, such as Chevrolets or Pontiacs) and to use its trademark while selling these products.

The main advantage of franchising to franchisees is that each owner (franchisee) can own and operate his or her own business with a smaller capital outlay than would be possible without joining the franchise team. In addition, franchising breaks down a barrier to entry into the retail market by allowing the franchisee to sell established brand names and products. Franchisees can also achieve economies of scale through their association with a larger, more powerful buying group, thereby bringing down their cost per unit. Finally, the franchisee gets specialized training in the functional areas of

One of the reasons franchises are popular is that the franchisee benefits from the established brand name. Krispy Kreme is a quick-service restaurant franchise located in the United States.

retail operations, such as advertising (IMC), retail information systems (RIS), inventory control procedures, employee/managerial development and training, and the right to exclusivity in selling the national or regional product or service.

leased department A department in a large retail store in which space is "leased" or rented to an outside vendor that in turn operates under the larger retailer store's policies.

LEASED DEPARTMENTS. Another form of retail ownership is the leased department. A **leased department** consists of space in a larger retail store (such as JCPenney) that is rented to an outside vendor. The retail business that leases the space runs that area as if it were a small business within the larger business unit. It is generally responsible for all retail functions (in many cases including the fixtures of the leased area). In addition, the lessee pays rent for the space. Examples of leased departments often include jewelry and shoe departments in large department stores.

Because many larger stores lack the expertise for a given product line—for example, jewelry—they get the advantage of greater expertise within the store. The stores are also assured of having a product that their customers need or want. The lessee has the advantage of established customers and customer traffic for their products and services. In addition, many costs can be reduced for the lessee, such as security and parking.

COOPERATIVES. There are three major types of cooperative store arrangements (also called *co-ops*): retail-sponsored cooperatives, wholesale-sponsored cooperatives, and consumer cooperatives.

retail-sponsored cooperative A type of retail organization in which several retailers have banded together to create an organization that helps to overcome many of the problems associated with running a small retail operation.

To overcome many of the disadvantages associated with being a smaller, independent retailer, some retailers band together to create a **retail-sponsored cooperative,** an organization that allows centralized buying and overcomes other problems involved in running a small retail operation. Through centralized buying, member retailers can take advantage of the price savings that accompany large purchases from vendors. In addition, retailers can improve their operating efficiency by sharing methods developed by the cooperative organization. An example of a retail-sponsored cooperative is Carpet One, a national cooperative of independent floor retailers.[13]

wholesale-sponsored cooperative An organization that is developed, owned, and run by a group of wholesalers.

A **wholesale-sponsored cooperative** is developed, owned, and run by a group of wholesalers. The wholesaler groups generally offer integrated retail programs to smaller, independent retailers. The wholesalers may offer the independents services such as warehousing and transportation. In addition, members receive additional services (many fee based) such as site selection, store displays, and other merchandising methods. An example of a wholesale-sponsored cooperative is Blooming Prairie (*www.bpco-op.com*), which has been distributing natural foods throughout the Midwest since 1974.

consumer cooperative A retail establishment owned and operated by a group of consumers.

In a **consumer cooperative,** the consumers themselves own and operate the retail establishment. Generally, consumer cooperatives come about because members believe they can offer products and services at a lower price than traditional retailers. Often these consumers believe there is a need in the marketplace traditional retailers are not serving. It may be, for example, that a group of consumers believe a traditional retailer isn't being environmentally friendly and in response join forces and form a co-op more responsive to environmental concerns. In the banking industry, consumer cooperatives have emerged in response to a perceived lack of sensitivity to the consumer by traditional banks. These cooperatives are known as *credit unions.*

Suppose you and your classmates have been discussing the high cost of textbooks. You decide that you can offer textbooks cheaper than the traditional publishing houses, so you go into business. Your first job is to create a company and look for substantial company investment. Next, you elect company officers and establish the amount of time each "employee" needs to devote to running the business. You need managers and personnel to sell and buy the products (textbooks). In addition, you need an accountant and perhaps some retail and marketing professionals. Finally, you may want to hire a lawyer to make sure you are compliant with all laws and regulations involved in running your business. You need to find an acceptable site and negotiate rates for rent or purchase. In the end, you and your investors will share the profits you have earned through the development of this cooperative. You may discover that it takes a lot of time, effort, and money to sell textbooks through a cooperative and that they may not be as overpriced as you previously thought.

CLASSIFICATION BY STRATEGY

Retail stores are often classified by the types of strategies they employ in selling their goods and services. This section is divided into two major strategic categories: general merchandise retailers and food retailers. It covers only store-based retail strategies; nonstore-based retail strategies are covered in a later section.

GENERAL MERCHANDISE RETAILERS

general merchandise retailer A retailer involved in the sale of general, nonfood items.

General merchandise retailers are involved, obviously, in the sale of general, nonfood merchandise. Almost any nonfood item falls into this category. This section discusses the major types of general merchandise retailers. According to the U.S. Census Bureau, general merchandise sales in the United States were over $450 billion for the year 2002,[14] making general merchandise retailing a powerful retail institution.

department store A large retailer that carries a wide breadth and depth of products and is organized into departments.

DEPARTMENT STORES. Department stores are large retailers that carry a wide breadth and depth of products. In addition, they offer more customer service than their general merchandise competitors. Department stores are so named because they are organized by departments—such as juniors, men's wear, or lingerie. Each department acts as a "ministore." The department is allocated sales space and managers and sales personnel that pay particular attention to their departments. Often departments are responsible for their own IMC, which is coupled with the store's overall IMC executions.

Department stores often are the anchors of major shopping centers. Macy's, Nordstrom, Bloomingdale's, Saks Fifth Avenue, JCPenney, and Dillard's are some of the larger department stores. Most, but not all, department stores are part of a large chain.

Department stores have a perceptual advantage because they use IMC more than most other types of retailers. Department stores utilize newspapers, magazines, radio, television, and direct mail to deliver their marketing communications. Due to overstoring, most of the promotional budgets are geared to sale advertising. Couponing, historically used by grocery stores, has been used to generate sales.[15] Unfortunately, the use of coupons diminishes profits and creates a situation where consumers do not buy unless they receive some type of discount.[16]

In recent years, department store sales have slowed because of the appearance of specialty retailers and full-line discount stores such as Target, Kmart, and Wal-Mart. Strategies for success in department store retailing include expanded customer service, sales training for sales personnel, exciting IMC (especially at point of sale), and the elimination of nonproductive, slow-selling products. A movement is under way in department store retailing to generate more research in the area of consumer information to be used to create better customer relations. In addition, department stores have moved toward greater centralization in their buying and IMC areas. A key to successful retailing in department stores is the use of store brand names to develop customer loyalty.

In an attempt to retain and attract new customers, department stores are being more innovative. For example, Macy's invested $100 million to make over 42 of its stores. The renovations included shopping carts, bright signage, customer price-scanner stations, and lounges. Saks Inc. partnered with Smith & Hawken to set up garden boutiques in 243 stores, and Sears, Roebuck and Co. brought Lands' End clothing into its stores and changed its electronics department to include high-end items.[17]

DISCOUNT STORES. Full-line discount stores can also fall under the U.S. Census Bureau definition of a department store. The difference between a department store and a full-line discount store lies in the service and merchandise areas. **Discount stores** generally offer limited customer services but have merchandise priced below that of department stores. In addition, the products sold at some discount stores tend to be less fashionable than similar merchandise carried at larger department stores. Wal-Mart, Target, and Kmart are the world's largest discount retailers.

discount store A type of department store that offers limited customer services and has merchandise priced below that at department stores.

The main strategy employed by the discounter is to develop an image of high-volume, low-cost products. Since strong national discount retail chains began in the 1960s, they have taken a large share of the market away from traditional retailers. This trend continues. Discount retailers' sales climbed from $2 billion in 1960 to over $300 billion in 2001. Wal-Mart is the nation's leading discounter with 2001 annual sales of $220 billion, followed by Target ($39 billion) and Kmart ($37 billion).[18] The 2002 sales numbers were $280 billion for Wal-Mart, $40 billion for Target, and $36 billion for Kmart.[19]

A key factor spurring the growth of discount retailers is value consciousness. This change began in recessionary periods but has cut across all economic climates and income levels. The rise in discount retailers has been due in part to the attention they have paid to their core competencies, such as low

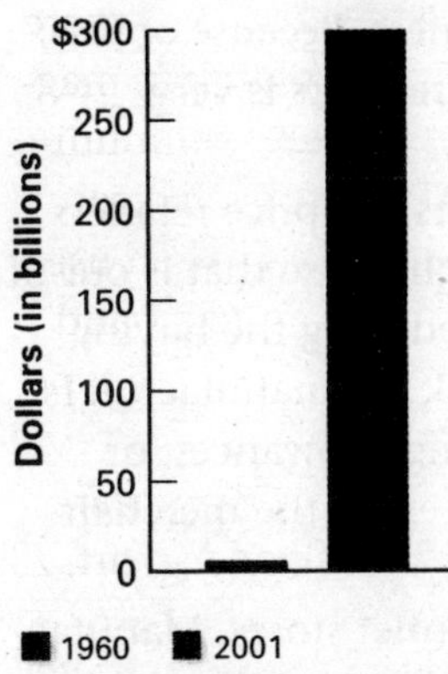

FIGURE 4.1

Discount Stores: An Industry Landscape Assessment (Source: Data drawn from "Discounters Survive Volatile Year," *Chain Store Age*, State of the Industry Supplement, August 1999.)

prices and a wide selection of products. Many customers no longer see any added value in paying higher prices at traditional department stores. The department stores have lost their differentiation of quality customer service. Thus, discount retailers have captured a significant share of the overall general merchandise market. Figure 4.1 gives a good picture of what is happening with today's discount retailers.

SPECIALTY STORES. Specialty stores carry a limited number of products within one or a few lines of goods and services. They are so named because they specialize in one type of product, such as apparel and complementary merchandise.

specialty store A store that carries a limited number of products within one or a few lines of goods and services.

Specialty stores utilize a market segmentation strategy rather than a typical mass marketing strategy when trying to attract customers. They tend to create a market niche for their product assortments. Although they do not carry a large number of product lines (*width*), they offer many products within each line (*depth*). Specialty retailers tend to specialize in apparel, shoes, books, toys, auto supplies, jewelry, and sporting goods.

Customers frequent specialty stores because of the extensive assortments and personal service provided. For example, the Great American Spice Co. boasts 3,200 items including Ashwagandha root powder and Kittens' Big Banana hot sauce. The online store has over 25,000 recipes.[20] Specialty stores' staff tends to be more knowledgeable about the products sold. In addition, specialty stores often offer a more physically comfortable shopping atmosphere.

The larger specialty stores include Borders Books, Toys "R" Us, Gap, Circuit City, Office Depot, and Best Buy. Smaller specialty stores include GNC (vitamins and other food supplements), Hallmark, The Body Shop, and The Rocky Mountain Chocolate Factory.

In recent years, specialty stores have seen the emergence of the category killer. **Category killers** (sometimes called *power retailers* or *category specialists*) are generally discount specialty stores that offer a deep assortment of merchandise in a particular category (books, toys, shoes, sports items, etc.). Blockbuster Video, for example, offers a large selection of DVDs and VHS tapes at a relatively low price. Other examples include Babies "R" Us and Toys "R" Us.

category killer Sometimes known as a *power retailer* or *category specialist*, a discount specialty store that offers a deep assortment of merchandise.

Some shoppers do not want a "huge" store atmosphere. Therefore, many category killers have created additional retail venues that carry some of the same merchandise but are downsized to give the customer a smaller, more intimate store. Home Depot, for example, has created a number of smaller stores (called Villager Hardware) to satisfy those customers who prefer the smaller store format.

OFF-PRICE RETAILERS. Off-price retailers resemble discount retailers in that they sell brand-name merchandise at everyday low prices (EDLP). Off-price retailers rarely offer many services to customers. The key strategy of off-price retailers is to carry the same type of merchandise as traditional department stores but offer prices that can be 40 to 50 percent lower.

off-price retailer A retailer that sells brand-name merchandise, which may include overruns or distressed merchandise, at 40 to 50 percent below traditional retailers.

To be able to offer lower prices, off-price retailers develop special relationships with their suppliers for large quantities of merchandise. Inventory turnover is the key to a successful off-price retailing business. Because of this, the buying strategy developed and executed by off-price retailers is very aggressive.

In addition to purchasing closeouts and canceled orders, off-price retailers negotiate with manufacturers to discount orders for merchandise that is out of season or to prepay for items to be manufactured, thus reducing the buying prices of those items. Because off-price retailers do not ask the manufacturers for additional services such as return privileges, advertising allowances, or delayed payments, they are often able to get reduced prices for the merchandise they purchase.

There are many types of off-price retailers, including outlet stores. Manufacturers, department stores, or even specialty store chains can own off-price stores. Stores owned by the manufacturer are usually referred to as *factory outlet stores. One-price stores,* such as dollar stores, are also considered off-price retailers. This type of store offers every product at the same price. Consumers like these stores because they know exactly how much each product costs. In each of these stores, most merchandise is discounted for the reasons stated earlier, or the merchandise has been specifically made to sell at a lower price.

closeout retailer A type of retailer that sells broad assortments of merchandise purchased at closeout prices.

flea market A retail format in which many vendors sell used as well as new and distressed merchandise.

In addition to outlet stores are **closeout retailers,** which sell broad assortments of merchandise that they purchase at closeout prices, and **flea markets,** where many vendors sell used as well as new and distressed merchandise.

FOOD RETAILERS

There are many types of food retailers. To make their classifications easier to understand, this section is broken down into the main types of food retailers that operate in the United States and around the world. Table 4.3 shows the twenty-five largest food retailers in the United States, ranked by sales.

The premier association for food retailing is the Food Marketing Institute (FMI). FMI conducts programs in research, education, industry relations, and public affairs on behalf of its member companies—food retailers and wholesalers.[21] To learn more about this important group, access their website at *www.fmi.org.* In addition, Saint Joseph's University, in Philadelphia, has a very strong academic program in food retailing and marketing, with a wealth of information and experts in the area of food marketing. For more information, write to Erivan K. Haub School of Business, Saint Joseph's University, 5600 City Avenue, Philadelphia, PA 19131-1395.

To remain competitive in the mature food retail business, many retailers are carrying merchandise outside their traditional lines. "As the mass merchandisers industry begins to mature, this channels vigorous focus on food as a vehicle for growth results in super centers that are beginning to look similar to conventional grocery stores. The conventional supermarket channel, in turn, has fought back with an expanded offering of general merchandise and various other peripheral departments that is beginning to look a lot like the super center format. The net result is a blurring of the retail channels."[22] Nevertheless, there are general categories into which food retailers fall.

TABLE 4.3

TOP 25 U.S. FOOD RETAILERS (BY 2002 GROCERY SALES)

1. Wal-Mart Supercenters Bentonville, AR $51,849,930,000 Stores - 1,258	**2. The Kroger Co.** Cincinnati, OH $51,419,000,000 Stores - 3,229	**3. Albertson's, Inc.** Boise, ID $36,700,000,000 Stores - 2,291
4. Safeway Inc. Pleasanton, CA $32,400,000,000 Stores - 1,798	**5. Ahold USA, Inc.**[1] Chantilly, VA $25,252,000,000 Stores - 1,623	**6. Costco Wholesale Group** Issaquah, WA $23,257,500,000 Stores - 405
7. Sam's Club Bentonville, AR $20,160,000,000 Stores - 522	**8. Publix Super Markets, Inc.** Lakeland, FL $16,046,280,000 Stores - 726	**9. Delhaize America**[2] Salisbury, NC $15,400,000,000 Stores - 1,485
10. Winn-Dixie Stores, Inc. Jacksonville, FL $12,334,353,000 Stores - 1,073	**11. Great Atlantic & Pacific Tea Co.** Montvale, NJ $10,880,000,000 Stores - 692	**12. H.E. Butt Grocery Co.** San Antonio, TX $9,900,000,000 Stores - 300
13. SUPERVALU, Inc. Eden Prairie, MN $9,604,000,000 Stores - 1,294	**14. Meijer, Inc.** Grand Rapids, MI $7,420,000,000 Stores - 156	**15. Shaw's Supermarkets, Inc.** West Bridgewater, MA $4,550,000,000 Stores - 185
16. BJ's Wholesale Club, Inc. Natick, MA $4,004,000,000 Stores - 142	**17. Pathmark Stores, Inc.** Carteret, NJ $4,000,000,000 Stores - 143	**18. Hy-Vee, Inc.** West Des Moines, IA $3,864,000,000 Stores - 188
19. Giant Eagle, Inc. Pittsburgh, PA $3,399,550,000 Stores - 213	**20. Raley's.** West Sacramento, CA $3,300,000,000 Stores - 128	**21. Aldi, Inc.** Batavia, IL $3,132,350,000 Stores - 626
22. Wegmans Food Markets, Inc. Rochester, NY $3,045,000,000 Stores - 64	**23. Whole Foods Market, Inc.** Austin, TX $2,690,500,000 Stores - 137	**24. Stater Brothers Markets** Colton, CA $2,666,300,000 Stores - 156
25. Fleming Companies, Inc. Lewisville, TX $2,248,277,710 Stores - 103		

[1]Ahold USA's sales include revenue from its U.S. subsidiaries.
[2]Delhaize America's sales include revenues from its U.S. subsidiaries.

Source: Directory of Supermarket, Grocery & Convenience Store Chains 2003 (Tampa, FL: Business Guides, Inc.). Prepared by Information Service, Food Marketing Institute, April 2003.

According to a study by the Food Marketing Institute,[23] a trend for food retailers is to offer one-stop convenience shopping. Offerings include:

- Delis (97.2 percent)
- Fresh, prepared foods for takeout (93.1 percent)
- Greeting cards (91.7 percent)
- Floral departments (79.2 percent)
- In-store banks (50 percent)
- In-store pharmacies (48.6 percent)
- Cooking classes (26.4 percent)
- Self-scanning of groceries (25 percent)
- Gas pumps (18.1 percent)
- Child care (16.7 percent)

conventional supermarket A self-service food store that generates annual sales of at least $2 million.

CONVENTIONAL SUPERMARKETS. Conventional supermarkets are essentially large department stores that specialize in food. According to the Food Marketing Institute, a **conventional supermarket** is a self-service food store that generates an annual sales volume of $2 million or more.[24] These stores generally carry grocery, meat, and produce products. A conventional food store carries very little general merchandise. Supermarkets first appeared in the 1930s, when food retailers found they could increase the size of their operations to persuade customers to make purchases by offering more products at lower costs. Piggly Wiggly was the first self-service store (opened in 1916); the first supermarket was King Kullen Grocery Company in New York (1930).[25]

In 2002, there were about 33,000 supermarkets in the United States, accounting for approximately $411.8 billion in sales. Average weekly sales per supermarket were $361,564.[26] Chain Supermarkets accounted for $340.5 billion in sales, representing 82.7 percent of the total $411.8 billion.[27]

impulse buying The purchase of products and services by consumers that was not planned in advance.

One benefit that accompanied the development of supermarkets was increased **impulse buying.** Impulse purchases are those that haven't been planned. Shoppers at conventional supermarkets generally prepare a list of items needed for their households. While in the supermarket, however, they may find some tempting items that weren't on the list and may purchase them on the spot, or by impulse.

The key to successful supermarket sales is high inventory turnover. Because supermarkets have a great deal of competition from convenience stores, warehouse stores, and superstores, they must develop an effective strategy to keep their customers coming back. To compete effectively, many supermarkets have developed intensive IMC programs that offer their customers many types of promotions—such as coupons, advertisements, fliers, free samples, and customer affinity cards. The strategic use of couponing, coupled with other promotions such as double or even triple manufacturer coupon values, is called *hi-lo pricing.*

everyday low pricing (EDLP) A retailing strategy that emphasizes consistently lower-priced merchandise.

Other supermarkets do very little promotion; instead they rely on consistently low-priced merchandise sales. By selling the merchandise at the basic same low price each day, they are utilizing a strategy known as **everyday low pricing,** or **EDLP.** On a day-to-day basis, the listed prices at an EDLP supermarket are lower than those at a promotional supermarket. At a promotional supermarket, customers must rely on their coupons and take advantage of the store's promotional activities to keep their overall purchase costs lower.

superstore A food-based retailer that is larger than a traditional supermarket and carries expanded service deli, bakery, seafood, and nonfood sections.

SUPERSTORES. One of the biggest trends over the past twenty years in food retailing has been the development of superstores. **Superstores** are food-based retailers that are larger than the traditional supermarket and carry expanded service deli, bakery, seafood, and nonfood sections.[28] Superstores vary in size but can be as large as 150,000 square feet. Generally they are no smaller than 20,000 square feet.

Wegmans Food Markets, Inc., is an example of a superstore, although the stores refer to themselves as supermarkets. Typical stores run 80,000 to 130,000 square feet and carry more than 60,000 products, compared to an average of 40,000 products for supermarkets.[29] Typically included in Wegmans stores are bakeries, ready-to-cook meat and seafood entrée sections, international foods, photo labs, floral shops, and a fun center for kids to play in while their parents shop.

The PETsMART chain is the nation's leading retail supplier of products and services for pets. The company operates more than 600 pet superstores in the United States and Canada as well as a pet supply catalog business and a website.

combination store A retail format in which food items are combined with nonfood items to create a one-stop shopping experience.

COMBINATION STORES. Because shoppers have been demanding more convenience in their shopping experiences, a new type of food retailer has been emerging. Called a **combination store,** this type of retailer combines food items with nonfood items to create a one-stop shopping experience for the customer. In general, customers can find general merchandise along with food products and can take all these products to a common checkout area. Combination stores emerged in the mid-1960s and early 1970s and grew rapidly. Combination stores can be as large as 100,000 or more square feet.

In 1934, Hendrik Meijer started one of the first combination stores in the United States, in Greenville, Michigan. Meijer (*www.meijer.com*) is a family-owned and operated retailer with 157 stores throughout Illinois, Indiana, Kentucky, Michigan, and Ohio.[30] Meijer customers can select from a full range of attractively displayed food products, as well as toys, sporting goods, clothing, health and beauty aids, domestics, furniture, gifts, small appliances, and other products.

super center A retailer that is a combination of a superstore and a discount store.

hypermarket A large retailer that carries many types of products in addition to foods; originated in Europe.

SUPER CENTERS AND HYPERMARKETS. A **super center** is a combination of a superstore and a discount store. Super centers developed based on the European **hypermarket,** an extremely large retailing facility that offers many types of products in addition to foods. In super centers, more than 40 percent of sales come from nonfood items. Super centers are the fastest-growing retail category and encompass as much as 200,000 square feet of area; Wal-Mart is the category leader with a 74 percent share of super center retail sales.[31] Wal-Mart is focusing on the food industry to spur growth. By 2005, Wal-Mart expects food sales to contribute more than 20 percent of total divisional sales.[32]

The key to a successful super center is sales of food products at very low prices to stimulate customer traffic and sales of nonfood items with higher markups. The *market area* for super centers is much greater than that for the other food retailer classifications. This means customers are willing to drive longer distances to visit super centers than to visit any other type of food retail center.

The major disadvantage of super centers is that customers may not want to frequent them for small purchases. Because the centers are so large, it is often difficult to find the exact product one is looking for in a reasonable period of time.

warehouse club A warehouse store that charges a membership fee to consumers or businesses who buy from the store.

warehouse store A retailer that offers a limited assortment of goods and services, both food and merchandise, to both end users and small to midsize businesses.

WAREHOUSE CLUBS AND STORES. **Warehouse clubs** and **warehouse stores** (also known as *club stores*) were developed to satisfy customers who want low prices every day and are willing to give up service needs. These retailers offer a limited assortment of goods and services, both food and general merchandise, to both end users and small to midsize businesses. The stores are very large and are located in the lower-rent areas of cities to keep their overhead costs low. Merchandising within the store is almost nonexistent, and pallets are used extensively. Steel shelving and concrete floors are common.

Generally, warehouse clubs offer varying types of merchandise because they purchase products that manufacturers have discounted for a variety of reasons

Sam's Club members pay a yearly fee to shop in exchange for lower prices and special services. Shown here is a family sampling a food product in one of the stores.

(overruns, returns, and so on). Warehouse clubs rely on fast-moving, high-turnover merchandise. One benefit of this arrangement is that the stores purchase the merchandise from the manufacturer and sell it prior to actually having to pay the manufacturer.

Typically, warehouse clubs and stores charge their customers an annual membership fee. These fees vary but generally are around $30 to $40. Warehouse clubs may require that customers be affiliated with a government or business entity, such as a credit union, local business, or university. Many warehouse clubs do not carry perishable items, or carry a limited amount, because of the costs associated with storing them. Among the larger warehouse stores are Costco Wholesale, Sam's Club, and BJ's Wholesale Club.

convenience store A small retailer that caters to a neighborhood and carries a very limited assortment of products.

CONVENIENCE STORES. As the name suggests, convenience stores are located in areas that are easily accessible to customers. **Convenience stores** (also called *c-stores*) carry a very limited assortment of products and are housed in small facilities. The major sellers in convenience stores are cigarettes, accounting for about 25 percent of in-store sales, and nonalcoholic beverages, which amount to about 15 percent.[33] Owners of convenience stores locate in neighborhoods and try to intercept consumers between their homes and places of employment.

The strategy convenience stores employ is "fast shopping": consumers can go into a convenience store, pick out what they want or need, and check out in a relatively short time. They don't have to search for the products they want, and they don't have to wait a long time in line to pay. The vast majority of products purchased at convenience stores are consumed within an hour after purchase.

Due to their high sales, convenience stores receive products almost daily. Because convenience stores don't have the luxury of high-volume purchases, and because many of the products are impulse purchases, most products are priced relatively high. In recent years, many convenience stores have added gasoline to their product mix; gasoline now accounts for the majority of sales for those stores carrying this product. In addition, convenience goods such as milk, eggs, tobacco, soft drinks, and beer are among the largest sales items.

limited-line store (box store) No frills food and merchandise discounters that offer a small selection of products.

LIMITED-LINE STORES. Limited-line stores, also known as *box stores* or *limited-assortment stores*, represent a relatively small number of food retail stores in the United States. Limited-line stores are food discounters that offer a small selection of products at low prices. They are no-frills stores that sell products out of boxes (or *shippers*). Limited-line stores rarely carry any refrigerated items and are often cash-and-carry, accepting no checks or credit cards. Limited-line store customers do their own bagging and frequently bring their own bags or purchase bags from the retailer. In a limited-line store, the strategy is to price products at least 20 percent below similar products at conventional supermarkets. Many of these stores focus on private labels, which eliminates the need for manufacturers to recoup the costs of advertising and sales promotions.[34]

Aldi is an example of a successful limited-line retailer. Located in Europe and the United States, Aldi has about 570 stores in the United States alone. Its product line includes a little more than 700 most-often-used products for the average home. In comparison, most full-line grocers offer more than 25,000 items.[35]

CENSUS CLASSIFICATIONS

As stated earlier, the U.S. Census Bureau has been converting its classification system for retailers from the SIC code system to the new NAICS codes, to ease additional international competition. Products and services are classified by assigning numbers to the various retail categories, such as toys or swimming pools and supplies. These categories make it easier for retailers to generate and gather information about the markets in which they compete.

In addition, the U.S. Census Bureau has established standard definitions for each type of retail business. For example, by U.S. Census definition, a retail establishment has to meet four minimum criteria to be considered a department store: (1) it must employ as least fifty people; (2) sales of apparel and nondurables (soft goods) must be at least 20 percent of total sales; (3) the merchandise mix must include at least some items of home furnishings, furniture, family apparel, appliances, radios and television sets, and linens and dry goods; and (4) sales of $10 million or less can have no more than 80 percent of the total sales coming from any single line the store carries. Regarding the last criterion, if sales exceed $10 million, the combined sales of the two smallest lines must equal at least 10 percent (equal to $1 million).[36]

CLASSIFICATION BY CHANNEL

brick-and-mortar store A traditional retail outlet that sells out of a physical location.

Although not a formal classification system, retailers and customers refer to retail stores based on the retailer's channel of distribution. Traditional retail outlets that sell out of a physical location are referred to as **brick-and-mortar stores.** The examples used earlier represent traditional brick-and-mortar retailers.

Some retailers do not sell out of traditional stores but instead offer products from nontraditional locations. These types of retailers are known as **nonstore retailers.** These retailers are covered in the following section.

nonstore retailer A retailer that offers products in a nontraditional format.

Finally, many retailers offer products both at a physical location and over the Internet. These retailers, known as **bricks-and-clicks,** have channels of distribution that allow for customer convenience, especially in the customer's shopping time. This type of retailer is also covered in the following section.

brick-and-click A retailer that offers products both at a physical location and online via the Internet.

NONTRADITIONAL RETAIL CLASSIFICATIONS

Nontraditional retailers offer products and services in many different venues and employ numerous strategies and tactics to reach and service their targeted markets. The 1990s and 2000s have seen a dramatic growth of these types of retail institutions. The major nontraditional retailers are direct marketers and cybermarketers (or "clicks"). These retailers could fall into other classification systems as well, but the wise retail student can see the nuances in operating or owning a nontraditional retail business.

direct marketing An interactive system of marketing that uses one or more advertising media to generate a measurable response or transaction at any location.

DIRECT MARKETING. **Direct marketing** is a form of integrated marketing communication as well as a classification system for retailing. It can be argued that this is also a form of advertising, because prospective and current customers are exposed to the retailer through some medium, such as the telephone, television, radio, newspapers, magazines, the mail, or the Internet. The largest trade association for direct marketing, the Direct Marketing Association (DMA), defines direct marketing as "any direct communication to a consumer or business recipient that is designed to generate a response in the form of an order (direct order), a request for further information (lead generation), and/or a visit to a store or other place of business for purchase of a specific product(s) or service(s) (traffic generation)."[37]

Many types of direct marketers exist. The scope of this book limits our discussion to direct-marketing retail institutions, however. There are both general merchandise and specialty direct retailers. General merchandise direct retailers include firms that utilize many different media, such as QVC and Bloomingdale's. Specialty direct retailers include Lands' End, L.L. Bean, and Audio Book Club. Direct retailers typically are nontraditional, but they may combine the classifications of nonstore and brick-and-click. Direct retailers may sell using catalogs, the telephone, magalogs, television, magazines, direct mail, or radio. In addition, they may employ fliers to provide customers with information about their products and services. The test of whether a retailer falls into the direct retailer category is to see if it meets all the basic tenets of the DMA definition.

direct selling A type of sales interaction that involves personal contact—via telephone, at the consumer's home, at an out-of-home location such as the consumer's office, and so on.

DIRECT SELLING. In contrast to direct marketing, which involves no personal contact with consumers, **direct selling** entails some type of personal contact. This contact can be at the consumer's home or at an out-of-home location such as the consumer's office. In addition, direct selling includes telephone sales. Examples of direct sellers include Avon, Mary Kay Cosmetics, Cutco (knives), and Amway.

vending machine A nonstore retailing format in which consumers purchase products through a machine.

VENDING MACHINES. Vending machines represent an additional class of retail institutions. Essentially, vending is nonstore retailing in which the consumer purchases a product through a machine. The machine itself takes care of the entire transaction, from taking the money to providing the product. Vending machine offerings range from typical products such as soft drinks and candy to insurance, cameras, phone calls, phone cards, books, paper, and pens. In the United States, pricing for vending machine products is typically $1.50 and under because of the number of coins involved in each transaction. Many vending machines accept dollar bills. These machines can also make change.

FIGURE 4.2

Unique Items Sold in Vending Machines Around the World

(Source: Raphael Carter, "Things That Have Been Sold in Vending Machines" [2002], www.chaparraltree.com/vending. Reprinted by permission.)

Hotels often have vending machines that provide personal necessities the traveler may have forgotten to pack, such as toothpaste, soap, and toothbrushes.

In other scenarios, vending machines allow the retailer to extend service after sales personnel have left. The U.S. Post Office, for example, has stamp machines and scales available to customers around the clock, in response to consumers' need for convenience.

The major drawback with vending retailing is the reverse-logistics process, in which the consumer wants to get a refund for a product that was unwanted or is defective. In addition, vending machines have a tendency to break, leaving the customer with no product after having paid for it. As a result, the consumer may develop a negative attitude toward the brand or vending machine owner.

Figure 4.2 provides a list of unique items that have been sold in vending machines around the world.

E-TAILING. Electronic retailing is referred to as *e-commerce, Internet retailing,* or *e-tailing*. In this retail classification, the retailer and customers communicate with each other in a typically nonpersonal way via some type of electronic, interactive system, generally a computer facilitated by the Internet.

E-tailing has been growing dramatically. Many firms now utilize both an e-tailing approach and a traditional approach to selling. Conversely, some companies that began as e-tailers are developing brick-and-mortar sites to facilitate sales and improve customer relations. Gateway computers is one example of this trend.

Many types of products and services have been sold over the Internet. This website sells sourdough bread. (Courtesy of Interstate Brands West Corporation.)

More than 100,000 companies have Internet addresses, and some 20,000 companies have homepages on the Internet.[38] E-tailing can effectively help a company establish synergy for its products or services. It can assist with retail research; it also can advance the communications a company has with other companies, its suppliers, and its customers, both current and potential. E-tailing can help with inventory and enable simultaneous exchange of information among many sources. Almost all retailing functions can be performed online except the physical delivery of goods. For some products, such as software downloads, however, delivery can be accomplished online.

E-tailing offers a relatively easy way to bring buyers and sellers together at a moderate cost. Although e-tailing has grown tremendously over the past decade, some companies still do not conduct business using e-commerce. As of 2000, nearly two-thirds of American manufacturers were still not conducting business electronically.[39] E-tailing can effectively increase a company's trading area by giving it access to people worldwide who may desire the offered product or service.

The greatest advantage of e-tailing is the speed at which retailers can make sales, process them, and follow through on delivery. For consumers, e-tailing provides access to a great quantity of products and services throughout the world. Consumers can find anything from "books and compact disks . . . to French bread."[40] You can access books and compact disks through Amazon.com (*www.amazon.com*) or French bread through *www.sourdoughbread.com.* You can also use a search engine to explore numerous other providers of these and other products.

Another advantage of e-tailing is the opportunity to save on costs associated with traditional retailing. Marketing, distribution, personnel, phone, postage, and printing costs can be reduced with an effective IRM plan. For example, all printing costs can be passed on to consumers—with their consent. E-tailing also helps eliminate a barrier to entry into the retail industry by

INTERNET IN ACTION

New E-grocer Succeeds Where Others Have Failed

The failures of early e-tailers of grocery products have not deterred Joseph Fedele from launching FreshDirect.com, an online grocery service catering to New York City's convenience-oriented consumer. The store offers 15,000 products at 10 to 30 percent below supermarket prices. Fedele saves money by buying his products directly from the farm. The company bakes its own bread and cuts its own steaks. Because there is no intermediary, FreshDirect.com earns margins of nearly 20 percent, more than double the industry average.

Fidele learned from some of the mistakes of the earlier online grocery retailers. Unlike the pioneers, Fedele has a minimum order price of $40 and a delivery charge on top of that. Fedele believes the success of FreshDirect will be attributed to cost savings realized by cutting out the intermediary and the technology the company uses to leverage knowledge.

The technology leveraged by FreshDirect.com includes sophisticated software that tracks and manages all food deliveries. At any given time, Fedele knows where an order is. In addition, FreshDirect's facility includes nine climate-controlled rooms that are set to the optimal temperature for the relevant types of food. Ice cream is stored at −40 degrees so that customers receive it still frozen. A central control system gets flagged when temperatures fall outside acceptable limits. By focusing on cost savings and technology, FreshDirect hopes to make online grocery shopping a routine activity.

Source: Reproduced from the September 24, 2002 issue of *Business Week* by special permission, copyright © 2002 by the McGraw-Hill Companies, Inc.

saving on the costs of a physical site. The costs associated with the opening of a physical store are very high, but with an e-tail venue costs are greatly reduced.

Finally, e-tailers can create virtual inventories by placing virtual products into large databases. When a customer orders a product, the computer can search for its availability through the e-tailer's many suppliers, thus reducing the amount of inventory the e-tail business must carry itself.

E-tailing also has some disadvantages. The biggest drawback is consumers' perceived or real lack of privacy and security. Because anything sent over a computer goes through a series of computers before reaching its destination, a series of firewalls are needed to assure the buyer of privacy in purchase decisions. To combat this perceived (or real) disadvantage, e-tailers have begun using encryption to increase the safety of doing business over the Internet.

Another disadvantage is that Internet users have become accustomed to receiving many types of free products and services. Because of this, much of the business conducted over the Internet has been funded utilizing a nontraditional business model—*i.e.,* through sponsorships or advertising. With the reduction in advertising expenditures by major advertising agencies for Web advertising, e-tailers have had to reassess their business model. Now they are returning to the more traditional model of having users pay for more services.

Business must be careful to avoid some common pitfalls associated with e-tailing. Because setting up a website can be very inexpensive, businesses can create websites that are not adequately customer friendly. In addition, once the websites are up and running, they can quickly become out of date. Consumers get bored with the same site day after day. Products become obsolete, and businesses close. E-tailers must maintain attractive, up-to-date websites to convince customers that they are technologically advanced and committed to providing timely products and services.

E-tailing will constantly evolve. Banking and online trading will continue to utilize Internet technologies and expand by doing so. People will find new uses for the computer, and retail industries will find more effective ways to create and maintain large customer bases. In the future, the role of e-tailing will become clearer and more defined.

COMPETITIVE ANALYSIS

Armed with the classifications of retail institutions, a retailer can develop a competitive analysis to gain an understanding of the environment in which it does business. Because retailing has reached a mature phase in its life cycle, one of the only ways to increase business is to take away market share from competitors. While one retailer is trying to increase market share, so are its competitors. The successful retailer has a thorough understanding of its retail environment. Information on the retail environment should be included in the situational analysis and become part of the retail strategy. Data for a complete competitive analysis can be accessed from the retailer's retail information system (RIS). Any data generated during the analysis should be placed in the RIS.

TYPES OF COMPETITORS

The major types of competitors are intratype, intertype, and divertive.

intratype competitors Retailers that compete for the same customer bases or households.

INTRATYPE COMPETITORS. Intratype competitors compete for the same customer bases or households. To be considered intratype competitors, the competing retailers must fall under the same NAICS classification. In other words, JCPenney competes with Sears for the same consumer dollars, and both retailers have the same NAICS number. Kmart competes with Wal-Mart and, to a large extent, Target for the same household dollars. Wal-Mart, Kmart, and Target all have the same NAICS number.

intertype competitors Different types of retailers that compete by selling the same lines of products and compete for the same household dollars.

divertive competitors Retailers that compete by selling the same type of merchandise or services; they do not necessarily specialize in that merchandise.

INTERTYPE COMPETITORS. Intertype competitors compete by selling the same lines of products and compete for the same household dollars. To be defined as intertype competitors, retailers cannot be of the same type (as determined by their different NAICS classifications). Intertype competition has increased with the advent of e-tailing.

DIVERTIVE COMPETITORS. Divertive competitors sell the same type of merchandise or services but do not necessarily specialize in that merchandise or service. Divertive competition occurs when the customer is lured

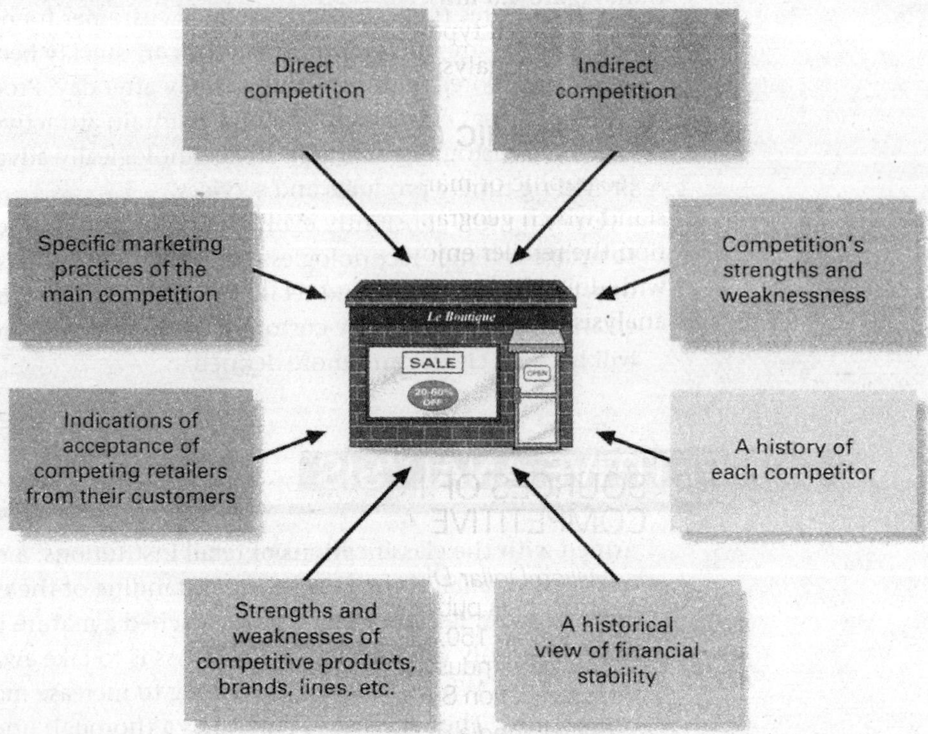

FIGURE 4.3 A Competitive Analysis Outline

away from a competitor. Divertive competition can be either intratype or intertype.

Divertive competition can be best described using an example. Assume your sister is ill and you want to get her some flowers. You are planning to send her a bouquet to brighten her day. Before you go online or set out for the florist shop, you stop by the supermarket to pick up some needed grocery items. You notice that the supermarket has a small floral area with less expensive but pretty bouquets. You decide to buy the flowers there, thus avoiding the hassle of going to the florist or searching online. The supermarket has just diverted you from going to its competitors and has pocketed the additional sales dollars.

It is important that all three types of competitive situations be included in an overall competitive analysis and situational analysis.

COMPETITIVE AND INDUSTRIAL ANALYSES AND EVALUATIONS

Competitive and industrial analysis is helpful in gaining insights into the competitive environment. In addition, the retail planner needs to know how, why, and when the competition will respond to changes in retailer tactics and executions. Other retailers that compete directly, and those that compete indirectly, should be included in the analysis, with emphasis on direct competition. Figure 4.3 illustrates the elements of a competitive analysis, and Table 4.4 lists several types of sources that are helpful in generating an in-depth competitive analysis.

GEOGRAPHIC (OR MARKET) ANALYSIS

A geographic or market analysis is undertaken by the retail planner to understand which geographic areas are key areas—either because of the strong position the retailer enjoys in a particular area or because of problems associated with doing business in that area. In addition, the data gathered in the market analysis provide the retail planner with geographic information that facilitates

TABLE 4.4

SOURCES OF INFORMATION FOR CONDUCTING A COMPETITIVE ANALYSIS

1. *Million Dollar Directory: Leading Public and Private Companies.* This directory is published by Dun & Bradstreet and offers brief summaries of more than 150,000 U.S. companies. The information is based on SIC (Standard Industrial Classification) and NAICS (North American Industrial Classification System) codes, thus allowing access to a particular industry.
2. *Encyclopedia of Associations.* This publication lists information on around 22,000 U.S. and worldwide organizations. The retail planner should pay particular attention to the listings of trade and professional organizations.
3. *Brands and Their Companies and Companies and Their Brands.* This directory provides limited information on specific brands by company.
4. *The Thomas Register* (*www.thomasregister.com*). This publication lists suppliers of products indexed by product category.

Miscellaneous Sources

The Encyclopedia of Business Information Resources
Wasserman's Statistics Sources
Statistical Abstract of the United States
County and City Data Book
County Business Patterns

U.S. Census Bureau Publications

The Census of Transportation
The Census of Population
The Census of Mineral Industries
The Census of Agribusiness
The Census of Retail Trade
The Census of Wholesale Trade
The Census of Service Industries
The Census of Manufacturers (also, the *Annual Survey of Manufacturers*)
The Census of Housing

dollar allocation (budgets). Many of the data gathered in the market analysis can be directly utilized in the consumer evaluation. (For that matter, the data gathered for any purpose of the retail plan may be generalizable to another section.)

COMPETITIVE MODELS

As mentioned in previous and subsequent chapters, the successful retailer understands the nature of competition. To achieve a good understanding of what is occurring in the competitive environment, the retailer must identify what the competitive environment looks like from both the supply and demand sides of retail management.

In retailing, it is general practice to compete for customers within a given market area, usually regional or local in nature. The exceptions to this rule are those retailers involved in e-tailing or direct retailing. Thus, it is important to note the product preferences of customers in a local market. National trends are not always the norm for regional or local market areas. Think of a friend who lives in a different state. She or he may wear clothes that are different from the ones you wear, so you think they aren't "cool." But in fact, your friend's clothes may be the "coolest" in his or her geographic region. For example, in New Mexico many people are wearing a new shoe called Z-Coil. Z-Coils have a spring heel that is not covered by any fabric, leather, or plastic. In New Mexico, it is common to see this product, but in other parts of the country people may stop the wearer to inquire about "those weird shoes." Regional differences among customers can occur in almost any product category.

In addition to paying heed to local and regional markets, the savvy retail professional understands the structure of the market in which the retailer does business. Economists describe four economic situations labeled pure competition, monopoly, monopolistic competition, and oligopolistic competition.

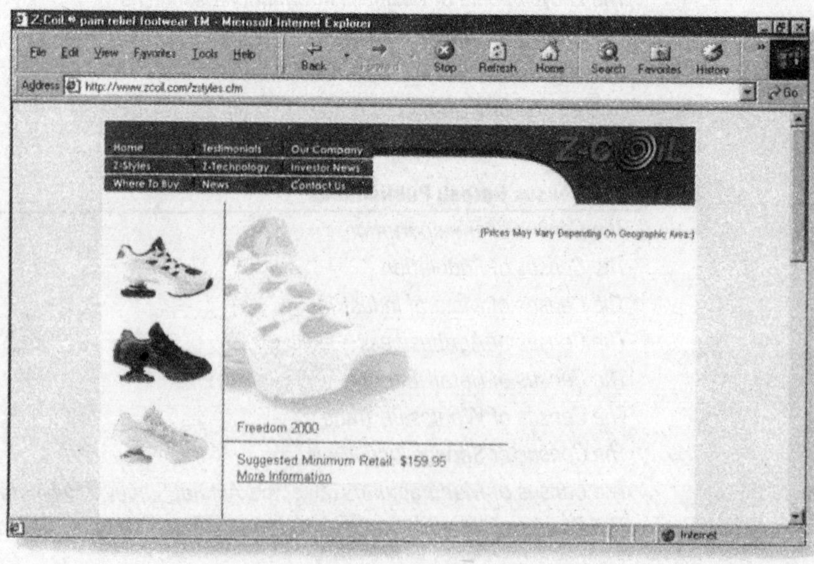

Regional differences among customers can occur in almost any product category. Z-Coil shoes are commonplace in New Mexico but may draw stares and questions in other states and countries.
(Courtesy of Z-Tech, Inc.)

Blunders or Best Practices?

Initial Marketing of Products

It's always interesting to learn about the origins of particular products. Read below for some interesting ways in which these products were first marketed. Do you think these marketing plans would be effective today?

Corn Flakes. Originally this breakfast cereal staple was sold by mail order only.

Ragu. The famous spaghetti sauce was originally sold door to door.

Tea. Tea was originally sold wrapped in silk bags.

Perforated toilet paper. Can you imagine buying perforated toilet paper on the street, where it was first sold?

Tabasco Sauce. "This Tabasco sauce has a certain smell to it . . ." Perhaps this is what customers said when they first purchased Tabasco Sauce in used cologne bottles.

Source: "Chex in the Mail," *Morning Call* (Allentown, PA), September 18, 2002, p. E1.

pure competition A market in which there are many different buyers and sellers.

Pure competition occurs when there are many different buyers and sellers in the market area. Entry into the market by other retailers is relatively easy, and the retailers sell similar products. Information about products and sellers is freely available.

monopoly A market in which there is only one seller selling a specific good or service.

A **monopoly** exists when there is only one seller selling a specific good or service in a given market area. The retailer can set any price it wants for the product, assuming there is enough demand to warrant the price. Thus, if there is a large want or need for the product, the retailer can set high prices to create a better profit margin. Because of the costs needed to compete effectively, barriers to entry are substantial when a monopoly is in control of a given market.

monopolistic competition A market in which there is a limited amount of competition from other retailers for consumer dollars.

Monopolistic competition occurs when there is a limited amount of competition from other retailers for consumer dollars. Even when retailers are selling different products in the marketplace, the consumer may perceive the products as "substitutes" and be willing to buy them to satisfy their need or want even if the products are different from those they planned to purchase. Thus, in a monopolistic competitive environment, a retailer that is the only one selling a particular product brand still faces competition from others selling substitute product brands.

As an illustration of a monopolistically competitive market, suppose your town has only one car lot. To buy a car locally, you need to go to that particular dealer. This appears to be a monopoly, but it may not be. If you are willing to purchase a car from a used-car dealer, or if you will accept a motorcycle or bicycle as a form of transportation, that market is probably a monopolistically competitive market rather than a true monopoly.

oligopoly A market characterized by similar products and very few sellers.

Finally, an **oligopoly** exists when there are very few sellers and similar products. Generally one firm is the market leader. Whenever the market leader changes a strategy or tactic, the other retailers fall in line and make the same adjustments to their tactical executions or strategies. Thus, if you live in a small town that has only two or three fast-food restaurants, and if the largest restaurant raises the price of a basic burger and the other two restaurants raise their prices, the competitive environment is most likely an oligopoly.

In an oligopolistic situation, most of the prices for the same types of products will be close to the same. Think of the gas prices in your town. Are all of the gas retailers selling products at close to the same price? If they are, you may be experiencing an oligopolistically competitive market.

Overall, most competitive market situations are monopolistic competition, but not all. Therefore, retail professionals must understand the market in which they are competing. In addition to the competitive models, a retailer needs to analyze and understand the market indicators for each level of competition, such as employment, interest, and inflation.

SUMMARY

To fully comprehend and develop an IRM plan, retail professionals must have a good understanding of the environment in which they are operating. This chapter looked at the many competitive situations retailers can face. These concepts should be carried over to the many different areas of the overall retail plan.

An understanding of retail institutions is essential for building strategies and tactics that allow the retailer to gain competitive advantage over other retailers. Different classifications for retail institutions help retailers develop a synergistic plan that makes them successful.

A competitive analysis gives retailers a more thorough understanding of the competition they face in the marketplace. By understanding the competition, retailers can create IRM plans that respond to competitive threats. Armed with knowledge of competitors' products and services, retailers can differentiate their businesses from those of their competitors, giving consumers a reason to select their outlets.

KEY TERMS

company analysis (86)
product history and analysis (87)
Standard Industrial Classification (SIC) (88)
North American Industrial Classification System (NAICS) (89)
independent retailer (90)
strategic clarity (92)
chain store (92)
economies of scale (92)
franchise (93)
franchisor (93)
franchisee (93)
product franchising (95)
business franchising (95)
trademark franchising (95)
leased department (96)
retail-sponsored cooperative (96)
wholesale-sponsored cooperative (96)
consumer cooperative (96)
general merchandise retailer (97)
department store (97)
discount store (98)
specialty store (99)
category killer (99)

off-price retailer (99)
closeout retailer (100)
flea market (100)
conventional supermarket (102)
impulse buying (102)
everyday low pricing (EDLP) (103)
superstore (103)
combination store (104)
super center (104)
hypermarket (104)
warehouse store (104)
warehouse club (104)
convenience store (105)
limited-line store (box store) (106)
brick-and-mortar store (106)
nonstore retailer (107)
brick-and-click (107)
direct marketing (107)
direct selling (107)
vending machine (108)
intratype competitors (111)
intertype competitors (111)
divertive competitors (111)
pure competition (115)
monopoly (115)
monopolistic competition (115)
oligopoly (115)

QUESTIONS FOR DISCUSSION

1. Why is it important for retailers to analyze the retail environment?
2. What are the types of retailers by ownership?
3. What advantages does the NAICS system have over the SIC system?
4. What type of information do retailers collect to conduct a competitive analysis?
5. What future challenges do you see for businesses involved in e-tailing?

E-TAILING EXERCISE

Go to the U.S. Small Business Administration website at *www.sba.gov* and do the following or answer the following questions:

1. Browse through the website to get a good idea of the information available.
2. What information is offered that could prove valuable to a small-business owner?
3. What potentially useful information is *not* included on the website?
4. What are the most common types of information requested from this site by small-business owners?

Continuing Case 4.1

Sherwin-Williams Company: A Competitive Analysis

Although it is one of the largest manufacturers and retailers of paints and wall coverings, Sherwin-Williams must still be keenly aware of its retail environments. As such, Sherwin-Williams regularly identifies the strengths and weaknesses of all its competitors in both the retail and business-to-business areas. The company gathered the following information to identify its largest competitors:

Valspar Corporation. Valspar concentrates on consumer, packaging, and industrial coatings. It is also involved in resins and emulsions (used in coatings and colorants). The main brands for Valspar are Laura Ashley and Magicolor. Valspar sells to home centers, farm stores, and specialty paint stores.

RPM, Inc. RPM concentrates on brand-name coatings and chemicals. The best-known brands are Rust-Oleum and Day-Glo paints. In addition, RPM is involved in the do-it-yourself (DIY) markets, manufacturing home and automobile decorations and projection products as well as marine coatings and hobby paints.

E.I. du Pont de Nemours and Company. DuPont is the world's largest chemical company. Its best-known brands are Dacron, Teflon, and Lycra. In addition, DuPont manufactures pigment and paint as well as automotive lacquers.

Imperial Chemical Industries PLC. Imperial is thought to be the world's largest producer of paints and industrial coatings. Its main brands include Glidden, Alba, Devoe, Dulux, ICI Autocolor, and Maxlite. Imperial also manufactures halochemical products such as chlorine, refrigerants, and caustic soda.

Akzo Nobel N.V. Akzo is involved in the manufacture of paints and chemicals. The Akzo coatings group makes automotive finishes, inks, and paints.

These firms are the main competitors for Sherwin-Williams as manufacturers. The following brands are the primary competitors for Sherwin-Williams's contractor and DIY markets:

Local/regional paints
Glidden
Benjamin Moore
K-Moore
Duron
Pittsburgh Paint

In addition, Sherwin-Williams perceives home markets or centers to be competitors, even though many also carry the Sherwin-Williams brands.

Questions

1. Given the above data, plan a competitive analysis for Sherwin-Williams Company.
2. What other data does Sherwin-Williams need to create an effective analysis?
3. Utilize the above data, plus outside resources, to create a SWOT (strengths/weaknesses/opportunities/threats) analysis for Sherwin-Williams.
4. Do you think Sherwin-Williams should create competitive analyses for all of its divisions or just for its retail businesses?
5. Given the above information and your competitive analysis, what recommendations would you make to help strengthen Sherwin-Williams's marketing efforts?
6. Using the above information as a base, create a table showing the approximate market share for Sherwin-Williams and its main competitors.

This case was developed from information supplied by Sherwin-Williams Company, as well as data and information generated from the various companies' homepages. Additional data were generated from the APMP Superior Fund, Michigan Technological University, School of Business and Economics (www.sbea.mtu.edu/APMP/reports/sherwin.pdx), July 8, 2002.

Case 4.2

Target Enters the Super Center Competition

In 1962, Dayton Company entered discount merchandising with the opening of the first Target stores. In 2000, Dayton Hudson Corporation changed its name to Target Corporation to reflect the dominance of Target stores in generating revenue for the company.

Target Corporation operates more than 1,400 stores under the trade names of Mervyn's, Marshall Field's, Super Target, and Target Greatland. The Target name stores compete against Wal-Mart and Kmart but try to attract a more upscale clientele.

Wal-Mart, Target's largest competitor, has about 1,100 super centers. To be more competitive, Target has opened 82 superstores and plans to open more. By the year 2010, the company plans to have 300 locations across the United States. According to Target's president, Gregg Steinhafel, due to changing consumer preferences the combination of general merchandise store and food store is growing.

Target is taking Wal-Mart super centers head on by locating the majority of its Super Targets in the same geographical area, sometimes directly across the road or highway from a Wal-Mart super center. Management at Target believes the power of the Target brand will guarantee success.

In comparison to Target discount stores, which earn on average $30 million a year in revenue, the average Super Target makes only half as much. The reason is that the superstore format is less productive. Conventional Target stores average $635 per square foot in annual sales, whereas Super Targets average only $500 per square foot. The grocery items carried by Super Targets have a lower margin than other items.

A competitive advantage for Wal-Mart is its twenty-five grocery warehouses in the United States. Target's practice of buying its groceries through wholesalers adds about 21 percent to costs. Wal-Mart's warehouse expense is about 16 percent of costs.

Questions

1. Do you agree with Target's decisions to open more Super Targets? Why or why not?
2. What changes in the retail environment are making department stores rethink their strategy?
3. How important is a company's brand to the success of the business?
4. What would you do differently if you were Target's president?
5. How do you think Wal-Mart will respond to Target's location of its super centers?

Sources: "Target Corporation," Hoover's Online Company Capsule, retrieved September 2002 from www.hoovers.com; Target Corporation homepage at www.target.com; Kemp Powers, "Kitchen-Sink Retailing," *Forbes*, September 2, 2002; "Food for Thought: Discount Stores Eat into Supermarket, Drug Store Sales," *Chain Store Age*, May 2000, pp. 49–52, "Target Leverages Brand in Expansion Strategy," *Home Textiles Today*, July 11, 2001; Carole Sloan, "In Great Shape and on Target," *Home Textiles Today*, June 26, 2000.

Evaluation and Identification of Retail Customers

Chapter

5

The secret is to know your customer. Segment your target as tightly as possible. Determine exactly who your customers are, both demographically and psychographically. Match your customer with your medium. Choose only those media that reach your potential customers, and no others. Reaching anyone else is waste.

Robert Grede,
Naked Marketing:
The Bare Essentials

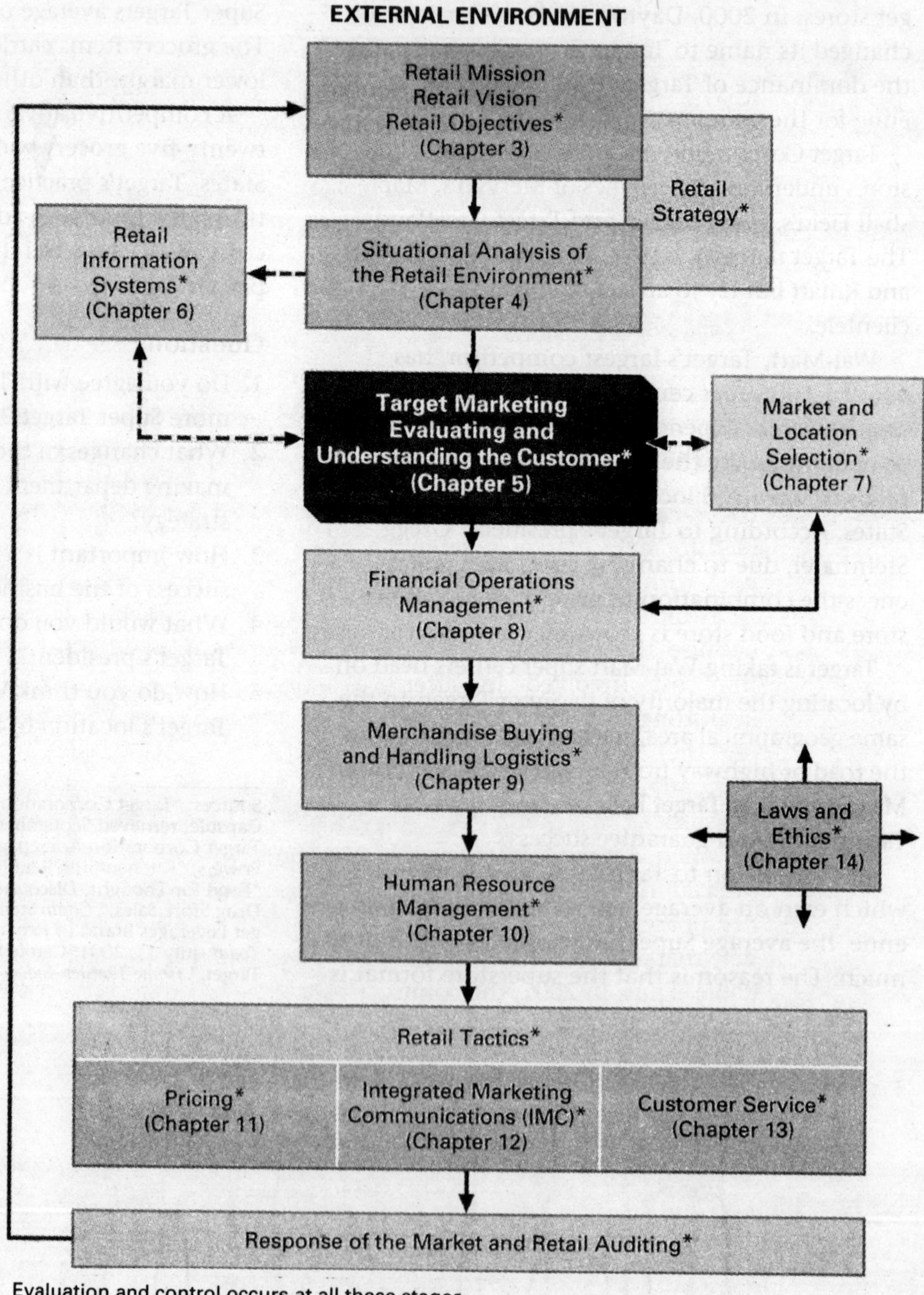

Evaluation and control occurs at all these stages.

CHAPTER OBJECTIVES

After completing this chapter, you will be able to:

1. Discuss the importance to retailers of understanding customers.
2. Discuss the four general means used to describe customers: demographics, psychographics, geographics, and behavioristics.
3. Explain why it is important for retailers to study consumer decision processes.
4. Describe the consumer decision process.
5. Describe the models that attempt to explain consumer behavior.

Dell Targets a Younger Market

Dell Computer Corporation is ranked number 2 in *Business Week*'s "Info Tech 100 list."[1] Part of Dell's success is its ability to identify new market segments and to connect with its customer base. Prior to 1997, Dell did not target the final consumer because the company was concerned with the cost involved in after-sale support. Beginning in 1997, as more people were buying their second or third computers, the company began direct marketing to the final consumer.

When computer sales began to decline, an indication that the industry was in the maturity phase of the life cycle, Dell had to find new markets in order to continue to be profitable. Thus, in 2001, the company targeted a younger segment[2] and hired a new media spokesperson, Ben Curtis.[3] The advertising campaign featured Curtis playing the role of Steven, the young surfer type who ended every commercial with the catchy phrase "Dude, you're getting a Dell!" This campaign was a big success for Dell, and sales of Dell computers skyrocketed.[4] However, the campaign got a bit tarnished with the arrest of Curtis in February 2003 on charges of purchasing marijuana from an undercover cop.[5] The negative publicity did not affect sales, but the company decided not to renew Ben's contract and instead turned to an inexperienced but eager cast of interns in their commercials.[6]

Dell continues to analyze its target market. As of 2003, Dell was the largest online retailer in terms of revenue (excluding travel sites). Dell's success is closely related to its knowledge of customers' wants and needs and its effective targeting of those customers.

INTRODUCTION

In retailing, the customer is the reason for existence. The people who enter a retailer's store (or visit its website) and make purchases are the ones who drive the business. In a service economy, the relationships the retailer builds with customers determine its success.[7] Any successful retail establishment understands its customers, including how they think and behave, where they live, and their demographic characteristics. All retailing tactics should be directed toward those individuals who will inevitably purchase the products and services offered.

Customers have a wide choice of businesses to patronize. The retailer that understands its customers' needs and wants is able to provide the products and services that will best satisfy those customers. In addition, the retailer is able to price the product at an appropriate level and at the same time generate a profit. The retailer can have an effective product mix available to customers when and where they want it if, and only if, there is effective communication with those customers.

This chapter discusses the many variables used to identify and understand the retail customer. The retailer that integrates this information into its retail plan is more likely to achieve profitable sales levels than those that are unaware of their customer base.

The retailer's target market should consist of consumers who have specific needs for its services or products. Consumers may wish to purchase the products as gifts, for daily family use, or for personal consumption. To be able to "talk" to these consumers using integrated marketing communications tactics, the retailer must know precisely who they are.

There is an old saying in advertising, "We have met the consumer and he ain't us." In other words, retailers need to research *who* their customers are and how their customers make decisions. Retailers cannot rely only on intuition; they must employ outside research methods to gain insights into how and why consumers shop.

Retailers can use a number of methods to obtain a good picture of their customer base. The behaviors consumers exhibit when shopping for goods and services, for instance, can teach the retailer a great deal. The information generated can be easily placed into the target marketing section of the integrated retail management plan, which deals with evaluating and understanding the customer. These data can then be used to help select the target market and are instrumental in the retailer's site selection activities. It is important to include all consumer data in the retail information system (RIS). This gives all retail decision makers access to the data at the push of a button and significantly reduces the work required to research these data manually.

Information about consumers usually falls into one of four categories (called the "four *ics*"): (1) demographics, (2) psychographics, (3) geographics, and (4) behavioristics. Often a clearer picture of the customer base emerges when these areas are combined. For example, when retailers analyze the demographics and geographics of a consumer base, the result is a consumer's geodemographics. It is important for retailers to understand the link between the four categories and consumers' responses to marketing efforts.[8] We will consider the first three areas (demographics, psychographics, and geographics) first, followed by a look at behavioristics and the practice of combining the categories.

DEMOGRAPHICS

demographics Statistics about any given population base.

Demographics are statistics about any given population base. These variables are used to help the retailer better select target markets, or market segments, for its business. In addition, the retailer uses these data to help forecast product or service sales and to develop better communication with its customers.

Demographics may include data on population sizes, numbers of households in given market areas, household sizes, income levels, levels of educational attainment, gender, age distributions, and occupation and other employment data. Of utmost importance to the retailer is information on marital and family status: Are the current and potential consumers married? Are they single? Are they divorced? Do they have children? If they have children, how many do they have? The various demographic categories generally indicate differing customer needs and wants. By identifying those differences, the retailer will find it easier to generate profits.

Retailers can also use demographic data in selecting the appropriate market areas in which to operate. For a business selling an expensive, upscale product (for example, a Rolls-Royce), the physical location should be close to those customers who have a need or want for that product.

Collection of demographic data is the most popular method of identifying customers, perhaps because this type of data is the easiest to obtain.[9] Demographic data can tell retailers what potential customers like to read, what television shows they watch, where they work, and many other habits that increase the effectiveness of the retail plan. Demographic data alone may not provide a complete picture, but when tied to a product or buying situation, they provide useful information on consumer preferences.[10]

All demographic data gain importance depending on the application. The three most common demographic variables are age, ethnicity, and income.

AGE GROUPS

generational marketing The study of age groups and how they behave in the consumer market.

The study of age groups and how they behave in the consumer market is called **generational marketing.**[11] Generational marketing is based on the premise that people of a similar age tend to behave similarly and respond to marketing in a like manner. Marketers have generalized the U.S. population into what are termed *generations*. Based on one's particular age, one may exhibit certain behavioral characteristics.

- People born prior to 1946 have been called *seniors, the silent generation, matures, the World War II generation,* and *the greatest generation.*[12] The people in this age group endured the hard times of war and the Great

Dockers is the number one khaki pant in the United States. This advertisement depicts a new style that allows the wearer more flexibility.

Depression. Consequently, they believe in hard work, are economically conscious, and trust government more than other groups.

- People born between 1946 and 1964 are part of the *baby-boom generation* (also known as *baby boomers*), so named because of the great number of births (the boom) following World War II. With over 78 million members (about 29 percent of the U.S. population), it is a difficult group to understand due to the diverse consumer behavior and attitudes that exist within it.[13] This group is also called the *me generation*, because of its focus on accomplishment. Baby boomers are said to hate aging and love nostalgia.[14]
- People born after the baby boom, between 1965 and 1976, fall in a group called *generation X*. Members of generation X that are attending college are considered nontraditional students because they are older than the average student. The approximate 40 million Gen Xers (about 16 percent of the U.S. population) celebrate diversity and individuality. This group tends to have more trouble than other groups trusting network news, political parties, and corporate America.[15]
- People born between 1977 and 1995 are considered members of *generation Y* (also called *echo boomers, generation why,* and *millennials*). There are about 74 million people in this group, representing 27 percent of the U.S. population.[16] Members of this generation are described as materialistic, selfish, and disrespectful, but technologically capable and aware of world issues.[17]
- Marketers have not yet named the generation born after 1995.

Although marketers generally identify people as being in one of the generational categories, the U.S. Census Bureau created the following categories for the U.S. population: children and teens, young adults, middle agers, olders, elders, and the very old.

The overall concept for retailers in looking at these age categories is to gain insight into the market. Levi Strauss & Co. saw a need in the 1980s for a line of clothing that could be worn anywhere. It introduced Dockers® Khakis in the United States in 1986. This product served as a link between jeans and dress slacks, and brought a shift to casual clothing in the workplace. In 1988, it launched Dockers® for Women, with a line of clothing designed to fit a variety of body types and sizes, and today the brand has expanded to include a wide range of products for consumers in more than forty countries. Over the years, Levi Strauss & Co. has tried many different products, including the "leisure suit" of the 1970s. Today the Dockers® brand is the number one khaki pant in the United States.[18] Levi Strauss & Co. developed a product that its retailers were willing to carry, its customers were willing to buy, and that returned sizable sales to the company.

Several research companies analyze consumers by their age grouping. Table 5.1 is an example of research on generations conducted by Yankelovich, a research and consulting services company. The next time you go shopping or watch television commercials, observe how various retailers target their marketing toward the different generations. For instance, manufacturers and retailers appeal to the senior generation by using older models. Seniors understand that they are aging and generally appreciate that they cannot fight this natural process. The strategy in selling to seniors is to depict them as active

TABLE 5.1

EXAMPLE OF RESEARCH CONDUCTED ON GENERATIONS

Things you do when you feel nervous and upset about what's happening in the world (top 10 responses)

	Total	Echo Boomers	Xers	Boomers	Matures
Turn to family and friends.	54%	56%	55%	58%	43%
Listen to music.	46	67	49	44	31
Pray or meditate.	37	30	36	39	40
Keep busy around the house.	37	26	38	38	42
Turn to something light or funny.	37	41	39	39	29
Get as much news/ information as possible.	32	21	29	34	38
Stick closer to home.	29	27	32	30	25
Exercise.	24	35	21	24	20
Eat comfort foods.	22	27	27	21	15
Sleep/nap more.	19	32	23	17	12

Source: 2002 Yankelovich *Monitor.*® Reprinted by permission.

and attractive. Think of all of the television commercials for new pharmaceuticals or fiber-enriched products that feature healthy, energetic seniors urging consumers to buy the products to enrich their lives.

According to Ken Dychtwald, gerontologist and author of several books on aging, people over the age of 55 control nearly two-thirds of U.S. financial assets.[19] One can understand why many retailers want to capture the senior market.

Now contrast seniors' wants and needs with those of the baby-boomer generation. Demographic data about boomers indicate they are concerned with maintaining youthfulness. Thus the appearance of numerous products that "erase wrinkles," "color that gray," or even grow hair. The number of health-related items has increased to serve baby boomers concerned about health issues—more low-fat, low-carbohydrate products; more exercise machines; and more prescription and nonprescription drugs that promise healthfulness.

Generation Xers were the first "latchkey" group, meaning that many grew up without a substantial parental presence at home. Having had to fend for themselves, they are highly independent yet desire personal contact with others. The divorce rate among parents of generation Xers has been more than 50 percent. For this generation, a work/life balance is very important. As a group, generation Xers are cynical consumers. They were raised on convenience and thus demand accommodations in their shopping excursions. They want a lot of product information and expertise when making purchase decisions. For generation Xers, the use of technology, particularly the computer, is essential in buying decisions.

Generation Y has never known a world without cell phones, compact disks, computers, or MTV; as a result, they are highly educated, creative, and technologically competent.[20] In contrast to generation X (latchkey kids), generation Y grew up with overly attentive parents. This group has been described as "generation X on fast forward, with self-esteem."[21] These consumers have more money to spend than did the generations before them. They also have a major influence on family spending and household consumption. As shoppers, generation Yers like to have interactive shopping experiences and are very concerned about the environment. They also desire "in" products and services.

RACE AND ETHNIC GROUPS

As you can see, it is essential to have a good grasp of the data that reflect various customer groups. As the twenty-first century continues, race and ethnicity are playing larger roles in defining the consumer. A **race** is a group of individuals sharing common genetic traits that determine physical characteristics. An **ethnic group** is "any group that is defined or set off by race, religion, national origin, or some combination of these categories."[22] It is important to observe the similarities and differences of behavior within and among races and ethnic groups.

race A group of individuals sharing common genetic traits that determine physical characteristics.

ethnic group Any group defined by race, religion, national origin, or some combination of these categories.

The major ethnic groups in the United States are referred to as Hispanic, African American, and Asian American. To avoid confusion, note that these are ethnic classes and not races. According to the U.S. Census Bureau, in the United States there are five racial classifications: White; Black; American Indian (also called Native American); Eskimo and Aleut; and Asian and Pacific Islander. Ethnic groups are based on origin or nationality; thus, Hispanics may be correctly classified as any of the five races. That is why you sometimes see results reported as "white (non-Hispanic)" to indicate that the data do not include people of Hispanic or Latin American origin.

Many people understand the Hispanic identifier but are confused about the race identifier. This confusion prompted a change in the way the 2000 census data were collected. In the 2000 census, respondents were given the option to select one or more racial categories as well as asked about Hispanic origin. Among Hispanics, 48 percent reported their race as "white" and about 42 percent reported "some other race."[23]

In terms of race, three-quarters of the U.S. population is White (75.1 percent); Blacks account for 12.3 percent; Asians 3.6 percent; American Indians .7 percent; and Eskimo, Aleut, and Pacific Islanders about .3 percent.[24] In the year 2050, African Americans, Japanese Americans, and Hispanic Americans within the United States are expected to make up approximately 50 percent of the total U.S. population. In June 2002, the Hispanic community, at 38.8 million, became the largest minority group.[25] Researchers show that in the United States, ethnic groups are outspending white households.[26]

Census 2000 marked the first time that information on people who identify themselves as more than one race (multiracial) was collected. In the United States, 2.4 percent of the population is classified as multiracial. More than half of multiracials identify white along with another race. Multiracials tend to live in large metropolitan areas and in states with a diverse population.[27]

The retailer needs to understand the racial and ethnic demographics of its market(s) so it can better develop an effective product mix and communication strategy. The accompanying Global Retailing box gives an example of how the paint industry undertook a major research study to find out how, why, and what its Hispanic market wanted in paint and wall coverings.

INCOME

An additional demographic important in retailing is income level. People in different income brackets demand different types of products and services. For example, many companies have developed unique stores to serve the upscale consumer.

Classifying income levels is often difficult. What is meant by "middle class," for example? Some marketers use income quintiles and consider the middle three (60 percent of U.S. household distribution) to represent the middle class. Others suggest that "middle class" is a feeling. Still others say it depends on the number of people in the household and the state in which one lives, due to geographical differences in the cost of living.[28]

Despite these difficulties, many retailers use income classification to help them understand consumer spending habits. Lower-income consumers, for instance, are more likely to eat in the home than other groups. These

GLOBAL RETAILING

Hispanic Consumers and the Do-It-Yourself Paint Segment

The do-it-yourself (DIY) paint segment is a subcategory in the architectural coatings industry. Architectural coatings are used for on-site application to interior and exterior surfaces of commercial, industrial, and residential buildings. Most architectural coatings are bought by DIY consumers and professional painter/contractors.

According to a 1999 report by the National Paint and Coatings Association, architectural coatings represented 50 percent of total paint gallons sold in the United States. The annual growth rate of this market was 2.5 percent. In 2000, U.S. architectural coating sales amounted to $6.7 billion; they are expected to grow to about $7.5 billion by 2005. Consumers purchase approximately 40 percent of architectural paints, and contractors and maintenance crews purchase the remainder.

In 2001, the National Paint and Coatings Association conducted a study to find out more about how Hispanics who migrate to the United States from Latin American countries adapt to the U.S. consumer environment and, in particular, how they make decisions regarding paint purchases. A national telephone survey was conducted comparing Hispanic consumers with Anglo consumers. Several aspects of consumption and buying habits were analyzed. Results showed that for most purchase decisions, there were no differences between Hispanics and their Anglo counterparts. Differences were found in preferences for spokespersons in advertisements and language usage: Hispanics generally preferred Hispanic spokespersons and the use of Spanish in product literature.

This information will be used to better meet the needs of Hispanic consumers. The research helps support the findings from the Yankelovich research firm's "2000 Hispanic Monitor" report, which found that Hispanics place greater emphasis, compared to other immigrants, on language and culture.

Sources: Denise T. Ogden and J. R. Ogden, *The Hispanic Consumer and the United States Do-It-Yourself (DIY) Paint Segment*" (Washington, DC: The Paint Consumer Research Panel, 2002); "2000 Hispanic Monitor," Yankelovich Research, retrieved July 2002 from www.yankelovich.com; *Paint & Coatings 2000: Review and Forecast*, 3d ed. (Little Falls, NJ: Kline & Company, Inc., 1999); Ivan Lerner, "Architectural Coatings Survive Bad Economic Times," *Chemical Market Reporter* (August 20, 2001).

consumers are less likely to buy luxury items and tend to be more practical in their purchases than other income groups. Finally, in their quest for value, more low-income consumers shop at department stores than do people in other income levels.[29]

The largest concentration of individuals in middle-income brackets is in the Midwest. This class is dominated by people who identify themselves as White (82 percent). Given that there are about 26 million households in this group, further segmentation becomes necessary for retailers.[30] Generally, middle-class consumers are college educated and spend more on vacation and meals outside the home than lower-income people do. Like lower-income people, middle-class consumers tend to search for higher-quality merchandise at lower prices.

People in the upper-income category, often referred to as *the affluent*, more than any other group, are likely to buy luxury items, spend on travel, eat meals outside the home, be college educated, and own a house. A *super-*

affluent subgroup has also been identified. The super-affluent are households earning more than $200,000 per year; they represent only 2 percent of the population.[31]

All of the demographic data discussed in this section can be turned into useful information for the retailer. It is essential to incorporate these data into the integrated retail management plan.

PSYCHOGRAPHICS

psychographics Lifestyle analysis data used to determine "what consumers do" over specified time periods.

Psychographics simply refers to lifestyle analysis. Psychographic data provide insights into "what consumers do" over a period of days, weeks, or even years. These data may include information on activities, interests, and opinions (AIOs). In addition, retailers can utilize VALS™ (**v**alues **a**nd **l**ife**s**tyles) information. A consumer's lifestyle often gives the retailer more accurate and detailed information on the purchasing pattern of that consumer.[32]

Although psychographic studies are typically undertaken by, or for, a specific client such as a retailer, there are general categories of psychographics that provide helpful guidelines for the retailer. For example, AIOs include numerous areas the retailer can use to develop a direction for its strategies or tactics. Table 5.2 lists some areas included in the study of AIOs.

VALS™ is a consumer classification model that was developed by the Stanford Research Institute (SRI) (see Figure 5.1). In VALS, a number of categories attempt to classify consumers' lifestyles (see Figure 5.2).

In addition to VALS and AIO data, other psychographic data important to retailers are related to culture, social class, reference groups, the family life cycle, and consumers' personalities. The important task for retailers is to develop a customer profile that allows them to reach consumers in the most efficient way possible.

TABLE 5.2

ACTIVITIES, INTERESTS, AND OPINIONS (AIOs)

Activities	Interests	Opinions
Work	Family	About themselves
Hobbies	Home	Social issues
Social events	Job	Politics
Vacation	Community	Business
Entertainment	Recreation	Economics
Club membership	Fashion	Education
Community	Food	Products
Shopping	Media	Future
Sports	Achievement	Culture

Source: Del I. Hawkins, Roger J. Best, and Kenneth A. Coney, *Consumer Behavior: Implications for Marketing Strategy,* 6th ed. (Chicago: Richard Irwin, 1995), p. 329. Reproduced with permission of the McGraw-Hill Companies.

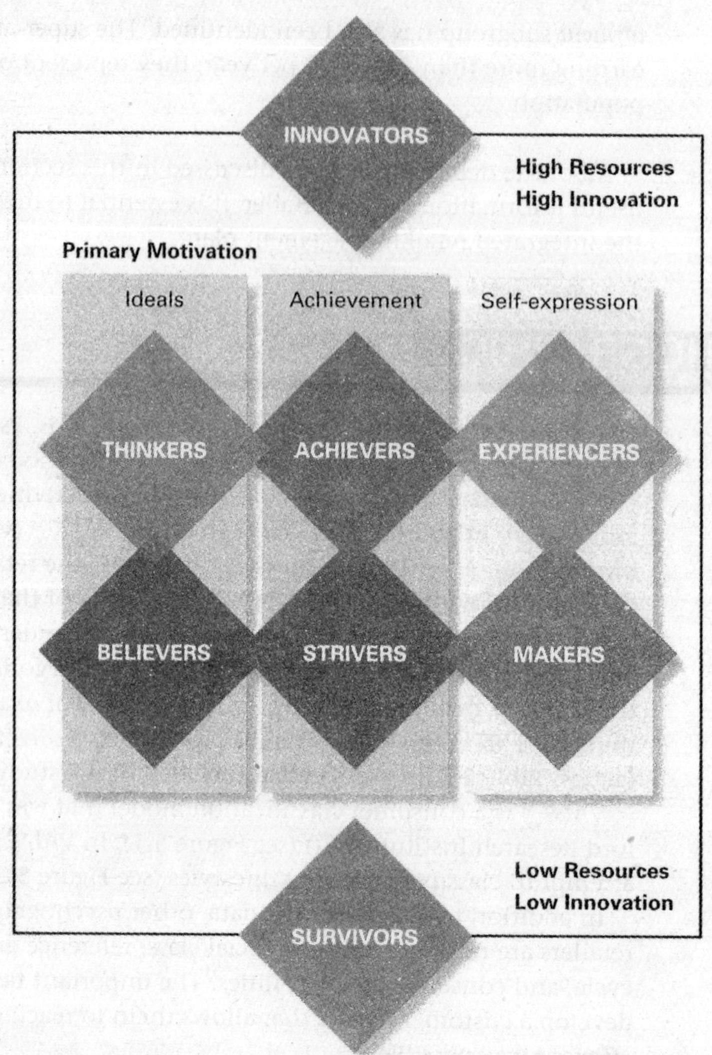

FIGURE 5.1 VALS™ Framework (Source: SRI Consulting Business Intelligence, www.sric-bi.com/vals/types.shtml. Reprinted with permission.)

GEOGRAPHICS

geographics Analysis that helps the retailer find out where customers are physically located.

Analyzing **geographics** helps the retailer find out where customers are physically located. The various retail markets are divided into separate geographic areas. An area may consist of a nation, a state, a region, a county, or a few small blocks in a neighborhood. The principle is that buyers in the various geographic areas behave differently than those in other areas. For example, a retailer may not want to retail ski apparel or equipment in a state that does not have mountains for skiing. Conversely, it might want to locate some of its

Thinkers

Ideals-motivated consumers. Well educated, high income, value oriented, with leisure activities centered within the home. Well informed about current events.

Believers

Ideals-motivated consumers. Conservative, modest incomes, favor established products and brands, with lives and leisure activities centered around their families, churches, communities, and nation.

Achievers

Achievement-motivated consumers. Successful, work oriented, politically conservative, favoring established products, with their satifaction coming from their jobs and families.

Strivers

Achievement-motivated consumers. Very similar to achievers but with fewer ecomomic resources. Style is important, and they like to emulate people they admire.

Experiencers

Self-expression motivated consumers. High energy, like physical exercise, very social, younger, adventurous. They spend heavily on clothing, fast food, and music, and they like youthful activities.

Makers

Self-expression motivated consumers. Practical, self-reliant, focus on family, work, and physical recreation. Interested in material possessions if they have a practical or functional use.

Survivors

Consumers with low resources and low innovation. Brand loyal.

Innovators

Consumers with highest resources and high innovation. Strong self-esteem, change leaders. Image is important, and they buy the finer things in life.

FIGURE 5.2 VALS™ Classifications (Source: www.sric-bi.com/vals/. Reprinted by permission of SRI Consulting Business Intelligence.)

ski retail business in a state such as Colorado, with its physical proximity to mountains and ski resorts.

Marketing communication vehicles may differ in different geographic areas, as may price and the physical good or service. Therefore, obtaining an in-depth understanding of the customer's location is essential for retailing success.

BEHAVIORISTICS

behavioristics The subdivision of a retailer's current or potential markets based on buying responses, product usage patterns, product loyalty, or store loyalty.

The idea underlying the use of **behavioristics** is to subdivide the retailer's current or potential markets based on buying responses, product usage patterns, product loyalty, or store loyalty. User profiles are developed to help explain who the customer is and how he or she responds to the various elements of the retail mix.

80/20 rule A guideline stating that 20 percent of a retailer's customers make up 80 percent of its sales volume.

One key finding of behavioristics is that a small number of customers may provide the majority of business for the retailer, a marketing concept called the *80/20 rule.* The **80/20 rule** states that 20 percent of a retailer's customers provide 80 percent of the retailer's sales volume. This rule was established for industrial marketers, but many retailers are finding that it holds for retail products as well. In response to this rule, these retailers have developed programs to treat this group of customers in a special way. Blockbuster, for example, developed a program that rewards shoppers with free rentals and added benefits based on their rental behaviors. Those shoppers who spend a lot of money

INTERNET IN ACTION

VALS™ Online Survey

In 1980, a survey was conducted to capture psychological traits from a national sample of people residing in the forty-eight contiguous United States. The survey asked more than 800 specific questions on a wide number of topics. More than 1,600 people over eighteen years old took the survey. Based on this information, the VALS (values and lifestyles) system was further developed. VALS classifies adult consumers into mutually exclusive groups. Instead of using only demographics or geographics, VALS is unique because it uncovers factors that explain consumer buying behavior from a psychological perspective.

VALS was originally designed by consumer futurist Arnold Mitchell, who created VALS to explain changing U.S. values and lifestyles. In 1978, SRI International, a nonprofit research organization based in Menlo, California, incorporated VALS into its product line. Over the years, changes in VALS occurred that placed more emphasis on measuring personality traits in relation to consumer behavior, rather than on social values that change over time. The most recent survey is the third version of the original.

You can take the survey online from the SRI Consulting Business Intelligence website (*www.sric-bi.com/vals/*). Don't worry: the survey has been condensed to about forty questions. Here is a sample question:

I follow the latest trends and fashions.

- ☐ Mostly disagree
- ☐ Somewhat disagree
- ☐ Somewhat agree
- ☐ Mostly agree

Sources: Arnold Mitchell, "The VALS Typology," article 13 in *Marketing Classics,* ed. Ben M. Enis and Keith K. Cox (Boston: Allyn and Bacon, 1991), pp. 192–207; www.sric-bi.com/vals/surveynew.shtml.

Frequent Blockbuster shoppers are awarded a card that gives them free rentals and added benefits based on their rental behaviors.

at Blockbuster stores are rewarded with free rentals and Blockbuster Rewards Gold Membership. Similar programs are in effect at Hallmark, CVS, the major airlines, and a host of other retail businesses.

GEODEMOGRAPHICS

geodemographics The combination of geographics and demographics used to describe the customer more clearly.

In recent years, marketers have found it useful to create a hybrid of the "four *ics*" (geograph*ics*, demograph*ics*, psychograph*ics*, and behavioris*tics*) to obtain an even clearer picture of the customer. The most commonly used hybrid is termed *geodemographics*. The basic premise of **geodemographics** is that people who are located in similar geographic areas behave similarly and share some demographics. Many companies specialize in providing geodemographic data based on neighborhoods or postal zip codes. These companies break the markets into clusters and then provide useful psychographic and demographic information based on the clusters' geographic locations. Table 5.3 provides a select list of some of those companies.

Research also shows that certain demographics are associated with location. The 2000 census data indicate that baby boomers, currently in their late

TABLE 5.3

SELECTED PROVIDERS OF GEODEMOGRAPHIC DATA

Tools Used for Segmentation

Company	Product	Description
Claritas	PRIZM (**P**otential **R**ating **I**ndex by **Z**ip **M**arkets)	One of the most widely used neighborhood target marketing systems in the United States
CACI	ACORN (**A** **C**lassification **o**f **R**esidential **N**eighborhoods)	Analyzes and profiles customers based on demographic and geographic data
Donnelly Marketing and Simmons Market Research Bureau	ClusterPlus	Divides the mass market into 47 distinct lifestyle clusters

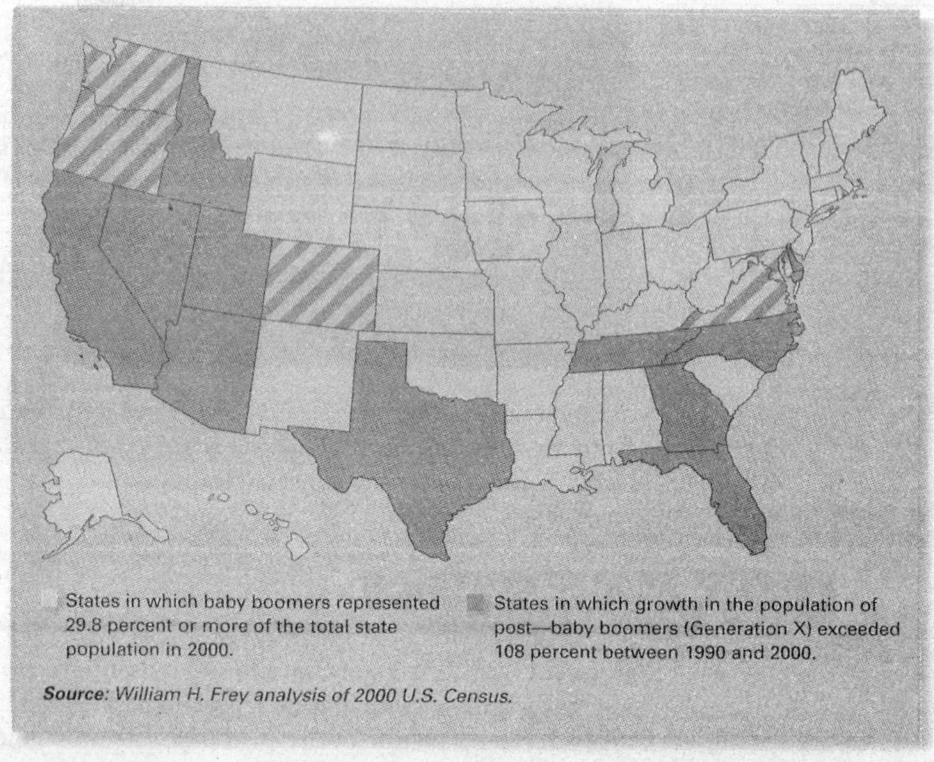

FIGURE 5.3 **Locations of Baby Boomers versus Generation Xers**
(Source: William H. Frey, "Boomer Havens and Young Adult Magnets," *American Demographics*, September 2001, pp. 22–24.)

thirties to mid fifties, are in the nesting stage of their lives. Consequently, in 2002, only 1.9 percent of this group made a residential move across states. Baby boomers live mostly in New England and the eastern seaboard, the upper Midwest, the upper Rocky Mountain West, and the Pacific Northwest. In contrast, post–baby boomers (or generation Xers) are more heavily concentrated in the South and most of the West (see Figure 5.3).

Geodemographics paint a picture of widening geographic differences leading to increasing demographic differences between cities, suburbs, and rural areas and the growth of distinctive regional markets. For example, the minority population is higher in central cities (49 percent) than in rural areas (18 percent).[33] These trends indicate that retailers may have to rely on tailored messages to reach consumers, rather than national marketing efforts.

CONSUMER BEHAVIOR

consumer behavior The study of how customers buy products.

Consumer behavior is a classification of marketing that is applied to consumers. As it relates to retailing is essentially the study of how customers buy products. Jacob Jacoby, Merchant Council professor of retail management and consumer behavior at New York University, provides a more in-depth definition of consumer behavior: "Consumer behavior reflects the totality of consumers' decisions with respect to the acquisition, consumption, and disposition of goods, services, time, and ideas. . . ."[34]

By getting a clear picture of their customers' behavior, retailers can increase product, brand, or product category sales significantly. Specifically, they can increase sales by studying the *hows*, *whys*, *whens*, and *wheres* of consumers' shopping behaviors.

To understand shopping behaviors, retailers need to know how consumers make purchase decisions. In retailing, purchase decisions are made at two stages of the shopping experience. First, the consumer selects a retailer with which to conduct business. Second, the consumer enters the store and goes through a second decision process related to selecting merchandise. The process used for both of these decisions is essentially the same.

Sometimes the consumer first decides on a product or brand that she or he wants. After choosing the product or brand, the consumer selects a retail outlet based on store service, product price, or perhaps convenience. This scenario is common with potential customers who use the Internet to shop and obtain product information.

THE CONSUMER DECISION PROCESS

The consumer decision process consists of problem awareness, information search, evaluation of alternatives, purchase, and post-purchase evaluation (see Figure 5.4). Knowledge of these stages helps retailers plan effective marketing communication plans to reach their targeted markets.

need Something the consumer perceives as required for his or her well-being.

PROBLEM AWARENESS. A consumer makes a purchase decision only after becoming aware of a problem or **need.** Problems are associated with unsatisfied consumer needs. Need recognition can be conscious or subconscious. Imagine this is the beginning of the semester and you have started a new course in integrated retail management. The professor tells you on the first day of class that all examinations will be out of the textbook. Realizing that you haven't purchased the book yet, after class you head straight for the bookstore. This book represents a conscious need.

Next, imagine you have been sitting in a three-hour class for about two hours. The professor begins to talk about food retailing, and your stomach

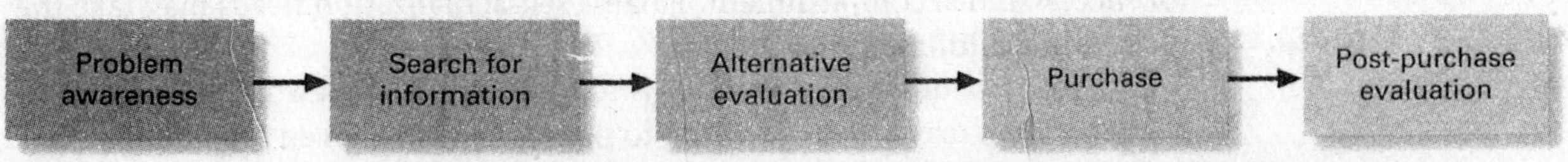

FIGURE 5.4 **The Consumer's Decision-Making Process** (Note: Additional factors affect the consumer's decision, such as demographics, psychographics, behavioristics, and geographics. In addition, the various retail mixes from the retail business and competitors affect the overall process.)

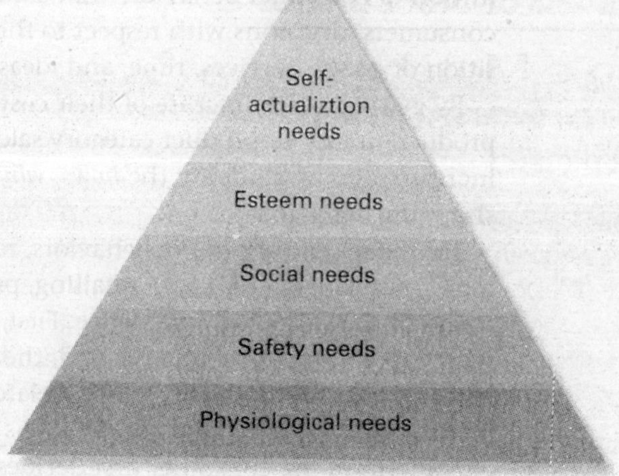

FIGURE 5.5 **Maslow's Hierarchy of Needs** (Source: Abraham H. Maslow, *Motivation and Personality,* 2d ed. [New York: Harper and Row, 1970].)

growls. Thanks to an internal reminder, you realize that you are hungry. This is an example of an unconscious need. You didn't realize you were hungry until your stomach "told you" or you were prompted by an outside source such as a marketer (in this case, your professor).

Abraham Maslow's hierarchy of needs model, depicted in Figure 5.5, suggests that five levels of needs exist for each individual: (1) physiological needs, (2) safety needs, (3) social needs, (4) esteem needs, and (5) self-actualization needs. Any unsatisfied need creates tension, which in turn helps motivate the individual to action. Thus, many times the individual attempts to find some way to relieve the tension caused by the unfulfilled need.[35] As a person's needs are met at one level, starting with the lowest, he or she seeks to fulfill the next level on the hierarchy.

Retailers are very concerned with the lower-level needs. Physiological needs include the need for food, air, water, sleep, and sex (not necessarily in that order, depending on mood and time of day). Safety needs include the need for physical well-being, shelter, and protection. Social needs include aspects such as the desire to fit into a particular group, for affection, or for friendships. Esteem needs include the need for recognition for work well done or the need for success and accomplishment. Finally, self-actualization needs may take the form of self-fulfillment.

The goal in studying these needs is to formulate a framework for understanding what drives the consumer to purchase from a given retail outlet. In reality, needs are never fully satisfied; therefore, customers go through a constant process of need fulfillment.

Some researchers criticize the use of Maslow's hierarchy because it is too general and has not been supported by sufficient empirical research. Maslow's

Blunders or Best Practices?

McDonald's Matches Strategy to Consumer Wants Abroad

Imagine a hamburger with no bun! In Thailand, where consumers' wants in a hamburger differ from Americans' desires, McDonald's is giving customers what they want. The "bunless burger," a first for McDonald's, was introduced in 2002 and is made from roast pork patties. Instead of being sandwiched within a bun, the burger is served between two patties of sticky rice. To announce the menu item, the local paper's headline read, "McDonald's Drops Its Buns For Thailand!" In addition to the Sticky-Rice Roast Pork burger, diners can order the McSomtam Shaker, a fiery green papaya salad that is a popular Thai accompaniment to sticky-rice dishes.

In India, which has a large Hindu population, people can buy McVeggie burgers and, instead of fries, feast on McAloo Tikki, a fried, potato-based patty. In Singapore, breakfast customers at McDonald's dine on traditional Chinese rice porridge called Chicken SingaPorridge. Kids are not forgotten at a McDonald's in Singapore. They can enjoy an ice cream cone topped with a mustard-yellow durian dip. (A durian is a tropical fruit that is banned from Singapore's public transportation system for its putrid odor.) Additional dessert toppings include water chestnuts, lotus seeds, and red beans . . . Yummy!

Source: Daniel B. Haber, "Culture & Thought—Culture Clash: Fast Food (Con)Fusion—Shaping Up McDonald's Buns," *Asian Wall Street Journal,* May 24, 2002, p. P13. Copyright 2002 by Dow Jones & Co., Inc. Reproduced with permission of Dow Jones & Co., Inc.

model does provide a valuable guide for retailers, however, in that it is easy to apply. Even so, it is important to avoid adhering to it too strictly. Sometimes more than one need influences a consumer's behavior. For example, a consumer looking for a quick snack may pick a Hershey bar because her father works at Hershey Foods and she wants to support his employer. Clearly more than just a physiological need (hunger) motivates this consumer's purchase decision. In addition, a consumer may skip one or more levels based on the purchase situation. For example, a consumer shopping for a gift for his best friend's wedding may bypass the physiological and safety levels and move right to the social-needs (love and belongingness) level.

Because needs have so much impact on the consumer's behavior, retailers and marketers study and research needs to get a better understanding of customer motivations. The problem is, as mentioned earlier, a consumer may not be aware of a need. The challenge for retailers and marketers is to turn the consumer's needs into wants. We talk a lot about needs and wants in retailing and marketing; what is the difference? Essentially, a **want** is simply a learned need. We *need* to eat because we're hungry, but we *want* a Big Mac!

want A learned need.

SEARCH FOR INFORMATION. Once the consumer has recognized that he or she has a problem, the consumer will begin to search for information to solve the problem. Depending on the time, effort, and cost associated with the problem, the information search may take a long time or have a short duration.

When you go to a vending machine to purchase a soda, you spend little time looking for a particular product that will quench your thirst. The products are all familiar to you, and you have made this purchase decision before. But what if you are planning to make a first-time purchase—say, a new car—and you know you will spend a lot of money for the purchase? In this instance, you most likely will spend considerable time and effort considering various purchase options. As a first step, you may get brochures and fliers from the many car dealers in your area, to compare options and costs.

internal search A process in which the consumer looks inwardly or internally for product or service information.

In your search for information, you will perform either an **internal search,** in which you ask yourself, "Do I have experience with this product?" or an *external search,* in which you gather information from outside sources, such as car dealers or the Internet. Once again, the type of search you perform will be based on your experience with the product or service, the cost of the product or service, and the time required to gain additional outside information.

It is up to the retailer to ensure that it provides information about itself and its location, so that consumers have that awareness when they attempt to satisfy their needs and wants. In addition, the retailer needs to provide information on the types of products it carries and how they can satisfy consumers' needs and wants.

ALTERNATIVE EVALUATION. After searching for and gathering all the information needed to solve the problem, the consumer must make a decision as to the best alternative or solution. This is the *evaluation of alternatives* step in the decision-making process. As stated before, if the purchase is a routine one, the consumer will spend little time in this phase (maybe only a few seconds). If it is an important and new decision, however, the evaluation phase may be relatively long term. It is during this phase that the retailer must ensure that the consumer has been supplied with all relevant information that will lead to selection of its store. The retailer needs to show the consumer that it can satisfy his or her wants and needs better than any other source can.

PURCHASE. Having evaluated the alternative solutions to the problem, the consumer then actually purchases (or does not purchase) the product or service. Ideally, of course, the retailer wants the individual to make a purchase; sometimes a person makes a conscious decision not to decide or not to purchase, however. The purchase phase consists of something of value being traded for something else of value. In retailing, it is generally a trade of money from the consumer for a durable or nondurable good provided by the retailer. At this time, the consumer becomes concerned with the place of business, the cost and terms of the transaction, and the availability of stock. Consumers always choose the most desirable place (for them) to shop. They want to feel welcome and comfortable in their surroundings.

Before making a final decision to purchase a car, consumers go through a decision process that includes problem awareness, information search, and evaluation of alternatives. After the car is purchased, a post-purchase evaluation occurs.

POST PURCHASE EVALUATION. Finally, after the purchase, the consumer makes a post-purchase evaluation of the process. If the consumer is happy with the overall shopping experience, including the product and location of purchase, she or he will make further purchases. If the consumer is not happy, he or she will likely reevaluate the purchase decision. Customer service is very important during this phase of the decision cycle. Happy customers will tell their friends, family, and associates about how much they enjoyed the store and the shopping experience, and may even recommend the retail outlet. Unhappy customers will also tell their friends, family, and associates about the experience, but will throw a negative light on it. Not only will the customer not come back to the store, but chances are that those individuals who were told about the bad experience won't patronize it either.

buyer's remorse (cognitive dissonance) A consumer's doubt associated with a purchase.

Retailers and marketers refer to customer dissatisfaction as **buyer's remorse** or **cognitive dissonance.** Specifically, this refers to the consumer's doubt about the purchase, which creates discomfort and prompts reassessment of the purchase to alleviate the negative state.[37] It is important that the customer be able to alleviate this doubt, or dissonance. Warrantees and guarantees are good ways to let consumers feel positive about their purchases. They know that if they don't like the product, they can return it.

The best way to relieve dissonance about the retail store and shopping situation, however, is to make sure it doesn't occur in the first place. Research and customer feedback are excellent tools for retailers in coming to understand customers and what they look for in a retail outlet, whether a brick-and-mortar store or a cyberstore.

While the consumer is going through the purchase decision cycle, other factors may influence the consumer. The family is a big influence on a consumer's decisions about what to buy, where and when to shop, and how many items to purchase. Consumers also look to reference groups (people they turn to when developing a basis for feelings and beliefs about something), cultures, and subcultures as aids in their decision making.

IN-STORE DECISION MAKING

Once the consumer is in the store, the retailer needs to know how the consumer shops.[38] Figure 5.6 presents a model of in-store decision making. The model was developed for use in understanding consumers in a food retailing environment, but it is also relevant to just about any type of retailer that wants to know how shoppers perceive the store.

trip type A classification to determine why a particular shopping trip was initiated.

In breaking down the model, some of the terms may need additional explanation. **Trip type** refers to why the shopping trip was initiated. Was the trip

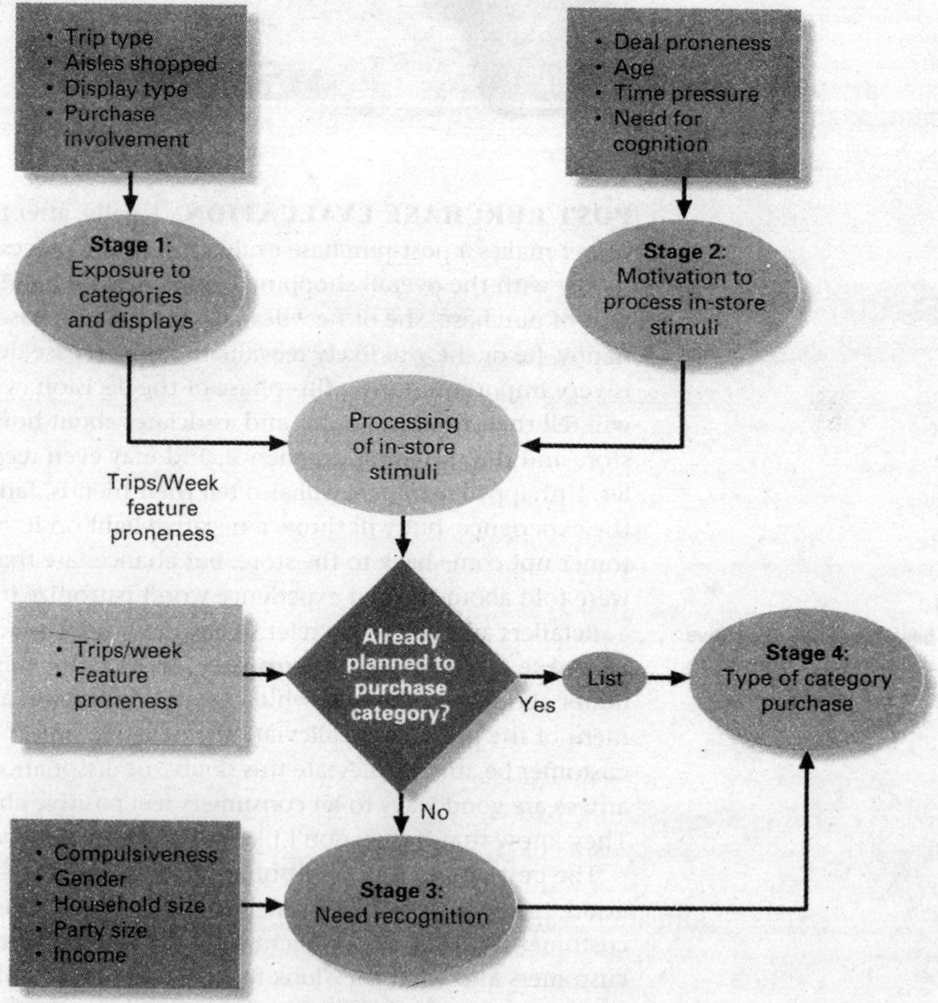

FIGURE 5.6 **The Inman and Winer Model of In-Store Consumer Decision Making** (Source: J. Jeffrey Inman and Russell S. Winer, "Where the Rubber Meets the Road: A Model of In-Store Consumer Decision Making," working paper [report no. 98–122], Marketing Science Institute, October 1998, p. 6.) Reprinted by permission.

display type and location The exact in-store locations of products and the type of display used to sell the products.

deal proneness The shopper's propensity to purchase products that are on sale or where some type of "deal" for the product is offered.

feature proneness The tendency of shoppers to use or not to use coupons or other promotional items in their shopping decisions.

purchase involvement The consumer's involvement in the overall shopping experience.

compulsiveness The degree of openness shoppers have to impulse purchases.

for a convenience product, or was it a major shopping excursion? **Display type and location** refer to the exact in-store locations of products and the types of displays used to sell them (end-of-aisle display, shelf, and so on). **Deal proneness** refers to the shopper's propensity to purchase products that are on sale or where some type of "deal" is offered. This could include frequent-shopper points, discounts, and other types of motivation. **Feature proneness** refers to shoppers' use or nonuse of coupons, freestanding inserts (FSIs), and/or newspaper circulars in their shopping decisions.

Purchase involvement refers to the consumer's participation in the overall shopping experience. **Compulsiveness** represents how open shoppers are to impulse purchases. The need for cognition deals with the consumer's thought process. The pressing question is: Does the shopper need to spend a great deal of time processing and thinking about all the information collected during the search-for-information phase of the decision-making model? Is the shopper a systematic thinker?[39] The key here is that the more information retailers have about their customers, the greater their chance for success.

SUMMARY

This chapter covered the evaluation and identification of retail customers. Although customers are diverse, they can be placed into similar categories where they have a propensity to respond in a like manner to the retailer's strategies and executions. In categorizing customers, retailers collect data using geographics, psychographics, demographics, and behavioristics, as well as geodemographics. Such information helps the retailer develop strategies that they then incorporate into the integrated retail management plan.

Consumers behave in different ways when deciding on where to shop and what to buy. The consumer decision process consists of (1) problem awareness, in which the need or want of a product is identified; (2) information search, in which the consumer searches for information on how to solve the problem identified in the awareness stage; (3) evaluation of the choices brought about by the information search; (4) purchase, in which the consumer decides whether or not to buy the product or service; (5) post-purchase evaluation, in which the consumer reflects on his or her decision. Knowledge of these stages helps retailers plan effective marketing communication plans to reach their targeted markets.

The models of the consumer decision process attempt to describe the consumer's decision-making process, both prior to deciding on a store and once in the store. These models give the retailer another tool to use in its quest to exceed customer wants and needs.

KEY TERMS

demographics (123)
generational marketing (123)
race (126)
ethnic group (126)
psychographics (129)
geographics (130)
behavioristics (132)
80/20 rule (132)
geodemographics (133)
consumer behavior (134)
need (135)
want (137)
internal search (138)
buyer's remorse (cognitive dissonance) (139)
trip type (140)
display type and location (141)
deal proneness (141)
feature proneness (141)
purchase involvement (141)
compulsiveness (141)

QUESTIONS FOR DISCUSSION

1. You have heard the saying "the customer is always right." Do you agree or disagree with this statement? Why?
2. What are the four general categories used to describe customers?
3. Describe the steps involved in the consumer decision process.
4. Think of a recent purchase you made. What steps did you go through before making the final purchase?

E-TAILING EXERCISE

Visit the following companies' websites and find a description of the retailers' target markets. This description is usually in the About Us section of the site.

JCPenney (*www.jcpenney.com*)
Nordstrom (*www.nordstrom.com*)
Avon (*www.avon.com*)
Animal Crackers (*www.k9gifts.com*)

Answer the following questions:

1. Which of the four "*ics*" (behavioristics, demographics, psychographics, and geographics) does each company use to define its customers?
2. Do you think the style of the websites would appeal to the types of customers the retailers are targeting? Why or why not?
3. Are there any other customer segments that you believe could be a target market for these companies?

Continuing Case 5.1

Sherwin-Williams Company: Target Marketing

In the late 1990s, Sherwin-Williams reassessed its target market profile. After looking at its situational analysis and environmental scanning, company executives decided that they needed to update the current market profile for their retail market divisions. The decision to change markets was a tough one because it meant major changes in a strategy that had worked for more than 100 years. Following are some of the data Sherwin-Williams looked at in reaching its decision:

- In the United States, women influence the purchase of 80 percent of all consumer goods.
- The number of minority-owned businesses has increased to 1.2 million, employing more than 800,000 workers and generating in excess of $100 billion in sales.
- Overall, woman-owned businesses account for more than $2.3 trillion in sales and employ more than 18.5 million people.
- Among the top-growth industries for women are construction and manufacturing.

Given these data, why was Sherwin-Williams not selling its products to women rather than exclusively to men?

Sherwin-Williams utilized some of the above data, along with internal research, to develop a new marketing program aimed at women. Instead of focusing on selling paint and paint-related products to men, Sherwin-Williams began to sell home decorating ideas, wall coverings (including wallpaper and paint), and related products to women. Sherwin-Williams also brought in a talented marketing communications (MARCOM) professional, Bob Wells, to spearhead the change. (Wells's past marketing successes included being responsible for putting the baby in Michelin tires in what the advertising and automobile industries perceived to be a very effective IMC campaign.) Thus, the advertising campaign theme of "Ask How, Ask Now, Ask Sherwin-Williams" was created.

Of course, men will always be a part of Sherwin-Williams's target, but the environmental scanning pointed to a new opportunity that had never been explored.

Questions

1. Do you think Sherwin-Williams made the right decision in downplaying its male market to concentrate on women?
2. Do you think the change in the marketing strategy will be long term? Why or why not?
3. What other data would you suggest Sherwin-Williams use to better define its new target market?
4. What do you believe female customers really want in wall-covering products and services?
5. Develop an effective customer profile for Sherwin-Williams's new retail market. Be sure to include the "four *ics*" (demographics, geographics, psychographics, and behavioristics).
6. Do you think all female customers of Sherwin-Williams will respond to its marketing communications in the same way? Explain your answer.
7. How does Sherwin-Williams's evaluation of its customers affect its mission and vision? Will this evaluation have an impact on the situational analysis?
8. What might be a better method for creating primary and secondary target groups for the company?

Sources: Sherwin-Williams's homepage at www.sherwin.com; internal company information at www.pbs.org/ttc/economics/marketing.html, www.pbs.org/ttc/economics/minoritywomen.html, and www.pbs.org/ttc/economics/minoritybusiness.html.

Case 5.2

eCraft Furniture and the Internet Marketing Dilemma

"I think it's a totally insane idea!" exclaimed Lori Abrams, the marketing manager. "People buy our furniture because they know it holds up and we are flexible about putting any fabric on any style. We're price competitive, but people have to see the product and talk to us to appreciate it." Craig Julio, the information technology manager, leaned back in his chair and rolled his eyes. Lori just didn't seem to understand how technology was taking over business—as far as he was concerned, *all* business, even this one.

Background

eCraft Furniture was not yet an actual business; rather, it was a concept that the management of Craft Guild Furniture Corporation had been considering for the past six months. Craft Guild, with annual sales just shy of $10 million, was founded in the early 1950s by Lori's grandfather, Austin Trexler. For nearly fifty years the family-controlled company maintained an outstanding reputation throughout the Northeast for both a quality product and superior customer service. Craft Guild was not only a manufacturer but also a direct marketer that owned its own retail stores in several urban and larger suburban areas. The typical customer came from lower- and middle-income families who were interested in affordable but durable furniture. Most advertising was by word of mouth, and it wasn't uncommon to have a third generation of the same family as customers.

Austin Trexler had insisted that the company produce only six different product styles, each containing a chair, a loveseat, and a sofa. However, each piece could be upholstered in any of more than 750 different fabrics representing various patterns, colors, fibers (natural and synthetic), and protective treatments such as Scotchgard™.

Business had been profitable, but revenue growth was modest. Senior management had challenged everyone in the company to find ways to improve the situation. The ideas had run the gamut from increased television advertising to billboards to coupons, but the one truly innovative idea had been Craig Julio's. After considering the success of Michael Dell's business model in which personal computers could be sold over the Internet, Craig believed a parallel situation might also work for Craft Guild. Dell was widely known for being a tough competitor to Compaq, Hewlett-Packard, Gateway, and IBM because it built personal computers to customer order rather than building for inventory. The results spoke for themselves as Dell continued to put product into customers' hands within a week, provide outstanding return on assets employed, and be the "darling of Wall Street" among the PC makers.

For starters, Craig designed an interactive website that would allow customers to try any fabric on any style and get immediate pricing, including shipping to their door. From a cash flow standpoint, customers would pay in full by credit card at the time of the order—a much better arrangement than the 20 percent down that the retail stores insisted on when taking a factory order. Moreover, there was no finished-goods inventory.

Total Marketing

Craig was not alone in advocating that Craft Guild expand into e-commerce. With so many other industries making some attempt at it, most of the other managers were starting to accept the idea. Lori Abrams clearly was the most vocal opponent. There has to be some way to win her over, Craig thought. But what can that be?

The Next Management Meeting

At the next management meeting, the topic of eCraft came up again. Lori remained adamant about the importance of customer contact, and not only by the sales staff at the time of the initial sale. "Everyone at Craft Guild is a marketer," she explained. "Even the delivery personnel are always willing to do some of the little things, like getting a sofa into a third-story loft or rearranging existing furniture in an elderly customer's apartment." Craig again rolled his eyes, but she continued, "Everyone knows that our delivery people are so skilled that there have been times when they've removed doors from their hinges and window sashes from their frames to make a delivery! Who's going to do that when we're Web based and having some unknown trucker delivering to an otherwise unknown customer thousands of miles away?"

"Lori, we've got to change with the times if the company is to survive. You just don't get it," Craig burst out, startling everyone in the room. "*I* don't get it? *You* don't get it!" Lori retorted. "You don't know why we have the customers we do. It's a good thing you want to call this new venture eCraft, because I'm not so sure that I want such a faceless concept contaminating the good name of Craft Guild!"

After a few more minutes of exchanging accusations about not understanding the business, the meeting moved to other agenda items without reaching any closure on the eCraft concept. The gridlock was nothing new, as the group had agreed to disagree many times previously in the hope that in the interim some new insight would generate a compelling argument one way or the other.

Questions

1. What is eCraft's target market?
2. How does this market differ from its traditional market?
3. What product attributes of upholstered furniture would suggest that it is or is not well suited for selling over the Web?
4. Assuming management comes back with a decision to try the eCraft venture, what risks might there be for Web customers who want the same services that in-store customers want?
5. How might the interactive website that Craig designed for eCraft help improve sales through the traditional channels?
6. If Craft Guild goes through with the concept, should it call itself by its own distinct name, eCraft? Explain your answer.
7. Make and support a detailed recommendation to management that endorses or rejects the long-debated eCraft concept.

Source: This case was prepared from actual business situations by Richard R. Young, Ph.D., associate professor of business logistics, Penn State Berks-Lehigh Valley. It is intended to foster class discussion and not to suggest either good or inappropriate administrative behavior.

Internal Planning

and Management

Part 3 examines internal retail planning and management. Chapter 6 covers research activities and retail information systems (RIS). Market selection and location decisions that retailers face are the focus of Chapter 7.

Chapter 8 outlines the financial aspects of operations management, including analysis of financial statements. Chapter 9 looks at the dynamic areas of merchandise buying and handling. Chapter 10 addresses human resource decisions that are made in the retailing environment.

Retailing Information Systems and Research

Chapter

6

The ability to "listen in" on conversations about you or your competitors may represent one of the best market-research values of the Internet, simply because it's unique to the medium. I'm talking, of course, about the newsgroups and discussion groups so prevalent in the Usenet section of the Internet.

Susan Greco,
articles editor, Inc.

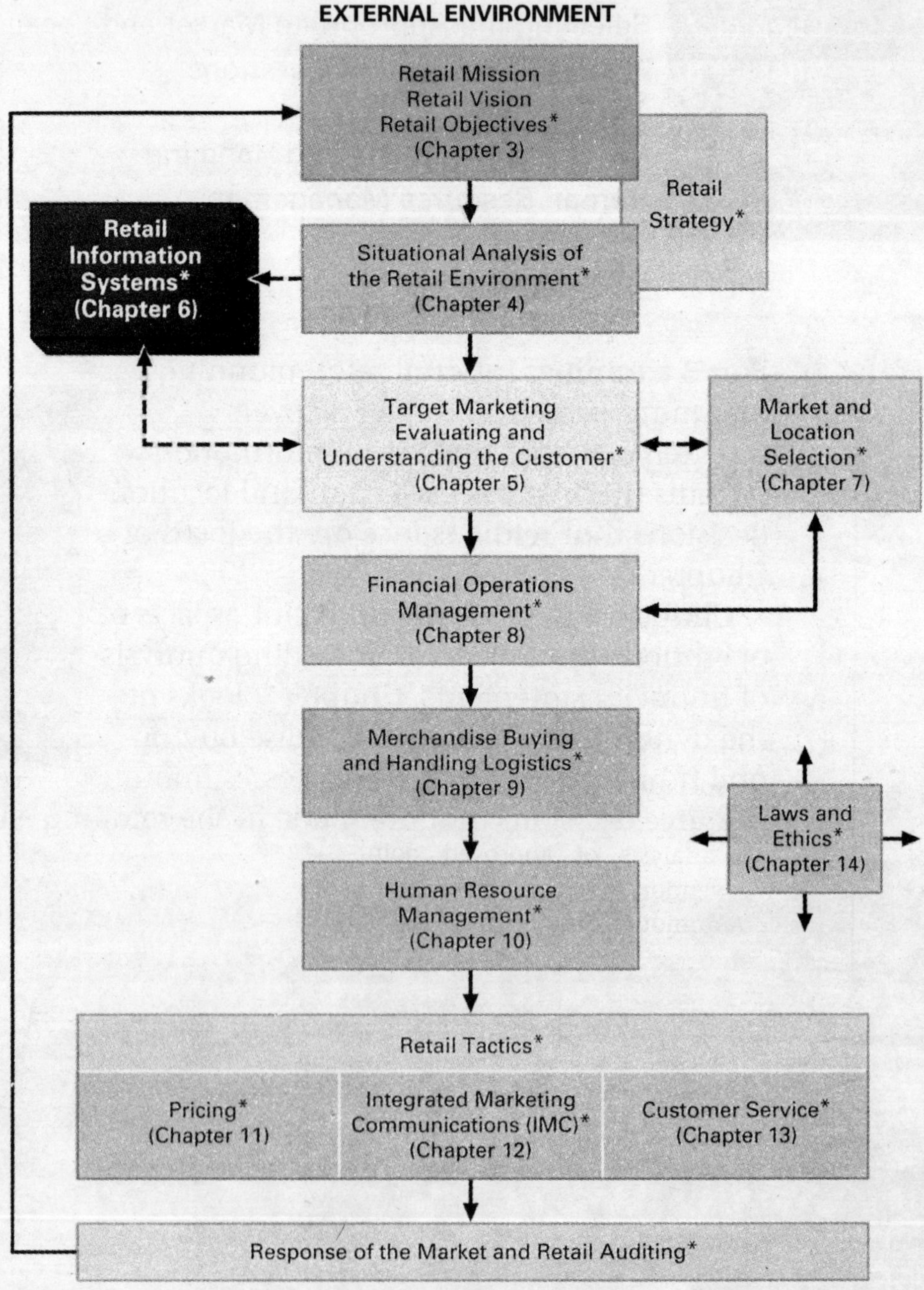

CHAPTER OBJECTIVES

After completing this chapter, you will be able to:

1. Define and explain the purpose of a retail information system (RIS).
2. Explain the steps in conducting marketing research.
3. Describe the difference between secondary and primary data and identify some tools for collecting data.
4. Discuss the role of technology in gathering data.

Midas Revamps Its Retail Information System

In an effort to develop a common information technology infrastructure for the Midas chain of automotive repair stores, a team of Midas representatives led by Ron McEvoy, chief information officer, undertook a two-year journey to choose a vendor for the project. In addition to Midas staff, the computerization team consisted of the International Midas Dealers Association president and a group of franchisees.

An analysis of approved point-of-sale (POS) vendors was completed, and Progressive Automotive Systems of Houston, Texas, was chosen as the supplier. The Internet-based system allows for electronic ordering from headquarters. Other data management features include the integration of estimating and sales processes, vehicle maintenance schedules, labor charges, and technicians' compensation.[1]

In January 2001, Midas, Inc. acquired Progressive Automotive Systems. According to Wendel H. Province, Midas's chairman and chief executive officer, "By acquiring Progressive Automotive, we are assuring the continuing availability and development of software to enhance our ability to serve customers and to improve the profitability of our dealers."[2] Acquiring the company has allowed Midas to develop and implement systems that fit its operations and also ensure the security of the data collected.

INTRODUCTION

Retail managers must make decisions about handling data and information while ensuring that customer needs are met. Before they can do this, though, they must distinguish between data and information. Data represent raw numbers that have no meaning unless attached to other relevant information. According to one source, "**Data** are news, facts, and figures that have not been organized in any manner. **Information** is a body of facts organized around some specific topic or subject."[3] Thus, once raw data are gathered and organized, useful retail information results. Once retail managers have made this distinction, they must determine the best way to gather and disseminate the needed data.

data News, facts, and figures that have not been organized in any manner.

information A meaningful body of facts organized around some specific topic.

When beginning the IRM planning process, retail managers need to arm themselves with sufficient information and data to make the best decisions possible. In some decision-making situations, retail managers react from their "gut," drawing on their many years of retail experience. For the majority of decisions, however, retail managers rely on data that have been generated from customers, the marketplace, the retail environment (both internal and external), employees, and the competition. After gathering the data and the information the data reveal, managers must apply them to solve the problem at hand. These problems can occur at any step in the IRM process.

This chapter discusses the systems used to collect and store retail data and the research process used by retailers to better understand the market and their customers. As discussed earlier in the text, retailers need to assess the environments that affect their business. This analysis is research based and is accomplished through environmental scanning. Likewise, retailers need to identify and respond to issues that arise in market segmentation, site selection, financial operations, logistics, pricing and service levels, and many other areas.

RETAIL INFORMATION SYSTEMS

A **retail information system (RIS)** is the method for systematically gathering, analyzing, storing, and utilizing valuable retail information and data gathered in the market research process. An RIS facilitates the process of finding solutions to problems. The process of collecting, organizing, analyzing, and disseminating data related to a particular area is called **market research.** An RIS is often used to facilitate the market research process. The major logistical problem in this phase of the development of an IRM plan is the building and usage of the system.

retail information system (RIS) A method for systematically gathering, analyzing, storing, and utilizing valuable retail information and data.

market research The process of data collection, organization, analysis, and dissemination of data relating to a particular area.

RIS can be as low tech as a handwritten log used to record a small retailer's inventory or as high tech as a database warehouse that ties smaller databases together (as in the Midas example earlier in this chapter). Today, most retailers have some type of computerized system.

Because the RIS will be used in virtually all areas of the retail operation, the system should be general enough to be accessible to all users but specific enough to help create solutions to any retail problems that develop. Generally, the communication process for the RIS needs to flow in all directions; that is, the RIS should be able to gather data and at the same time send the data to the many internal and external stakeholders in the retail business. The RIS need not release all information to stakeholders who have only limited information needs. Information may be shared among store groups, vendors, internal buyers and planners of merchandise, members of the distribution channels, and customers. Some of the information may be proprietary; thus, a system for ensuring the confidentiality of these data needs to be developed.

Several retailers, including Albertsons, Inc. and The Yankee Candle Company, Inc., have upgraded their RIS with better technology. In 2003, Albertsons, one of the world's largest food and drug retailers, implemented a system to serve as a central repository of data on more than one million grocery and pharmaceutical items sold by its 2,300 retail stores in 31 states. The result will be higher accuracy of the massive amount of item information that the company manages.[4] The Yankee Candle Company, manufacturer and retailer of premium scented candles, updated its manual collection of employee data by implementing a common database that provides an enterprisewide view of the workforce. The database allows Yankee Candle centrally to collect workforce data from over 4,000 employees in its 260 retail stores in 42 states while at the same time allowing local store managers to edit employee information. The database will save the company both time and money.[5]

A properly developed RIS will be used in the management of the supply chain; in the finance department(s); in data warehousing; and in distribution, pricing, merchandising, integrated marketing communications, and product acquisition. In addition, the data may become part of the retailer's logistics system, including inventory planning and control. The data may also be used to make sound, scientific decisions in regard to planning, strategy, and tactical executions.

multichannel retailer A retailer that uses more than one means of distribution for products and services.

As more businesses become **multichannel retailers** (utilizing more than one channel to sell products and services), integration of RIS between stores, websites, and other channels becomes important. The ability to combine online data with data from other sources, such as demographics, behavioristics, and in-store and catalog purchases, allows a retailer to turn these insights into action.[6] As can be seen, an effective RIS is a very important part of managing information. The RIS must be developed in a systematic manner with input from all users of the system, along with the research data that have been gathered.

Figure 6.1 shows the various elements to be included in a comprehensive RIS.

BENEFITS OF USING AN RIS

The development of an effective RIS helps ensure that the system is fully integrated into the overall retail management plan. In addition, an effective RIS should allow for continuous updating of important data. Prior to the

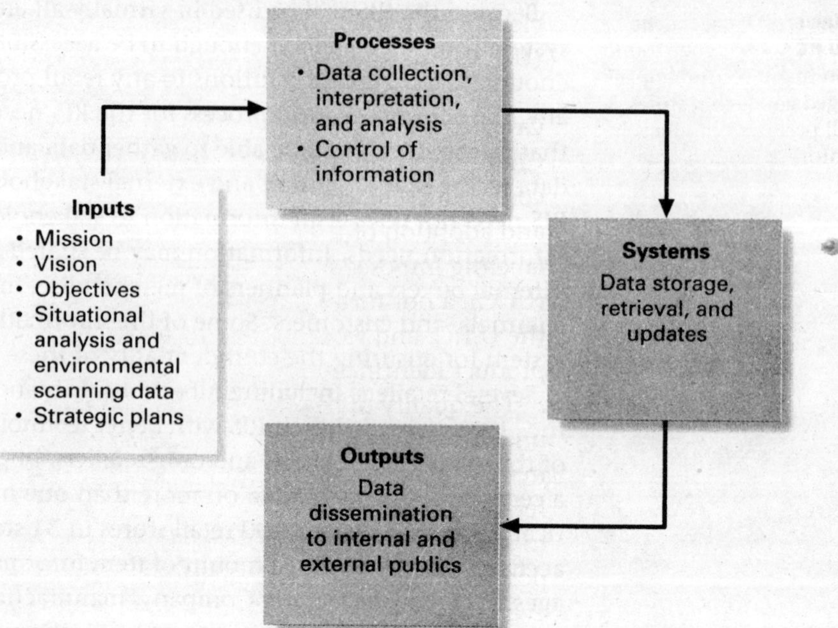

FIGURE 6.1 Input and Output Elements for a Retail Information System

development of high-technology retail information systems, much day-to-day operational work was done by hand. For example, the retailer did not know immediately when it had sold the last product or unit in the store until a physical inventory was performed. Through the use of Universal Product Code (U.P.C.) and point-of-sale (POS) scanning, retailers can capture price data in milliseconds and send it to other systems via **electronic data interchange (EDI).** In addition, merchandise optimization technology, another example of an RIS, allows the retailer to identify the most profitable merchandising decisions and determine, in real time, approximately how many units remain in stock, when to order more inventory, and how much inventory to order (called the **economic order quantity**).[7]

electronic data interchange (EDI) A system that enables the transfer of data from one computer to another.

economic order quantity A calculation of how much merchandise to reorder.

Retailers use an RIS to access data regarding which items have the highest turnover rates and where the economic order quantity points are. In addition, RIS databases can aid in understanding consumers' behaviors, in customer response management, and in the development of customer loyalty programs.

An effective RIS is necessary to be competitive in today's retail environment. The function of retail information has become so important that many retailers have created positions for heads of RIS departments. Generally, these responsibilities fall under the guidance of the chief information officer (CIO).

THE UNIVERSAL PRODUCT CODE (U.P.C.)

Think of the last time you visited a supermarket. Each of your purchases was probably run through an optic scanner, either by you or by the store checkout

Universal Product Code (U.P.C.) A bar code found on many consumer packaged goods that stores all pertinent product information.

clerk. This optic scanner reads the bar code, or **Universal Product Code (U.P.C.),** on the package and records all the pertinent data from the U.P.C.

The idea for the U.P.C. system came about in 1969 when members of the Grocery Manufacturers of America and the National Association of Food Chains met and determined there was a need for an "interindustry product code." In 1973, the linear bar code was chosen as the symbol for the U.P.C., and adoption of the U.P.C. was swift due to new requirements for nutritional labeling imposed by the federal government. The Uniform Code Council, Inc. (UCC), a not-for-profit standards organization (*www.uc-council.org*), oversees the U.P.C. and works to establish and promote multi-industry standards for product identification and related electronic communication.[8]

The quality of bar codes is a major concern for retailers. An erroneous or unscannable bar code can create additional expense because incorrect information may be fed into the RIS, resulting in a ripple effect throughout the retailer's supply chain.[9] Many state governments conduct routine inspections to make sure that the prices charged to consumers are the same as those posted. To ensure quality, many retailers use price verification software and even hire a service to verify prices.[10]

A typical U.P.C. has a company identifier built into it. There are also additional numbers assigned by the retailer to identify a specific product stock-keeping unit (SKU). The cost for participation in the U.P.C. program varies with the size of the retailer.

The United States and Canada use a 12-digit U.P.C. Over 100 other countries use the EAN.UCC system, which utilizes 8-digit (EAN-8) and 13-digit (EAN-13) symbols. Due to the differing systems, many system translation problems arise in international trading situations. In an effort to simplify worldwide commerce, the Uniform Code Council announced the "January 1, 2005 Sunrise harmonization initiative." In addition to the 12-digit U.P.C. symbols, by January 1, 2005, all U.S. and Canadian companies must be capable of

The quality of Universal Product Codes (U.P.C.s) is important because an erroneous or unscannable bar code can create additional expense. Incorrect information may be fed into the RIS, resulting in a ripple effect throughout the retailer's supply chain.

scanning EAN-8 and EAN-13 symbols at point of sale.[11] The change will facilitate global retail communication.

POINT-OF-SALE TERMINALS

The data embedded in the U.P.C. are sent to a centralized location for analysis. The interpreted results are then sent back to the store manager (often in a matter of seconds), who uses the results to make decisions on merchandising, advertising, accounting, and ordering, among other functions. In this process, the store manager is using the organization's point-of-sale terminal to facilitate the retailer's RIS function.

point-of-sale (POS) terminal A computer workstation designed to collect information from sales of products and services.

A **point-of-sale (POS) terminal** is a computer workstation designed to collect information from the sales of products and services. Each workstation can support optional peripherals such as bar code readers and scanners, invoice printers, magnetic strip readers (for credit or debit cards), modems, and so on, depending on the retailer's needs. POS terminals can be fixed (positioned at a specific, predetermined location), hand-held, or both. POS terminals are effective in providing data used to generate useful retail information.

One company that develops research for retailers is IRI. IRI data provides information regarding specific products, brands, and product categories. The data are amassed through the use of U.P.C.s and POS scanners that input the information about specific product purchases into a database. The database holds information such as how many products were purchased, where the purchases were made, when they were made, and how they were made (*i.e.,* cash versus credit or debit). The use of effective POS systems can greatly increase the quantity and quality of retail research.

RADIO FREQUENCY IDENTIFICATION (RFID)

radio frequency identification (RFID) Wireless technology that uses radio waves to read product information.

A new wireless technology that may revolutionize RIS is **radio frequency identification (RFID).** Like bar codes, RFID captures price and inventory data; unlike bar codes, however, RFID does not need to be in the line of sight of a scanner and does not require a human to scan an item.[12] A basic RFID system consists of an antenna, a transceiver, and a tag (also called an RFID tag or a smart tag). The antenna on the RFID microchips emits radio signals to activate the tag. These data are sent to a transceiver, which reads the data from the RFID tag into the computer.[13]

Gap Inc. has piloted RFID technology. RFID tags were placed on denim apparel throughout its stores, and antennas were built into the shelves. In tests, the RFID system helped improve tracking accuracy to a level as high as 99.9 percent. Because RFID allows for mass scanning of items, the technology speeded checkout and returns of merchandise and facilitated in-store pickups from Internet sales. In addition, the technology provided real-time inventory tracking.[14]

To accommodate adoption of RFID technology, the Uniform Code Council and EAN International established AutoID, Inc., a not-for-profit organization that will develop and oversee commercial and technical standards for the Electronic Product Code (EPC) Network. The EPC, used in conjunction with RFID technology, allows products to be identified.[15] The biggest obstacle to rapid adoption is the price of the tags. The electronic tags cost about 30 cents each, significantly more than the 5 cents typically paid by retailers for tags.[16]

SELF-CHECKOUT SYSTEMS

self-checkout system A format in which shoppers scan, bag, and pay for their own purchases.

Self-checkout systems let shoppers scan, bag, and pay for their own purchases. In 1999, only 6 percent of grocery stores had self-checkouts; by 2003, 30 percent of food retailers had the systems in place.[17]

Many systems operate similarly. Consumers scan each item. The self-checkout machine reads the bar code and identifies the product's price and weight. Next, shoppers place the items in a bag that sits on a scale. The scale validates each item's weight. A screen displays the list, the individual prices, and a running total of scanned items. If an item is sold by weight, the customer uses a touchscreen to tell the computer what they are buying. Various codes differentiate between items sold by weight, such as grapes and potatoes. At most stores there is an attendant who aids consumers in the process.

Drug stores, convenience stores, and office supply stores are also adopting the self-checkout format. Home Depot, the chain of home improvement stores, has installed self-service checkout counters. According to Home Depot's CEO, Home Depot is spending 12 times as much on technology as it did three years ago.[18] Typical systems cost on average about $100,000 for four checkout lanes, about twice the cost of traditional systems. According to industry experts, however, retailers recoup the cost in labor savings and higher sales in a little more than one year.[19]

OUTSOURCING

Questions managers face when developing an RIS relate to what type of information needs to be collected, how it will be collected, how it will be stored, and how it will be disseminated. They also need to decide whether to spend time and effort developing the RIS in house or to outsource the development work. **Outsourcing** is the practice of hiring an individual, a group, or an organization outside the company to perform the necessary work on the system. The individuals or companies that provide this service typically are consultants. If outsourcing is chosen, the retailer must be sure that the system to be developed can be tailored to meet the specific needs of the retail organization. It is typical practice for retailers to perform some of the work on the RIS but to outsource other areas where they have little or no expertise. For example, a retailer might like to undertake some exploratory research, such as a focus group, for the purpose of data collection but might lack the expertise to do so. This is a task that could be outsourced to a consultant. Security and management of theft are other functions that are frequently outsourced.[20]

outsourcing The practice of hiring an individual, a group, or an organization outside the company to perform certain work.

BALANCING DATA NEEDS

The overall goal of an RIS is to collect useful data, whether performing tasks in house or outsourcing. Retail managers must generate enough data to be meaningful in decision making, but not so much that it entails excessive cost in terms of time and capital. In addition, too much data may have the adverse effect of overwhelming managers, who have very little time to devote to any one decision-making problem. What they need is easy access to *relevant* data only.

MANUAL VERSUS COMPUTERIZED SYSTEMS FOR AN RIS

How does a retailer choose between a manual or a computerized RIS? Certainly manual systems can be, and are, used. They have limitations, however, especially in terms of the time it takes to access and disseminate data. Computerized systems, particularly for larger retailers, are generally the better choice. Given the abundance of inexpensive computer hardware and software, computerized systems need not be cost prohibitive. In fact, many software packages were developed for retail decision making and are very affordable, even for smaller retailers

The most popular systems are Retailer Technologies International's *Retail Pro* (*www.retailpro.com*) and MicroStrategy Incorporated's *MicroStrategy* (*www.microstrategy.com*). Retail Pro is used by small to midsize retailers and can be found worldwide in over 22,000 stores.[21] MicroStrategy is generally used by larger retailers such as Best Buy and Lowe's Home Improvement Warehouse[22] because of its higher cost and more sophisticated capabilities. Many software companies also build personalized software designs to meet the needs of a specific retail application. Of course, retailers must pay a higher price for this specialized software.

An RIS would not be possible without the data gathered in the market and marketing research processes. These stages are vital to the effective development of an integrated retail strategy.

MARKETING AND MARKET RESEARCH

marketing research
Research conducted to identify and define marketing opportunities and problems; generate, refine, and evaluate marketing actions; monitor marketing performance; and improve understanding of marketing as a process.

Marketing research and market research are distinctly different. **Marketing research,** by definition of the American Marketing Association (AMA), is "the function which links the consumer, customer, and public to the marketer through information—information used to identify and define marketing opportunities and problems; generate, refine, and evaluate marketing actions; monitor marketing performance; and improve our understanding of marketing as a process."[23]

Market research, on the other hand, is a subfunction of marketing research. In market research, the retailer or marketer is concerned only with information about the retailer's market(s) or potential market(s). In brick-and-mortar retailing, market research often concerns itself with geographically defined markets. However, with e-tailing, the market researcher may be concerned with other aspects of the cybermarket, including its size. Thus, market research refers to research about a retailer's market, whereas marketing research deals with the research generated for and from the entire marketing program or for underlying theoretical issues such as consumer behavior.

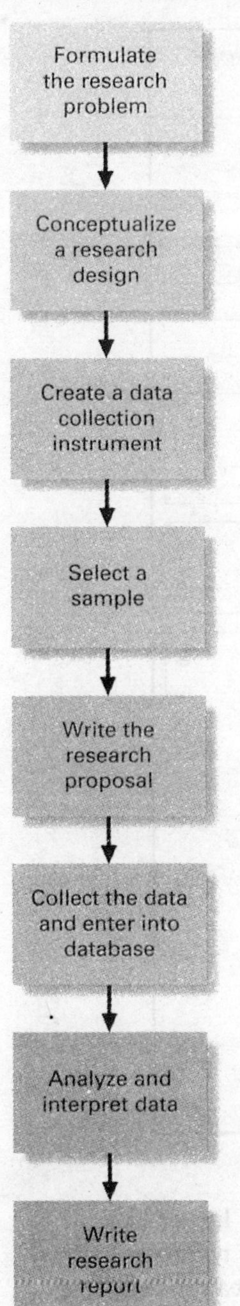

FIGURE 6.2

The Marketing Research Process

(Source: Ranjit Kumar, *Research Methodology* [Thousand Oaks, CA: Sage Publications, 1999].)

THE MARKETING RESEARCH PROCESS

To understand marketing research, it helps to have a basic grasp of the process used to gather data. The research process is composed of a series of eight steps to achieve the overall goal of generating usable information.[24] Figure 6.2 illustrates a typical marketing research process.

STEP 1: FORMULATE THE RESEARCH PROBLEM. This is often the hardest step in executing the research program. The researcher looks for underlying causes of the problem. Often certain symptoms are incorrectly identified as the problem. Solving a symptom does not solve the underlying problem. For example, a retail manager of a gym finds that sales figures are a little low compared to those of the same time the previous year. The question she should ask is: "Are lower sales the primary problem?" The answer is most likely "no"; rather, the lower sales are probably a symptom of the primary problem. To uncover the primary problem, the appropriate question is: "What caused the sales decrease?"

When distinguishing symptoms from problems, the manager may find that sales are low for other retailers and that her gym's sales decrease is actually the smallest of all competitors'. This may be due to a slumping economic environment. Thus, there is no internal problem; instead the problem is industry-wide. Managers may need to develop response strategies to counter retail environmental issues.

Problem formulation is difficult for beginners because they are used to being given problems. Think about your last college examination. If it was a multiple-choice test, the professor gave you a series of problems or questions, along with a series of possible solutions. This is not the way it happens in the retail world, however. In professional retailing, you are not given the original problem to be solved (and far less a series of potential solutions from which to choose). Critical, analytical thinking must come into play.

In retailing, the research problem usually comes about because retail objectives are not being met. When this is the case, the first question to ask is: "Why?"

To uncover the problem, the researcher must search for data in the specific area of interest to avoid collecting an excessive amount of useless data. A secondary data search helps develop a better understanding of the retail environment under study. In addition, a comprehensive secondary data review may actually solve the problem and avoid the need to develop a more formalized approach to getting the necessary information. If the secondary data help solve the problem, the research process is complete. If it does not offer solutions to the problem, the research process must continue.

Once the research problem has been clearly defined—in other words, once the question "What needs to be accomplished or solved by undertaking the research process?" has been answered—the researcher is ready to continue. During this step, it is wise to identify variables that may alter the findings: What environmental issues and variables may have an impact on the final solution?

A data collection instrument, such as the data collection form shown here, is used to provide structure to the research process.

LMTSK Limited

Study # 5687

Time Began: ______

Time Ended: ______

Total Time: ______

Screener

Name: ______

Address: ______

City: ______ State: ______ Zip Code: ______

Phone: ( ) ______

Phone Number Listed Under: ______

Interviewed By: ______ Date: ______

Validated By: ______ Date: ______

Sex	
Male	1
Female	2

Age	
18-34	1
35-54	2

City:

Massapequa	1	Austin	9	Louis Joliet	17	Miami	25
Ft Myers	2	Goodlettsville	10	Hawthorn	18		
Melbourne	3	Charleston	11	Akron	19		
Orlando	4	Detroit	12	Denver	20		
Tampa	5	Kansas City	13	Phoenix	21		
Coral Square	6	Bannister	14	Portland	22		
Greenspoint	7	St Louis	15	Tyler Galleria	23		
Gwinnett	8	Mall of America	16	Tracy	24		

Hello, my name is ______ from ______. We are conducting a survey today and would to include your opinions.

Q1 Which group best describes your age? (Read the list)

Under 18	1	**(Terminate and record below)**
18-24	2	
25-34	3	**Check Quotas**
35-44	4	
45+	5	
Refused	6	**(Terminate and record below)**

Term Q 1 | 1 2 3 4 5 6 7 8 9

OQ Age | 1 2 3 4 5 6 7 8 9

STEP 2: CONCEPTUALIZE A RESEARCH DESIGN. In step 2, a choice needs to be made among the many available types of research designs (observation, survey, longitudinal study, and so on). The research design is used as a guide throughout the entire research process and is dependent on the type of data to be collected and how they are to be collected. Thus, a thorough understanding of the problem is needed to choose the research design that will be most effective in solving the problem.

STEP 3: CREATE A DATA COLLECTION INSTRUMENT. Based on the identified problem, methods of data retrieval and collection are chosen. When creating a data collection instrument, options include a questionnaire, an observation feedback form, or a personal interview feedback sheet. For example, a retailer has ordered 100,000 pens to be used in the retail promo-

LMTSK Limited — Study # 5687

Q2 How often, if ever, do you go out to lunch or dinner at a casual restaurant? (Read the list)

Once a week or more	1	
2-3 times a month	2	
Once a month	3	
Less than once a month	4	**(Terminate and record below)**

Term Q 2 — 1 2 3 4 5 6 7 8 9

Q3 (Record by Observation)

Male	1	**Check Quotas**
Female	2	

Term Q 3 — 1 2 3 4 5 6 7 8 9

Q4 How often, if ever do you eat either lunch or dinner at each of the following restaurants? (Read the list)

	Once a month or more	Once every 2-3 months	Once every 4-6 months	Once every 6-12 months	Less often or never
Applebee's	1	2	3	4	5
TGI Friday's	1	2	3	4	5
Bennigan's	1	2	3	4	5
Ruby Tuesday's	1	2	3	4	5
Chili's	1	2	3	4	5

(Respondent must have at least 2 answers circled in the boxed area otherwise terminate and record below)

Term Q 4 — 1 2 3 4 5 6 7 8 9

Q 5 Which group best describes your total household income, before taxes? (Read the list)

Less than $25K	1	**(Terminate and record below)**
$25K to 35K	2	
$35K to 50K	3	
$50K or more	4	
Refused	5	**(Terminate and record below)**

Term Q 5 — 1 2 3 4 5 6 7 8 9

Q6 We would like to get your opinon of a new restaurant opening up in your area. It will only take 10 minutes of your time, are you willing to participate?

Yes	1	
No	2	**(Terminate and record below)**

Term Q 6 — 1 2 3 4 5 6 7 8 9

tions department. When the shipment arrives, the retailer does not want to look at every single item to determine how many are defective. In this case, the retailer uses an observation feedback form to record defects. To save time, the retailer chooses a sample of pens and then extrapolates, or projects, the number of defective units from that sampling. In this case, a "piece of paper," is the research instrument and, for this retailer, is sufficient to record the data pertaining to the problem.

STEP 4: SELECT A SAMPLE. To use statistics correctly, the selection of a sample must be somewhat scientific. One needs to understand the concept of sampling and to know whether a probability sample or a nonprobability sample is called for to complete the research project.

STEP 5: WRITE THE RESEARCH PROPOSAL. It is not within the scope of this text to discuss the development of research proposals. Briefly, the proposal needs to cover the secondary data search, the problem, what is to be accomplished from the work, the hypothesis(es), the study design, and methodologies to be used in generating responses from the sample. The proposal should also include a section on how and to whom the findings will be communicated.

STEP 6: COLLECT THE DATA AND ENTER INTO DATABASE. In this step the data are collected and placed into some type of database to allow for analysis. The data collection process must be conducted in a sensitive and ethical manner. In most instances, subjects need to be "briefed" about the intent of the research.

Once the data are collected, the analyst codes the data. Coding involves assigning the data numbers and/or titles to help the computer read them. Not all researchers code data, but data coding helps organize and interpret the data, which is done in the next step. After coding, the data are then entered into the appropriate database.

STEP 7: ANALYZE AND INTERPRET DATA. In this step, statistics are used to analyze the data. After statistics have been applied, an interpretation of the data is made.

STEP 8: WRITE THE RESEARCH REPORT. There are several things to keep in mind when writing the research report. Most important is to understand the audience that will read the report. Are they practitioners who have little time or use for every detail of the project? Are they researchers who will be very interested in the methods used to collect and present the data? Should the report include a "works cited" section, a reference section, or a bibliography section, or perhaps all three? Regardless of the audience, it is standard practice to include the conclusions and recommendations within the body of the report.

executive summary An abstract of an entire paper.

Often it is necessary to complete an executive summary at the beginning of the research report. An **executive summary** is essentially an abstract of the entire report. It should identify all the activities performed in the research process, including recommendations on how to solve the problem or issue, in a page or less.

GATHERING INFORMATION

Because of capital resource and time constraints, it is not always possible to undertake a grand-scale research project in retailing. Just as retailers sometimes outsource their RIS function, they also sometimes outsource the research function to consultants or other facilitators (such as advertising agencies). In addition, retailers often rely on secondary data to help solve their problems.

SECONDARY DATA

secondary data Published data that have already been collected for some other purpose.

Secondary data are published data that have already been collected for some other purpose. Secondary data may be internal to the organization, such as sales reports and receipts, or external, such as government reports or privately circulated reports. Trillions of pieces of data are available; thus, the acquisition cost in terms of dollars and time can be very high if the process is not well planned. To cut down on acquisition time, a manager should retrieve only secondary data that are relevant to the specific retail problem. Fortunately, the finding and storage of secondary data are fairly inexpensive when compared to the primary data collection process.

Trade associations, most notably the National Retail Federation (NRF) (*www.nrf.com*), provide a wealth of information and data for retailers. In addition, the research and education arm of the NRF, the NRF Foundation, is involved in the development and execution of studies undertaken specifically to benefit retailers and retail researchers. Each type of retailer can utilize data that were generated specially for a specific retail industry (booksellers, landscapers, food marketers, footwear retailers, apparel retailers, and so on).

Blunders or Best Practices?

Database Marketing Tips from an Expert

Using databases to collect information is becoming increasingly important to retailers in their competitive environment. Bob Donath, of Bob Donath & Company, Inc., White Plains, NY, provides several tips for successfully developing a database:

1. *Metrics need not be bulletproof to be enlightening.* A database may not be able to tell retailers why a particular customer is shopping with them, but with time the database can be used to spot trends. These trends can help companies determine the most effective media to reach their customers.
2. *Modest amounts of supplemental field research produce valuable insights.* Use sampling methods to query suppliers and end users. The data collected can be used to estimate total usage.
3. *Marketing should have a lagging effect.* Database marketing is an investment and it is often difficult to measure long-term success due to the lag in response. Impact may not be seen for months or sometimes years. Use the database to spot potential lagging effects.
4. *Set specific, measurable objectives.* When objectives are more specific, they are easier to measure. A "25 percent increase in sales in a two-month period" is a specific objective compared to an objective that states "to increase sales."
5. *Hold program elements accountable for the right effects.* Make sure the right information is collected to measure the effects of a program. In other words, do not look at advertising alone to measure effectiveness. Other effective measures may be customer calls, website visits, or changes in brand awareness.
6. *Measure marketing effects among key market segments.* Limit data collection to specific segments. Concentrated efforts will make results more meaningful.

Source: Bob Donath, "Resolve to Add Database to Marketing," *Marketing News*, December 3, 2001, p. 8. Reprinted by permission of the American Marketing Association.

ADVANTAGES OF SECONDARY DATA. The major advantage of utilizing secondary data to solve problems is that such data can be gathered quickly and at a low cost. Most libraries offer a wealth of books and periodicals as sources of secondary data. Using the Internet, data can be accessed almost instantaneously. In contrast, setting up a formal primary research project necessitates creating the data collection instrument, hiring people to help generate the data, and so forth. The costs associated with a primary research project are very high compared with those for a secondary data search.

A second advantage of secondary data is that they can be highly accurate. Large research companies and many government divisions such as the U.S. Census Bureau develop and provide valid and reliable data and information. Marketing research companies base their reputations on the types of data they generate. Two well-known research companies are Yankelovich and Nielsen Media Research. Yankelovich (*www.yankelovich.com*) is best known for its research on lifestyle trends and customer targeting, whereas Nielsen Media Research is best known for its television audience measurement research.

DISADVANTAGES OF SECONDARY DATA. Secondary data can often be incomplete or overly general for the specific research problem. For example, a retailer may want information on the number of thirteen-year-olds who drink Pepsi because of the packaging but may be unable to find any data generated for this specific problem. There may be data on how many thirteen-year-olds drink soft drinks, and in particular colas, or on how many thirteen-year-olds live in given targeted areas. But to find out how many thirteen-year-olds buy Pepsi because they like the packaging may require undertaking a primary research project.

Another major disadvantage of using secondary data is that for the most part, such data may be outdated. Although older data can be useful for certain situations, when making decisions in an ever-changing environment such as retailing, the more current the information, the more effective the research and problem solving.

INTERNAL SECONDARY DATA. There are many sources of internal retail information. By utilizing a systemized process of searching for data or records, researchers can gather **internal secondary data,** which are secondary data available from within an organization. This information might be generated from the retailer's accounting system—such as operating statements, balance sheets, profit and loss statements, expense reports, accounts receivable data, accounts payable data, inventory records, purchasing records, and information from the logisticians (*e.g.,* information on the supply chain). Departmental sales data may be researched to check for patterns in sales. In addition, by accessing "reverse logistics" data (see Chapter 9), the researcher can ascertain which items consumers are returning.

internal secondary data
Sources of data and information that are internal to the firm.

Many retailers find that inventory records provide a great deal of information on product- and brand-specific problems that come up as part of the day-to-day retail operations. Often overlooked sources of internal data include the company's annual reports, internal publications such as newsletters, and the prospectus.

external secondary data
Sources of data and information that are external to the firm.

EXTERNAL SECONDARY DATA. External sources of information are numerous. As stated earlier, many organizations compile data that are useful to the retail researcher. **External secondary data** include all sources of data and information that are obtained outside the firm. These data may come from the library, the government, trade associations, competitors, and commercial information providers.

Because retailers want to keep their research confidential, it is recommended that researchers undertake an internal search for information as the first step in the research process. When external sources of data are used, competitors may learn that a particular issue is being researched. Often this cannot be avoided, and the retail researcher needs to go to the next step, generating external data. Because of the low costs associated with external secondary data, retailers should conduct an exhaustive search for these data before moving to primary data collection techniques.

One resource for data collection efforts are reference guides. Reference guides are readily accessible and help the researcher focus on just the data applicable to the current retail problem. Some examples of reference guides include:

Wall Street Journal Index

Census Catalog and Guide (U.S. Census Bureau)

Books in Print

Funk and Scott Index of Corporations and Industries

Business Periodicals Index

In addition, numerous computerized databases are available to the researcher. We will discuss these resources in the section on using technology to gather data and information.

A useful source of information is the U.S. government's census data. The U.S. government provides a variety of public information (as do many other governments worldwide). The most useful of these publications for retail researchers is the census. The U.S. census is broken down into many different censuses, all of which have application in the retail setting. Table 6.1 shows the various government and census websites. These data can be accessed through requests via mail or online.

In addition to the census publications, the government publishes *U.S. Retail Trade, American Fact Finder, Monthly Retail Sales and Inventory,* and *Statistical Abstract of the United States.* Many government agencies, such as the Federal Trade Commission (FTC) and the Small Business Administration (SBA), publish numerous pamphlets, books, and other publications that assist in solving retail problems. A particularly informative source is *U.S. Business Advisor,* published by the FTC.

External data for determining trade area are also available. The U.S. Census Bureau offers TIGER® (Topologically Integrated Geographic Encoding and Referencing). TIGER (*www.census.gov/geo/www/tiger*) is a digital database that contains images of geographic features of the United States. Information such as the locations of roads, rivers, lakes, and political boundaries is available, as

TABLE 6.1

USEFUL GOVERNMENT PUBLICATIONS

Source	Website
U.S. Census of Retail Trade	www.census.gov/econ/www/retmenu.html
U.S. Census of Service Industries	www.census.gov/econ/www/servmenu.html#services
U.S. Census of Population	www.census.gov/population/www/index.html
U.S. Census of Housing	www.census.gov/hhes/www/housing.html
U.S. Census of Governments	www.census.gov/govs/www/index.html
U.S. Census of Construction	www.census.gov/mcd/index.html
U.S. Census of Manufacturing	www.census.gov/mcd/index.html
U.S. Census of Transportation	www.census.gov/econ/www/tasmenu.html
U.S. Census of Wholesale Trade	www.census.gov/econ/www/retmenu.html
American Fact Finder	www. factfinder.census.gov/servlet/BasicFactsServlet
Monthly Retail Sales and Inventory	www.census.gov/econ/www/retmenu.html
Statistical Abstract of the United States.	www.landview.census.gov/prod/www/statistical-abstract-us.html
U.S. Business Advisor	www.business.gov/
Small Business Administration publications	www.sba.gov/library/pubs.html

Note: Website addresses may change in the course of business. Try the homepage of the U.S. Census Bureau (www.census.gov) if you have trouble with the above websites.

well as address ranges for most streets and other related information. Because the files in TIGER are not digital images of maps, a company must have geographic information system (GIS) software to import the data into its system.

Many trade associations offer their members different types of information and data that are specific to the industry. The American Marketing Association (AMA) (*www.ama.org*) has numerous publications aimed toward its membership of academics, practitioners, and students of marketing. In addition, the AMA publishes or supports the publishing of numerous academic and practitioner-oriented journals and periodicals. Point-of-Purchase Advertising International (POPAI) (*www.popai.com*) has generated many research articles of interest to retailers involved in point-of-purchase advertising. POPAI also regularly holds workshops and conferences. In addition, many colleges and universities, such as Santa Clara University, Brigham Young University, and California State University, have institutes of retail management that can serve as a source of information. Finally, as mentioned earlier, the National Retail Federation (NRF) (*www.nrf.com*) is an excellent source for data and retail information.

Organizations of all sizes are involved in the marketing of data and information to assist retail managers in their decision making. An online source of general information on companies is Hoover's Online (*www.hoovers.com*). Hoover's provides general background information on companies and their competitors and financial information free of charge or for a subscription fee. Financial information about competitors, suppliers, and government agencies is available through Standard and Poor's and Moody's. Table 6.2 shows the various resources offered by Moody's and Standard and Poor's.

One of the best sources of data for the retail research specialist or the retail manager trying to solve tough problems is a publication put out by *Sales and Marketing Management (SMM)* magazine. Titled *SMM Survey of Buying Power and Media Markets,* this useful product serves as a guide for researchers interested in data on U.S. populations, effective buying income, and various other measures of consumer purchasing. The data are shared with Claritas, Inc. (a sister organization to SMM). In addition, *Survey of Buying Power* has recently begun offering data on metro and media market information.

Many companies specialize in providing consumer data. Demographic data can be accessed through either the Simmons Market Research Bureau (SMRB) or Mediamark Research, Inc. (MRI). Both these companies offer data online, in print, or on CD-ROM. SMRB and MRI also provide psychographic data, as does the Standard Rate and Data Service (SRDS). SRDS publishes *The Lifestyle Market Analyst,* which contains a host of useful information. SRI Consulting developed a product called VALS™ that is available to researchers, and CACI Marketing Systems publishes *Sourcebook of ZIP Code Demographics* (among others), which offers useful psychographic and other data.

Geodemographic data can be accessed using SRI's GeoVALS, Donnelly Marketing Information Services' ClusterPLUS, and Claritas's PRIZM (Potential Rating Index by Zip Markets). Nielsen Media Research, A. C. Nielsen, Information Resources, Inc. (IRI), and the Gallup organization (*www.gallup.com*) offer a great deal of data and information useful to the retail researcher. IRI data are particularly helpful when generating data regarding specific products or product categories.

TABLE 6.2

MOODY'S AND STANDARD AND POOR'S MANUALS

Moody's	Standard and Poor's
Contact information: Moody's Investors Service 99 Church Street New York, NY 10007 212-553-0300 (www.moodys.com)	Contact information: Standard and Poor's 25 Broadway New York, NY 10001 212-208-8690 (www.standardandpoors.com)
Moody's Industrial Manual	Standard and Poor's corporation records
Moody's Transportation Manual	Standard and Poor's over-the-counter regional exchange reports
Moody's OTC Unlisted Manual	Standard and Poor's New York Stock Exchange reports
Moody's Municipal and Government Manual	Standard and Poor's American Stock Exchange reports
Moody's Public Utility Manual	
Moody's Bank and Financial Manual	

As we have seen, a wealth of external secondary data are available to the retail researcher, and a retailer can benefit from conducting secondary data searches before or in place of primary data collection. Some of these data are inexpensive or free, but some come with a high price. It is the researcher's job to find as much pertinent data as possible and to turn those data into information that is useful to everyone involved in the management of the retailing organization. Advances in technology have made it much easier to utilize the Internet in data collection.

PRIMARY DATA

If the secondary data search does not yield the desired results—in other words, if the search fails to solve the retail problem—primary data collection will be needed. **Primary data** have not yet been published and are gathered for a specific purpose, in this case to solve a specific retail problem. The primary data collection process is outlined in Figure 6.2. The major disadvantage of using primary data is that the collection process is very time consuming and expensive. The information is current and meets the retailer's specific needs, however, thus creating advantages that frequently outweigh the disadvantages. The data are confidential and proprietary, meaning the information is not available to the general public or, significantly, to competitors.

primary data Data that are gathered for a specific purpose and have not yet been published.

In collecting primary data, the retailer should engage the experts within the organization to help plan and execute the research. The systems used in retail research are somewhat complex. Each phase of the research process needs to be tested to ensure that the results have sufficient validity and reliability on which to base decisions. For this reason, retailers often outsource their research to consultants and research specialists. In doing so, the retailer still keeps the data proprietary and is assured that the information will be of high quality. Outside specialists can also offer the retailer a new perspective on the problem and solution.

SAMPLING. Another important decision in the primary data collection process relates to sampling. **Sampling** is the process of choosing a subset of the population of interest from which to collect problem-specific data. The researcher must make sure to draw the data from a representative sample of the most relevant populations. For example, if the retailer wants to study differences between Hispanic children's versus Anglo children's influence on their parents' purchasing behaviors, the sample should come from populations of Hispanic and Anglo children.

sampling The process of choosing a subset of the population of interest to collect problem-specific data.

The most accurate type of sampling is probability sampling. In **probability sampling**, each and every member of the population has an equal and known chance of being chosen for the sample. Although probability sampling is the preferred choice, in some instances the researcher has neither the time nor the money to undertake a probability sample. In that case, the researcher uses nonprobability sampling. In **nonprobability sampling,** no member of the population has an equal and known chance of being selected for the research study. This type of sample is generally taken on the basis of convenience and is often used when the researcher does not have sufficient knowledge of more accurate methods.

probability sampling Sampling in which each and every member of the population has an equal and known chance of being chosen for the sample.

nonprobability sampling Sampling in which no member of the population has an equal and known chance of being selected for the research study.

sampling frame A list of all population members from which a sample will be drawn.

A **sampling frame,** or a list of all relevant population members, needs to be identified. Imagine you are a student at Eastern Michigan University in Ypsilanti, Michigan, doing a research project for the student newspaper, *The Eastern Echo*. You want to find out what percentage of the student body actually reads the newspaper. To do this, you decide to pull a sample out of the university's database of currently enrolled students. This database would be your sampling frame. As another example, suppose you are a member of Alpha Kappa Psi, a professional business fraternity, and the national office has asked you to find out what student members think about the national fraternity office. A useful sampling frame would be the fraternity's membership directory.

In addition to decisions regarding the types of samples to be taken and the sampling frame, the researcher needs to decide how large a sample to pull from the relevant population. This can be done with a formula or simply through the researcher's judgment. Researchers benefit from using a sampling formula until they develop the experience to estimate the sample size that would return the most accurate results. The "correct" sample size generates adequate data while meeting budget constraints. As a rule of thumb, as the sample size increases (to a point), so does the accuracy of the research.

Small samples frequently produce excellent results. It is certainly possible to have too large a sample. Such samples sometimes generate false results because they show statistically significant findings that are due solely to the large sample size. When in doubt, retailers should consult market research experts or statisticians about sampling issues.

DATA COLLECTION. After choosing the sample, the researcher must create a method for collecting the data. Surveys, or questionnaires, are by far the most often used type of data collection instrument. The survey is convenient, allowing the researcher to gather the data either in person, by mail, online, or over the phone. Researchers also use observation or experimental settings to generate data.

A very popular technique for internal marketing research is an observational method of research involving mystery shoppers. Retailers hire firms that specialize in mystery shopping to assess how well employees handle customers. Mystery shoppers can help determine whether the retailer is meeting its vision and mission of, for example, exceeding customer expectations through service. The mystery shoppers pose as consumers to help managers rate their employees (or vice presidents and assistant vice presidents to rate their managers). Dale Mingilton, a senior vice president of the 1st Bank of Colorado, is in charge of the mystery shoppers program at the bank. He uses the results of the research to help him make decisions regarding his personnel. Decisions may range from pay raises to additional training to the feared "career readjustment," in which an employee is encouraged to look for employment elsewhere.

scaling technique A method used to measure attitudes, knowledge, opinions, or perceptions on a given topic or issue.

It is important to note that the data collected are only as good as the forms developed to collect those data. Questions should be structured in a way that will not bias the respondents. Scaling techniques often help in the collection of data. **Scaling techniques** are methods used to measure attitudes, knowledge,

"Fascinating. The rats choose chocolate over vegetables nine times out of ten, but they always feel guilty about it later."

opinions, or perceptions on a given topic or issue. Different types of scales can be used to collect data. Two of the most popular are the Likert-type scale and the semantic differential scale.

A *Likert-type scale* uses a rating scale to determine the degree to which an individual agrees or disagrees with a statement or an issue. For example, a survey may state, "I think the customer service at this store is better than the competition's." The respondent chooses among several options, such as Strongly Agree, Agree, Neither Agree nor Disagree, Disagree, and Strongly Disagree. With a *semantic differential scale,* the choices for measuring agreement might be in the form of a 5- to 7-point bipolar scale. Thus, instead of using a range of Strongly Agree to Strongly Disagree, the individual would indicate his or her level of agreement by choosing a number between 1 and 5.

In both types of scaling techniques, a series of statements is used to measure a particular characteristic by asking for a response that usually involves choosing from among two or more response categories to indicate the extent of the agreement or disagreement with each statement.

DATA ANALYSIS. Once the data have been collected, they must be analyzed. Generally speaking, data are subject to a number of statistical tests. The statistics yield an estimate of how the overall population will respond to a given situation. Remember that the more current the research is, the better its predictability will be for the general population under study.

RECOMMEND AND REPORT. The last phase in the research process is to make recommendations based on the interpretation of the data. The easiest way to understand the process, the statistics, and ultimately the data is to take coursework or workshops in statistics and research methodologies and then practice, practice, practice! The projects your professor gives you may seem tough at the time, but once you are out in the professional retail world, you will look back and be glad you had the opportunity to practice conducting research before actually applying it in a retail environment.

USING TECHNOLOGY TO GATHER DATA AND INFORMATION

Data and information collected utilizing the Internet are generally gathered faster than those gathered using the more traditional methods. Almost anything that can be accomplished face to face can be accomplished in cyberspace.

One of the best research uses for cyberspace is the collection of secondary data. The job of data acquisition becomes easier and faster. In addition, more data can be gathered over the World Wide Web than from other sources. When writing a term paper, you can spend your time going to the library to access the stacks of information and data on the shelves. However, you may find that your time is better spent in your home, your dorm room, or the library using targeted search engines to find secondary data that will help you write an even better term paper.

Technology has made our lives both easier and harder. Although it may be easier to research using computers, the disadvantage is that today more data and information exist than ever before. Thus, advances in technology have outpaced the human capacity to analyze and use the data for maximum impact.[25] To secure a marketing advantage over competitors, a retailer needs access to as much data and information as possible. Although more sources of information may be needed to solve a research dilemma, sifting through and finding the best data can be difficult.

SEARCH ENGINES

As much data as there are in print, much more are available in cyberspace. The researcher should become familiar with the many search engines available to help access data and information. The three main types of search engines are general directories, search engines based on algorithms, and specialized search engines.[26]

GLOBAL RETAILING

Focus on Technology: Island Pacific, Inc.

Island Pacific, Inc. (IP; formerly SVI Solutions, Inc.), headquartered in Irvine, California, provides multichannel technology solutions to retailers. In addition to its U.S. location, IP has a presence in the United Kingdom. One way the company helps retailers is by replacing outdated cash registers with point-of-sale (POS) and retail management systems.

Island Pacific specializes in merchandise management and applications and provides advanced POS applications that are retailer specific. According to its website, its vision is "to become the world's leading provider of low cost, high value, multichannel, end-to-end solutions for retailers worldwide." One company that uses IP's OnePointe POS solution is Silver Dollar City, a regional theme park operator with five properties in Branson, Missouri, along with Dollywood in Pigeon Falls, Tennessee. Silver Dollar City used IP products to combine its POS and inventory management systems. Before using IP technology, the company had to maintain separate systems. Other companies that use IP's products and services include Toys "R" Us, NIKE, Dollar General, OfficeMax, Crate & Barrel, American Eagle Outfitters, and The Limited.

Sources: Island Pacific, Inc. homepage at www.islandpacific.com; Hoover's Online, "Island Pacific, Inc.," www.hooversonline.com; "SVI Teams with European Multi-media Courseware Developer to Test and Certify European Computer Users," *Business Wire*, August 25, 2000, p. 1; "SVI Store Solutions Signs POS Contract with Silver Dollar City," October 16, 2002, retrieved January 2003 from www.svisolutions.com.

TABLE 6.3

USEFUL SEARCH ENGINES CATEGORIZED BY TYPE

General Search Engines

Yahoo!	www.yahoo.com
AOL	www.aol.com
NBCi	www.nbci.msnbc.com/ nbci.aspi.com
About	www.about.com
DMOZ	www.dmoz.org
MetaCrawler	www.metacrawler.com
Ask Jeeves	www.askjeeves.com

Search Engines Based on Algorithms

Google	www.google.com
Alta Vista	www.altavista.com
Dogpile.com	www.dogpile.com
Hotbot	www.hotbot.lycos.com
Lyco	www.lycos.org
Iwon	www.iwon.com
AllTheWeb	www.alltheweb.com
MSN	www.msn.com
NorthernLight	www.northern.light.com
OneSearch	www.onesearch.com
Mamma	www.mamma.com

Targeted Search Engines—Pay per Click

7search	www.7search.com
Aha	www.ah-ha.com
Xuppa	www.Xuppa.com
Espotting	www.espotting.com
Kanoodle	www.Kanoodle.com
Looksmart	www.looksmart.com

Specialized Search Engines

EDGAR	www.sec.gov/edgar/shtml
Hoover's Online	www.hoovers.com
ProQuest Direct ProQuest includes the following databases: • ABI Inform (business trade and research journals) • Periodical Abstracts (general and research journals) • National newspapers and research library newspapers	Available on a subscription basis (usually available through college/ university libraries)
Predicasts F&S Index: Europe	
EconLit	
Info Trac	
Dialog Information Retrieval Service	
LEXIS/NEXIS Academic Universe	
National Trade Data Bank	
Dow Jones Interactive	
Emerging Markets (International Business)	

GENERAL DIRECTORIES. The content in general directories is managed by a system of categorized lists instead of an automated database. With these types of directories, submissions to the search engine are evaluated and then included in the directory based on a human review.

SEARCH ENGINES BASED ON ALGORITHMS. An algorithm that calculates how a site rates against certain criteria and places the entry in the appropriate position determines rankings in these search engines. Each website creates its own criteria.

SPECIALIZED SEARCH ENGINES. These search engines specialize in a particular area such as business- or company-specific information. These search engines are most useful when writing projects for business classes. Some require a password for access. Table 6.3 lists some of the more useful engines.

INDUSTRY-SPECIFIC SEARCHES

When trying to access company-specific information and data, one way to begin the Internet search is by accessing the government's Internet EDGAR (Electronic Data Gathering Analysis and Retrieval) system. All public companies must file paperwork required by the Securities and Exchange Commission

TABLE 6.4

AN ABBREVIATED LISTING OF EXTERNAL DATA SOURCES

Advertising Age	www.adage.com
American Demographics	www.demographics.com
American Marketing Association	www.marketingpower.com
Business Week	www.businessweek.com
Commodity Yearbook	www.investorsoftware.com/products/7498.htm
Consumer Goods Technology	www.consumergoods.com
Direct Marketing Association	www.the-dma.org
Discount Store News	www.discountstorenews.com
E-commerce Times	www.ecommercetimes.com
E-tailer's Digest	www.etailersdigest.com
Emarketer	www.emarketer.com
Forbes	www.forbes.com
Fortune	www.fortune.com
Fortune Directory	www.fortune.com
Franchise Handbook	www.franchise1.com
Information Please Almanac	www.infoplease.com
International Franchise Association	www.franchise.org
Internet News	www.internetnews.com
Library of Congress	www.loc.gov
Marketing Research Association	www.mra-net.org
New York Times	www.nytimes.com
Point-of-Purchase Advertising International	www.popai.com
Progressive Grocer	www.progressivegrocer.com
Promo (magazine)	www.promomagazine.com
Retail Merchandiser	www.retail-merchandiser.com
Sales and Marketing Management	www.salesandmarketing.com
Stores	www.stores.org
U.S. Census Bureau	www.census.gov
U.S. Department of Commerce	www.doc.gov
U.S. Small Business Administration	www.sba.gov

through EDGAR. Table 6.4 gives an abbreviated list of the various types of external secondary data sources.

When looking for a specific census document, additional information is required to gain access. For example, to access the U.S. Census of Retail Trade, enter *www.census.gov/econ/www/retmenu.html*. Each of the various census publications is available at *www.census.gov,* but an additional search is required.

In addition to online databases, researchers can access data placed on CD-ROM. The major data collection companies generally have data available in this format. For example, SMRB's Choices CD contains psychographic data on consumers, and D&B's RollCall has demographic information.

Whether primary or secondary research is used, chances are that a great deal of data, which must be turned into useful, actionable information, can be found in cyberspace.

SUMMARY

Thus far, we have explored several aspects of the development of an integrated retail management plan. In this chapter, retail information systems (RIS) and the marketing research process were covered. RIS help retailers gather, store, and analyze data. Use of the Universal Product Code (U.P.C.), point of sale technology, self-checkout, and radio frequency identification (RFID) aid in the RIS process. Some retailers choose to outsource data collection, verification, and analysis.

Research processes help ensure the IRM process is successful in all aspects of retailing. This chapter looked at a research process used to generate data and to turn those data into useful, actionable information that allows managers to make better retail management decisions. There are many different approaches to marketing research. The goal is to provide useful, relevant, and current information to retail managers and other employees.

The chapter discussed the differences between market and marketing research. Market research is a subset of marketing research that aims to generate data from which retail managers can make intelligent choices to solve the organization's problems.

Retail research is used throughout the development of the integrated retail management plan. The research can be used to help develop strategies or tactical executions. In addition, it can help the retailer solve day-to-day retail management problems such as forecasting, inventory buying, selling, training, and market development and segmentation. Without good research, retail decisions will be inferior to those that are research based.

Secondary data are relatively easy and inexpensive to obtain. There are many sources of secondary data, including U.S. government sources, directories, and journals. In addition, internal secondary data such as balance sheets, sales records, and inventory information may be useful to retailers. Primary data, although more expensive, can provide more retailer-specific information than secondary sources of information.

KEY TERMS

data (150)
information (150)
retail information system (RIS) (150)
market research (150)
multichannel retailer (151)
electronic data interchange (EDI) (152)

economic order quantity (152)
Universal Product Code (U.P.C.) (153)
point-of-sale (POS) terminal (154)
radio frequency identification (RFID) (154)
self-checkout system (155)
outsourcing (155)
marketing research (156)
executive summary (160)
secondary data (161)
internal secondary data (162)
external secondary data (163)
primary data (166)
sampling (166)
probability sampling (166)
nonprobability sampling (166)
sampling frame (167)
scaling technique (167)

QUESTIONS FOR DISCUSSION

1. What are the benefits of utilizing an RIS? What are the disadvantages?
2. Identify some companies that you believe have a competitive advantage in the storage and collection of retail information.
3. What are the distinctions between marketing research and market research?
4. Why is marketing research important to the retailer?
5. Explain the difference between primary and secondary data. When should a retailer employ primary data collection?
6. If you had to find out what your competitors are doing, what type of research would you undertake?
7. When is it appropriate to outsource retail research projects?
8. What sources of information do you use to decide which stores to patronize? Do you trust some stores more than others? If so, why?
9. What role does technology play in the gathering of data?

E-TAILING EXERCISE

Many retailers are combining their physical locations and Internet systems to better address their customers' needs. Two retailers that are recognized for this multichannel integration approach—allowing customers to order online and pick up the merchandise at a local branch location—are Sears and Circuit City. Go to *www.sears.com* and *www.circuitcity.com* and answer the following questions:

1. Search for information on how to order online and pick up at a local store (sometimes called *store pickup*). How long did it take you (in seconds or minutes) to find this information?
2. On which of the two sites was it easier to locate this information?
3. Were the instructions for store pickup clear? Why or why not?
4. What, if anything, would you change to make the site and its navigational capacities more user friendly?

Continuing Case 6.1

Sherwin-Williams Company: Technology with a Customer Focus

At Sherwin-Williams, technology is adopted with the customer in mind. For example, in 1996 the Consumer Brands Division of Sherwin-Williams was looking for a better way to manage customer information from its Customer Financial Services Group (CFSG). The CFSG services Sherwin-Williams's home center, independent paint store, and discount store retail customers. The amount of paperwork required to process customer requests was causing problems with lost and misplaced documentation. As a result of these problems, Sherwin-Williams implemented a new release of its Credit and Account Receivable Management System (CARMS), as well as a Feith Document Database (FDD) document imaging system. With the combined systems, all faxed, scanned, and system-downloaded information resided in a single electronic file folder. The new process enabled Sherwin-Williams to eliminate costly errors and to serve its customers more effectively.

More recently, in an effort to overhaul the information technology infrastructure of its retail stores, Sherwin-Williams announced that the Linux operating system would replace Unix. According to IBM Company, which will coordinate the migration, the new Linux-based system is expected to lower information technology costs, provide more flexibility for future upgrades, and improve the stores' customer service.

About 9,700 IBM desktop PCs running Turbolinux's operating system will be installed in 2,500 stores in the United States, Canada, and Puerto Rico. New printers, hand-held scanners, signature pads, and modems will also be installed. The rollout, one of the world's largest involving Linux in a chain of stores, was completed in 2003.

Questions

1. Do you think Sherwin-Williams made the right decision in adopting the new system? If so, what were the advantages of installing the system?
2. What problems, if any, do you foresee at Sherwin-Williams as a result of the new system?
3. Can you recommend a better way to access data and service the company's customers?
4. Are there any retail organizations that may not benefit from a system such as that developed at Sherwin-Williams?
5. Why is it important to have a centralized system such as the one Sherwin-Williams is using?
6. Do you think Sherwin-Williams should look at what its competitors are doing in terms of internal information technology related to a research system?

Sources: Juan Carlos Perez, "Sherwin-Williams Picks IBM and Linux for Stores," IDG News Service, May 23, 2002, retrieved July 2002 from Network World Fusion at www.nwfusion.com/news/2002/0523sherwinit.html; IBM Global Services press release, "Flexibility Key to Paint Company Relying on IBM for Its Store Technology Infrastructure," May 23, 2002, retrieved July 2002 from www.ibm.com; Feith Case Studies, "Manufacturing—The Sherwin-Williams Company," retrieved July 2002 from www.feith.com/kstudy/sherwin.htm.

Case 6.2

Circuit City, Multichannel Retailing, and Online RIS

According to the National Retail Federation's Internet division, a growing percentage of Internet retailers are starting to show a profit. The Internet has a market share of 5 percent or greater in each of seven areas, including computer gear, books, event tickets, music, and travel. In a recent survey of 270 Internet retailing executives, respondents admitted they are not performing well in the areas of helping customers return products, making sites easier to navigate, and setting up accounts for customers. Merchants scored themselves highest in helping customers place orders.

Seamless multichannel retailing is becoming increasingly popular as more and more large retailers adopt the practice. During the next few years, multichannel retailers will strive to integrate their inventory and point-of-sale (POS) systems with their Internet sites.

When integration occurs, a customer can buy from the Internet site and pick up the merchandise at a local store. Only a few retailers have this capability because of the complexity involved in integrating these RIS. Integration is difficult because a company must have the space to store items that consumers have reserved when using its website. In addition, bricks-and-clicks need an infrastructure in place that allows them to transfer sales from one store to the next.

A pioneer in achieving seamless multichannel retailing is Circuit City, the number two electronics retailer in the United States. Circuit City Stores, Inc. has more than 620 stores, composed mainly of Circuit City Superstores. In July 1999, Circuit City introduced a system allowing customers to order online and pick up or return merchandise at a local Circuit City store. One advantage Circuit City had is called *alternate-location sales*. This arrangement allows the chain to sell the inventory of one store to another store within the chain. Even with this advantage, however, Circuit City had some minor problems during the initial rollout of the system.

One problem was that no procedures were in place for dealing with inventory issues between online and in-store components. If a customer ordered a computer, the computer that was available during online ordering may have been sold from the store in the time it took the salesperson to retrieve it from storage. To solve this problem, Circuit City implemented a fifteen-minute rule. This rule gives a store associate fifteen minutes to put merchandise aside when an order is initiated from the online site. If the task is not completed, the point-of-service (POS) terminal beeps to remind the employee to complete the task. If the task is not completed within thirty minutes after the initial beep, a manager is alerted to complete the task. About half the company's online sales involve orders that are picked up at stores. The service is definitely growing in popularity.

Questions

1. What can other retailers learn from Circuit City's experience?
2. What types of retailers might not benefit from multichannel integration?
3. What else can retailers do to ensure customer service and satisfaction with multichannel efforts?
4. What are the competitive advantages for companies that implement multichannel integration?

Sources: Leslie Walker, "Online Shopping Grows Popular, But Not Easier," *Seattle Times*, September 2, 2002, p. C3; Meridith Levinson, "Your Place or Mine? You Want Customers to Be Able to Buy Online and Pick up at Your Store. But Figuring out How to Do That Is a Major IT Challenge," *CIO*, 15, no. 20 (2002), pp. 62–69; "Circuit City Stores, Inc.," Hoover's Company Capsules, retrieved November 2002 from www.hoovers.com; Bob Tedeschi, "Buy It Online and Pick It up at the Store? Many Consumers Are Doing Exactly That to Speed Delivery," *New York Times* (East Coast edition), December 24, 2001; p. C5.

Selecting the Appropriate Market and Location

Chapter

7

Location, location, location.
William Dillard, founder, Dillard's department stores

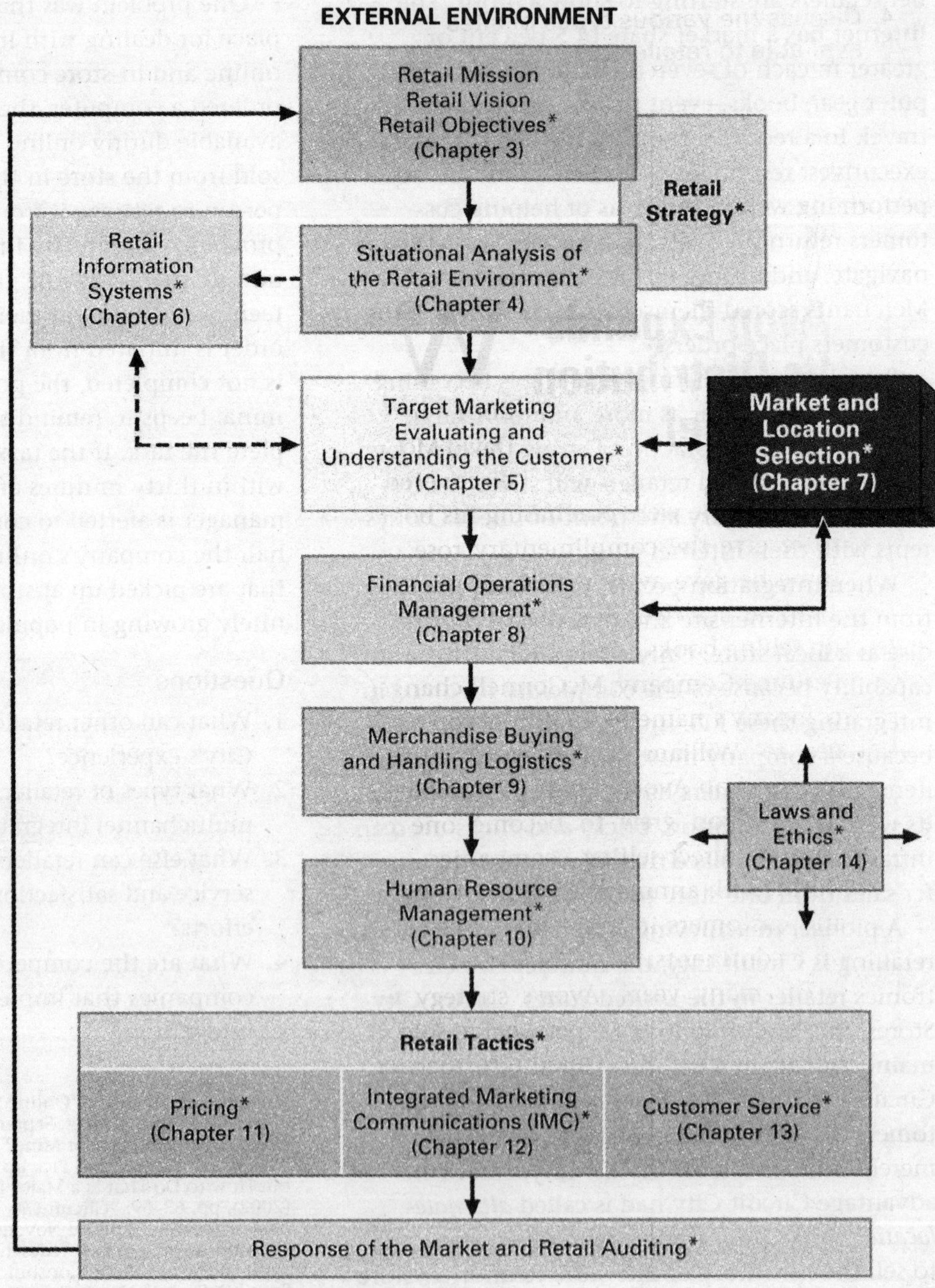

CHAPTER OBJECTIVES

After completing this chapter, you will be able to:

1. Define *target customer group.*
2. Describe the processes involved in selecting a retail market and site.
3. Analyze a retail trading area.
4. Discuss the various types of sites available to retailers.
5. Explain the difference between a planned and an unplanned shopping district.
6. Describe the various characteristics that influence a retailer's site selection.

Avon Expands Its Distribution Channel

While selling books door to door, David McConnell discovered that some people were purchasing his books just to receive the complimentary rose oil perfume he gave away with each purchase. In 1886, at age twenty-eight, McConnell gave up selling books and founded the California Perfume Company. McConnell changed the company's name in 1939 to Avon as a tribute to William Shakespeare's birthplace, Stratford on Avon.[1] From its humble beginnings, Avon grew to become one of the biggest direct-selling companies in the world, with annual sales of nearly $6 billion and customers in more than 143 countries on 6 continents.[2]

For many years, Avon's strategy was to recruit women who personally sold Avon products using direct methods, such as selling to friends or door-to-door selling. Then, in 1999, Avon decided it needed a new strategy to reach more potential customers. Avon's management decided to use kiosks, or "beauty centers," as a showcase for the company's products. They believed this move would shed Avon's grandmotherly image and appeal to a younger consumer segment.

To determine where to locate kiosks, Avon used mapping software from Tactician Corporation. The software enabled the company to overlap representative territories and sales information with population data from the U.S. Census Bureau. By examining where Avon was selling best and finding areas for opportunity, managers were able to choose malls that would help them achieve their objectives. The software also helped identify population trends that could signal necessary strategy changes.[3]

The kiosks are located in areas where the average income is higher than the company's traditional target market. Avon must ensure that the kiosks do not cannibalize the business of its field sales representatives. To placate field representatives, beauty centers do not offer the sales that are featured in brochures, and shoppers who request other products are referred to a field representative.[4]

INTRODUCTION

Selecting a market area and a specific location are two of a retailer's most important decisions. To get to the best market area available and choose the best location possible, the retailer must consider many variables. The ultimate goal is maximum customer access. Accomplishing this goal is a time-consuming, research-based process. The selection of a physical location, or even an e-tailing site, requires training and practical experience.

Although many retailers attempt site location on their own, many others choose to hire site location specialists to lead them through the extensive process of market and location planning. Depending on the retailer's knowledge, a specialist may be the best way to go.

This chapter explores how to evaluate the external and internal variables inherent in the process of site selection. In general terms, the process begins by targeting the group toward which the retailer plans to aim its marketing efforts. Next, the retailer assesses and analyzes the characteristics of the trading area from which it will operate. After defining the trading area, the retail specialist moves to the analysis and selection of a physical and/or Internet site from which to operate.

DECIDING ON A TARGET CUSTOMER GROUP

Chapter 1 focused on the value to a retailer of a situational analysis. The situational analysis can be accessed via the retail information system (RIS) to help the retailer identify an effective target customer group. Of particular value is undertaking an **environmental analysis,** which helps the retailer understand the various market environments prior to deciding on a target area and a target customer group (or target market segment).

environmental analysis A study of the various market environments prior to deciding on a target area and a target customer group.

The data compiled for the integrated retail management (IRM) flow chart should be consulted when developing the overall site location plan. Two key areas of the flow chart with reference to site planning information are the *situational analysis* and data collected on the *market and location selection.* These analyses should guide the selection of the retailer's customer group(s).

A **target market** is composed of all the customers toward whom the retailer decides to aim its marketing efforts. To be included in the overall target market, customers must meet four basic criteria:[5]

target market All of the customers toward whom a company decides to aim its marketing efforts.

- They must need or desire a particular product. If they do not, that aggregate is not a market.
- They must have the ability to purchase the product. Ability to purchase is a function of their buying power, which consists of resources such as money, goods, and services that can be traded in an exchange situation.
- They must be willing to use their buying power.
- They must have the authority to buy the specific products.

GLOBAL RETAILING

La Ciudad de Los Niños (Kids City International)

Do you remember when you were young and pretended you were a doctor, firefighter, lawyer, or other great professional? Thanks to a Mexican business, many kids will get to engage in more realistic role-playing in a new theme park. *La Ciudad de Los Niños* (or Kids City International, as it will become known in the United States), is a theme park, targeted toward children ages two through twelve, that allows kids to pretend they are adults. The theme park recreates a city complete with a town square, a hospital, and even an airport. Upon entering the park, kids are given a "check" for 300 *pesitos*. Their first stop is the bank, where they can cash the check for "money" that they will spend on food, merchandise, and "grown-up" activities. Kids can pretend to be doctors, dentists, television producers, car dealers, and much more.

According to Ruben Cors, a principal of Kids City International (Mexico City), customers fall into four market segments, each of which uses the facility at different times: families with children go to the park on Friday nights and weekends; school trips occupy the park on weekday mornings; birthday parties are held on weekday afternoons; and corporations rent out the park on weeknights for their company celebrations.

The first park opened at the Santa Fe Business, Commercial, and Shopping Center in Mexico City in September 1999, with 52,000 square feet. The company also plans to open a theme center in Nyack, New York. After analyzing data on many other trading areas, the company decided that other potential U.S. sites include Atlanta, Chicago, San Francisco, and Washington, DC. Location decisions are very important in developing a marketing strategy, especially in understanding markets located in countries other than the host company's headquarters.

Source: Debra Hazel, "Export Child's Play for Mexican Theme Park," Copyright 2003, International Council of Shopping Centers, Inc., New York, NY. Published in *Shopping Centers Today,* dated July 2002. Reprinted with permission.

After assembling all the information and data about the consumer, a "typical customer profile" can be developed to help identify and understand the customer and his or her buying behaviors. An inclusion of the customer's needs and wants is essential. The retailer should keep in mind who its current customers are, who its competitors' customers are, and who makes up the potential customer bases. Table 7.1 provides some suggestions for what to include in a typical customer profile.

In conducting marketing research, professionals tend to quantify all data, generating numbers that describe the market group on paper. In reality, of course, retailers sell to people, not to numbers. If the retailer can put a face to the numbers, the job of understanding the customer becomes a lot easier.

The data collected for target market and customer profiles is used to help select the best possible market and location. In addition, these data allow the retailer to recognize not only current needs and wants in the market but also needs and wants that are not being met. The result will be additional differentiation for the retailer and, in the long run, additional sales. Data collected should include benefits for products and/or services and shopping experiences that consumers are seeking.

TABLE 7.1

SELECTED VARIABLES FOR INCLUSION IN THE TYPICAL CUSTOMER PROFILE

Variable	Example
Demographics	Education, marital status, ethnicity, income
Geographics	Physical location, where customers live, physical boundaries
Psychographics	Lifestyle analysis, psychology of target market
Behavioristics	Buyers' behaviors toward different types of products and services, usage rates
Geodemographics	Population demographics for a particular geographic area
Type of buyer	Consumer, industrial, business, not-for-profit

It is essential for the retailer to first identify its markets before trying to reach the customer base. It would not make sense for the retailer to establish an outlet for ocean-racing boats in Paris, Illinois, or Alamosa, Colorado, since these cities have no access to oceans.

With advances in technology, it is possible to reach customers with products and services from a physical location (brick-and-mortar) or from a nonstore location (clicks, catalogs, and so on). Thus, it is important to look at the entire target market before selecting a site or market location. People are not spread randomly throughout the world. People who are alike tend to live near one another and have similar behavioristic and psychographic traits. The site selection specialist must identify the target market and then identify the geographic areas throughout the world where this market lives.

Because e-tailers may have customers in locations around the world, they pose a special problem for site selection personnel. An effective, integrated RIS will make this task somewhat easier. Why does geographic location matter at all in e-tailing? There are two important reasons: (1) because cost-effective product delivery options must be selected and (2) because it is necessary to adapt websites to fit local market interests, needs, wants, and concerns. Lands' End, for example, has two distinct websites—one for the United States and one for the United Kingdom (*www.landsend.com* and *www.landsend.co.uk*). In addition, the company had to develop different methods for handling payments coming from Japan.

Let's look at how a retailer can undertake the task of choosing the right market and location.

CHOOSING THE RIGHT LOCATION

Retailers can use a three-step process, based on geographics, when assessing where to locate their businesses. These steps traditionally have been labeled *regional analysis, trading area* (or *trade area*) *analysis*, and *actual site analysis*.

E-tailers must also assess their markets, but in a somewhat different manner than brick-and-mortar retailers. Both types of retailers need to decide whether to pursue a global retail reach or stay within a given national market.

REGIONAL ANALYSIS

Whether located in the United States or another country, retailers must decide in which region to operate. A region represents a large geographical area. It could be the part of the country in which a retailer has decided to study, a state, a city, a designated market area (DMA), or a metropolitan statistical area (MSA).

DMAs and MSAs reflect actual trading areas that traditional city or county boundaries do not capture. These designations provide nationally consistent definitions for collecting, tabulating, and reporting purposes.[6] Although the designations tend to follow county lines to determine a particular area, the two types of designations are not identical, so one must be careful when analyzing data from multiple sources.

DESIGNATED MARKET AREA (DMA)

designated market area (DMA) A designation developed by A. C. Nielsen to describe a particular geographic area that serves a specific market.

A **designated market area (DMA)** is composed of counties (or split counties, where necessary) assigned exclusively to that market area. For example, the Atlanta, Georgia, DMA encompasses over forty-five counties, including two located in the state of Alabama.

DMAs were developed by the A. C. Nielsen Company to help with measuring media reach. In part, DMAs are defined according to a population's total television viewing hour percentages.[7] DMA designations are updated annually by Nielsen Media Research (the current company name). As of 2003, there are 210 DMAs throughout the United States, none of which overlap.[8]

METROPOLITAN STATISTICAL AREA (MSA)

metropolitan statistical area (MSA) A government designation of an area within the United States that has a minimum of 50,000 permanent residents.

A **metropolitan statistical area (MSA)** is an area within the United States that has at least one urbanized area with a population of at least 50,000.[9] (It does not include college students unless it is their permanent residence.) MSAs are based on the U.S. government designations, specifically those of the Office of Management and Budget (OMB), and are reviewed every ten years to coincide with the decennial census. In 2003, the OMB announced the creation of 49 new MSAs, bringing the total number to 370 (362 in the United States and 8 in Puerto Rico). In addition, many existing MSAs were revised.[10] For example, the Lehigh Valley (Pennsylvania) MSA consisted of Allentown, Bethlehem, and Easton. After the revision in 2003, Warren County (New Jersey) was taken from Newark's MSA and added to the Lehigh Valley MSA. With the change, the population of the Lehigh Valley MSA grew 16 percent and the demographics of the area also changed considerably—toward a younger, wealthier, and better-educated group.[11]

Wal-Mart has operations in many countries and attempts to cater to local tastes. This photo shows a Wal-Mart employee from Germany holding a promotional poster.

GLOBAL EXPANSION

A very small percentage of retailers pursue strategic global expansion. Having mentioned that the retailer has a choice of global retailing, a few comments about global retailing are in order. Many international firms decide to enter the U.S. retail market because of the average American family's buying power. There are a few rules of thumb the retailer should follow when entering the global retailing arena.

First, the retailer has to make sure that the targeted international destination has adequate spending power. It would be unwise to pursue an international focus for retailing if the nation, or the region within the nation, could not support the retailer. Second, the retailer needs to conduct an exhaustive research study of the potential market. The retailer must cater to local tastes, needs, and wants to succeed. In addition, all countries have unique customs, laws, regulations, and ethics by which the retailer must abide.

Finally, the retailer must gain country-specific or local expertise. Generally, the easiest and most effective way to do so is through the acquisition of local retailers, joint ventures, strategic alliances, and franchising. One strategy many international retailers use as they expand globally is to create retail branding. Many companies create brand positioning and take the retail operation global based on this positioning. For example, as Wal-Mart continues its globalization, the company has decided to hold to its retail brand differentiation of low price. To effectively offer a low price, Wal-Mart must rely on outside suppliers from the countries in which it operates. Thus, Wal-Mart creates a presence in its markets, yet relies on the countries' national brand suppliers to be members of its overall channel of distribution.

Gaining an understanding of the local retail markets is essential during the planning process. For example, Wal-Mart acquired local chains in Germany and Great Britain. Instead of using the Wal-Mart name, the company decided to continue using the local chain names.

An additional example further illustrates the need to fully understand global markets. In 1992, there was a couple that wanted to open a bookstore in Beijing. They developed a major retail management plan prior to researching the area's problems and issues. They were ready to open for business when they discovered that at that time, all retailing in China was being done through state-owned stores.[12] Because they failed to discover this crucial information during the planning process, their business could not move forward.

TRADING AREA ANALYSIS

Once the regional analysis step has been completed, the next step is to assess the retail trading area. A **trading area** is defined as "a geographical area containing the customers of a particular firm or group of firms for specific goods or services."[13] The trading area should account for more than 50 percent, and usually higher, of the retailer's sales and/or customers. A trading area can be as large as a nation or even international (especially for bricks-and-clicks). Conversely, a trading area can be as small as a single neighborhood block. The size of the area depends on the retailer's objectives. How many customers are needed to achieve profitability? How much sales volume needs to be generated to establish a breakeven point? It is the overall job of the retailer or site selection specialist to select the most potentially profitable trading area from the numerous alternatives available.

trading area A geographical area containing the customers of a particular firm or group of firms for specific goods or services.

Ray Kroc, founder of the McDonald's food empire, knew the importance of trading area analysis. He insisted that franchisees live in their trading areas so they would understand the local market. He also hired regional advertising firms as opposed to a national advertising agency, because he felt regional firms better understood their trade areas. Kroc felt that each restaurant was a part of the local business community and recognized that the neighborhood is where retail wars are won and lost. From the beginning, he insisted that restaurant managers get involved in community programs.[14]

When assessing the retail trading area, it should be noted that advances in technology have led to two types of retail outlets for reaching targeted markets: **store-based retailers,** which have physical locations, and **non-store-based retailers,** which have no physical location but do have a presence in the retail arena through cyberspace, catalogs, vending machines, or other nontraditional places of business, including the home. Many retailers have both store and non-store locations, thus using more than one type of sales channel. These are called **multichannel retailers.**

store-based retailer A retailer that has one or more permanent, fixed physical location(s).

non-store-based retailer A retailer that has no physical location but sells via cyberspace, catalogs, vending machines, or other nontraditional places of business, such as a home.

multichannel retailer A retailer that uses more than one means of distribution for products and services.

The type of retail establishment is important, but the retailer must have a good understanding of the target market and customer base. In addition, unless the entire market can be furnished with goods and services, the retailer should identify the number of potential or current customers in the market. It

Kiosks found in the aisles of malls are one of many forms of nonstore retailing.

angers customers when they come to a store for a specific advertised product only to find that the item is out of stock and the retailer expects a new shipment in the near future or—worse yet—has no idea when the product will be available again. If this happens often enough, the retailer may lose its customer base.

DETERMINING THE TRADING AREA

Armed with knowledge about the target market and the typical customer profile, how does the retailer go about analyzing the trading area? Often retailers break the area down into primary and secondary areas. In some cases, retailers also utilize tertiary, or fringe, areas for those customers and sales unaccounted for in the primary and/or secondary trading areas. A primary area should produce at least 60 percent of the retailer's business, the secondary area an additional 15 to 20 percent of sales, and the tertiary or fringe areas the remainder.

It is important to note that even though the retailer is located in a specific geographic area, its business may come from outside that area. A sporting goods store located in southern Colorado provides an example. This store was trying to assess its trading area. For years the owners had assumed their business was coming from the southern Colorado area, but after a careful analysis they found that more than 70 percent was coming from Texan tourists and around 60 percent of them were from Dallas. In response, the owners readjusted their retailing tactics, including changes in the integrated marketing communications mix, in particular advertising and store signage. Customer needs that were previously unknown were identified, and a different product mix was developed that appealed to the newly identified target group; they began ordering and selling more top-of-the-line fishing rods and reels, for instance. The end result was a substantial increase in business.

The main thing to look for in a trading area is a customer base that matches the target market. Other variables to be studied in the assessment include:

- Population (both size and characteristics) of the potential trading area
- Availability of a labor force for clerical, management, and line workers
- Rules, laws, and regulations that govern the area
- Types of schools
- State of the area's economy
- Number and size of competitors
- Communications or promotion network
- Types of transportation available (to facilitate shipping and receiving product)
- Proximity of suppliers

INTERNET IN ACTION

A Company Specializing in GIS

ESRI started operations in 1969 as Environmental Systems Research Institute, a company specializing in land use analysis. The firm evolved into one of the largest GIS consulting companies in the world. In 1981, ESRI introduced the first commercial GIS software, ARC/INFO. The software combined computer display geographic features, such as points, lines, and polygons, with database management tools. Today ESRI's GIS products are on personal digital assistants, desktops and networks, and the Internet. According to owner Jack Dangermond, "We at ESRI believe that better information makes for better decisions. Our reputation is built on contributing our technical knowledge, our special people, and our valuable experience to the collection, analysis, and communication of geographic information."

ESRI sponsors the Geographic Information System site (*www.GIS.com*), which serves as a portal to GIS information on the Web. The site educates interested people in geographic technology systems and applications of these systems.

Sources: "ESRI—GIS & Mapping Software," retrieved October 2002 from www.esri.com; "Geographic Information Systems," retrieved October 2002 from www.gis.com.

GEOGRAPHIC INFORMATION SYSTEMS

All the information needed for the trading area analysis is available through either secondary data searches or primary research. These data can be purchased, downloaded, or entered by hand into the RIS. One excellent tool used by retailers and site selection specialists in deciding on specific trading areas is a geographic information system. A **geographic information system (GIS)** is a computer-based tool for integrating and analyzing spatial data from multiple sources.[15]

geographic information system (GIS) A computer-based tool for integrating and analyzing spatial data from multiple sources.

Retailers use a GIS to help in determining the trading area and in making location decisions. Various GIS software programs allow retailers to identify key geographic areas and to combine each of those areas with psychographic and demographic information.[16] The data may include information on competitors, consumer purchase behaviors, numbers of consumers, effective buying incomes, and other data that help in the trading area decision. Geographic barriers such as bridges, tunnels, and rivers (or the lack thereof) are also included in many systems.

A company must evaluate its specific needs when choosing among available GIS programs. Companies that provide software include:

- Claritas, Inc. (*www.claritas.com*)
- ESRI, Inc. (*www.esri.com*)
- GIS Solutions (*www.gissolutions.com*)
- GeoSystems Global Corporation (*www.mapquest.com*)
- MapInfo Corporation (*www.mapinfo.com*)
- Microsoft (*www.microsoft.com/mappoint/net*)

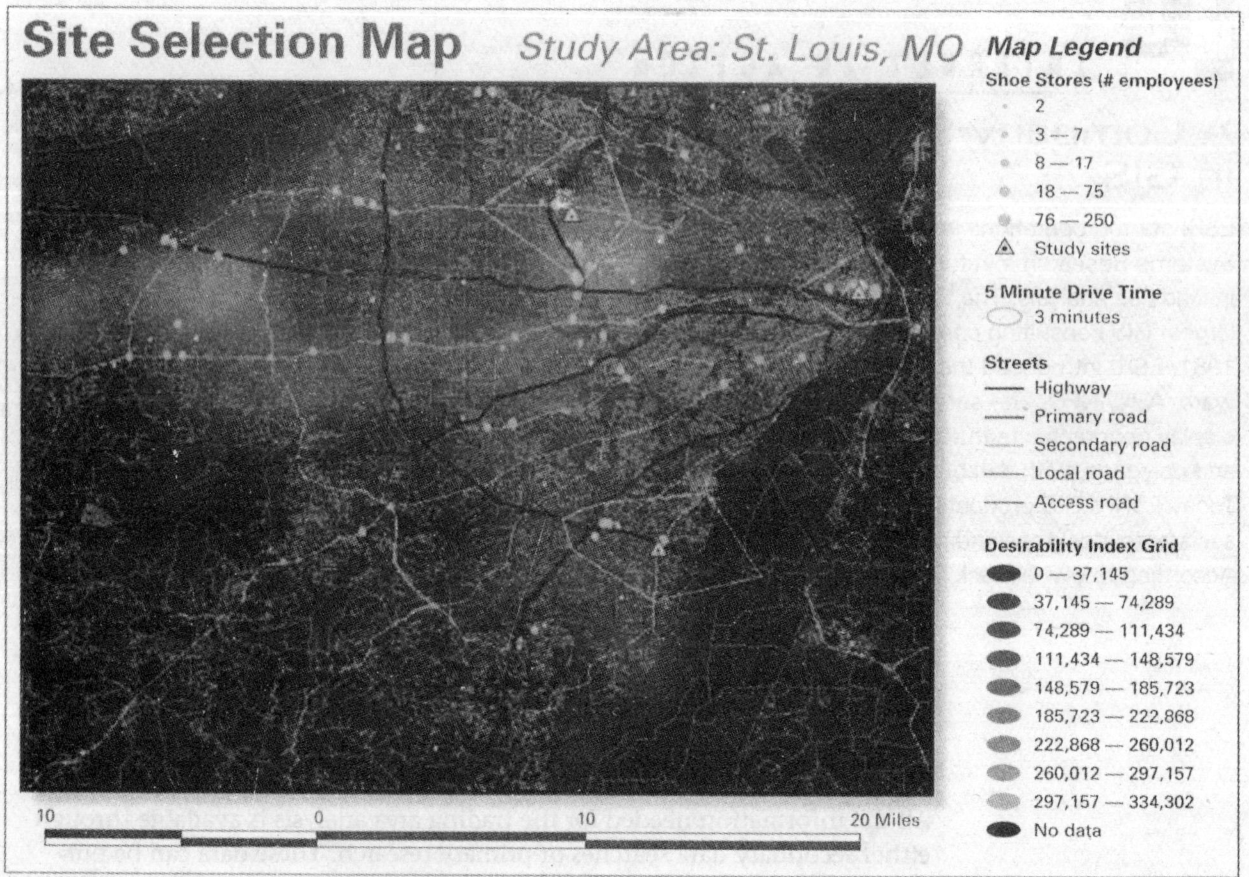

FIGURE 7.1 GIS Map (Source: www.dsslink.com/gallery.htm.)

- Northwood Geoscience Ltd. (*www.northwoodgeo.com*)
- Sites USA (*www.sitesusa.com*)
- Total Systems Inc. (*www.totalsystemsinc.com*)

ESRI software, called ARC/INFO, is very popular in retailing. ARC/INFO works with UNIX systems and with Windows NT. The GIS industry offers a trade publication called *Business Geographics,* which focuses on how GIS can be effectively used by businesses (contact GIS World in Fort Collins, Colorado, for additional information). GIS software has been developed for use in many countries.

Figure 7.1 shows an example of the output from a GIS system. This GIS contains data that allow the program to draw a geometric shape. That shape corresponds to any unique area in the world. Data can then be linked to that geographic area, allowing the retailer to access the data for more informed trading area decisions. This particular map was one of a set used in a retail site analysis to determine which of three sites in the St. Louis market represented the best potential for success. First, a series of grids were run to produce a desirability index across the St. Louis market. This index was derived in part from target household counts, consumer expenditures, and access to existing competitors. Next, drive-time polygons were run for each potential site and the potential aggregated to this theoretical trade area from the underlying grid.[17]

Thus, a GIS helps the retailer visualize the trading area as well as assisting with the analysis of trading area data. Many retailers also utilize a GIS when they make corporate presentations, to allow the audience to better "see" what the trading area looks like. The retailer or site specialist can enter specific data into the software to create a customized GIS for any given subsidiary or division of the retail business. Use of GIS software can cut the length of the site selection process from weeks to days.[18]

geolocation Technology that uses Web geography to determine where an online buyer is located.

Online retailers can use a technology, called **geolocation,** that uses Web geography technology to determine where an online buyer is located. Geolocation technology instantly identifies the originating Internet service provider's address to determine the location of the site visitor down to the city level. This doesn't invade the user's privacy, because personal information is not collected.[19] Knowing customers' locations allows online retailers to customize their products and services to fit the needs of their trading areas.

Industry specialists foresee that the costs of GIS will decrease and that continued improvement in the hardware and software will result in much wider applications of the technology. In the future, GIS will have more animated and 3-D images, which will allow retailers to view sites in ways never before imagined.[20]

INCLUSION OF NONSTORE RETAILERS AND CUSTOMERS

In analyzing a trading area, it is extremely important for the retailer to ensure that trading area analysis data include nonstore retail activities and customers. For e-tailers, the job of trading area definition and analysis may differ somewhat from that for brick-and-mortar retailers. The trading area for nonstore retailers may take on a different shape, but data are still needed to develop effective channels of distribution and communications links with the customer. In addition, the analysis must include consideration of customers' attitudes about e-tailing and other forms of nonstore retailing.

Some argue that there is no need for nonstore retailers to develop a trading area. However, the majority of academicians and practitioners believe nonstore retailers require trading area analysis. It is not possible for a retailer to be all things to all customers. The more the retailer tries to please everyone, the more the retailer ends up pleasing no one. It is essential that the nonstore retailer identify from which areas its customers are coming.

As we have seen, nonstore retailers include many different types of retailers, not just e-tailers. For example, some retailers sell from mobile locations, such as pushcarts. If you have visited New York City, Los Angeles, or Philadelphia, you probably noticed the large number of nonstore vendors selling products and services "on the street." You may have purchased a hot dog in New York, a gyros sandwich in L.A., or a cheesesteak in Philadelphia. When traveling internationally, you will likely see a large number of street vendors peddling their products to their markets. For example, in Caribbean nations such as the

Retailers that have both store and nonstore locations are called multichannel retailers. Primarily a mail-order retailer, Lillian Vernon mails out about 150 million copies of its eight catalog titles each year. Lillian Vernon also sells online through about fifteen outlet stores in Delaware, New York, South Carolina, Tennessee and Virginia.

Virgin Islands, Jamaica, and Aruba, you can get your hair braided. In the Bahamas, many tourists line up at the straw markets to purchase souvenirs. Countless other products, from T-shirts to books to candy, can be purchased from such nonstore retailers.

Different types of large retailers have embraced the concept of nonstore retailing and sell products not only from their brick-and-mortar locations but also from various nonstore venues such as catalogs or websites. The strategy of creating many different retail channels of distribution (multichannels) is well founded. By understanding who the customers are and the trading area for these customers, a retailer will be able to reach them through numerous channels. The location of retail outlets, whether store based or nonstore based, is an important decision that can rest on the analysis of the trading area and the customer base.

Without an understanding of the customer base, the site decision is doomed to fail. Although it would be intuitive to assume that nonstore customers come from "all over the globe," the fact is that information and data on nonstore customers are also available and essential in the trading area decision process. Customers tend to live in distinct geographic areas. By understanding the customers and their behaviors, demographics, and lifestyles, a retailer can find the MSAs that provide the majority of the retail business—in sales and in number of customers.

For e-tailers, the following information is helpful in the analysis of trading areas:

- *The size of the market.* Specifically, how many potential customers have a need or want for the products and services provided by the e-tailer?
- *Levels of product or service consumption and usage.* The higher the level of product or service usage for a given market area, the better the market

value. The e-tailer needs to know which areas have heavy users, average users, and light users.

- *Customer characteristics*. The e-tailer must develop a comprehensive database on the individuals in the market area, including a customer profile for the area.
- *Market area trends*. E-tailers need to have a thorough grasp of what the online customer looks for. As each generation becomes more Web savvy, it brings new needs, wants, and attitudes that are important to the e-tailer.
- *Customers' e-travels*. E-tailers must find out what types of websites their customers typically visit. This information can be placed in the e-tailer's database and used to design websites and promotions that meet or exceed customers' needs and wants.

Thus, the e-tailer (or other nonstore retailer) develops market areas by cultivating market segments whose customers are similar in behaviors with others in the segment but different from those in other segments. Such data assists the retailer in developing a successful venture for each market area chosen.

SOURCES OF INFORMATION FOR THE TRADING AREA

Characteristics such as populations, the economic climate, competition, physical geography, and lifestyles are very important in the trading area decision. When assessing populations, the retailer should include all the necessary demographic data. Whether or not a GIS is employed to assist in a trading area analysis, data and information about consumers within the area are still needed. A wealth of such information and data are available. See Table 7.2 for sources of information for selecting a trading area.

There are also a number of sources of data that can help with competitive analysis. One excellent source is D&B (formerly Dun & Bradstreet), which

TABLE 7.2

SOURCES OF INFORMATION FOR SELECTING A TRADING AREA

U.S. Census of the Population
Sales and Marketing Management's *Survey of Buying Power*
Demographics USA's *Buying Power Index (BPI)*
Editor and Publisher Market Guide
American Demographics
Standard Rate and Data Service's *Lifestyle Analyst*
Rand McNally's *Commercial Atlas & Market Guide*
GIS providers such as Claritas, Inc., ESRI, Inc., and GeoResearch, Inc.
Equifax/National Decision Systems (in particular, the MicroVision program)
Commercial list providers such as D&B and ABI

TABLE 7.3

SOURCES OF COMPETITIVE INFORMATION FOR SELECTING A TRADING AREA

Source	Where to Find Information
U.S. Census of Retail Trade	www.census.gov/econ/www/index.html
U.S. Census of Wholesale Trade	www.census.gov/econ/www/retmenu.html
U.S. Chamber of Commerce	www.uschamber.org
Trade associations (check membership directories for location data)	Check your library for the *Directory of Associations,* or use a search engine to find a particular trade association
International Council of Shopping Centers	www.icsc.org
Standard Directory of Advertisers (also known as the "Red Book")	Available at most libraries
Local colleges and universities	Seek out professors of retailing, research, and geography
Local (and national) clubs and organizations	Local business clubs such as city chamber of commerce, the Kiwanis club, or the Rotary organization
Small Business Administration	www.sba.gov

offers business information reports (BIRs) that give basic information about businesses. In addition, D&B provides data via many other products and services ranging from credit to marketing. Many businesses such as D&B charge for information, but several sources provide information free of charge. See Table 7.3 for additional sources.

Because the profiles of e-tail customers may not be accurately represented by current census data and data from other print sources, e-tailers often look online for trading area information. Table 7.4 lists several online sources that provide various levels of marketing information to e-tailers.

customer spotting An observational technique in which the retailer utilizes various types of already-acquired data to try to ascertain where customers are located.

TECHNIQUES. Numerous quantitative and qualitative techniques can aid in the choice of a trading area. One easy technique is **customer spotting,** an observational technique in which the retailer utilizes various types of already acquired data to try to ascertain where customers are located. The technique is generally applied to existing retail locations; it can also be used with new locations, however.

In customer spotting, location data (such as the customer's city and state) are usually gathered by looking at credit card receipts or delivery orders.[21] In addition, many retailers have set up customer relationship management (CRM) programs. These programs offer a wealth of information to help retail-

TABLE 7.4

MARKETING INFORMATION FOR THE E-TAILER

Source	Website
CyberDialogue	www.cyberdialogue.com
IntelliQuest	www.intelliquest.com
USADATA	www.usadata.com
Datamart on America (Claritas, Inc.)	www.claritas.com
Forrester	www.forrester.com
Jupiter	www.jup.com
Electronic Journal Miner (searchable engine for e-journals and e-magazines)	http://ejournal.coalliance.org

ers make more informed judgments on trading areas. Vendors such as PeopleSoft, SAP, and Oracle offer certified and effective CRM software.

Finally, to spot geographical customer origins at a prospective site, the retailer can simply walk around the parking lot and record the license plate numbers of the vehicles. The retail researcher must be careful to follow all applicable state and local laws regarding the use of this technique. This type of spotting should be done in a longitudinal manner (*i.e.,* over time) to ensure there is a good base of license plates for the sample. Finally, the sample size for the license plate count should be more than 500.

After generating the plate numbers, a list of the plate owners is needed to uncover where the owners live. Many states assign plate numbers by county and have a listing of which numbers correspond to which counties. In addition, many states physically place the county name on the license plate, thus making the job a little easier. If the plate data cannot be accessed through the local or regional government offices, the retailer may have to pay for the data. Many companies offer to match plate numbers against their databases for a fee. One such organization is R. L. Polk and Company, which has a specialized division, the Motor Statistical Division, that provides this service.

An additional spotting technique is the use of zip codes. The retailer simply asks customers for their zip codes and uses this information to generate trading area data on its customer base.

DEFINING THE TRADING AREA

The last step in the trading area analysis is to make an educated guess as to what the trading area physically looks like. To create synergy, this is a good time to employ a GIS, physically draw the trading area on a piece of paper, or outline the trading area on a map. It is important to pay attention to physical barriers such as rivers, highways, and train tracks. A number of theories and methods are available to help define the trading area. In the following sections, we discuss a few of the more popular approaches.

REILLY'S LAW OF RETAIL GRAVITATION. Developed by William J. Reilly, Reilly's law of retail gravitation is used to establish a "point of indifference" between two cities' locations that helps the retailer project the physical trading area.[22] Reilly suggests that a consumer living between two cities will consider both trading areas for shopping based on the distance of each area from the consumer's home and the size of each area. Reilly suggests that inventory and selection may be more important to shoppers than distance; therefore, the consumer will travel a little farther to get to the bigger city. The travel distance being equal, Reilly posits that the consumer will choose the city with more population because she or he will assume more product assortment is available there.

point of indifference The distance at which the choice between two shopping destinations is equal.

Reilly's law was amended to include a point of indifference between cities. The **point of indifference** is the distance at which the consumer is indifferent about shopping at either location. In other words, if you live between Dallas and Fort Worth, how close to Dallas, in miles, would you have to live to have a propensity to shop in Dallas? Is there a distance beyond which you would decide to shop in Fort Worth instead? Where is the point at which you would become indifferent about which city to shop in? The algebraic expression of Reilly's law is as follows:[23]

Reilly's law of retail gravitation

$$D_{ab} = \frac{d}{1 + \sqrt{P_b / P_a}}$$

where

D_{ab} = breakeven point, or point of indifference, in miles, between cities a and b

P_a = population of city a

P_b = population of city b

d = distance along the most-traveled route between cities a and b

An Example You live between Fort Collins, Colorado, and Greeley, Colorado. The closest route between Greeley and Fort Collins is approximately 36 miles. The population of Greeley is approximately 61,000, and the population of Fort Collins is around 90,000. Where would the point of indifference lie? Represent Fort Collins as city a, so P_a equals 90,000. Let Greeley be city b, so P_b equals 61,000. The distance (d) between the cities equals 36. Thus, the point of indifference can be calculated as follows:

$$\begin{aligned} D_{ab} &= 36/(1 + \sqrt{61{,}000/90{,}000}) \\ &= 36/(1 + 246.98/300) \\ &= 36/(1 + .823) \\ &= 19.75 \text{ miles from Fort Collins} \end{aligned}$$

and

$$
\begin{aligned}
D_{ab} &= 36/(1 + \sqrt{90{,}000/61{,}000}) \\
&= 36/(1 + 300/246.98) \\
&= 36/(1 + 1.215) \\
&= 16.25 \text{ miles from Greeley}
\end{aligned}
$$

Reilly's law of retail gravitation assumes that both cities are accessible from a major thoroughfare and that population data represent differences in the amounts of goods and services available from each city (that is, the larger the population, the greater the amount of goods and services available to the consumer). Thus, consumers are attracted to the cities based on the amounts of goods and services available to them, including product lines, product assortment, and better facilities, and are not attracted simply by a larger population.

HUFF'S GRAVITY MODEL. Huff's gravity model, or Huff's law of shopper attraction, states that consumers will shop at a store or shopping center more often if the size of the store or center is increased and the distance to the shopping area is decreased.[24] It is much like Reilly's law of retail gravitation; in fact, it is based in part on Reilly's early research. Huff's model can be used to help estimate sales for a particular trading area as follows:

Huff's gravity model (Huff's law of shopper attraction)

$$
P_{ij} = \frac{\dfrac{S_j}{(T_{ij})^{\lambda}}}{\displaystyle\sum_{j=1}^{n} \frac{S_j}{(T_{ij})^{\lambda}}}
$$

where

P_{ij} = probability of a consumer traveling from origin (i) to any given shopping center or store (j)

S_j = square footage of selling space in the shopping location, represented by j, that is expected to be devoted to the particular product or product category being sold

T_{ij} = travel time from the consumer's origin (i) to the shopping location (j)

λ = an exponent reflecting the effect of travel time on different kinds of shopping trips made by the consumer (*i.e.*, one may be willing to travel a greater distance for a heart transplant than for a soda)

n = number of different shopping locations available

In plain English, Huff says that the larger the shopping center relative to competing centers, the higher the probability that a consumer will patronize that center. The theory states that because the center is larger, it probably has a larger and wider assortment of goods and services. In addition, distance has the opposite effect on probability of patronage: the farther away the shopping center is from the consumer, the smaller is the probability that the consumer will shop there. All things being equal, the consumer wants a shopping area that is close to home.

INDEX OF RETAIL SATURATION THEORY. Reilly's and Huff's models deal with the role of consumers' wants and needs in their decisions to patronize a given shopping location. What about the competition? It is strategically sound to assess how deeply competitors are entrenched in a given market area. The index of retail saturation (IRS) theory was developed to help the retailer assess the levels of supply and demand in various trading areas.

retail saturation The point at which consumers' needs are just being met with the existing retail facilities.

understored A situation in which a trading area has too few stores (or too little selling space).

overstored A situation in which too many stores (or too much selling space) are devoted to a product or product line.

index of retail saturation (IRS) A formula used to assess the saturation levels of various trading areas.

A trading area in which supply and demand are in equilibrium exhibits a condition referred to as *retail saturation*. **Retail saturation** means consumers' needs are just being met with the existing retail facilities. When that trading area has too few stores (or selling space), the area is said to be **understored.** If too many stores or too much selling space is devoted to a product or product line, the area is said to be **overstored.** Thus, when assessing trading areas, the retail site specialist looks for areas that are minimally saturated, but a better scenario would be areas that are understored. Following is a formula to assess the saturation levels of various trading areas. This ratio is called the **index of retail saturation (IRS).**[25]

Index of retail saturation

$$IRS = (H \times RE)/RF$$

where

IRS = index of retail saturation for any given trading area

H = number of households in the given trading area

RE = annual retail expenditures for the retailer's line of products per household in the trading area

RF = retail square footage of a particular product or product line for the trading area (including the proposed square footage)

Thus, the IRS is simply the sales per square foot of retail space for a trading area for a given product or product line. If the IRS is high, the area is understored; if it is low, the area is overstored. Experienced retail site selection personnel also assess trading area saturation in terms of the number of employees per retail establishment, average sales per store (both overall and by department), average sales per employee, and average sales per retail store category.

Numerous other methods can be used to assess trading areas for the retail location. We looked at the most popular models. Other models include *Sales and Marketing Management*'s buying power index (BPI), the analog approach,[26] and multiple regression analysis (for use only in chains with more than twenty stores).

Which of these methods is the best one to use? It depends. It is a good idea to try more than one, or all, of the methods and utilize the ones that work best. As stated in Chapter 6, the more data and information available to make a sound, research-based decision on the trading area, the better the decision. Only through academic and professional training, as well as pragmatic experience, can one decide which method will yield the best results.

ACTUAL SITE ANALYSIS AND SELECTION

After selecting the trading area, the next task is to select a specific site. Basically, three types of sites are available: freestanding (or isolated), planned, and unplanned sites.

FREESTANDING SITES

Although freestanding sites are generally planned, they do not fall into the planned business sites category because they are, by definition, isolated. In other words, these sites are not districts but individual stores.

With a *freestanding site* (also referred to as an *isolated location*), the retailer moves into an area with no other retailers in the immediate vicinity. Generally, the store is located off of a main road, highway, or street.[27] Based on the theories dealing with retail gravitation, retailers have a hard time attracting consumers to a freestanding site, because the absence of other retailers may lead consumers to decide not to bother making the trip.

Thus, large retailers and convenience store retailers are the types of retailers that usually take advantage of freestanding sites. In addition, many types of medical retailers utilize isolated sites. A consumer may not be willing to drive 20 miles to buy a taco but be more than willing to make the trip if the best cancer doctor in the state has an office that distance away.

An obvious advantage of a freestanding site is that there is no, or limited, competition. Because of this, the retailer can usually negotiate lower rental, leasing, or purchasing prices for the property. On the other hand, it is harder to attract traffic to a freestanding site. Costs associated with integrated marketing communications tactics may be higher in a freestanding area. Also, the retailer needs to be aware of the laws and regulations in effect for the site. Zoning laws in particular may keep a retailer from opening a store in an isolated site location.

PLANNED BUSINESS SITES

A *planned business site* is just what the name suggests: an area of business that is planned. Generally, each planned business site or district is centrally managed and/or owned. The key to a successful planned business district is a balanced tenant mix, or tenancy, which allows the business district to offer complementary merchandise to the consumer. Tenancy is based in part on population data from the trading area. In general, planned business districts are shopping centers developed to attract consumers from greater distances. Part of the planning process for planned business districts includes the development of some type of parking area. Most planned sites have at least one anchor store large or distinct enough to attract traffic to the center.

The three major types of planned business sites are regional centers, community centers, and neighborhood centers. A new entry to the neighborhood center is the lifestyle center.

regional center A retail site that provides general merchandise and is typically enclosed with parking surrounding the center.

REGIONAL CENTERS. Think about that mall where you usually go to shop for electronics, clothes, CDs, or DVDs. Most likely it is a regional center. A regional center attracts customers from an area of about 5 to 15 miles. A **regional center** provides general merchandise and is typically enclosed with parking surrounding the center. The first enclosed regional center, the Southdale Center, was built in Edina, Minnesota, in 1956 by Dayton's (formerly Dayton-Hudson, and now Target Corporation). This concept caught on quickly, and shopping malls began springing up all over America. Retailers found malls were effective for generating traffic because they had a balanced tenancy, convenient and free parking, and a vast selection of stores. In addition, an enclosed mall gave shoppers protection from the weather. These advantages helped create a concept that has lasted more than forty-five years.

A regional center has at least one anchor store, and usually many more. A typical anchor store is a large, full-size department store, such as Macy's, JCPenney, Dillard's, or Nordstrom, that attracts shoppers on its own merit and, when combined with additional tenants, generates traffic from a greater distance. Generally at least fifty stores, in addition to the anchor store, make up a regional center. As a rule of thumb, a center should have at least 400,000 square feet of gross leasable area (GLA), though most regional centers are much larger than this.

megamall A mall that is often several times larger than a regional center; also known as a *superregional center.*

The concept of a regional mall was so successful that larger malls began to be developed all over North America. These giant malls are a subset of the regional center and are called **megamalls,** or *superregional centers.* Two of the largest megamalls in the world are the West Edmonton Mall in Canada and the Mall of America in Minneapolis. At a cost of more than $650 million to build, the Mall of America (*www.mallofamerica.com*) has 2.5 million square feet of GLA and more than 4 million square feet in total. According to Mall of America authorities, if a shopper spent just 10 minutes browsing at every store, it would take more than 86 hours to complete the visit.[28] In addition, Cedar Fair operates a 7-acre theme park, Camp Snoopy, in the middle of the mall.

community shopping center A retail center typically between 100,000 and 400,000 square feet in size. Tenants often include smaller stores, branch department stores, and a large discount store.

COMMUNITY SHOPPING CENTERS. Community shopping centers are substantially smaller than regional centers or megamalls. Community shopping centers tend to be between 100,000 and 400,000 square feet. They may house a smaller, branch department store as an anchor. Sometimes the anchor is a large discount store, a category killer, or a combination of these retailers. In addition to the anchor store(s), the community center has a number of smaller stores. Some community centers also have convenience stores as tenants.

Like the larger regional centers, community shopping centers generally have a diverse mix of tenants. The mix includes businesses that support service needs, such as banks, pharmacies, and hair salons. The centers also have

Blunders or Best Practices?

The Biggest Mall in the World

Spanning the equivalent of forty-eight city blocks, West Edmonton Mall in Edmonton, Alberta (Canada), is the largest mall in the world. It has 5.3 million (yes, *million*) square feet. The mall calls itself "the world's largest entertainment and shopping centre." The mall is listed in the *2003 Guinness Book of World Records* for the "largest shopping centre in the world" and "world's largest parking lot" (room for over 20,000 vehicles). There are over 23,500 employees at the mall. Besides shopping, the mall houses seven attractions: Galaxyland Indoor Amusement Park, World Waterpark, Deep Sea Adventure (an indoor lake that offers submarine rides), Professor Wem's Adventure Golf, Ice Palace skating rink, Dolphin Lagoon (which houses two Atlantic bottlenose dolphins), and Sea Life Caverns. Other diversions include a 3D IMAX theater, a live dinner theater, twenty-six movie theaters, a Las Vegas–style casino, more than 800 stores and services, and over 100 restaurants.

The complex was built in four phases opening in 1981, 1983, 1985, and 1998. The total cost to build the mall was $1.2 billion (Canadian). The planned site was developed to increase drawing power and trading area size. From the looks of it, the developers made a good choice of site.

Prior to the presence of the West Edmonton Mall, the city was known to outsiders mainly for oil and hockey. Since the mall was built, tourists have numbered over 20 million annually. About 39.9 percent of the visitors come from Alberta, 17.2 percent from British Columbia, 20.9 percent from other western Canadian cities, 11.6 percent from eastern and central Canada, and 10.5 percent from outside Canada. The primary visitors to the mall are families with school-aged children, followed by teens and seniors. The primary markets are women between the ages of 18 and 34 and teens.

The West Edmonton Mall is an example of best practices in choosing a location and analyzing trading areas.

Source: West Edmonton Mall website at www.westedmontonmall.com; " 'Eighth Wonder of the World' West Edmonton Mall Has It All," retrieved June 2003 from www.wheredmonton.com; Anna Elkins, "Did You Know?" *News Sentinel*, June 18, 2003, p. A11.

specialty stores that are suited to a specific community. The community centers work hard at promoting their image; thus, they pay a lot of attention to their tenant mix.

power center A type of community center that includes at least one category killer with a mix of smaller stores.

As community centers began to show retail success, some centers' creators developed **power centers,** community centers that include at least one category killer with a mix of smaller stores. Toys "R" Us, Best Buy, Circuit City, and Sports Authority stores are category killers located in power centers.

neighborhood center A planned shopping district with a smaller anchor store.

NEIGHBORHOOD CENTERS. Neighborhood centers are planned shopping districts with a smaller anchor store. Generally, a neighborhood shopping center has a supermarket or large drugstore, such as Phar-Mor, as its anchor store. Neighborhood centers focus more on convenience goods than do regional or community centers.

Neighborhood centers generally draw their clientele from a limited distance (no more than 10 minutes away). Most neighborhood centers are laid out in a strip configuration: they tend to be outdoors and in a straight or curved line.

According to *Shopping Centers Today,* neighborhood centers are a good investment because even when the economy is down, people go to strip centers an average of three times per week. "We're catering to basic necessities of people: dry cleaning, banking, dentists, and so on," says Chaim Katzman, CEO of North Miami Beach–based REIT Equity One, an investor in neighborhood centers. In addition to location, large populations, high incomes, and growth potential, investors seek a stable, strong anchor, preferably one of the dominant grocers in a given area.[29] (If the neighborhood center's anchor were to shut down, a domino effect could result, as other retailers in the center also shut down due to lack of business.)

LIFESTYLE CENTERS. Lifestyle centers are gaining momentum. According to the International Council of Shopping Centers (ICSC; *www.icsc.org*), a **lifestyle center** "caters to retail needs and 'lifestyle' pursuits of consumers in its trading area."[30] A lifestyle center is a "souped-up neighborhood center."[31] Targeted to upper-income shoppers, lifestyle centers are typically outdoors with a "Main Street" type of ambience, have tenants that sell nonessential items, building and landscaping costs that are higher than those of other retail developments, and parking available in front of the stores.[32]

lifestyle center A planned shopping center targeted to upper-income shoppers. Typically outdoors with a "Main Street" ambience, tenants that sell nonessential items, higher building and landscaping costs than those of other retail developments, and parking in front of the stores.

Although the concept has been around for awhile, the number of lifestyle centers has been growing nationwide only during the last few years. Presented as an alternative to the big, enclosed shopping mall, the lifestyle center is typically one-third the size of a traditional regional center.

Although many types of retail developments have used the term *lifestyle center,* as of 2002 only thirty true lifestyle centers existed in the United States, according to the ICSC. Locations such as Aspen Grove (Littleton, Colorado), Deer Park Town Center (Deer Park, Illinois), CocoWalk (Coconut Grove, Florida), Mount Pleasant Towne Center (Mount Pleasant, South Carolina), and Alamo Quarry Marketplace (San Antonio, Texas) qualify as lifestyle centers.

The term *lifestyle center* is attributed to Poag & McEwen Lifestyle Centers, Memphis, Tennessee, one of the earliest and most active developers of the centers. According to Terry McEwen, president of Poag & McEwen, lifestyle centers offer shoppers convenience, safety, an optimal tenant mix, and a pleasant atmosphere.[33]

Typical tenants of a lifestyle center include apparel stores such as Ann Taylor, Gap, and Banana Republic; home goods retailers such as Pottery Barn and Williams-Sonoma; and book and music stores such as Barnes and Noble and Borders. Restaurants and entertainment establishments are also included in the tenant mix, as are special-interest businesses such as needlework shops.

OTHER TYPES OF PLANNED SHOPPING CENTERS. Planned shopping centers include several other types. Among the primary types are outlet centers, cybermalls, and airport malls.

outlet center A type of community center that brings together retail establishments for manufacturers and retailers of consumer goods. These centers increase drawing power by providing deep discounts on brand-name products.

Outlet Centers Originating in Reading, Pennsylvania, **outlet centers** began as employee stores where manufacturers would sell flawed or overstocked merchandise to their own workers at deep discounts.[34] Eventually, outlet stores expanded to welcome the general public and became "outlets" for retailers as well as manufacturers of consumer goods. Outlet centers are essentially community centers that offer off-price merchandise and draw from a larger area, including tourists. Some outlet centers are enclosed, and some are laid out in a strip configuration. Other developers have tried to create a town- or village-type atmosphere. Outlet centers have primary (weekly) customers who come from a distance of 25 miles, secondary (monthly) customers who travel as far as 150 miles to shop, and tourist customers, who travel over 150 miles.[35]

Vanity Fair (VF) was among the first to convert old manufacturing facilities into an outlet for its products. When other manufacturers saw how successful VF's retail outlets were, they followed suit and opened their own.

The Mills Corporation, a self-managed real estate investment trust (REIT), based in Arlington, Virginia, has become the largest developer of outlet centers in the United States. People who live near a trading area with a large population probably live near a Mills Corporation outlet center. Sawgrass Mills (near Fort Lauderdale), Franklin Mills (near Philadelphia), and Gurnee Mills (near Chicago) are a few examples.[36] In 2003, The Mills Corporation had several retail destinations under construction, including six new malls in the United States and two in Toronto, Canada.[37]

cybermall (virtual mall) A "mall" whose "tenants" are usually brought together online or through a catalog or newspaper ads.

Cybermalls Retailers have found that they can create a planned shopping district in cyberspace. Many communities are now seeing the formation of cybermalls. In a **cybermall** (or **virtual mall**), "tenants" are usually brought together online or through a publication such as a catalog or newspaper ads. Cybermalls have a planned tenant mix and are created by some type of

Outlet malls have increased in popularity as consumers search for off-price merchandise.

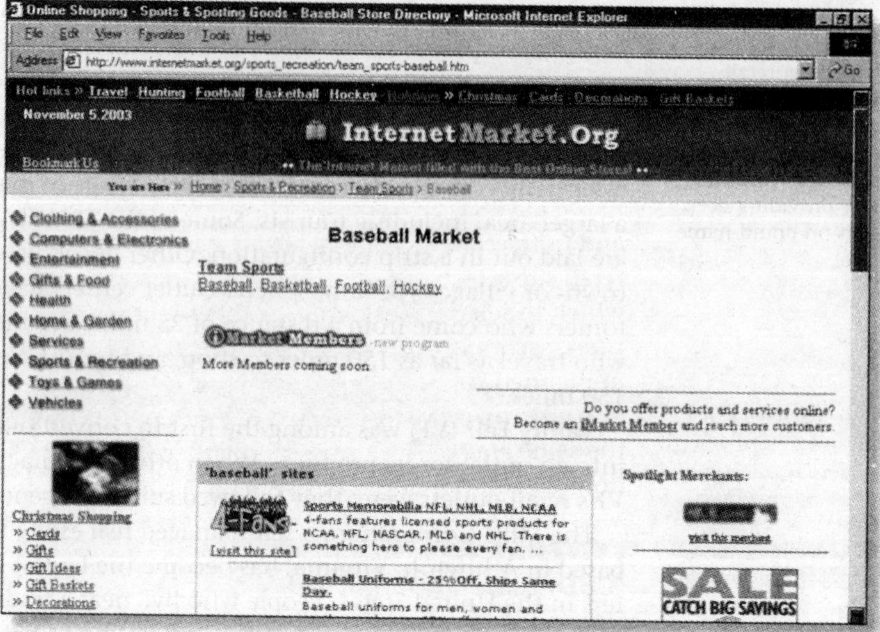

This website is an example of a cybermall. Cybermalls are like traditional malls in that several retailers share the sales environment. (Courtesy of InternetMarket. Org.)

cyberdeveloper. An example of a cybermall is the SkyMall (1-800-SkyMall or *www.skymall.com*), developed for Delta Airlines. Delta retails products and services to consumers through its *SkyMall* catalog, found on all Delta flights, or through the website. SkyMall has products from Alsto's, Frontgate, Hammacher Schlemmer, Plow and Hearth, and others. Another example is a company called Cybermall.com, which provides products and services through its webpage. MyPoints (*www.mypoints.com*), a service designed to reward shoppers, offers points that members can redeem for merchandise by performing activities such as taking surveys, reading e-mail, visiting websites, and making purchases from one of the participating e-tailers.

airport mall A community shopping center located in an airport.

Airport Malls There are many planned retail operations in airports around the world. An **airport mall** is a community shopping center located in an airport. Whereas some of the older retailing in airports was unplanned, there now appears to be a trend toward planned shopping districts for airports.

There are two models for airport malls: the prime model and the developer model. In the prime model, the airport is responsible for management of retail facilities, whereas in the developer model, an outside company serves as the mall manager and works to draw top retailers to the airport. The shops in the latter model are owned and operated by individual retailers, who do their own hiring.[38]

Pittsburgh International Airport, praised as having one of the best airport malls in the United States, was the first U.S. airport to try the developer model. Since moving to the developer model in 1992, its retail revenue has increased from $2.40 per airport passenger to $9.02.

The developer model tends to work best for large airports.[39] Each airport has to weigh the pros and cons of the two models in deciding which is the better choice.

UNPLANNED SHOPPING SITES

As we have seen, a large number of retailers operate in planned shopping sites and in freestanding sites. However, when making a site selection decision, the retail site selection specialist has a number of unplanned shopping sites from which to select as well. Among the unplanned sites are central business districts, secondary business districts, neighborhood business districts, and unplanned strip or string districts.

unplanned shopping site A site that develops when two or more retailers move into the same area or in close proximity to each other. These sites are a function of evolution; they are not planned but develop over time.

Unplanned shopping sites result when two or more retailers move into the same area or in close proximity to each other. Unplanned sites are a function of evolution; thus, they are not planned but develop over time.

central business district (CBD) An unplanned shopping site in the downtown area of any city.

CENTRAL BUSINESS DISTRICTS. The **central business district (CBD)** is the downtown area of any city. Some states, particularly on the East Coast, describe the CBD as the *center city*. Because the CBD is the hub of the city, it draws a great deal of pedestrian and automobile traffic. In addition, many of the city's public transportation systems have a link with the CBD.

Most of the growth of traditional department stores occurred in the CBD of the city. Examples include Marshall Field's in Chicago, J. L. Hudson in Detroit, Macy's in New York City, Denver Dry Goods in Denver, Eaton's in Toronto, and Neiman Marcus in Dallas. In addition to department stores, CBDs traditionally have many specialty stores.

CBD growth came from merchants who wanted to move into a central location to trade their wares. Little advance planning was involved in the development of the CBD. When looking at the CBD as a possible site for a retail business, the retailer needs to take into account the many advantages and disadvantages of this type of unplanned district. Among the advantages of moving into a CBD are:

- Easy access to public transportation
- A wide assortment and variety of products available to the consumer
- A variety of price points for products
- Close proximity to other businesses and government offices
- Proximity to social activities and facilities
- A high level of automobile, bus, subway, and pedestrian traffic

Disadvantages of a CBD site include:

- Expensive and inadequate parking for employees and customers
- High crime rates in some CBDs
- Relatively high rent, lease, or own costs for the physical store location

- Older buildings, thus older stores, indicating that the site may need substantial renovation before it is ready to open
- Inner-city decay rates, leading to an overall deterioration of the area
- Perception of consumers that downtowns lack good shopping
- Congestion caused by inner-city traffic and deliveries
- High tax rates
- Lack of a balanced tenancy
- Long travel times for consumers wishing to shop at a center-city location

Although the CBD began as the major trading area in developing towns and cities, it has seen its best days. Many CBDs are in need of major renovation and repair. Over the past couple of decades, however, many governments and private groups have attempted to revive center-city areas. These cities have paid attention to details that make shoppers want to return to CBDs. Increased security; more parking; a better tenant mix; and physical renovations such as brighter colors, enhanced building facades, walkways, pedestrian malls, and improved parking areas are among the improvements cities are making to create more appealing CBDs.

Many CBDs are fine alternatives from which to select a site. New York City, particularly Times Square, is an excellent example of a rejuvenated CBD. Toronto's Eaton Center, Crowne Center in Kansas City, Circle Center in Indianapolis, and Peabody Place in Memphis are other excellent examples.

secondary business district (SBD) An unplanned shopping site (smaller than a CBD) that is located around the major transportation intersections of cities. A typical SBD has at least one department store or variety store, coupled with a number of smaller stores.

SECONDARY BUSINESS DISTRICTS. A **secondary business district (SBD)** is generally a miniature CBD. SBDs are usually located around the major transportation intersections of cities. A typical SBD has at least one department store or variety store, coupled with a number of smaller stores.

Although not as large as that of a CBD, the trading area of an SBD is usually substantial. A wide variety of products are available in an SBD, but there is less product width and assortment compared to a CBD. Generally, an SBD has a few convenience stores, or the larger stores carry an assortment of consumer convenience goods. Advantages of an SBD include less congestion and better service offerings than exist in a CBD. Generally, an SBD has adequate parking for employees and customers. On the down side, rent and lease costs are often fairly high. In addition to having a smaller trading area relative to a CBD, adequate parking and space for store deliveries may be a problem in some cities. Finally, many SBDs are aging, making them less attractive to retailers, and the tenant mix is unplanned and weak.

neighborhood business district (NBD) An unplanned shopping site that provides shopping for a neighborhood rather than a larger trading area.

NEIGHBORHOOD BUSINESS DISTRICTS. The **neighborhood business district (NBD)** generally relies on convenience products as the main product mix. The NBD provides shopping for a neighborhood rather than a larger trading area; thus, many NBDs have several service retailers in addition to product retailers. It is not uncommon to have a hair salon, a spa, a beer and liquor store, one or two restaurants, a few smaller specialty stores, a drugstore, and a smaller supermarket in an NBD. The drugstore and supermarket perform the function of an anchor store within these business districts.

Advantages to selecting an NBD include good neighborhood locations, expanded hours of operation, adequate parking, and less traffic congestion than in the larger centers. Because of the limited number of products sold, the prices at an NBD tend to be higher than in other locations. The key to product and service offerings in an NBD, however, is convenience.

strip (string) shopping district An unplanned shopping site with stores that are visible from the road and arranged in a strip.

STRIP SHOPPING DISTRICTS. **Strip** (or **string**) **shopping districts** have stores that are visible from the road and arranged in a long "strip." Strips are unplanned shopping districts consisting of a series of retailers that sell comparable goods and services. Strip districts probably began as freestanding, or isolated, sites, followed by an influx of competition. Because the stores in strips generally have the same types of products, consumers often give strips special names, such as Automobile Mile or Furniture Row.

Strip districts tend to have lower rents or lease costs. Store visibility is generally high. Parking is above average, and the overall cost of operation is lower than at many other potential sites. In addition, consumers seeking a wide variety within a product line, such as an automobile, are willing to come from a distance because they know they will have a large choice of products in a relatively small area.

Disadvantages of strips include problems with zoning laws, higher advertising costs, limited availability of established locations (often the retailer is forced to build rather than rent, buy, or lease an existing facility), and a lack of flexibility in pricing (due to the competition selling the same or similar products and services and customers' ability to compare prices).

SITE ANALYSIS SUMMARY

In addition to the many different types of freestanding, planned, and unplanned sites, some have suggested other types of sites, including fashion centers, specialty centers, theme centers, and festivals. Other potential sites could include kiosks, mixed-use developments (such as offices in retail outlets), and other nontraditional locations (such as antique and craft malls and shows that allow small retailers/dealers to enter the market without having to staff a store). Whichever site is pursued, the retailer must have a thorough understanding of the nature and location of the site and the benefits and disadvantages associated with each alternative.

CHARACTERISTICS OF THE AVAILABLE SITE

As stated earlier, it is important to find the site that best suits the retailer's needs, generates competitive advantage, yet keeps overall costs low. To make the soundest decision, the retailer must look at the physical location and characteristics of the alternative sites. A number of variables are important in the selection of a site; the remainder of the chapter describes these variables.

TRAFFIC

There are two types of traffic patterns to look for when assessing and evaluating retail sites: vehicle and pedestrian. By studying traffic patterns, the retailer can make an educated guess as to the value of the site for potential sales. In addition, the retailer must make a decision regarding the kinds of customers that the site generates. Although higher-volume traffic is generally preferred, the traffic may not be of the type the retailer wants. Consider a convenience retailer, for instance. If it is evaluating a site within the CBD, it will find that traffic is at a higher volume than at a community center. But the traffic at the CBD may consist of consumers who are seeking specialty goods and services, not convenience, making the CBD an inappropriate choice.

VEHICLE TRAFFIC. To gauge the vehicular traffic pattern, the retailer should look at not only the number of vehicles that pass by the site but also the types of vehicles. In addition, the vehicles should have ready access to the potential retail site. Is the site located on a one-way street? If so, will this affect its accessibility? Is the potential site accessible to and from all major highways in the area? The easier it is to get to the site, the more business it will generate.

Another important variable is the quality of the infrastructure surrounding the site, in particular the quality of the streets and roads. What is the level of congestion in the street that abuts the potential site? If the traffic backs up, is this good or bad for the types of products or services the retailer will be selling? Will a traffic light allow easy turns into and out of the site?

Parking is a big consideration for a retail location. The retailer must assess the parking situations at and around the potential site. Are there adequate parking spaces for the number of customers contemplated? The retailer answers this question based on the size of the potential retail outlet, the types of products or services that are to be sold, the frequency of consumer visits to the store, the length of the visits, and the proximity of public transportation to the store's entrance.

When assessing parking at a large retail center, there should be about ten parking spaces for each 1,000 square feet of selling area within the center, because customers tend to stay longer at regional centers than at other types of retail districts. In an SBD or community shopping center, a retailer may need only five parking spaces per 1,000 square feet of selling area. Parking requirements may be determined by local zoning codes.

Physical barriers to store entry should also be assessed. Are there any bridges that limit the traffic flow in and around the site? Are there one-way streets that could deter potential customers?

PEDESTRIAN TRAFFIC. In analyzing pedestrian traffic, retailers consider the types of people that pass by the store in addition to the sheer numbers of passersby. Sites with heavy pedestrian traffic patterns make excellent choices for a retail location. It is important to determine, however, whether the people passing by the store are actually consumers of products or are just on their way elsewhere. Pedestrian traffic patterns should be segmented for each alternative location.

Other variables to consider are the gender of the pedestrians, their ages, and the number of shopping bags they are carrying. What are they wearing? Are they walking by themselves or with others? Much of these data can then be "matched" against the defined target market to see if a good fit exists between the pedestrian traffic and the retailer's targeted market customers.

Many retailers develop research methodologies and actually interview pedestrians to learn more about them. Retailers may research which shops pedestrians enter and the amount of time they spend in them. Information can also be generated based on whether the customer purchased or did not purchase products from the store. In some cases, the retailer simply checks whether the shopper leaves the store with a shopping bag.

When checking the pedestrian traffic patterns of a particular site, the retailer needs to ensure there is good accessibility to the site. Customers must be able to get in and out of the shopping district in the least restricted way possible.

TRANSPORTATION CONSIDERATIONS

Another major consideration when assessing a site is availability of transportation. Can trucks deliver inventory with ease? The transportation in and around the site should allow for smooth delivery of the retailer's products to the location. Many roads prohibit trucks because of the damage caused by the trucks' weight. In addition, turns are often too sharp to allow a truck access to the delivery docks.

Mass transportation is also an issue. When assessing the site, the retailer should find out if public transportation is available for customers. This is especially important in a CBD. Many people who live in CBDs do not own cars and rely on other means of transportation to get them where they need to go. For example, the cost of owning and operating a car in New York City and Boston is extremely high; therefore, many residents of these cities rely on buses, subway systems, and cabs to get around. It is also important to make sure the site is visible from the major thoroughfares that surround it.

SITE AVAILABILITY

Site availability is the final variable to look at when deciding on a specific site. The retailer must not only establish that the site is physically available (unoccupied and ready for renting, buying, or leasing) but also research the conditions required to secure the site. The terms of the rental agreement, lease, or purchase agreement should be studied carefully.

If the retailer decides not to purchase the property, is it available for rent? If so, what will the basic lease payment be? When is the rent due? What length of time is the owner asking for in the duration of the lease? How much does the current owner pay to maintain the property? What are the operating costs? How much are the taxes? Are there requirements such as membership in various merchants' associations? If a retailer moves downtown, does the business have to become a member of the downtown revitalization committee? Are dues required? What happens if a breach of contract occurs and one of the parties wants to get out of the agreement? Lawyers generally write terms of occupancy in legal jargon, but they can be called on to explain the terms in plain English.

Finally, what do the retail location's neighbors look like? Are they desirable or undesirable neighbors? Do they offer complementary products, or are they direct competitors? Do they keep their properties looking well groomed or uncared for? Is new construction going on that blocks the retail site's visibility? Answers to these questions are important to the attractiveness of a retail site.

SUMMARY

The retailer or site selection expert is interested in one main result when searching for the best location and market: profitability. The site should have the potential to add to the retailer's bottom line. Thus, the retailer needs to pick the best site available by asking all the right questions and being sure they are answered.

This chapter explored the many variables involved in the process of site selection. The importance of creating a unique group of customers that will make up the retail target market was examined. The chapter presented several methods for analyzing trading areas, as well as tools, such as a geographic information system, that can assist in the analysis. The specific characteristics of trading areas were covered in detail.

The chapter discussed the various types of sites available, including freestanding sites, planned business districts, and unplanned shopping districts. In addition, it looked at how to assess locations and the nature of potential retail sites. Also discussed were site characteristics such as traffic patterns (vehicular and pedestrian), availability of mass transportation, and site availability.

Armed with this information, and hints on where to find additional information and data for making correct decisions, the reader can march to the next goal: that of studying the actual operations management of the retail business.

It should become clear that the processes used for the development of an integrated retail management plan overlap. Information gathered for the initial part of the plan is now used for decisions on site selection. Target markets are used over and over, and the availability of sites is related to the distribution function. Certainly the key to effective retailing has to do with the development of a retailing plan, its integration among all of the retailing functions, and the synergy that is created by understanding the whole retail planning process, the "big picture" of retailing.

KEY TERMS

environmental analysis (178)
target market (178)
designated market area (DMA) (181)
metropolitan statistical area (MSA) (181)
trading area (183)
store-based retailer (183)
non-store-based retailer (183)
multichannel retailer (183)
geographic information system (GIS) (185)
geolocation (187)

customer spotting (190)
point of indifference (192)
retail saturation (194)
understored (194)
overstored (194)
index of retail saturation (IRS) (194)
regional center (196)
megamall (196)
community shopping center (196)
power center (197)
neighborhood center (197)
lifestyle center (198)
outlet center (199)
cybermall (virtual mall) (199)
airport mall (200)
unplanned shopping site (201)
central business district (CBD) (201)
secondary business district (SBD) (202)
neighborhood business district (NBD) (202)
strip (string) shopping district (203)

QUESTIONS FOR DISCUSSION

1. What are the four requirements for inclusion of a customer in a retailer's target market? Should a retailer refuse to do business with someone who does not fit the criteria? Why or why not?
2. What are some types of retail sites located in a city? Are these sites planned or uplanned? How do you know?
3. How can the use of computers aid in site selection?
4. Describe the various types of traffic patterns. Why are they important to site selection?
5. Choose a company in your local area and analyze its location strategy. What are the strengths and weaknesses of the location?

E-TAILING EXERCISE

Go to the TIGER website sponsored by the U.S. Census Bureau (*www.census.gov/cgi-bin/gazetteer*). This site gives users the opportunity to view maps that they choose by typing in the city and state or the zip code. Then do the following:

1. Locate the place on the site where you can find a particular city either by name or by zip code. Choose a city to view.
2. Pull up the map for the city you chose. Does this map appear to be accurate?
3. What other information does this website provide?
4. How can retailers use this website?

Continuing Case 7.1

Sherwin-Williams Company: Location Decisions

In the year 2000, Sherwin-Williams opened ninety-two new retail stores that generated $3.2 billion in net sales. In 2001, Wal-Mart discontinued a paint line under the Thompson brand. In addition, Sherwin-Williams lost its licensing contract with Ralph Lauren. Partly in response to those developments, and with the increase in demand for Sherwin-Williams products, the company planned to open sixty new stores in 2001, with additional openings foreseen for the next few years.

Research had revealed that women purchased or influenced the purchase of 80 percent of all consumer goods. In response to this trend, Sherwin-Williams changed its marketing program to target women. Instead of stating that the company sells paint and accessories, Sherwin-Williams altered the wording to state that it sells "home decorating ideas," a phrase more acceptable to women. Wall coverings, both wallpaper and paint (and accessories), are its primary products.

Given the new locations and other changes in the environment, Sherwin-Williams is assessing new sites. International expansion is a possibility if the global market responds as the domestic market has.

Questions

1. Where would you recommend that Sherwin-Williams locate its new retail stores?
2. Do you think Sherwin-Williams would do better in an unplanned or a planned site? Why?
3. Do you think a lifestyle center would be a good location for Sherwin-Williams?
4. Would a geographic information system be a good tool to use to identify the best possible locations for the new stores? Why or why not? How could a GIS be used? Give examples.
5. Create a site location plan for Sherwin-Williams using the information in the chapter and any other current data you can gather.
6. Explain the ideal location and nature of a site for Sherwin-Williams. Do you think the company needs to look at pedestrian traffic? Explain your answer.
7. Given all of the Sherwin-Williams data from the preceding cases, do you think the company should become involved in e-tailing? Why or why not?
8. How could Sherwin-Williams most effectively utilize the Internet?
9. Would Huff's gravity model or Reilly's law of retail gravitation be useful to Sherwin-Williams in its site location decisions? Explain your answer.

Source: PBS, "To the Contrary," retrieved October 27, 2002, from www.pbs.org/ttc/economics/marketing.html; "Paint and Home Décor," *National Home Center News*, May 21, 2001.

Case 7.2

Retailer on the Go: Homier Mobile Merchants

Homier Mobile Merchants sells thousands of brand-name tools, general merchandise, furniture, and collectibles at prices the company says are 30 percent below the competition. The concept behind the company is to eliminate the middleman and pass the savings directly to the customer. The company targets the "average Joe," people looking for discounted merchandise.

Homier Mobile Merchants began as a small auction business in Andrews, Indiana, in 1958. Much of Homier's success was due to its ability to recognize trends and capitalize on them. In the winter of 1978, a blizzard caused the roof of the Homier warehouse to collapse. The entire inventory, at the time worth $500,000, was destroyed. Because the company had no insurance coverage for natural disasters, it had to start over.

Shortly after that incident, the founder, Charles Homier, Sr., became disabled in an automobile accident. His son, Chuck Homier, had just completed his college degree and began to explore some new opportunities within the family business. The competition was fierce, and consumers' wants and needs were changing.

In 1979, a man who attended the Homier auctions asked Chuck Homier if he could sell some of Homier's excess inventory at fairs and flea markets throughout the area. That winter, to pare down the inventory, Homier rented a banquet room at a hotel for three days in Warsaw, Indiana. He took out a full-page ad in the local paper, and on opening day there was a line to get into the sale. By the end of the day Homier was sold out. This success prompted the family to give up the auction business and start Homier Mobile Merchants.

The company grew at an average rate of 25 to 30 percent per year. As it grew, so did inventory storage needs. Currently, the company has a site in Huntington, Indiana, that will be 270,000 square feet after renovations. Although the primary product is tools, Homier also sells products from leather jackets to dining room sets. The company holds sales in all forty-eight contiguous states. Typically, it rents a convention center or places tents in a parking lot to sell its products. Homier is in a town for typically one to five days before moving on to the next location.

The mobile retail concept is not new—most people are familiar with more traditional mobile merchandising such as hot dog and beverage vendors who sell from carts. They are much less accustomed to tractor-trailer trucks loaded with merchandise coming to town for a few days, however. Homier Mobile Merchants maintains more than fifty trucks and twenty-four sales and service crews. Nationwide, Homier conducts sixty sales per week, fifty weeks per year, on average. Customers who are dissatisfied with merchandise after purchase can call a toll-free customer service line. Homier's refund policy is "no questions asked." Customers can also buy from the online catalog at *www.homier.com.*

Questions

1. Why is Homier so successful?
2. Describe Homier's location strategy.
3. Would Homier be able to sell products to people who are in upper-income brackets?
4. What disadvantages does Homier's strategy have?
5. How can Homier use geographic information systems?
6. What is the advantage or disadvantage of a "no questions asked" return policy?

Sources: "Innovation at Work: The History of Homier," retrieved September 2002 from www.homier.com; Natalie Morris, "Under the Big Top: Homier Offers Everything from Drill Presses to Oil Paintings at Its Tent," *State Journal Register* (Springfield, IL), July 22, 2000, p. 17; Howard Riell, "Boldly Going Where Customers Are," *Foodservice Equipment & Supplies,* May 1999, pp. 77–78; Don Nelson, "Homier Mobile Merchants," *Knight Ridder Tribune Business News,* April 16, 2002, p. 1; "Business Briefs," *Knight Ridder Tribune Business News,* March 31, 2002, p. 1.

Financial Aspects of Operations Management

Chapter

8

The buck stops with the guy who signs the checks.

Rupert Murdoch

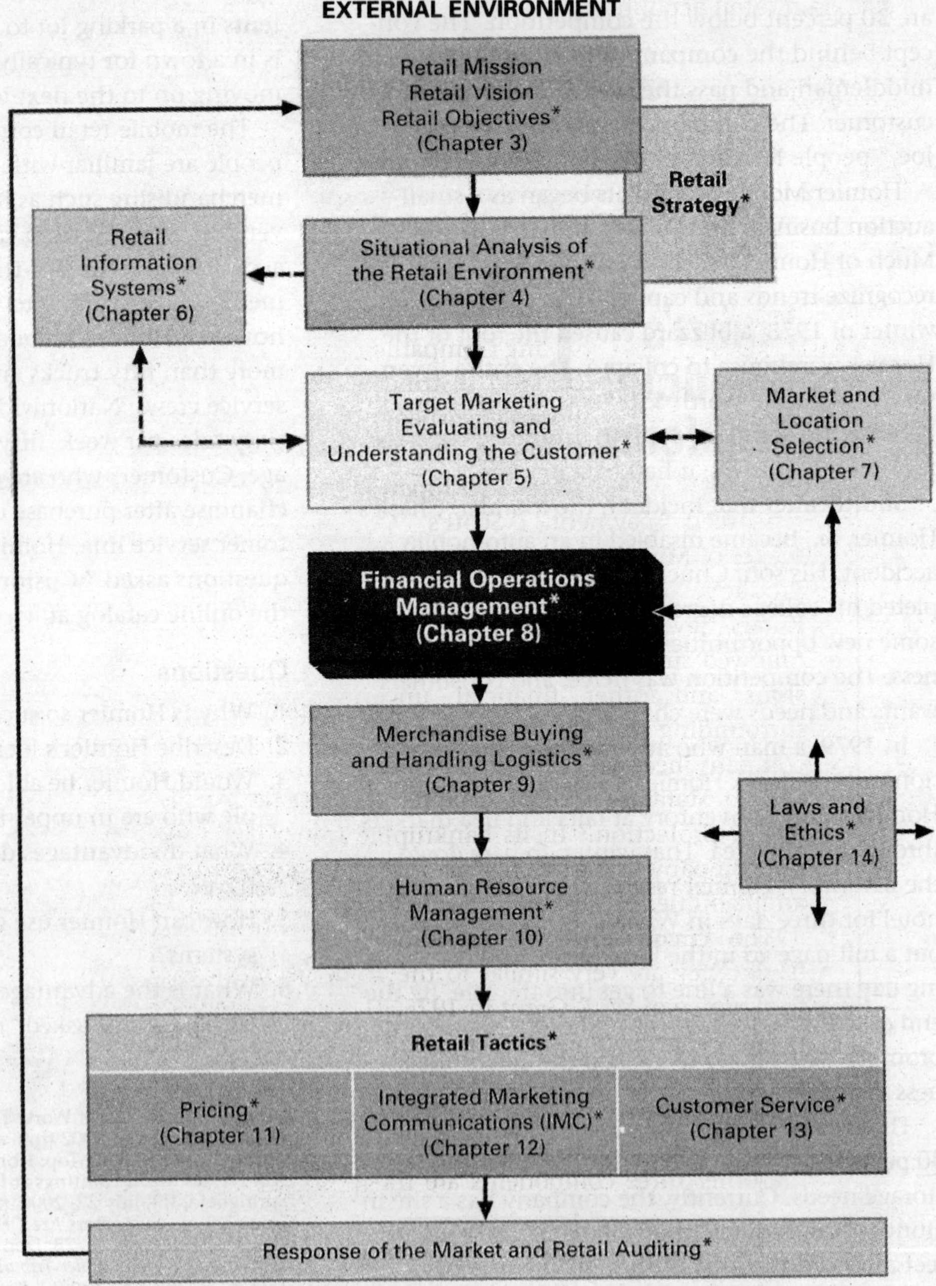

*Evaluation and control occurs at all these stages.

The authors wish to thank Dr. Craig Latshaw, Ph.D., CPA, for his expertise in helping to write and edit this chapter. Dr. Latshaw is assistant accounting professor at St. John's University (300 Howard Avenue, Staten Island, NY 10301).

CHAPTER OBJECTIVES

After completing this chapter, you will be able to:

1. Explain why it is important for retailers to plan for profit and to develop a financial plan.
2. Describe the main types of reports found in a retail accounting system.
3. Calculate inventory values at cost and retail price.
4. Determine how to allocate retail resources.

Kmart's Financial Problems

In January 2002, Fleming Companies, Inc., a food distributor, temporarily suspended shipments to all 2,114 Kmart stores after Kmart missed a scheduled payment.[1] Scott's Company, maker of Miracle-Gro plant food and similar products, also suspended shipments to Kmart. Several other suppliers immediately followed suit. With these shipment suspensions and other financial uncertainties surrounding Kmart, in January 2002, the company became the largest retailer in the United States to file for Chapter 11 bankruptcy protection.[2] In its bankruptcy filing, the company listed total assets of $17 billion and liabilities of $11.3 billion.[3]

The circumstances surrounding Kmart's bankruptcy are very similar to the landmark bankruptcy of W. T. Grant in 1975. The W. T. Grant bankruptcy was instrumental in the development and integration of the statement of cash flows as one of the four major required components of a set of financial statements; the other three components are the balance sheet, income statement, and notes to financial statements.[4] Prior to 1975, an evaluation of a company's cash flow position was not considered a necessary element in evaluating a company's financial stability. Since then, the importance of a company's cash position, particularly for retailers, has continued to grow.

As Kmart's situation illustrates, a company's cash position can have a significant impact on the firm's stability and even its viability. A company can have millions of dollars in revenues and assets, yet still not have enough cash to pay current bills. Unlike its predecessor, W. T. Grant, Kmart emerged from bankruptcy in May 2003. During the reorganization of the company, Kmart closed 600 struggling stores nationwide. In 2003, the company owned 1,500 locations and had 180,000 employees.[5] Analysts are confident that Kmart will regain its strength.

Other retailers that have successfully reorganized after Chapter 11 bankruptcy include Federated Department Stores Inc., which owns Macy's and Bloomingdale's, and Toys "R" Us. Those that were not so lucky include Montgomery Ward and Ames Department Stores.[6]

INTRODUCTION

Up to this point in our study of integrated retail management, the retailer has effectively developed retail mission and vision statements. It has also performed a situational analysis that includes an ongoing system for scanning the retail environment. A retail information system (RIS) has been developed to help with the gathering, analyzing, and dissemination of important retail information. The retailer has developed a sound retail strategy by researching a viable target market based on extensive consumer data. The retailer has developed and extensively studied the target market and weighed the advantages and disadvantages of brick-and-mortar, brick-and-click, and click-only channels of distribution. Retail locations have been carefully selected. The

INTERNET IN ACTION

More Companies Placing Financial Information on Websites

The two main reasons companies post financial information on their websites are that it saves them time and that it saves them money. Companies find that the number of phone calls to the investor relations department decreases dramatically when information is posted online. The investor relations link for company websites most often features financial statements, SEC filings, stock quotes, press releases, and information request forms.

According to *Investor Relations Business,* about 93 percent of the top 100 Fortune 500 companies include financial information on their websites. Many smaller companies are following the trend, but some are unclear about what information to include. The result is many discrepancies in the reporting of financial information on the Internet.

The Financial Accounting Standards Board (FASB) is in the process of developing guidelines to help companies decide what information to post and how to present that information. The FASB reports that companies that direct investors to a website for information instead of faxing or mailing the data have significantly reduced costs. Investors that initially complained about online distribution of investor information have grown to accept the Internet as the primary medium for financial information. With both the consumer and the company benefiting, financial information on the Web will become increasingly prevalent.

The cover of Target Corporation's annual report, as it appears online.

Sources: Financial Accounting Standards Board website (www.fasb.com), accessed October 2002; "IR Web Sites Get Guidance from FASB," *Investor Relations Business,* March 6, 2000, pp. 1, 14–15.

next step in the integrated retail management plan is to actually manage the retail business.

The management function of retailing consists of two main components: operations management and human resource management. Because these concepts encompass many different areas, the remainder of Part 3 is divided into three chapters. This chapter focuses on the financial aspects of operations management. Chapter 9 deals with merchandise buying and selling, including the logistics functions. Chapter 10 covers human resource management, the effective management of the store's personnel.

Operations specialists develop plans that enable the integrated operation of the entire retail business. This operation must be seamless and create synergies wherever possible. Accounting systems, budgets, and inventory management are all part of the overall operations management plan. In addition, monies for the development of the retailer's tactics are allocated based on the information contained in the operations management plan. This plan is then integrated into the overall integrated retail management plan to give retail managers and owners the big picture of what is going on within their stores.

operations management A planning function dealing with the implementation of store policies, tactics, and procedures.

Essentially, **operations management** (also known as *ops management*) deals with the implementation of store policies, tactics, and procedures. Resources must be allocated and monitored to accomplish every function. The plan should be directed by the marketing concept of satisfying customer wants and needs while earning a profit. Operations managers generally have the responsibility of overseeing the human resource functions of the retail establishment; purchasing, accounting, and inventory systems; supply chain management and logistics; and various areas of marketing, such as sales and service.[7]

PLANNING FOR PROFIT: DEVELOPING A FINANCIAL PLAN

Understanding the concepts involved in developing an integrated retail management plan is the basis for the development of the financial plans. Financial plans encompass three major objectives:

- To generate profits for the retailer
- To manage cash such that obligations can be satisfied as they come due
- To manage company growth so that it does not outpace the company's ability to obtain the cash necessary to maintain current operations

Financial reporting can be complicated. The way a company presents its financial information affects how the marketplace receives it. Most of the information needed to develop a financial plan and monitor the company's financial performance can be gathered by constructing budgeted financial statements (financial plans) and comparing those statements to actual results (financial statements). The financial statements allow the retailer to monitor the organization's financial performance and to evaluate and control those activities that are not producing the desired results. The past performance of a retailer can provide a basis for future planning. It is wise, therefore, to refer to the financial statements when developing retail objectives. Communication and exchange of information is critical in the financial reporting process. Conflicting department goals often interfere with the data collection and can create "silos."

RETAIL ACCOUNTING SYSTEMS

retail accounting system (RAS) A method for systematically gathering, analyzing, storing, and utilizing financial information and data.

A subsystem of the RIS, **retail accounting systems (RAS)** are the methods used for systematically gathering, analyzing, storing, and utilizing the financial information and data that guide firms in their financial planning. An understanding of the financial condition of the business is necessary to effectively control the overall business functions. Primary reports found in most retail accounting systems are the balance sheet, income statement, and statement of cash flows. Information from these documents aids in the analysis of ratios and asset management. Retail accounting systems are computer based, paper based, or a combination of both. Integration of the RAS with the primary RIS provides a competitive advantage when in comes to developing strategy and tactics.

THE BALANCE SHEET

balance sheet A financial statement that itemizes the retailer's assets, liabilities, and net worth as of a specific point in time.

The first step in controlling and evaluating a retailer's performance is the construction of financial statements. The first and most often discussed financial statement is the balance sheet. A **balance sheet** itemizes the retailer's assets, liabilities, and net worth at a specific point in time. Thus, a retailer can develop a balance sheet for any day of the year. Typically though, balance sheets are constructed for the end of the month, quarter, or year. The basic concept underlying the balance sheet is:

Assets = Liabilities + Net worth

assets Anything of value that a retailer owns.

current assets Cash and other items that can be converted to cash quickly.

long-term assets Property, equipment, and other fixed assets used to operate a business.

ASSETS. **Assets** are anything of value that the retailer owns. Generally assets are broken down into two distinct groups: current and long-term assets. **Current assets** are cash and other items that can be converted to cash quickly, such as inventory and accounts receivable. **Long-term assets** (also known as *fixed assets*) are property, equipment, and other assets that are used to operate the business.

Let's take a look at your personal assets. Any cash you have in the bank right now—say, $500—is a current asset. This cash is considered to be liquid because you can access it whenever you need to. Now suppose your friend Steve owes you $45 that he borrowed last week to purchase a textbook. This $45 is also a current asset and is referred to as an *account receivable*—money that is owed to you. Thus, with the inclusion of the account receivable, you have a total of $545 in current assets.

To continue, suppose your generous parents have bought you a car to use for college. The price of the car was $14,000. Since you cannot immediately access that $14,000, the car is a long-term, or noncurrent, asset. In other words, it is "fixed."

total assets Current assets plus long-term assets.

Your **total assets**, therefore, are $14,545: $545 in current assets and $14,000 in fixed assets.

liabilities Financial obligations owed by a retailer.

current liabilities Financial obligations that must be paid back within the upcoming year.

long-term liabilities Financial obligations due in more than a year's time.

total liabilities Current liabilities plus long-term liabilities.

LIABILITIES. Unfortunately, you also have financial obligations, referred to as **liabilities.** Like assets, liabilities are divided into two distinct groups: current and long-term liabilities. **Current liabilities** include any debt that must be paid back within the upcoming year. **Long-term liabilities** include debt that needs to be satisfied in more than a year's time. Added together, current and long-term liabilities equal **total liabilities.**

Suppose you borrowed $34 from Sylvia last week. She expects you to pay her back on payday (next Friday). You have incurred a short-term debt, or current liability, of $34. In addition, you recently took out a student loan for $10,000 to cover your mounting college costs. You have 25 years to repay the loan; thus, this debt is a long-term liability. Combined, these two figures amount to total liabilities of $10,034.

net worth (owner's equity) Assets minus liabilities; represents the net value of a retail business on a cost basis.

NET WORTH. Net worth is the third major component of the balance sheet. **Net worth,** often referred to as **owner's equity,** is simply assets minus liabilities. Net worth represents the net value of a retail business on a cost basis. Using the preceding example, your net worth is $4,511: your assets of $14,545 minus your liabilities of $10,034.

Figure 8.1 depicts balance sheets for D & D Bookstore, a hypothetical company.

THE INCOME STATEMENT

Essentially, an income statement has nine main categories: (1) net sales, (2) cost of goods sold (COGS), (3) gross profit, (4) operating expenses, (5) net income from operations, (6) other income (expenses), (7) net income before taxes, (8) income taxes, and (9) net income after taxes.

net sales All gross sales a retailer earns during a specified period of time, minus sales discounts given to customers to promote sales and minus returns and allowances given to customers for returned items or defective products.

NET SALES. **Net sales** represents all gross sales the retailer earns during a period of time (usually monthly, quarterly, seasonally, or yearly) minus sales discounts given to customers to promote sales and minus returns and allowances given to customers for returned items or defective products. In other words, net sales is the gross sale price of the products the retailer sold for cash, or on account, to customers during a specified period of time, subtracting out returns, discounts, and any markdowns taken during that specified period.

cost of goods sold (COGS) The amount a retailer pays for its merchandise.

COST OF GOODS SOLD. **Cost of goods sold (COGS),** or *cost of sales,* represents just what it says: the cost the retailer pays for its merchandise. This includes the actual purchase price of the goods and services plus the freight-in costs associated with getting the products physically to the retail warehouse or

D & D Bookstore
Balance Sheets
As of December 31, 2005 and 2004

	2005 Amount	2004 Amount
Assets:		
Current Assets:		
Cash	$45,320	$35,000
Accounts receivable	12,900	22,000
Inventory	197,633	100,000
Total Current Assets	$255,853	$157,000
Property, Plant, and Equipment:		
Land	$250,000	$250,000
Furniture	60,300	60,300
Shelving	51,000	51,000
Accumulated depreciation	(25,000)	(15,000)
Property, Plant, and Equipment Net	$336,300	$346,300
Total Assets	$592,153	$503,300
Liabilities:		
Current Liabilities:		
Accounts payable	$96,500	$65,000
Salaries payable	6,000	10,000
Interest payable	7,000	3,500
Payroll taxes payable	2,000	1,400
Other payables	19,450	12,200
Line of credit payable	130,275	3,000
Current portion Mortgage payable	2,500	2,500
Total Current Liabilities	$263,725	$97,600
Long-Term Liabilities:		
Mortgage payable	$197,500	$200,000
Long-term debt	100,000	100,000
Total Long-Term Liabilities	$297,500	$300,000
Total Liabilities	$561,225	$397,600
Net Worth	$30,928	$105,700
Total Liabilities and Net Worth	$592,153	$503,300

FIGURE 8.1 D & D Bookstore Balance Sheets

outlets. Purchase discounts are subtracted from the merchandise cost and freight-in costs are added to come up with the actual COGS. **Purchase discounts** are reductions in the payment amounts vendors are willing to accept to satisfy the amount due if the payments are made earlier. Purchase discounts are discussed in more detail later in this chapter.

purchase discount Reduction in the payment amount a vendor is willing to accept to satisfy the amount due if the payment is made earlier.

GROSS PROFIT. Gross profit, or *gross margin,* is the difference between the retailer's net sales and the cost of goods sold. In other words, this is the amount the retailer has left to cover expenses related to the operation of the retail business.

gross profit The difference between the retailer's net sales and the cost of goods sold.

OPERATING EXPENSES. Operating expenses are the normal costs associated with doing business, not including the cost of the merchandise for sale. They may include lease or mortgage costs, personnel costs (wages), insurance costs, and utilities expenses. Often retailers prefer to see the costs associated with sales and break up the personnel costs into selling expenses, general expenses, and administrative expenses. By doing so, the retailer gets a much better idea of where the costs of running the business actually come from.

operating expenses The normal costs associated with doing business, not including the cost of the merchandise for sale.

NET INCOME FROM OPERATIONS. Net income from operations is the gross profit minus the operating expenses; it represents the extent to which the retailer is generating profits from its major business operations.

net income from operations Gross profit minus operating expenses.

OTHER INCOME (EXPENSES). Other income (expenses) includes income and expense items such as interest income, dividend income, interest expense, and gains or losses on disposal of assets such as fixtures or a store location. These types of income and expense are not considered part of the business operations and are therefore separated from the sales and expenses directly related to operations.

other income (expenses) Income and expense items such as interest income, dividend income, interest expense, and gains or losses on disposal of assets.

NET INCOME BEFORE TAXES. Net income before taxes (NIBT) (also called *net income before income taxes*) is the difference between net income from operations and the net effect of other income (expenses).

net income before taxes (NIBT) The difference between net income from operations and the net effect of other income (expenses).

INCOME TAXES. Income taxes are federal and state taxes on the net income before taxes.

income taxes Federal and state income taxes on net income before income taxes.

NET INCOME AFTER TAXES. Net income after taxes is the difference between net income before taxes and income taxes. Figure 8.2 shows the 2005 and 2004 income statements for our hypothetical retailer, D & D Bookstore. As you can see, D & D had a very profitable year in 2004. It started out with sales of $1.5 million and subtracted the cost of the merchandise, or $1.0 million (freight costs are high for many of its products). D & D showed a gross profit of $500,000. From that $500,000, D & D subtracted the operating expenses of the business. Because D & D has a small operation, it had only $349,450 in operating expenses. After subtracting the $349,450 from the gross profit, D & D had a net income from operations of $150,550. After other

net income after taxes The difference between net income before taxes and income taxes.

D & D Bookstore Income Statements For the Years Ended December 31, 2005 and 2004	2005 Amount	2004 Amount
Net Sales	$1,250,000	$1,500,000
Cost of goods sold	950,000	1,000,000
Gross Profit	$300,000	$500,000
Operating Expenses:		
Sales commissions	$125,000	$150,000
Salaries expense	22,000	45,000
Payroll tax expense	5,350	6,750
Fringe benefits expense	10,400	13,200
Rent expense	32,000	48,000
Insurance expense	6,000	5,000
IMC expense	27,000	46,000
Maintenance expense	3,200	4,500
Utilities expense	9,200	9,000
Advertising expense	20,000	16,000
Depreciation expense	10,000	6,000
Total Operating Expenses	$270,150	$349,450
Total Operating Income	$29,850	$150,550
Other Income (Expenses):		
Interest income	$500	$1,000
Interest expense	(30,000)	(25,000)
Total Other Income (Expenses)	($29,500)	($24,000)
Net Income Before Income Taxes	$350	$126,550
Income Taxes (assume 35%)	123	44,293
Net Income After Taxes	$228	$82,258

FIGURE 8.2 D & D Bookstore Income Statements

income and expenses of $24,000 and $44,293 in income taxes, D & D was left with a net income after taxes of $82,258.

The same cannot be said about 2005. D & D had lower net sales than in 2004, and its cost of goods sold was close to the previous year's, leaving the company with a gross profit of $300,000 instead of the $500,000 in 2004. With operating expenses of $270,150, the company was left with an operating profit of only $29,850. Subtracting other income and expenses of $29,500 and income taxes of $123, D & D's net income after taxes was only $228 for the year ended December 31, 2005.

THE STATEMENT OF CASH FLOWS

statement of cash flows A financial statement showing cash receipts and cash payments during a given period.

The **statement of cash flows** is relatively new to financial statements. It wasn't until 1987 that the Financial Accounting Standards Board (FASB), the accounting regulatory body, issued its statement (Number 95), which mandated that the statement of cash flows be a required component of financial statements.[8] The statement of cash flows has three components: (1) cash flow from operating activities, (2) cash flow from investing activities, and (3) cash flow from financing activities.

cash flow from operating activities Cash received or disbursed from all of the activities involved in a company's operations.

CASH FLOW FROM OPERATING ACTIVITIES. Cash flow from operating activities includes the cash received or disbursed from all of the activities involved in the company's operations. All activities that are a component in determining net income are included in the cash flow from operating activities. Therefore, any cash receipts from sales of goods and services are considered cash inflows from operations. At the same time, any cash disbursements resulting from those transactions are included as cash outflows. Finally, interest and dividend income received and interest expenses paid are included in cash flow from operations.

The difference between cash inflows and cash outflows is considered the net cash inflow or outflow from operations. For example, a department store's sales from merchandise are cash inflows and monies owed on the merchandise, as well as amounts paid for supplies, are cash outflows. Companies prefer to have more cash inflows than outflows because cash inflows increase their profitability.

cash flow from investing activities Cash received or disbursed from extending or collecting loans and acquiring or disposing of investments or long-term assets.

CASH FLOW FROM INVESTING ACTIVITIES. Cash flow from investing activities is the cash received or disbursed from extending or collecting loans and acquiring or disposing of investments or long-term assets. For example, if a company owns the building in which it operates but rents out a portion to another business, those proceeds are cash inflows. As stated previously, interest or dividends received are not considered investing activities; rather, they are included in operating activities.

cash flow from financing activities Cash received or disbursed from activities dealing with a company's own debt and capital instruments.

CASH FLOW FROM FINANCING ACTIVITIES. Cash flow from financing activities includes activities that deal with the company's own debt and capital instruments. In other words, cash receipts from a company issuing its own debt or capital instruments are included as financing activities. Cash disbursements would include the reacquisition of a company's stock or repayment of its own bonds or debt instruments. In addition, dividends paid to stockholders are included as a financing activity cash disbursement.

The statement of cash flows is particularly important to the retailer because it identifies which activities are generating cash and which are using cash. Some rules of thumb apply in evaluating a statement of cash flows. For example, there should be at least enough positive cash flow from operations to cover cash outflows from investing and financial activities. There should be cash outflows from investing activities for property, plant, and equipment and from financing activities for repayment of debt and dividend disbursements to stockholders. These are only guidelines and could differ depending on the retailer's organizational objectives. For example, if a retailer is utilizing a high-growth strategy, the net cash outflows may not be sufficient to finance the investing activities necessary for property, plant, and equipment. Therefore, cash inflows will be required from financing activities to cover the difference in cost.

Figure 8.3 shows the statement of cash flows for D & D Bookstore for the years ended December 31, 2004 and 2005.

NOTES TO THE FINANCIAL STATEMENTS

notes to the financial statements The section that provides supplemental information about the balance sheet, income statement, and statement of cash flows.

The **notes to the financial statements** provide supplemental information about the financial statements. If there are any concerns about the financial statements, they will be found in these notes. The main purpose of the notes to the financial statements is to provide readers with the information necessary to fully understand and interpret the financial statements. Reviewing financial statements without also reviewing the notes could lead to misinterpretations.

FINANCIAL STATEMENT ANALYSIS

Financial statements report the historical financial results for a company. The objective of financial statement analysis is to use historical information and data to predict the company's future. Investors and prospective employees can also use these statements to evaluate the firm's financial health. In addition, financial statement analysis can be used for asset and liability management.

Types of financial statement analysis include (1) horizontal analysis, (2) vertical analysis, and (3) ratio analysis. No matter which type of analysis is performed, no single measure means much when analyzed alone. Each measure must be compared to some other measure. For example, company measures can be compared to prior years' company results, industry averages, or industry leaders' measurements. To illustrate financial statement analysis, we will use a set of financial statements for D & D Bookstore.

horizontal analysis An analysis that uses comparative financial statements for two consecutive years.

comparative financial statement A financial statement that reflects more than one year of financial information, to show changes over time. The information is typically presented in a side-by-side columnar format.

HORIZONTAL ANALYSIS. Horizontal analysis uses **comparative financial statements** for two consecutive years, allowing managers to compare the changes in dollar amounts and percentages in each item measured over the two-year period. The objective of horizontal analysis is to determine the year-to-year change in each financial statement item, why it changed, and whether the change is favorable or unfavorable. Figures 8.4 and 8.5 depict comparative balance sheets and income statements, respectively, for D & D Bookstore for the years ended December 31, 2004 and 2005.

vertical analysis An analysis that concentrates on the relationships among items within the same set of financial statements.

VERTICAL ANALYSIS. Vertical analysis concentrates on the relationships among items within the same set of financial statements. Often managers evaluate the dollar relationships; however, in many cases the percentage relationships are more revealing. On the balance sheet, individual dollar amounts are often converted to percentages of total asset dollars. On the income statement, individual dollar amounts are often converted to a percent-

D & D Bookstore
Statement of Cash Flows
For the Years Ended December 31, 2005 and 2004

	2005	2004
Cash Flow from Operating Activities:		
Cash Receipts:		
Cash receipts from customers	$1,259,100	$1,550,000
Cash receipts from interest income	500	1,000
Total Cash Inflows (Outflows) from Operating Activities	$1,259,600	$1,551,000
Cash Payments:		
To supplies of merchandise	$1,016,133	$956,000
To employees	151,000	185,000
For payroll taxes	4,750	7,000
For fringe benefits	10,400	13,600
For rent	29,334	45,333
For insurance	6,000	13,600
For IMC	21,532	46,000
For maintenance	3,200	4,500
For utilities	9,200	85,000
For interest	26,500	15,000
For income taxes	123	51,993
For advertising	20,883	15,000
Total Cash Payments	$1,299,055	$1,438,026
Net Cash Inflows (Outflows) from Operating Activities	(39,455)	112,974
Cash Flow from Investing Activities:		
Purchase of furniture and shelving	0	(26,700)
Total Cash Inflows (Outflows) from Investing Activities	0	(26,700)
Cash Flow from Financing Activities:		
Proceeds from increase in long-term debt		19,000
Payments to owners	(75,000)	(142,000)
Contributions by new owners	0	20,000
Decrease in long-term debt	(2,500)	0
Increase in line of credit	127,275	0
Total Cash Inflows (Outflows) from Financial Activities	49,775	(103,000)
Net Increase (Decrease) in Cash	10,320	(16,726)
Balance in Cash Beginning of the Period	35,000	51,726
Balance in Cash End of Period	$45,320	$35,000

FIGURE 8.3 D & D Bookstore Statement of Cash Flows

D & D Bookstore
Comparative-Size Balance Sheet
As of December 31, 2005 and 2004

	2005 Amount	2004 Amount	Increase or (Decrease) Amount	Percent
Assests:				
Current Assests:				
Cash	$45,320	$35,000	$10,320	29.49
Accounts receivable	12,900	22,000	(9,100)	(41.36)
Inventory	197,633	100,000	97,633	97.63
Total Current Assets	$255,853	$157,000	$98,853	62.96
Property, Plant, and Equipment:				
Land	$250,000	$250,000	$0	0.00
Furniture	60,300	60,300	0	0.00
Shelving	51,000	51,000	0	0.00
Accumulated depreciation	(25,000)	(15,000)	(10,000)	66.67
Property, Plant, and Equipment Net	$336,300	$346,300	($10,000)	(2.89)
Total Assests	$592,153	$503,300	$88,853	17.65
Liabilites:				
Current Liabilities:				
Accounts payable	$96,500	$65,000	$31,500	48.46
Salaries payable	6,000	10,000	(4,000)	(40.00)
Interest payable	7,000	3,500	3,500	100.00
Payroll taxes payable	2,000	1,400	600	42.86
Other payables	19,450	12,200	7,250	59.43
Line of credit payable	130,275	3,000	127,275	4242.50
Current portion Mortgage payable	2,500	2,500	0	0.00
Total Current Liabilites	$263,725	$97,600	$166,125	170.21
Long-Term Liabilities:				
Mortgage payable	$197,500	$200,000	($2,500)	(1.25)
Long-term debt	100,000	100,000	0	0.00
Total Long-Term Liabilites	$297,500	$300,000	($2,500)	(0.83)
Total Liabilites	$561,225	$397,600	$163,625	41.15
Net Worth	$30,928	$105,700	($74,773)	(70.74)
Total Liabilites and Net Worth	$592,153	$503,300	$88,853	17.65

FIGURE 8.4 D & D Bookstore Comparative Balance Sheets

ratio analysis The computation of several financial ratios derived from the financial statements.

D & D Bookstore Comparative-Size Income Statement For the Years Ended December 31, 2005 and 2004				
	2005	2004	Increase or (Decrease)	
	Amount	Amount	Amount	Percent
Net Sales	$1,250,000	$1,500,000	($250,000)	(16.67)
Cost of goods sold	950,000	1,000,000	(50,000)	(5.00)
Gross Profit	300,000	$500,000	($200,000)	(40.00)
Operating Expenses:				
Sales commissions	$125,000	$150,000	($25,000)	(16.67)
Salaries expense	22,000	45,000	(23,000)	(51.11)
Payroll tax expense	5,350	6,750	(1,400)	(20.74)
Fringe benefits expense	10,400	13,200	(2,800)	(21.21)
Rent expense	32,000	48,000	(16,000)	(33.33)
Insurance expense	6,000	5,000	1,000	20.00
IMC expense	27,000	46,000	(19,000)	(41.30)
Maintanence expense	3,200	4,500	(1,300)	(28.89)
Utilities expense	9,200	9,000	200	2.22
Advertising expense	20,000	16,000	4,000	25.00
Depreciation expense	10,000	6,000	4,000	66.67
Total Operating Expenses	270,150	349,450	(79,300)	(22.67)
Total Operating Income	$29,850	$150,550	($120,700)	(80.17)
Other Income (Expenses):				
Interest income	$500	$1,000	($500)	(50.00)
Interest expense	(30,000)	(25,000)	($5,000)	20.00
Total Other Income (Expenses)	($29,500)	($24,000)	($5,500)	22.92
Net Income Before Income Taxes	$350	$126,550	($126,200)	(99.72)
Income Taxes (assume 35%)	123	44,293	(44,170)	(99.72)
Net Income After Taxes	$228	$82,258	($82,030)	(99.72)

FIGURE 8.5 D & D Bookstore Comparative Income Statements

common size financial statement A financial statement in which common size ratios are used to compare financial statements of different size companies. For balance sheet items, ratios are typically expressed as a percentage of total assets. For income statement items, ratios are expressed as a percentage of total revenue.

age of sales. These converted statements are called **common size financial statements.** Vertical analysis allows managers to identify the magnitude of different items on the balance sheet and income statement. Figures 8.6 and 8.7 present common size financial statements (balance sheets and income statements) for D & D Bookstore.

RATIO ANALYSIS. Ratio analysis involves the computation of one or more financial ratios that are derived from the financial statements. Ratio analysis can provide extensive insights into the company's financial position

D & D Bookstore
Common-Size Balance Sheet
As of December 31, 2005 and 2004

	2005		2004	
	Amount	**Percent**	**Amount**	**Percent**
Assests:				
Current Assets:				
Cash	$45,320	7.65	$35,000	6.95
Accounts receivable	12,900	2.18	22,000	4.37
Inventory	197,633	33.38	100,000	19.87
Total Current Assests	$255,853	43.21	$157,000	31.19
Property, Plant, and Equipment:				
Land	$250,000	42.22	$250,000	49.67
Furniture	60,300	10.18	60,300	11.98
Shelving	51,000	8.61	51,000	10.13
Accumulated depreciation	(25,000)	(4.22)	(15,000)	(2.98)
Property, Plant, and Equipment Net	$336,300	56.79	$346,300	68.81
Total Assests	$592,153	100.00	$503,300	100.00
Liabilities:				
Current Liabilities:				
Accounts payable	$96,500	16.30	$65,000	12.91
Salaries payable	6,000	1.01	10,000	1.99
Interest payable	7,000	1.18	3,500	0.70
Payroll taxes payable	2,000	0.34	1,400	0.28
Other payables	19,450	3.28	12,200	2.42
Line of credit payable	130,275	22.00	3,000	0.60
Current portion Mortgage payable	2,500	0.42	2,500	0.50
Total Current Liabilites	$263,725	44.54	$97,600	19.39
Long-Term Liabilities:				
Mortgage payable	$197,500	33.35	$200,000	39.74
Long-term debt	100,000	16.89	100,000	19.87
Total Long-Term Liabilites	$297,500	50.24	$300,000	59.61
Total Liabilites	$561,225	94.78	$397,600	79.00
Net Worth	$30,928	5.22	$105,700	21.00
Total Liabilites and Net Worth	$592,153	100.00	$503,300	100.00

FIGURE 8.6 D & D Bookstore Common Size Balance Sheets

D & D Bookstore
Common-Size Income Statement
For the Years Ended December 31, 2005 and 2004

	2005		2004	
	Amount	**Percent of Sales**	**Amount**	**Percent of Sales**
Net Sales	$1,250,000	100.00	$1,500,000	100.00
Cost of goods sold	950,000	76.00	1,000,000	66.67
Gross Profit	$300,000	24.00	$500,000	33.33
Operating Expenses:				
Sales commissions	$125,000	10.00	$150,000	10.00
Salaries expenses	22,000	1.76	45,000	3.00
Payroll tax expense	5,350	0.43	6,750	0.45
Fringe benefits expense	10,400	0.83	13,200	0.88
Rent expense	32,000	2.56	48,000	3.20
Insurance expense	6,000	0.48	5,000	0.33
IMC expense	27,000	2.16	46,000	3.07
Maintenance expense	3,200	0.26	4,500	0.30
Utilities expense	9,200	0.74	9,000	0.60
Advertising expense	20,000	1.60	16,000	1.07
Depreciation expense	10,000	0.80	6,000	0.40
Total Operating Expenses	$270,150	21.61	$349,450	23.30
Total Operating Income	$29,850	2.39	$150,550	10.04
Other Income (Expenses):				
Interest income	$500	0.04	$1,000	0.07
Interest expense	(30,000)	(2.40)	(25,000)	(1.67)
Total Other Income (Expenses)	($29,500)	(2.36)	($24,000)	(1.60)
Net Income Before Income Taxes	$350	0.03	$126,550	8.44
Income Taxes (assume 35%)	123	0.01	44,293	2.95
Net Income After Taxes	$228	0.02	$82,258	5.48

FIGURE 8.7 D & D Bookstore Common Size Income Statements

that would not be detected in any other manner. To illustrate ratio analysis, we will use Figures 8.3 and 8.4 for the calculations. At the same time, we will use Perfect Bookstore, a major competitor of D & D, to generate competitive ratios for comparative purposes.

liquidity ratios Ratios that reflect management's control of current assets and current liabilities.

Liquidity Ratios The first group of ratios, called **liquidity ratios,** reflect management's control of current assets and current liabilities. Generally, current assets are considered to be those assets that are expected to turn into cash within the year. Current liabilities can be defined as debts that are to be paid back within the year.

current ratio Current assets divided by current liabilities.

Current Ratio The first liquidity ratio is the **current ratio,** the ratio of current assets to current liabilities. D & D Bookstore's current ratios for 2005 and 2004 are computed as follows:

2005

Current ratio = $255,853/$263,725 = 0.97 to 1

2004

Current ratio = $157,000/$97,600 = 1.61 to 1

As we can see, D & D's current ratio declined over the one-year period. If this trend continues, D & D may have trouble paying current liabilities as they come due.

A common rule of thumb is that the current ratio should be 2 to 1, meaning a company should have twice as many current assets as it does current liabilities. This is a general guideline; in reality, appropriate current ratios can vary widely among industries and companies.

The current ratio has a limitation. A company whose current assets consist mainly of cash and accounts receivable might be considered much more liquid than a company with small amounts of cash and accounts receivable and a large amount of inventory. Of all current assets, inventory normally takes the longest to convert into cash. Also, market changes can lower inventory value in unforeseen ways.

acid test ratio (quick ratio) Quick assets divided by current liabilities.

Acid Test Ratio The second liquidity ratio is the **acid test ratio,** or **quick ratio.** The acid test ratio is a better indicator of a retailer's ability to meet short-term obligations as they come due. Due to sales and markdowns, inventories sometimes are not worth what they are listed for on the balance sheet. Therefore, many analysts use the acid test ratio as an indication of a company's ability to meet short-term needs.

The acid test ratio is calculated as follows:

Acid test ratio = Quick assets/Current liabilities

or

Acid test ratio = (Current assets − Inventory)/Current liabilities

Quick assets include cash, accounts receivable, and current notes receivable. These assets can usually be converted quickly into cash. Inventory and prepaid expenses are not included because they require a longer time to convert into cash.

The computations of D & D Bookstore's acid test ratios for 2005 and 2004 are as follows:

2005

Acid test ratio = $58,220/$263,725 = 0.22 to 1

2004

Acid test ratio = $57,000/$97,600 = 0.58 to 1

By using the acid test ratio instead of the current ratio, D & D shows a considerable decline in its ability to meet current obligations as they become due. A general rule of thumb for this ratio is 1 to 1. Managers may need to consider cash-generating tactics such as sales and/or loans.

activity ratios Ratios used to determine how well a firm manages current assets, pays off current liabilities, and uses assets to generate sales.

accounts receivable (A/R) turnover in days A measurement of the number of days, on average, it takes to convert accounts receivable into cash.

Activity Ratios A second set of ratios, **activity ratios,** are used in cash management.

Accounts Receivable (A/R) Turnover in Days The first activity ratio, **accounts receivable (A/R) turnover in days,** measures the number of days, on average, it takes for accounts receivable to turn into cash. In retailing, A/R turnover should be calculated using two different methods. The first is to determine the number of days required, on average, for credit sales to turn into cash. Using this method, A/R turnover in days is calculated as follows:

$$\text{Accounts receivable turnover in days} = \frac{365}{\text{Sales on account/Average accounts receivable balance}}$$

To compute D & D's A/R turnover in days for 2005 and 2004, we must include certain assumptions not available in Figures 8.3 and 8.4. First, credit sales are $100,000 in 2005 and $80,000 in 2004. Second, 2004's beginning accounts receivable equals $15,000. Based on these assumptions, the calculations for D & D's A/R turnover in days for 2005 and 2004 are as follows:

2005

$$\text{A/R turnover in days} = \frac{365}{\$100{,}000/[(\$22{,}000 + \$12{,}900)/2]} = 64 \text{ days}$$

2004

$$\text{A/R turnover in days} = \frac{365}{\$80{,}000/[(\$15{,}000 + \$22{,}000)/2]} = 84 \text{ days}$$

Based on these calculations, D & D appears to have reduced the number of days needed for its credit sales to turn into cash by 20 days. This calculation is important for two reasons. First, the longer accounts receivable are outstanding, the greater the chance that they may not be collected. Second, the faster the cash is collected, the more cash is available to pay current liabilities.

The second method of calculating A/R turnover in days is used to help determine the overall cash collection cycle from the time inventory is received until it is converted into cash (the cash conversion cycle). This cycle is an important part of cash management. The major difference in the two approaches is that instead of using credit sales in the denominator, total sales are used. This difference is important for retailers if the vast majority of their sales are cash. In other words, the conversion of sales into cash is immediate. Following are examples of the ratio using this method:

2005

A/R turnover in days =

$$\frac{365}{\$1{,}250{,}000/[(\$22{,}000 + \$12{,}900)/2]} = 5.1 \text{ days}$$

2004

A/R turnover in days =

$$\frac{365}{\$1{,}500{,}000/[(\$15{,}000 + \$22{,}000)/2]} = 4.5 \text{ days}$$

By including cash and credit sales, these ratios indicate that, on average, it took 5.1 days to convert sales into cash in 2005 and 4.5 days in 2004. These calculations, added to inventory turnover in days, are an estimate of the total cash cycle.

inventory (I/V) turnover in days A measurement of the number of days, on average, from the time a retailer receives inventory to the time the inventory is sold to the customer.

Inventory (I/V) Turnover in Days The second activity ratio, **inventory (I/V) turnover in days,** measures the amount of days, on average, from the time the retailer receives inventory until the time the inventory is sold to the customer. Inventory turnover in days is computed as follows:

Inventory turnover in days =

$$\frac{365}{\text{Cost of goods sold/Average inventory balance}}$$

To determine D & D's I/V turnover in days, the only assumption is that $110,000 is the beginning inventory for 2004. By adding this assumption, we can calculate the I/V turnover in days as follows:

2005

I/V turnover in days =

$$\frac{365}{\$950{,}000/[(\$100{,}000 + \$197{,}633)/2]} = 57.2 \text{ days}$$

2004

I/V turnover in days =

$$\frac{365}{\$1{,}000{,}000/[(\$110{,}000 + \$100{,}000)/2]} = 38.3 \text{ days}$$

A comparison of these ratios for 2005 and 2004 indicates that D & D's conversion of inventory into sales, on average, has increased significantly, which further restricts the availability of cash for paying obligations as they become due. The cash cycle is the total number of days from the time a company receives goods until the goods are converted into cash. In D & D's case, the total cash cycle is A/R turnover in days of 5.1 plus I/V turnover in days of 57.2, or 62.3 days for 2005. In 2004, the total cash cycle is 4.5 days plus 38.3 days, equaling 42.8 days.

efficiency ratios Ratios that provide evidence of how effectively management is running the business.

Efficiency Ratios Efficiency ratios comprise the third set of ratios. **Efficiency ratios** provide evidence of how effectively management is running the retail business.

return-on-assets ratio Net income plus interest income, net of its tax effect, divided by average total assets.

Return-on-Assets Ratio The first efficiency ratio is the **return-on-assets ratio.** The higher the return on assets ratio, the better management appears to be using the retailer's assets efficiently to generate net income. Return on assets can be calculated as follows:

$$\text{Return on assets} = \frac{(\text{Net income} + \text{Interest income}),\ \text{net of tax effect}}{\text{Average total assets}}$$

Interest expense net of tax effect is added because management of assets should be separated from the means by which those assets are financed, which is a financial management decision. If retail financial managers decide to finance some assets by incurring debt rather than contributing capital, interest income will be incurred, which in turn will reduce net income. The interest expense is added back to net income net of tax effect because the total interest expense reduces net income before taxes, which is used to calculate income taxes. Thus, if total interest expense were subtracted from net income before taxes, income taxes would be higher and net income after taxes would not increase by the total of the interest expense.

To determine D & D's return on assets, the only assumption needed is that the beginning total assets for 2004 are $387,000:

2005

$$\text{Return on assets} = \frac{(\$228 + \$30{,}000) \times (1 - 0.35)}{(\$503{,}300 + \$592{,}153)/2} = 3.60\%$$

2004

$$\text{Return on assets} = \frac{(\$82{,}258 + \$25{,}000) \times (1 - 0.35)}{(\$387{,}000 + \$503{,}300)/2} = 22.13\%$$

return-on-equity ratio Net income available to owners divided by average owner's equity (net worth).

Return-on-Equity Ratio The second efficiency ratio is the **return-on-equity ratio.** This ratio views the efficiency of management from the common stockholder's position. The ratio indicates how well management is using owner's equity to generate net income that could be available to owners. It is calculated as follows:

Return on equity = Net income available to owners/ Average owner's equity (net worth)

To determine D & D's return on equity, the only data not available in the financial statements is the beginning net worth for 2004, which we will assume to be $120,000:

2005

Return on equity = $228/[($105,700 + $30,928)/2] = 0.33%

2004

Return on equity = $82,259/[($105,700 + $120,000)/2] = 72.89%

return-on-sales ratio Net income divided by sales.

Return-on-Sales Ratio The third efficiency ratio is the **return-on-sales ratio.** This ratio indicates how well the retailer is converting sales dollars into net income. It is computed as follows:

Return on sales = Net income/Sales

D & D's return on sales is calculated as follows:

2005

Return on sales = $228/$1,250,000 = 0.02%

2004

Return on sales = $82,258/$1,500,000 = 5.48%

debt-to-equity ratio Total liabilities divided by total owner's equity.

Debt-to-Equity Ratio The final efficiency ratio, the **debt-to-equity ratio,** is a capitalization ratio because it indicates whether financial managers have financed the retailer's assets with debt or with owner's net worth. The debt-to-equity ratio is calculated as follows:

Debt-to-equity ratio = Total liabilities/Total owner's equity (net worth)

The debt-to-equity ratio for D & D is computed as follows:

2005

Debt to equity = $561,225/$30,928 = 18.15 to 1

2004

Debt to equity = $397,600/$105,700 = 3.76 to 1

The 2005 debt-to-equity ratio is probably the most troublesome of all the ratios for D & D. As a rule of thumb, the debt-to-equity ratio should be around 1 to 1. At 18.15 to 1.00, D & D could shortly find itself in a situation where it will be unable to obtain additional financing from lenders or investors. The ratio of asset financing using debt, which must be paid when due, is so high that the risk of default on those liabilities is also extremely high. Financing using owner's equity carries less risk because companies are not required to repay owners' contributions or financing charges associated with those contributions.

TABLE 8.1

RATIO EQUATIONS

	LIQUIDITY RATIOS
Current ratio	Current assets/Current liabilities
Acid test (quick) ratio	Quick assets/Current liabilities *or* (Current assets − Inventory)/Current liabilities
	ACTIVITY RATIOS
Accounts receivable turnover in days	365/(Sales on account/Average accounts receivable balance) *or* 365/(Total sales/Average accounts receivable balance)
Inventory turnover in days	365/(Cost of goods sold/Average inventory balance)
	EFFICIENCY RATIOS
Return-on-assets ratio	Return on assets = [(Net income + Interest income), net of its tax effect]/Average total assets
Return-on-equity ratio	Return on equity = Net income available to owners/ Average owner's equity (net worth)
Return-on-sales ratio	Return on sales = Net income/Sales
Debt-to-equity ratio (net worth)	Debt to equity = Total liabilities/ Total owner's equity (net worth)

Table 8.1 summarizes all the ratios discussed in this section.

ASSET MANAGEMENT: INVENTORY. To ensure that the retail business is using its assets to their fullest potential and to implement control systems for revenues generated, the retailer must engage in asset management. A prime example of asset management is management of inventory. Inventory is usually one of the retailer's most important assets, because it typically represents the largest dollar value on the balance sheet.

To illustrate the importance of inventory management, consider apparel retailers. Because of such factors as changing fashion trends and seasonality, apparel retailers need to be concerned about their inventory becoming obsolete. A second concern is **carrying costs,** the costs of storing and maintaining inventory. Carrying costs can include the rent or depreciation on the warehouse, warehouse utilities, and insurance, as well as personnel costs for safeguarding the inventory. Some estimates of the carrying costs of inventory are as high as 20 to 30 percent of the cost of the average inventory on hand. The following example illustrates the impact of carrying costs and obsolescence of inventory.

carrying costs The costs of storing and maintaining inventory.

A clothing retailer has a winter dress that cost $70 and has a list price of $120. The retailer is unable to sell the dress, so it decides to warehouse the product until next year. The following year, the dress has gone out of style and the retailer is again unable to sell it. This time the retailer decides to dispose of the dress. The impact on the retailer is as follows:

Cost of dress	$70.00
Carrying cost of dress for one year (assume 30%)	21.00
Total loss	($91.00)

If the retailer had sold the dress in the first year at a 30 percent discount off the list price of $120, the result would have been as follows:

Sales price of dress	$84.00
Cost of dress	70.00
Total gross profit	$14.00

FINANCIAL STATEMENT FRAUD

Clearly, many formulas are available for organizing and maintaining a retailer's financial environment. Though laws bind retailers to maintain lawful and truthful records, some retailers choose to ignore them. The unfortunate result is financial statement fraud. Determining the impact of financial statement fraud is difficult because many fraudulent practices go undetected. Most companies, when given the choice, will hide incidences of fraud by quietly dismissing those involved.[9] According to Joseph T. Wells, CPA and CFE, five types of financial statement fraud schemes exist:[10]

1. *Fictitious revenues.* This is the most common way to make up sales figures that place the company in a positive light.
2. *Fraudulent asset valuations.* The most frequent instances of fraudulent asset violation occur in inventory valuations. Companies inflate the value of inventory, double-count inventory, or create inventory on the books that does not exist in reality.
3. *Timing differences.* Companies may overstate assets and income by taking advantage of the accounting cutoff period to boost sales and/or reduce liabilities and expenses.
4. *Concealed liabilities and expenses.* To pull off this type of fraud, companies hide their bills or other paperwork that shows liabilities. The rationale for this fraud is: If the accountants don't see the liabilities, they don't exist.
5. *Improper disclosures.* Generally accepted accounting principles (GAAP) require companies to disclose all changes in accounting procedures in the financial statements or accompanying footnotes. Businesses commit fraud when they knowingly omit information that would affect the analysis of financial reports.

The lesson to be learned from the fall of Arthur Andersen, one of the world's largest financial auditing firms, is that unethical business practices, no matter how small, can have a devastating effect on a business.

GLOBAL RETAILING

International Accounting Standards

One roadblock to conducting business in foreign countries is the differences in financial standards. Companies in the European Union (EU) are considering the adoption of international accounting standards (IAS). The adoption of IAS would make expansion to European markets more attractive for U.S. retailers. Without IAS, it is difficult for U.S. companies to compare U.S. accounting standards to the various European accounting standards. For example, bribes are expected (and deductible) expenses in some countries, but not in the United States. The adoption of standards will also make accounting practices easier for investors to understand.

European companies have until 2005 to adopt IAS. This process is not without challenges. One problem is that only some countries, such as Austria, Belgium, and Germany, permit companies to file IAS financial statements in lieu of the individual countries' accounting standards. In other European countries, IAS is allowed only as a supplement to the local reporting standards. Fortunately, uniformity will likely be reached by the EU's deadline of 2005.

Many accounting firms believe it is a good idea for the United States to follow the EU's lead and adopt global accounting standards. After the accounting scandals that rocked the U.S. economy in the early 2000s, international standards would help restore investor confidence.

Sources: Suzanne Kapner, "S.E.C. Chief Promises to Cooperate with Europe," *New York Times*, October 11, 2002 (East Coast edition); "EU Agrees to Adoption of IAS by 2005," *Accountancy* (London), July 2002; "Global Rules May Draw U.S. Capital: Local Accounting Standards Hinder Early IAS Adoption in Europe," *Investor Relations Business*, July 1, 2002, retrieved July 2003 from Proquest.

BUDGETING FOR MERCHANDISE AND FORECASTING

Armed with an understanding of these accounting systems, as well as legal and ethical issues, the retailer is prepared for the ambitious task of merchandise allocation. This section discusses the various methods used in budgeting for merchandise and forecasting the right amounts to purchase. The process of visual merchandising is one of integrated marketing communication and is covered more fully in Chapter 12.

merchandise Products or services a retailer currently offers, or plans to offer, for sale.

commercial merchandise Articles for sale, samples used for soliciting orders, or goods that are not considered personal effects.

merchandising Activities involved in organizing the display of products and services.

Merchandise consists of the products or services the retailer currently offers, or plans to offer, for sale to customers. The U.S. Customs Service defines **commercial merchandise** as "articles for sale, samples used for soliciting orders, or goods that are not considered personal effects."[11] **Merchandising** refers to activities involved in organizing the display of products or services.[12] In a buying sense, *merchandising* refers to the process of buying and selling goods and services to generate profits from the consumer and business markets. To plan for current and future products and services, the retailer needs a good understanding of the costs involved in merchandising and an idea of what consumers will want in the future. These requirements are key to establishing effective merchandise budgets.

To effectively utilize the budgeting process, the retailer needs a fairly comprehensive financial merchandise plan that includes a section on performance objectives for finance personnel. In addition, the retailer needs to know which products are to be purchased and in what quantities (forecasting). Many retailers establish plans that allow them to see both the physical product purchases and the dollars spent on those purchases. Although these concepts are covered briefly in the next chapter, the data generated at this point can ease the process of merchandise buying. Inventory valuation, discussed in the next section, should be integrated into the merchandise budgeting process.

BUDGETS. Budgets can be prepared for any length of time; the standard is yearly. Many retailers, however, generate budgets on a monthly, quarterly, seasonal, or every-four-week basis. Some retailers prepare budgets on a rolling basis, meaning that if a retailer is budgeting on a four-week basis, another week is added to the budget as one week of the budget period expires. In this way, the budget always includes four weeks.

Although not common, budgets can be prepared for four-month and six-month periods. The time period is left to the discretion of the retailer and the company's financial analysts. Retailers often have to purchase inventory six to twelve months in advance, so an inventory plan may be completed well in advance of receipt and stocking of the inventory merchandise.

The beginning point for establishing a budget is to set responsibility: Who, specifically, will be responsible for the process? Many retailers use budgeting committees or ask for input from several departments. Some retailers use a **bottom-up approach** to budgeting. In this method, each retail department supplies data for the budget; these budgets are then scrutinized and passed on to the next level, until the budget finally goes to the individual who is primarily responsible for the budgeting process. Other firms elect a more **top-down approach,** wherein upper management personnel prepare a budget and pass it down to their various departments. The departments are then instructed to try to "stay within budget" when making merchandise-buying decisions. It is possible to combine the bottom-up and top-down approaches to ensure adequate input from the retailer's employees, yet leaving the final decision making to the financial merchandise expert.

bottom-up approach A method of budgeting in which each retail department supplies data. The budgets are passed up to the next levels of management until all budgets reach an individual who is responsible for the budgeting process.

top-down approach A method of budgeting in which members of upper management prepare budgets and pass them down to departments to follow.

The retailer needs to determine a timeline for putting the budget into effect. Unfortunately, many retailers must order merchandise three to six months, or even a year, before the goods are received and ready for sale. Therefore, a six-month or one-year budget may be necessary. Even if the budget is for six months or a year, the retailer may want to break it into monthly or even weekly components due to the constantly changing retail environment. In this way, the accuracy of the budget can be determined by comparing the weekly or monthly budgeted amounts to the actual amounts. This approach allows the retailer to either change the product mix, purchase more products that are moving quickly, drop products that are not moving, reduce the price of slow-moving merchandise, or increase the price of fast-selling merchandise, to name but a few strategies. Whatever the reaction to the budget, developing a budget gives the retailer a method of control and evaluation on an ongoing basis. Therefore, a key to effective budgeting is flexibility.

Numerous methods have been developed for merchandise budgeting. Most of the methods have common inputs, or variables, that are essential to the retailer and financial planner. The following elements are generally included in the budgeting process:

- Planned monthly sales
- Planned beginning-of-month (BOM) stock
- Monthly retail reductions
- Planned end-of-month (EOM) stock
- Planned purchases for the month at retail price
- Planned purchases for the month at cost
- Initial markup for the month
- Planned gross margin for the month

To develop a budget, the retailer must forecast planned sales. Sales should be estimated for the entire budget period, but also on a weekly or monthly basis. There are numerous methods for inventory forecasting. The easiest is to look at the past year's performance. Another method is to examine the average of the last two years, the last five years, and so on. This is a good method as long as adjustments are made for changes in the environment that may affect the purchases and forecasts, such as inflation, marketing changes, and the economy.

A forecast should include as many external variables as possible. These variables may include changes in the population mix for a particular retail market, changes in the economy of that market, and changes in any of the environments identified in the situational analysis. Larger firms use computer models (programs) that combine environmental inputs with past sales data. Small firms use a more informal approach, but still take new industries, population changes, and similar factors into account when deciding how much to purchase.

The next step is to assess planned beginning- and end-of-month stock. Because of changes in demand for products, retailers generally carry additional supplies of products called **safety stock.** In retailing it is generally better to carry an additional, "small" amount of merchandise to keep from experiencing a stockout situation, in which the retailer runs out of products for which demand still exists. For example, Apple Computer builds in safety stock when forecasting inventory levels.[13]

safety stock Extra merchandise carried to keep a retailer from running out of a product.

It is important to reassess optimal stock levels on a frequent basis. Calculating safety stock once a year instead of several times a year is a common mistake. More frequent calculations help maintain more efficient stock levels.[14]

An excellent method of determining beginning-of-month (BOM) and end-of-month (EOM) stock balances is to calculate a stock-to-sales ratio. A **stock-to-sales ratio** allows a comparison of stock levels to levels of sales. In other words, the ratio indicates how much stock is needed during a given sales period—say, one month—to prevent a stock shortage. This ratio supports the retailer's forecast. A good way to assess BOM and EOM inventory levels is

stock-to-sales ratio A measurement that compares a retailer's stock levels to levels of sales.

TABLE 8.2

FINANCIAL MERCHANDISE BUDGETING AND FORECASTING

SELECTED FORMULAS ON A MONTHLY BUDGETING BASIS
Planned monthly sales = Planned sales percentage for the month × Planned sales for the month
BOM stock = Planned monthly sales × Planned BOM stock-to-sales ratio
Planned retail reductions = Planned monthly sales × Planned retail reductions in percentages
EOM stock = BOM stock (for the upcoming month)
Planned purchases (at retail) = Planned monthly sales + Planned reductions + Planned EOM stock − Planned BOM stock
Planned purchases (at cost) = Planned purchases at retail × (100% − Initial markup percentage estimates)
Planned initial markup = Planned monthly purchases × Planned markup percentage
Gross margin = Initial markup − Planned reductions

through the use of point-of-sale (POS) databases. In addition, training and practice helps in the execution of this task.

Recall that carrying inventory costs the retailer in two ways. First, the inventory takes up valuable selling space and capital (carrying cost of inventory). Second, slow-moving or nonselling merchandise occupies space that could be given to more current or faster-moving products. Walgreens is an example of a company that used technology to decrease inventory costs. The drugstore chain improved its strategic inventory management system and thereby cut safety stock and cycle times in its warehouses and stores from 53 days in 2002 to 44 days in 2003. As a result, inventory carrying costs were reduced by 1.5 billion over three years (2003–2006).[15]

The retailer needs to plan for any retail reductions that may occur during the budget period. As stated earlier, retail reductions are any stock shortages, markdowns, or employee discounts that accrued during the budget forecast period. Next, purchases must be planned at the selling price and at cost amounts. Finally, the gross margin needs to be added, allowing the retailer to generate profits. Table 8.2 shows some formulas the retailer can use in determining the merchandise budget.

To acquire the data necessary to create a budget, the retailer needs to understand the system of inventory valuation used by the company's accountants. The next section takes a close look at methods used to determine inventory value and the advantages and disadvantages of each of the methods.

INVENTORY VALUATION

Retailers use two methods to place a value on their merchandise: inventory valuation based on merchandise costs (the cost method) or inventory valuation based on the merchandise's retail price (the retail method). This section looks at each method in detail.

THE COST METHOD OF INVENTORY VALUATION

Although most large retailers have moved toward the retail method of inventory valuation because of advances in technology, especially off-the-shelf POS systems, many smaller retailers still use the *cost method of inventory valuation.* This method consists of recording the value of the merchandise at cost and adding in the cost of shipping (in-bound freight). The retailer must value each item in the inventory as it is purchased, when it is sold, and whenever the retailer undertakes a physical inventory.

A key to successful cost accounting is to assign a code to each product or product line. The easiest and most common coding method is simply to turn the letters of the alphabet into numbers so that the numbers can be entered into the RIS and accessed when needed. Because the letters are arbitrary, it does not matter which letters are used, as long as there are ten letters representing numbers 0 through 10. For example, if letters A through J are used, A becomes 1, B becomes 2, C becomes 3, and so forth, until J becomes 10. Thus, a product coded DADE would have an associated cost of $41.45. Many firms use ten-letter words such as *Charleston* for coding prices, because the ABC code may be too easy for customers to decipher.

A cost accounting system of valuation works well with both physical and book inventories. Slightly different methods of cost accounting are used, such

Blunders or Best Practices?

Playing with the Books: An Unwise Strategy

"I'm Crazy Eddie. . . My prices are INSANE!" Eddie Antar, chairman of Crazy Eddie's, a New York consumer electronics retailer who committed one of the most infamous financial statement frauds of all time, may be giving accounting lessons to some of the nation's biggest retailers. Crazy Eddie fooled accountants by moving inventory from one store to another so the same inventory was being counted over and over again. Antar eventually was caught and served prison time for fraud, having bilked investors out of more than $100 million.

More recently, in July 2002, former Rite Aid executive Timothy J. Noonan pleaded guilty to a felony charge of withholding information from the company's internal investigators. Under the terms of a plea agreement, Noonan agreed to work undercover to help the SEC build a case against other executives. Three other former senior executives—Martin L. Grass (former chairman and CEO), Franklin Brown (former chief counsel and vice chairman), and Franklyn Bergonzi (former executive vice president and chief financial officer)—and a current executive, Eric S. Sorkin (vice president for pharmacy services), were also arraigned on criminal charges from accounting irregularities. In 2003, Grass, Bergonzi, and Sorkin pleaded guilty to various charges. As a result, they may spend time and prison and be required to pay several million dollars in fines and forfeitures.

Sources: Pete Hisey, "The State of Retail Ethics," *Retail Merchandiser,* May 1, 2002, retrieved July 2002 from www.retailmerchandiser.com; John L. Micek, "Former Rite Aid Chief Noonan Pleads Guilty," *The Morning Call,* July 11, 2002, p. A11; Tom Dochat, "One Former Rite Aid Executive Pleads Guilty, Another Waits," *Knight Ridder Tribune Business News,* June 27, 2003.

as periodic or perpetual inventory systems, which are dependent on the retailer's specific needs.

periodic inventory system A cost accounting system in which sales are recorded as they occur but inventory is not updated.

PERIODIC INVENTORY SYSTEM. In a **periodic inventory system,** sales are recorded as they occur but the inventory is not updated. Therefore, a complete inventory must be taken periodically. Retailers using a periodic inventory system need to calculate sales receipts for the period under study. The merchandise costs are recorded, at cost, for the required time period. Let's assume a skateboard retailer is costing on a monthly basis, so the merchandise, at cost, is recorded monthly. The retailer then calculates all purchase invoices (those purchases that have already been made and billed). The retailer then counts up the merchandise value at the end of the month (EOM) and enters that value. The gross profit can then be calculated, at cost:

Gross profits = Sales − (BOM merchandise value [at cost] + Purchase invoices) − EOM merchandise value [at cost]

Keep in mind that with this type of system, the actual gross profits cannot be calculated until after a physical inventory has been performed. Again, many retailers have opted for inventory systems that allow for more frequent, electronic inventories to keep track of their merchandise. Physical inventories are generally undertaken infrequently—such as once or twice a year. Thus, the retailer may be unable to uncover any theft or other shortages until the physical inventory is finished.

PERPETUAL INVENTORY SYSTEM. A perpetual inventory system can give the retailer a fairly accurate idea of the merchandise value on a constant basis. With a **perpetual inventory system** (or *book inventory system*), calculations for shortages can be made without a physical inventory; purchases are added to the books when they are made, and sales are subtracted as soon as they occur. This gives the retailer an idea of the current value of the inventory at cost. When developing a perpetual inventory system, it is important to recognize that there are several ways to account for sales of merchandise, depending on the sophistication of the retailer's accounting system. Because of the affordability of sophisticated POS hardware and software, most large retailers use specific identification in determining the items sold and their inventory value by using a perpetual inventory system. Each time an item is scanned for sale, the information system subtracts it from inventory.

perpetual inventory system A cost accounting system that shows the level of inventory on hand at all times.

FIFO AND LIFO. Less sophisticated retailers may use the FIFO or LIFO method of accounting. The **FIFO** (**f**irst **i**n, **f**irst **o**ut) method assumes that older stock is sold before newer stock; in other words, the first products the retailer receives are the first products to be sold. "First come, first served" is a FIFO method of valuation. For example, when you buy a new gallon of milk and store it in your refrigerator, you place the new gallon behind the already opened gallon (or so you should) so that the older milk is consumed first.

FIFO (first in, first out) An inventory costing method that assumes older merchandise is sold before newer stock is sold.

LIFO (last in, first out) An inventory costing method that assumes newer merchandise is sold before older stock is sold.

The **LIFO** (**l**ast **i**n, **f**irst **o**ut) method assumes that newer merchandise is sold first; older merchandise stays in inventory or on the shelves until the newer merchandise is gone. Under the LIFO method, current sales are matched with current rather than noncurrent costs. FIFO does the opposite, matching inventory values with costs. If the inventory values are rising, using LIFO can generate tax advantages.

The cost method may be difficult without automated and POS inventory systems. In the case of manual accounting systems, the cost method may favor retailers who have low inventory turnover and high-priced products. These types of retailers have limited merchandise assortments and do not change prices on a daily, or frequent, basis. In addition, a cost system does not allow the retailer to adjust inventory values. The retail value of the inventory may increase or decrease during any given time period, but with a cost system the retailer cannot account for such fluctuations in price. The bottom line is that the retailer may get an inaccurate assessment of what the merchandise is worth. For example, suppose the inventory increases in value, but the retailer has not received an updated estimate of its worth and fails to obtain additional insurance coverage. In the event of a disaster, the retailer may stand to lose a great deal due to being underinsured. What if the inventory value decreases? In this case, the retailer may be paying too much for the merchandise, space, and insurance. To alleviate some of these disadvantages, retailers often use the retail method of inventory valuation.

THE RETAIL METHOD OF INVENTORY VALUATION

Retailers who wish to value merchandise at current retail values, or prices, use the *retail method of inventory valuation*. This method virtually eliminates the disadvantages associated with the cost system. The retail method of inventory valuation requires a number of interrelated steps because the retailer has to convert from cost to retail price and then convert back again. The steps are as follows.

cost complement Total value at cost divided by total value at retail.

1. Calculate the cost complement (the total value at cost divided by the total value at retail). In retail costing, the values of all merchandise are recorded at both cost and retail value, allowing the retailer to calculate the relationship between the two values. The beginning-of-period (BOP) inventory is shown at cost and at retail. Net purchases (the total purchases the retailer makes, plus freight-in, less purchase discounts, returns, and allowances) equal the total net cost of purchases. The purchases are also valued at the retail sales price. The formula for the cost complement is as follows:

Cost complement = Total value at cost/Total value at retail

For example, assume the beginning inventory is worth $25,000 at cost and $40,000 at retail. Now assume purchases of $56,000 at cost and $188,000 at retail. Freight-in costs are $6,990. The additional markups to merchandise (usually due to an increase in demand for the product or to cover inflation), at retail, are $7,000. Here is the computation:

	At Cost	At Retail
Beginning inventory	$25,000	$40,000
Purchases (net)	56,000	188,000
Additional markups	—	7,000
Freight costs (in-bound)	6,690	—
Total inventory for sale	$87,690	$235,000

The cost complement is equal to the total cost value of $87,690 divided by the total retail value of $235,000. Thus, the cost complement equals $87,690/ $235,000, or 0.373.

2. Record any reductions made in the physical inventory levels. Reductions to inventory come from the sales of products, but they also come from other areas that have reduced the level of inventory, such as markdowns on damaged, seasonal merchandise. The retailer may have reductions due to discounts given to students, senior citizens, or employees (and any other discounts allowed during the given time period). A good chance exists that there is lost inventory due to theft by employees or store customers. Finally, more reductions to inventory may be needed because of damage to the goods (or, in the case of a food retailer such as a supermarket, spoilage).

Although the retailer has a grasp of how much inventory has been marked down and discounted, there is no such knowledge of stock shortages, such as those due to theft. The only way to get an accurate financial picture of stock shortages is to take a physical inventory, which involves actually counting the merchandise. This is an expensive and time-consuming process, usually done only once or twice a year. For this reason, the retailer needs to estimate the stock shortages, typically by using historical data from the RIS. Because of the estimation process, the retailer must correct the estimates by inserting the actual stock shortage values *after* taking each physical inventory. The following calculation shows what the input would look like for step 2:

Available merchandise at retail		$235,000
Less reductions:		
Sales	$208,000	
Markdowns	6,700	
Discounts	1,300	
Total reductions		216,000
Ending (book) retail value of inventory		$ 19,000

3. Convert the ending retail (book) value of inventory to the cost value. This allows the calculation of the closing inventory value at cost. This step is fairly simple: multiply the cost complement by the ending adjusted retail inventory value to get the cost value. Remember, the ending retail book value of inventory must be adjusted after a physical inventory to allow for an accurate costing of stock shortages. Thus, the books may look something like the following:

	Cost	Retail
Ending retail book value of inventory	—	$19,000
Physical inventory	—	18,500
Stock shortages	—	500
Adjusted ending retail book value of inventory	—	$18,500

One of the ways a retailer determines the value of its inventory is to take stock of it periodically. One method of taking inventory is using an optic scan device to read product information into a hand-held machine. The machine then transmits the data to a database for further analysis.

The closing inventory at cost is equal to the adjusted retail book value of inventory (in the example, $18,500) multiplied by the cost complement (in the example, 0.373):

$\$18,500 \times 0.373 = \$6,900.50$

This calculation is not exact, so the retailer must use a cost complement that represents an average. The actual number calculated for the ending cost inventory value is an approximation, not the actual closing inventory at cost. Figure 8.8 shows what the profit-and-loss statement for D & D Bookstore would look like following the retail inventory valuation steps.

Although the retail method of inventory valuation overcomes most of the problems associated with the cost method, it has some shortcomings. The biggest disadvantage involves the use of averages. Indeed, accounting statements can be generated for any point in time; however, these statements are based on approximations, not on definite numbers. In addition, as discussed earlier, closing inventory is valued on the cost complement, which is an average of the relationship between costs and retail values. If there are many different lines of products, a cost complement will be needed for each individual product line (or department). In addition, a great deal of bookkeeping is required to keep the figures up to date. Each time a retailer purchases and sells merchandise; it must record the retail price and cost information associated with these purchases. These and many other disadvantages can be overcome with POS computer systems and computerized inventory systems.

Remember, inventory value is a dollar amount. It is also important to understand the numbers of units of products processed through the retail outlet. Chapter 9 delves into this topic.

D & D Bookstore
Income Statement
For the Year Ended December 31, 2006
Fiscal Year 2005

Sales		$208,000.00
COGS		
Inventory available for sale (at cost)	$87,690.00	
Adjusted ending inventory (at cost)	6,900.50	
COGS		94,590.50
Gross Margin (Profit)		$66,590.50
Operating Expenses		
Sales commissions	6,500.00	
Rent	6,000.00	
Insurance	1,000.00	
IMC	9,500.00	
Maintenance	1,500.00	
Other, misc.	500.00	
Total Operating Expenses		25,000.00
Profit Before Taxes (NET)		$41,590.50

FIGURE 8.8 D & D Bookstore Income Statement

RESOURCE ALLOCATION

Once the retail manager has a firm grasp of the organization's financial operations, she or he uses the information to make allocations for the firm's various resources—both capital resources and human resources. Although human resource management is discussed in subsequent chapters, the wise manager uses the information presented in this chapter to help make allocation decisions. The overlap between the elements comprising the integrated retail management plan means that many decisions link to other areas, and sometimes simultaneous decisions must be made to ensure consistency.

In terms of generating information for financial decisions in operations management, the retail manager makes a number of decisions regarding resource allocation. Depending on the size of the organization, the retail manager must decide how the various retail forecasts needed for effective financial management will be organized. For example, a decision must be made as to how many different forecasts should be undertaken. Are data needed for the store as a whole, or is it better to create forecasts for product lines, departments, or retail divisions? Sales forecasts help ensure that the retailer will have enough of the "right" stock to satisfy consumers' needs, wants, and desires.

The retail manager must determine the levels of stock needed on hand. To achieve this goal, the manager must be informed about the turnover rates for

Popular books, such as the Harry Potter *series, can generate good sales for book retailers. In an effort to generate traffic and increase market share, many retailers offer best-sellers at a reduced price and allow customers to place orders for them before their release dates.*

the various departments, divisions, and product lines and for the store as a whole. Department managers are likely to want increased resources. Thus, allocation receives close attention and concern in every department.

To meet sales objectives, the retail manager needs to pre-plan for reductions from the retail price of merchandise. Many things happen throughout the year that may make merchandise obsolete. Food retailers have the additional problem of spoilage; food products often need to have their prices reduced to move them off the shelves in a timely manner. The retail manager can look at the accounting systems, particularly previous years' income statements and balance sheets, to estimate how much in retail reductions will be necessary to move merchandise and meet sales objectives. Remember, these estimates are forecasts, or guesses, as to how the product inventories will perform. In the case of fast-moving merchandise, the retailer may have to plan for additional purchases to ensure an adequate supply of the "hot" products. For example, whenever a new video game system comes on the market, many electronics stores make extra efforts to have enough inventory to satisfy demand. Some stores allow customers to order ahead when a new product launch has been announced.

It is important to establish cost categories for the retail business. Many retailers use standard categories such as fixed costs or direct costs. Some retailers set up the categories as capital costs versus operating costs. Others use costs associated with departments. The National Retail Federation (NRF; *www.nrf.com*) has developed standardized categories that are used by many retailers to set cost categories. One advantage of using the NRF's categories is that it allows for direct comparisons between the retailer's products and those of competitors and the industry averages.

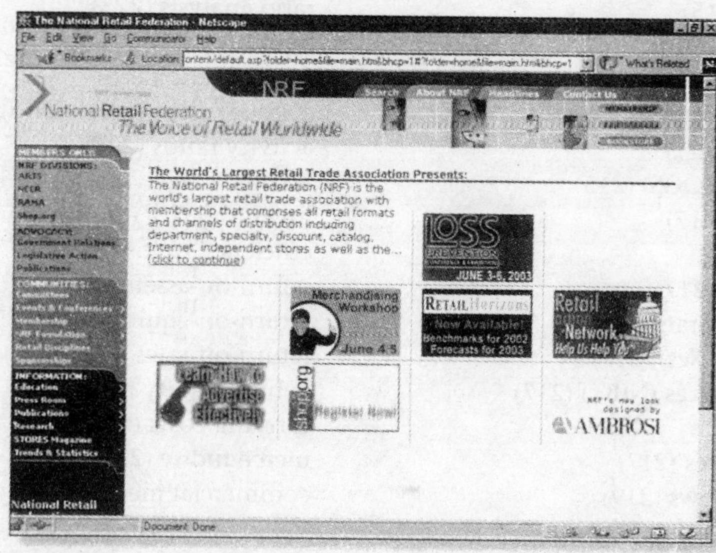

The National Retail Federation (NRF) is a trade association for retailers. Members use the information provided by the NRF to assist them in financial statement preparation and other areas pertaining to operations management, such as competitive analysis and developing strategy.
(Source: National Retail Federation website, www.nrf.com. Reprinted with permission.)

SUMMARY

This chapter explored issues and processes in financial planning for inventory and operations. The data gathered during financial planning allow the retail manager to make more effective decisions. The financial operations management function is particularly important when designing the integrated retail management plan because cash management and financial statement analysis allow retailers to evaluate various aspects of the organization's performance.

Because one of the main goals of retailing is to turn a profit, the retail manager devotes a great deal of time to planning. All activities need to be integrated so that everyone knows why and where the retail dollars are going. In addition, because a finite number of dollars are available to the retailer, the allocation of those dollars is crucial in retail decision making.

Important financial statements were discussed and illustrated, including the balance sheet, the income statement, and the statement of cash flows. The chapter then discussed financial fraud and the importance of budgeting for merchandise.

Next, the chapter focused on inventory valuation using the cost and retail systems, with special emphasis on the LIFO and FIFO methods. Systems for monitoring inventory were discussed. These systems enable the retailer to generate forecasts for product sales. Allocations of resources to achieve the forecasted sales goals are undertaken when the retailer has a good grasp of the company's cash flows.

KEY TERMS

operations management (213)
retail accounting system (RAS) (214)
balance sheet (214)
assets (214)
current assets (214)
long-term assets (214)
total assets (215)
liabilities (215)
current liabilities (215)
long-term liabilities (215)
total liabilities (215)
net worth (owner's equity) (215)
net sales (215)
cost of goods sold (COGS) (215)
purchase discount (217)
gross profit (217)
operating expenses (217)
net income from operations (217)
other income (expenses) (217)
net income before taxes (NIBT) (217)
income taxes (217)
net income after taxes (217)
statement of cash flows (219)
cash flow from operating activities (219)
cash flow from investing activities (219)
cash flow from financing activities (219)
notes to the financial statements (220)
horizontal analysis (220)
comparative financial statement (220)
vertical analysis (220)
common size financial statement (223)
ratio analysis (223)
liquidity ratios (225)
current ratio (226)
acid test ratio (quick ratio) (226)
activity ratios (227)
accounts receivable (A/R) turnover in days (227)
inventory (I/V) turnover in days (228)
efficiency ratios (229)
return-on-assets ratio (229)
return-on-equity ratio (229)
return-on-sales ratio (230)
debt-to-equity ratio (230)
carrying costs (231)
merchandise (233)
commercial merchandise (233)

merchandising (233)
bottom-up approach (234)
top-down approach (234)
safety stock (235)
stock-to-sales ratio (235)
periodic inventory system (238)
perpetual inventory system (238)
FIFO (first in, first out) (238)
LIFO (last in, first out) (239)
cost complement (239)

QUESTIONS FOR DISCUSSION

1. Why is it important for retailers to understand financial statements?
2. Why is cash management so important to retailers?
3. What is the difference between current assets and long-term assets? Between current liabilities and long-term liabilities? What other information is needed to interpret these ratios?
4. Why are budgets important in retailing?
5. What is the difference between the cost method and retail method of inventory valuation?
6. What is the major difference between the LIFO and FIFO methods of inventory valuation?
7. What type of financial information should be available to investors?
8. What are the consequences for companies that cheat when reporting their financial status?

E-TAILING EXERCISE

All public companies are required to file paperwork required by the Securities and Exchange Commission (SEC) through EDGAR (Economic Data Gathering and Retrieval). Go to the SEC website (*www.sec.gov*). Use the "Filings and Forms" section of the website to do the following:

1. Complete the tutorial on EDGAR.
2. Use EDGAR to find recent filings for three retailers of your choice.
3. From the list of recent filings, choose one or two reports for each retailer.
4. In a written report, summarize the information found for each retailer.
5. Analyze the implications of the information for that retailer.

Continuing Case 8.1

Sherwin-Williams Company: Reporting Financial Information on the Web

The Sherwin-Williams website (*www.sherwin-williams.com*) offers a wealth of information about the company's financial condition. There is a link for investor relations that sends visitors to other links offering financial information from the company's balance sheets.

Many companies follow the guidelines provided by the Financial Accounting Standards Board (FASB) to prepare their financial reports. Since 1973, FASB has been the provider of standards of financial accounting and reporting for the private sector. Both the SEC and the American Institute of Certified Public Accountants (AICPA) recognize FASB as the authority for financial accounting and reporting (*www.fasb.org.facts*).

In the first quarter of 2002, Sherwin-Williams adopted the Statement of Financial Accounting Standard No. 142 (SFAS No. 142), "Goodwill and Other Intangible Assets." Intangible assets are nonphysical factors and assets, such as the company's brands, trademarks, or reputation in the marketplace. Whereas goodwill previously would have been amortized to earnings up to 40 years, SFAS No. 142 no longer requires companies to charge goodwill against their earnings. Companies can instead use an impairment of value test to determine the value of goodwill, whereas other intangible assets are to be amortized over their useful lives. An impairment of value test determines how much an asset has declined in value. Sometimes value drops so suddenly that large write-offs are recorded. According to the 2002 first-quarter results for Sherwin-Williams, the company recorded an after-tax transitional impairment charge of $183.1 million ($1.21 per share). The charge was recorded as a cumulative effect of the change in accounting principle in accordance with SFAS No. 142. The net loss after the cumulative effect of change in accounting principle was $148.4 million in the quarter ($.98 per common share).

As other retailers adopt SFAS No. 142, similar statements will appear in their financial analyses.

Questions

1. What is the impact on retailers of an accounting change that decreases their profitability?
2. Do you think companies do enough to educate their investors on changes in accounting practices? Explain your answer.
3. Is there an advantage for Sherwin-Williams in adopting SFAS No. 142 before its competitors do? Why or why not?
4. What do you think will be the long-term impact of SFAS No. 142 on companies?

Sources: Sherwin-Williams Company 2002 First Quarter Report, April 18, 2002, retrieved July 2002 from www.sherwin-williams.com; Financial Accounting Standards Board, "Summary of Statement No. 142," retrieved July 2002 from www.fasb.org; Max Gottlied, "Impairment of Long-Lived Assets: Recognition, Measurement and Disclosure," 1992, *The CPA Journal Online*, retrieved January 2003 from www.nysscpa.org/cpajournal.

Cal Corporation's Ratio Analysis

Cal Corporation (Cal Corp), a publicly held company, is a leading retailer of cellular phone components. Three individuals—a banker, a potential investor, and a member of the board of directors—have asked you to evaluate Cal Corp and make recommendations on the company's performance.

You were able to gather the following information concerning the operations of Cal Corp for the last seven years and those of SJL Corporation, Cal Corp's major competitor, for the last six years. Prepare the ratios for Cal Corp; then compare Cal Corp's ratios with those of SJL Corporation.

Questions

1. What can you say about the financial condition of each company?
2. Which ratios of the two companies are similar? Which are different?
3. What other information would be valuable in assessing these companies?
4. Which company has a higher inventory turnover? What are the implications of this ratio?

Source: This case was developed by Craig Latshaw, Ph.D., CPA.

RATIO ANALYSIS: CAL CORP

Cal Corp Ratios	**2006**	**2005**	**2004**	**2003**	**2002**	**2001**	
Current Ratio							
Acid Test							
A/R Turnover in Days							
Inventory Turnover in Days							
Return on Assets							
Return on Equity							
Debt to Equity							
Cal Corp Data– ($ thousands)	**2006**	**2005**	**2004**	**2003**	**2002**	**2001**	**2000**
Total Cash	150	200	250	300	350	360	380
Total Receivables	225	200	215	190	118	115	95
Total Inventory	350	200	100	50	30	30	25
Total Assets	2218	2312	2059	1200	1000	900	850
Total Current Liabilities	650	285	375	185	199	203	210
Total Stockholders' Equity	649	527	614	634	450	500	400
Net Sales	850	990	950	1300	1100	900	850
Cost of Goods Sold	430	460	680	790	630	570	450
Operating Expenses	220	223	180	185	200	155	145
Interest Expense	85	75	60	45	35	10	8
Income Tax Rate	0.30	0.30	0.30	0.30	0.30	0.30	0.25
SJL Corporation Ratios	**2006**	**2005**	**2004**	**2003**	**2002**	**2001**	
Current Ratio	2.50	2.40	2.20	2.00	1.80	1.90	
Acid Test	2.35	2.30	2.10	1.70	1.60	1.55	
A/R Turnover in Days	30	34	36	36	40	44	
Inventory Turnover in Days	41	46	42	38	43	40	
Return on Assets	0.07	0.08	0.06	0.05	0.04	0.05	
Return on Equity	0.10	0.12	0.10	0.06	0.07	0.08	
Debt to Equity	0.95	0.90	0.80	1.20	1.10	1.00	

Merchandise Buying and Handling

Chapter 9

Different is what sells. Our customers want to go into a place of business that's different. They want to shop at stores that stock diverse merchandise and have diverse promotions. It's the key to not only staying ahead, but staying in business.

Rick Segel, retail consultant and founder of Rick Segel and Associates

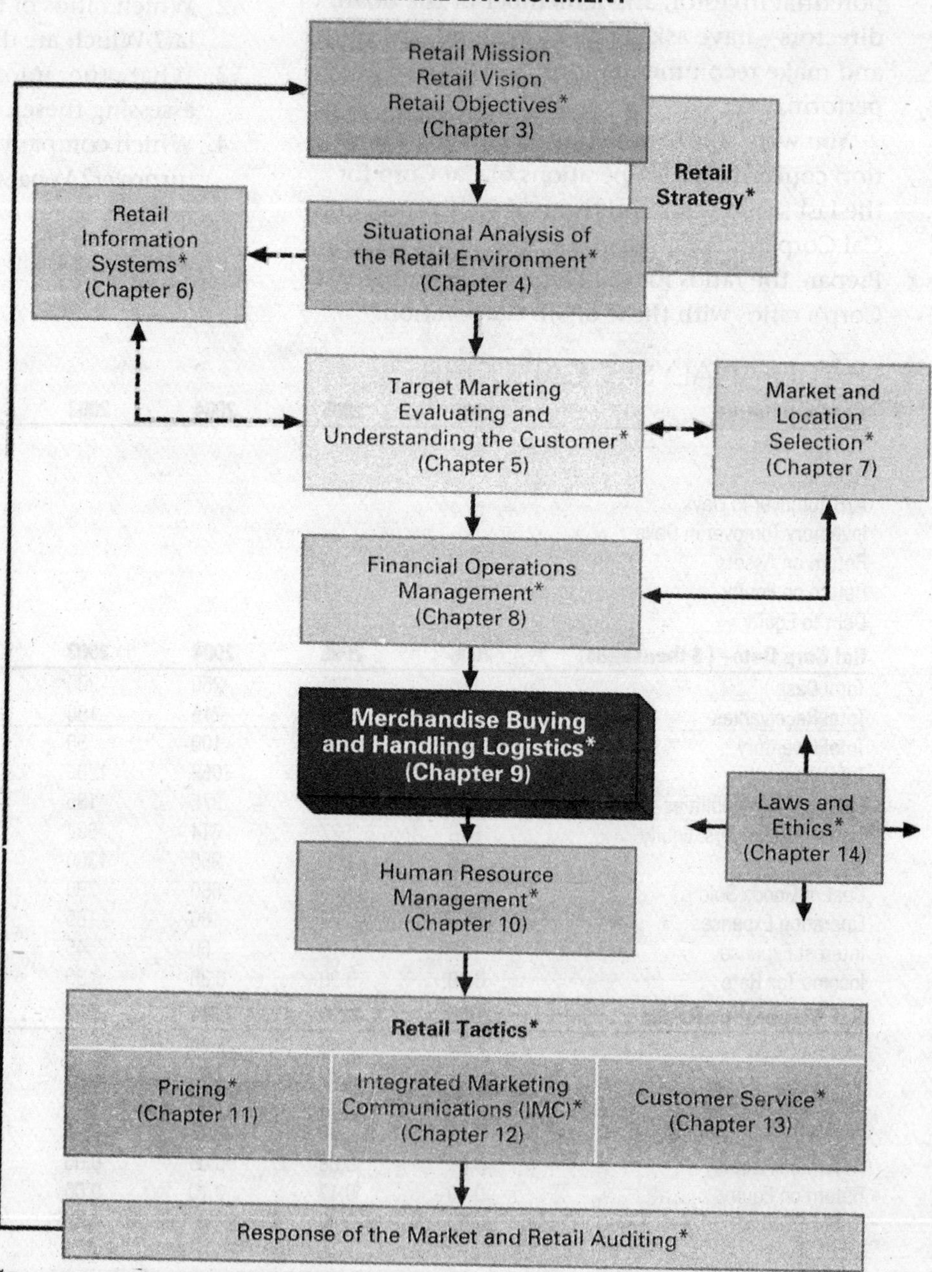

*Evaluation and control occurs at all these stages.

CHAPTER OBJECTIVES

After completing this chapter, you will be able to:

1. Explain the process of dollar merchandise planning and forecasting.
2. Discuss how a retailer returns its investment in inventory.
3. Calculate the formulas related to inventory planning.
4. Describe the various aspects of the merchandise mix.
5. Discuss the variables that affect the merchandise mix.
6. Explain the process used to identify vendors and the negotiation interactions that occur with vendors.
7. Explain the importance of logistics and supply chain management.

Using Merchandising to Attract Markets

Discount retailers pursue differing strategies to attract a particular market. Target attempts to appeal to upscale, higher-income consumers, whereas Wal-Mart markets to price-conscious consumers. While emerging from Chapter 11 bankruptcy, Kmart revisited its target market and found an underserved market segment in urban areas where there is a more diverse customer base.

In June 2003, the Census Bureau announced that Hispanics had overtaken African Americans to become the largest minority group in the United States.[1] Within the Hispanic and African-American segments, Kmart is often the first or second department store choice. Because both groups are known to have high levels of shopper loyalty, Kmart believes it will get a return on its investment in these segments.

One area where Kmart has a competitive edge is in ethnic merchandising. For example, in the Aurora, Colorado, SuperK, the store includes 96 feet of Mexican specialty food. The hair care aisle stocks a sizable variety of products that appeal to the African-American segment.[2]

One of the successes of Kmart's merchandising strategy was the development of the Estilo brand (*estilo* means "style" in Spanish.) This line was developed from Kmart's Puerto Rican division, and the brand is gaining popularity in other ethnic segments besides the Hispanic segment.[3] Kmart also named a fashion line after the Mexican pop star Thalia Sodi in the hopes of attracting younger Hispanics.[4] According to industry experts, Kmart will face competition for ethnic markets as Wal-Mart moves more heavily into urban areas.[5]

Because of Kmart's past problems, the company has an urgent need to succeed. For now, Kmart hopes its new strategies will provide the differentiation it needs to survive in the fiercely competitive retail environment.[6]

INTRODUCTION

Recall that, with reference to the integrated retail management (IRM) flow chart, we are within the operations management section. The operations management function of retailing consists of two main components: operations management and human resource management. The two areas that fall under operations management are financial management (Chapter 8) and merchandise decisions (this chapter). Human resource management is covered in Chapter 10.

merchandise buying and handling The physical purchase of products and services and how those products and services are brought to the retail outlet, handled, and finally placed ready for sale.

Merchandise buying and handling includes the physical purchase of products and services and how those products and services are brought to the retail outlet, handled, and finally placed ready for sale. The merchandise buying and handling process is vital and must complement the strategic focus of the firm. When merchandising decisions are inconsistent with strategy, it can damage the retailer's image and confuse customers. The decisions made in buying are significant because they help determine the consumer's perception of the retailer. Consequently, many retailers employ specialists who purchase products and services for the retail organization.

This chapter begins with a discussion of dollar merchandise planning and forecasting and the integration of those concepts with unit buying. Various formulas for use in retailing are presented. The chapter covers four primary methods of inventory planning: the basic stock, percentage variation, stock-to-sales, and weeks' supply methods. Because of their importance throughout the retailing process, stock turnover and return on investment (ROI) to the retail owners are also examined.

The chapter also reviews concepts related to the merchandise mix and provides information about interactions that take place with vendors. The chapter ends with a discussion of merchandise logistics management.

DOLLAR MERCHANDISE PLANNING AND FORECASTING

buyer The employee whose basic responsibility is to make purchases.

A **buyer** is an employee whose basic responsibility within the retail organization is to make purchases. When buying, the retailer's (or retail buyer's) goal is to make the best possible purchases for the store. In years past the buying function was less complicated; but advances in technology, rapid changes in consumers' wants, needs, and desires, and new venues in retailing such as e-tailing have made the buying process far more sophisticated than it was even ten years ago. It is important that the retail buyer have access to vendors for both physical- and non-physical-site retail stores.

Integration and consistency of merchandise across locations are also paramount. In addition to buyers, many large firms have merchandise planners who work in cooperation with the buyers. Merchandise planning and forecasting merges quantitative analysis with qualitative assessment, making the process a science as well as an art. The marriage of quantitative assessment and intuition has been coined "rocket science retailing."[7]

The merchandise planner's job is to provide an analysis of potential merchandise for the store. The merchandise planner is responsible for decisions concerning the merchandise assortment. Assortment decisions may include styles, price points, quantity, quality, variety, and sizes. The buyer's job is to purchase the products according to the budget. In addition, the planner devotes time to planning for the merchandise and the handling and control of the merchandise. Buyers are expected to know the number of units and the types of products to order, and at what prices they should be ordered. They are also expected to know when to order and how much stock is necessary to avoid a premature stockout situation.

Developing a winning merchandise mix is exciting. It's very satisfying to guess the next fad—and be right. Unfortunately, retail buyers sometimes make wrong guesses, resulting in excess, slow-moving stock. To ensure greater accuracy in retail merchandise planning, the astute retail buyer develops a good understanding of the concepts and methods necessary to create "great buys," as well as knowledge of customers' current and future wants and needs.

It is essential that the buyer understand the type of retailer for which he or she is buying. For example, buying for a consumer electronics chain such as Circuit City involves different buying decision criteria from those for an independent, one-store retailer. In addition, the buyer needs to understand the industry in which the retailer competes. For example, a department store and a food retailer require different merchandise mixes. Similarly, buying for a physical-site retailer differs considerably from buying for a non-site retailer such as an e-tailer, a catalog retailer, or a home shopping network. Finally, the buyer must be familiar with the dollar volumes for a particular market. Most buyers have at least some duties and responsibilities in common, but the type of merchandise being purchased will influence the buying methods used.

A retailer that demonstrates differences in merchandise buying decisions is Chico's FAS, Inc., headquartered in Fort Myers, Florida. The company has two chains of stores, Chico's and Pazo. Chico's stores offer exclusively designed classic fashions targeted to women aged 35 to 55. In contrast, Pazo carries trendier fashions aimed at women aged 25 to 35.[8] Both chains train sales associates to put together entire assemblies for their customers, including clothing, shoes, and accessories. But Chico's products are more expensive than Pazo's, averaging $50 to Pazo's $40. In an effort to keep the chains distinct, they have different staff and product sources and are run out of different buildings. Pazo also uses a different set of factories for its clothing as well as different sizing.[9]

The duties and responsibilities of the retail buyer are discussed later in the chapter. The next section focuses on the information that goes into the merchandise plan.

RETURN ON INVENTORY INVESTMENTS AND STOCK TURNOVER

gross margin return on inventory (GMROI) A calculation of how much investment is being returned for each type of merchandise purchased.

Inventory represents a large investment for retailers. Therefore, retailers want to know what kind of return they are getting from their merchandise. To do this, retailing professionals have developed a method to assess the return on investment (ROI) from inventory investment. This method is called the **gross margin return on inventory (GMROI).** The GMROI is particularly helpful to retailers because it brings together the concepts of other performance measures such as return on assets, asset turnover, profits, and sales. The formula used to calculate GMROI (see Table 9.1) shows how these performance measures are incorporated into the calculation.

The gross margin percentage provides an idea of how much investment is being returned for each type of merchandise purchased. The retailer can compare and contrast the figures with those of competitors, the retailer's historic margins, and the industry averages. Calculating the GMROI helps retailers generate more profitable inventory decisions and gain a clearer picture of how their inventory is performing. To see how effectively their investments in inventory are performing, retailers utilize inventory turnover formulas.

INVENTORY TURNOVER

inventory turnover A measure of how many times a store sells its average investment in inventory during a year.

Inventory is typically a retailer's largest asset. To measure the productivity of the merchandise being purchased, retailers use a concept known as **inventory turnover,** a measure of how many times a store sells its average investment in inventory during a year. The faster the merchandise turns over—that is, is bought, marked, stocked, and sold—the more money is generated for the retail outlet. It is important to know how to measure inventory turnover, because this shows how quickly each product is moving. For example, an inventory turnover ratio of 15.15 means that, on average, every $1.00 invested in inventory generates $15.15 in sales. There are two basic ways to calculate inventory turnover, shown on the next page.

TABLE 9.1

CALCULATING GMROI

GMROI = Gross margin percentage × Stock-to-sales ratio

Gross margin percentage = Gross margin (in dollars)/Net sales

Stock-to-sales ratio = Net sales/Average inventory (at cost)

Thus,

GMROI = Gross margin/Average inventory (at cost)

Inventory turnover = Net sales (at retail)/Average inventory (at retail)

and

Inventory turnover = Cost of goods sold (COGS) (at cost)/
Average inventory (at cost)

These computations allow the retailer to measure stock productivity.

In addition to dollar amounts, the retailer may want to know the inventory turnover in units. This calculation is as follows:

Inventory turnover (in units) = Number of units sold for the year/
Average inventory (in units)

Using these formulas the retailer can track, analyze, and compare the turnover rates for its store to competitors' rates.

It is also important to know the average amount of inventory being carried. The average inventory is used in numerous formulas to determine merchandise performance. To calculate the average inventory, the retailer first determines the number of months to use for the average inventory period. For example, a music store calculating average inventory for the year's first quarter would use the first three months of inventory. (Note that any number of months up to twelve can be used to calculate the average inventory for a year.) The calculation for the music store example is as follows:

Average inventory = (Month 1 + Month 2 + Month 3)/3

Thus, if the music store had $25,000 in inventory in month 1, $15,000 in month 2, and $50,000 in month 3, the average inventory would be $30,000.

point-of-sale (POS) terminal A terminal or computer workstation designed to collect information from sales of products and services.

Smaller retailers use the preceding formula more often than larger ones do. Large retailers can calculate their inventory data utilizing high-tech, **point-of-sale (POS) terminals.** Recall that POS equipment consists of a terminal or computer workstation designed to collect information from sales of products and services. Advanced POS systems scan and input daily sales figures into a database that the retail manager can access at any time to get an average inventory (on-hand) figure. Thus, the retailer can know its levels of turnover at any point in time. POS systems are excellent tools for developing product assortments and determining amounts of shelf space for products. In addition, POS systems can help retailers track sales and measure the effectiveness of integrated marketing communication (IMC) tactics such as coupons, contests, point-of-purchase promotions, and other in-store activities. They can also help retailers decide which products to feature within stores and flag those products that are underperforming.[10] POS terminals can be linked to other databases to generate interconnected information on demographics, geographics, and psychographics. The generated data are valuable to retail buyers for decisions on order size and customer types. The effective use of a POS system relies on the analytical skills of the retail manager.

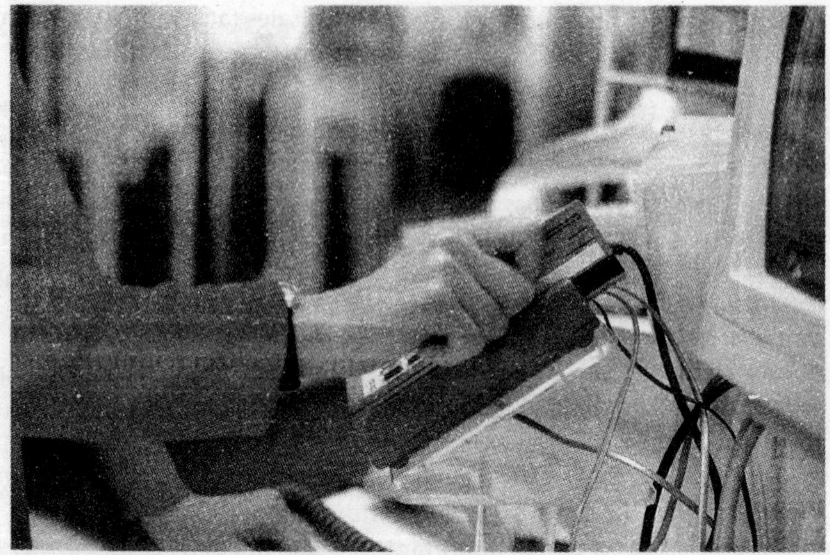

Point-of-sale (POS) equipment consists of a terminal or computer workstation designed to collect information from sales of products and services. Shown here is a salesperson scanning a credit card into a POS terminal.

A well-developed POS system can be tied in to many inventory management programs, such as vendor-managed inventory (VMI), quick response (QR), effective customer response (ECR), just-in-time (JIT), and other forms of electronic data interchange (EDI) (discussed later in the chapter).

CASH CONVERSION CYCLE

Financial managers often assert that "cash is king." This is true for all internal business operations and certainly true for retailers. In fact, outside analysts evaluate retailers based on the effectiveness of the retailers' cash management. One method used to evaluate cash management is the cash conversion cycle. The **cash conversion cycle (CCC)** indicates how many days it takes to turn purchases of inventory into cash (see Figure 9.1). Retailing success is tied to a company's ability to manage this cycle.[11] If a retailer does not effectively manage the cash conversion cycle, the firm may find it necessary to borrow money to maintain operations, thus increasing debt and limiting the range of opportunities available to the retailer.[12]

cash conversion cycle (CCC) A measure of how many days it takes to turn purchases of inventory into cash.

The CCC incorporates accounts receivable, inventories, and accounts payable into a single figure. The smaller this figure, the better the cash management situation. The CCC is calculated by adding days sales outstanding (DSO) to days inventory outstanding (DIO) and subtracting days payables outstanding (DPO):

$$\text{CCC} = \text{DSO} + \text{DIO} - \text{DPO}$$

where

$$\text{DSO} = \text{Accounts receivable}/(\text{Sales}/\text{Number of days in cycle})$$

$$\text{DIO} = \text{Inventory}/(\text{Cost of sales}/\text{Number of days in cycle})$$

$$\text{DPO} = \text{Accounts payable}/(\text{Cost of sales}/\text{Number of days in cycle})$$

The DSO and DIO should be as low as possible, indicating a fast collection of receivables (the DSO calculation) and a fast inventory turnover (the DIO calculation). The DPO should be as high as possible without damaging the company's credit rating. A high DPO indicates that the retailer is taking advantage of the interest-free loans (*i.e.,* payables) from its suppliers.[13]

The cash conversion cycle is important for merchandise managers because to effectively manage cash, the retailer must turn over inventory as quickly as possible, avoid stockouts that may lead to lost sales, collect accounts receivable quickly, take advantage of cash discounts, and pay accounts payable as late as possible without damaging its credit rating.[14] The last factor requires careful timing: the retailer wants to take advantage of cash discounts usually given for prompt payment, yet make the payments at the latest possible moment.

According to John Cravenho, managing director of Excel Consulting, one of the best ways to improve the cash conversion rate is to focus on faster collections of receivables. Some areas to concentrate on are as follows:[15]

- Train team members on the entire cash conversion cycle so they understand how cash flow is maximized and how they play a role in improving the cycle.
- Prioritize the largest receivables outstanding and problem accounts on a daily basis. Be proactive in contacting these accounts before they fall behind on payments.

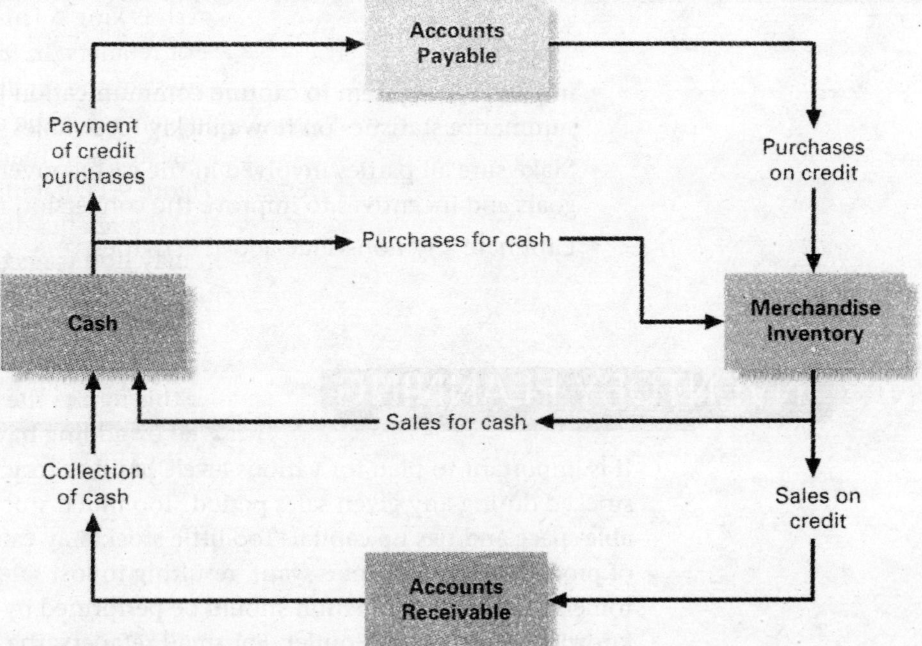

FIGURE 9.1 **The Cash Conversion Cycle** (Source: Jane M. Cote and Klaire Kamm Latham, "The Merchandising Ratio: A Comprehensive Measure of Working Capital Strategy," *Issues in Accounting Education,* May 1999, pp. 255–267.)

Blunders or Best Practices?

Dell and the Cash Conversion Cycle

One of the biggest players in the computer market is Dell Computer Corporation. Much of Dell's success is due to its cash management. In 1998, Dell had a cash conversion cycle (CCC) of −8, meaning that Dell was paid by its customers eight days before it had to pay its suppliers. Dell continues to focus on negative cash conversion cycles as a business strategy. In 2002, Dell posted a record cash conversion cycle of −36 days! In 2003, the record was broken again, with a −40 day CCC. Whereas most companies struggle to balance their receivables and payables, Dell consistently outperforms other companies in this area.

Dell then uses its financial strength to pass on savings to the customer or further invest in the company. "Because the company keeps only five days' worth of inventory, manages receivables to 30 days, and pushes payables out to 59 days, the Dell model will generate cash—even if the company were to report no profit whatsoever," one observer notes. The company is collecting its receivables faster than it is paying out monies that it owes. Because Dell carries no finished goods inventory and only seven days of inventory comprising components and work in progress, it doesn't have the large investment tied up in inventory that other companies do. Dell has been praised as one of the best companies when it comes to managing the cash conversion cycle.

Sources: Kate Walker, "E-Business Clicks for Consumer, Stockholders," *Purdue News*, December 1998, retrieved July 2002 from www.purdue.edu/UNS/html14ever/9812.Duparcq.e-com.html; J. William Gurley, "The Smartest Price War Ever," News.com, June 25, 2001, retrieved July 2002 from www.news.com; "Finance Opportunities at Dell," retrieved July 2002 from www.dellapp.us.dell.com/careers/professionals/finance/index.asp; "Dell Computer Corp. (Dell) Annual Report (SEC form 10-K)," 2002, retrieved January 2003 from http://biz.yahoo.com; William Schaff, "Taking Stock: Dell Succeeds Where Competitors Lag," *InformationWeek*, February 24, 2003, retrieved July 2003 from www.informationweek.com.

- Implement a system to capture communication and track reports that summarize statistics on how quickly receivables are being collected.
- Make sure all parties involved in the cash conversion cycle have shared goals and incentives to improve the conversion rate.
- Eliminate any non-value-added activities.

INVENTORY PLANNING

It is important to plan for various levels of inventory that will need to be stocked during any given sales period. Too much stock costs the retailer valuable space and ties up capital. Too little stock may cause the retailer to run out of products that customers want, resulting in lost sales and unhappy customers. The buying function should be performed by individuals with a good knowledge of the retail outlet. For small retailers, the function may be performed by the owner or manager, who may also make pricing decisions. Large firms often have buying centers or purchasing agents.

Most retailers utilize beginning-of-month (BOM) and end-of-month (EOM) inventory figures to evaluate their stock conditions. These numbers provide a method to effectively assess inventory turnover rates. The most commonly used techniques in planning inventory levels are the basic stock method, the percentage variation method, the stock-to-sales method, and the weeks' supply method. To help with inventory planning, the open-to-buy is calculated. The **open-to-buy** is the amount the buyer has left to spend for a given time period, typically a month. Each time a purchase is made, the open-to-buy amount decreases.

open-to-buy The amount the buyer has left to spend for a given time period, typically a month. Each time a purchase is made, the open-to-buy amount decreases.

BASIC STOCK METHOD

basic stock method Inventory planning tool that allows the retailer to include a few more items (*basic stock*) than were forecasted in an order for a given period of time. BOM stock (at retail) = Planned sales (monthly) + Basic stock.

The **basic stock method** is used to help estimate required inventory levels. It is very useful to the retail merchandise planner. The basic stock method involves calculating inventory levels *after* the retailer has developed a viable sales forecast. The inventory levels must match the sales forecast, allowing for potential changes in the environment that might create inaccuracies in the forecast.

Remember, the only constant in the universe is change; in other words, no sales forecast will be 100 percent accurate; the astute retail buyer understands this and builds a "fudge factor," or a small amount of additional inventory, into orders for merchandise. The basic stock method was developed to allow the retailer to include a few more items (called *basic stock*) than were forecasted in the order for a given period of time. This method provides a cushion should the merchandise shipments be delayed for any reason (labor strikes, weather conditions, lost orders, etc.).

The basic stock method is best for retailers who have a somewhat low inventory turnover or who experience erratic sales over the specified sales periods.

Using the basic stock method, stock levels are estimated as follows:

Basic stock (at retail) = Average monthly stock for the sales period (at retail) − Average monthly sales for the sales period

Average monthly sales for the sales period are calculated as follows:

Average monthly sales for the sales period = Total planned sales for the sales period/Number of months in the sales period

Average monthly stock for the sales period is computed as follows:

Average monthly stock for the sales period = Total planned sales for the sales period/Inventory turnover for the sales period (estimated)

From this result, the amount of beginning-of-month (BOM) stock is calculated using the following formula:

BOM stock (at retail) = Planned sales (monthly) + Basic stock

Thus, the BOM stock is simply the planned, or forecasted, sales for the month added to the basic stock amount.

As an example, assume Weston Wire Service has forecasted its sales to be \$95,000 per month. Owner Jim Weston would like to have at least 5 percent more stock on hand because of historical fluctuations in sales. Weston's largest sales usually occur during the month of July, and he is projecting sales of \$108,000 for July of this year. How much stock should he plan to have for the beginning of the month of July? Here is the calculation:

Weston's basic stock (at retail) = (\$95,000 × 1.05) − \$95,000 = \$4,750

Weston multiplies \$95,000 by 1.05 because he wants an extra 5 percent of stock on hand. Thus, Weston wants the total amount (or 1), plus the additional "fudge factor" stock (.05). Using the result from the basic stock formula, Weston calculates the BOM stock level for July as follows:

Weston's beginning-of-July level = \$108,000 + 4,750 = \$112,750

Note that these are dollar amounts that should be spent on inventory, not units that are needed in the store.

PERCENTAGE VARIATION METHOD (PVM)

percentage variation method Inventory planning tool in which the beginning-of-month planned inventory during any period (typically a month) differs from planned average monthly stock by half of that month's variation from average monthly sales. BOM stock (at retail) = Average stock for the sales period (at retail) × ½ [1 + (Planned monthly sales/ Average monthly sales)].

Perhaps the retailer has stable inventory turnover rather than erratic turnover. Or maybe the retailer has a somewhat high inventory turnover rate—as a rule of thumb, more than six times per year. The **percentage variation method** reduces the BOM stock for retailers with annual inventory turns greater than 6. If the turnover rate is 6 or less, the basic stock and percentage variation methods will yield approximately the same results. The percentage variation method also assumes that stock percentage fluctuations each month will be no greater than one-half of the average stock on hand. The percentage variation method (PVM) uses the following formula:

BOM stock (at retail) = Average stock for the sales period (at retail) × ½ [1 + (Planned monthly sales/ Average monthly sales)]

Remember that the planned monthly sales and the average monthly sales are estimates of the population parameters. Therefore, these methods should only be used as guidelines in inventory planning.

Suppose Weston Wire Service wants to have at least \$95,000 worth of stock per month, on average. Jim Weston estimates his sales for the month of July to be about 2 percent under the average of \$91,000 per month. What would Weston's planned inventory level be for July?

BOM July inventory level (at retail) = \$95,000 × ½ [1 + (\$89,180/91,000)]
= \$94,050

Because planned monthly sales were expected to be 2 percent less than usual for the month of July, the planned monthly sales would be 1 − .02 = .98, and .98 × 91,000 = \$89,180.

STOCK-TO-SALES METHOD

stock-to-sales method Inventory planning tool in which the amount of inventory planned for the beginning of the month is a ratio of stock to sales. BOM stock = Stock-to-sales ratio × Planned sales.

stock-to-sales ratio Used to calculate beginning of the month stock in the stock to sales method. Stock-to-sales ratio = Value of stock/Actual sales.

The **stock-to-sales method** helps retailers establish costs for their inventories; it is a good tool for retailers who want to maintain a level of inventory that correlates directly to sales. The investment in inventory is measured at cost rather than at retail. To assess the return on the investment in inventory, the retailer can use the **stock-to-sales ratio,** calculated as follows:

Stock-to-sales ratio = Value of stock/Actual sales

For example, if a retailer had inventory stock valued at $50,000 at the beginning of the month and sales were $44,000, the stock-to-sales ratio would be (50,000/44,000), or 1.136. This 1.136 value suggests that for each dollar of product sold, there should be approximately $1.136 worth of products in stock. Thus, an inventory investment of $1.136 for every dollar of sales is needed.

This ratio gives the retailer an idea of how much inventory is needed at the beginning of the month to support the month's sales. A retailer that knows what the stock-to-sales ratio is for the store, or even for a given department, can multiply planned sales by the stock-to-sales ratio and calculate the BOM stock budget. The formula for calculating the BOM stock figure is as follows:

BOM stock = Stock-to-sales ratio × Planned sales

If a retailer knows the stock-to-sales ratio is 1.136 and plans for $50,000 in sales, BOM stock will equal 1.136 × 50,000, or $56,800. Thus, the retailer needs $56,800 in beginning-of-month merchandise.

Utilizing this calculation, the stock-to-sales ratio allows the retailer to maintain a required ratio of goods or services on hand to sales. The ratio is used in the stock-to-sales method to tell the retailer how much product is needed at the beginning of the month to achieve that month's sales forecast. For example, a stock-to-sales ratio of 1.5 indicates that the beginning of month inventory should be one and one-half times that month's expected sales. The retailer should be able to retrieve the data for the ratio from the retail information system (RIS). If a good RIS is unavailable, the retailer can get average ratio data from external sources, such as trade associations, or may want to use a different ratio for comparison. Sources of external information are suggested at the end of this section.

Suppose Weston Wire Service has developed a stock-to-sales ratio of 1.15. This means Weston must have $109,250 worth of inventory for the month of July to have planned sales (at retail) of $95,000 (1.15 × 95,000). A stock-to-sales ratio of 1.5 would require $142,500 in inventory (1.5 × 95,000).

The major problem with the stock-to-sales ratio is that it attempts to adjust the retailer's inventory to a greater extent than the retailer's sales may require. This may cause too much fluctuation in inventory levels. In other words, in the months in which sales increase, inventory levels also increase, but at a slower rate than sales, and the stock-to-sales ratio decreases. In months with large sales decreases, inventory levels also decrease, but at a slower rate than sales, causing the stock-to-sales ratio to increase. This disadvantage can be overcome if the retailer uses subjective judgments during times of large sales increases or decreases. In addition, the retailer should make the adjustments when major, unforecasted changes occur in the retail environment. For example, after the debut of *Finding Nemo,* the Disney/Pixar Studios animated movie about fish, aquariums throughout the country were inundated with requests for clown fish. Sales of clown fish were as high as 10 to 15 percent over average. Sales of other aquarium fish also increased significantly. Although some aquarium retailers anticipated the fad, many were caught off-guard and experienced inventory shortages.[16] Retailers that experience stockouts may lose sales, customers, or both.

The advantage of the stock-to-sales ratio is that the retailer can generate comparison data from external sources, such as the following:

Robert Morris Associates (Philadelphia), *Annual Statement Studies*

D&B (Murray Hill, NJ), *Industry Norms and Key Business Ratios*

National Retail Federation (NRF) (New York), *Merchandising and Operating Results of Retail Stores*

WEEKS' SUPPLY METHOD

weeks' supply method Inventory planning tool in which beginning of the month inventory equals several weeks' expected sales. BOM (at retail) planned inventory = Average weekly sales (estimated) × Number of weeks to be stocked.

Many supermarkets and other food marketers utilize the **weeks' supply method** of inventory planning because these businesses have a relatively fast turnaround on their inventory and consequently plan inventory levels more frequently than other types of retailers. Many supermarket managers, such as the produce manager, plan sales on a weekly basis rather than monthly, quarterly, or yearly. In addition, sales levels at a supermarket do not fluctuate nearly as much as they do at other retail outlets. Thus, with the weeks' supply method, the retail merchandise planner needs to estimate how many weeks' supply of merchandise is needed. The inventory level is then set to equal that amount. The weeks' supply is directly correlated with the inventory turnover. The method assumes the retailer's inventory is in direct proportion to sales. The sales estimates are usually generated from previous months' sales. The weeks' supply of inventory is calculated as follows:

BOM (at retail) planned inventory = Average weekly sales (estimated) × Number of weeks to be stocked

Assume Weston Wire Service has forecasted weekly sales to average $25,000 for the last quarter of the year (October 1 to December 31, for a total of 13 weeks). How much inventory does Weston need to have on hand at the beginning of this period?

BOM stock = $25,000 × 13 = $325,000 (at retail)

Thus, Weston needs to have $325,000 (at retail) in beginning inventory for the quarter.

If the retail buyer is looking for additional information on the number of weeks to be stocked and the average weekly sales, the following calculations can be used:

Number of weeks to be stocked = Number of weeks in sales period/ Stock turnover rate (for sales period)

Average weekly sales estimate = Estimated total sales (for sales period)/ Number of weeks in sales period

By performing these calculations prior to calculating the BOM stock for the weeks' supply method, the retailer can keep track of where the numbers are coming from and use them for other ratio calculations.

OPEN-TO-BUY

As explained earlier in this chapter, open-to-buy is the amount the buyer has left to spend for a given time period, typically a month. Open-to-buy planning helps the retailer keep track of how much money has been expended on inventory for any given period, plus the amount of inventory on hand. In some instances unplanned purchases may come up and the buyer must check open-to-buy records to make sure there is money left in the budget for those purchases. Reasons for unplanned purchases include the introduction of new products into the market and opportunities to buy at substantial discounts, such as when a supplier is trying to move merchandise to clear its warehouses for new shipments.

The retailer must have resources left in the budget to take advantage of sales and markdowns by suppliers. To calculate open-to-buy, the retailer simply takes the planned purchases and subtracts out any commitments to purchase products (already committed orders):

Open-to-buy (at retail) = Planned purchases − Purchase commitments

Weston Wire Service has the following situation:

Inventory needed for July:		
EOM inventory	$20,000	
Estimated sales	5,000	
Markdowns (planned)	500	
Needed merchandise		$25,500
Available inventory:		
BOM	$10,000	
Purchase commitments	5,000	
Available merchandise		$15,000
Open-to-buy		$10,500

Weston has an additional $10,500 in the budget to allow him to take advantage of new styles, new products, supplier sales, and so on.

Many businesses have seasonal cycles and buy merchandise based on those cycles. Shown here is an example of seasonal advertising from Home Depot.

A retailer can determine its open-to-buy on any day of any year by accessing the RIS, whether computerized or manual (assuming the open-to-buy system has been placed in the RIS). Numerous software packages are available to help both small and large retailers calculate open-to-buy.

The inventory planning methods presented so far cover the retail plan from a cost perspective (because that basis really defines the amount of investment in inventory). Keep in mind, however, that the retailer puts units, not costs, on the shelves. At some point, the retailer needs to convert those all-important dollar values into units to get a bigger picture of what is and is not moving. Products, not dollars, are stocked and sold.

Most staple merchandise that retailers stock does not immediately lose its value. However, for products such as apparel, sporting goods, and fad items, the season will end and the fad will dissipate, and markdowns on this merchandise will be necessary to clear them from the selling floor. Methods of discounting merchandise to ensure it is cleared prior to acquiring new supplies of inventory are discussed later in the chapter.

Inventory must match the needs of the retailer's target market. Thus, the retailer needs to consider several factors when developing the merchandise mix, the subject of the next section.

THE MERCHANDISE MIX

merchandise mix The combination of merchandise variety, assortment, depth, quality, and price points.

The retailer looks for a number of things when purchasing inventory for the store. These include the variety, assortment, and quality of merchandise and the merchandise price points, which in combination are referred to as the **merchandise mix.** The overall key to effective merchandise planning is to ensure that the merchandise mix meets or exceeds the needs and wants of the retailer's market. Once again the retailer should access the situation analysis and target market data to verify that the merchandise is indeed a good fit for the targeted customers.

VARIETY

product line A category of products with similar characteristics.

variety (breadth) The number of different lines of product a retailer stocks.

The number of **product lines** (or categories) the retailer stocks is referred to as the **variety,** or **breadth.** Breadth can also refer to the number of brands carried within a product line. For example, shoe retailers need to decide whether to carry just athletic shoes, work shoes, and boots or to offer a wider variety of products including dress shoes. They also must decide whether to carry a limited assortment of shoe accessories or a full line of shoe accessories.

Breadth is often described along a continuum of narrow or broad. A store that offers twenty lines of shoes may be said to have broad variety (breadth).

One of the things retailers look for when purchasing inventory is merchandise variety. The retailer in this photo has many types of products to offer the customer.

In contrast, a store that offers only one line may be said to offer a narrow variety (breadth).

The merchandise variety must be consistent with the retailer's mission and vision, and should be developed with the retailer's objectives in mind. The customer will make a number of decisions about the retailer based on the merchandise mix.

ASSORTMENT

assortment (depth) The number of SKUs (brands, colors, and sizes) that the retailer stocks within each product line carried.

Merchandise **assortment**, or **depth**, consists of the stockkeeping units (SKUs) within a category (this could include types of brands, colors, and sizes that the retailer stocks within each line it carries). Depth is often described along a continuum of shallow to deep.

stockkeeping unit (SKU) The smallest unit of measure that is used to inventory products.

Merchandise depth is directly related to quality, assortment, and variety of merchandise offered. To monitor merchandise depth, retailers use **stockkeeping units,** or **SKUs,** to determine the average quantity of merchandise carried for each of the various brands sold in their stores. An SKU (pronounced a letter at a time or as one word) is the smallest unit of measure used to inventory products. SKUs are established by the retailer and are typically an alpha-numeric combination. For example, a shirt of a particular style and color could have an SKU of 091766-B, meaning "style number 091766, in blue." An SKU tells the retailer exactly what product is in inventory. The SKU may or may not be visible to the customer.

The retailer must let the buyer know the assortment policy so that the buyer can develop a merchandise mix that is in line with the retailer's mission, vision, and objectives.

Figure 9.2 shows the relationship between variety and assortment. By cross-classifying assortment (deep or shallow) by the variety (narrow or broad), a

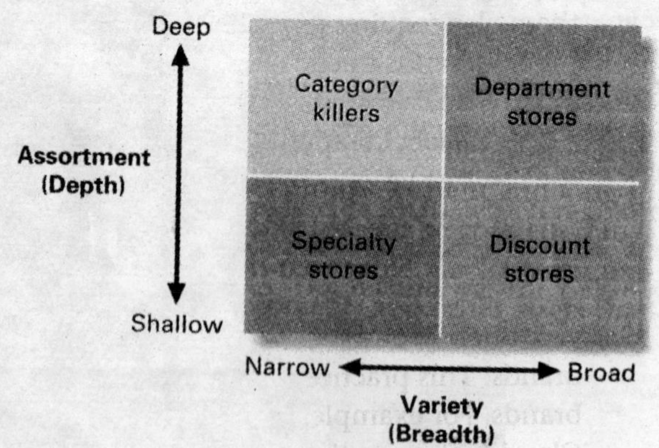

FIGURE 9.2 The Merchandise Mix: Variety and Assortment

two-by-two dimensional matrix is formed, as depicted in the figure. The four cells in the matrix may be described as follows:

1. Deep and narrow: many types of goods in one or a few product lines. Examples: category killers (*e.g.*, Toys "R" Us, PETsMart).
2. Shallow and narrow: few types of goods in one or few product lines. Examples: specialty stores (*e.g.*, Rocky Mountain Chocolate Factory, Kaufman's Tall and Big Men's Shop).
3. Deep and broad: many types of goods in each of many different product lines. Examples: department stores (*e.g.*, JCPenney, Macy's, Sears).
4. Shallow and broad: few types of goods in each of several different product lines. Example: discount stores (*e.g.*, Wal-Mart, Kmart, Target).

Each individual brand can have its own level of depth. For example, consider a shoe retailer that carries the Z-Coil shoe. For each brand of Z-Coil (such as Freedom 2000 and the Cloudwalker), the retailer must decide which sizes, or depth of offering, to include. Many retailers carry only the most popular sizes and colors of Z-Coils so they can have faster inventory turnover (shallow assortment). Other retailers that focus on customer service may carry the whole depth (deep assortment) of sizes and colors so that all customers will be able to find a particular brand of Z-Coil shoe in their size and preferred color.

PRIVATE VS. NATIONAL BRANDS

One problem retailers face when developing their merchandise assortment is achieving an appropriate balance between their own brands (private labels) and the national assortment of products (national brands). This balance is important because the retailer has to allocate shelf space for each of these products. National brands generally have a smaller profit margin for the retailer but are supported with national advertising and IMC from the supplier. Thus, there is consumer demand for these products. In contrast, private labels provide higher margins—an advantage to the retailer—but carrying them also requires associated additional costs and tasks, such as communicating the brands to consumers and developing consumer brand loyalty to the private labels.

Private label brands have grown nearly twice as fast as national brands over the last five years.[17] JCPenney is an example of a retailer that carries both private brands and national brands. Its private brands include Arizona Jeans, Hunt Club, Stafford, and St. John's Bay.[18] National brands include Levi Strauss's Dockers, Adidas, Lee, and Ocean Pacific.

A recent trend is toward retailers buying previously established national brands. This practice blurs the distinction between national and private brands. For example, in 1999, Wal-Mart picked up the rights to sell White Cloud bathroom tissue. Target, another discounter, is the only retailer with the rights to sell Tupperware. Industry experts predict that the retailing industry may see more conscious acquisitions of national brands.[19]

QUALITY

Suppliers of merchandise provide varying levels of quality in their merchandise assortments. Therefore, retailers must decide what level of quality they want when purchasing inventory. A consumer shopping at an electronics store, for example, may find television sets priced hundreds or even thousands of dollars apart, based on product quality.

Consumers have developed firm attitudes and opinions regarding the quality of products. Thus, the retailer needs to be clear about what its consumers want from a product (long life, low price, and so on) and to offer the appropriate merchandise mix of high-quality and/or lower-quality products.

Once again the retailer should look to the retail mission and vision to determine what to offer the consumer in terms of quality. The merchandise quality should be consistent with all other messages communicated to the consumer about the retail operation. A retailer that is located in an upscale area, uses high-quality communication vehicles, and offers an elegant shopping atmosphere complete with top-notch customer service should carry only high-quality merchandise. Conversely, a discount retailer's customers look primarily for value for their dollars. Therefore, the discount retailer should concentrate on merchandise that can be offered at a lower price. As a result, the overall merchandise mix should contain lower-quality products.

PRICE POINTS

price points The range of prices for a particular merchandise line.

Price points are another consideration when selecting merchandise assortments. (Pricing is covered in detail in Chapter 11.) **Price points** are the range of prices for a particular merchandise line. Price points help attract the retailer's target market into the store. Retailers must decide if they want to have market-average, above-average, or below-average price points for the products they offer. Price points generally have a fairly wide range. For example, the price points for the various types of Z-Coils may run from $89 to $289. The benefit of establishing price points early in the merchandise mix development process is that it helps the retailer select the market for the product. Consumers who are not interested in expensive, high-quality shoes will probably not be attracted to a shoe store that markets Z-Coils.

VARIABLES THAT AFFECT THE MERCHANDISE MIX

In creating the merchandise mix, a number of variables have an impact on merchandise purchases. These variables can hinder the retailer's ability to achieve merchandise mix goals and objectives. The main variables are budget constraints, space limitations, product turnover, and stock replenishment.

BUDGET CONSTRAINTS. One problem encountered by many firms is that the retail buyer is constrained by the amount of money available to make purchases. In an ideal world, buyers are able to purchase everything they desire, provided a customer need for those products exists. In the real world, the retailer's budget may not be large enough to generate the price points, variety, assortment, quality, and depth of product the buyer would desire. The retail buyer must make the best decisions possible given a limited budget.

SPACE LIMITATIONS. Another problem is that the retailer's selling venue (store, catalog, etc.) has inherent space limitations. Thus, the retailer has to decide which products will most appeal to consumers and at the same time return a good investment to the owners of the retail outlet.

In an e-tailing environment, there is also limited space to display products. Therefore, the e-tailer has to determine which types of merchandise to feature given the limited amount of cyber–selling space. In addition, e-tailers, like traditional retailers, cannot inventory all the products available for sale. However, the e-tailer has the advantage of being able to quickly place their customers' orders with its suppliers, thus avoiding the need to stock all the items offered for sale.

PRODUCT TURNOVER RATES. Closely related to the problems of budget and storage limitations are product turnover rates. The more variety of merchandise a retailer carries (in other words, the greater the depth), the lower the turnover rate for all products. Although some products turn over faster than others, many retailers need to carry a lot of depth to ensure customer satisfaction. In addition, carrying too few units of a product may lead to a stockout situation. Department stores typically buy only a few units of an item in small and extra-large sizes and buy the bulk in the most popular sizes (medium and large). Because of this, department stores may experience stockouts on the small and extra-large sizes. The lack of variety in these sizes creates a niche position for retailers specializing in small sizes as well as those specializing in larger sizes. The 5-7-9 shops and Petite Sophisticate stores cater to the smaller-size woman, whereas Lane Bryant and Avenue focus on women who need larger-size clothing.

STOCK REPLENISHMENT. Finally, the retailer needs to know when the various levels of stock for the stores must be replenished. By establishing these stock levels, the retailer will know when to reorder the various products. Reorder points are calculated using software specifically developed for that purpose. The POS system scans the product data and, when it detects that inventory levels are becoming depleted, triggers the main database to ship more merchandise. However, the retailer has to input these levels into the computer. To get accurate information on the reorder point, the retailer needs to know the order lead time, the product usage rate, and the amount of safety stock required within the retail unit.

When a retailer places an order for merchandise, a certain span of time is required for the order to be fulfilled. The order has to be sent to the supplier. The supplier then develops a payment plan and fills the order through its warehouse. In addition, the supplier has to transport the load to the retailer. This time span between placement and fulfillment of the order is the **order lead time.**

order lead time The span of time required to fulfill an order.

Department stores typically buy only a few items in extra-large sizes. This practice creates opportunities for specialty retailers who cater to niche customers' needs. Shown here is a Lands' End ad targeting women who wear larger sizes.

usage rate Average sales per day of a specific product in units.

safety stock Extra merchandise carried to keep a retailer from running out of a product.

The product's **usage rate** is the average sales per day of the specific product in units, *not* in dollars. To avoid an out-of-stock situation, the retailer needs to build in some additional stock in case the merchandise shipment is damaged or lost or some other emergency occurs. This additional stock is known as **safety stock.** The retailer should establish a customer service level that will help determine how much safety stock to keep on hand. If the retailer is customer focused and aims to have merchandise available for sale at all times, the service level will be high. However, as mentioned earlier, the cost of carrying merchandise can be high, and carrying high levels of safety stock can be even more costly.

The following formula shows how to calculate the required reorder time, or point, for merchandise:

$$\text{Reorder point} = (\text{Usage rate} \times \text{Lead time}) + \text{Safety stock}$$

economic order quantity (EOQ) A calculation of how much merchandise to reorder.

ECONOMIC ORDER QUANTITY

Another important decision is how much merchandise to reorder. This concept is called the **economic order quantity (EOQ).** Deciding on the amount of merchandise to reorder will influence the decision on when to reorder. Remember that the larger the order, the lower the unit costs for the merchandise. Also, the cost of stocking the products—inventory costs—will be higher with larger shipments of merchandise.

The retailer wants to minimize the costs of ordering and carrying inventory. The EOQ is derived by finding the lowest point on the total inventory cost curve. A retailer's economic order quantity is determined by four variables: demand for the product, the costs associated with order placement, the percentage of carrying costs to unit costs, and the unit cost of an individual item. The formula to determine EOQ is as follows:

$$EOQ = \sqrt{\frac{2DS}{IC}}$$

where

D = Annual demand for the products (in units)
S = costs to place the order (not including the merchandise cost)
I = percentage of carrying costs to unit costs (annually)
C = unit cost of an item

Suppose Weston Wire Service needs to order watches for sale in its stores. Jim Weston has estimated that the company will sell 1,000 watches per year, and the per-unit cost of the watches is $100. Weston has accessed the RIS and found that the cost of carrying the watches (including insurance, warehousing, sales space, and shoplifting) is 35 percent. Every time Weston places an order, it costs the company $2, mostly for time. Thus, Weston wants to estimate the EOQ and calculates it as follows:

$$EOQ = \sqrt{2(1{,}000)(\$2)/(.35)(\$100)} = \sqrt{\$4{,}000/\$35} = \sqrt{\$114.28} = 10.69$$

Weston Wire Service needs to order 10.69 units every time it places an order for the watches. Because watches are not fractional—that is, you cannot order ⁶⁹⁄₁₀₀ of a watch—Weston would use an EOQ of 11 watches. By ordering 11 watches at a time, Weston will order 91 times per year (1,000/11), or approximately every four days (365/91).

VENDOR INTERACTIONS

In 2003, a study of more than 130 leading retailers and manufacturers was conducted by ChainLink Research, Inc. to identify gaps between winning and losing companies. One of the findings of the study was that disconnects in interactions with trading partners were a major cause of problems and competitive disadvantages. The study found that although there will always be tension in retailer-supplier relationships, suppliers and retailers that understand each other's goals have a higher likelihood of success.[20] Thus, vendor

GLOBAL RETAILING

Armani Sets Up Shop in Moscow

Images of Moscow conjure up open-air markets where cheap goods are bartered. Enter Giorgio Armani, the world-famous designer. When Armani visited Moscow, he was intrigued by the city's potential. He believed the people desired the image he could provide.

Armani translated the potential he saw into a "boutique"—(although at 7,500 square feet, the boutique description is a little surprising). The store is experiencing great success as Russians look for ways to enjoy their newfound prosperity.

Moscow is adapting to the fall of communism by adopting many capitalist ideals. The economy has produced wealth for a privileged few. In Moscow you will see black luxury cars in the high-fashion district, while just a short distance away you will see stalls where people barter for shoes and food and where you can buy the best fake Armani merchandise in the area.

After an interview at Armani's Moscow boutique, a reporter from Russia's NTV television station presented the designer with fake Armani jeans and sunglasses bought at a Russian market. Said Armani, "Actually I am very glad that people can buy Armani—even if it's a fake."

Sources: Michael Wines, "The Empire Has New Clothes," *Fashions of the Times* (supplement to the *New York Times*), August 18, 2002, section 6, p. 169; "Armani Accepts Phony Jeans, Sunglasses," Associated Press, June 22, 2002, retrieved January 2003 from Lexis Nexis news database.

interactions are a very important part of the merchandise buying and handling process. Three important areas of focus are (1) the identification of vendors, (2) technology used by vendors, and (3) vendor negotiations and discounting.

VENDOR IDENTIFICATION

Once a merchandise order has been planned, the retailer must identify potential vendors to supply merchandise to the retail operation. Many variables need to be assessed during the vendor identification process. The retail buyer should compare the types of merchandise offered by various vendors with the types of products the retail outlet carries. Does the vendor's merchandise align with the retailer's mission statement? Does the merchandise fit with the overall image that will be communicated to customers? The buyer then compares the retailer's current products with potential products offered by vendors, in terms of price points, brand names, styles, and depth and width of the product lines. The buyer also looks for discounts available for buying larger quantities.

A second variable to look at is the vendor's distribution policies. Does the supplier offer the same merchandise to geographically close competitors? For an e-tailer, does the vendor offer competitors the same products? At what price points? For retailers selling merchandise that has intensive distribution (that is, products that are sold everywhere they can be placed, such as convenience goods), the vendor's distribution policies may not matter. If exclusive or even selective distribution is important to the retailer, however, it may want to go with a vendor that limits sales of products to given geographic areas.

A third consideration is the vendor's IMC. In particular, the retailer should look for vendors who provide promotional assistance such as advertising allowances. Many vendors have product lines that are overruns or are distressed (such as "seconds"). Depending on the retailer's strategy, the retailer may wish to take these vendors into consideration when selecting suppliers. Closeouts, overruns, and distressed merchandise allow the retailer to offer its customers product sales throughout the year. Sales attract a wide range of customers, and suppliers that give the retailer the opportunity to take advantage of these types of products offer the retailer a better margin when sales times roll around.

Much of the handling of merchandise goes on behind the scenes. Shown here is a conveyor system that streamlines the receiving and processing of products.

The retail buyer also needs to be aware of the shipping arrangements the supplier uses. Many suppliers ship only large quantities of product to their retailers, whereas others are willing to ship in smaller quantities. Merchandise buyers decide which of the suppliers provide the "best fit" for their particular organizations.

An imperative for retail buyers is to compare various vendors' product prices. Generally, numerous suppliers offer the same products. Product price may end up being the deciding factor in the choice of vendors.

Following are some questions the retailer considers when identifying potential vendors:

- Is the vendor reliable?
- If the vendor has promised products or services to the retailer, has it fulfilled its promise?
- Can the supplier expedite orders when needed?
- Can the supplier handle special orders?
- What is the vendor's order-processing record?
- Can the vendor get the products to the store in the shortest time possible?
- How much risk is the retailer to assume as the buyer? (This is particularly important in food retailing.)
- What are the rights of the buyer? (Is the retailer being offered exclusive rights to the products?)
- Will the vendor customize orders and products?
- How does the vendor provide product and company information to its retailers?
- Do warrantees or guarantees accompany the products' purchase?
- Does the supplier offer credit? If so, what are the terms?
- Does the vendor have a reputation for running an ethical business?
- What is the vendor's return policy?

The answers to these questions will help the retailer acquire the best merchandise fit at the least cost. In addition, by asking and answering these questions up front, retailers can save themselves a great deal of time and trouble and create a mutually rewarding relationship with their suppliers.

Retailers have many resources available to assist them in identifying potential vendors. Following is a list of some of these resources:

- Trade shows
- Chambers of commerce
- Resident buying offices
- Trade organizations

- Vendor's place of business
- Wholesale market centers
- Manufacturers
- Raw producers (In the case of food marketers, the store can often buy products directly from the producers, such as chicken farms, dairy farms, and so on.)
- Internet buying services
- Directories (such as the *Thomas Register*)

Sometimes vendors seek out retailers and set up appointments to show their products and services.

TECHNOLOGY (VMI AND EDI)

An important consideration in vendor interactions is the use of technology. Vendors that have a good electronic inventory system may get products into the retailer's hands in a more timely fashion. If it is decided to use an inventory system such as **just-in-time (JIT) inventory,** the retailer should select a vendor that has the capabilities for vendor-managed inventory (VMI) or electronic data interchange (EDI).

just-in-time (JIT) inventory A process in which a supplier delivers products to a retailer right before they are needed, thus saving the retailer storage costs.

What do JCPenney, Kmart, and Wal-Mart have in common? They all use a software/hardware technology called **vendor-managed inventory (VMI).** VMI is a basic technology that allows vendors to track sales of their products through their various retail outlets using scanner data. With VMI, the responsibility for inventory management is shifted to the suppliers. E-tailers, direct retailers (especially catalog retailers), and brick-and-mortar retailers can rely on this technology to replenish their inventories and create additional data for the RIS and communications within the channel of distribution.

vendor-managed inventory (VMI) A technology that allows a vendor to track sales of its products through its various retail outlets using scanner data.

With VMI, it is common for vendors and retailers to share pertinent data. This data sharing helps create and solidify a mutually beneficial vendor-retailer relationship. Companies adopting VMI have achieved significant benefits in scheduling and inventory control.[21]

In addition, the use of **electronic data interchange (EDI)** enables retailers to conduct business with vendors electronically. Often the retailer uses EDI to access information about various vendors and their products. Whenever possible, the retailer should select vendors that have an EDI or VMI system, so that long-term goals and objectives for merchandising buying and planning can be met.

electronic data interchange (EDI) A technology that allows retailers to conduct business with vendors electronically.

VENDOR NEGOTIATIONS AND DISCOUNTING

The final step in the merchandise buying and planning process is the negotiation process between the retailer and its suppliers. Vendor negotiation revolves around the cost of merchandise. Suppliers offer products and services to retailers at different price levels. Of course, the supplier wants to make a return on its investment, just as the retailer does. To facilitate the buying

list price The price given in the vendor's price list.

process, the negotiations generally begin with the products' list prices. A **list price** is the price given in the vendor's price list. Before the advent of computerized databases, vendors carried lists of their products and entered a corresponding price for each inventoried item.

Vendors adjust their list prices based on what the retailer negotiates in return for a reduced price. Vendors can also adjust their prices upward if there is nothing of value in the deal for them. A vendor can create discounts for its products or even create add-ons, which involves a price increase. Several types of discounts exist.

trade discount An offer by a vendor to reduce the price of merchandise if the retailer provides the vendor with a service in return for the discount.

TRADE DISCOUNTS. Probably the most common discount is the trade discount. A **trade discount** is an offer by the vendor to reduce the price of the merchandise if the retailer provides the vendor a service in return for the discount. For example, a vendor may offer a retailer a 10 percent discount if the retailer takes responsibility for picking up the product from a distribution center.

quantity discount A discount offered to retailers that purchase in large quantities.

cumulative discount A discount that runs for an entire purchase period and allows the retailer to order several times until the agreed-on discount level is reached.

QUANTITY DISCOUNTS. Quantity discounts are given to retailers who purchase inventory in large quantities. Quantity discounts can be one-time, or noncumulative, discounts, or they can run for the entire purchase period (a cumulative discount). A **cumulative discount** allows the retailer to order several times until the amount of the total of all orders equals some figure predetermined by agreement between the retail buyer and the vendor. The more products a retailer purchases cumulatively, the greater the discount it receives for the purchases.

To illustrate, suppose Great Toys, Inc., a toy vendor, offers its retailer customers a 2 percent discount if they purchase at least $100,000 of product a year. A 4 percent discount is given for orders of $150,000 to $200,000 per year. One of Great Toys' customers is Fun Toys, a small, independent retailer. Fun Toys used to purchase products four times a year in lots of $20,000. To take advantage of the cumulative discount, Fun Toys has decided to purchase $150,000 in products per year.

If a retailer decides to carry a certain brand of paint, but the retail store has a small (but steady) volume of customers, the retailer can ask the supplier to "add" or cumulate the amount of products that are purchased over time. When the retailer gets to that predetermined number—say, $10,000 worth of product, or 500 units—the vendor reduces the cost by a certain percentage or dollar amount. Vendors often use this type of discount to encourage additional retailer purchases and to create a relationship between themselves and the retailers. In addition, a vendor may offer retailers "free" merchandise after they purchase a minimum quantity of goods or services.

seasonal discount A discount given to retailers for making purchases out of season.

SEASONAL DISCOUNTS. Seasonal discounts are given to retailers for making purchases out of season. If the retailer is willing to store and pay for off-season merchandise, the vendor may reduce the cost of the products to the retailer. The benefits to the vendor are that it has a sure order for those products, and it does not have to store all the products it is manufacturing until the appropriate sales season. The vendor saves money on storage and overrun costs; the retailer, for its part, performs the storage function for the vendor but gets a reduced price for the merchandise it will sell in season. For example, if a sporting goods retailer purchases baseball bats during the off-season, the manufacturer may provide the sporting goods store with a discount.

cash discount A discount offered to retailers to encourage them to pay early or pay with cash.

CASH DISCOUNTS. **Cash discounts** are sometimes given to retailers to encourage them to pay early or pay with cash. Thus, the terms of a vendor-retailer contract may read "2/10, net 30," indicating that a 2 percent discount will be provided to the retailer if the merchandise is paid for within a ten-day period. If the retailer does not pay within the specified limit, there is no discount. In any case, the total amount due is payable in 30 days. Many retailers take advantage of this type of discount to save money. Even good investments do not return that much money to investors (2 percent for 10 days).

allowance A discount offered to retailers that agree to participate in the vendor's marketing efforts.

slotting allowance An allowance given to retailers to get the vendor's products and/or services on the shelves or in choice locations in the retailer's stores.

ALLOWANCES. Often suppliers provide retailers with discounts called **allowances** for retailer cooperation during IMC executions. For example, if a retailer advertises the vendor's products in its retail ads, the vendor may provide the retailer with an advertising allowance. Or the vendor may give the retailer a discount for preferred product placement within the retail store. Vendors give retailers **slotting allowances** to get their products and/or services on the retailer's shelves or in choice locations in its retailer's stores. About $9 billion a year is paid out in slotting fees to supermarket retailers.[22] In addition, many vendors provide the retailer with display materials for certain products or with other types of promotional materials. Slotting allowances can be extremely expensive for vendors—often costing $25,000 or more to get shelf space for new products—making it difficult for small vendors to introduce their products in larger chains.[23] Slotting allowances have generated some controversy because some view this practice as a bribe paid by suppliers to retailers to get the best shelf position. Retailers support slotting fees as insurance for taking the risk of carrying new products, most of which fail. Vendors sometimes provide retailers with free merchandise in exchange for the performance of some channel function such as advertising or sales promotion.

In addition to the various types of discounts and allowances, the vendor-retailer negotiation process includes coming to agreement about the transportation of merchandise. Who pays for the freight charges—the retailer or the vendor? In addition, the retailer and vendor need to negotiate where the title to the merchandise changes hands, who must file claims on lost or damaged merchandise, and who is responsible for obsolete or damaged merchandise.

In the vendor-buyer relationship, almost everything is negotiable. Good retail negotiators can save their organizations a great deal of money, time, and responsibility if they are practiced at the art of negotiation.

Finally, the retail buyer must establish a method for buying the products and for the receiving and handling of all merchandise. This function is often referred to as *merchandise logistics*. The following section deals with the logistics necessary to get merchandise into the store and out to the customers.

MERCHANDISE LOGISTICS AND LOGISTICS MANAGEMENT

Merchandise logistics and logistics management include all aspects of a company's logistical systems. In retailing, some of the main functions included in logistics planning include logistics management; selecting modes of transportation; receiving, checking, and storing merchandise; and supply chain management.

reverse logistics The development of policies and procedures for the return of merchandise purchased by customers to a store or to a vendor or manufacturer.

Retailers have the additional burden of the development of a **reverse logistics** process, wherein policies and procedures for the return of merchandise by customers are developed. The reverse logistics process also includes steps to return products back to the vendor or manufacturer of the product. Reasons to send products in reverse through the chain include attempting to recapture value or properly disposing of returned or damaged goods.[24]

LOGISTICS MANAGEMENT

logistics management (logistics) Every action taken to ensure that products and services get from the point of origin to the final customer.

Many retailers once defined the functions of getting the product to the retail store and then to the end user as *materials management (MM)* or *purchasing*. These terms are often used interchangeably. **Logistics management** is often called **logistics** and is defined by the Council of Logistics Management as "that part of the supply chain process that plans, implements, and controls the efficient, effective flow and storage of goods, services, and related information between the point of origin and the point of consumption in order to meet customers' requirements."[25] In other words, logistics is every action taken to ensure that products and services get from the point of origin to the final consumer.

Logistics management is a broad term referring to the entire process of materials acquisition, receiving, labeling, and physically moving goods and services to customers.[26] It is not uncommon for some of the merchandising functions described earlier to be included in the retailer's logistical system. Although many experts consider logistics to be the heart of supply chain management,[27] we cover the supply chain in a separate section of this chapter.

The success or failure of a business can depend on the efficiency of its logistics methods. One company that has improved logistics methods is the Raymour and Flanigan Furniture chain (Liverpool, New York). The furniture industry historically has been slower than others in their product delivery. Typical delivery times can range from two to ten weeks.[28] Raymour and Flanigan guarantees a three-day delivery for items displayed in its stores. Their sophisticated automated logistics system tallies and reorders inventory on a

TABLE 9.2

SELECTED ADVANTAGES AND DISADVANTAGES OF TRANSPORTATION MODES

Transportation Mode	Advantages	Disadvantages
Trucking	• Door-to-door delivery • Fast delivery speed • High frequency of deliveries	High costs
Rail	• Lower to average costs • Good for hauling extremely heavy materials	• Services to small retailers not as good as for large retailers • No access to cities without rail • Low shipment frequency
Water	Very low costs	• Services not available in cities without access to waterways • No door-to-door delivery • Slow delivery speed • Low frequency of deliveries
Air	Fast delivery speed	• High costs • No door-to-door delivery

daily basis.[29] Improvement in their logistics management has allowed the company to gain a competitive advantage.

MODES OF TRANSPORTATION

There are many facets to creating an effective logistical system. A major advantage of a well-planned logistical system is increased profitability. Vendors and retailers, by working in collaboration, can help satisfy each other's needs and wants, which increases all the companies' bottom lines. Effective integrated and coordinated logistical systems reduce the time and costs associated with the delivery of products. Suppliers work to physically move products to a retailer's venue in a timely matter. The movement of these goods is achieved through one of four basic modes of transportation: trucks, railway, water carriers, and air transportation. Each of these modes has advantages and disadvantages (see Table 9.2).

RECEIVING MERCHANDISE

The receipt of merchandise, including order processing and fulfillment, has recently become more automated. Larger retailers such as Wal-Mart have created positive vendor-retailer relationships and have eased the process of receiving and checking products through the use of EDI, QR, and VMI programs. Smaller retailers use these systems less often. Whether small or large, all retailers must receive and check merchandise. The process is generally handled by centralized receiving departments, decentralized (district or regional) receiving centers, or a single store.

Centralized receiving departments receive, check, and mark merchandise at one central location. They offer greater physical merchandise control compared with decentralized systems. Centralization helps ensure consistency among many branch sites. Central receiving also offers better financial control than decentralized receiving, because the company can record inventory more efficiently when it is handled in one location instead of several. District or regional receiving centers perform the same functions but place the merchandise closer to the stores where the merchandise will be sold. Decentralization has the advantage of having more flexibility in tailoring merchandise to local tastes.

Single-store receiving also involves the same functions, but these are handled at the store where the merchandise will be sold. Of the three methods, single-store receiving has the greatest flexibility in catering to the tastes of the local market. Independent retailers generally use single-store receiving, whereas larger retailers and chains may use any of the three methods.

Specialized equipment, including many different types of conveyors, is needed for merchandise receiving. In addition, records must be kept indicating the vendor, shipper, date and time of arrival, total units in the shipment, cost, and other invoice information. The quality and actual quantities of merchandise must also be checked.

Once received, the merchandise must be marked either by hand or through an automated system. Today most marking is computerized. POS terminals coupled with the use of uniform product codes (UPCs) have provided for efficient merchandise marking. By using POS systems, individual merchandise information can be placed in a database that may include department names, vendor information, product information, and price. Most of the information is coded by the retailer; customers do not have access.

The retailer stores the physical merchandise on the floor, in a small in-store warehouse, or at a regional or central location, depending on the distribution method. Larger chains often use central locations and handle their own distribution. Many retailers still have merchandise delivered and stored at the store where it will be sold.

As merchandise is sold, the retailer needs to track it. Tracking involves recording which products were sold, how often, how many units, and at what price. Tracking allows for more efficient product replacement.

supply chain management The coordination of a retailer's vendors and trading partners for the purposes of improving the long-term performance of the individual companies and the supply chain as a whole.

SUPPLY CHAIN MANAGEMENT

Although made up of logistics functions and systems, **supply chain management** is defined as coordination within a supply chain for the purposes of improving the long-term performance of the individual companies and the supply chain as a whole.[30]

FIGURE 9.3 Example of a Supply Chain

supply chain The group of vendors and trading partners, including the retailer, that a retail business uses to create and stock supplies for the company.

A **supply chain** generally refers to the chain of vendors the retailer uses to create and stock supplies for the retail store. A supply chain consists of retailers and suppliers, such as manufacturers and wholesalers. To fully understand the supply chain process, it is important to know all the key parties in the chain, from the raw material producers to the end user. By understanding each party's goals, constraints, and environmental issues, a retailer can identify which issues are likely to affect product availability. Most retailers involved in supply chain management also include the intermediaries that provide support for the overall supply chain, such as providers of transportation, order fulfillment houses, and others. Last but by no means least in the supply chain are the customers. As stated earlier in the discussion of reverse logistics, the customer plays a large role in the retailer's supply chain. Figure 9.3 depicts an example of a supply chain.

Supply chain management specialists and academicians have developed systems to create a "seamless" supply chain that satisfies all members of the chain, in particular the customers. Techniques such as JIT and QR are very popular with retailers (and others involved in the movement of goods and services). It is common to include the supply chain management functions, as well as the logistical systems, in the RIS to allow retail decision makers instant access to important data and information.

channel captain The company or person that plays the biggest role in the supply chain.

Because the supply chain is made up of many individuals and organizations, it becomes a task to delineate which member is in charge of the supply chain. Though the process can be formalized, in practice leadership often falls to the most dominant power in the chain. The company or person that plays the biggest role in the supply chain is deemed the **channel captain.** The channel captain can be a wholesaler, manufacturer, or retailer. The captain organizes and controls the chain. For example, suppliers of Wal-Mart understand that the large discount giant is the channel captain and dominates supply chain processes. Consequently, Wal-Mart systems should (and often must) be used to develop an effective supply chain.

The retailer, being on the "front line" between the business organizations and the buyers, is in a unique position to generate relationships with consumers. Hence the retailer can gather important data and information from consumers that can be used by all members of the supply chain. This situation gives the retailer somewhat more leverage in its buying and selling of goods and services and in negotiations with vendors and other members of the supply chain.

SUMMARY

Once major issues regarding retail strategy have been incorporated into the integrated retail management plan, merchandising decisions are made that complement the strategic focus of the firm. This chapter discussed the processes that a retailer uses in developing its merchandise buying and handling functions. Incorporating the merchandising functions into the integrated retail management plan is essential to creating an effective IRM plan.

This chapter discussed the value of merchandise planning and forecasting. It described and gave examples of four basic methods for generating stock levels for the retailer. In addition, the chapter looked at several performance measurements the retailer can utilize to ensure its investments are performing well and to make adjustments to its merchandise mix should some unforeseen circumstances arise. Then the chapter examined issues involving vendor interactions, including vendor identification and the negotiation process. The chapter concluded with a discussion of the concepts of logistics and supply chain management as they apply to retailing.

KEY TERMS

merchandise buying and handling (250)
buyer (250)
gross margin return on inventory (GMROI) (252)
inventory turnover (252)
point-of-sale (POS) terminal (253)
cash conversion cycle (CCC) (254)
open-to-buy (257)
basic stock method (257)
percentage variation method (258)
stock-to-sales method (259)
stock-to-sales ratio (259)
weeks' supply method (260)
merchandise mix (263)
product line (263)
variety (breadth) (263)
assortment (depth) (264)
stockkeeping unit (SKU) (264)
price points (266)
order lead time (267)
usage rate (268)
safety stock (268)
economic order quantity (EOQ) (268)
just-in-time (JIT) inventory (273)
vendor-managed inventory (VMI) (273)
electronic data interchange (EDI) (273)
list price (274)
trade discount (274)
quantity discount (274)
cumulative discount (274)
seasonal discount (274)
cash discount (275)
allowance (275)
slotting allowance (275)
reverse logistics (276)
logistics management (logistics) (276)
supply chain management (278)
supply chain (279)
channel captain (279)

QUESTIONS FOR DISCUSSION

1. Identify some companies that you think do a good job of merchandising. What makes their merchandise appealing? What about stores whose merchandise you don't like? Why doesn't the merchandise appeal to you?
2. What is the advantage to the retailer of calculating the GMROI?

3. Explain the techniques for determining inventory planning. Under what circumstances should one method be chosen over another?
4. What are the components of the merchandise mix?
5. What are the responsibilities of a retail buyer? Does the position of retail buyer appeal to you? Why or why not?
6. Explain the differences in the following inventory planning methods: basic stock, percentage variation, and weeks' supply.
7. Define *logistics*. What is the difference between logistics and supply chain management?
8. J.&J. Retailers wants to have extra stock on hand at the end of the month equal to 5 percent of its average monthly stock of $55,000. Sales for the next month are estimated at $47,000. What would the BOM stock level be for next month?
9. Billy's Budgies is a pet retailer. Billy just found out about a great sale on neon tetra fish. Billy has planned to purchase $10,000 worth of merchandise and has made purchase commitments of $7,000 for the month. What is Billy's open-to-buy? Can he purchase the neon tetras? If so, how many?
10. Do you think Wal-Mart is primarily concerned with its depth of product assortment? Why or why not? Would Bloomingdale's have the same concern? Why or why not?

E-TAILING EXERCISE

Go to the Bloomingdale's website (*www.bloomingdales.com*). Browse the catalog and answer the following questions:

1. Comment on the merchandising mix.
2. What do you think is the rationale for Bloomingdale's choices of products to place on its site?
3. What are the price points for the merchandise that you viewed? Are these price points above or below the national average? Why?
4. What would you change regarding the merchandising mix online?
5. After analyzing the merchandise mix and price points, what can you say about Bloomingdale's target market?

Continuing Case 9.1

Sherwin-Williams Company: Merchandise Systems

In the mid-1990s, Sherwin-Williams decided to upgrade the technologies used by its stores to improve productivity in transportation and in inventory management and control. Sherwin-Williams's director of strategic information applied the following information technologies:

- Bar codes on all Sherwin-Williams paint cans at the point of manufacture
- Bar codes on shipping containers and pallet loads for distribution purposes
- Electronic data interchange (EDI) with all of the company's partners and customers
- Integrated radio frequency data communications (RFDC), incorporated with other information strategies into the RIS for warehouses

Along with these changes, Sherwin-Williams also instituted the use of quick-response (QR) inventory systems and utilized point-of-sale (POS) terminal scanning for its retail outlets.

The changes appear to be helping Sherwin-Williams with its merchandise buying and handling. The company enlarged its customer database and generated more accurate and timely flows of information and product to customers. Only time will tell if these changes will have an impact on Sherwin-Williams's bottom line.

Questions

1. Why do you think Sherwin-Williams spent the time, effort, and money to install the new systems?
2. How do you think the new tools can be integrated into Sherwin-Williams's inventory control processes?
3. Give a few examples of how the new systems may help in the evaluation and execution of Sherwin-Williams's inventory turnover.
4. Will the new systems help Sherwin-Williams to better understand its open-to-buy? Why or why not?
5. What will be the overall impact of the new systems on Sherwin-Williams's supply chain? Will they facilitate logistics management? If so, how?
6. Will the new systems be effective for in-store ordering and reordering of merchandise? Explain your answer.
7. What will be the impact of the changes on Sherwin-Williams's customers?
8. What do you think will happen to the prices for Sherwin-Williams's products? Justify your answer.

Sources: "Driving Paint to the Marketplace," *Industry Week*, September 18, 1995; Sherwin-Williams homepage at www.sherwin-williams.com, accessed July 9, 2002.

Case 9.2

Veterinarians and Merchandising Decisions

All types of retailers, even nontraditional ones such as veterinary practices, must consider merchandising. Veterinarians are engaged in debate about whether or not to sell merchandise in their practices. For a veterinary hospital, *merchandising* refers to nearly everything that is not part of the professional services, such as dietary products and supplements, over-the-counter and prescribed medications, and ancillary animal supplies such as collars and pet toys. Some veterinarians have started selling ancillary products because they have a strong customer focus. During the course of examining people's pets, other animal care issues may become known, resulting in a recommendation for a specific product. It is more convenient for the customer to buy the product while at the veterinarian's office than to make a separate trip to a retail store.

Although many veterinary hospitals like the one-stop shopping concept, it raises merchandising issues with which veterinary hospital managers are unaccustomed to dealing, such as reverse logistics and making sure an item is in stock when the customer wants it. The debate as to whether or not veterinary clinics and hospitals should even consider selling products to begin with will continue, but the trend in the industry appears to be toward selling a limited line of products.

Some financial issues for veterinarians include tax consequences, choice of accounting method, tracking and management of inventory, payment of invoices, payment terms offered to customers, electronic ordering technologies, markups and markdowns on merchandise, and compensation of staff for sales.

Questions

1. If you were a veterinarian, what stance would you take in the debate on whether or not your practice should retail supporting products?
2. What are the advantages and disadvantages of selling ancillary products?
3. What ethical questions arise when considering whether or not to pursue ancillary selling?
4. What advice would you give to a veterinarian who is considering selling other products in his or her practice?

Source: Marsha Heinke, "Financial Considerations Critical to Successful Merchandising," *DVM,* March 2002, pp. 25–29. Reprinted by permission of the author.

Human Resource Management

Chapter 10

Appreciate everything your associates do for the business. Nothing else can quite substitute for a few well-chosen, well-timed, sincere words of praise. They're absolutely free and worth a fortune.

Sam Walton, founder, Wal-Mart Stores, Inc.

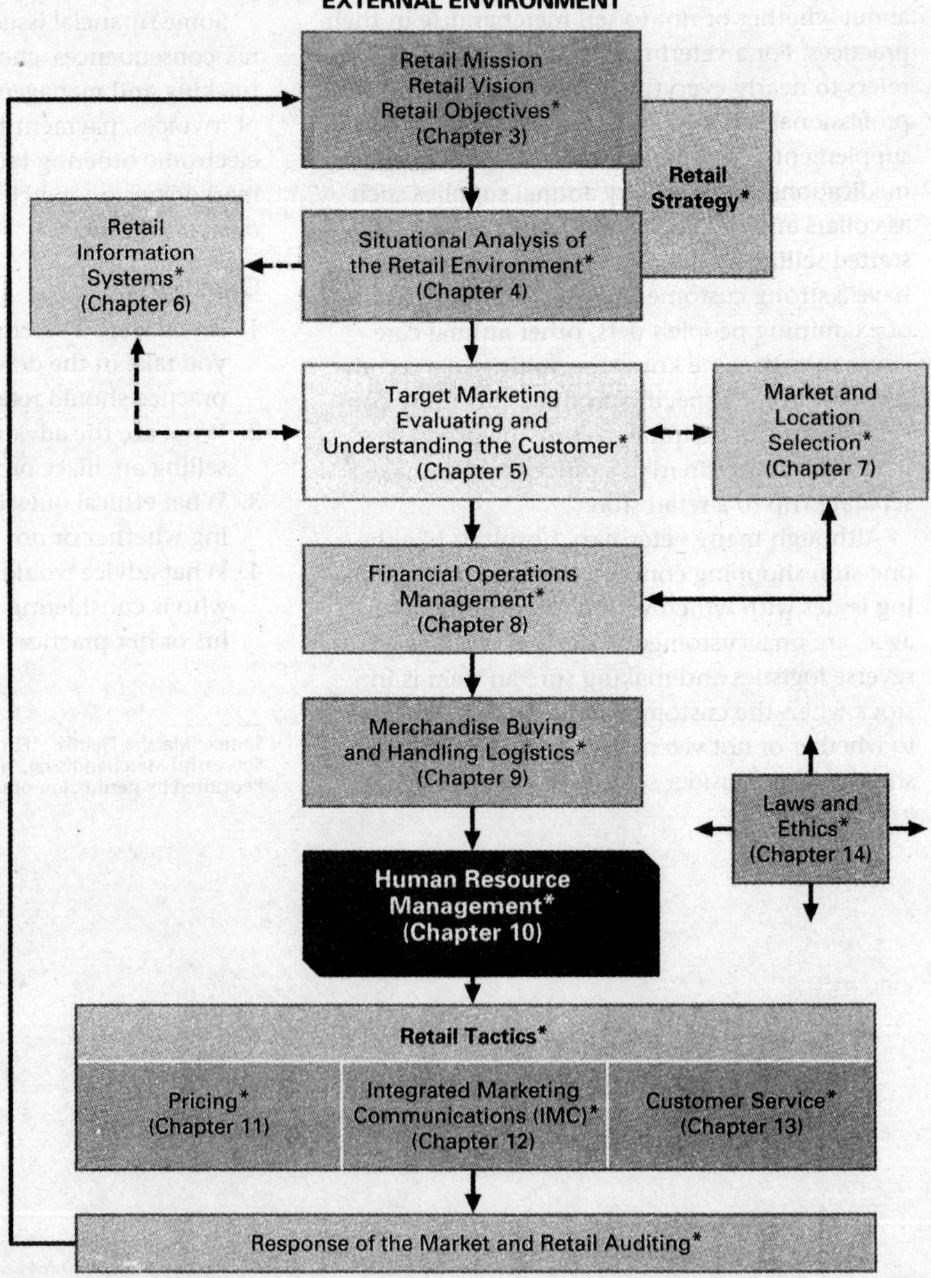

*Evaluation and control occurs at all these stages.

CHAPTER OBJECTIVES

After completing this chapter, you will be able to:

1. Describe the types of information to include in a human resource management plan.
2. Explain the differences between short-term and long-term human resource planning.
3. Explain how tasks and positions within a retail organization are developed.
4. Describe the major types of organizational charts and discuss the purpose of each type.
5. Explain the processes involved in hiring and firing employees.
6. Give examples of effective training and human resource management techniques for retailers.

FleetBoston Financial's Employee Management

Headquartered in Boston, FleetBoston Financial is one of the ten largest banks in the United States. The bank operates about 1,500 branches in the Northeast through its principal subsidiary, Fleet National Bank. Through its Personal Financial Services franchise, Fleet offers retail banking, wealth management, and investment services.[1]

Fleet National Bank has more than 55,000 employees. Recruiting, retention, and management of all these employees is a challenge. To help ease the challenge, Fleet installed integrated work force management and online recruiting application software from Deploy Solutions Inc. Fleet hopes the new system will help in the recruitment and retention of its work force. The director of recruitment and staffing believes the tool will improve communication between managers and potential and existing employees.[2]

The system is customized for Fleet. Some of the portal's capabilities include allowing interested employment prospects to search for jobs online based on criteria they choose, such as location and function. The system also allows existing employees to manage their personnel files and have access to internal job postings.[3] Fleet is attempting to improve its management of human resources. All retailers face similar issues and hope to discover the best methods to recruit and retain employees.

INTRODUCTION

Up to this point, we have dealt with the development of managerial tools for all functions in retailing except the management of personnel. Management of personnel is one of the most important functions a retailer performs. According to Sandy Kennedy, president of the International Mass Retail Association, one of the greatest challenges retailers face is attracting and developing employees.[4] The retailer's employees have direct contact with customers. Sales and customer relations employees are generally the first and last individuals with whom customers interact.

human resource management (HRM) Policies, practices, and systems that influence employees' behavior, attitudes, and performance.

The process of managing the retailer's employees is called *human resource management.* **Human resource management (HRM)** is the "policies, practices, and systems that influence employees' behavior, attitudes, and performance."[5] This chapter discusses the various policies, practices, and systems retailers use to run their operations efficiently.

Retailers, and especially individuals involved in HRM, need to be knowledgeable about the legal and ethical issues associated with this function. Laws and ethics are discussed in Chapter 14; for now, note that HRM personnel face ethical decisions in many areas, such as employee health and safety, drug and alcohol use, discipline, dismissal, discrimination, privacy, working conditions, and pay.

PLANNING FOR HUMAN RESOURCES

The retailing industry employs one in five Americans.[6] Because of the global nature of the industry, the planning for human resources can be complex. One of the many roles a retail manager fills involves the development and implementation of a comprehensive human resource management plan. The plan should attempt to take advantage of the various skill sets and abilities of the retailer's employees. The HRM plan—whether for large or small retailers—follows the same pattern as the integrated retail management (IRM) plan: the retailer needs to create an overall mission and vision for human resources, followed by a series of objectives to guide human resource personnel in their day-to-day operations.

task A duty to be performed in a given job.

The HRM plan needs to specify the **tasks** to be performed, the jobs that will fulfill those tasks, an organizational chart showing reporting relationships, hiring guidelines for the retailer, and possible causes for employee dismissal. In addition, HR is responsible for personnel compensation and benefits packages. If unions operate within the organization, the HR department may also be responsible for ensuring that the retailer complies with union contract(s).

In a small, independent retail firm, the owner of the firm performs most of the HR duties or assigns the tasks to an employee within the organization. In larger chains, the general practice is to develop a separate department that handles all the HR functions. In either scenario, the HR functions must be

TABLE 10.1

HUMAN RESOURCE FUNCTIONS

- Job analysis and job design
- Recruitment and selection of retail employees
- Training and development
- Performance management
- Compensation and benefits
- Labor relations
- Managerial relations

Source: Adapted from C. Fisher, L. Schoenfeldt, and B. Shaw, *Human Resource Management,* 5th ed. (Boston: Houghton Mifflin, 2003), pp. 14–27.

carefully defined and efficiently managed. Table 10.1 lists the functions performed by most HR departments.

The key point when developing a human resource management plan is to include all tasks that will help the retailer satisfy or impress customers. HR's job is to make sure retail personnel have a good understanding of the retailer's customers. The HR manager should access the retail information system (RIS) databases to become familiar with the target consumers' behaviors, lifestyles, demographics, and geographics prior to the development of the HR plan.

The HR manager should begin the planning phase by creating a list of tasks that need to be undertaken within the retail environment. In addition, HR personnel should talk to the managers and employees of other functional areas to confirm the list and allow them to add additional tasks to it.

human resource information system (HRIS) A method for systematically gathering, analyzing, storing, and utilizing information and data related to personnel management.

To assist with the collection and dissemination of HR-related information, HR managers utilize **human resource information systems (HRIS).** Recently *HR Focus,* a leading publication for HR professionals, asked HR managers to share their top concerns regarding HRIS.[7] Their responses were as follows:

- Integration of various HR applications
- Making information available electronically to employees
- Developing and improving intranets
- Self-service implementation
- Accomplishing HRIS goals with limited or reduced resources

SHORT- AND LONG-TERM ANALYSIS AND PLANNING

One of the HR manager's responsibilities is to identify all the tasks to be performed by the retailer and members of the channel of distribution. These tasks are divided into long-term and short-term plans. *Long-term* generally refers to a plan with a scope of more than one year, whereas *short-term* refers to a plan that is in effect one year or less.

LONG-TERM ANALYSIS AND PLANNING. To pursue a long-term approach to HR planning, the retailer should focus on the overall growth of the organization. In other words, the retailer needs to be knowledgeable about the organization's growth patterns and then project future growth. Generally, growth is documented by sales volume.

Company growth affects all areas of the business, especially HR. If the projected growth for the retailer is high, the organization may want to expand by increasing the number of stores or pursuing other retail formats such as e-tailing, catalog retailing, or direct retailing. Based on the retailer's projected growth, the HR staff needs to ensure that adequate numbers of employees are available to staff the expansion. Also, it needs to train the new (and possibly current) employees in their new positions.

Often a retailer is unable to expand due to an insufficient number of employees or a lack of employee skill sets. The retailer must monitor where company growth will occur—to develop an understanding of the customers within that geographic market and, in turn, to train the employees who will service those customers.

SHORT-TERM ANALYSIS AND PLANNING. Although long-term planning is important, in this age of "we want it *now*," larger retailers are emphasizing short-term analysis. As stated earlier, *short-term analysis* refers to plans that are less than one year in duration. Generally, it is a good idea to break the short-term plan into smaller units that are aligned with merchandise seasons, quarters, or months. During the Christmas season, for example, the need for different functional areas, and especially for additional employees, is usually high.

PART-TIME EMPLOYMENT. A final issue the retail HR specialist must plan for is the number and type of part-time employees. Retailers use many part-time employees to accommodate heavier customer traffic during peak buying periods.

Restaurant retailing has day-parts (different times of the day) that are more popular than others. Most people prefer to eat during their "regular" at-home dining hours. Thus, the most popular customer times are the day-parts of breakfast, lunch, and dinner. In some instances, employees are needed for late-night meals, such as at a bar and grill or at a diner. These patterns vary from country to country and even region to region. For example, in Boca Raton, Florida, where the seasonal elderly population is high, most restaurants commonly have a surge of dinner patrons from 4 to 5 P.M. In contrast, in Spain dinner is usually served no earlier than 9 P.M. It is the job of HR professionals to make sure enough full-time and part-time employees are "on the clock" to meet or exceed customers' expectations.

INCREASED SKILL SETS FOR E-TAIL EMPLOYEES

E-tailing poses some additional challenges for retailers. The human resource department needs to be aware of the different skill sets needed for employees

TABLE 10.2

POSITIONS IN AN E-TAIL ENVIRONMENT

- Network technicians
- Network administrators
- Network designers
- Systems administrators and technicians
- Programmers
- Systems analysts
- Web programmers
- Database managers, administrators, analysts, and programmers
- Management, marketing, and sales positions
- Customer service
- Web designers, writers, and editors

of an e-tail firm. In addition to having basic business skills, e-tailing personnel need a background in technology. Skills in computing and networking are important. E-tail employees should also have training in applicable hardware and software management, maintenance, and development. Table 10.2 lists some potential career areas for people interested in the e-tail field.

Although many specialized positions exist, e-tailers follow the same processes in hiring employees that brick-and-mortar retailers do. The special challenge is to find individuals qualified to staff these positions. The e-tailer also needs human resource personnel with a background in both e-tailing and technology to be able to manage employees effectively.

After dealing with the planning process, the retail HR manager can move on to other areas to be included in the HR plan, such as task development, job creation, development of organizational charts, hiring and firing processes, and employee compensation.

DEVELOPING TASKS

Task development is an essential part of the overall HR plan. Figure 10.1 provides a list of general tasks. Some tasks are specific to a particular retailer, such as insurance negotiations for delivery businesses. Delivery firms, such as UPS and FedEx, hire numerous employees to take retailers' products directly to customers' homes or businesses. For these types of retailers, it is the task of the HR manager to make sure that insurance coverage is in place.

advertising allowance A price concession given by a manufacturer of a product to a retailer to defray the retailer's costs associated with advertising the product.

Frequently, other members of the channel of distribution, such as a vendor, can perform a number of the tasks associated with running a retail business. This is important to a retailer involved in negotiations with merchandise vendors. For example, the retailer may be able to negotiate a liberal advertising allowance with a manufacturer. An **advertising allowance** is a price concession given by a manufacturer of a product to a retailer to defray the

GLOBAL RETAILING

The Retail Council of Canada's National Retail Certification Program

The Retail Council of Canada (RCC) is a not-for-profit, industry-funded association started in 1963. RCC has more than 8,500 members from various retail types, accounting for two-thirds of Canada's general merchandise retail market.

In an effort to improve the career image of retailing, the RCC developed the National Retail Certification Program. The program benefits employers by

- Reducing turnover by retaining a more talented staff
- Creating a positive and professional work environment
- Helping identify employees who want to advance
- Making the company more attractive to career seekers
- Allowing for cost-effective training
- Providing recognition of employees who successfully complete the course

The National Retail Certification Program defines career paths and provides training for employees to develop the skills they need to achieve their goals. Individual self-esteem is improved, as well as the image of the retail industry.

Certification as a Retail Sales Associate or First Level Manager involves completing a self-directed workbook and, after skills are mastered, taking a certification examination. After the candidate passes the certification examination, a trained evaluator assesses the person's skills and knowledge on the job. The certification signifies that the participant has met the national occupational standard for the occupation.

Sources: Retail Council of Canada homepage at www.retailcouncil.org, retrieved October 2002; "Retail Certification Improves Image for Industry," *Canadian HR Reporter*, July 15, 2002, p. 8.

MAJOR PERSONNEL DECISIONS RELATED TO:

The Retail Site	Marketing	Merchandising	Administration	Customer Service
Who will: • Determine site locations • Handle security • Manage store appearance	Who will: • Develop IMC components • Sell	Who will: • Handle shipping and receiving • Handle pricing • Mark merchandise • Handle inventory warehouse and storage • Handle damaged/returned merchandise	Who will: • Develop store and credit policies • Handle budgeting • Purchase supplies and equipment • Manage site	Who will: • Handle customer contact • Develop customer services • Handle complaints

FIGURE 10.1 General Tasks in the Development of the HR Plan

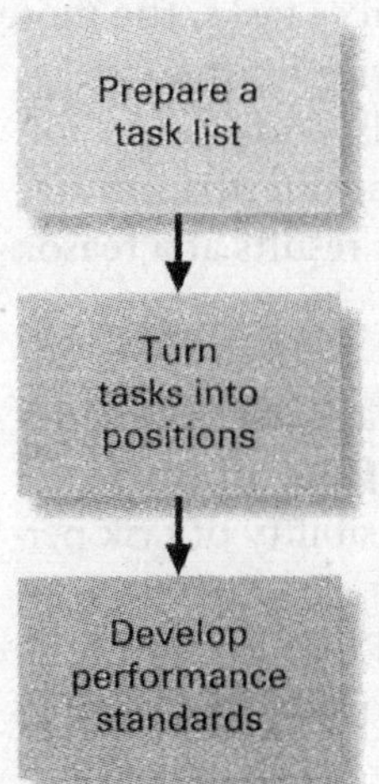

FIGURE 10.2
Stages in Task Analysis

task analysis A technique used to facilitate the listing of tasks.

retailer's costs associated with advertising the product. Depending on the agreement, in some cases, the manufacturer performs many of the advertising activities that would typically fall on the retailer. The amount of the allowance is negotiated between the buyer and seller. When another channel member performs activities for the retailer, the amount of capital and human resources the retailer would need to perform that function is reduced.

Often tasks can be outsourced. Many retailers, such as Home Depot, have in-house advertising and integrated marketing communication (IMC) professionals that work on tasks associated with those areas. However, some retailers may want to outsource those tasks—not only to reduce expenses, but also to take advantage of various areas of expertise that are unavailable in-house. For example, an advertising agency may be better equipped than the retailer to achieve large media purchases at a reduced cost.

TASK ANALYSIS

Whether the retailer chooses to outsource tasks or not, the retailer still needs to develop a complete list of the tasks required to efficiently run the retail operation. **Task analysis** is one method of facilitating the listing of tasks.

Figure 10.2 illustrates the steps involved in task analysis. To perform a task analysis, the retailer (or HR manager) first identifies the tasks believed to be essential to the smooth, integrated operation of the retail business. The HR manager then determines which employee positions will be responsible for the tasks. Finally, performance standards for each position are developed.

IDENTIFY TASKS. In this step, the retail manager lists all the tasks needed to run the business. Additionally, decisions are made about whether any tasks can be assigned to other members of the channel of distribution. If so, the tasks are assigned to those members. For example, the advertising task may be assigned to an internal employee who has the responsibility of working with the retailer's advertising agency (another member in the channel) in the development of the necessary functions of integrated marketing communication.

Retailers should not overlook customers as potential sources of task performance. If one retail task is home delivery of products, the retailer may be able to negotiate with a customer to have the customer assume the task of home delivery. To assign this task to the customer, the retailer may need to offer the customer a concession, such as a percentage off the product's price or a discount on future purchases. Many retailers find that customers like this idea and are willing to perform the delivery task if given some incentive. The incentive should be in line with the amount of money the retailer would save by not having to perform the task itself. This practice is fairly common in the do-it-yourself (DIY) industry, factory outlets, and home improvement retailers.

Retailers need to keep in mind that *the customer is the reason they are in business*. This means that if a customer refuses to perform a task, the retailer should respect the customer's feelings and perform the task itself. The retailer must use critical-thinking skills to determine who can best perform the task to meet the customer's expectations.

A final consideration is that the more the retailer outsources tasks, the more control the retailer gives up. Because no one provides a service for free, the retailer needs to understand channel members' wants, needs, and reasons for task performance. When a task is critical to a retailer's operation, performing it in-house may be the only way to ensure reliable, efficient results at a reasonable price.

job (position) A general category used by managers to assign responsibility of task performance to members of a retail organization.

TURN TASKS INTO POSITIONS. In this step of the task-development process, the retailer groups the tasks into jobs or positions. **Jobs** (or **positions**) are general categories managers use to assign responsibility of task performance to members of the retail organization.

In this step, tasks developed in the first step are classified into positions within the organization. Each task can be broken down into subtasks, or steps taken to accomplish a particular task. Similar tasks/subtasks are assigned to one person or group of people. The key in turning tasks into positions is to make sure that both the tasks and the positions are clearly defined. Employees need to know exactly what they are doing and why they are doing it.

job description An explanation of the tasks involved in the performance of a given position in an organization.

One method for clarifying tasks is to create **job descriptions,** also known as *job classifications, job specifications,* or *position descriptions*. The chief characteristic of job descriptions is that they tell employees exactly what needs to be accomplished. A good job description includes the job's title, the employee's immediate supervisor, the overall objective of the job, and the specific duties and responsibilities. This communicates to the employee, as well as other retail personnel, who is accountable for the completion of various tasks and who reports to whom.

A potential negative aspect of job descriptions is that they can limit employee performance. Most people have experienced the "it's not part of my job description" attitude from an employee at one time or another. If an employee finishes his or her work before other employees, that employee, due to the limitations of the job description, may have down time—nonproductive time that could be better spent helping other employees accomplish their tasks. Thus, the specificity of a job description can hinder maximum productivity.

Many retailers agree that job descriptions can be restrictive for their employees. Others argue that the only good job description is one that states, "Your job is to make sure the customer is happy while at the same time providing a return on investment to all of our stakeholders." The way to achieve appropriate specificity may be to include in the job description a statement that the employee has primary responsibility for a given area but is also expected to perform other tasks as assigned by her or his manager. Figure 10.3 shows a job description for D & D Bookstore.

Keep in mind that one retail institution may have many tasks another does not. Therefore, the tasks and jobs developed must be specific to the particular retailer. Also, small "mom and pop" retailers may not have written job descriptions simply because they do not need them. This is especially true with family-run businesses in which every family member grew up working in the store and takes on tasks as needed. The bigger the organization, the more likely it is to have written human resource policies and job descriptions.

JOB TITLE	CUSTOMER SERVICE AND SALES CLERK
Summary description	The people hired for these positions are responsible for providing all D & D customers with exceptional service. Duties include the following: • Answering customer questions • Assisting with customer checkout • Use of POS terminals • Use of database for searches • Stocking shelves This position requires exceptional customer service skills.
Provide exceptional customer service (50%)	The following are the tasks associated with providing exceptional customer service: • Maintain a record of typical customer questions • Become familiar with store stock • Smile whenever working with customers • Learn how to use the database to locate books and inventory for the customer • Keep the store attractive by returning books and other products to their proper positions • Maintain adequate stock levels on the sales floor • Assist other employees when needed
Customer checkout (35%)	The following are the tasks associated with customer checkout duties: • Efficient use of POS terminals • Ask customers if they found everything they needed • When customers seek help in finding something, walk them to where the product is located • Smile • Thank the customers for their patronage • Keep the work area clear • Ask customers if they would like to become members of the D & D Loyalty Program
Other (15%)	The following are other possible duties: • Prepare products to be shipped to customers • Wrap gifts • Stock shelves • Train other employees • Assist with special events

FIGURE 10.3 Job Description for D & D Bookstore

Developing job descriptions is an iterative process; it is necessary to analyze tasks periodically to incorporate changes into the design. The task analysis process can be time-consuming and involve many hours of research. An online source available from the Bureau of Labor Statistics can aid in this task. The *Occupational Outlook Handbook* (*www.bls.gov/oco/home.htm*) is a nationally recognized source of career information that is revised every two years. The

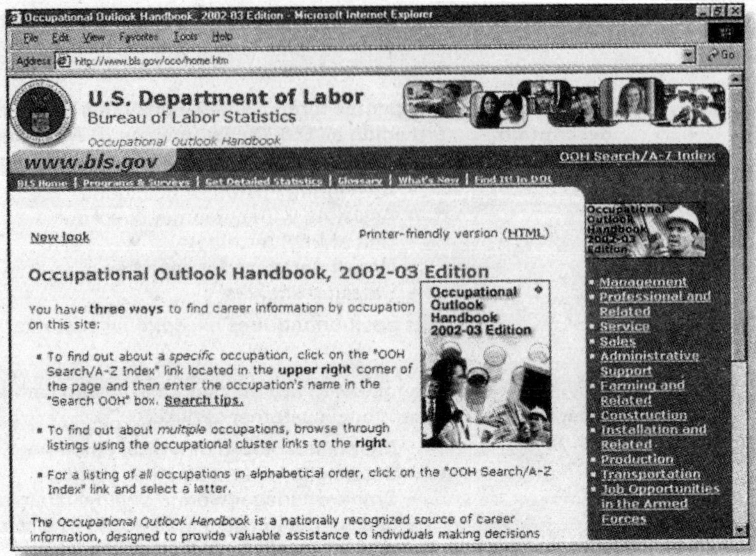

The Occupational Outlook Handbook *is an online source available from the Bureau of Labor Statistics. This source can be useful to students in their career search and can also aid in task development for retail managers.*

searchable handbook describes the tasks performed for specific jobs, working conditions, necessary training and education, earnings, and trends.[8] It offers guidelines for preparing job descriptions and for determining salary and training requirements. In addition, individuals seeking employment can use the website's resources to find information related to their career search.

DEVELOP PERFORMANCE STANDARDS. The third step in the task-analysis process is to develop performance standards for the tasks listed in the job description. These standards document the level of proficiency required to meet quality and quantity expectations. The performance standards can be used to identify training needs as well as to provide feedback to employees.

Based on the short-term and long-term human resource plans and, in particular, the tasks and positions created, the retailer creates an organizational chart, the subject of the next section. The organizational chart presents the hierarchy of the company in a graphical form.

ORGANIZATIONAL CHARTS

organizational chart A graphical display that delineates who is responsible for the various areas of the firm.

Organizational charts delineate who is responsible for the various areas of the retail firm. The chart provides a visual display of what the retail organization looks like. Software programs such as PowerPoint make it easy to produce organizational charts.

Small, independent retailers may have a simple organizational chart or, for that matter, no chart at all. It may be understood that the owner is "the boss" and responsible for the entire operation. If the organization does have a hierarchy, it may grow out of previous family arrangements. Figure 10.4 depicts a typical organizational chart for a small, independent retailer.

Owner, Manager

Merchandising manager | Human resources manager | Operations manager

FIGURE 10.4 Typical Organizational Chart for a Small Clothing Store

Larger retailers, particularly the big chains, need organizational charts to inform employees about who has responsibility and authority for the various retail departments or product lines. Organizational charts usually fall into functional, regional, divisional, or product/brand structures. Each retailer determines the type of chart that best meets the organization's needs. Figure 10.5 depicts the four types of organizational charts generally used by larger retailers.

TYPES OF ORGANIZATIONAL CHARTS

functional chart An organizational chart based on the company's functional activities.

regional chart An organizational chart based on geographic designations.

divisional chart An organizational chart based on the divisions or business units within an organization.

product/brand chart An organizational chart based on the products or brands an organization carries.

The **functional chart** is based on the retailer's functional activities, including marketing, human resources, and customer service. **Regional charts** are based on geographic designations. These charts contain titles such as Manager—East Coast Division or Vice President of Asian Operations. **Divisional charts** are based on particular divisions or business units within the organization. **Product/brand charts** are based on the products or brands the organization carries. These charts contain designations such as Apparel Manager, Automotive Manager, or Sporting Goods Associate. Retailers may combine these chart structures. For instance, one may find titles such as Eastern Division Manager—Men's Apparel or Vice President of Customer Relations—U.S. Division.

Each type of retailer finds that a specific type of chart best fits the organization. Hospitals set up their organizations differently than food retailers. In addition, an organization may have a number of different structures, including, for instance, one for its corporate offices and one for its franchise divisions.

ORGANIZATIONAL DESIGN

Although tasks and jobs often vary among different retailers, some organizational design issues are universal to all retail organizations. Every retailer should strive to match its organizational structure to its mission, vision, and overall strategic direction.

Another universal consideration is that employees within the hierarchical structure need to have a clear understanding of where responsibility and authority lie within the organization. The organizational chart illustrates the chain of command. Additionally, by attaching authority and responsibility to the job description, the retail store manager or firm CEO knows who is or is not performing as expected.

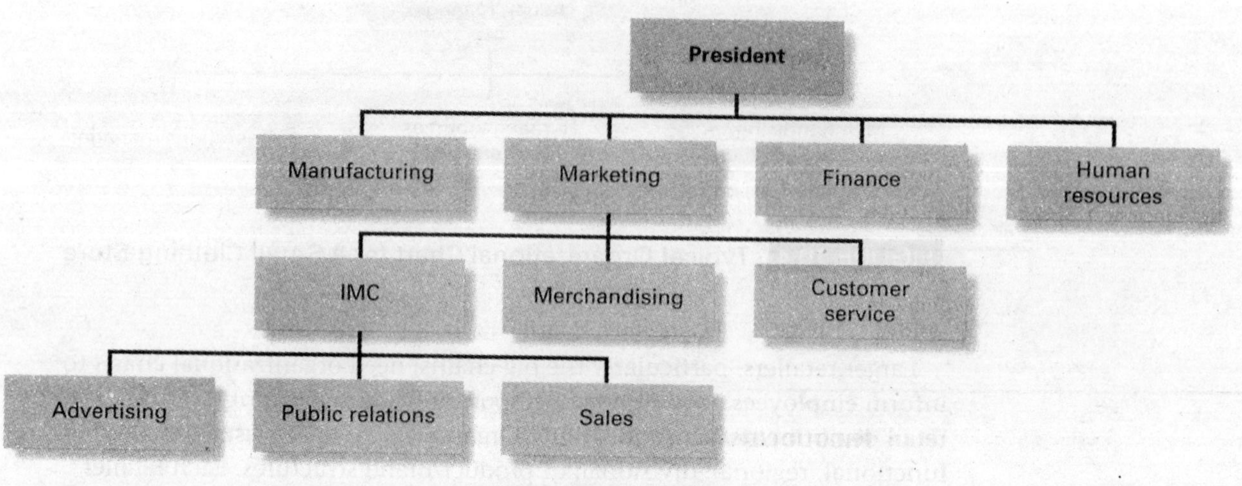

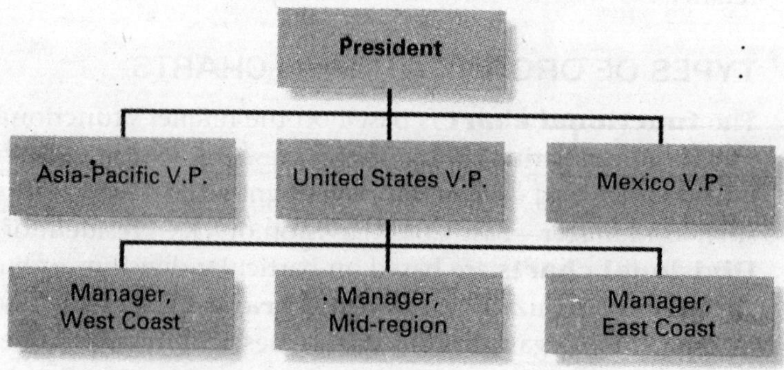

FIGURE 10.5 Types of Organizational Charts

Finally, appropriate reporting structures are essential to any type of organizational structure. There needs to be an effective mix of employees who directly report to any given manager. Too many direct reports result in lost productivity because a manager cannot devote enough time to the individuals who report to him. Too few direct reports will also result in lost productivity because the manager may have too much time on her hands. Thus, achieving balance in this area is important.

The organizational design should take into account the type of work being performed. Is the work specialized or general in nature? One may argue that store managers should be retail generalists. Retail generalists have an understanding of all functions within the retail organization but may be unable to perform all of them equally well. Retail specialists, on the other hand, focus on a specific type of task or job. Researchers, for example, are generally specialists. The store manager may understand the researcher's output but not

DIVISIONAL ORGANIZATION CHART

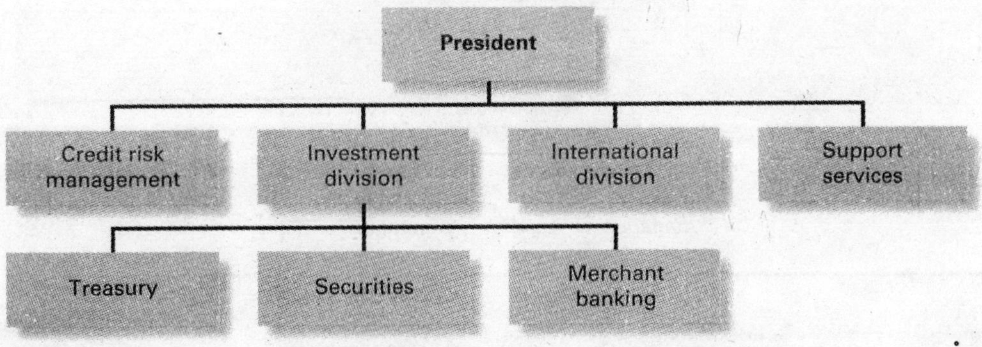

PRODUCT/BRAND ORGANIZATION CHART

President

General manager

Marketing manager

Women's clothing manager

Home furnishings manager

Men's clothing manager

Toys manager

Supervisor

Salesperson

Salesperson

Salesperson

Salesperson

have a good grasp of what is required to initiate and execute a research project. The store manager may not know how to calculate the various statistics or even which statistics to use to get the information required, whereas the research specialist is trained in that specific task.

ORGANIZATIONAL DESIGN FOR RETAILERS' SPECIFIC NEEDS

Different types of retailers use different organizational designs. Department stores tend to use a functional organizational structure. Retail researcher and author Paul Mazur developed an organizational design in the form of a chart in the 1920s that is still used by many retailers today, especially department store chains.[9] Mazur's chart has been updated to reflect current operations. The basic structure is depicted in Figure 10.6.

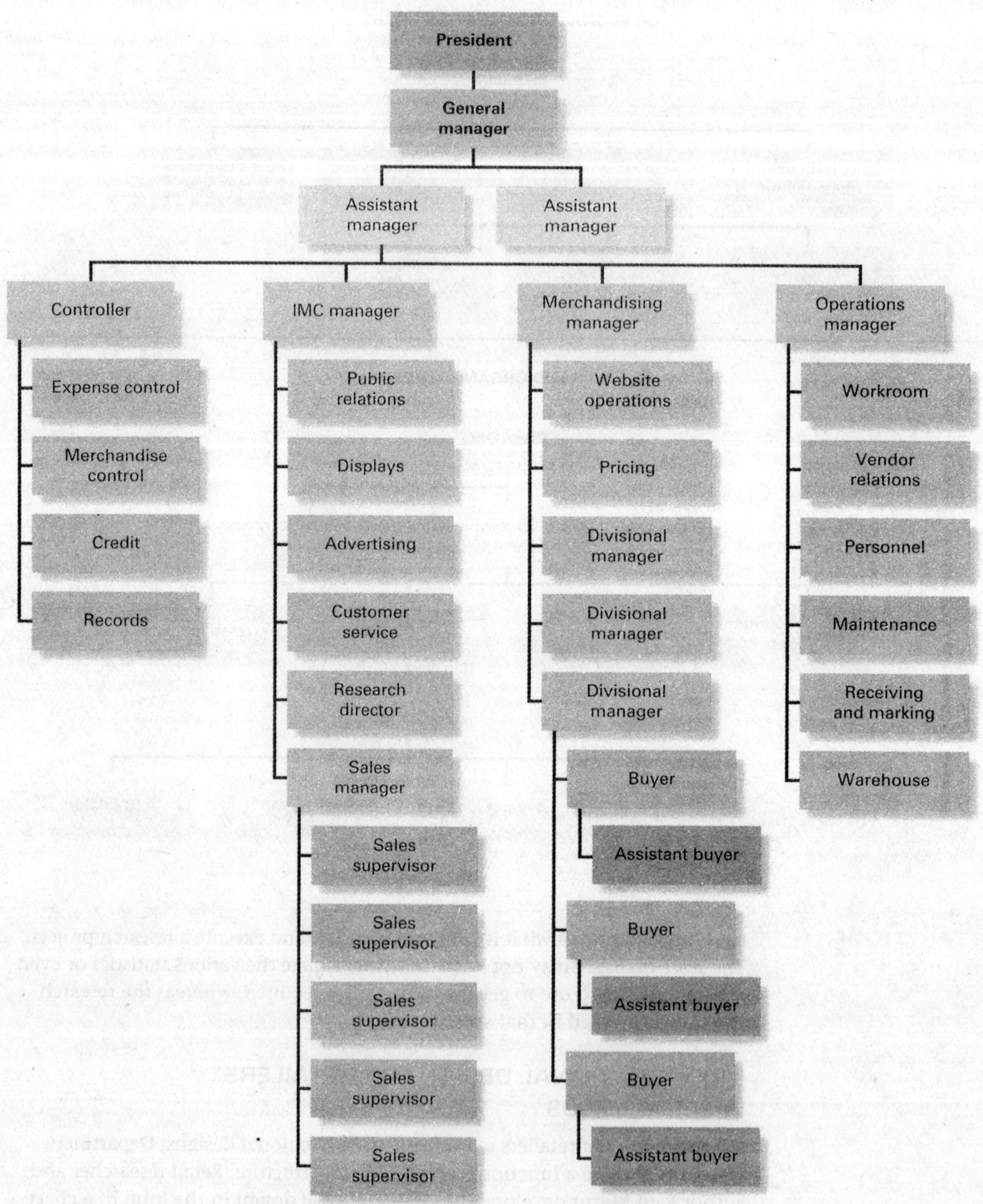

FIGURE 10.6 Sample Organizational Chart for a Department Store
(Adapted from Paul Mazur, *Principles of Organization Applied to Modern Retailing* [New York: Harper & Brothers, 1927].)

When designing the organization, the retailer should address structural issues that affect the retail group. For example, is the retailer centralized in terms of decision making? In a **centralized organizational structure,** decisions are made from one central location, often termed *headquarters* or *the home office*. The primary advantage of a centralized organizational structure is that it makes integration and coordination easier to achieve when compared to a decentralized organizational structure.

centralized organizational structure An organizational structure in which decisions are made from one central location, often termed "headquarters" or the "home office."

In a **decentralized organizational structure,** decisions are made at the local level instead of from a central location. In a chain store operation structured in this way, for example, each store makes decisions regarding its own operation with little or no coordination among other branches. The primary advantage of decentralization is that it allows retailers to cater to the needs of the local market. Decentralization is preferred by firms that are very diverse in their business offerings. Whether centralized or decentralized, the key is to choose a structure that best fits the company's overall design.

decentralized organizational structure An organizational structure in which decisions are made at the local level, such as at individual stores.

After the organizational design and charts have been developed, the retailer needs to determine who is best qualified to fill the positions within the organization. The next section focuses on how human resource personnel recruit and hire qualified job applicants.

THE HIRING PROCESS

Recruitment is an often-overlooked yet critical function of human resource personnel. Potential employees must be a good fit for the organization. Sometimes the criteria for "good fit" can be surprising, as shown in the following example.

A graduating senior went for an interview for an entry-level position at a large retail firm. When the student returned from the interview, her professor asked her for the details. She explained that she thought she had done her homework by studying the retailer and the types of people the retailer was seeking for its work force. She had also given a lot of attention to her personal appearance. She purchased an "interview suit," appropriate shoes, and understated jewelry. The morning of the interview, she took particular care that her hair and makeup looked appropriate. When she entered the interview, she felt confident. At the end of the interview, however, the interviewer politely told her that she would not be asked back for a second interview.

The professor, who could vouch for the student's extensive retail and marketing knowledge, wondered what had gone wrong in the interview. Curiosity got the best of him, so he decided to call the personnel manager (who, coincidentally, was a former colleague). When he asked why the student had not been invited back, he got a surprising answer. The interviewer assured him that the student had done a wonderful job preparing for the interview and that he was impressed with her company and industry knowledge. However, the one defining feature of the interviewee was that she didn't smile enough. The personnel manager explained that this particular retailer was extremely customer focused and that each employee was expected to communicate this fact to customers through the simple act of smiling. He went on to explain that the appearance of being happy was the number one attribute they were looking for and this student just wouldn't fit with the overall organizational culture.

When the professor relayed this conversation to the student, the importance of studying the corporate culture prior to applying for a position was clearly driven home.

Many retailers have specific wants in terms of their employees. It may be that some positions within the retail organization require different types of people than others do. Doing homework on the retail firm's organizational culture may be the most advantageous step for the retail job applicant. Frequently information about a firm's culture is not found in published reports. A good way to find out about a firm is to talk to current or former employees When visiting a retail site, one employee was asked if she liked her job. She smiled and enthusiastically replied, "I love my job!" This is the type of employee retailers want.

The Internet has become a widely used resource for job searches. Shown here is an advertisement from Career-Builder.com designed to recruit retail salespeople.

In hiring, HR personnel look for the best match between the employee and the organization. Numerous techniques can be used to determine which potential employees are best suited to the job. When performing the hiring function, the main task is to recruit the best possible employees. Effective recruitment saves valuable time and effort in training and can even avoid the need to fire an employee who does not fit well with the organization.

HUMAN RESOURCE RECRUITMENT

Hiring retail employees can be a challenging task. The field of retailing is known to have lower starting wages than many other industries. In addition, there are many more part-time employees in retailing than in other industries. Consequently, benefit packages may be less attractive for part-timers. Long and varied hours of work are not unusual, especially in the hospitality and tourism segments.

human resource recruitment The process of identifying and attracting the best potential employees to an organization.

Human resource recruitment is the process of identifying and attracting the best potential employees.[10] To ensure effective management, recruitment activities can be broken down into the following tasks: (1) determine the number of potential employees who will be attracted to the position, (2) clarify the type of potential employees desired, and (3) identify those potential employees who will accept the job offer.[11]

The first task is to recruit as many applicants as possible, provided they are qualified. A large number of applications is not helpful if the applicants are not qualified to do the job. Therefore, it is important to generate a large pool of qualified applicants.

The second task is to clarify the type of employee that is desired. The student in the preceding example would have been better prepared for her job interview had the hiring firm communicated clearly that the organization was looking for enthusiastic, upbeat people. Finally, the retailer needs to identify the candidates most likely to accept the job offer. The HR professional should consider what potential employees may want prior to searching for qualified individuals. It is pointless to recruit potential employees who will turn down the offer. People look for certain things in a career. Certainly compensation is a key factor. An applicant whose objective is to receive a starting salary of at least $35,000 upon graduation may not want to interview with a retailer for a position offering only $20,000. Other things many applicants look for include excellent benefits, a satisfying quality of life, and working in a given geographical location. All of these factors may influence a candidate's decision to accept or reject an employment offer.

COMPANY POLICIES AND PRACTICES

Company policies and practices provide guidance to managers on how to recruit. For example, company policy may require HR professionals to recruit employees from particular sources. Many retailers have policies that call for internal recruitment prior to taking the recruitment process out of house. *Internal recruitment* refers to the act of promoting people from within the company. An internal recruitment policy might state that 80 percent of open positions should be filled through internal promotion. In other words, the policy would be that internal employees (those already working for the retailer) are given preference over external (outside) candidates for eight out of ten open positions.

Some retailers have more general policies. For example, Target stores have a policy of promoting from within. They do hire new college graduates as manager-trainees, but once employed these trainees are given the first shot at any new openings within the store.[12]

A company's pay policies and practices can also play a role in recruiting personnel. How does the retailer's pay structure compare to that of the industry? Does the retailer have better benefits than its competitors do? Do desirable employees prefer straight salaries or salaries with commissions? Are bonuses given? How rapidly are raises earned? The retailer should strive to create competitive advantage when recruiting potential personnel.

Another practice with regard to recruitment is to use image advertising. **Image advertising** is a type of advertising that attempts to enhance the retailer's overall standing in the eyes of the consumer (or in this case, the potential employee). Instead of, or in conjunction with, a detailed position vacancy ad, the retailer may advertise the advantages of working for the company. This practice helps recruitment efforts because it portrays the retail operation as a great place to work with a superior work environment.

image advertising A type of advertising that attempts to enhance the retailer's image.

Other common practices in recruiting employees are requiring potential employees to submit an application form and/or résumé, requiring references from the applicant, conducting interviews for the most preferred candidates, and administering various types of tests to ensure the applicant is a good fit. These areas are discussed in greater detail below.

THE APPLICATION FORM/RÉSUMÉ. The application form and/or résumé helps ensure that the applicant has at least the minimal required qualifications. Through the application form, the firm can gather information for use during the recruitment process or later during the employee's tenure with the retailer. The application or résumé becomes a permanent record if the applicant is hired. Many firms use the application or résumé to screen out unsuitable candidates. This is an advantage if the retail organization has openings for popular jobs or if the job pays above the market average, resulting in a large influx of applications and résumés. For example, if an application or résumé contains spelling or grammatical mistakes, or if the candidate has obviously lied about something in the document, the retailer can immediately weed out that candidate.

REFERENCES. For those applicants that will be called in for an interview, the HR professional should check the applicant's background through the references the candidate has supplied. This can be done before or after the interview, depending on time constraints and past practices. It is suggested that written recommendations be required, because they provide documentation and can be distributed more easily to those involved in the hiring process.

One of the first steps to employment in retailing is filling out a job application, as this job candidate is doing.

Through the candidate's references, the retailer can obtain information helpful to the recruitment and hiring processes. Information about work habits and motivation level are often uncovered from references, for example. In addition, a reference check allows the retailer to verify the honesty and accuracy of the employment application and résumé.

INTERVIEWS. Interviews are usually face-to-face meetings between job applicants and retail personnel. For the HR professional, the interview is the best opportunity to get to know the applicant prior to his or her employment. An interview can be formal or informal. Formal interviews place the candidate "on guard." Because they can anticipate typical questions, candidates can prepare for the interview ahead of time. In a more informal setting (such as dinner, lunch, or after the formal interview), the candidate may speak a little more freely, allowing the interviewer to further assess the applicant's abilities.

TESTING. Many retailers utilize various testing methods to get a better picture of potential employees. Often hard decisions must be made regarding whom to hire. If the field has been narrowed down to two equally qualified candidates, a test may help the HR manager break the tie. Employment tests vary in their applications and uses, but personality tests, psychological tests, and achievement tests are common in the retail industry.

Tests should be performed only on those applicants the retailer intends to hire. Tests are often set up to identify leadership skills and ability, intelligence level, or critical-thinking skills. Other tests help assess the applicant's physical strength. Many retail jobs require some degree of physical strength and endurance, especially jobs in the loading zones or on the docks.

Many retailers require drug tests for certain employees. A drug test should be considered if the job is such that the use of drugs or alcohol makes it dangerous not only to the potential employee but also to other employees and the public at large. In administering a drug test, the retailer must take care not to infringe on the applicant's basic rights. The courts generally hold that a drug test is permissible if the use of drugs or alcohol would impair the employee's job performance and/or endanger other people. A job involving delivery is an example of a position that would call for drug and/or alcohol testing.

SOURCES OF JOB APPLICANTS

Once the recruitment policies and strategies have been established, HR personnel need to find sources of potential employees. The search may be limited by the retailer's hiring policies. Internal searches are somewhat easier than external searches. Generally, with an internal search, job announcements can be posted in common areas around the retail outlet. In addition, HR personnel can insert job postings in the retailer's internal correspondence, such as

Many retailers take out advertisements as part of their recruitment strategy. Shown here is a full-page ad from Best Buy.

The Internet is one of the many sources of career information. Shown here is the website for Monster.com, which allows potential employees to post their résumés and search for jobs. (Courtesy of Monster.com.)

the company newsletter or intranet. In the search for employees from external sources, the HR manager may want to employ one of the following methods:

1. Local, regional, or national newspapers' help-wanted listings
2. Trade association publications, such as *Supermarket News*
3. Direct applications (job seekers often send in unsolicited application letters and résumés)
4. Referrals (either internal or external)
5. Contracts with private employment agencies (sometimes called *headhunters*) for high-level internal positions
6. Recruitment at colleges and universities, especially those with majors or courses in retailing, marketing, or related areas
7. Postings on electronic bulletin boards or recruitment companies such as monster.com

Once the best candidates have been identified and have passed all of the necessary screenings, they can be hired for employment. One word of caution concerns the numerous laws governing the hiring of employees, particularly laws that pertain to discrimination in the hiring process. These include the Vocational Rehabilitation Act (1973) and the Americans with Disabilities Act (1991), which extends the Vocational Rehabilitation Act. In addition, the Age Discrimination in Employment Act (1967), the Civil Rights Act (1964), and the Civil Rights Act (1991) provide guidance to HR professionals in hiring decisions.

Finally, a number of excellent candidates have been hired to work in the retail firm. Now that they are on board, they need training and management, topics to which we turn next.

TRAINING AND MANAGEMENT

At this point, the retailer's task is to attempt to retain its best employees. This can be achieved by developing an outstanding training program. Frequently, especially during down sales periods, retailers cut their training programs as a quick, short-term financial fix. This action, however, can set up employees and the entire organization for future failure. Training is crucial. It provides new employees with valuable information about the organization's culture, as well as information about the company's products, services, and policies. Training also helps make new hires feel at home in the organization. Training for current employees provides retail personnel with new information and innovative ways to get tasks performed faster, more accurately, and with less stress.

TRAINING

It is preferable to break down training information into two areas. First, the retailer provides to current and new employees information about the organization as a whole so that employees will understand how what they do affects the larger organization. Employees should have information about the organizational structure and the retailer's policies and procedures, rules, objectives, and expectations. In addition, it is helpful to give employees (especially new employees) historical information about the retailer.

A second area of training is functional training. The retailer needs to generate training programs for each of the company's functional areas. It is important that employees receive training in basic skills such as customer relations, selling techniques, inventory control methods, reorder methods, and POS operation, among others, to maximize the likelihood that they will perform their jobs successfully.

The two main venues for conducting training are on-the-job training and off-the-job training.

ON-THE-JOB-TRAINING. *On-the-job training (OJT)* occurs at the location where the employee works, such as on the sales floor, in the office, or at the delivery docks. The employee is under direct supervision from his or her manager or supervisor, and the manager provides positive reinforcement as well as helpful hints on areas of needed improvement.

OFF-THE-JOB TRAINING. *Off-the-job training* occurs in conference rooms or classrooms specifically set up to provide intensive training for employees. Off-the-job training is more formal than on-the-job training. The trainers use various methods to dispense the necessary information to employees, including PowerPoint presentations, flip charts, cases, simulations, role playing, and any other technique that allows the employees to learn about the retailer's products, services, and brands, as well as areas such as inventory management or new and other applications for the retail operation.

TRAINING INFORMATION. Training information can be provided in many formats. Generally the formats are referred to as *individual, programmed, group,* and *mentor training.* With **individual training,** employees take the responsibility to train themselves. This approach resembles a trial-and-error system. Employees are allowed to ask questions and are encouraged to observe other successful employees and managers. Most retailing experts do not recommend this method because the feedback loop is not formalized and new employees may model themselves after a system or method that is unproductive. In addition, because existing employees have other functions to perform, the new employee may be forced to "fly solo."

individual training A trial-and-error approach to training in which employees take responsibility for training themselves.

Methods of programmed learning can be very effective. **Programmed learning** is a structured, formal process that allows employees to study important material pertaining to the retailer's operation and then respond to questions about the material. It is much like taking a course and then having an examination covering the material of study. Employees can check their answers to questions from a "teacher's manual" or answer key. If they respond incorrectly to most of the questions, they can repeat the first two steps in the training process, study and examination, and take the test again after they have done so. If they still have not mastered the material, they repeat the process until they get it right.

programmed learning A structured, formal training process that allows the employee to study material pertaining to the retailer's operation and then respond to questions about the material studied.

Group training involves more than one employee. Employees are placed in groups that have similar training needs. Thus, cashiers may be included in one group, managers in another group, soft-line clerks in another group, and so forth. In group training, lectures and demonstrations, role playing, and case studies may be used to effectively convey information to employees. Group training also allows employees to get to know one another and share questions and information. It instills the value of teamwork and the need for integration within the retail organization.

group training A type of training offered to groups of employees with similar training needs.

Mentoring is another method of training employees. The retailer identifies employees who are ambitious, hard workers who exemplify the retailer's corporate culture. These employees are then assigned a new hire for whom they serve as role models. The difference between individual training and mentoring is that in mentoring, an existing employee takes responsibility for the development of a new employee. With individual training, the new employee is responsible for training himself or herself. Because hard-working role models have been identified as mentors, the mentor training method is very effective. Each of the skill sets needed for effective selling, buying, and customer relations can be taught and role-modeled for the new employee. This method also helps the new employees feel like they are part of a family.

mentoring A type of training in which an experienced employee is assigned to train and act as a role model for a new employee.

Retailing executives and managers may require additional training not provided to other employees. Large department stores and chain stores in particular utilize a training method for upper-level employees labeled **executive training programs (ETP).** ETP may also be used for ambitious employees who are working their way up the corporate ladder.

executive training programs (ETP) Training available to the company's managers or executives.

ETP training is sometimes outsourced. Sometimes retailers provide funding for executives and managers to take coursework at various colleges and

Mentoring is an effective method of training new employees. An existing employee is assigned to serve as a mentor and helps the new employee adapt to the company.

universities. In addition, retail trade associations frequently offer seminars or courses that award *continuing educational units (CEUs)* upon completion. The educational value of these programs includes the opportunity for employees to interact with others in the industry.

Whichever training method is chosen, the goal is to offer employees additional education about basic skills and functional skills areas. Training in reading, mathematical ability, and cognitive abilities is not uncommon. The training needs to focus on the teaching of transferable skills (skills that can be used in almost every area of the retail operation). Feedback is an important component of training programs. If employees do not know what they are doing right or wrong, the training will be useless.

ASSESSING THE OUTCOME OF TRAINING. At some point, the outcomes from the training sessions need to be assessed. What were the cognitive outcomes? Were the skills learned effectively? What benefits did the employee gain from the training?

A final application of training is to assess on-the-job results. It would be beneficial to develop a method of tracking employees to see if the training paid off. A tracking system can provide management with a return-on-training investment and allow for changes in areas that need them.

The training process involves certain legal issues. The trainer needs to be up to date on issues dealing with injury, confidentiality, copyrights for training materials, and other potential problems. Legal training for the trainer is generally an expense that pays off in the long run.

MANAGEMENT

Retail management can be broken down into three areas: supervision and evaluation, motivation, and compensation.

supervision An area of management in which managers direct employees in various tasks and monitor employees' productivity.

evaluation An area of management that involves assessing an employee's performance in relation to goals and objectives designated for that employee's position.

SUPERVISION AND EVALUATION. Supervision involves the retail manager directing employees as they perform their tasks to ensure the tasks are completed. In addition to overall direction of employees, the manager must ensure that employees are performing at a productive level.

Evaluation of employees is generally tied to minimum performance levels or objectives designed for each position in the firm. It is the role of a supervisor to determine the objectives for a given position. The objectives, or goals, should be based on the overall retail objectives, divisional objectives, and departmental objectives. Having established objectives helps the retailer ensure that everyone in the organization is working toward the same goals and that employees' tasks have been coordinated to minimize duplication.

As a rule of thumb, performance appraisals should be fair, systematic, and formal, and should contain quantifiable criteria. Even though performance appraisals are done on an individual basis, all employees performing the same tasks should be evaluated using the same criteria.

One way to appraise individual employee performance is to provide ongoing informal evaluations plus formal evaluations that become part of the employee's record. Time periods for formal evaluations should be based on the retailer's schedule. Usually formal evaluations occur yearly; some retailers evaluate more often, but rarely more than quarterly.

The formal evaluation should enlighten the employee regarding his or her job performance. The employee should leave the formal evaluation with a firm understanding of what she or he did right and where there is room for improvement. The criteria used to evaluate employees should be provided to them prior to their evaluations. It is a good idea to give employees a detailed list of the tasks they are expected to perform and the level at which they are expected to perform them. The various levels of performance should also be included in the performance evaluation.

To illustrate, consider a retail sales clerk who is scheduled for an evaluation. The criteria or objectives that are developed should include how the clerk will be assessed. For example, the retailer may have developed an overall corporate culture of consumer service and friendliness. This objective needs to be quantified. What is meant by "friendliness"? How can this employee know whether she is performing as she is expected to? For example, a retail manager may use mystery shoppers as part of the evaluation process, to help quantify performance. In this scenario, one part of the evaluation would read, "number of mystery shoppers who complained about employee X," or "number of mystery shoppers who complimented the work of employee X." The principle is that the evaluation of employee X should be as specific as possible.

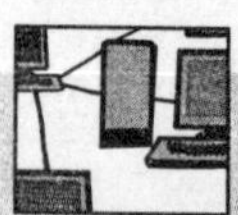

INTERNET IN ACTION

Surfers Beware: Employers May Be Monitoring Your Computer Use

According to an *Information Week* research survey, more than 50 percent of large companies, 38 percent of mid-size companies, and 20 percent of small firms are using software to monitor employee Web use. Companies are also monitoring e-mail and instant-messaging activity.

Most companies report monitoring computers for inappropriate use of Internet and messaging technology. Surveillance also occurs to keep up productivity and protect proprietary company information from accidental dissemination. A virtual learning agent added to an e-mail filter "learns" what proprietary information looks like and prevents the information from being sent out.

Other features of monitoring software include the ability to block out certain sites completely and to set time quotas that limit the time employees can spend on particular sites, such as sports and shopping sites. Some companies are installing features that allow workers to see what their managers are recording in terms of sites visited and time spent on the Internet. The idea behind the monitoring is to help companies better manage their employees' time and to increase productivity.

Words of advice to employees: Don't overuse the Internet for personal use, and beware of what you write in e-mails!

Source: Sandra Swanson, "Employers Take a Closer Look," *Information Week*, July 15, 2002, pp. 40–41.

Let's say the number of complaints for an "average" rating on the appraisal is between 3 and 5; for an "above average" rating, complaints fall between 1 and 2; and an "outstanding performance" rating is zero complaints. An employee with more than five complaints would know that his or her job performance is below average. Some quantitative measure must be tied to the employee's performance evaluation.

Often formal evaluations are directly tied to employee compensation. Employees may receive bonuses or even pay raises based on their overall performance in meeting or exceeding the retailer's objectives.

motivation A basic drive of all humans; in business, it is usually associated with the need to create personal or job satisfaction.

MOTIVATION. Motivation is a basic drive of all humans. The motivational drive is usually associated with unsatisfied needs or the desire to create personal or job satisfaction. Individual employees have different levels and types of motivation. For this reason, the motivational process is sometimes difficult for managers. The key to successful motivation is to develop an overall organizational culture for the retailer. The **organizational culture** is "the pattern of shared values and beliefs that help individuals understand organizational functioning and thus provide them norms for behavior in the organization."[13] Many believe that culture is the most important factor accounting for the success or failure of a company.[14]

organizational culture The pattern of shared values and beliefs that helps employees understand how their organization functions and provides guidelines for behavior on the job.

The organizational culture should evolve from the retailer's vision statement and should include the organization's values, traditions that have developed over time, and customs or practices. The organization's culture is *not* written, other than the information contained in the vision statement. It is generally passed verbally or by example from employee to employee within the organization. The members of the retailer's channel of distribution usually understand the organization's culture, as well, by having worked with its employees.

intrinsic motivation The desire to achieve something that comes from within the individual (happiness, satisfaction, etc.).

Two types of motivation exist: intrinsic and extrinsic. **Intrinsic motivation** comes from an employee's internal feelings. Someone who says "I work because it makes me happy" is indicating that he or she is intrinsically motivated. In other words, intrinsic motivation is an internal reward the employee receives for doing a good job. External rewards such as awards, trips, and a pat on the back help develop intrinsic motivation. In fact, intrinsic motivation often can be tied to extrinsic motivational processes, such as bonuses. The retail manager must motivate employees to want to perform.

extrinsic motivation The desire to achieve something that comes from outside the individual (money, acknowledgment, etc.).

Extrinsic motivation comes from outside the individual. The most common types of extrinsic motivators are monetarily based incentives: the employee is rewarded for good work with cash or other prizes. Commissions and bonuses are the main types of incentives used in retailing. Commissions are tied to productivity and typically represent the amount of money an employee will earn for each individual sale—a fixed amount derived from a predetermined formula. For example, a retail furniture salesperson may receive an additional 10 percent of the selling price for each piece of furniture he sells over $500.

A bonus is compensation, in addition to base salary and commissions, given to the employee for reaching additional levels of performance. For example, the furniture salesperson might be rewarded with additional amounts of money if he reaches certain objectives in terms of customer service and product sales. Bonuses are generally given for a specified period of time. They may be tied to the employee's job appraisal or evaluation, to a department's overall sales performance, to the store's performance, or to the retailer's overall performance.

It is wise to use both extrinsic and intrinsic motivational tools to encourage employees to work to their fullest potential. The retail manager needs to be a cheerleader, a frenzied fan, or a coach, as appropriate, when it comes to employee motivation. Above all, the manager must be fair and impartial in attempting to generate high levels of employee motivation.

COMPENSATION. One key factor in attracting and retaining employees is the method used to compensate and otherwise reward them. *Employee compensation* refers to both the payment of money for services performed (commissions, salaries, hourly rates, bonuses) and any benefits the employee is to receive from the retailer, such as health insurance, life insurance, paid personal days, paid vacation days, retirement benefits, and perhaps a car allowance for out-of-store retail salespeople. Whatever the method chosen to reward employees for their work, the compensation plan should be fair to all employees as well as to the retail organization.

Traditional compensation structures work for any type of retail organization from brick-and-mortar to brick-and-click to click-only retailers. Following are descriptions of the various compensation plans.

Hourly Wage Under an hourly wage compensation system, the retailer and employee agree on an amount of money the employee is to be paid for each hour of work. The retailer may predetermine the wage, or it may be negotiable with input from the employee.

Straight Salary Straight salary is an agreed-on, fixed amount paid to the employee for a specified period of time at work. A salary can be stated in quarterly, weekly, or monthly periods, but is almost always yearly.

Straight Commissions A straight commission is compensation for the amount of sales an employee generates, in either units or dollars. Employees who are individualists and hard workers often prefer the commission structure because it rewards them with payments based on their own performance. It is a good fit for those employees who are highly extrinsically motivated.

Salary Plus Commission In a salary-plus-commission arrangement, the employee gets a fixed salary but also receives commissions for sales of products (either units or dollars) above what is expected during normal performance of his or her duties. The salary-plus-commission system allows the retailer some control over employees, but it also generates a strong level of employee motivation.

Salary Plus Bonus Many executives and upper-level managers prefer a system that gives them a salary but also provides a bonus for extraordinary work. Under this system, the employee receives a straight salary but also gets periodic bonuses (weekly, monthly, quarterly, or yearly) for extraordinary sales or behavioral performance. This system allows the employee to earn a good living while also having the opportunity to work harder and earn more money. Bonuses are not given to employees who fail to meet their basic retail objectives. Job appraisal and evaluation decisions should be separate from whether or not an employee receives a bonus, however.

In addition to the above plans, retailers often provide employees with fringe benefits. These benefits allow employees to have a satisfying lifestyle without additional out-of-pocket costs for necessities such as health and life insurance. Table 10.3 lists the major types of benefits.

In some instances, benefits are paid for directly by the retailer. Recently, however, it has become more common for employee and retailer to share the cost of fringe benefits. For example, the employee may pay the first $250 to $300 of health insurance, with the employer paying 100 percent of the remainder.

Many retailers use a "smorgasbord" or "cafeteria plan" approach to benefits. A cafeteria plan allows employees a certain amount of money for benefits; then, from a prepared list, employees select those benefits that are most bene-

TABLE 10.3

MAJOR FRINGE BENEFITS

1. *Insurance:* Insurance may include both health and life insurance. The insurance may be for the employee only or for the employee's immediate family.
2. *Sick leave:* This is paid time off given to employees because of illness. Many retailers allow employees to take "sick time" for members of their immediate families as well as for themselves.
3. *Personal time off:* In many instances, the retailer allows employees to take time off, with pay, to take care of family or household needs. Thus, an employee can take a "personal day" for almost any reason without having to report that reason to the employer.
4. *Recreational facilities:* Many retailers offer employees facilities to relax or work out. This may come in the form of health club memberships or an exercise room.
5. *Employee discounts:* Employees are often awarded discounts at the retail outlet for products they purchase from the retailer. These discounts are good for both the employee and the employer. It shows customers that the employee is also a patron of the retailer because, for example, she or he is wearing clothing from the store. In service retailing, it is common to let employees take advantage of the service or service facilities as a benefit of working for the retailer. An example is the airline industry, which allows employees to fly for free if they follow the restrictions for this program.
6. *Pension or retirement plans:* Often the retailer contributes to the employee's retirement program.
7. *Profit sharing:* Profit sharing programs allow employees to share in the retailer's overall profit. When e-tailers were starting up, they utilized profit sharing and stock options as a method of recruiting good employees. Because they couldn't afford to pay new employees the amount those employees were making in the brick-and-mortar stores, the e-tailers developed these plans, which enabled them to pay employees less, but at the same time allowed employees to buy back into the organization through the use of stock options or to get additional monies at the end of the period through profit sharing.
8. *Holiday paid leave:* Many retailers designate certain national holidays as days off. In most cases, employees are paid for their time.
9. *Paid vacations:* The retailer designates the number of days off, usually per year, that the employee can take with pay. As a general rule, the longer the employee has been with the retailer, the more vacation days with pay he or she receives.

ficial to them, up to the paid amount. They are then allowed to purchase additional benefits for themselves or their family members out of their own pockets. The out-of-pocket costs are usually affordable because the health care provider has given the retailer a quantity discount that is passed on to employees. Thus, the retailer incurs no expenses from the employees' additional benefits. Generally, the retailer deducts these payments directly from the employees' paychecks.

INVOLUNTARY EMPLOYEE TURNOVER

The two main reasons for involuntary employee turnover are termination and downsizing. Termination most often occurs due to unsatisfactory performance. Because of the costs associated with employee turnover, the retail

Blunders or Best Practices?

Supervisor Portals Use Technology to Help Manage HR Functions

Timera Inc. (*www.timerasolutions.com*), a leading provider of work force management solutions, introduced new Web-based work force interaction portals. These portals enable retailers to more effectively manage their human resource functions by providing secure, online access to work force management tools based on the employee's role in the organization. For example, employees can view actual and scheduled start times, end times, and total hours, print schedule assignments, enter requests for time off, review and respond to supervisor-to-employee messages, and access bulletin boards. Supervisor portals allow a manager to develop budgets, approve or deny employee requests, review timesheets, review forecasted sales activity, create schedules, and define access privileges for the employees they supervise.

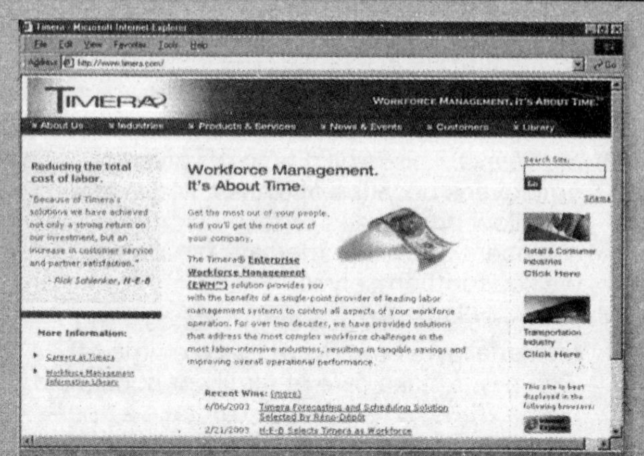

Timera is a company that provides software and equipment to help companies manage human resource issues. (Courtesy of Timera.)

Source: "Timera Introduces Workforce Interaction Portals at Annual National Retail Federation Convention and Expo," *Business Wire*, January 10, 2002, retrieved July 2002 from the Proquest database.

manager should strive to retain good employees and at the same time help poor to average employees boost their performance. There are varying reasons that an employee may underperform. Reasons such as poor training or an unsatisfactory employee-task fit can be corrected. When it becomes evident that an employee is not a good fit for the organization, however, it is to the benefit of both retailer and employee to sever the relationship.

The step of terminating an employee should not be taken unless the employee cannot be "turned around" into a positive, contributing member of the retail organization. Employee **termination,** or firing, is one of the hardest tasks a retail manager faces. After all, the terminated employee may have a family to support or other pressing financial obligations.

termination The legal dismissal of an employee.

The employee should have been given numerous warnings about the possibility of termination; it should not come as a surprise. Many laws deal with employee firing or termination. The key is to develop and implement a system that is in line with all laws and regulations applied to human resource management. Terminated employees often blame the system that was developed to assess their performance, claiming it was discriminatory or unjust. The wise manager has a tried-and-true system in place prior to firing any employee. Unjust dismissal and discrimination dominate legal cases against retailers.

downsizing The planned elimination of a group of employees to increase organizational performance.

Downsizing is another form of involuntary employee turnover. **Downsizing** (also call*ed rightsizing, reduction in force, layoff,* and *reengineering*) occurs when a company eliminates large numbers of employees, typically to boost financial performance.[15] Downsizing often occurs after a company merges with or gets acquired by another company. In an unstable economy, employees lose jobs more to downsizing than to termination.[16]

Downsizing poses challenges to human resource managers, who must decide who to let go and whether or not to offer severance packages. After the downsizing, the managers must attend to the motivation of those who remain with the company. In an effort to assist downsized employees with the process of finding other employment, many retailers turn to outplacement services.

outplacement A process in which a business hires experts to offer support, personal assessments, and job-search skills training to employees who are being downsized.

Outplacement is a process in which a business hires experts to offer support, personal assessments, and job-search skills training to employees that are being downsized.[17] Outplacement firms offer services that range from résumé writing to providing phones and computers for job seekers.[18] Outplacement has many benefits to the organization, including lessening the likelihood of litigation and creating a caring reputation. On the downside, outplacement services can be very expensive.

VOLUNTARY EMPLOYEE TURNOVER

In addition to involuntary employee turnover, most retailers experience numerous situations of voluntary employee turnover. Employees leave their companies because they wish to retire, want to change careers, have personal issues, have found other job opportunities outside the organization, or are simply unhappy with the retail organization. If possible, the retailer should set up **exit interviews** with departing employees to find out why they are leaving.

exit interview An interview conducted when an employee leaves an organization, for the purpose of determining the reasons behind the departure.

Information gained in exit interviews should be used to help the retailer develop managerial processes and systems that will better retain good employees. The cost associated with attracting and retaining employees is high; thus, retention directly affects the firm's profitability. Many firms, such as Chick Filet, offer college scholarships to employees who stay with the company for a minimum period of time. The costs associated with this practice are offset by the low employee turnover.

SUMMARY

This chapter focused on the human resource function of retailing. The chapter covered processes used in planning the overall human resource functions. These functions, and the overall plan, must be tied into the comprehensive IRM plan.

The chapter looked at two methods of analyzing the human resource function: short-term analysis and long-term analysis. Then it discussed the development of retailing tasks and managers' responsibility for turning tasks into positions.

Next, the chapter discussed the development and types of organizational charts. It examined the creation of authority and responsibility within the retail organization.

The chapter then turned to recruitment and evaluation of employees. Problems associated with attracting qualified employees and creating job readjustments for employees who are performing poorly were examined. Some methods used to assess employee performance, such as job evaluations and ratings, were also provided.

Next, the chapter looked at various methods of compensation for retail staff, including hourly wage, straight salary, straight commission, salary plus commission, and salary plus bonus plans. It then discussed employee benefits such as insurance, sick leave, profit sharing, and paid time off.

One of the most difficult aspects of human resource management is termination. The chapter covered the two main types of termination: involuntary (such as termination through firing or downsizing) and voluntary.

KEY TERMS

human resource management (HRM) (286)
task (286)
human resource information system (HRIS) (287)
advertising allowance (289)
task analysis (291)
job (position) (292)
job description (292)
organizational chart (294)
functional chart (295)
regional chart (295)
divisional chart (295)
product/brand chart (295)
centralized organizational structure (299)
decentralized organizational structure (299)
human resource recruitment (301)
image advertising (301)
individual training (307)
programmed learning (307)
group training (307)
mentoring (307)
executive training programs (ETP) (307)
supervision (309)
evaluation (309)
motivation (310)
organizational culture (310)
intrinsic motivation (311)
extrinsic motivation (311)
termination (314)
downsizing (315)
outplacement (315)
exit interview (315)

QUESTIONS FOR DISCUSSION

1. What are the qualities of a good human resource manager? What are the potential consequences of ineffective HR management?
2. Name some methods retailers use to recruit employees. Are there other methods that could be used to recruit more effectively?
3. Do you think e-tailers need to use nontraditional approaches to finding employees to staff their organizations? If so, what approaches would you recommend?
4. What are the differences between the HR functions performed by an e-tailer and those performed by a typical brick-and-mortar retailer?
5. What do you believe is the most important aspect of retail training?

6. What rewards motivate you to work harder? Are intrinsic rewards more important to you than extrinsic rewards? Why or why not?
7. What methods of compensation can be used to motivate an employee who prefers to work in groups? An employee who prefers to work alone?

E-TAILING EXERCISE

Go to the *Occupational Outlook Handbook* at *www.bls.gov/oco/home.htm*. Answer the following questions:

1. What are the three ways to find information on a particular occupation?
2. Look up the following occupations on the website and write a paragraph that describes each position:
   a. Purchasing manager
   b. Retail manager
   c. Retail salesperson
   d. Human resource manager
3. What are the typical salaries for the positions listed above?

Continuing Case 10.1

Sherwin-Williams Company: Facing Competition for Employees

The do-it-yourself (DIY) paint industry is expected to continue its pattern of rapid growth, thus requiring more products and services for customers. Sherwin-Williams has been opening new stores every year. In 1999 the company opened 142 stores, in 2000 it opened 92 stores, and the growth continues today. Duron, one of Sherwin-Williams's competitors, is also enjoying rapid growth. Duron established a strategy of growth during the late 1990s and into the 2000s. Duron markets to professional painters, with only 5 percent of its business coming from the DIY market.

To keep up with this booming industry, Sherwin-Williams has stepped up its HR function. The company recruits from many colleges and universities, as well as through the SIFE (Students in Free Enterprise) organization. Sherwin-Williams puts new hires into management training programs to educate them on the company's background and policies. The trainees receive management, customer service, and product information. Once the training process is completed, the recruits are qualified to work in the industry.

To generate enough employees to staff its new stores, Duron has developed a different strategic approach to staffing. Its method is to entice competitors' employees to join its work force. Duron uses targeted recruitment practices and offers of a better working environment. Although Sherwin-Williams and Duron employ different methods of attracting new hires, their final goal of hiring and retaining the best-trained employees is the same.

Questions

1. Is Duron's approach to finding qualified applicants ethical? Would you use this method if you owned or managed your own company?
2. How do you think Sherwin-Williams will react to Duron's recruitment tactics?
3. What are some good sources of potential employees for both Sherwin-Williams and Duron?
4. Develop an employee-training program that would work equally well for Sherwin-Williams and Duron.
5. Develop a SWOT analysis that Sherwin-Williams could use in its attempt to retain top-performing employees.

Sources: Yuki Noguchi, "At Duron Inc., Paint with a Personal Touch," *Washington Post,* September 22, 1999, p. M16; Terry C. Evans, "Growth in Tough Times," *National Home Center News,* 27 (October 22, 2001), p. 14; Darrin M. Brogan and Stanton G. Cort, "Industry Corner: DIY Home Products: A Global Perspective," *Business Economics,* 32 (January 1997), pp. 58–61.

Case 10.2

The Container Store: Consistently One of the Best Places to Work

In 2000 and 2001, The Container Store was the number one firm on *Fortune* magazine's list of "Best Companies to Work For." In 2002 and 2003, it was number two on the list. The company was founded in 1978 by Kip Tindell (CEO and president) and Garrett Boone (chairman), who shared a vision of selling multifunctional products that would save customers space and, ultimately, time. Headquartered in Dallas, the company has more than twenty stores, located mostly in big cities in California, Colorado, Georgia, Illinois, Maryland, New York, and Texas. Each store carries up to 10,000 items. Major competitors are Bed Bath & Beyond and Linens 'N Things.

Kip Tindell believes that if the company hires one great person, that person can do the work of three good people. Its strategy of attracting outstanding employees works well and fits its goal of "fewer, better people." Most employees are college educated, and most were first customers of the company.

The following are some of the benefits employees receive:

- Wages far above the industry average
- A 40 percent merchandise discount
- Full-time, part-time, and flexible positions
- Security in a financially stable company
- An environment that values communication
- Extensive training programs
- Individual and team-based incentive programs
- Health and dental benefits
- Vacation for all full-time and part-time employees
- A 410(k) savings plan, with dollar-for-dollar matching company contributions

Many retail companies experience turnover rates as high as 100 percent. The Container Store's rate is only 15 to 18 percent for full-time staff and 50 to 60 percent for part-time staff. The company's "Golden Rule" is a quote by Andrew Carnegie: "Fill the other guy's basket to the brim. Making money then becomes an easy proposition." The Container Store serves as a role model to other retailers on how profitability increases when employees are treated respectfully and compensated fairly.

Questions

1. What qualities of The Container Store would a potential employee find appealing?
2. What is The Container Store's primary human resource strategy?
3. If the strategy implemented by The Container Store is so successful, why aren't other retailers copying it?
4. What effect do you think the HR strategy has on other areas of the company?
5. How does a happier work force give a retailer a competitive advantage?

Sources: The Container Store homepage at www.containerstore.com, retrieved July 2003; Verne Harnish, "The Right People—Why One Great Hire Is Better Than Three Good Ones," *Fortune Small Business,* April 12, 2002, retrieved July 2003 from fortune.com; "A Principled Approach to Retention and Service," *HR Focus,* October 2001, pp. 6–7; Hoover's Online, "Company Capsule—The Container Store," retrieved October 2002 from www.hoovers.com; "Fortune Magazine Names Best Employees," January 7, 2003, retrieved July 2003 from CNN.com.

Retail Tactics, Laws,

Part

4

and Ethics

Part 4 deals with the retail tactics necessary to execute the integrated retail management plan, the laws and ethics that help guide these decisions, and some of the trends that are developing in the retail environment.

Chapter 11 covers the development of pricing tactics. Specific focus is on the need for price integration as well as the development of pricing objectives and policies and the actual establishment of retail price. Chapter 12 focuses on the development of an effective integrated marketing communication mix for retailers. Chapter 13 centers on the development and execution of customer service in retailing. The chapter stresses the importance of customer service throughout the retail firm and describes some methods for creating effective customer service. Chapter 14 discusses the legal and ethical environments that affect retail decision making. Chapter 15 focuses on diversity in the retail environment and explores current trends and issues in retailing.

Pricing in Retailing

Chapter 11

People want economy and they'll pay almost any price to get it.

Lee Iacocca, chairman, Chrysler Corporation

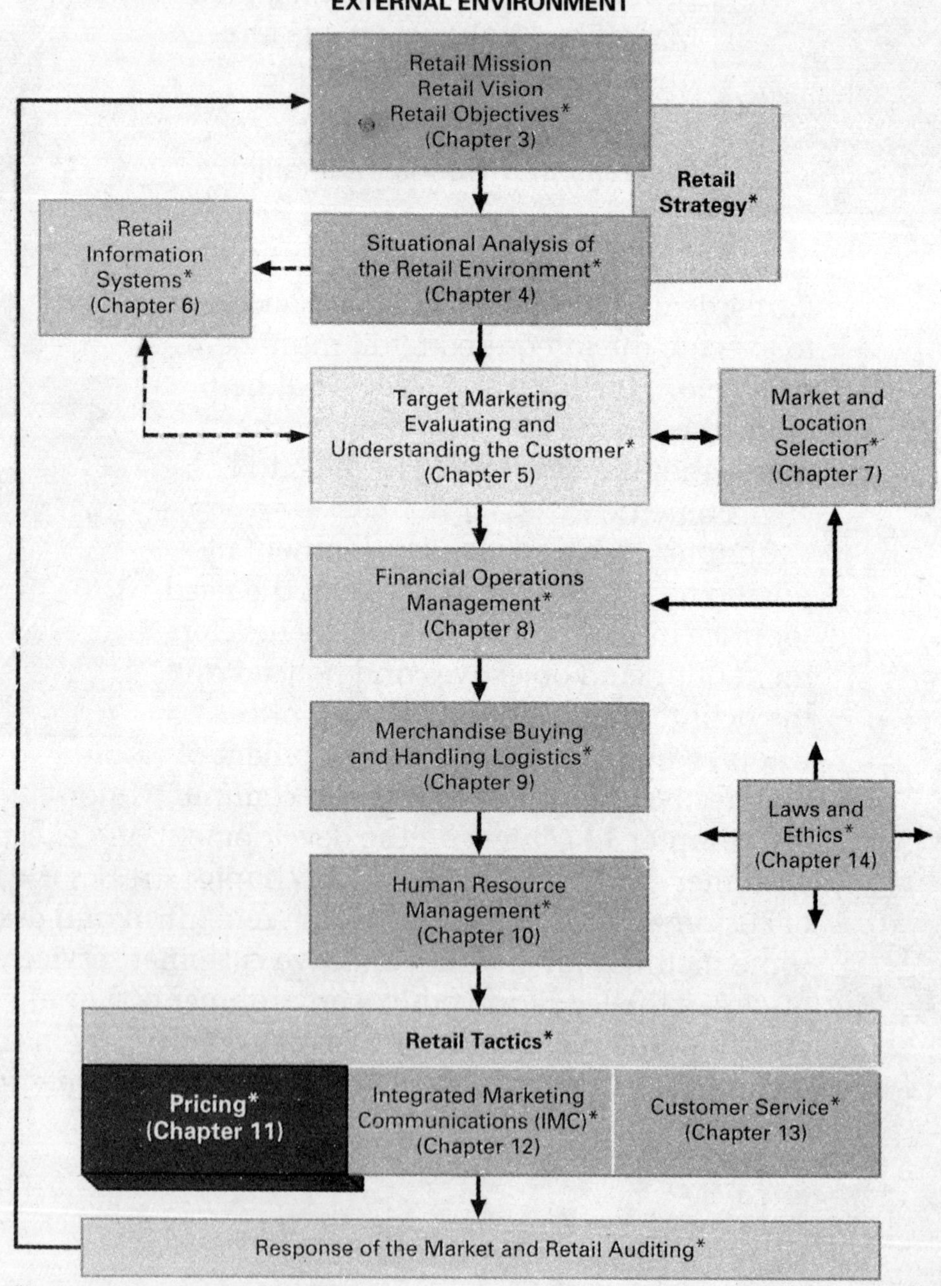

CHAPTER OBJECTIVES

After completing this chapter, you will be able to:

1. Explain and create pricing objectives for retailers.
2. Outline the main types of pricing policies.
3. Develop retail prices for products and services.
4. Explain why and how prices are adjusted.

Adjusting Container Size Instead of Price

Ice cream is often touted as a favorite dessert. Standard container sizes for ice cream are a pint, half-gallon, and gallon. Most people are accustomed to buying a "brick," or half-gallon container. In 2001, Breyers, a leading ice cream manufacturer, boosted its half-gallon price by 30 cents. Breyers claimed that prices of butterfat and other ingredients had skyrocketed. Costs also increased because consumers were demanding more assortments in flavor and the extra ingredients were often more expensive.

Other ice cream manufacturers have grappled with higher costs (and, as a result, lower profits) as well. Some responded by making their ice cream packages smaller but keeping the same price (called *weight out*). This strategy is frequently employed when customers are especially concerned about price increases for products.[1]

Often customers initially don't notice the smaller package size, typically 1.75 quarts. But when they realize they are getting less product for the same amount of money, they may feel cheated, and retailers carrying the merchandise may receive complaints.[2] Even so, this doesn't stop many consumers from buying ice cream. One reason is that consumers see ice cream as a luxury and will "splurge" for their favorite flavors. These consumers are less concerned when prices go up or package size decreases.

When costs for raw materials rise, manufacturers basically have two choices: increase prices or reduce unit size. According to the International Ice Cream Association, about 75 percent of ice cream is still sold by the half-gallon size. Will more manufacturers adopt the package-downsizing strategy? Only time will tell.[3]

INTRODUCTION

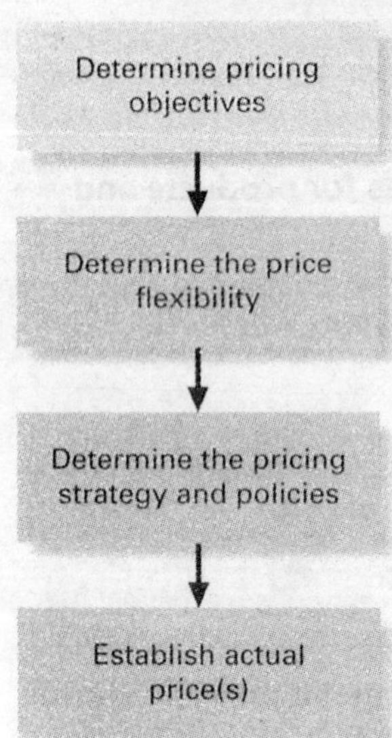

FIGURE 11.1
A Typical Pricing Decision Flow Chart

Up until now, we have concentrated on the functions of setting up and organizing the retail establishment. In the next few chapters, we focus on how to execute and coordinate the functions of the IRM plan, particularly on the pricing, integrated marketing communication (IMC), and customer service **tactics** necessary to generate a comprehensive retail program.

tactics Specific actions undertaken by a retailer to achieve its overall strategy.

This chapter examines the pricing decisions retailers make to satisfy customer wants and needs at a profit. As with the overall IRM plan, pricing follows some clearly established steps, including the development of objectives and strategies, and tactical executions. Figure 11.1 depicts major pricing decisions that will be covered in this chapter.

The following internal and external variables influence pricing and are discussed throughout the chapter:

- *Pricing objectives* Goals for pricing products and services
- *Price flexibility* The range of prices consumers are willing to pay for a particular product or service
- *Pricing policies* Overall retail guidelines for price setting
- *Competition* The retailer's competitive environment
- *Demand* How much of a product consumers want
- *Price adjustments* Changes to price based on sales results

DETERMINING PRICING OBJECTIVES

The retailer must develop a pricing strategy in a systematic manner, starting with the identification of overall pricing objectives. Objectives are necessary to achieve effective **price points** (or *price levels*). In pricing, the objectives should follow the same rules that apply to other areas; that is, they must be measurable and realistic. The primary types of pricing objectives are described next.

price points Different levels of prices set for products and services.

CATEGORIES OF POTENTIAL PRICING OBJECTIVES

Product Quality Objectives **Product quality objectives** center on recouping costs associated with retail research and development. In addition, product quality objectives can be used in conjunction with IMC tactics to create the perception of high product quality, and thus high retail store quality, in the consumer's mind. This objective is often used together with a skimming objective by high-end retailers.

product quality objective A type of pricing objective that focuses on recouping costs associated with retail research and development or to develop a desired product image.

Example: A retailer prices items at 300 percent above cost to ensure that its prestigious image is firmly established in the consumer's mind.

Skimming Objectives With **skimming objectives** (also called *skimming strategies*), the retailer sets an initial relatively high price for a product. A skim-

skimming objective A type of pricing objective in which the price for a newly introduced product is set high. After competitors enter the market, the price is adjusted down.

ming strategy is often used to recoup costs incurred when selling a new product—costs associated with research, development, and marketing, for instance.

The term *skimming* comes from dairy farms, where personnel skim the high-quality cream from the top of the milk. The cream is more valuable than the milk and can be sold at higher prices. Likewise, the product marketer skims the market with an initial high price to sell to customers who are relatively unconcerned about price. The price may be lowered later to attract additional customers who are more price conscious. With this strategy, the customer must be somewhat price insensitive and view the product or service as premium quality.

Example: A retailer initially prices a DVD player at $750. After a period of six months, the cost will be lowered to $500. Once competitors enter the market, the price will be set to remain competitive.

market penetration objective A type of pricing objective in which product prices are initially set low to attract large numbers of buyers. The resulting increase in sales volume offsets the lower introductory price.

Market Penetration Objectives **Market penetration objectives** are the opposite of skimming objectives. Prices are initially set lower to attract large numbers of customers. Market penetration objectives are effective when the retailer's customers are price sensitive. The key to an effective market penetration strategy is to increase sales volumes to offset the low product price. As a general rule, after a certain point, retail costs do not increase very much when sales volume increases. Market penetration objectives have the added benefit of allowing the retailer to discourage competition from entering the trading area because of the lower prices the retailer has already established for the market. In addition, market penetration may help establish a new product as a popular alternative for the consumer, thus creating social pressure to own the product as well as an economic benefit.

Example: A retailer sets prices at lower levels for the first two months of operation to increase market share and discourage competition.

market share objective A type of pricing objective in which the retailer adjusts price levels based on competitors' changes in price, with the goal of gaining market share.

market share The proportion of sales of a particular product (or brand) to the total sales of that product (or brand) in a given area.

Market Share Objectives **Market share objectives** allow the retailer to adjust price levels based on competitors' changes in price, enabling the retailer to create additional **market share** or reduce market share in relation to the competition. This can be done for the entire retail operation (that is, all stores), for a division, or for a specific store. The retailer can also set a market share objective for each department, product line, or product and brand.

Example: To stand by its "we will not be undersold" policy, a retailer sets its average prices below those of its three main competitors.

survival objective A type of pricing objective in which the retailer increases price levels to meet sales expenses.

Survival Objectives **Survival objectives** allow the retailer to increase price levels to meet sales expenses. This type of objective is generally used to match sales volumes to overall store (or company) expenses.

Example: A retailer sets pricing to cover expenses and increase store profitability over last year's by 5 percent.

return on investment (ROI) objective A type of pricing objective in which the retailer attempts to meet or exceed stated return on investment figures.

Return on Investment (ROI) Objectives **Return on investment (ROI) objectives** are created to help the retailer meet or exceed stated return on investment figures. Management creates a target return figure it thinks will be satisfactory to stakeholders (primarily stockholders). Then the price is set to reach that targeted return level.

Example: A retailer sets prices to deliver a 15 percent return on investment within one year.

profit objective A type of pricing objective in which the retailer attempts to meet or exceed projected profit levels.

Profit Objectives **Profit objectives** are like ROI objectives, except that target profit levels rather than ROI levels are the goal. If management uses a profit maximization approach to retailing, there is a good chance that profit objectives will be set.

Example: A retailer sets prices to increase profits by 15 percent within one year.

status quo objective A type of pricing objective in which the retailer attempts to maintain the current situation.

Status Quo Objectives **Status quo objectives** embody the attitude that "Everything is going well—let's not rock the boat." A retailer that wants to stabilize sales will probably utilize a status quo objective.

Example: In the upcoming year, a retailer will price items to match last year's sales.

cash flow objective A type of pricing objective in which the retailer attempts to generate money quickly.

Cash Flow Objectives **Cash flow objectives** allow the retailer to generate money quickly. These objectives are designed to encourage additional sales volumes. Generally, they are short-term objectives.

Example: During any given month(s), a retailer sets prices lower to encourage sales volume and increase cash flow.

Market share and product quality have a major impact on the retailer's profitability and are therefore often used to help set pricing objectives. For example, when management at Quaker Oats Company received complaints from food retailers that its line of cereal products was overpriced compared to the competition, the company decided to reduce their prices to appease the retailers and hopefully generate additional market share. To offset the lower price, Quaker Oats changed the product's packaging: instead of using the traditional box, Quaker Oats placed cereal into bags, thus allowing the company to reduce the cost of the product to food retailers. The change increased Quaker Oats's market share while meeting pricing objectives.[4] In this example, both manufacturer and retailers achieved their pricing objectives. As a result, Quaker Oats increased its market share by 2 percent.

Pricing objectives are set for many reasons. Additional factors that are often considered when developing pricing objectives include development of customer traffic (both online and in a brick-and-mortar store), movement of slow-selling products, an attempt to desensitize consumers to price, creation or enhancement of the retailer's image, avoidance of legal and ethical problems associated with price, and attempts to dissuade other competitors from cutting or reducing their prices. Retailers can use multiple pricing strategies simultaneously while keeping all of these concerns in mind.

DETERMINING PRICING FLEXIBILITY

pricing flexibility The range of prices consumers are willing to pay for a particular product or service.

Although the step of determining pricing flexibility comes after that of setting price objectives in Figure 11.1, in practice pricing flexibility for goods and services helps the retailer establish its pricing objectives. **Pricing flexibility**

Competition and Customer Demand $

The Retailer's Variable and Fixed Costs $

FIGURE 11.2

Pricing Ranges Based on Demand and Cost

refers to the "best" range of prices that the retailer can set. Two factors retailers consider when determining pricing flexibility are the costs associated with running the business and selling the products (both fixed and variable costs) and the demand by the store's existing or potential customers. These factors help the retailer develop the range over which to set its final retail prices. The costs help set the floor, or lower limits, of this range, whereas the competitors and consumers (product demand) set the upper pricing limits. Figure 11.2 illustrates this relationship.

There are three steps in determining pricing flexibility. The first is to determine the costs associated with the retailing operation. Data that will help the retailer determine costs are located in the retailer's financial documents and in the retail information system (RIS). The second step is to estimate the demand for the products and services, taking the competition into account. The demand estimate helps set the upper price limits for the products. The greater the difference between the upper and lower limits, the more flexible the price is said to be. Finally, in the third step, the retailer estimates the elasticity of price for its products and product lines.

INTERNET IN ACTION

BLS Releases Key Data Too Early

With the advent of the Internet, information has become more readily available than ever before—so readily that many companies have at one time or another inadvertently released incorrect or untimely information. Such was the case with the U.S. Bureau of Labor Statistics (BLS).

In the last quarter of 1998 and first quarter of 1999, the BLS committed a major blunder when it prematurely released key economic data over the Internet. The information was from the department's report on prices charged by producers of finished goods during 1998. The information was not supposed to be published until January 13, 1999, but it was released one day early, on January 12, 1999. The information was worth millions of dollars to stock and bond traders who spotted it. According to the BLS, the information was available to the public for about ninety minutes before the mistake was caught. Although the agency removed the information, management decided to release it later in the day.

The blunder was the second time in four months that the BLS released data prematurely. In November 1998, the department prematurely released October unemployment figures. Computer glitches were to blame for the error.

It's important that sensitive information not be released early because changes in the data can affect the value of stocks and bonds, and traders who access the information will act on it. Stock traders and rating services use these data to develop profiles of various retailers. Based on the data, orders are issued to customers, advice is given on which stocks to purchase, and ratings are determined that consumers use to assess the value of a given retailer and its products.

Source: Tim Smart, "Glitch Causes Early Release of Key Data: Producer Prices Posted on Net," *Washington Post*, January 13, 1999, p. F1. **© 1999, The Washington Post. Reprinted with permission.**

PRICE ELASTICITY

price elasticity of demand A measurement of the responsiveness of quantity demanded to a change in price, with all other factors held constant; also called *price elasticity*.

Price elasticity of demand (also called *elasticity*) is a measure of the consumer's sensitivity to price. It is important to understand the relationship between price and consumer purchasing habits. Consumers make many decisions based on price; thus, the elasticity of price may change during the course of a given sales period. In addition, there is a high correlation between price and consumer perceptions and, thereby, purchases.[5]

price elastic A term referring to consumers who are sensitive to changes in price.

price inelastic A term referring to consumers who are relatively insensitive to price changes.

Price elasticity of demand measures the responsiveness of quantity demanded to a change in price, with all other factors held constant. In some cases, a decrease in price results in an increase in demand or, conversely, an increase in price results in a decrease in demand. In each case, consumers are price sensitive; put another way, demand is relatively **price elastic.** When a price reduction or a price increase occurs and demand remains relatively the same, consumers are less sensitive to price changes, and demand is said to be **price inelastic.** When assessing price elasticity of demand, one of three situations can occur: price elasticity, price inelasticity, or unitary elasticity of price.

1. Price Elasticity In this situation, when the retailer raises price, a relative decrease in total revenue occurs. Conversely, when the retailer lowers price, a relative increase in total revenue results. The elasticity of price and demand coefficient (E_p) would be greater than 1 ($E_p > 1$). This situation most often occurs when there is low urgency to purchase products or services and when substitutes for the products or services are available. An example is a shirt that one can buy at several other retailers at a competitive price.

2. Price Inelasticity In this situation, when the retailer increases price, a relative increase in total revenue occurs. Conversely, when the retailer decreases price, a relative decrease in total revenue results. Thus, the elasticity of price and demand coefficient is less than 1 ($E_p < 1$). In this situation, consumers are not sensitive to a change in price; they are willing to pay the current price and possibly a higher future price. This situation typically occurs when purchase urgency is high and no acceptable substitutes exist. A life-saving drug is an example of a product that would exhibit price inelasticity.

unitary elasticity A situation in which the percentage change in price equals the percentage change in quantity demanded.

3. Unitary Elasticity In a situation of **unitary elasticity,** the percentage change in price equals the percentage change in quantity demanded. This rarely occurs, because the marketplace is extremely dynamic. The retailer can use unitary elasticity to create a midpoint, or mean, for the inelastic and elastic pricing situations. In unitary elastic situations, a price change has no impact on total revenue; thus, E_p is equal to 1 ($E_p = 1$).

When comparing elasticity of price quotients (*i.e.,* E_p), the quotients should be compared only for a given store, product, or product line. In other words, there are no benchmarks defining a "good" or "bad" elasticity of price quotient. Thus, in the example that follows, the E_p is calculated as 4.0. Is this high or low? On the surface it appears low; however, when compared to the quotient in the second example ($E_p = 1.5$), it is actually high.

The formulas used to calculate the elasticity of price are as follows:

Elasticity of price = E_p

E_p = Percentage change in quantity demanded/Percentage change in price

or

$$E_p = \frac{\text{Absolute change in demand at new price/Demand at old price}}{\text{Absolute change in price/Old price}}$$

or

$$E_p = \frac{\Delta Q/Q}{\Delta P/P}$$

where Q = quantity sold and P = relative price.

As an example, suppose a retailer wants to check on its price elasticity because it is considering a drop in price. The price of the product may be dropped from \$20 to \$15 (a 25 percent reduction). Research reveals, however, that if the price is dropped from \$20 to \$15, demand will increase from 100,000 units to 200,000 units (a 100 percent increase). Is this situation price elastic, price inelastic, or unitarily elastic? If you answered *price elastic,* you are correct. To see this, let's plug in the numbers given in the following formula:

$$E_p = \frac{(200{,}000 - 100{,}000)/100{,}000}{(20 - 15)/20}$$

$$E_p = \frac{100{,}000/100{,}000}{\$5/\$20} = 4.0 \text{ or } 100\%/25\% = 4.0$$

This is a highly elastic situation.

Let's take another example using some of the same numbers. Suppose the price increases from \$15 to \$20, thus reducing demand from 200,000 units to 100,000 units. Though the numbers being used are the same, the situation is quite different. Let's see how elastic this situation may be:

$$E_p = \frac{100{,}000/200{,}000}{\$5/\$15} = 1.5 \text{ or } .5/.333333 = 1.5$$

In this example, the price is still elastic, but not quite as elastic as in the prior situation. The coefficient of elasticity of price and demand is 1.5 compared to the coefficient of 4.0 calculated earlier. In this example, the elasticity of price is closer to unitary elasticity and is less elastic than in the previous situation, where the calculation was 4.0.

When assessing elasticity of price, it is important to monitor the competition and the legal and ethical constraints placed on retailers in the United States (or other countries, if the retailer does business there). Numerous laws and regulations—international, national, regional, or local—govern price levels. It is essential that the retailer understand the rules, laws, and regulations affecting price. Important laws in the United States are the Sherman Act (1890), the Clayton Act (1914), and the Federal Trade Commission Act (1914). These laws are covered in more detail in Chapter 14.

DETERMINING PRICE ELASTICITY

In real-world problem solving, the elasticity of price coefficient needed to determine price is usually known and used in decision making about raising or lowering price. Based on the formula used to generate the coefficient of elasticity of price and demand (E_p), it is necessary to know the elasticity coefficient. This can be obtained in two ways. The first is to use the retailer's historical sales and pricing data to forecast the level of price elasticity. The second, and probably more accurate, method is to undertake research by sampling a group of consumers from the targeted market segment with regard to various price/quantity relationships. Both methods produce fairly crude estimates, but those estimates are useful when calculating the value of E_p. An example using a hypothetical retail firm follows.

> The owner of Computers, Inc., has estimated overall price elasticity to be 1.5 (E_p = 1.5). The owner wants to know if a price reduction of $100 for each fully loaded computer system would be profitable. Currently, the average price for a computer system is $2,500 per unit, with a forecasted sales volume of approximately 1 million units. A price reduction of $100 would generate a reduction of 4 percent ($2,500 − $100 = $2,400; $100/$2,500 = 4%).
>
> The price elasticity of 1.5 would thus generate an increase in sales of 6 percent. This is because an increase of 4 percent times the elasticity figure equals a 6 percent increase in unit sales (1.5 × 4% = 6%). Because the price is elastic, reductions in price increase total revenues. The owner of Computers, Inc., wants to know the amount by which revenues will increase. Based on these data, the new sales volume would increase from 1.00 million units to 1.06 million units. Here is how that number was derived:
>
> 1,000,000 × 1.06 = 1,060,000
>
> At the old price of $2,500 per unit, revenues would be $2.5 billion (1 million units × $2,500 per unit = $2.5 billion). At the new price of $2,400, anticipated sales revenues would increase to $2.544 billion ($2,400 × 1.06 million units = $2.544 billion). Thus, revenues would increase by $44 million by lowering the price from $2,500 to $2,400.

The above scenario does not take into account other costs associated with the sale of additional computer models, such as transporting, storing, shipping, increased sales staffs, and so on. It assumes that everything stays the same. In real life, however, additional costs associated with the acquisition and sale of so many additional computers would exist. In addition, government regulations could limit some of the activity, or rivals may respond with price reductions and other competitive tactics.

After implementing pricing flexibility, the retailer needs to develop pricing policies that will guide the actual price determination. The pricing strategy is derived from the pricing objectives, pricing flexibility, and pricing policy phases of the overall pricing plan.

DETERMINING PRICING STRATEGY AND POLICIES

pricing policies General rules or guidelines for price development based on company strategies.

Pricing policies help create the overall pricing strategy. Therefore, the retailer must establish general guidelines for price development. Because prices are influential in consumers' perceptions of the quality of the retailer's products[6] and stores, retailers must pay special attention to pricing tactics and the integration of these tactics into the overall IRM plan. Because product quality and pricing are so interrelated, it is vital that the retailer be consistent when developing and implementing pricing policies. It would be inconsistent for a high-end retailer to offer products and services at a discounted price. Neiman Marcus would not sell a no-name or off-brand perfume at $3 a bottle. Conversely, if a low-end retailer such as Wal-Mart offered expensive, prestigious products such as Rolex watches, consumers might become confused about the retailer's image.

Common factors involved in establishing pricing policies include the need for short-term profits, competitors' prices, product and supply-chain costs, and historical actions.[7] Several pricing policies are particularly widespread in the retailing industry, including price variability, promotional pricing, price leveling, life cycle pricing, price lining, price stability, and psychological pricing.

PRICE VARIABILITY

price variability The practice of varying price of merchandise or services based on established criteria.

In setting a **price variability** policy (also known as *differential pricing*), the retailer asks, "Do we want to charge the same price for our product(s) to all our customers, or do we want to charge different prices to different customers?" Although there are some legal restrictions on price variability, retailers have the option to offer the same product to customers at different prices. Sometimes this policy can anger or confuse consumers; thus, an understanding of consumer perceptions is paramount. Price variability used to be referred to as *price discrimination,* but due to the negative connotation of the term *discrimination,* it is rarely used today.

Federal, state, and local laws impose limitations on price variability. These regulations discourage retailers from varying their prices for "classes" of buyers. The laws relating to price discrimination are not clear-cut and are often open to interpretation. For example, in 1991, a complaint was issued against a California nightclub because the club did not admit people whose clothes and appearance were not considered trendy.[8] The California Department of Alcoholic Beverage Control sued nightclub owners under civil rights laws. A judge ruled that the nightclub had to change its ways to stay open.

The nightclub's stance was that it was attempting to create demand for the establishment by being selective in admittance policies.[9]

In general, it is legal to develop different prices for the same product as long as there is no discrimination against a class of buyer (Hispanics, African Americans, men, women, people with disabilities, and so on). Because most of the pricing antidiscrimination laws are mandated by state or local governments, challenges often arise in state or local courts. Typically, if no one is injured by the differences in price, a formal complaint is not registered.

There are many examples of price variability policies. Car dealers utilize price variability in selling cars. Most people don't pay the same price for a "like" model of automobile; rather, the price is determined based on many factors, such as credit, down payments, trade-in allowances, discounts, the consumer's ability to negotiate, and so on. Airlines also offer variable pricing to customers. Most passengers on a given flight have paid different prices for their seats. Those who travel in the first-class or business-class section have paid premium prices for the extra service and legroom. Also, travelers can expect to pay more during the holiday season, when demand is relatively high, than during "off-peak" times. Similarly, the price of a ticket to a major concert varies based on the location of the seat. Senior citizen discounts have become more common as more retailers offer discounts to this group.

It is important for retailers to educate customers on their pricing policies. When consumers understand the basis for price variability, they are usually more accepting of these policies. If they perceive the variability to be valid and equitable, they are less likely to harbor negative feelings toward the product, service, or retailer.

promotional pricing The practice of coordinating pricing with the promotion variable of IMC.

leader pricing A type of promotional pricing in which products are priced below the usual markup, near cost, or below cost. Also called *loss leader pricing*.

special-event pricing A type of promotional pricing in which advertised sales, typically coinciding with a major holiday or event, are used to generate store traffic.

price leveling The practice of setting prices on products and services so that prices remain stable for a defined period of time. Also called *customary pricing*, products are generally priced above, below, or at market prices.

PROMOTIONAL PRICING

In **promotional pricing,** a retailer coordinates pricing with the promotion variable of IMC. Because the two areas are interrelated, many times the pricing policy becomes tied to promotions. Two main types of promotional pricing are leader pricing (often called *loss leaders*) and special-event pricing. **Leader pricing** occurs when products are priced at less than the usual markup, near cost, or below cost. Leader pricing is used to increase traffic. In the process of buying the sale item, the customer typically picks up items at regular prices, thus offsetting the lower revenues from the price leaders. With **special-event pricing,** advertised sales are used to generate store traffic. Typically, sales coincide with a major holiday or event, such as Valentine's Day or an inventory clearance.

PRICE LEVELING

Under a **price leveling** policy, the retailer attempts to maintain price levels for the long term. Also called *customary pricing*, this type of policy is typically implemented prior to the actual opening of a retail facility. Retailers use price leveling to communicate to their publics the type of business they are operating. A discount retailer such as Wal-Mart may choose to set lower prices for all

In an effort to capture the Hispanic market, Wal-Mart has developed ads in Spanish. Whether in English or Spanish, Wal-Mart touts its low prices—"Always" ("Siempre").

of its products (everyday low pricing, or EDLP), thus supporting its image of a low-price retailer.

When using price leveling, retailers take into account many variables, including the organization's vision and mission statements, corporate culture, and product line objectives; competitors' strengths, weaknesses, and prices; and the state of the economy. The retailer should refer to the situational analysis before setting a price-leveling policy.

It is difficult to change a price strategy once it has been established in consumers' minds. For example, in 1988, department store Sears, Roebuck & Co. changed its pricing strategy from promotional pricing, which emphasized sales and specials, to "everyday low pricing."[10] Its customers were confused with the change and falsely assumed that it meant prices would go down. In fact, many product prices moved up, as they were priced somewhere between former sales prices and regular prices.[11] The strategy did not improve profits, and in 1990, Sears abandoned the EDLP strategy and returned to offering sales prices.[12]

Most retail stores have a level at which they set prices. This level may be based on an overall skimming strategy or on a market penetration strategy. The thing to remember is that overall prices may be set at market, below market, or above market prices.

LIFE CYCLE PRICING

life cycle pricing Price planning based on the stage of the product (or store) life cycle that the product (or store) has reached.

Pricing may be planned based on the product or store life cycle. Under **life cycle pricing,** price points are set based on the stage of the product life cycle (introduction, growth, maturity, and decline) that the product (or store) has reached. For example, a retailer may use a penetration strategy to enter the market with low prices when it first opens the store. As consumers demand more products (during the growth phase), the retailer raises the prices slightly. As the product reaches maturity, the retailer levels off the price to current market prices. Finally, during the decline phase, the retailer either raises or lowers the price because demand and sales have decreased significantly.

When a new product, such as an MP3 player, is introduced, the initial price may be very high. One reason may be that the manufacturer is trying to recoup research and development costs. Another possible reason is that the manufacturer wants to capitalize on retailers' desire to carry the new, hot product and therefore sells the product at a higher price. After more competitors start building MP3 players and more people start buying the product, the price typically decreases. In the decline phase of the product life cycle, retailers offer products at substantial discounts. The videocassette recorder has entered this stage; in the late 1990s, one could buy a VCR for less than $100.

In other situations, new products are introduced at a lower price, to gain market share or acceptance; this is especially true when a similar product already exists in the marketplace. As the product moves through the life cycle, the price is usually adjusted.

Life cycle pricing is uncommon in retailing because of the time and costs associated with preparing and planning prices for each individual product or product line. A retailer would need to know in advance when discounts or sales would occur; therefore, prices would need to be preplanned throughout the cycle. The retailer would need to know at what moment the product would be entering another stage of the life cycle and then would need to decide whether to raise or lower prices in response. Life cycle pricing is contingent on the pricing strategy and the type of product.

PRICE LINING

price lining A policy in which various products and prices are offered to match competitors' offerings for a particular product category.

A retailer using a **price lining** policy offers various products and prices to match its competitors' offerings for a particular product category. Price lining is also referred to as the *development of price points*. Therefore, each line of products receives special pricing. This allows the retailer to compete at different levels within a given product line. The goal in a price lining strategy is to maximize profits for the whole line versus focusing on only one product's profitability.

The Chevrolet division of General Motors (GM) is a good example of a retailer supplier that utilizes a price lining strategy. GM offers luxury, full-size, mid-size, compact, subcompact, and sport-utility vehicles, as well as other products, to appeal to each type of consumer who has a need or want for an automobile. Chevy's Trailblazer, for example, allows Chevrolet to compete in

cannibalization A situation in which a company introduces a product that takes away sales from an existing product.

the SUV market. In addition, price lining helps avoid **cannibalization** of each product; that is, GM can achieve different levels of competition by attracting additional buyers from the market rather than moving current GM customers from product to product. The price of each product type is often a signal of the quality of the merchandise.

The cosmetics industry also utilizes price lining, allowing retailers to have many different types of cosmetics at different prices to appeal to different consumers. For example, Procter & Gamble offers the Olay line, which is priced highest; Covergirl, which is average priced; and Max Factor, which is the least expensive line. Thus, a consumer looking to purchase cosmetics can choose among three differently priced lines.

Price lining helps position products as good, better, and best.[13] The consumer is willing to pay more for the perceived "better" product and less for the perceived "generic," or low-cost, product.

PRICE STABILITY

At times, retailers try to create a stable price, or a "one-price policy," for certain products, to avoid price wars with the competition. The popular dollar store formats operate under this **price stability policy.** These stores do not have to run frequent sales because their customers know prices will remain stable.

price stability policy A practice in which the retailer attempts to create a one-price policy for individual products.

A good way to create a stable price is to negotiate with suppliers for exclusive product rights for a given geographic territory. Because of the costs associated with exclusivity, retailers often negotiate selective distribution clauses that allow them to be among a handful of retailers that carry the product or service for each territory. If a company is an upscale retailer, management will not want to charge a lot of money for a product that can be purchased a block away from a retailer that charges 20 percent less. Pottery Barn, a home decoration retailer, is an example of a company that pursues price stability.

Although by law retailers cannot be required to adhere to minimum retail prices set by manufacturers, many suppliers maintain price stability by dealing only with retailers that traditionally adhere to the manufacturers' suggested retail prices.

In some cases, in exchange for agreeing to minimum retail prices, manufacturers provide promotion money to assist the retailer. Such was the case in the music industry in the mid 1990s. In an effort to avoid price wars, record manufacturers instituted a minimum advertised price policy, known as MAP. Under the policy, record labels gave retailers millions of dollars to be spent on promoting new releases. Retailers who took the money agreed to adhere to minimum advertised prices set by the major record labels. This meant that retailers could not sell new releases and other popular music below a specified price. In 2000, the Federal Trade Commission issued a cease and desist order because the MAP policies were a form of price-fixing. To avoid a federal lawsuit, the record labels dropped MAP policies.[14]

consignment selling A method in which the retailer sells goods for the supplier and receives a commission on sales instead of taking title to the merchandise.

Another way to establish price stability is to sell by consignment. In **consignment selling,** a retailer sells goods for the supplier and receives a commission on sales instead of taking title to the merchandise. Under this method, the retailer bears less risk in terms of product sales. If the products fail to move, they are simply returned to the supplier. If they do sell, the retailer gets a percentage of the sales price and the supplier keeps the rest. Many suppliers sell only to retailers with a reputation for good customer service, because the products' prices tend to remain stable with these retailers.

PSYCHOLOGICAL PRICING

psychological pricing A method of pricing in which the retail takes into account consumer's perceptions and beliefs.

Because consumers make a correlation between the price of a product and the product's quality, many retailers set prices using psychological pricing. **Psychological pricing** takes into account the consumer's perceptions and beliefs. The three main types of psychological pricing are odd/even pricing, reference pricing, and prestige pricing.

odd/even pricing The practice of using prices that end in either an odd or an even number.

ODD/EVEN PRICING. The retailer using **odd/even pricing** places prices on individual products that end in either an odd or an even number. Consumers often perceive the price to be lower if it falls below an expected threshold. For example, a product that is priced at $39.99 is perceived as less expensive than one priced at $40.00. In many cases, consumers expect prices to end in an even number. For example, for products sold from a vending machine, an even price such as $1.00 is more practical than an odd price such as $0.49.

Many retailers, including grocery stores, use a psychological pricing tactic called odd pricing. *This tactic is based on the premise that consumers often perceive a price to be lower if it falls below an expected threshold.*

Odd/even pricing allegedly began in grocery retail outlets. Before the development of effective point-of-sales instruments such as POS terminals and cash registers, grocery retailers hired employees to work as cashiers. Retailers had to put their trust in the cashiers, but sometimes employee theft occurred. Theft was easy because many products had an even price on them (this was prior to the taxing of food products in many states). Because an even price was associated with the products, cashiers didn't have to make change. They didn't even have to open the cash register to show that a transaction had taken place. The cashier could just set the money on the cash register, wait until the customer left, and then pocket the money. To combat this practice, food retailers changed the pricing structure of their products to odd numbers, forcing cashiers to make change. Making change required opening the cash register and recording the transaction into the retailer's records.

Odd/even pricing continues to be used today, despite the advent of POS systems. Why do food retailers still offer most food products with odd-numbered prices? They do so because consumers expect them to. Consumers may see a food product with an even price as being too expensive.

Gasoline is also priced using an odd-number pricing strategy. The price for a gallon of gas nearly always ends with 9/10 of a cent. Therefore, an advertised price of $1.67 per gallon is really $1.67 and 9/10 of a cent, or closer to $1.68 per gallon. In retailing (and marketing), the consumer's perception is reality. If the consumer thinks a price that ends in an odd (or even) number is more affordable, retailers should price the product accordingly.

reference pricing A concept of what the price of a product should be based on the consumers' frame of reference.

just noticeable difference (JND) The price at which consumers believe they are paying more or less than the norm or reference price.

REFERENCE PRICING. Reference pricing uses a consumers' frame of reference to help set price. A frame of reference is established through information searches or previous experience purchasing other like products.[15] To uncover customers' expectations, it is important that the retailer survey customers to determine the **just noticeable difference (JND)**. This is the price at which consumers believe they are paying more or less than the norm or reference price. The key is to find out the magnitude of change necessary for a change in price to be noticed by the consumer.[16]

A retailer would not want to raise the price of a product above the JND, because the customer may perceive the price as unfair. For example, let's say a consumer's experience tells her that popcorn should be priced at $1.50 for a medium-size bag and she complains about paying $4.50 for a similar-sized bag in a movie theatre. In this case, the JND was surpassed. Many times retailers raise prices gradually, thinking that consumers are less likely to notice gradual price changes than drastic price increases.

Prestige pricing involves selling products at high prices to establish a reputation of quality, a tactic employed by Mercedes-Benz in selling its cars.

prestige pricing The practice of selling products at high prices to build a reputation for quality.

PRESTIGE PRICING. Selling products at high prices to establish a reputation of quality is called **prestige pricing.** This pricing strategy aims to create "snob appeal."[17] Manufacturers that spend a great deal of time and money developing their brands often sell high-end products to retailers that are associated with prestige. The products demanded by these retailers' customers generally carry a higher, or prestige, price. Think about the last time you shopped for clothes. What stores did you visit? Did you shop at Abercrombie and Fitch rather than Kmart for your jeans? Your decision to shop at either one of those stores shows that you are brand or price sensitive.

Car manufacturers and retailers often use prestige pricing for their top-of-the-line models. BMW and Mercedes are good examples of companies that utilize prestige pricing. Other examples are the makers of Rolex watches, Mount Blanc pens, Tiffany's fine jewelry, and Vermont Teddy Bears.

Once pricing policies have been established, specific product prices must be determined. Retailers can use many methods to create a final price for products. The next section discusses the most popular of these methods.

Blunders or Best Practices?

Kohl's Pricing Policies Under Fire

Due to a four-month inquiry into Kohl's pricing policies by the *Boston Globe* in 2002, the Massachusetts attorney general investigated Kohl's Department Stores' pricing policies. In October 2002, Kohl's was informed by the state that its pricing policies appeared to be in violation of state law and asked Kohl's management to bring the company's thirteen Massachusetts stores into compliance.

Kohl's pricing strategy is to position itself as a budget department store (instead of a discounter) and use promotions to stress the chain's value. Kohl's appeals to its target market by offering quality national-brand merchandise at affordable prices in easily accessible and convenient retail outlets.

Kohl's aggressive sales pricing is at the heart of the state's complaint. According to the complaint, Kohl's appears to offer some items "on sale" throughout most of the year. This means these items never have a "regular" price to which consumers can compare other retailers' prices. This practice creates fictitious "regular prices," percentage discounts that do not reveal the original prices, and sales tags that do nothing to clarify the item price. According to Kohl's management, the chain is in compliance in Massachusetts.

Kohl's pricing strategy also created problems for the company in Kansas during 2000 and 2002. Although Kohl's did not admit to guilt, the company paid $500,000 in fines.

As this example illustrates, retailers must be very careful in developing and implementing a pricing strategy.

Sources: Brent Felgner, "Kohl's Under Fire in MA," *Home Textiles Today,* November 11, 2002, pp. 1, 23; Bruce Mohl, "Kohl's Told to Act on Pricing Policies: AG Asks Chain to Comply with State Law on Sale Advertising," *Boston Globe,* October 22, 2002, p. C1; Joanne Kimberlin, "Area Retailers Beware: Kohl's to Be a Major Player: Incoming Chain Will Challenge Discounters and Department Stores," *Virginian–Pilot* (Norfolk, Virginia), January 12, 2003, p. D1.

ESTABLISHING PRICE

The three major categories of methods used to establish product prices are cost-oriented pricing, competition-oriented pricing, and demand-oriented pricing. A retailer may use one or a combination of the methods. The most common is cost-oriented pricing.

COST-ORIENTED PRICING

cost-oriented pricing A pricing method in which a fixed percentage is added to the cost of products; also called *cost-plus pricing.*

To generate a profit, product costs *must* be covered. **Cost-oriented pricing** (also called *cost-plus pricing*) has two approaches: markup pricing (the more common) and breakeven pricing. The retailer needs to determine its markup percentage; one way to do this is to look at traditional product markups within the industry and at the manufacturer's suggested retail price. The retailer must also consider the product's average turnover, the amount of competition for the product, the levels of service required, and the amount of sales time and effort involved in selling the product. All these factors, along with the inclusion of the expected or targeted profit margin, determine the **markup.**

markup The dollar amount added to the cost of a product to determine its final price.

MARKUP PRICING. In markup pricing, two options exist for determining the markup percentage: markup based on the retail, or selling, price of the product, and markup based on the product's cost. The chosen method is generally selected based on the accounting systems the retailer employs.

The vast majority of retailers use *markup based on selling price,* because expenses and profits for the product's sales are calculated as a percentage of sales. In addition, this method keeps the markup percentage from exceeding 100 percent. Manufacturers and other suppliers most often quote discounts and price reductions from the retail selling prices they provide to the retailer. Finally, retail sales information is easier to acquire than cost information is; thus, it is easier to compare sales to those of competitors (and other stores) than it is to compare costs. The general formula for developing a markup based on the retail price of the product is as follows:

Amount of markup = Selling price (retail price) − Cost

If a product's selling price is \$100 and the cost is \$40, the markup is calculated as \$100 − \$40 = \$60. To calculate the markup percentage, use this formula:

Markup percentage = Amount of markup/Selling price

Using the example above, the percentage markup at retail would be \$60/\$100, or 60 percent.

To calculate the selling price rather than the cost, use the following formula:

SP = C + M

or

Selling price = Cost/(1 − % of SP)

where SP = selling price, C = cost, and M = markup.

Assume the cost associated with the product is $100 and a markup percentage, based on the selling/retail price, of 40 percent is desired. Then:

SP = C + M; SP = $100 + .40(SP); SP − .40(SP) = $100 + .40(SP) − .40(SP)
.60(SP)/.60 = $100/.60 = $166.67, or $100/(1 − .40) = $100/.60 = $166.67

Thus, the selling price (or retail price) = $166.67.

In addition, the cost of the product can be calculated given the selling price and markup percentage based on selling price using the following formula:

SP = C + M, so C = SP − M

Assume the product has a cost of $1,000 and a markup percentage based on selling price of 60 percent. Then:

$1,000 = C + .60(1,000); $1,000 = C + $600; therefore, C = $400

Finally, both the cost and the selling price of the product can be calculated using the following formula:

Markup percentage based on retail (selling) price
× Retail price (selling price) = Amount of markup

Suppose the desired markup percentage on the retail/selling price is 55 percent and the amount of markup is $200. The cost and retail price are calculated as follows:

.55 × SP = $200.00; .55(SP) = $200.00; SP = $200/.55 = $363.64

Now we have the retail price of $363.64, so SP = C + M, or $363.64 = C + $200.00. Therefore, cost = $163.64 ($363.64 − $200.00).

Another markup method is based on the *cost of the product.* The following formulas will guide you through the steps to calculate markup based on product cost:

Retail price = Cost + Markup

If the retail price is $1,000 and the cost for the product is $600, the markup based on cost is $400, or $1,000 − $600. The percentage markup based on the product's cost can be calculated by taking the amount of the markup and dividing it by the cost, as follows:

$400/$600 = 66.67 percent

To calculate the selling price for a product using a cost basis, see the following example (remember, SP = C + M, or cost/[1 − % of selling price]).

> If a product costs $25 and a markup percentage on cost of 30 percent is desired, what will be the selling price? The calculation is as follows:
>
> SP = $25 + .30 ($25); SP = $25 + $7.50; thus, SP = $32.50
> or 1.30 × $25 = $32.50
>
> The retail price for the product would be $32.50.

The product's cost can also be calculated. Consider the following example.

> A product's selling price is $50 and the markup percentage, based on cost, is 65 percent. If SP = C + M, then SP/(1 + markup) will give the cost. Let's calculate this problem using both methods:
>
> SP = $50.00; M = 65 percent of the cost
>
> SP = C + M; thus $50.00
> = C + (.65)C (keep in mind that the cost is equal to 1 × C)
>
> $50.00 = 1.65C; thus, $50/1.65 = Cost (again) = $30.30

Finally, let's calculate both the retail price and the cost for a product. See the following example.

> Assume a markup percentage of 20 percent on cost (C = .20). Also assume that the amount of markup for the product has to be $32 (M = $32). The calculation is as follows:
>
> Markup percentage on cost x Cost = Amount of markup
>
> If the markup percentage is 20 and the amount of markup is $32, then:
>
> .20 × Cost = $32; Cost = .20C/.20 = $32/.20 = $160
>
> SP = C + M; thus, SP = $160 + .20(160) = $160 + $32 = $192

Keep in mind that the cost of goods equals the cost, per unit, of the merchandise (invoice price) plus the inbound freight costs associated with getting the merchandise. In addition, any discounts received from the trade as part of a purchase (including quantity discounts) are also taken out.

breakeven pricing A pricing method in which pricing is based on the breakeven point for a given product.

breakeven point (BEP) The level of activity at which income from sales (total revenue) equals total costs.

BREAKEVEN PRICING. Breakeven pricing is the other method used in the creation of a cost-oriented pricing system. With breakeven pricing, the retailer determines the **breakeven point (BEP),** or the level of sales needed to cover all the costs associated with selling the product. The breakeven point is calculated using the following formula:

> BEP (in quantity) = Fixed cost/Unit price − Unit variable cost

This formula can be modified to calculate the BEP in dollars bv multiplying the BEP (in quantity) by the selling price of the item.

GLOBAL RETAILING

Wal-Mart and Mexican Retailers

Wal-Mart, the biggest retailer in the world, is facing intense competition in Mexico. Wal-Mart de Mexico, SA de C.V. operates several apparel stores and restaurants as well as Wal-Mart supercenters. The supercenters compete against a hypermarket called Soriana. The Mexican unit of Wal-Mart has sales of about $10 billion, whereas Soriana's sales are in the $3 billion range.

Although Soriana has fewer locations, the company will not back down in the competitive arena. Soriana invested $250 million in 2002 to open twelve new stores in northern Mexico. This hardly compares with Wal-Mart's plans to open sixty-three new grocery stores, wholesale club outlets, and restaurants over the same time period.

Wal-Mart's strategy of everyday low pricing (EDLP) is one area of competitive advantage for the giant chain. Many other supercenters use frequent promotions to lure consumers to their locations. One of Wal-Mart's competitors, Comerci, decided to copy Wal-Mart's pricing strategy by instituting its own version of EDLP. Comerci has less bargaining clout with suppliers than Wal-Mart does and is less efficient with cost controls, so this strategy may backfire.

Although Wal-Mart has boosted Mexico's economy, the company is facing criticism for its alleged pressure tactics on suppliers to lower their prices. In 2002 through 2003, Wal-Mart was under investigation by Mexico's Federal Competition Commission for allegations that its stores were removing products from the shelves to sanction some suppliers for participating in promotions organized by Wal-Mart's competitors. In 2003, the Federal Competition Commission offered to close the investigation on the condition that Wal-Mart adopt a new code of conduct with its suppliers that would ensure fair competition.

Sources: Reproduced from the September 16, 2002 issue of *Business Week* by special permission. Copyright © 2002 by the McGraw-Hill Companies, Inc.

COMPETITION-ORIENTED PRICING

competition-oriented pricing Pricing of products based on the industry leader's prices.

In **competition-oriented pricing**, the retailer identifies the industry leader and then replicates the leader's prices. In using this method, the retailer assumes that the industry leader is best equipped to select appropriate price levels for its products.

Retailers often "shop" the competition to ascertain competitors' price structures. A representative from the retailer's organization visits a competitor's store to see what prices are set for the product mix. Shopping the competition is not always welcomed by retailing competitors, especially when done in person. It is understood that environmental scanning should be an ongoing, not sporadic process, however, so many retailers see these actions as necessary. Particularly in service retailing, the same information often can be obtained from phone calls to competitors. For example, a large hotel chain in southern Colorado regularly has disguised "shoppers" call competing hotels and ask for a list of prices for the various rooms. Different rates, such as state rates, government rates, AAA rates, and frequent-traveler rates, are checked. The chain then adjusts its prices based on the competitor's rates.

If competitors raise or lower their prices, the retailer follows suit with price increases or decreases. Competition-oriented pricing assumes that costs, demand, competition, and other factors external to the retail firm remain fairly constant. Therefore, it is safe to follow the leader or follow the general trends within the industry.

DEMAND-ORIENTED PRICING

demand-oriented pricing Pricing of products based on consumer demand.

Under the **demand-oriented pricing** method, prices are set based on consumer demand. In this approach, retailers often raise prices based on unusual environmental changes. These changes might include unusually high customer demand (*e.g.,* for fad products), events such as natural disasters, or conflicts in other countries that affect supplies of various products such as gas or oil.

price gouging A tactic wherein a retailer takes advantage of high demand and limited supply to raise the price of a good or service beyond customary amounts.

In some instances, retailers raise their prices to exorbitantly high levels, a tactic called **price gouging.** Although this tactic may appear to be a sound business practice, it is an ethical gray area. Customers may pay the demanded price initially, but they may harbor negative feelings toward the retailer, thus decreasing long-term business and goodwill.

The three major types of demand-oriented pricing are modified breakeven, consumer market, and industrial market pricing.

modified breakeven pricing A method wherein the retailer estimates the market demand for a product and then applies it to the breakeven point.

MODIFIED BREAKEVEN PRICING. Modified breakeven pricing assumes the retailer estimates the market demand for the product and then applies it to the breakeven point. In so doing, the retailer can estimate, or forecast, sales at different price points or levels.

consumer market approach A method in which a retailer generates data about prices based on controlled store experimentation.

CONSUMER MARKET PRICING. When using a **consumer market approach** to pricing, the retailer generates data about prices based on controlled store experimentation. Many techniques can be applied here, but the general idea is that consumers enter the store and are allowed to make product purchases. The prices on the various products are changed, and the retail researcher tracks the price points that are most popular with the consumers. The retailer then implements these price points throughout its locations.

industrial market approach An approach in which the retailer sells its products to other businesses in addition to the final consumer. Prices for products or services may be different for business customers than for nonbusiness customers.

INDUSTRIAL MARKET PRICING. A technique much like the consumer market approach is the **industrial market approach.** With this approach, the retailer sells its products to other businesses in addition to the final consumer. The retailer performs a wholesaling function aimed toward other businesses. If the retailer is reselling products to intermediaries or industries (such as Home Depot, Office Depot, or Office Max may do), the retailer identifies the benefits of its products compared to competitors' products and sets prices accordingly. The assumption is that industrial buyers do not buy as much on emotion as ultimate consumers do. Rather, industrial buyers, or intermediary buyers, purchase more on a need basis. Consequently, by identifying the benefits these buyers are seeking, the retailer is better able to set price. This technique is also used when responding to government bids; in this situation, the government agency purchasing products is treated like another business.

Once product and service prices have been set, retailers need to prepare for the possibility that they will not sell all the products at the established prices.

initial markup The price set on a product less the cost of the merchandise.

maintained markup The amount of markup the retailer attempts to sustain for a particular product or product grouping. Calculation: Net sales – COGS.

initial markup percentage The initial markup expressed in percentage form.

maintained markup percentage The maintained markup expressed in percentage form.

gross margin The total cost of goods sold subtracted from net sales.

Retailers must develop **initial markups, maintained markups,** and gross profit margin projections for the store inventory. In addition, retailers must consider creating markdowns for products, to move slower-selling items off the shelves. In the next section, we will look at how an initial markup percentage is developed.

INITIAL MARKUP PERCENTAGE

The **initial markup percentage** is a starting point for setting individual product prices. After calculating an initial markup percentage, the retailer can calculate the impact of markups, markdowns, and discounts. Initial markup percentages are usually calculated based on the retail selling price. Initial markups are calculated by taking the estimated retail expenses, adding them to the planned retail profit, and adding that figure to the planned reductions. This figure is then divided by the planned net sales plus the retail reductions:

$$\text{Initial markup percentage} = \frac{\text{Planned expenses} + \text{Planned profit} + \text{Reductions}}{\text{Net sales} + \text{Reductions}}$$

The markup is based on the original retail values placed on the merchandise after subtracting out the costs associated with the merchandise. By looking at the actual prices the retailer paid for the merchandise and again subtracting out the costs associated with that merchandise, the retailer can calculate its **maintained markup percentage:**

$$\text{Maintained markup percentage} = \frac{\text{Retail operations expenses (actual)} + \text{Actual profit}}{\text{Actual net sales}}$$

Another method is to take the average retail prices of products and then subtract out the costs associated with the merchandise and divide by the average retail price:

$$\text{Maintained markup percentage} = \frac{\text{Average retail price} - \text{Product costs}}{\text{Average retail price}}$$

Finally, the retailer may want to know what its gross margin will look like. The **gross margin** is the total cost of goods sold (COGS) for the retailer subtracted from the retailer's net sales:

$$\text{Gross margin in dollars} = \text{Net sales} - \text{COGS}$$

Gross margin allows the retailer to adjust for cash discounts and other expenses associated with sales of goods and services. The retailer may still have to adjust the prices on some merchandise. The process of changing prices is called *price adjustment*.

VARIABLES IN THE INITIAL MARKUP PERCENTAGE. Variables in the initial markup percentage can affect the initial price. One variable is the influence members of the retailer's channel of distribution can have on the organization. In distributor relationships, members of the channel of distribution have expectations of the other channel members. One expectation may be that the retailer adheres to the manufacturer's suggested retail price. The amount of influence a given channel member has is based on the type of supply chain used and the dominance of the channel member. For example, because Wal-Mart purchases in very large quantities, its suppliers give the discounter a smaller markup than they would give other retailers that purchase less. Wal-Mart then passes on those savings to its customers, thus creating a competitive advantage.

Related to the influence of channel members are the variables of quantity discounts and shipping arrangements. These variables are negotiated with suppliers and consequently have an impact on the price the retailer sets. In their infancy, e-tailers got into trouble by failing to factor in the shipping and handling costs associated with retailing products to end users. This was one of the significant factors that contributed to the failure of a number of dot-com companies.

Pricing for cyberspace sales can be a difficult task. Although e-tailers have an advantage over brick-and-mortar businesses in that they have lower physical location expenses and a less labor-intensive environment, in other ways they are at a disadvantage: customers can access the prices of competitors with the click of a button.[18] Thus, e-tailers should avoid using price as a main tactic in attracting customers. They should also stay away from price wars with well-established retail outlets that have deeper pockets than they do.

PRICE ADJUSTMENTS

No matter how thoroughly the retailer plans for the execution of pricing, some change in the retail environment is bound to alter the product's value to the consumer. These value changes can take two forms. In one case, an environmental change increases the value of the product. More frequently, however, changes in the environment decrease the product's value.

To respond to these changes, retailers make two major types of product adjustments: additional markups and markdowns. If the retail environment changes or the economy weakens, prices may have to come down (markdowns). In some situations, additional markups may be warranted. During the holiday season, for example, if demand for a particular item is high, retailers often raise the price on that item because its demand exceeds its supply.

As seasons change, so do consumers' desires for certain types of products. Price adjustments allow the retailer some flexibility in its day-to-day business operations. It is important for retail managers to understand the concepts of additional markups and markdowns.

This photo pokes fun at the high price of gas.

ADDITIONAL MARKUPS

At times retailers will see an increase, or a spike, in the sales of a particular product. When this occurs, the retailer may be able to increase its profits and margins by adding additional dollar amounts to the product's retail price. These additions are called **additional markups** (or, sometimes, *markons*).

additional markup An increase in the retail price of a product in addition to what has already been added as a markup.

Trendy or fad products often lend themselves to additional markups. Remember, an additional markup is an increase in the retail price of a product in addition to what was already added as a markup. Popular toys may be subject to increases in selling price during the holidays. Popular car models may also carry additional markups to increase the retailer's bottom line. When creating additional markups, the retailer should pay particular attention to the demand functions of economics, particularly the law of supply and demand.

Sometimes during pricing periods, unexpected rises occur in the costs of merchandise purchased from suppliers. When costs rise, the retailer needs to pass the increases on to the consumer. The retailer may utilize an additional markup for this purpose. For example, when suppliers' prices for gas increase, the retailer can no longer generate the required markup percentage, so it adds an additional markup to help make up for the added costs associated with carrying the product.

MARKDOWNS

Retailers can rarely sell all the merchandise they carry at the established original prices. Frequently the retailer needs to encourage consumers to purchase products so the retailer can move the products out of the store to make way for newer products or products and services that will yield a higher return. In these cases, the retailer initiates **markdowns,** or decreases in the overall markup percentage (or dollar amounts).

markdown A decrease in the initial retail price, typically expressed as dollar amounts or a percentage.

Markdowns are regular practice for many types of retailers. For example, in promotional apparel retailing, almost 76 percent of clothing in department stores is sold at lower-than-retail price through the use of markdowns.[19] Markdowns can be calculated in much the same way as markups. To calculate the dollar markdown amount, subtract the new product retail price from the original or regular retail selling price:

Markdown (in dollars) = Retail selling price − New selling price

Consider an owner and operator of a small retail business. He wants to know what his markdown is on a product he was selling for $50. His new selling price is $30. His markdown is $50 minus $30, or $20. In addition, he wants to know what his markdown percentage was. To calculate the markdown percentage, he needs to take the dollar amount of the markdown and divide it by the new selling price. He can calculate the markdown percentage using either the new retail price or the old retail price. Each calculation yields a slightly different percentage:

Amount of markdown (new retail price) = Percentage of markdown on new retail price

Amount of markdown (old retail price) = Percentage of markdown on old selling price

Using the numbers given in the example, if the new retail price is $30 and the old retail price is $50, the markdowns are as follows:

Amount of markdown = $20, so $20/$30 = .66666, or approximately 67% of the new retail price

Amount of markdown = $20, so $20/$50 = .40, or 40% of the old retail price

Which method is better? It depends on the retail mission, vision, and philosophy. It also may depend on which accounting method the retailer uses. Either calculation is correct. A consumer, however, obviously would prefer a 67 percent markdown over a 40 percent markdown. Thus, consumer perception may have an impact on which method is chosen for creating markdowns. Next time you go shopping, pay attention to the fine print under the sales signs; your savings may not be as much as you think they are!

The pricing tactic is very useful for retailers, but pricing policies and strategies are often downplayed or outright ignored by retail managers.[20] Pricing is the marketing mix variable that has the most direct impact on revenues and therefore can substantially influence the bottom line for all retailers. The deputy executive director for the Pennsylvania lottery wrote an article for *Lottery Insights* about the value of pricing and the fact that its importance is sometimes ignored. In his article, he calls for an increase in lottery ticket prices because although the costs of running state lotteries have gone up, the price for lottery tickets has remained relatively unchanged for decades.[21]

As we have seen, many variables affect price, and the approaches used to set prices vary depending on the type of retailer and the other tactical areas. Retailers must not overlook the importance of pricing in retail management. In the words of Mark Bergen, marketing professor at the University of Minnesota, "It's easy to set a price. It's hard to set a good price."[22]

SUMMARY

In the IRM planning process, there are many issues that relate to pricing of products and services. In addition to integrated marketing communication (IMC) and customer service, price is one of the three main tactics retailers use to help them communicate with their target market. This chapter covered the development of overall pricing objectives and how those objectives can help create specific pricing objectives, including product quality, market share, survival, ROI, profit, status quo, cash flow, penetration, and skimming. Next, the chapter focused on the pricing policies of price variability, price leveling, life cycle price , price lining, price stability, and psychological pricing. When establishing pricing objectives, integration with the other tactical areas in the IRM structure is important.

The chapter provided a number of formulas to determine retail prices for products. It discussed how to mark up a product at both selling price and product cost, along with various methods used to adjust price after the initial price has been set. Finally, the chapter examined the concepts of initial markup and maintained markup and provided formulas to calculate these important numbers and percentages. Although retailers tend to favor one method over others, they often use more than one approach, depending on their accounting methods.

KEY TERMS

tactics (324)
price points (324)
product quality objective (324)
skimming objective (324)
market penetration objective (325)
market share objective (325)
market share (325)
survival objective (325)
return on investment (ROI) objective (325)
profit objective (326)
status quo objective (326)
cash flow objective (326)
pricing flexibility (326)
price elasticity of demand (328)
price elastic (328)
price inelastic (328)
unitary elasticity (328)
pricing policies (331)
price variability (331)
promotional pricing (332)
leader pricing (332)
special-event pricing (332)
price leveling (332)
life cycle pricing (334)
price lining (334)
cannibalization (335)
price stability policy (335)
consignment selling (335)
psychological pricing (336)
odd/even pricing (336)
reference pricing (337)
just noticeable difference (JND) (337)
prestige pricing (338)
cost-oriented pricing (339)
markup (339)
breakeven pricing (341)
breakeven point (BEP) (341)
competition-oriented pricing (342)
demand-oriented pricing (343)
price gouging (343)
modified breakeven pricing (343)
consumer market approach (343)
industrial market approach (343)
initial markup (344)
maintained markup (344)
initial markup percentage (344)
maintained markup percentage (344)
gross margin (344)
additional markup (346)
markdown (346)

QUESTIONS FOR DISCUSSION

1. What do you think are the most difficult aspects of determining prices for products?
2. What are some reasons a retailer might choose a particular pricing strategy?
3. Assume you have been given the responsibility of setting prices for Macy's department stores. Which of the following policies would you choose to implement, and why?
   a. Price variability
   b. Price leveling
   c. Life cycle pricing
   d. Price lining
   e. Price stability
   f. Psychological pricing
4. Is it fair to consumers when a retailer manipulates prices? Why or why not?
5. What types of retailers attract price-sensitive customers?
6. What types of retailers have customers who are less price sensitive?
7. Which types of retailers make frequent price adjustments?

E-TAILING EXERCISE

To complete this exercise, do the following:

1. Use your local town paper to find advertisements for three or four items.
2. Use the Internet to comparison-price shop for the items selected in step 1.
3. Compare the online prices to the prices found in the print advertisements.
4. Answer the following questions:
   - What were the differences in price for each item?
   - Are there factors other than price that would make you choose one retailer over another? If so, what are they?
   - When shipping and handling were added to the online price, how much did the total price increase?

CHAPTER PROBLEMS

1. If the price of a product drops from $50 to $25, resulting in an increase of demand from 1,000 units to 1,500 units, what is the elasticity of price?
2. If the retail price of a new cell phone is $150 and the cost of each phone is $90, what is the dollar amount of markup? What is the percentage markup on the phones?
3. A new watch costs a retailer $25. If the retailer wants to generate a 50 percent markup on the watch, at what selling, or retail, price should the retailer set the watch?
4. An e-tailer wants to generate a markup percentage, on retail, for a new DVD set. If the amount of markup is $100, what is the cost for the product, and for how much should the DVD set retail?
5. A video game retailer wants to generate a markup percentage of 35 percent on a new video game *at cost*. The amount of this markup is $64 (at cost). At what price should the merchant sell the new game? What is the cost of the game to the retailer?

Continuing Case 11.1

Sherwin-Williams Company: Variable Pricing

Sherwin-Williams Company, with approximately 2,573 stores within North America, has two major customer groups: the do-it-yourself (DIY) group and the contractor group. In addition, Sherwin-Williams sells its products through its company-owned retail stores, and it sells to other channels of distribution partners, such as K-Mart. Total yearly sales for Sherwin-Williams are approximately $5 billion, with the paint stores generating just over half of all sales.

Sherwin-Williams wants to sell as much product as possible to its current and potential customers. Because of the differences in its customer base, Sherwin-Williams has found it useful to create variable pricing. Thus, for the many different customers that Sherwin-Williams services, there are differing prices for the core product: paint. Customers at K-Mart, for example, may pay less for a can of paint than those who shop at the company-owned stores. K-Mart shoppers also have the option of spending a little more money to purchase Martha Stewart brand paints.

Sherwin-Williams can afford to create differing prices for its products by reducing the amount of binders included in the cheaper products or by varying the pigments in the paints (the lower the pigmentation, the cheaper the cost to produce). Also, contractors receive a quantity discount for the paints they purchase.

Questions

1. Do you think that price variability is a good policy for Sherwin-Williams? Why or why not?
2. From a pricing perspective, why do you think Sherwin-Williams sells its products in outlets other than its company-owned stores?
3. Do you think that the average paint consumer perceives higher quality for higher prices? Why or why not?
4. In addition to the price variability policy, what other pricing policies would you think Sherwin-Williams employs?
5. Would you be angry if you found that you spent $1.00 more per gallon for your paint purchase than your friend did for the same paint? $5.00 more? $10.00 more? Would this situation cause you to change brands?
6. Is it fair for a DIY consumer to pay more for paint than a contractor does? Why or why not?
7. Suggest an overall pricing strategy for Sherwin-Williams.

Sources: *Sherwin-Williams 2002 Annual Report*; Robert Lowes, "The Anatomy of Paint" retrieved July 22, 2003, from Paint and Wallpaper Contractor Magazine website at www.paintstore.com/archives/misc/14.html; Howard Upton, "Martha Living Under the Microscope," *Tulsa World*, November 3, 2002, p. G4.

Case 11.2

Online Auctions Pose Competitive Threat to Retailers

Online auction houses were never considered a threat to the average brick-and-mortar retailer until they became more prevalent. Numerous success stories have prompted consumers to take a closer look at buying merchandise via online auctions. For example, in the travel industry, websites such as Expedia.com and Travelocity.com returned profits through their practice of auctioning airline seats. Amazon.com has also achieved success in its online auction in which visitors sell their used or rare books to other visitors.

Of course, there is the forerunner of e-auctions, eBay, which started in 1995 and, as of press time, had more than 50 million registered users throughout the world. In the past, eBay has come under scrutiny due to individuals using its website to commit fraud by selling goods online and not delivering the products.

Although consumers are familiar with auction sites in which they bid for products and services, a new trend, called the "reverse e-auction," is emerging, where retailers can bid for suppliers' goods and services. Some suppliers don't like reverse e-auctions because they believe their products should be bought on attributes other than price. Also, many suppliers believe these auctions push down prices, which in turn lowers the suppliers' margins. Apparently, the Internet is changing pricing strategies for suppliers and retailers—but the winner in the price wars may be the consumer.

Questions

1. What can brick-and-mortar retailers do to compete against online auctions?
2. Why do you think online auctions are so popular?
3. What do you predict for the future of online auctions?
4. How are the concepts of markups and markdowns applied in an online auction environment?
5. What are the advantages and disadvantages of reverse e-auctions?
6. What can online auctions do to reduce fraud?

Sources: Kim Bayne, "Online Auctions Are Changing the Way We Buy and Sell," *Colorado Springs Gazette-Telegraph,* August 2, 1999, p. IB9; Carol Draeger, "New eBay Fraud Case Under Investigation; Mishawaka Police Find Second Set of Deceptions in Three Months," *South Bend Tribune* (South Bend, IN), November 1, 2002, p. 1; Maria O'Daniel, "Locating Rare and Used Books on the Net," *New Straits Times* (Kuala Lumpur), November 11, 2002, p. 32; Amon Cohen, "The Changed Face of Buying Online—E-Auctions," *Financial Times* (London), November 8, 2002, p. 4.

Developing an Effective Integrated Marketing Communications Mix

Chapter 12

Integrated marketing's primary objective is to break through the clutter. The challenge is that consumers get roughly 650 advertising/brand impressions a day . . . to create a singular and compelling message across all touch points has to be the marketer's competence.

Bob Gamgort, general manager for chocolate, Masterfoods USA[1]

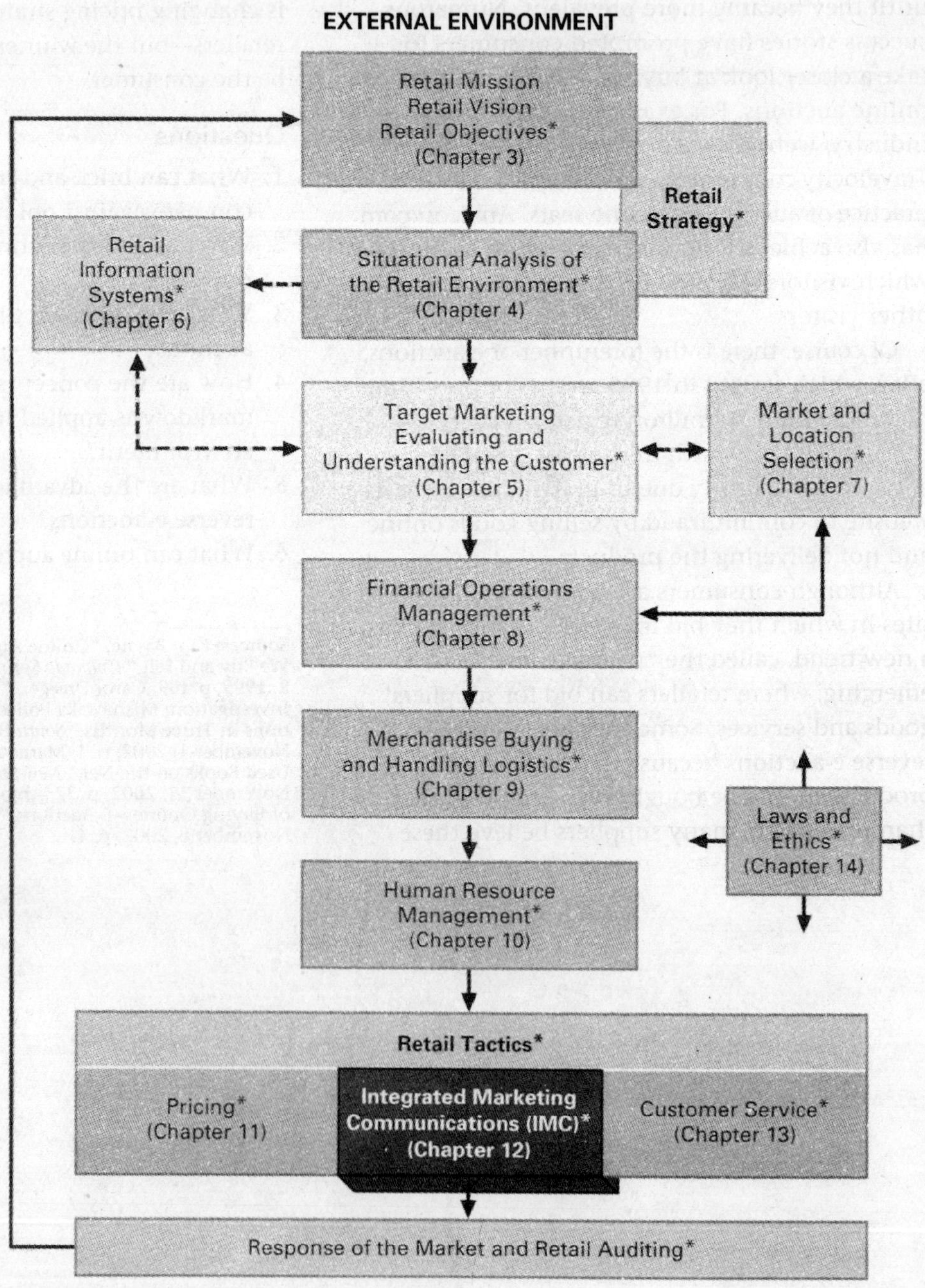

CHAPTER OBJECTIVES

After completing this chapter, you will be able to:

1. Define the concept of integrated marketing communications (IMC).
2. Explain the differences among all tactical elements of the IMC mix, including advertising, sales promotion, direct marketing, cybermarketing, personal selling, public relations, and publicity.
3. Describe the importance of effective customer communications.
4. Explain how a store's layout can be an effective tool in communicating with customers.

Hanes Company Introduces the Tagless T-shirt

In October 2002, Hanes Company, one of the biggest manufacturers of underwear, unveiled its tagless T-shirt. In an effort to appeal to the comfort-seeking consumer, Hanes replaced the tag with the same information, heat-applied directly to the shirt.[2]

To introduce the tagless merchandise, the company held tag "retirement" parties and sponsored a parade in Comfort, Texas.[3] Hanes also hired Michael Jordan as the spokesperson for its "go tagless" advertising campaign. To help spread the word about the tagless shirts, Hanes took out its first Super Bowl ad since 1985. The spot showed action hero Jackie Chan whipping himself into numerous contortions trying to remove the irritating tag on a brandless shirt before Michael Jordan comes to rescue him with tagless Hanes. Chan ends the spot by flipping for joy.[4]

There is much at stake in the campaign. The undergarment industry is in the maturity phase of the product life cycle. Apparel sales were down 4 percent in 2002 compared to the previous year, and price wars with retail discounters have reduced profitability. Any growth in sales will be cause for celebration. Consumer response to the tagless tee has been positive, with a 15 percent sales increase five months after the launch, compared to the previous year.[5] Hanes is even considering going tagless on all its products.[6]

INTRODUCTION

integrated marketing communications (IMC) A customer-focused philosophy in which all communications a company delivers are integrated and consistent with corporate strategies. Also called *mar*keting *com*munications, or *MARCOM*.

The process of communicating with various publics is known as **integrated marketing communications (IMC).** Although relatively new, the concept of IMC (also called *mar*keting *com*munications, or *MARCOM* for short) is catching on with many retailers. Individuals involved in the communications process have seen a need to integrate all the communications functions to create a synergistic, seamless incorporation of all of these activities into the IMC process. According to faculty at the Medill School at Northwestern University, "the IMC process starts with the customer . . . and then works back to determine and define the forms and methods through which persuasive communications programs should be developed."[7]

Consumers do not see all the various functions that businesses provide; rather, they see only the resulting product and/or brand and the physical retail store or e-tail site. They do not care about any of the functional areas required to bring them products or services; they care only about how those products or services satisfy their needs and wants. The satisfaction of these needs and wants generates sales for the retailer.

To effectively reach customers with a consistent message, everyone involved with internal and external customer communications must tell the consumer the same thing. Often the biggest challenge in IMC is executing the plans to meet marketplace demands while at the same time meeting company goals.[8] How many times have you seen an advertisement for a product you want only to find out that the store does not carry the product, the salesperson has never heard about the sale, or the price of the product is higher than in the advertisement? These inconsistencies could have been reduced or eliminated had the retailer used some type of system to integrate all its communications functions.

This chapter discusses the various methods and issues involved in the creation of an effective IMC mix for the retailer. In addition, the chapter examines the use of the store itself as an effective tool in customer communications.

DEVELOPING AN INTEGRATED MARKETING COMMUNICATIONS PROGRAM

The primary purpose for developing a retail IMC program is to generate consumer traffic—that is, to draw consumers to the retail site, whether a physical or an e-tail site. To attract consumers to the site, the retailer must inform them about items on sale, the location of the site, the reasons the consumer should shop there, and so on. The communications program should also inform consumers about the retailer's product and service offerings and any other areas that differentiate the retailer from competitors. In addition, the IMC program can develop customer loyalty that will yield repeat business for the firm.

Large retailers may develop different communication plans for specific geographic markets to take advantage of geographic differences. Plans may also be developed to take advantage of differences among the retailer's target market segments. For example, in 2003, Office Depot launched the company's first Hispanic-focused IMC campaign.[9] The back-to-school campaign integrated retail, direct marketing, catalog, e-commerce, public relations, and advertising efforts. To create consistency in the program, several advertising agencies had to work together.

IMC mix All the communications activities undertaken in an integrated marketing communications approach, including personal selling, advertising, public relations, direct marketing, sales promotions, and cybermarketing.

Several tactics are used to communicate with the retailer's internal and external publics. Together these tactics are known as the **IMC mix.** Components of the mix are advertising, sales promotions, direct marketing, cybermarketing, personal selling, public relations, and publicity. An argument can also be made to include the brand or product itself in the overall mix.

What makes you want to shop at a particular retailer? Are you searching for hard-to-find products or brands? Are you trying to find a particular brand? How did you hear about the brand? How did you hear about the retailer? IMC can help determine the answer to all of these questions. Many communications variables may influence the decision to shop at a particular retailer. Given the thousands of product offerings and the thousands of retailers offering them, retail marketers must ensure that their communications with their customers are "clear, concise, and integrated."[10]

Retailers invest a lot of time and money developing a positive image of their business and stores. This image carries a certain value, called *equity*. An effective communications plan builds and enhances equity for the retailer. IMC is essential for the continued operations of the retail organization. One example of a company that used its established image and brand equity to break into retailing is the General Motors Corporation (GM). In February 2002, GM opened its first branded retail store, at the Detroit airport. The store sells a variety of merchandise such as clothing and die-cast toys, all featuring GM brands such as Chevrolet, Corvette, and Hummer.[11] GM also sells similar merchandise from its website.

In developing an IMC plan, communications specialists (*i.e.,* marketing communications managers) conceive of a plan and then execute it so that the consumer is exposed to the end result of this planning process. Essentially the same steps are taken in developing an IMC program as in developing the integrated retail management (IRM) plan: creating objectives, then strategies, and then tactical executions.

Costs associated with IMC are often high. Therefore, the IMC plan includes a budget that allows management to see where money is being spent and determine whether the budget allocations are effective. A typical plan includes the following elements:

- The IMC mission or vision
- A situational analysis, including profiles of current users, a competitive analysis, and the geographic locations of the retail outlets and their customers
- Overall objectives

- The budget
- The overall strategy
- The tactical executions—including personal selling, direct marketing, sales promotions (which include point-of-purchase advertising), cyber-marketing, public relations and publicity, advertising, and in some instances, the packaging and branding of the products sold in the store
- Resource allocations (including human and capital resources)
- Methods of evaluation

IMC MISSION OR VISION

The IMC mission or vision is written in exactly the same manner as the overall retail mission and vision statements, except that it focuses on MARCOM only. The mission explains why the retailer is using IMC to communicate with customers. Specifically, it explains where the MARCOM function fits into the overall IRM plan.

SITUATIONAL ANALYSIS

Most of the information for the situational analysis can be generated from the retailer's general situational analysis. With MARCOM, however, there should be a fairly comprehensive analysis of the company, including the level of retailer "aggressiveness" in the marketplace, sales and profits from the past few years, the corporate culture, the mission and vision, market share for each product line and for the retailer as a whole, and sales trends. The analysis should also include corporate resources, such as technology and human resources, that are available for use in integrated marketing communications.

In addition, the situational analysis should include the environments within which the retailer operates, product and service histories, a competitive analysis, a current user analysis, and geographic data. Data for the situational analysis come from the same sources provided in our discussions of the retail information system (RIS) and site selection (see Chapters 6 and 7). The more information and data available to facilitate IMC executions, the more effective the executions will be.

DEVELOPING OBJECTIVES

General IMC objectives are developed to provide a basis for determining the extent of the IMC program's success. Like the objectives for other parts of the IRM plan, IMC objectives should be measurable and realistic. In creating MARCOM objectives, the retailer needs to have a good understanding of who the target audience is, when the objectives should be met, and specifically what the retailer wants to accomplish by undertaking the executions. The objectives can be either long term, short term, or both. The idea is to provide motivation and direction for the entire campaign. Typical categories of retail IMC objectives are described next.

POSITIONING OBJECTIVES. The purpose of positioning objectives is to create an image in consumers' minds about the retailer, typically in relation to the competition. Positioning objectives help build the retailer's brand name. This is also called *brand building.*[12] Retailers can also position by attributes, price, or quality.[13]

Example: "Our objective is to become the number one retailer in the children's shoe category, as measured by market share, within the greater Los Angeles, CA, area by the year 2008."

INCREASED SALES. The purpose of increased-sales objectives is to stimulate the sales of certain products (or all products) during a given time period.

Example: "Our objective with this advertising campaign is to increase sales of women's apparel by 10 percent in one year."

COMMUNICATIONS OBJECTIVES. Communications objectives usually deal with the influence of the retailer's communications on consumers over a period of time. Communications objectives tend to be both long and short term, to try to persuade consumers to do something (continue buying products from the retailer, learn that the retailer is open twenty-four hours a day, and so on).

Example: "To create awareness of the company's website such that at the end of three months, 20 percent or more of a random sample of 100 surveyed customers indicate knowledge of our website and 10 percent or more have accessed the website at least once during the three-month measurement period."

TRAFFIC OBJECTIVES. Traffic objectives aim to draw increasing numbers of customers to the retailer's store over time. These objectives may be particularly useful in an e-tailing environment.

INTERNET IN ACTION

Malls Begin Using the Internet for Communications to Customers

The next e-mail you receive may be from your local mall. Many mall owners are harnessing Web capabilities to generate sales. In this communication format, consumers interested in receiving information about promotions sign up for an e-mail notification program. When various retailers from the local mall are having sales or special deals, the consumer gets an e-mail notification.

One company achieving success with e-mail notifications to customers is Taubman and Johnstown of Bloomfield Hills, Michigan. Taubman and Johnstown has an "e-bulletin" program that informs subscribers about sales, promotions, and new merchandise at the stores in the company's malls. More than 450,000 shoppers receive the bulletin. According to Taubman and Johnstown, more than 90 percent of its 4,000 retail tenants participate in the program. Many retailers believe the program has contributed to an increase in sales.

Source: Donna Mitchell, "Mall Owners Harnessing Web to Generate Sales," *Shopping Centers Today,* September 2002, p. 32.

Example: "The objective is to increase store traffic by 10 percent over a one-year period and to increase website traffic by 30 percent over the same period."

IMAGE. Image objectives focus on developing the overall image of the retailer (as opposed to product or sales revenue objectives).

Example: "The long-term objective is to, within the next five years, change our image from the 'lousy customer service retailer' to the 'we respond quickly to customers' needs retailer,' as necessitated by customer image surveys."

Objectives are usually specific to each type of retailer. Although there is no one "right" IMC plan for each and every retailer, some elements are common to all plans and must be included in the retailer's IMC mix. The following sections discuss budgeting for IMC and the tactical areas of the IMC mix.

THE IMC BUDGET

Once the objectives are developed, the budget for the MARCOM executions should be determined. A number of techniques can be used for MARCOM budgeting, but our discussion focuses on the most popular methods. Dollar amounts for any type of IMC campaign must be included in the budget. Often retailers are given advertising allowances or are encouraged to create cooperative advertising or IMC with their suppliers. These additional incentives must be included in the overall IMC budget.

Developing a budget can be a difficult process because decision makers often deal with competing pressures such as long-term objectives versus short-term needs, personal success versus company success, and risks versus rewards.[14]

Although there are many different ways to calculate a budget, most retailers and IMC professionals choose among the percentage-of-sales method, the percentage-of-profit method, the objective-and-task method, follow-the-leader budgeting, the all-you-can-afford method, and the best-guess method.

percentage-of-sales method A method of budgeting in which the retailer allots a basic percentage amount for the store and, in some cases, for each of the store's brands or products (or product lines).

PERCENTAGE-OF-SALES METHOD. With the **percentage-of-sales method** of budgeting, the retailer or IMC specialist allots a basic percentage amount for the store and, in some cases, for each of the store's brands or products (or product lines). This basic percentage is usually based on a past trend or a researched forecast for the retailer's sales. Thus, the retailer decides on a basic percentage amount—say, 3 percent of total sales—and that amount of money is placed in the MARCOM budget. This is the easiest budgeting method and thus is fairly popular. However, the percentage-of-sales method does have some drawbacks.

The first problem occurs when sales are decreasing. In a period of declining sales, one potentially effective communication tactic is to expand rather than reduce the amount of communication or advertising. With the percentage-of-sales method, however, the retailer would budget *less* money for IMC when sales decrease.

Another problem occurs when competitors increase their advertising and promotional budgets to achieve a stated objective or to follow a planned strategy. When the competition increases its budgets, a retailer following the percentage-of-sales method may not follow suit. Consequently, this retailer may face a loss of market share. For example, if the retailer planned a special event to introduce some new products or services, the percentage-of-sales method would restrict the retailer's ability to implement these events. Because of these shortcomings, the percentage-of-sales method is usually used in conjunction with one or two of the other budgeting methods discussed next.

percentage-of-profit method
A method of budgeting in which the retailer determines a basic percentage amount to be used for IMC based on overall profits.

PERCENTAGE-OF-PROFIT METHOD. The **percentage-of-profit method** of budgeting is very similar to the percentage-of-sales method. With the percentage-of-profit method, the basic percentage amount to be used for IMC is created based on the retailer's overall profits, rather than sales. This can be done division by division, for specific product lines, or for the retail operation as a whole. The percentage-of-profit method of budgeting has the same disadvantages as the percentage-of-sales method, so it too is usually coupled with one or two other budgeting methods.

objective-and-task method
A method of budgeting in which the retailer specifies the role IMC will play and the outcomes desired in the overall operation.

OBJECTIVE-AND-TASK METHOD. The **objective-and-task method** of budgeting for IMC is probably the best method of those described here because it requires a more thorough analysis of the role of the IMC components in achieving objectives. The retailer specifies the exact role the IMC program is to play in the overall retail operation. In addition, the retailer clearly defines the desired outcomes of the IMC plan. The retailer's budget is then based on the stated outcomes.

The objective-and-task method of budgeting consists of five steps:

1. The retailer specifies the retailing objectives to be achieved (profit increases, heightened consumer awareness, increased sales, increased market share, and so on).
2. The retailer specifies which variables are required to achieve the stated objectives.
3. The retailer defines the role each IMC variable is to play in achieving the objectives (*e.g.*, the retailer decides whether point-of-purchase advertising, print advertising, or more salespeople would be required).
4. The retailer specifies the levels of response required to achieve the overall goals.
5. The retailer assigns budgeted dollar amounts based on the first four steps and by taking into account the time and costs associated with meeting the objectives.

follow-the-leader budgeting
A method of budgeting in which the retailer generates estimates of competitors' IMC budgets from outside sources and attempts to match the industry leader's budget.

FOLLOW-THE-LEADER BUDGETING. In **follow-the-leader budgeting** (also known as the *competitive match*), the retailer generates estimates of competitors' budgets (possible sources of information are the *Standard Directory of Advertising Agencies*, the *Standard Directory of Advertisers, LNA [Leading National Advertisers]* listings, or some of the sources discussed in Chapter 6). Because most IMC data are proprietary, the retailer may have to make an educated guess as to the amount budgeted for IMC functions by competing retailers. The retailer can then either match the industry leader's IMC budget or budget higher or lower amounts, depending on the organization's overall needs.

In addition to the problem of trying to generate accurate budget data for competitors, follow-the-leader budgeting takes a reactive rather than proactive stance in customer communications. This method also assumes all competitors have the same communications needs when in fact each retailer's needs are unique. Retailers differ in size, have different target markets, and generate different types of communications. Thus, follow-the-leader budgeting may be ineffective for many types of retailers.

all-you-can-afford method A method of budgeting in which the retailer allots all the money it can manage to bear toward the IMC functions.

ALL-YOU-CAN-AFFORD METHOD. The **all-you-can-afford method** is exactly what the name implies: the retailer allots all the money it can afford to IMC functions. Although it is not recommended, with the all-you-can-afford method the retailer develops the other retailing budgets and allots the leftover amounts to the IMC budget. This is not an effective budgeting method because it assumes IMC is the least relevant function in running a business when in fact IMC is critical to the success or failure of the organization. IMC activities should receive a great deal of emphasis, but this budgeting method precludes that. In times of decreasing sales, it is important to increase rather than decrease customer communications. All-you-can-afford budgeting is common in small to mid-size retailers that are conservative in their attempts to increase market share and company sales.

best-guess method A method of budgeting in which the retailer makes a subjective guess at how much to allocate to IMC.

BEST-GUESS METHOD. The **best-guess method** is most often used by retailers that have very little experience or training in budgeting. In essence, the retailer has no idea of how much to allocate and therefore develops a subjective estimate ("guesstimate") as the budget figure. Because this method is largely subjective, it is inefficient.

THE OVERALL IMC STRATEGY

The IMC strategy should emanate from the first few phases of the IMC and IRM plans. The mission and vision provide direction in determining the strategy for achieving the overall goals. In addition, the situational analysis should provide information about competitors and customers. These data help frame the IMC strategy.

Two steps should be completed before undertaking the development of an IMC strategy. The first is to identify the main consumer or store problem (or opportunity) for which the IMC plan can provide a solution. This key fact may explain why consumers prefer a particular retailer over its competitors. It may deal with product offerings, customer service, responsiveness to the customer, and so forth. The key fact should be stated in the consumer's language, not in the language of retailing or marketing. For example, instead of saying, "We offer the largest number of stock keeping units related to spices in our geographic trading area," it would be better to say, "We offer a greater variety of spices than any other retailer in the world."

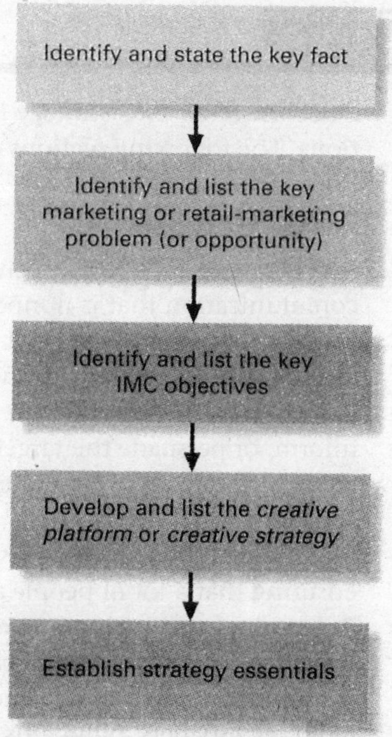

FIGURE 12.1 Developing an Effective Retail IMC Strategy

The second step is to identify and list the key marketing problems (or opportunities). This problem or opportunity should be based on prior research and approached from the point of view of the retail IMC specialist. For example, an opportunity may be stated as, "According to a survey taken last month, brand recall is up 10 percent within our primary target market compared to the same period last year, but down 30 percent within our secondary target market and 50 percent within our tertiary target market. An opportunity exists to increase brand awareness in our secondary and tertiary target markets."

Once these two steps are completed, the retailer is ready to identify the key IMC objectives from which the desired outcomes of the IMC executions are developed. If the objective-and-task method of budgeting is being used, this information already exists. Then the retailer should develop and document the **creative platform** (or creative strategy). The creative platform includes the target market, major competitors, reasons that consumers should purchase from the retailer, and a promise to consumers (*i.e.*, a solution to the problem or opportunity identified in step 2).

creative platform The creative strategy of a selected IMC tactic; includes the promise, creative objectives, and reasons the customer should buy. Also called *copy platform* or *creative strategy*.

Finally, the retailer is ready to establish the essential components of the creative strategy, including both creative and noncreative information (legal requirements, tag lines, logos, etc.). The strategy represents the "big picture" for IMC personnel, guiding them as they develop IMC campaigns for the retail outlet(s). It is also used to plan the tactical executions.

Figure 12.1 outlines the process for developing the IMC strategy.

IMC TACTICS

Once the retail IMC strategy is in place, the retailer concentrates on executions. The following sections describe the variables in the tactical executions.

ADVERTISING

advertising A form of either mass communication or direct-to-consumer communication that is nonpersonal and is paid for by an identifiable sponsor to inform or persuade members of a particular audience.

Advertising is "a form of either mass communication or direct-to-consumer communication that is nonpersonal and is paid for by various business firms, nonprofit organizations, and individuals who are in some way identified in the advertising message and who hope to inform or persuade members of a particular audience."[15] The retailer generally uses advertising to remind, inform, or persuade the targeted market to act. A retailer also might use advertising to create an overall retail image (information and persuasion for the consumer).

Whatever the reason for using advertising, the key to effective advertising is ensuring that a lot of people are reached in a relatively short period of time. Per-product advertising is relatively inexpensive; in contrast, the cost for an overall advertising program can be quite high. Advertising allows a business to communicate with a large audience through various media such as television, radio, newspapers, billboards, magazines, the Internet, and so on.

Author Lisa Fortini-Campbell compares successful advertising to hitting the "sweet spot." In sports, the sweet spot is the special place on a baseball, tennis

Kohl's integrated marketing communications strategy stresses availability of brand names, a customer-friendly environment, and low prices. Unlike many department stores, Kohl's avoids the use of heavy discounts. Shown here is a store interior.

FIGURE 12.2 Developing an Advertising Campaign

racket, or other piece of equipment that makes the ball travel faster with less effort. Advertising's sweet spot is the place in the consumer's mind where a connection is made between consumer insight and brand insight.[16]

When assessing what type of advertising to undertake, the retailer creates an advertising plan. This plan should give direction to IMC employees and should be integrated into all other functions as well, so that everyone understands the purpose of the advertising.

Establishing an advertising plan includes six major steps[17] (see Figure 12.2):

1. Review the IRM plan.
2. Restate the target market, taking care to include information that will help develop the best advertising plan. Data that are irrelevant should be ignored.
3. Develop and list the advertising communications objectives. Included within this step should be the key fact, the marketing problem, and the communications objectives. Like all objectives, the advertising objectives must be realistic, measurable, specific, cost effective, and timely. Each objective should be worded to allow for a specific outcome (and only one outcome).

4. State the advertising strategy. The strategy should contain information about the target markets and audiences, the principal competition, the consumer promise, and the reason that the consumer should purchase from the retailer. In other words, the advertising presents the rationale for shopping at a particular retail outlet. Advertising agencies usually create *copy platforms,* or creative strategies, that speak to all of these issues.
5. Develop samples of creative executions that will be pursued. These examples may be in the form of sample print layouts, television storyboards, radio scripts, or other samples of the creative work.
6. List all media recommendations. In this step, all the available media should be assessed to choose the best methods for communicating to targeted audiences. The media recommendations should include the key media problem and the objectives to be achieved. Media objectives are usually expressed in terms of **reach, frequency, continuity,** geographic weighting, costs per thousand exposures (CPM), and **gross rating points (GRPs).**

reach The percentage of a target audience that is exposed to an advertising message at least one time during an advertising campaign.

frequency The number of times a target audience is exposed to an advertising message over a particular time period.

continuity One of the attributes of media objectives, indicating a stable level of IMC activity.

gross rating points (GRPs) An advertising measurement taken by multiplying reach by frequency.

Each time an advertising choice is recommended, management or the readers of the advertising plan should be given a rationale for that choice. This makes it easier for managers to see at a glance why various methods, objectives, platforms, and so on were developed.

All advertising should be dynamic, strategic, based on consumer needs and wants, creative, integrated, persuasive, and informative. There are short-term and long-term results from advertising. Short-term results include increased sales, brand awareness, and traffic. Long-term results include increases in market share, customer loyalty, and brand equity.[18]

Each retailer has specific advertising needs. In addition, each retailer has certain times or periods that are more effective for its advertising programs.

TABLE 12.1

THOSE STRANGE MEDIA TERMS

- **Reach** refers to the percentage of a target audience that is exposed to an advertising message at least one time during an advertising campaign. Generally, reach is calculated based on a four-week period. Various advertising research companies generate reach figures. For example, Nielsen Media Research Company researches how many people watch television shows during different times of the day. The rating is simply a statement of the reach of that program.

- **Frequency** refers to the number of times the target audience is exposed to an advertising message over a particular time period (usually a four-week period).

- **Gross rating points (GRPs)** are a measurement advertisers use to integrate the concepts of reach and frequency. GRPs are calculated by multiplying the advertisement's reach by the frequency of the ad:

  GRPs = Reach (r) × Frequency (f)

  Example: If a retailer places three advertisements on a television show that has a Nielsen rating of 30, its GRPs are calculated as follows:

  30 (reach) × 3 (frequency) = 90 GRPs

For example, Wednesdays and Thursdays are good times for supermarkets to advertise their products. Shoppers look at the ads on those days and begin writing shopping lists for the weekend trip to the supermarket. They also clip coupons and note any special sales occurring over the advertised period. Large department stores usually begin advertising back-to-school products during the end of July and early August rather than spending the bulk of advertising dollars on weekly ads. Because advertising budgets are fixed, retailers must make sure they get the most reach and frequency out of their budgets (for an explanation of *reach* and *frequency,* see Table 12.1).

When using advertising, retailers have a choice of many media. The most popular medium used by retailers is newspapers, which provide geographic and demographic coverage of the retailer's marketplace. In the fall of 2003, Gap Inc. chose newspapers, magazines, and television to unveil its pop-star spokesperson, Madonna.[19]

sales promotion A short-term activity that enhances or supports other IMC variables.

point-of-purchase (POP) communications A type of sales promotion that includes in-store materials such as posters and displays designed to influence consumer purchases. Also called *point-of-purchase advertising.*

SALES PROMOTIONS

Tactical executions can also take the form of sales promotions. **Sales promotions** are used to complement the other IMC tactical areas. The overriding purpose of a sales promotion is to stimulate customer purchases with various nonrecurring sales efforts. In a study conducted by the department of integrated marketing communications at Northwestern University, it was found that promotion marketing results in significant contributions to the corporate bottom line.[20]

Although initially used to stimulate short-term sales, sales promotions today play a much bigger role in the IMC process. They can be used to tie in a branding strategy with a product in the retail store. They can be used to generate customer databases for use with site location planning or with direct-marketing campaigns.

Consumers can benefit from sales promotions, as well. These benefits include contributing to shopping enjoyment, increased satisfaction with the retail experience, and monetary savings.[21]

In an effort to revitalize the retailer, Kmart reintroduced its bluelight specials in 2001, after a ten-year hiatus. Many of Kmart's in-store promotions, such as the one shown here, incorporate the familiar blue light.

An example of a successful sales promotion is the Walt Disney Company–Hallmark partnership. The partnership was launched to the public in 2001 when the two companies shared title billing as hosts of a prime-time television show on skating. The promotion included a contest in which the winner and twenty-five friends got to go to Disney World. There was also a "watch-and-win" promotion on the Disney Channel.[22]

When planned properly, sales promotions can stimulate both short-term sales and long-term demand. Table 12.2 lists the most common types of sales promotions.

The most popular form of sales promotion among retailers in general is **point-of-purchase (POP) communications** (also called *point-of-purchase*

TABLE 12.2

THE MOST COMMON TYPES OF SALES PROMOTIONS

- Trade shows
- Business cards
- Contests and sweepstakes
- Trade allowances
- Vendor support programs (including displays and shippers)
- Training programs supplied to customers
- Specialty advertising (pens, pencils, caps, jackets, shirts, etc.)
- Cooperative advertising
- Sampling
- Point-of-purchase (POP) communications
- In-pack or on-pack coupons
- Premiums
- Direct-mail coupons (or other incentives)
- Price-off promotions
- BOGOs (**b**uy **o**ne, **g**et **o**ne free)
- Tie-in promotions, including licensing
- Warranties and guarantees

advertising). Point-Of-Purchase Advertising International (POPAI) is a trade association devoted to the execution of POP communications. POPAI created a trade publication called *Marketing's Powerful Weapon: Point-Of-Purchase Advertising* as a guide for the retailer in the development of effective POP communications.[23]

DIRECT MARKETING

direct marketing An interactive system of marketing that uses one or more advertising media to generate a measurable response or transaction at any location.

Many types of retailers, including e-tailers, use direct marketing to reach customers. Through **direct marketing,** retailers use one or more advertising media to generate immediate action from consumers (*i.e.,* the purchase of products and services). The idea behind direct marketing is to solicit from customers an order or a request for additional information about the store or products being sold, or to increase traffic to the retailer's place of business (including online sites). Referred to as "customized persuasion,"[24] direct marketing attempts to create immediate sales. Frequently, direct marketing is integrated into the other IMC tactical executions, especially advertising.

Direct-response advertising, direct-mail advertising, membership programs, and telemarketing are examples of direct marketing. Direct marketing can be used to reward frequent customers through loyalty programs that provide incentives for shopping at a particular retailer. It is estimated that half of all Americans belong to at least one customer reward program.[25]

The use of direct mail is growing due to recent limitations imposed on telemarketing. Tie-ins with sales promotion activities, such as coupons, have

Blunders or Best Practices?

McDonald's IMC Blunders

In 1997, after six consecutive quarters of declining domestic same-store sales, McDonald's needed to jump-start the business. Thus, the Campaign 55 promotion was launched. Named for the year the company was founded, Campaign 55 featured 55-cent rotating sandwich offerings for breakfast, lunch, and dinner.

Several mistakes led McDonald's to cancel the campaign after six weeks. First, the campaign was introduced by a full-page story in the *Wall Street Journal* before franchisees had voted on the plan. Second, some franchisees raised prices on fries and drinks to maintain margins lost by lowering sandwich prices. When consumers found out about this, many thought the company had misled them. Third, the corporation wanted franchisees to guarantee orders would be delivered within 55 seconds or the customer would get a coupon for a free sandwich. Franchisees rejected this plan. In general, the promotion was confusing to consumers and was not supported by all franchisees.

Other IMC blunders have included failed product introductions such as the Arch Deluxe, pizza, and the first Beanie Baby promotion, in which the company greatly underestimated demand. McDonald's has learned a great deal from its blunders. In 2002, McDonald's introduced a new discount campaign touting a Dollar Menu in which all items cost $1 or less. So far, this promotion has been well received by the public and by franchisees.

Sources: Richard Gibson, "With Egg on Its Face, McDonald's Cuts the 55-Cent Specials to Breakfast Only," *Wall Street Journal*, June 4, 1997 p. B7; Louise Kramer, "More Nimble McDonald's Is Getting Back on Track," *Advertising Age*, January 18, 1999,p. 6; Jim Kirk, "McDonald's Discount Menu Hits West Coast," *Chicago Tribune*, North Sports Final Edition, January 4, 2002, p. 3.

increased the effectiveness of direct mail. Consumers are often more willing to open direct-mail pieces that provide additional value, such as coupons, than those that don't. In addition, many brick-and-mortar retailers have nonstore divisions that specialize in direct mail, such as catalog retailers. These divisions focus on the use of mail to get their product offerings into consumers' hands.

Like the other tactical areas, direct marketing requires a plan. Because of the nature of direct marketing, the plan must show how it integrates with the other IMC variables. For the most part, the objectives behind direct marketing include customer retention, product trial, brand switching, increased sales, or sales through direct response (as in catalog sales). Database marketing is a form of direct marketing, although it is also used to create nondirect sales.

CYBERMARKETING AND E-TAILING

Many people think all business conducted online is cybermarketing. However, cybermarketing also includes any form of communication that is undertaken in cyberspace. Such communications certainly include those transmitted via the Internet, but other sources are used as well, such as videos, DVDs, CDs, e-mail marketing, and electronic data interchange (EDI). The IMC plan should include a rationale for the method(s) chosen. For retailers, the most common tactics in this method of communication are the establishment of e-tail outlets and the dissemination of product/store/customer information via cyberspace.

In addition to commerce, Barnes & Noble uses the Internet to communicate with its customers about its products and services. (Courtesy of Barnes & Noble.)

There is some overlap between cybermarketing and the other areas of IMC. Certainly advertising and sales promotions can be executed within this venue. Many argue that the sales functions can also be accomplished using cybermarketing. Like the other areas of IMC, cybermarketing requires developing a comprehensive plan. The plan should integrate this format with the retailer's other methods of communication.

Keep in mind that cybermarketing and e-tailing are two different concepts. Although the e-tailing venue is cyberspace, it deals primarily with the sale of products. Cybermarketing is much broader in that it includes advertising, information/communication, logistics, inventory, and other activities as well as e-tailing. When developing the IMC mix, the question to answer is "Does this method communicate to our customers in an effective and integrated manner?"

ISSUES IN THE USE AND EXPLANATION OF TECHNOLOGY. As we have seen, electronic technology can be used for a number of retailing functions. Therefore, it is best to deal with the use of these technologies from a functional rather than a general perspective. Certainly the Internet can be used as a channel of distribution, but that function is entirely different from using the Internet as a marketing communications tool. Thus, if the Internet is used as both a channel of distribution and a means of communication, the purpose for each function should be made clear in planning documents. Uses of electronic technologies are expanding rapidly; new applications of these powerful tools are found every day. IMC specialists focus on technology's power to communicate.

PERSONAL SELLING

Personal selling is the oldest form of communicating with customers. It is the salesperson at the retail level who can most effectively close sales. The importance of this function is often underestimated. In IMC, it is one of the most effective tools for creating retail sales. **Personal selling** involves face-to-face, or person-to-person, communication. The seller attempts to persuade customers to buy the retailer's products. The primary advantage of personal selling is its one-on-one nature, which allows the salesperson to be flexible when finding products or services to satisfy or exceed the customer's needs and wants.

personal selling Selling to a customer by face-to-face communication.

Often salespeople are the only contact a customer has with a retail store. The customer may then look upon the salesperson as the retailer. Customers come to retail salespeople with specific needs and wants, and a well-trained salesperson makes sure that those needs and wants are met or exceeded. The downside to personal selling as a communications vehicle is that it is very expensive when looked at on a per-customer-contact basis.

To increase the chances of success, a sales plan is needed for the sales function. Salespeople should receive ongoing training to ensure they have the answers to customers' questions, or at least know where to go to get those answers.

Personal selling entails a great deal of integration among the retailing functions. Human resource personnel train salespeople, customer service depends on personal customer contact, managers supervise salespeople, and all IMC functions rely on salespeople to close many sales. It can be argued that personal selling is the most important aspect of retailing.

Retailers often have different hiring criteria for the sales staff than for employees in many of the other areas. Demographic characteristics, prior work experience, and personality are important considerations when selecting sales personnel.

Examples of using demographics in the hiring of salespeople are found at Nordstrom department stores. If you have shopped at a Nordstrom store, you may have noticed that the salespeople in each department mirror the department in which they work. For example, the salesperson working in the women's petite clothing department is usually a petite person. This approach allows the salesperson to better understand customers' needs.

On a recent trip to Nordstrom, two retail consultants were looking around in each department. One thing that caught their attention was the age demographic of the salespeople. In the junior department, salespeople were younger. In the women's departments, salespeople were older than those in juniors, and all the sales clerks were women. Similarly, male sales personnel staffed the men's departments. This pattern held throughout the store. Consumers are likely to feel more confident about their purchases when they relate to salespeople who "look" like them. Other retailers can learn from the Nordstrom example by hiring and training salespeople who understand customers' concerns. The salesperson wearing a suit is probably more effective in his job—selling men's suits—than he would be if he worked in the athletic apparel section.

Training for sales personnel takes a slightly different approach than that for employees in other IMC areas. Selling techniques and product knowledge are the main issues in sales training. Many retailers rely heavily on role playing to enforce the processes being taught to sales staff.

Once again, it is the retail manager's job to ensure that personal selling is integrated with the other IMC variables. No customer likes to be confused by a retailer's communications process. If advertisers tell consumers that the retailer is "friendly," consumers expect to see friendly employees. To them, "friendly" may mean being greeted by smiling employees who thank them for their business. If shoppers do not experience friendliness, they may get confused and the IMC message will get lost in the execution. Sales employees should be trained to follow the "golden rule": "Treat customers as you would want to be treated were you to shop at the store." Chapter 13 addresses customer relations in greater depth.

PUBLIC RELATIONS

public relations (PR) The efforts of an organization to win the cooperation of various publics.

Public relations (PR) is an organization's efforts to win the cooperation of various publics.[26] The basic task of the PR department is to generate goodwill toward the retail organization, creating long-term, profitable relationships with the retailer's community. In particular, the PR department needs to create and maintain positive relationships with the various media, including newspapers, radio and television stations, and regional or local magazines. The task of internal employee communications also generally falls on the shoulders of the PR office.

Although the Internet has improved the speed of communication with various publics, there is also a risk in doing so, due to increasing expectations of accuracy.[27] PR professionals must learn to balance the time pressure to get information out on the Internet with the need to check facts before posting content on the retailer's website.[28]

The area of public relations requires a plan, so that it will be integrated with the other IMC functions. It is very important that the PR department be connected to the RIS. The PR manager has the added responsibility of monitoring the publicity that the retailer seeks to generate.

Thomas L. Harris, management consultant and author of a book about public relations, calls PR the secret weapon of IMC because PR can make the other IMC components (*e.g.*, advertising, cybermarketing, and sales promotion) more credible.[29] For retailers, credibility in the eyes of the customer translates into increased sales and loyalty.

PUBLICITY

publicity A subfunction of public relations in which the organization attempts to attract attention through various media.

Publicity is a subfunction of public relations in which the organization attempts to attract attention through various media without paying for the time or space to do so. The attention can be controlled or uncontrolled and can be positive or negative. Publicity might be about a retailer's employees, its customers (a very good idea), or the retailer as a whole (perhaps, for instance, about the retailer being the largest contributor to a town beautification project).

In general, publicity is seen as more credible than advertising. The reason for this is that in many instances publicity comes from an objective source as opposed to an advertisement paid for by the retailer.[30]

Publicity is referred to as being "free," because media time and space are not purchased. There are many costs associated with PR, however, such as those for hiring people to write press releases, purchasing supplies, and so on. One example of the costs associated with publicity involves the Harry Potter book craze. In the summer of 2003, due to the publicity surrounding the release of *Harry Potter and the Order of the Phoenix*, retailers had to adopt increased security measures to guard against theft of the book before its release.[31]

Retailers must attempt to control and plan publicity, and it must be integrated with all the other areas of the IMC mix. Unplanned publicity must be limited or eliminated completely. All communications vehicles should provide customers with the same ongoing message, to achieve continuity and thereby more communications power for the retailer.

There are two types of publicity: good and bad. Obviously, no retailer wants to generate any bad publicity for its operations. Unfortunately, due to the number of media outlets, misinformation about a retailer can spread rapidly and have a radical effect on an organization.[32] For example, in June 1993, consumer electronics retailer Best Buy got some bad press when the retailer helped *The Eagles* release their new single. The band wanted to bypass major record labels in releasing the song. They needed a fast method to get the song into the retail venue and used Best Buy because of its distribution channels and ability to promote the release. In exchange, Best Buy got to sell the single exclusively for the first 30 days of it release. The exclusivity agreement infuriated other retailers. The Coalition of Independent Music Stores began a press war that called into question the integrity and fairness of the band and made Best Buy appear to be a corporate bully.[33]

When planning for publicity, one or more of the following objectives is generally pursued:

- Reputation management (*e.g.*, consider Qwest, Arthur Andersen, or Martha Stewart)
- Publications (annual reports, brochures, manuals, other house organ–type publications)
- Speech writing (for the CEO or other members of the executive staff who do not have the time to write their own speeches)
- Special-events management (sports marketing, sponsorships, etc.)
- Lobbying (also known as *public affairs management*)

Some methods of generating publicity, in conjunction with the PR department, would be through news releases, photographs, event marketing, posters, exhibits, free sampling, and fact sheets or media kits.

RESOURCE ALLOCATION

The biggest challenge for those involved in IMC tactical executions is to fully integrate them with one another; the overall IRM plan; and the retail mission, vision, and objectives. Once the tactics have been integrated, resources for executing the tactics need to be allocated.

The IMC manager is responsible for allocating both dollars and human resources to each tactical area. Effective plans facilitate the allocation process;

those with the best rationales for their tactical executions generally get the lion's share of the resources.

EVALUATION

The final step in the overall IMC plan is the development of methods to assess the effectiveness of the company's communications. Although deemed the "final step," in practice the evaluation process should occur on an ongoing basis. Many methods can be used to assess communication effectiveness, but the most popular is simply to track sales. If outstanding advertising and promotions are created, sales should increase. However, evaluating the effectiveness of an IMC program is not always that easy.

Many variables affecting customer communications are beyond the control of the retailer and IMC planner (the economy is a major example). Therefore, in evaluating IMC, estimates are used to assess how well the programs are working. Because there are objectives for each tactical area, the first step in evaluation is to ascertain whether the objectives have been met. If they have not been met, the next step is to try to figure out why not.

Advertisers and IMC specialists use many techniques to test IMC effectiveness, such as pretest/posttest research, concept tests, copy tests, and tracking studies, among others. Different methods are used to measure the effectiveness of each of the IMC variables. Generally, direct marketing tends to be the easiest to monitor, because there is an immediate response to the marketing effort.

When putting the IMC program together and evaluating the outcomes, it is wise to keep in mind the words of the first large department store owner, John Wanamaker: "I know that half of my advertising is wasted; I just don't know which half." He was referring to the difficulties encountered when attempting to evaluate the effectiveness of IMC programs.

USING STORE LAYOUT AND DESIGN TO INCREASE THE EFFECTIVENESS OF THE IMC PROGRAM

In addition to the concepts discussed earlier, the store itself can be used as an effective method of customer communications. The store's design should evolve through planning and integration, not through a haphazard approach. Ideally, the store layout and design is planned prior to leasing or building a physical location. If e-tailing is a component of the business, the e-tail outlet must also have a creative layout and design that are integrated with the other communications tactics.

The store layout and design can help the retailer create differentiation for its products and services. Think about a restaurant that you visit frequently. What makes that particular restaurant attractive to you? The answer may be that you enjoy the atmosphere, the restaurant is close by, the customer service is excellent, and you enjoy the food. To attract consumers to a particular retail venue, the retailer needs to ensure that the overall store design is appealing to its target market groups.

In a physical store, the retailer has the means to make patrons comfortable. For example, when women shop for clothes with a male companion, chances are that he will want to take frequent breaks. An aware retailer can create a comfortable area for people who are waiting while their shopping partners try on clothes. A simple couch may be just what is needed to appeal to customers. Customers will return to a retailer that has treated them well.

DESIGN AND LAYOUT OBJECTIVES

To ensure that the store's layout and design are communicating the same message as other IMC variables, a plan is required. Within that plan are objectives, strategies, and tactics. The three main objectives in design and layout development are related to (1) creating an appropriate overall atmosphere, (2) designing the store to allow easy shopping, and (3) creating a design and layout that allots retail space to maximize the store's productivity.

Each time selling space is used to provide customers with added amenities, valuable selling space is lost. Thus, the question to ask is: How much do the design and layout add to overall sales? Another question is: Do the layout and design generate repeat business by bringing consumers back to the store?

atmospherics The attempt to create an overall positive atmosphere in a retail outlet.

ATMOSPHERE. The first objective is to create an overall positive atmosphere in the retail outlet; retailers refer to this as **atmospherics.** The retail store's physical characteristics affect the overall communications that are sent to the target market. They also contribute to the overall store image. When you hear the words "Hard Rock Café," you can picture in your mind the atmosphere of that restaurant. You may even be able to "hear" the music played there or recall the smells of a Hard Rock Café you have visited. These elements help define a retailer and create continuity in all IMC attempts.

If you have ever been to a mall that had a Cinnabon store, you can probably recall the fragrance of the fresh cinnamon rolls baking. Similarly, people who have shopped at a Victoria's Secret store tend to remember the smell of perfume that permeates the store. The smells associated with Cinnabon and Victoria's Secret help create an overall image for these retailers.

E-tailers and other types of nonstore retailers also rely on consumers' senses as they develop images for their companies and products. For example, many websites use audio or pop-up banners that make them memorable to visitors. A music e-tailer may include sounds on its websites to create not only an image but also the continuity needed when communicating to customers. Many catalog direct marketers use smells to help create an overall retail image by inserting "scratch and sniff" products or free product samples within their catalogs.

visual merchandising An attempt to inspire customers to purchase through the use of design techniques that enhance the overall buying experience.

To develop an overall store image, retailers use lighting, fixtures, point-of-purchase displays, music, smells, and other tools to enhance the customer's buying experience. This technique is often referred to as **visual merchandising.** The objective is to inspire the customer to purchase through the use

Bergdorf Goodman, located on Fifth Avenue in New York City, is a high-end retailer that is well known for its window displays.

of design techniques that enhance the overall buying experience. The store's windows are also important communications vehicles that add to the store's ambiance. The image can convey or reinforce the retailer's product mix.

Some elements used to create an overall store atmosphere involve the use of the store's exterior. The storefront must make the store look like an attractive place to shop. A marquee can also help the retailer create an overall store atmosphere. **Marquees** are generally large signs that include the retailer's name. They can be manufactured or purchased as stock pieces. Marquees come in many different styles and can be flashy (especially when used in conjunction with neon lights or other decorative lighting) or subdued.

marquee A large exterior sign that includes the retailer's name.

The key to an effective marquee is that it generate interest and traffic. The use of the AIDA model (*a*ttention, *i*nterest, *d*esire, and *a*ction) fits in well with the selection of a marquee. A sign that attracts attention and creates interest in the retail store should be selected. Once the store has captured potential customers' attention and instilled interest in the store, the marquee can help develop customers' desire to visit the store. Finally, the marquee causes action when customers enter the store.

EASE OF SHOPPING. A store's interior should allow customers to shop with ease. It is important to understand how the customer shops and then to plan a store design that facilitates the shopping process. Many supermarkets and smaller grocery stores use a "ring-of-perishables" design, in which perishables are placed in a semi-ring around the back part of the store's interior. When customers enter the store, they turn to the right and find themselves in the bakery. After the bakery, they may find themselves in produce. As they proceed around the far walls of the store, they may find dairy, deli, flowers, fresh meats, poultry, and other product types that are perishable. Customers have been "trained" to shop this way at a grocery store; thus, they feel comfortable knowing where various products are located.

PRODUCTIVITY. In terms of the third objective, the retailer needs to assess which of the many design options to choose for displaying merchandise. The productivity of the store's selling space is called **efficiency.** The retailer should select displays that create the most efficiencies. For example, clothing retailers may want to display clothes on waterfall fixtures. A *waterfall fixture* is usually a standalone fixture (although many can be attached to walls) that holds the same product at different eye levels. Thus, the customer can see each item easily, from first to last.

efficiency The productivity of a store's selling space.

The question, then, is: Does this display generate enough sales to be placed at this particular location? Compare the standalone waterfall display to one that connects to the wall. Which one provides more efficiencies? A retailer may find that the wall display uses less selling space, yet is equally appealing to customers.

The earlier ring-of-perishables example shows how the design and layout objectives can be integrated with each other. Although the ring of perishables can be used to influence the customer to shop and buy, it has a secondary function in terms of efficiency. Because most perishables require refrigeration, special fixtures are needed that not only refrigerate the products but also display them. With this display comes an added cost for electricity. Because of the internal refrigeration, the displays emit a great deal of heat. Thus, if displays are kept in the middle of the store, the retailer has to utilize additional air conditioning to offset the heat. With a ring-of-perishables technique, however, the additional energy costs can be reduced. In fact, the displays may actually help heat the areas to the back of them (including stockrooms), resulting in additional efficiency for the retailer.

In designing store layout, retailers must consider their target market. Shown here is the store layout for Costco Wholesale Corporation, which operates an international chain of membership warehouses.

When designing its store layout, the retailer needs to assess the outlet's floor space and plan for space allocation for merchandise storage, merchandise selling, store employees, and customers. It is also important to assess customer traffic patterns within the store. In creating traffic space, the retailer can have customers flowing in a straight line, a curved line, or a combination of the two.

Home Depot stores favor straight lines, as do most food retailers. This format allows customers to locate products easily and makes it easy for the retailer to stock. Department stores and boutiques prefer a curved format, because it encourages customers to browse and spend more time in the store. A downside to a curved pattern is that customers can get confused or be unable to find a product. When developing the store design, the retailer should begin with the traffic flow. Within the store, unique areas dedicated to certain types of product lines should be created. This approach enables a store manager or owner to create smaller store patterns within the overall design. This is effective if the retailer decides to create product groupings for its merchandise.

As an example, consider a situation in which a new Disney movie is playing at a local theater. A clothing retailer or a department store may want to "bundle" all the Disney merchandise into a single location, thereby giving customers a choice among the various licensed products.

Another possible store layout is to group products together based on their function. This can be accomplished using a functional grouping display (as an example, all over-the-counter drugs may be placed together within the store).

DESIGN WITH THE CUSTOMER IN MIND

Effective designs allow customers to make purchases easily. Store design must be set up based on what the customer expects. To facilitate sales, many IMC tactics, such as POP displays and store signage, can be utilized. In addition, the interior of the store can be changed through the use of freestanding fixtures. Finally, efficiencies can be created by using the walls of the store, end caps (displays at the end of an aisle), and exterior areas (such as sidewalk sales).

Nonstore retailers must also create a layout and design for their venues. Like brick-and-mortar retailers, nonstore retailers must also give attention to their storefronts (*i.e.*, webpages), their stores' exteriors and interiors (including displays), and their checkout areas. An advantage for nonstore retailers, especially e-tailers, is that they can change their displays much more quickly and inexpensively than can their brick-and-mortar counterparts.

Customers' judgments about a store can have a powerful effect on the store's image. Thus, the retailer must ensure that the layout and design of all the store's spaces are effective and regularly maintained. (This includes the design and cleaning of customer restrooms.) In addition, customers may begin to get bored with the store layout; thus, interior and exterior changes should be scheduled on a periodic basis. Signage and display fixtures should be updated. The retailer must strive to keep customers excited about their shopping experiences.

An important tool for the retailer is an evaluation program to assess the effectiveness of the overall store design and layout. Any time customer communications occur, both the IMC and the store layout and design must be integrated to send consistent messages and, in the long run, increase store sales and profitability.

SUMMARY

This chapter covered the overall communications process and its vital role in the integrated retail management plan. It discussed the different methods of communicating with customers and examined IMC objectives, budget creation, and strategy.

Next, the chapter looked at each element of IMC tactics, including advertising, sales promotions, direct marketing, cybermarketing, personal selling, public relations, and publicity. Each of these areas is extremely important to communications, and the messages conveyed by all areas must be consistent.

Finally, the chapter focused on some issues involved in store layout and design. The objectives of layout and design were discussed, along with the need to keep these important functions integrated with the IMC variables.

KEY TERMS

integrated marketing communications (IMC) (354)
IMC mix (355)
percentage-of-sales method (358)
percentage-of-profit method (359)
objective-and-task method (359)
follow-the-leader budgeting (359)
all-you-can-afford method (360)
best-guess method (360)
creative platform (361)
advertising (362)
reach (364)
frequency (364)
continuity (364)
gross rating points (GRPs) (364)
sales promotion (365)
point-of-purchase (POP) communications (365)
direct marketing (366)
personal selling (369)
public relations (PR) (370)
publicity (370)
atmospherics (373)
visual merchandising (373)
marquee (374)
efficiency (375)

QUESTIONS FOR DISCUSSION

1. Why is it necessary to create integration and synergy in communicating with current and potential customers? with internal employees?
2. What types of budgets do you think are used by market leaders such as Sears and Wal-Mart? Why?
3. Why is it important to develop an overall mission and vision for the IMC functional area?
4. Do you feel that there is some overlap in each of the tactical IMC variables? Explain and cite examples.
5. What type of store layout do you feel would be best for clothing boutiques such as Old Navy, Abercrombie and Fitch, and Delia's? Why do you feel this layout would be effective?
6. Develop a store layout and design for a new retailer of phones and related products. Provide the rationale for your layout.

E-TAILING EXERCISE

Visit the following websites (alternatively, choose three retailing sites that interest you), and answer the questions below.

- ***www.Kohls.com***
- ***www.Gateway.com***
- ***www.Pier1.com***

1. How is the website used to promote the retailer? How effective is the site in promoting the retailer?
2. Is the IMC message clear?
3. What changes, if any, would you recommend to enhance communications?

Continuing Case 12.1

Sherwin-Williams Company: Integrating IMC into Operations

To continue communicating with its changing customer base, Sherwin-Williams has introduced different colors and textures for its paint products. "The human eye can discern about 10 million colors in 'color space,' the three-dimensional color spectrum model," according to Lane Blackburn, vice president of quality and color at Sherwin-Williams. The three-dimensional color spectrum model allows the eye to view more colors than it would otherwise. Based on this technology, Sherwin-Williams is adding colors and offering customers thousands of choices in paint. One way Sherwin-Williams is communicating to its customers is through a two-part kit called American Accents. This kit stimulates people's creativity in an inexpensive and easy manner. This "one-package" solution to decorating is easy and has a unique look.

Sherwin-Williams is also adding more textures to its paint products. Texture in paint has become a hot trend in the industry, especially the marbleized, speckled, and crackled looks. Sherwin-Williams's American Accents kit enables customers to texture in a short time through the use of spray paints. The kit challenges the painter to come up with creative paint projects, promoted as fun, easy to complete, and less time consuming than other methods. It allows the do-it-yourselfer to save money by offering a cheaper and more hassle-free alternative to wallpapering.

Questions

1. Why did Sherwin-Williams introduce the American Accents kit?
2. Do you think this product is in line with Sherwin-Williams's mission and vision? Why or why not?
3. How does this new innovation fit into an IMC strategy?
4. Using the information in the case, create an IMC outline for promoting Sherwin-Williams's new product at the retail level.
5. Do you believe the American Accents product ties into the overall IMC direction in which Sherwin-Williams has been moving? Explain your answer.

Sources: www.sherwinwilliams.com, accessed July 2002; Annie Bowman, "Choose Cheery Colors for the Home," *San Francisco Chronicle,* November 15, 2000, p. WB6; Richard Halverson, "Paint Kits Brighten Accessory Sales," *Discount Store News,* January 4, 1999, p. 63; Debbie Howell, "Sherwin-Williams Premieres 1,000 New Colors," *Painting & Wallcovering Contractor,* March–April 2002, p. 16.

Case 12.2

Auntie Anne's Pretzels: From Small-Town Girl to Global Entrepreneur

Anne Beiler, CEO of Auntie Anne's, Inc., was raised in an Amish-Mennonite family in Lancaster, Pennsylvania. She married at age nineteen and in 1988, to raise money for a free family counseling store, she opened a pretzel stand at a farmer's market. In the beginning, Beiler bagged the pretzel mix in her garage. Since then her company has grown to a corporate staff of more than 100 employees and a franchise system that employs over 8,000 store owners, managers, and crew members. Auntie Anne's has franchises in Canada, Hong Kong, Indonesia, Japan, Malaysia, the Philippines, Singapore, Thailand, the United Kingdom, and Venezuela.

Integrated marketing communications (IMC) has several components, including sales promotions, direct marketing, advertising, cybermarketing, personal selling, and public relations. Auntie Anne's is an example of a company that relies heavily on public relations in its IMC planning. The cornerstone of Auntie Anne's business is active involvement in the community. Beiler believes Auntie Anne's success comes from three *P*s: purpose + product + people. With these three *P*s working together, everyone profits. Beiler believes companies have a duty to give back to their communities, and as such, Auntie Anne's donates 25 percent of the company's net profits to charitable organizations. The company has established a charitable foundation, called the Angela Foundation, which provides financial support to organizations that care for children of families in need. In addition, the owners of the company established the Family Resource & Counseling Center, Inc., and are a sponsor of the Children's Miracle Network, an international nonprofit organization.

One outcome of IMC is strong brand recognition. Auntie Anne's reputation for high-quality products, coupled with the company's community involvement, has made Auntie Anne's a strong global brand. The company did not intentionally focus on brand management in the early years. According to Sam Beiler, president, the company owners, without realizing it, protected the brand through communications with customers and potential business partners. This helped establish its global presence, even after imitators came on the scene. Auntie Anne's illustrates how using public relations as the focal point of an IMC program can often lead to success. The company's efforts helped build a brand that is recognized and accepted around the world.

Questions

1. How can community involvement enhance a retailer's image?
2. What must companies consider when marketing in different countries?
3. How can Auntie Anne's respond to competitive threats?
4. What is the value of a brand to a retailer?
5. Why doesn't Auntie Anne's advertise?
6. Why is consistent communication among the various franchises in the United States and other countries important?

Sources: "Auntie Anne's, Inc." (company capsule), Hoover's Online, retrieved December 2002 from www.hoovers.com; Auntie Anne's corporate website at www.auntieannes.com, accessed December 2002; Lee Kessler, "Malls' Favorite Aunt Hooks Shopper with Pretzels," *Shopping Centers Today*, September 2002, pp. 76–77.

Customer Service in Retailing

Chapter

13

Being on par in terms of price and quality only gets you into the game. Service wins the game.

Tony Alessandra, professional speaker on customer service

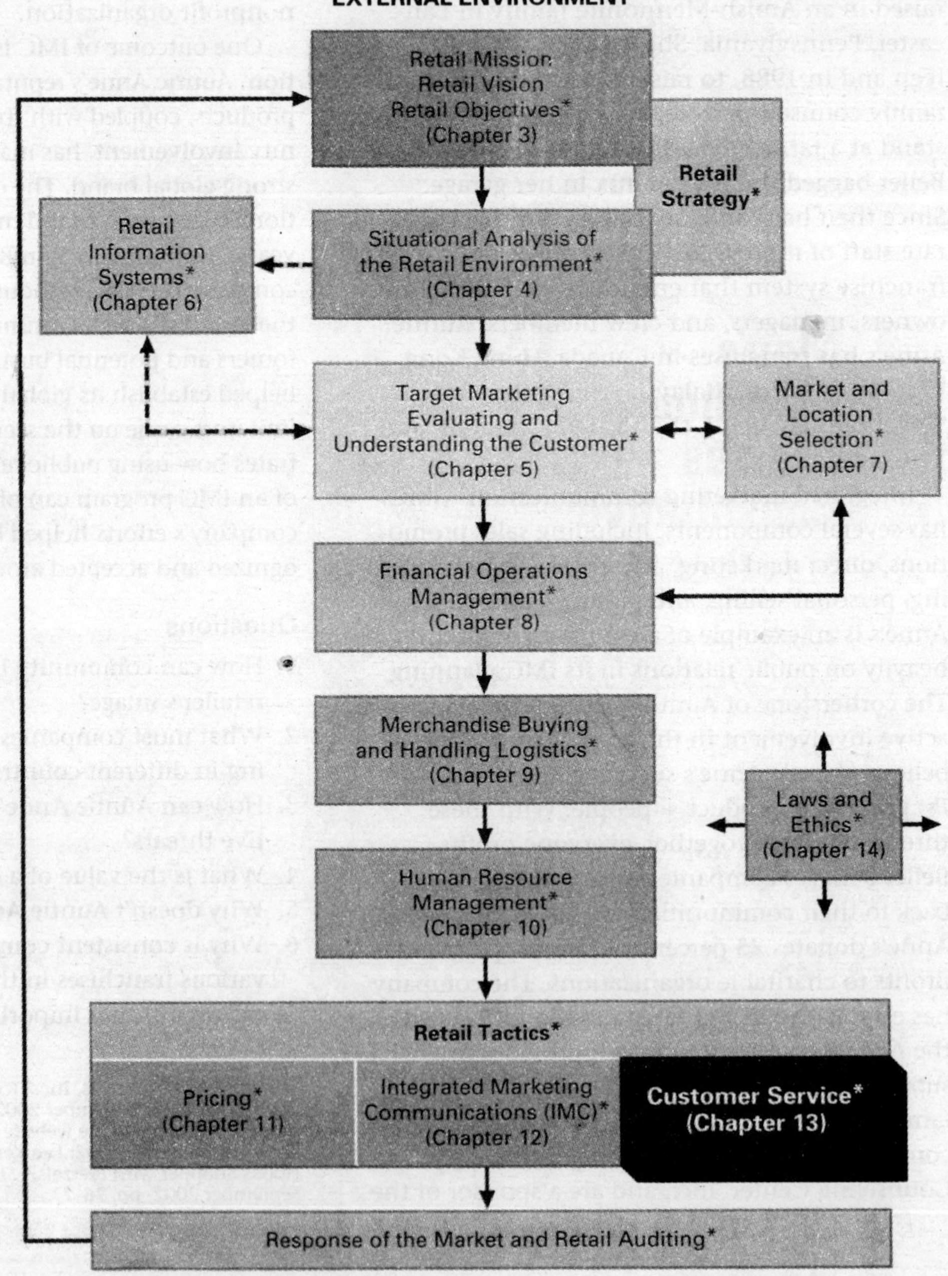

CHAPTER OBJECTIVES

After completing this chapter, you will be able to:

1. Explain why the targeted customer is always right.
2. Define *customer service* and explain the rater system.
3. List and explain the key customer service activities for retailers and e-tailers.
4. Explain customer response marketing and why it is important in retailing.
5. Identify and describe various customer service levels.

Men's Wearhouse Utilizes Consultative Approach

In past years, the men's clothing industry has experienced several changes. Many retailers specializing in men's clothing went out of business. One company that survived is Men's Wearhouse, Inc. The first sentence of Men's Wearhouse mission statement is "to maximize sales, provide value to our customers, and deliver top-quality customer service while still having fun and maintaining our values."[1] Men's Wearhouse has lived up to its mission and has become one of the largest discount retailers of men's business attire in the United States.[2] The company operates approximately 690 stores in 43 states and Canada. The chain sells suits, formal wear, casual clothes, and shoes priced at 20 to 30 percent less than competitors' products.[3]

The key to the company's outstanding customer service is the way it treats its own employees. "When you treat people as they should be treated, oddly enough, they're more productive," says Charles Bresler, executive vice president. Bresler believes happy employees translate into better customer service: "[Our employees] treat customers better partly because they're trained in customer service, but partly because they're just feeling better themselves and don't feel put down by the corporation. That energy translated to customer services sells more products and [results in] more repeat business. That's how you build a retail business, from our point of view."[4] Employees take the consultative approach, which focuses on building long-term relationships with customers, rather than the salesperson approach.

INTRODUCTION

customer services The additional practices, both tangible and intangible, that an organization provides in addition to its core product or service.

At this point in the IRM flowchart, we find ourselves at the third important tactical area: customer service. **Customer services** are the additional benefits, both tangible and intangible, that an organization provides in addition to its core product or service. Many retail firms live or die by their customer service. Everyone wants to be treated fairly and with respect. On the whole, customers are willing to pay a bit more for excellent customer service and will return to the retailer's venue if they receive it. It is also true that customers tell horror stories about bad customer service. These anecdotes are passed from person to person and can threaten the retailer's business.

Retailers need to be aware of the equity they have in their image and name. Most of this equity results from the way the retailer handles customers. In this chapter, we focus on the applications of customer service to both store-based and non-store-based retailing.

THE TARGETED CUSTOMER IS ALWAYS RIGHT

By definition, a customer is an individual who buys goods or services from a retailer. This definition can be expanded to say that there are two types of customers: good and bad. For our discussion, we will differentiate between good and bad customers, and conclude that the only "true" retail customers are the "good" customers. The astute retailer is able to generate classifications for its customers. Of course, not all people who visit a retail store are customers. In fact, the retailer has the opportunity to select customers; in other words, whom, specifically, does the retailer prefer as its customers? Will this group generate enough revenue to sustain the retail business? These are the questions this chapter addresses.

CUSTOMER PROFILES

Although it is a common belief among retailers that they have to satisfy the wants and needs of everyone who walks into their store, the retailer actually is in the position to choose the customers who appear to be a good fit for the store. This is done through the process of target marketing. Retailers look for those groups of people toward whom they wish to aim their marketing efforts. Unfortunately, not all people can be satisfied. A good method of identifying and understanding customers is to develop *customer profiles*. This approach is similar to that used in market segmentation, where a company chooses a target market and divides that market into segments that respond differently to the product, store, or brand.

In segmenting the market, the retailer creates some basis for dividing the various customer groups (psychographics, geographics, geodemographics, demographics, and/or behavioristics).[5] From each segmented group, the retailer then develops a "typical" customer profile.

Customers enter a store with different needs and wants as well as varying levels of needs or wants. The retailer's job is to identify those needs and wants and to develop different types and levels of customer service that will make these groups of customers happy. This approach may cost a little more up front, but it pays off in the long run.

Providing excellent customer service has become increasingly difficult. American shoppers have become more vocal and insistent on having their way. As one author puts it, America has turned into a "nation of whiners."[6] In the words of famous jazz musician Fats Waller, the retailer's job is to "find out what they [customers] like, and how they like it, and let 'em have it, just that way."[7] Once a retailer chooses a target market, "the customer is king" (or queen), and the old adage "the customer is always right" should become a top retail policy. As Jack Smith, former CEO of General Motors, once said, "Focus everything—all assets, all decisions—on your customers. They are the ultimate arbiters of success or failure." Smith was a successful CEO because he recognized the importance of the "customer is always right" credo.

UNDESIRABLE CUSTOMERS

Equally important to determining the target market is defining those customers that are not in the target market. Some people are simply undesirable customers. Many retailers tell stories of individuals who come into a store and make a purchase, only to return the goods to the store after using them. Consider a shoe retailer. Each year, just before the local high school proms, a number of teens flock to the store looking for shoes to complement their dresses or tuxedos. Although the vast majority of these customers are honest, some are not; they wear the shoes for just the one night and then return them with some complaint so they can receive a refund. Often the same people are actually good customers during the rest of the year. In this case, the retailer may want to keep them as customers. How does the retailer know which of these customers to retain? The retailer can use a database that includes the top customers in terms of their returns and purchases (by number of units and by dollar expenditures).

An example of a retailer that banned customers from its store comes from Filene's Basement. In May 2003, the retailer's parent company, Value City, sent a letter to two sisters from Newton, Massachusetts, banning them from all twenty-one Filene's Basement stores. The letter stated, "Given your history of excessive returns and chronic unhappiness with our services, we have decided that this is the best way to avoid any future problems with you and your sister."[8] According to James McGrady, chief financial officer at Value City, customer bans are "extremely rare." In this case, the company decided it didn't want customers who commanded a disproportionate amount of their employees' time and labor in handling the complaints. Because stores are considered private property, retailers can evict customers.[9]

Another type of bad customer behavior is entering a store with the intent to shoplift. Although shoplifters may purchase some products, they actually steal more than they purchase (if they buy at all). An estimated 23 million people shoplift on a yearly basis, costing retailers $25 million a day.[10]

Many service retailers choose to ban unruly customers. Such was the case when Dorney Park in Allentown, Pennsylvania, banned a person for physically assaulting a guard. (www.dorneypark.com)

In some instances, retailers refuse customers based on state or federal laws, such as laws prohibiting the sales of liquor and cigarettes to people under twenty-one years of age. Lowes, the home improvement retailer, had good intentions when it banned minors from buying products that might be abused as chemical inhalants. The stringent policy blocked minors from buying 2,000 products. Although other home improvement retailers, such as Home Depot, had similar policies, the other retailers applied them only in the seventeen states that regulate the sale of potential inhalants to minors. As a result of customer complaints, Lowe's was forced to cut back the list of banned products from 2,000 to 1,200 items.[11]

Finally, some individuals become verbally or physically abusive to a retailer's employees. Recently, at Dorney Park in Allentown, Pennsylvania, a "guest" was physically abusive toward one of the ride operators.[12] The abusive guest was waiting in line to get on a popular rollercoaster when the ride attendant noticed that the guest allowed some individuals to "line jump," or cut into the line, in front of some other guests who had been waiting for more than twenty minutes. The attendant explained that the park did not allow line jumping and that the guests would not be permitted to enter the ride unless they went to the back of the line. The party ignored the attendant and held their place in the line. When it was their turn to get on the ride, the attendant did not let them enter and reminded them of his warning. Then the original guest physically assaulted the ride operator. Dorney Park, to its credit, prosecuted the guest and barred him and his party from ever entering the park again. The guest was also barred from all parks owned by the parent company, Cedar Fair. The former guest was placed on an "unwanted" list, which was circulated to all the other properties. With the advances in technology, this tactic was not difficult to execute. The amusement retailer had decided that these individuals were not worth having as customers.

IDENTIFYING AND SEGMENTING CUSTOMERS

When developing strategies to provide excellent customer service, the place to start is with the customers themselves. Creating and accessing information about the customer base is greatly facilitated using the retail information system (RIS). The retailer first attempts to pull a "typical" customer profile from the RIS, which contains important data such as customers' purchases and product usage. If no profiles of customers are available, the retailer should build an information collection system to house these data. As stated earlier, a customer profile consists of data about various "groups" of consumers. From those data, the retailer creates an overall "average" customer profile.

Customer profiles can be created by segmenting. In terms of segmenting for customer service, customer usage rates are among the most useful data. The segmentation process can be simple (for example, categorizing customers as heavy versus medium versus light users of the store or its products or brands), or it can be far more complex. The reason a retailer would want to segment by usage is that heavy users generally supply the highest percentage of sales.

Pareto principle (80/20 rule) A guideline stating that 20 percent of a business's customers account for about 80 percent of its sales.

In marketing, there is a rule of thumb stating that 20 percent of a retailer's customers make up about 80 percent of its sales. This is called the **Pareto principle,** or **80/20 rule.**[13] Developed by Joseph Juran, the Pareto principle is based on the work of Vilfredo Pareto. Pareto's research uncovered an interesting pattern in the dispersion of wealth: 85 percent of the wealth in Milan, Italy, was owned by 15 percent of the citizens.[14] Although a general rule of thumb, the 80/20 mix is approximately accurate for many industries as well as individual companies within the industry. The Pareto principle mix varies among retailers depending on the type of retailer, the levels of customer services provided, and the customer mix.

In the airline industry, for example, 65 percent of all airline revenues are generated by 15 percent of the passengers. In the U.S. brewing industry, 20 percent of all beer drinkers consume approximately 70 percent of all beer. One can see the importance of segmenting customer groups to create outstanding customer service. By knowing their customer base, retailers can customize additional retail tactics to reach their most important customers. Likewise, they can greatly enhance customer service based on these customer groups and the typical customer profiles within each group.

Although many retailers believe all customers should be treated alike, it makes good business sense to treat the most important customers royally. This is not to say that the smaller customer segments should be ignored; rather, it means the retailer should invest more heavily in the loyal user groups. It is important to manage customer expectations so that customers understand why certain customers are receiving value-added services. Retailers can do this by communicating policies to current and potential customers and by applying services consistently based on the customer group. Loyalty programs, such as frequent flyer programs, can help solidify customer relationships.

CUSTOMER PERCEPTIONS

Customers have different opinions and perceptions about what good service is. Much has been written about the various types of services and levels of service that customers want. Retail customers are becoming more and more demanding in terms of the levels of service they expect from retailers. Research has found that these services can be classified into a finite number of categories of customer service wants and needs.

Keep in mind that there is a difference between offering *services* to customers and offering *service* to customers. Services deal with additions to the total product, whereas service is integrated into every aspect of the retailer's

TABLE 13.1

SERVICE QUALITY GAPS

1. Not knowing what customers expect
2. The wrong service-quality standards
3. The service performance gap
4. Promises do not match delivery

Source: Valerie Zeithaml, A. Parasuraman, and Leonard L. Berry, *Delivering Quality Service: Balancing Customer Perceptions and Expectations* (New York: The Free Press, 1990), pp. 15–33.

operations. Consider a services retailer that sells hairstyling services. Whereas cutting and styling hair is a service, the provision of a "no wait" policy for customers with reservations is a form of customer service. It adds value to the core product or service offered to the consumer.

Researchers think that consumers' perceptions of quality service are influenced by a number of "gaps."[15] The gaps are important because they give retailers a hint as to tactics and strategies that can help ensure a good service relationship (see Table 13.1).[16]

GAP 1: NOT KNOWING CUSTOMERS' EXPECTATIONS. To address this gap, the retailer needs to learn what customers value most in terms of service offerings. Once the retailer has segmented its market, it should develop a profile that shows the customers' value for each segment. It has been suggested that benchmarking and best practices are good tools for this research process. In addition, a competitive analysis such as a SWOT (strengths, weaknesses, opportunities, and threats) analysis helps identify the retailer's strengths and weaknesses, as well as those of its competitors.

GAP 2: PROVIDING THE WRONG SERVICE-QUALITY STANDARDS. To address this gap, the retailer should create a system for the planning and design functions. To ensure that the "correct" standards are set for service quality, it is important to capture standards in an easily accessible format. The information should be incorporated into the existing RIS, but in many instances it exists as a standalone document or computer file.

GAP 3: EXPECTED VERSUS ACTUAL SERVICE. The third gap deals with the difference between the quality standards promised to customers and the actual quality of service delivery and performance. The retailer must take care to avoid discrepancies between the service specifications and the performance of the service. This is a communications gap that centers on the retailer's standards for its product offerings.

GAP 4: ENSURING THAT DELIVERY OF SERVICE MATCHES PROMISES MADE BY THE RETAILER. The basic principle here is that retailers must be honest with their customers in regard to service guarantees. Thus, information should be provided to customers about the actual level and type of service a retailer provides. The retailer must then ensure that all promises are fulfilled.[17]

In 1998, in response to these gaps, three researchers developed a technique, called *SERVQUAL,* to measure service quality.[18] Although the initial research was developed for the service industry (*e.g.,* banking, long-distance telephone services, securities, credit cards, and product repair and maintenance), it has been generalized to include service-quality assessment for other industries. The researchers found that the majority of consumers' perceptions of quality fall into five main areas: reliability, assurance, tangibility, empathy, and responsiveness (RATER).[19]

reliability A component of quality that addresses the dependability of the retailer or its products and services.

RELIABILITY. From the customer's point of view, **reliability** means dependability: Does the retailer perform the promised service dependably and accurately? Because of the importance of reliability, retailers must take care not to promise anything they cannot deliver. This caveat applies not only to management but to the entire retail staff. Have you ever been promised something by a businessperson only to find out that he or she could not deliver on the promise? This incident probably made you angry with the service provider and perhaps led you to shop at a competitor.

assurance A component of quality that addresses a customer's satisfaction with the retailer or its products and services.

ASSURANCE. Assurance means customers must be confident that they made the right choice in buying the retailer's products and services. The entire retail staff needs to be courteous and have a thorough knowledge of the products and services available.

tangibility A component of quality that involves the physical characteristics of the retail store.

TANGIBILITY. Tangibility refers to the physical characteristics of the retail outlet. What will the customer's first impression of the store be? Are the physical facilities and equipment up to date, clean, and well maintained? How is the space utilized? Are restrooms clean and attractive? (Cleanliness of restrooms is a major issue in the tourism industry.) Are employees well groomed? If they wear uniforms, are the uniforms clean? Are backroom areas that are visible to customers also clean and organized?

empathy A component of quality that promotes understanding of the customer's needs.

EMPATHY. To convey **empathy,** the retailer needs to provide caring and individual attention for customers. Customers want to know that the retailer understands them and has had the same type of experiences they have. One good way for a retailer to express empathy is to use a customer's name. This makes the customer feel welcome and "closer" to the retailer.

Because of the vast numbers of customers who enter the stores, this tactic may be difficult to execute. However, if a retailer has done a thorough job of developing customer segments, a database of top customers (heavy users) will be available so that the retailer can concentrate on those individuals. If there is not a database, a simple way to create this relationship relates to customers who make purchases with a credit card. When a salesperson rings up an order for someone charging a purchase, the salesperson should look at the name on the credit card and simply call the customer by that name. Some airlines do this with their first-class travelers. To execute this superior customer service,

Customers want to know that the retailer understands them. One good way for a retail professional to express empathy is to smile and use a customer's name.

they provide a list of the first-class passengers to their flight attendants, who call each first-class traveler by his or her title (Dr., Mrs., Mr., Rev., Ms., etc.) and name.

responsiveness A component of quality that tells the customer the retailer is willing to provide high levels of prompt customer service.

RESPONSIVENESS. The retail staff must be **responsive** to customer needs. They must be willing to provide a high level of prompt customer service and assistance. For example, a salesperson at Meijer Thrifty Acres is trained not only to tell a customer where a product is but also to walk the customer to the area where the product is located and make sure the product is indeed the correct one.

To facilitate the above tactics, a programmed approach to meeting and helping customers should be developed. The first step in successful response is to greet the customer and make him or her feel welcome. Wal-Mart uses "greeters" to accomplish this task. The next step is to develop an understanding of the customer by asking questions. The retailer needs to help the customer find the desired product and ensure that she or he is satisfied with the "find." Finally, the retailer should confirm the customer's satisfaction in an effort to ensure a return visit. To make customers feel valued and appreciated, retailers should develop a philosophy of truly wanting to help customers.

RETAIL AND E-TAIL CUSTOMER SERVICES

Although there may be some differences in the delivery of e-tail customer service versus bricks-only service, the goal is the same: to make the customer happy. The key to offering customers high levels of service is a total organiza-

INTERNET IN ACTION

The Golden Rules of Online Customer Service

The number of Americans shopping online is growing every year. To lure more shoppers to this medium, online merchants must focus on providing stellar customer service. Based on several comprehensive studies, The E-tailing Group, an e-commerce research and consulting firm in Chicago, developed the "Golden Rules of Online Customer Service." The rules are as follows:

Rule 1: The role of customer service is to deliver a complete customer experience. The shopper experience includes all aspects of the site, including search functionality, completing the order, post-order communication, receipt of the goods, return, and post-order inquiries. All of these areas must be considered in developing customer service policies.

Rule 2: The goal of e-commerce is to motivate shoppers to buy. It's great to have visitors to a site, but unless the visitors are converted to buyers, the company will not be around for long. Ways to motivate customers to buy are free or reduced shipping charges and gift services.

Rule 3: Establish shoppers' expectations, from product availability to delivery costs—and then meet them. A great way to determine customers' expectations is to respond to customer queries within a twenty-four-hour time frame. A personalized response is the best method.

Rule 4: Respect shoppers and their privacy. A privacy policy should be developed and posted. In addition, accessible information about how to contact various departments should be posted.

Rule 5: Communicate with customers carefully and consistently. A best practice is to offer immediate order confirmation, post-order e-mail confirmations, and confirmations on the day the order is shipped.

Rule 6: Make shopping fast, easy, smart, and fun. Online customers are convenience oriented, so sites must be very user friendly. The experience must be fun for the shopper to ensure continued future purchases.

Source: Adapted from "Six Golden Rules of Online Customer Service" by Lauren Freedman from *Catalog Age* ®, April 2002. Copyright 2002, Primedia Business Magazines & Media, Inc. All rights reserved.

tional commitment. Lillian Vernon, founder and CEO of Lillian Vernon Corp., a specialty and online retailer, believes that the building blocks of happiness center around three things: selecting the right products, being honest with customers, and welcoming communications between the company and its customers.[20]

Retailers that provide superior service can use the service as a differentiation tool. High-quality service translates into repeat buyers. As stated earlier, services must be tailored to the identified customer profiles, and the levels of service must be applied by all employees. The level of customer service the retailer will provide should be included in the mission and vision statements. This section provides an overview of the many services a retailer can offer.

For e-tailers, some of the key customer service activities are (1) effective handling of complaints, (2) electronic confirmations of orders, and (3) developing cyber-relationships with customers. Because of the nature of e-tailing, customers and salespeople do not participate in face-to-face communications;

Customer service personnel should be enthusiastic about helping customers. Shown here is a telephone service representative ready to address a customer's concerns.

therefore, the task of providing customer service is somewhat more difficult. Service levels at brick-and-mortar retailers have declined significantly since the early 1990s, however; this decline has allowed e-tailers the opportunity to entice shoppers to try the Internet. One observer states, "Service in real-world stores leaves most shoppers cold . . . customer service is at its worst since . . . 1994."[21] What can retailers do to create higher service levels for customers?

CUSTOMER SERVICE ACTIVITIES

Numerous types of services can be offered to retail customers. Some work well for e-tailers; others work better for brick-and-mortar and brick-and-click retailers. Service offerings can range from basic to quite complex and luxurious.

BASIC SERVICE OFFERINGS. Although this can vary on an individual basis and by the type of retailer, basic services expected from any retailer include a convenient retail location, convenient hours of operation, clean facilities, and product availability. Security is also a consideration, especially for online retailing.

Customers must be able to easily access a physical or cyber retail location. The customer's time is a vital consideration. It is also good business practice to be open when the customer wants to shop. Many retailers understand this concept and have expanded the basic premise by keeping many of their stores open twenty-four hours a day. This practice not only provides shoppers with a service but also positions these retailers in consumers' minds as "a store that never closes." Thus, a customer who needs to go to a store at an odd hour knows that Wal-Mart or 7-Eleven will be open. In these cases, the benefits associated with continuous operation must be greater than costs.

Have you ever been to a bank on a weekend? Were you able to interact with the tellers? The answer is probably no, since banks generally are open only until 5 P.M. on weekdays and for limited hours on Saturdays. This can be quite frustrating for a bank's customers. Not surprisingly, when a large retailer that stays open twenty-four hours a day was asked about business traffic during that period, the busiest time reported was between 10:00 A.M. and 7:00 P.M. So why does this retailer operate twenty-four hours a day? Why not open from, say, 9:00 A.M. to 8:00 P.M.? The retailer's response would make any customer grin: the store is open to let the customer know that it is always open and available. This service actually increases business throughout the day. Although keeping the operation open at night may not be very cost effective, the increase in the customer base during other hours makes up for the costs.

In the 1990s, a small university in the Midwest was trying to attract nontraditional students. The school developed an IMC campaign that became very effective. During the implementation of the campaign, however, a problem became evident: although the number of nontraditional students (mostly working adults) who applied for admission to the night program increased nearly 30 percent, the retention rate for those students was much lower than that for traditional students.

When the school's marketing managers evaluated the problem, they found that it was based on the university's lack of student services. Because the university had previously serviced only traditional students, the bursar's and registrar's offices were open only until 5:00 P.M. In addition, the bookstore closed at 6:00 P.M. Therefore, a student who wanted to pay a bill in person or buy a book had to take time off from work to accomplish these tasks. The answer was obvious: keep the student services offices open when the students could access them.

Facility cleanliness is another basic service offering. Nothing turns off customers more than a dirty store. Researchers have found that cleanliness is one of the most important factors in choosing a restaurant.[22]

In addition, customers expect product availability. Outstanding retailers try to keep at least a 95 percent stock level. When customers come into the store, they know there is a high chance the product will be in stock. Have you ever gone into a store looking for a particular item only to find it was out of stock? Did you leave the store to shop at a competitor that was more likely to have the product in stock? This situation translates into lost sales for the first retailer and in fact may result in lost future customers and revenues. For very popular items, the retailer should have a stock level of higher than 95 percent.

Finally, security is another important basic customer service. Security for the store retailer could mean providing security guards, cameras, and computer systems to protect safety and privacy. For the online retailer, privacy and security are major concerns. In a study on customer satisfaction, online shoppers gave the lowest scores to online privacy.[23]

ADDITIONAL/LUXURY SERVICES. What about additional and luxury-type services? For any retailer, the most important service provider is the sales team. To the customer, the salesperson *is* the retail store. Poor service from a salesperson translates into unfavorable customer perceptions of the store. An adequately staffed service desk or toll-free service number should be available whenever the retail operation is open. There is nothing more frustrating than buying a defective product or service and having to wait in a long line to replace it or, worse yet, being unable to find someone who can help resolve the problem. All types of retailers need to decide which types of services to offer. Many retailers offer special services such as gift wrapping, product packaging and shipping, personalized orders, special orders, or personal shoppers.

Victoria's Secret offers two types of gift wrapping from its direct operations, even though the product is offered through a catalog or online. The costs associated with this service are self-liquidating; that is, the service costs pay for themselves through a charge to the customer for each gift box or wrapping order. The company takes care of its best customers by offering free gift wrapping during the holidays for large-dollar orders.

Buckle, the Kearney, Nebraska–based chain store, has a philosophy of providing the best selection and best service to their young, fashion-conscious customers. Some of the services they offer include free jean and T-shirt alterations, year-round free gift wrapping, layaways, and a frequent shopper reward program.[24] These services differentiate the retailer and keep customers coming back for more.

Most retailers offer delivery services as well as credit services. In addition, many retailers offer their customers product information. The key is for the retailer to consider its vision and mission, as well as its target market and market segments, to develop the desired level of customer service.

Different types of retailers need different types of services and service levels. For example, in 1998, the Ritz-Carlton, an upscale hotel, discovered that 35 to 40 percent of its business travelers were female. As a result of customer feedback, the chain started to include gender-specific amenities in the guestrooms. Women guests find items such as makeup-remover pads, Woolite for washing delicate clothing, skirt hangers, scented sachets, pantyhose, and nail polish remover in their rooms.[25] These additions exceed guest's expectations and add to the high levels of customer satisfaction.

Figure 13.1 illustrates the development of policies for a retail outlet while taking into account the types of products and their prices.

Thus, the choice of what types of services to offer depends on the type of retailer, the complexity of the product, and the product's price. In addition to the aforementioned services, many retailers offer the following: layaways, Christmas or holiday clubs, kiosks or touch-screens for bridal registry, a baby registry or other gift suggestions, automated teller machines (ATMs), shoppers' service (such as a concierge), coat and hat checking, package checking, valet parking, children's carts, multilingual salespeople and/or customer service personnel, complimentary beverages (sometimes including wine, champagne, and other hard and soft drinks), tourist maps, brochures or coupons, furniture for resting, guarantees, support salespeople (especially for do-it-yourself retailers such as Home Depot), parking shuttles, music, drinking fountains, classes, and workshops for customers (especially for technological products such as computer software and hardware), a store directory (both manual and computerized), a post office, bill-paying services, customer service reps for help with packages (especially at food retailers), drive-through services, special orders, restroom attendants, attached restaurants or coffee shops (such as in

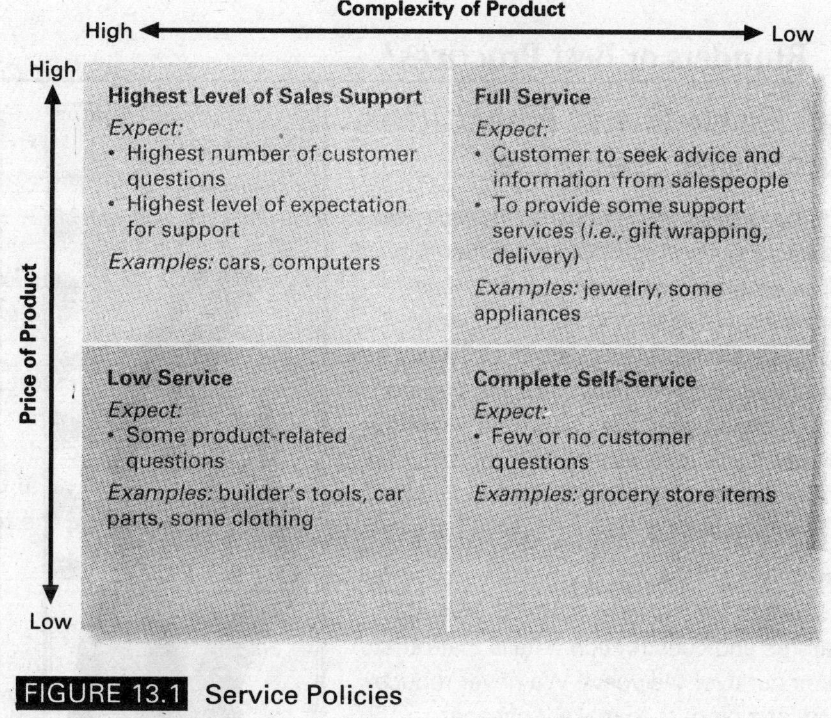

FIGURE 13.1 Service Policies

Barnes and Noble or Borders), child-care or child-play areas, free delivery, and delivery and shipping services (especially where the customer does not live near the retail site, such as tourism retailers).

CUSTOMER FOCUS

Types of services offered vary based on customers' wants and needs and the type of retail operation. The key to developing excellent service is to keep the customer as the focal point. The retailer must find out what the customer wants. Even simple actions, such as displaying the retailer's phone number and website address on all company-related information, sends a message that the retailer cares about customers' concerns.[26]

In an effort to get all employees focused on the customer, Bruce Leval, a former senior vice president at Disney, coined the term "guestology."[27] In practice, guestology means systematically uncovering key factors that determine quality and value from the customer's perspective. The ultimate goal is to keep customers coming back.

Some of the following tools can be used to generate more information about customers and the types of services they think should be offered to satisfy their wants and needs:

- Primary retailing research through surveys
- Bill-stuffer questionnaires

Blunders or Best Practices?

Lands' End: Best Practices in Customer Service

Lands' End, the largest online apparel retailer, owes much of its success to outstanding customer service practices. The emphasis on customer service is apparent when browsing through the company's website. Take, for example, its guarantee: "If you are not completely satisfied with any item you buy from us, at any time during your use of it, return it and we will refund your full purchase price." In addition, the site prints the company's principles of doing business, which are as follows:

Principle 1: We do everything we can to make our products better. We improve material, and add back features and construction details that others have taken out over the years. We never reduce the quality of a product to make it cheaper.

Principle 2: We price our products fairly and honestly. We do not, have not, and will not participate in the common retailing practice of inflating markups to set up a future phony "sale."

Principle 3: We accept any return for any reason, at any time. Our products are guaranteed. No fine print. No arguments. We mean exactly what we say: GUARANTEED. PERIOD.

Principle 4: We ship faster than anyone we know of. We ship items in stock the day after we receive the order. At the height of the last Christmas season, the longest time an order was in the house was 36 hours, excepting monograms, which took another 12 hours.

Principle 5: We believe that what is best for our customer is best for all of us. Everyone here understands that concept. Our sales and service people are trained to know our products, and to be friendly and helpful. They are urged to take all the time necessary to take care of you. We even pay for your call, for whatever reason you call.

Principle 6: We are able to sell at lower prices because we have eliminated middlemen; because we don't buy branded merchandise with high protected markups; and because we have placed our contracts with manufacturers who have proven that they are cost conscious and efficient.

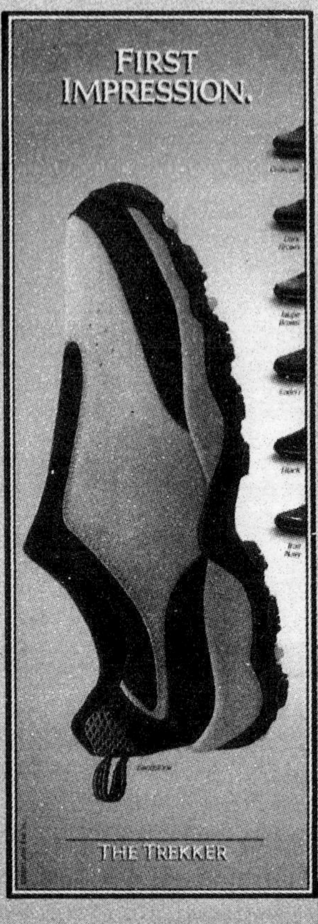

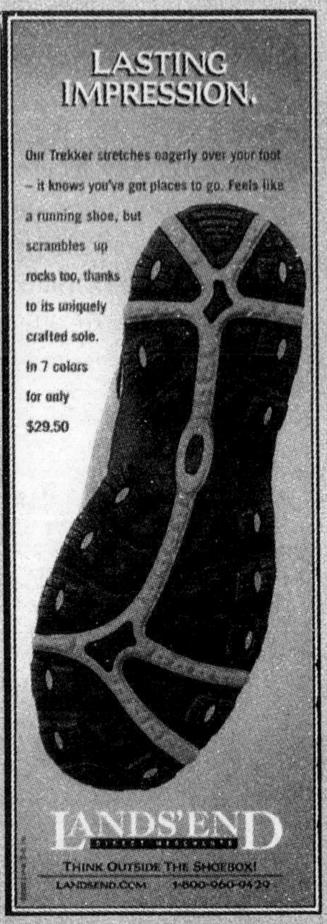

Principle 7: We are able to sell at lower prices because we operate efficiently. Our people are hard working, intelligent, and share in the success of the company.

Principle 8: We are able to sell at lower prices because we support no fancy emporiums with their high overhead. Our main location is in the middle of a 40-acre cornfield in rural Wisconsin.

It's easy to see why so many Lands' End customers are highly satisfied.

Sources: Robin Givhan, "When Khaki Meets Chichi; Land' End Makes Some Alterations to Its Conservative Image," *Washington Post,* June 18, 2002, p. C1; Lands' End website at www.landsend.com, accessed December 2002; Bob Lewis, "No Service with a Smile," *InfoWorld,* June 3, 2002, p. 58.

- Questionnaires accompanying warranty or registration cards
- Shopper-intercept studies (in which customers are asked, in person, what types of services they would like to see in the store)
- Focus groups
- A shopper's panel of six to twelve loyal customers who agree to serve as panelists for a longitudinal (long-term) study
- Trade associations
- Competitors' offerings
- Employee contact via suggestion boxes, continuous improvement initiatives, or other methods

Domino's Pizza conducts weekly phone surveys of customers. Questions are asked about response time, lumpiness of dough, freshness of pepperoni, and attitude of delivery people. Each retail outlet receives bonuses based on the outcome of the surveys.[28]

Remember that loyal customers are very valuable to retailers. The idea is to create equity in the retail operation by making customers want to come back to the site.

CUSTOMER RETENTION STRATEGIES

Because customers are valuable and have many choices available to them, retailers need to work hard to retain them. It is important to ensure that all customer-service programs are integrated with the overall strategy. In addition, customer service levels must be planned. In this planning process, there must be a top-down and bottom-up commitment to the customer service process.

The retailer must be willing to develop ongoing, intensive customer service training for all employees. A system must be developed to generate customer service ideas from retail stakeholders and customers themselves. In addition, the retailer must use selective hiring and reward outstanding employees to help reduce employee turnover. Investment in front-line employees pays off. For example, Taco Bell reports that 20 percent of its stores with the lowest employee turnover achieve double the sales and generate 55 percent more profit when compared to other Taco Bell stores.[29] Standards must be established to allow for evaluation and control of the customer service program.

Employees who are not committed to providing customer service must be allowed "career readjustment" (or termination). Electronic systems for service support should be developed and integrated into the overall RIS. Finally, and perhaps most important, customer service personnel, especially salespeople, must be empowered to deal with customer problems. For example, Dell Computer Corporation gives its call center employees powers that would normally be reserved for managers. They can offer discounts and modify products. In addition, sales call employees' incentives are tied to goals.[30]

Salesperson training requires a large amount of up-front and continuous investment in both capital and human resources. Like ROI (return on

GLOBAL RETAILING

IKEA Under Fire for Poor Service

Sally, a "typical" consumer, bought a "ready-to-assemble" desk from IKEA. She ran into trouble and looked for a toll-free number to call for help. There was none on the package or the instructions. Frustrated, Sally ended up calling her local IKEA store for help.

Nicole, a customer in London, bought a sofa from IKEA, which she took home herself. During assembly, she discovered two legs were missing. After many phone calls, IKEA agreed to send the parts. When the legs arrived several weeks later, they were the wrong ones. Once again the right legs were promised, but never showed up. To clear up the matter, IKEA decided to send a brand-new couch. After Nicole waited all day for the couch, she discovered there was no such order on the books. A new delivery date was made—and missed.

Ted, another customer, waited eight weeks for furniture. The delivery personnel who finally arrived realized the furniture was not on the truck. Somehow the furniture had gotten lost. Only when Ted's story about his poor customer service experience was published in a local newspaper did the furniture finally arrive.

IKEA is a Sweden-based home furnishings chain that operates 160 stores in about 30 countries. To save on transportation costs, IKEA uses flat packaging. Customers choose their furniture from a showroom and assemble it at home. In the past few years, IKEA has come under fire for poor customer service. Complaints include long checkout lines, insufficient staff at checkout stations or on the floor to advise customers, and failure to respond to customer feedback. Complaints have increased to the point where several websites have popped up to document them. Top management at IKEA must address this negative publicity to remain a competitive and respectable retailer.

Sources: " 'Ready to Assemble': How Hard Can It Be?" *Good Housekeeping*, November 2002, pp. 43–44; Allyson L. Stewart-Allen, "IKEA Service Worst in Its Own Backyard," *Marketing News*, April 23, 2002, p. 11; "It's the IKEA Way or No Way," *Discount Merchandiser*, 39, no. 1 (1999), pp. 51–53. Anna Tims, "Consumer: Dear Anna: Victims of IKEA," *The Guardian* (Manchester, UK), January 9, 2002, p. 18.

investment), this program is long term. The rewards for excellent customer service include increased sales and profitability and improved shareholder value.[31]

Although the same general concepts apply to both e-tailing and retailing, in e-tailing eight factors that help to create customer loyalty have been identified. These factors have been labeled the 8Cs: customization, contact interactivity, cultivation, care, community, choice, convenience, and character.[32]

Customization is "the ability of an e-tailer to tailor products, services, and the transactional environment to individual customers."

Contact interactivity is "the dynamic nature of the engagement that occurs between an e-tailer and its customers through its website." Factors here might include easy navigability of the website, high levels of product or store information, and zero delays in responding to customers via e-mail (or phone). A key to high interactivity is the creation of two-way customer communication.

Cultivation is "the extent to which an e-tailer provides relevant information and incentives to its customers in order to extend the breadth and depth of their purchases over time." This factor includes suggestion selling as well as cross-selling initiatives.

Care is "the attention that the e-tailer pays to all the pre- and postpurchase customer interface activities designed to facilitate both immediate transactions and long-term customer relationships." The customer should be provided with delivery information, tracking information, and notice of the availability of products (especially those the customer prefers). The e-tailer needs to take "care" to minimize any service interruptions to its customers.

Community is a system developed by the e-tailer to "facilitate the exchange of opinions and information regarding offered products and services." An example of community would be the ability of consumers to review books online; other consumers who are interested in these books can then access the reviews.

Choice refers to the range of products offered for sale. This includes offering not only a wider choice of product categories but also a wider range of products within product categories. Choice is a big competitive advantage for the e-tailer compared to the brick-and-mortar retailer.

Convenience refers to "the extent to which a customer feels that the website is simple, intuitive, and user friendly."

Character is "an overall image or personality that the e-tailer projects to consumers through the use of inputs such as text, style, graphics, colors, logos, and slogans or themes on the website."[33]

Figure 13.2 summarizes the 8Cs.

Whether a brick-and-mortar, click-only, or brick-and-click retailer, customer service is extremely important. The retailer must maintain a two-way, satisfying relationship with its customers to generate customer loyalty and, in turn, increased sales.

CUSTOMER RESPONSE MANAGEMENT (CRM)

customer response management (CRM) The management of databases that assist retail managers in identifying trends and responding to customer characteristics.

Customer service focuses on developing relationships with the retailer's customers. Ideally these relationships would be personal; however, given the large customer bases most retailers have, this is difficult to achieve. Many retailers utilize systems known as **customer response management (CRM)** (also called *customer relationship management* or *customer-responsive management*) to help them develop customer relationships that enhance customer service. CRM is a process in which databases are used to collect information from customers that the retailer can then use in developing programs designed to increase brand loyalty.[34] Although CRM systems were developed to assist in the logistics chain, they can be very effective when totally integrated into the IRM plan. The systems are particularly effective for e-tailers and direct retailers. To be successful, CRM must be integrated throughout the entire retailing process.

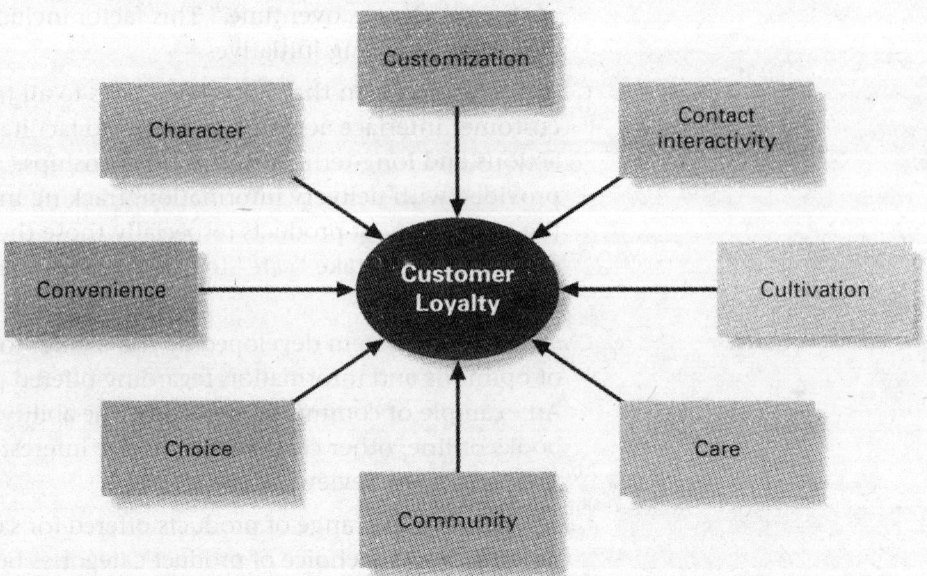

FIGURE 13.2 **The 8*C*s of Customer Loyalty in E-commerce** (Source: Adapted from Srini S. Srinivasan, Rolph Anderson, and Kishore Ponnavolu, "Customer Loyalty in E-commerce: An Exploration of Its Antecedents and Consequences," *Journal of Retailing,* Spring 2002.)

In the early 1960s, retail managers began to realize that their organizations needed to become more flexible to achieve higher levels of customer service. An increase in competition, often international competition, resulted in decreased overall market share for many U.S. retailers. Prior to the 1960s, firms had concentrated on larger, or mass, markets while ignoring smaller markets. Thus, in the 1960s, retailers determined that they needed to capture the smaller markets to maintain their levels of market share.

The result was market segmentation. Allied with these increases in competition were external environmental issues of high energy prices, increases in interest rates, and increased technologies. To deal with these environmental pressures, retailers and other businesses began to increase their managements' flexibility to adapt to the changes in the marketplace and allow them to respond to the smaller market segments.[35] Advances in technologies and the desire to increase market share through technology-based products led to the development of CRM. CRM allows a retailer to provide service that differentiates it from competitors.[36] In addition, CRM processes allow retailers to communicate with millions of consumers and at the same time make the communications appear personalized. This personalization of products and services is called *1:1 marketing,*[37] discussed in the following section.

1:1 marketing Using customer response management techniques to personalize products and services.

1:1 MARKETING

1:1 marketing (pronounced "one-to-one marketing") is a trend in retailing whose focus is not on accumulating more customers but on generating

TABLE 13.2

SELECTED INTERNATIONAL CRM EXAMPLES

Company	Method of Customer Relationship Management
RBC Royal Bank	Created a pilot program allowing for real-time awards redemptions at the point of sale for 5,500 Visa Classic II cardholders. Participants to redeem points for awards, in real time, at select Home Hardware and RadioShack Canada locations.
Red Robin, restaurant chain	Began an e-mail program that delivers promotions to customers. Promotions include welcome messages, birthday premiums/rewards, and a newsletter. Goal is to increase diner frequency and provide information to customers about the Red Robin menus.
Almacenes Siman, largest department store chain in Central America	Targeting the members of its loyalty program, Rombos De Oro, to replace its mass marketing emphasis with promotions and incentives based on individual customer profiles.

Source: Adapted from "crmwatch," *1to1 Magazine*, April 2002, p. 19.

increased business from current customers.[38] With 1:1 marketing, the CRM database is used to make products and services more personalized. For example, Sharper Image, a San Francisco–based retailer, identifies top customers by lifetime value in terms of how much these customers spend and how recent their last purchase was. Its best customers get special offers, preferred mailings, and gifts during the holiday season and sneak-preview e-mails about special new items.[39] 1:1 marketing has become successful not only in the United States but internationally as well. Table 13.2 gives some examples of global CRM.

Whether a retailer is domestic or international, CRM is a valuable tool for creating customer relationships and, in turn, excellent customer service. In a recent survey in *1to1 Magazine,*[40] readers were asked what they believed are the most important factors in the overall success of a customer-based strategy. The top three responses were (1) customer communications, (2) executive buy-in, and (3) maintaining a long-term focus for the execution of the strategy. The education and motivation of front-line employees were seen as a "building block for success."[41]

WHAT IS THE "RIGHT" CUSTOMER SERVICE LEVEL?

One problem retailers face when developing customer service programs is determining at what levels they should provide service to customers. Increasing sales is the overall objective of customer service programs. When retail executives cut back on customer services, the retailer's profits may increase in the short run. In the long run, however, the retailer runs the risk of losing a

Service retailers, such as amusement parks, must pay special attention to customer service because much of customers' satisfaction is based on their experience at the park.

significant number of previously loyal customers. Therefore, the question is: How should a retailer determine adequate customer service levels?

DEVELOPING THE CUSTOMER SERVICE LEVEL

A number of factors need to be addressed when attempting to develop the "right" customer service level for a retail business. The process involves identifying the appropriate match between customer expectations and retailer expectations.

CUSTOMER SERVICE COSTS. Perhaps the most important aspect of customer service leveling is the cost of providing the services. The retailer's financial statements should be accessed and a breakeven analysis performed regarding the cost of the services and the return on investment. In other words, how much of a sales increase can be expected from the customer service program, and what is the cost of providing the service(s)? The retailer needs to keep in mind that lost sales from poor customer service must be taken into account when developing the breakeven point (BEP). If the retailer reduces financial support for the customer service program, what will be the total amount of lost sales over the life of one customer or group of customers?

COMPETITIVE ANALYSIS. The second area to assess is the retailer's competition. When one competitor offers a service, consumers begin to wonder why another retailer does not offer the same service. There must be some tradeoff for lower service levels. Some retailers (*e.g.,* discount retailers) reduce the prices of their products to differentiate themselves from their competitors.

Some offer other lower-cost services to maintain their competitiveness. This additional service offering might be lower credit rates, free gifts with purchases, additional store hours, or any number of other amenities.

STORE CHARACTERISTICS. A third area to consider is the store's characteristics. For example, is the retailer an off-price retailer? A high-end retailer? As a general rule, the higher the retailer's prices, the more services should be offered. In addition, the store's location and size, and the type of retail institution, provide guidance in determining the appropriate service level.

The type of merchandise the retailer sells is an important consideration. Many types of products lend themselves to higher service levels. Entertainment retailers such as Disney World and Six Flags Over America have to offer additional customer services. Because sales associates contribute to the customer's positive or negative experience,[42] service retailers need to emphasize personal selling. They also need to create some degree of tangibility for the services they sell, to make customers believe they will receive value for the dollars they spend.

INCOME LEVEL OF TARGETED MARKET. The income of the retailer's targeted market will have an impact on the level of service developed. As a rule, the higher the income of the market, the higher the customer service level should be.

CUSTOMERS' WANTS AND NEEDS. Above all, the customer should be the focus when determining customer service levels. What does the customer want and need in terms of services?

The decision as to what customer service level to provide is a difficult one. Costs must be calculated and the retailer's overall image, the pricing structure, types of merchandise offered, the target market's income, and the competition must all be taken into account when determining a customer service level.

SUPPLIER CUSTOMER SERVICE LEVELS

In addition to determining the "right" customer service levels for its customers, the retailer needs to assess what kind of customer service it wants from its supply channel. In evaluating suppliers, many businesses use a supplier rating system that allows them to rate each supplier choice. In a survey of buyers, respondents ranked items according to their importance on a 1-to-10 scale. See Figure 13.3 for the results.

In a supply chain relationship, the retailer is dependent on the supplier to deliver products and services when they are promised. Thus, the supply chain becomes an important part of the overall customer service process for the retailer, and to build the retailer-supplier relationship, retailers must also practice good customer service. Sam's Club executive vice president of merchandising, Doug McMillon, was concerned that the warehouse club was losing out on obtaining new items because suppliers complained that store buyers

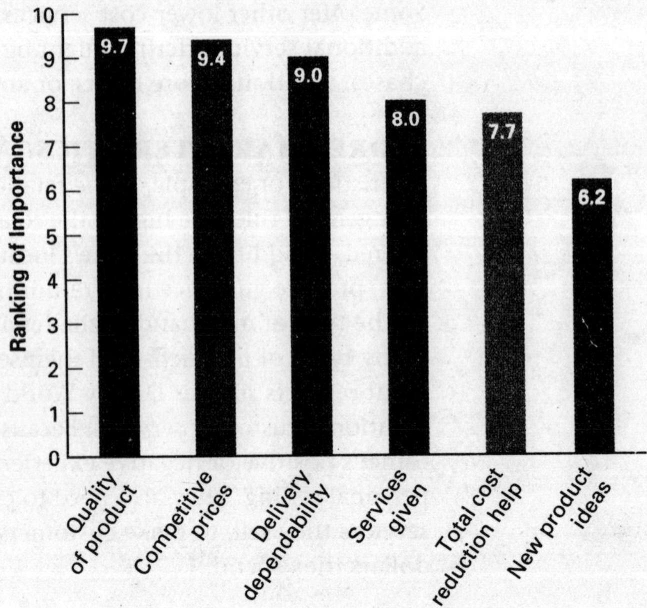

FIGURE 13.3 **Retailers' Top Criteria for Choosing a Supplier** (Source: Victor H. Pooler and David J. Pooler, *Purchasing and Supply Management* [New York: Chapman & Hall, 1997].)

were inaccessible. Sam's Club management started tracking when their employees were late for appointments, and everyone worked to improve their punctuality. The company realized that treating suppliers with respect causes the retailer-supplier relationship to improve.[43]

SUMMARY

This chapter focused on customer service in retailing. Customer service is an extremely important part of the integrated retail management process and should be consistent with the other strategic and tactical areas in design and implementation.

The chapter began with a discussion of who the retailer's customers are and how they are defined. Once targeted customers have been segmented, a profile for each group is developed. This process enables the retailer to assess who its best customers are and provides insights into how to better serve them.

Next, the chapter discussed different types of customer service programs for retailers and e-tailers. Discussed were customer characteristics. Those people that abuse a retailer's policies are undesirable as customers. One of the difficulties encountered by retailers is that each person has his or her own perception of good quality service. A retailer must find gaps in service and work to improve service levels by addressing the gaps.

Customer service offerings range from basic to additional/luxury services. Basic offerings may include a convenient location, clean facilities, security, and product availability. Additional and luxury services include anything over and above the services in the basic category.

The level of desired service was also analyzed, including the retailer's relationship with the supply chain. It is important to discover whether customers are satisfied with service levels by conducting surveys. Excellent customer service translates into happy customers, increased sales and profits, and higher stakeholder satisfaction.

KEY TERMS

customer services (382)
Pareto principle (80/20 rule) (385)
reliability (387)
assurance (387)
tangibility (387)
empathy (387)
responsiveness (388)
customer response management (CRM) (397)
1:1 marketing (398)

QUESTIONS FOR DISCUSSION

1. Why should retailers "bend over backwards" to ensure that their customers are happy with their shopping experience?
2. Why is it important to understand customers before developing customer profiles?
3. How is target marketing used in customer service?
4. What are the main differences between retail and e-tail customer services? What aspects are similar?
5. What are some uses for customer response marketing? What additional applications might become important during the next five years?
6. What service level do you believe discounters such as Target should offer? What about upscale retailers such as Neiman Marcus or Bloomingdale's?

E-TAILING EXERCISE

Choose three to five e-tailers and rate them on your perception of whether they satisfy the "golden rules" of online service (see Internet in Action, page 389).

Continuing Case 13.1

Sherwin-Williams Company: The Contractor Segment

Sherwin-Williams sells to numerous groups of customers. One of its customer groups is the contractor market. The contracting industry is very labor intensive; thus, the adage "time is money" is especially true for this group of customers. Because contractors are so busy, saving time is important to them. Customer services that save contractors time receive attention. For contractors, therefore, the key is to develop relationships with suppliers, including manufacturers and paint stores.

According to a late 1990s study, many aspects related to customer service rated high among the attributes contractors looked for in choosing a supplier. Specifically, the main attributes contractors considered when choosing a supplier were (1) staff product knowledge, (2) customer service, (3) delivery, and (4) payment terms.

Duron, a small, privately owned paint manufacturer with approximately $320 million in revenue, has responded to the needs of the contractor market. Duron has targeted the contractor segment and markets to this group exclusively. Duron pays special attention to its contractor customers by offering its products in five-gallon buckets. In addition, Duron concentrates on making prompt deliveries to contractors' job sites. Duron also pays for customers' lost time and wages if it is late in product delivery.

In contrast to Duron, Sherwin-Williams serves *all* painters. However, Sherwin-Williams may consider investing more effort and money in the contractor market to compete with Duron's increasing hold on this segment.

Questions

1. How can Duron effectively compete in this market, given the cost of customer service?
2. What can Sherwin-Williams do to halt the erosion of its market share in the contractor segment?
3. What other service ideas do you think would be appropriate to help Duron develop a larger market?
4. Do you think Duron can keep expanding its market based on its customer service philosophy? Why or why not?
5. At what customer service level do you think Duron operates?
6. Does Sherwin-Williams appear to have the same level of customer service as Duron? Explain your answer.
7. Are there tactics other than customer service activities that Sherwin-Williams could use to help the company compete with Duron?

Sources: Edward G. Marks, "Where Contractors Buy Price Is Nice, but Quality and Service Rule," *Painting & Wallcovering Contractor,* July–August 1999; Yuki Noguchi, "At Duron Inc., Paint with a Personal Touch," *Washington Post,* September 22, 1999, p. M16.

Case 13.2

Customer Service at AutoZone Stores

AutoZone, the number one auto parts chain in the United States, sells auto and light-truck parts, chemicals, and accessories through more than 3,000 AutoZone Stores in 44 states and 27 stores in Mexico. Founded in 1979 in Forrest City, Arkansas, AutoZone is on course to become a $10 billion company by 2010. Founder J. R. "Pitt" Hyde III retired in 1997, but his philosophies still drive the company. Meetings conducted throughout the year are filled with enthusiasm and a customer focus that has differentiated the company from its competitors.

Many of the strategies AutoZone employs are variations of Wal-Mart's strategies and tactics. From the company cheer to inventing its own acronyms, AutoZone has incorporated the practices that have made Wal-Mart successful. In addition to generating enthusiasm, AutoZone has adapted Wal-Mart's everyday low prices (EDLP) strategy, an inventory system that leverages technology, lower-cost ad strategies, international expansion, and emphasis on the customer.

According to the company's website, "AutoZone is built on customer service, spirit and pride . . . our ultimate goal is to exceed our customers' expectations." The company pledges to put customers first and to have the best merchandise at the right price. As an example of their dedication to customer concerns, AutoZone was the first in its segment to create a quality control program for parts. The company is regularly recognized for outstanding customer service. Although the competition is strong—Advance Auto Parts, Pep Boys, CSK Automotive, and O'Reily automotive, among others—AutoZone is confident that it will continue to beat the competition.

Questions

1. What elements have made AutoZone so successful?
2. What can competitors do to overtake AutoZone? Do you believe AutoZone will eventually be outdone by one of its competitors? Explain your answer.
3. How can AutoZone leverage its reputation for outstanding customer service?
4. At what point does a company such as AutoZone overdo its customer service efforts?

Sources: Tony Lisanti, "Maintaining the Winning Way," *DSN Retailing Today,* November 11, 2002, p. A3; "About Us," AutoZone homepage, retrieved December 2002 from www.autozone.com; Debbie Howell, "Charting a Course from 'Shack' to Empire," *DSN Retailing Today,* November 11, 2002, p. A3; "AutoZone Inc.," Hoover's Online company capsule, retrieved December 2002 from www.hoovers.com; Debbie Howell, "Pulling Away from the Pack," *DSN Retailing Today,* November 11, 2002, p. A4.

Laws and Ethics

Chapter 14

The reputation of a thousand years may be determined by the conduct of one hour.
Japanese proverb

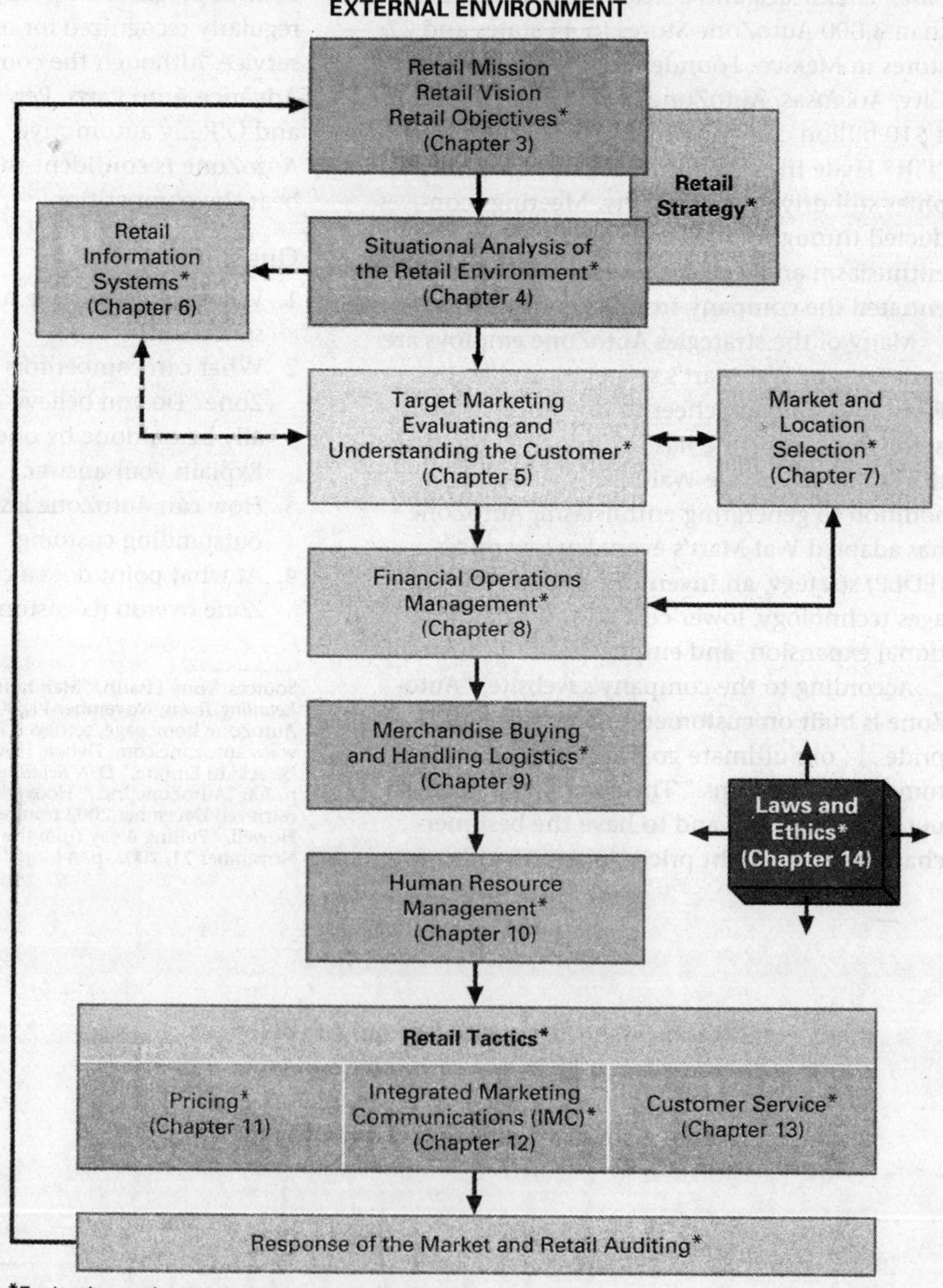

CHAPTER OBJECTIVES

After completing this chapter, you will be able to:

1. Explain the difference between laws and ethics.
2. Describe the different fields of ethics.
3. Explain how a company can incorporate ethics into its business operations.
4. Discuss specific laws governing the retail and e-tail industry.

Rite Aid Management Team Indicted for Fraud

In September 1962, Trif D Discount Center opened in Scranton, Pennsylvania. In 1968, after tremendous growth, the company went public and officially changed its name to Rite Aid Corporation. Today Rite Aid is the number three drugstore chain in the United States. The company operates about 3,400 drugstores in 28 states and Washington, DC.[1]

In the late 1990s and early 2000s, Rite Aid was investigated by the Securities and Exchange Commission (SEC) for accounting violations. Former chief executive Martin Grass, former chief counsel Franklin Brown, and former financial officer Frank Bergonzi were indicted for orchestrating a fraud that forced Rite Aid to restate $1.6 billion in profit, which at that time was history's largest corporate earnings restatement.[2] Grass faced thirty-six charges ranging from accounting fraud to witness tampering.[3]

Tapes recorded by Timothy J. Noonan, a former president of Rite Aid, revealed three executives discussing submitting false information to the Federal Bureau of Investigation, backdating documents, and destroying other evidence that would implicate them.[4] In 2003, Grass, Bergonzi, and Eric S. Sorkin, vice president for pharmacy services, pleaded guilty to various charges. As a result, they may spend time in prison and be required to pay several million dollars in fines and forfeitures.[5] Brown pleaded not guilty but was convicted by a jury in October 2003.

Despite the ethical violations, the company rebounded by installing a new management team and challenging them to create a new course for the company. In addition to the new executive team, the company hired twenty new officers in the hope of stabilizing the firm's financial situation and improving its image in the eyes of its customers and shareholders.

INTRODUCTION

As we can see from the integrated retail management flow chart, laws and ethics affect all the decisions that go into the development of the IRM plan. This chapter discusses the differences between laws and ethics, as well as methods for running an ethical business. The chapter also examines the consequences to retailers for breaking laws and addresses issues in e-tail law.

In October 2001, Enron, one of the world's leading energy companies, came under scrutiny for manipulating its financial statements. Enron is primarily a provider of energy, but it also has a retail division. As a result of these developments, the investing public lost so much faith in the company that Enron was forced to file for Chapter 11 bankruptcy on December 2, 2001.[6] Arthur Andersen LLP, once a highly regarded auditing firm, service retailer, and business-to-business service provider, had audited Enron's financial statements. Arthur Andersen was found guilty of obstruction of justice and as a result lost much of its auditing abilities, which were taken away by the SEC.[7] The negative publicity also affected the business operations. Enron continues to operate as it works through the legal backlash of past illegal and unethical practices.

In 2003, an SEC investigation revealed that J.P. Morgan Chase and Citigroup, two of the nation's largest banks, loaned Enron over $6 billion even though the banks knew that Enron was defrauding investors. In a settlement with the SEC, the banks agreed to pay $236 million in fines and to overhaul their loan practices. An additional $50 million settlement was paid to the state of New York.[8]

Since the Enron/Arthur Andersen fiasco, businesses and academicians have become more focused on laws and ethical decisions and their influence on corporate behavior. Laws and ethical decisions are intertwined with all aspects of retailing. This chapter provides an overview of the various laws that affect retailers and the ethical issues that management and employees encounter.

THE DIFFERENCE BETWEEN ETHICS AND LAWS

It can often be difficult to determine the line between right and wrong. Many activities that are unethical are also illegal. However, in some instances an act is legal but unethical and in others an act is illegal but ethical. If you are confused, you are not alone. Consider the following:

- According to the California State Floral Association, many California retail florists have lost business to telemarketers who use the florists' established business names to steal away customers. In defense, telemarketers claim they are introducing more competition. One telemarketer, Lower Forty Gardens, Inc., owns no stores, does not warehouse, and does not even ship flowers. Calls are taken by calling center representatives and sent to local florists, who fulfill the orders. The Society of American Florists wants laws that make it mandatory for florists to disclose whether or not they have a physical location.[9]

- The Kirby vacuum cleaner company came under fire in 1999 for its door-to-door sales practices. Many customers reported "hard-sell" techniques that coaxed them to buy a $1,500 vacuum cleaner. Fifteen out of twenty-two state consumer protection offices queried reported more than 600 complaints about Kirby's sales practices. According to Kirby, the company was in compliance with all laws and should not be held accountable for the independent sales force. The company claims that complaints represent only a small portion of its total sales.[10]
- In October 1999, Colt Manufacturing Company, one of the nation's largest gun manufacturers, decided to stop taking orders for retail handguns. At the time, Colt faced twenty-eight lawsuits from cities and counties blaming the company for violence caused by its products. As a result of increased legal pressures, Smith & Wesson, the nation's largest handgun manufacturer, began requiring its dealers to sign a code of ethics, which, among other actions, requires the dealers to obey firearms laws and to closely monitor buyers. The company believed this action would help prevent illegal sales of guns.[11]
- In 2001, human rights groups accused De Beers, a world leader in the production and sales of rough diamonds, of buying diamonds from African

Retailers have to be aware of the legal environment in which they operate. For example, as a result of public pressure, De Beers adopted a code that guarantees customers that "conflict diamonds" will not be sold by De Beers or its associates.

rebels who used the proceeds to finance their wars. As a result of intense pressure, De Beers adopted a code guaranteeing customers that "conflict diamonds" will not be sold by De Beers or De Beers associates.[12]

- In June 2002, Tyco's former chief executive officer, L. Dennis Kozlowski, was indicted for evading more than $1 million in New York sales tax on the purchase of $13 million in paintings. Because Tyco paid for several of Kozlowski's personal residences, the Securities and Exchange Commission considered charging Tyco for failing to fully disclose Kozlowski's compensation. As a result of the unfavorable publicity, Tyco's stock fell 54 percent, to $10.10.[13]

Retailers must consider both laws and ethics in running their businesses, but often, as the previous examples show, the "right" answer is not very clear. According to the *Internet Encyclopedia of Philosophy,* the field of **ethics** involves "systematizing, defending, and recommending concepts of right and wrong behavior."[14] The concept of what is right or wrong is often based on religious beliefs and moral codes of conduct. In contrast, a **law** is "a rule established by authority, society, or custom."[15]

ethics Concepts of right and wrong behavior.

law A rule established by authority, society, or custom.

THE FIELD OF ETHICS

The study of ethics is divided into three general categories: (1) metaethics, (2) normative ethics, and (3) applied ethics.[16] **Metaethics** is the study of the origin of ethical concepts and theories. **Normative ethics** involves deciding whether certain behavior is right or wrong. It tells us what a person should do when confronted with a particular situation. It also assumes there is only one criterion to guide right and wrong behavior. The criterion could be a single rule, such as the "Golden Rule" ("Do unto others as you would have them do unto you"). Alternatively, the criterion could be a set of principles that guides behavior, such as a code of ethics adopted by a retailer. **Applied ethics** involves analyzing specific ethical dilemmas. Retailing examples include deceptive advertising, buying from manufacturing firms that use child labor, recording assets and liabilities improperly, employee theft, inequitable pricing, and unfair competitive practices.

metaethics The study of the origin of ethical concepts and theories.

normative ethics The study of ethics using criteria to determine whether certain behavior is right or wrong.

applied ethics The study of ethics that involves analyzing specific instances of ethical dilemmas.

DIFFERENCES IN ETHICAL PERSPECTIVES

One problem in studying ethics is that people may not always agree on what is "right" and "wrong." A person faced with making a judgment about another person's moral conduct bases that decision on his or her own system of ethics; when these systems differ, disagreement arises about whether or not a particular action is moral.[17] To help explain these perspectives, a classification of ethical ideologies has been developed and is presented in Figure 14.1.

The *relativism* dimension describes the extent to which a person rejects universal moral rules in favor of relativism. On the high end of the relativism dimension, an individual rejects the idea that there are universal codes to which one must adhere. On the low end, an individual believes there are universal rules of conduct that apply to all people. The *idealism* dimension describes the extent to which a person is idealistic in anticipation of outcomes. On the high end of the idealism dimension, an individual believes one can always realize desirable consequences by making the "right" decision. On the low end, a person believes that undesirable actions are often mixed with desirable actions.

Blunders or Best Practices?

Giant Food Inc.: An Example of Professional Ethics

Founded in 1936 in Washington, DC, Giant Food Inc. operates more than 193 Giant and Super G supermarkets. The company is the number one food retailer in the metropolitan Baltimore and Washington, DC market. States in which the company operates include Delaware, New Jersey, Maryland, and Virginia.

In a world of ethical blunders, Giant is an example of a best practice. Several times in its history, Giant's professional ethics were put to the test. One example occurred when President Nixon placed price controls on beef. Although there were controls on beef for retailers due to pressure from cattle ranchers, no price controls were placed on wholesalers. As a result, wholesale prices were higher than allowable retail prices, and those supermarkets that sold beef did so at a loss. Many retailers chose to stop carrying beef, but not Giant. The president and CEO, Joseph B. Danzansky, believed the company was a merchant, not a banker, and continued to buy beef to meet customer expectations even though it had to sell the beef at a loss.

During this period, Ester Peterson, Giant's special assistant to the president for consumer affairs, took out a full-page ad in the *Washington Post* advising consumers not to buy beef because it was too expensive. The public was very surprised that a company would tell customers not to buy the company's own products. Giant got a lot of praise for its action and built public trust that helped make the company a market leader in sales and profits.

More recently, Giant Food Inc. voluntarily recalled beef in its supermarkets after a routine retail ground beef sample tested by the Food Safety Inspection Service of the U.S. Department of Agriculture proved positive for *E. coli* 0157:H7 (the numbers represent the strain of *E. coli*).

Giant's vision statement illustrates why Giant is the number one food retailer in its market:

Our goal is to be the best food and pharmacy provider in our market area:

We will delight our customers with a superior shopping experience, defined by quality, service, selection, value, and excitement, in a clean and friendly atmosphere.

We will provide our associates an environment where everyone can contribute and grow to their fullest potential.

We will be a leading corporate citizen in all of the communities that we serve.

We will conduct all our relationships with integrity and openness.

We will ensure our long-term viability through consistently strong growth in profitability and market share leadership.

Sources: "Giant Food Voluntarily Recalls Ground Beef for *E. coli* 0157:H7," PR Newswire, November 23, 2002; Paul S. Forbes, "Mrs. Murphy's Law . . . and Other Rules of Responsible Business from the Founder of Giant Foods," *Washington Post,* August 11, 2002, p. B8; "Giant Food Inc.," retrieved December 2002 from www.hooversonline.com; Giant Food Inc. homepage at www.giantfoods.com, accessed December 2002. Vision statement courtesy of Giant Foods, Inc.

		Relativism Dimension	
		High	Low
Idealism Dimension	High	Situationists	Absolutists
	Low	Subjectivists	Exceptionists

FIGURE 14.1 **Different Ethical Perspectives** (Source: Donelson R. Forsyth, "A Taxonomy of Ethical Ideologies," *Journal of Personality and Social Psychology,* 39:1 [1980] pp. 175–184.)

Situationists are high in both relativism and idealism. These individuals reject universal moral rules and advocate analysis of moral problems by considering the situation and context in which the behavior occurs. They also believe that with the "right" action, desirable consequences are obtainable. For example, a situationist would be optimistic about the outcome of the Rite Aid scandal if management comes clean. The situationist would also believe that the overall situation and context of the environment must be understood to explain why managers at Rite Aid committed fraud.

Subjectivists are high in relativism but low in idealism. People in this category reject universal moral rules in favor of personal values and perspectives

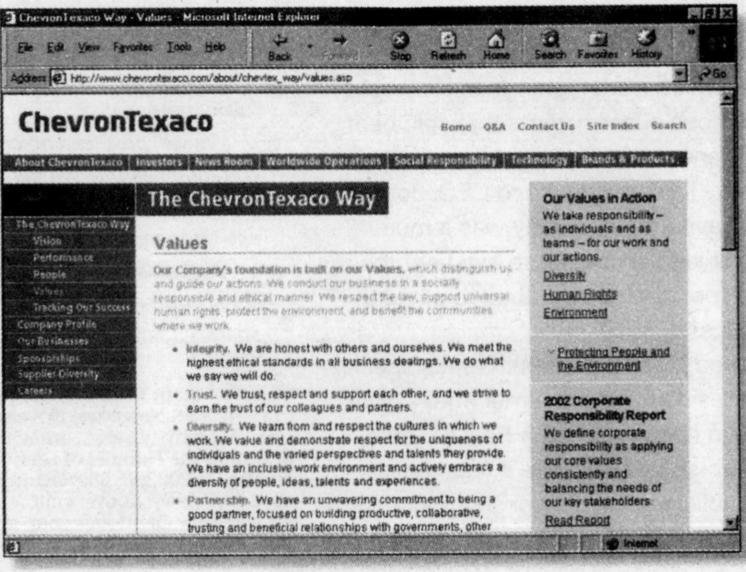

Many companies incorporate their ethical philosophies in a statement of values, such as the one displayed by CheveronTexaco on its website. (Reprinted with permission of ChevronTexaco Corporation.)

to guide behavior. They also believe that there are bound to be undesirable consequences mixed in with desirable consequences. Subjectivists would view the Rite Aid scandal in terms of the personal ethics that guided management's behavior. Individuals in this category do not believe there are universal rules of right and wrong. Instead, ethical behavior is guided by a person's perspective. Subjectivists would expect undersirable consequences, even when "right" actions are taken.

Absolutists are low in relativism and high in idealism. People in this category assume the best possible outcome can always be achieved by following universal rules. An absolutist would say that if the Rite Aid executives had followed the laws, the best outcome for the company would have resulted. This person does not believe that context is important.

Exceptionists are low in both relativism and idealism. These individuals believe that moral universal rules guide conduct but that the consequences of the action must also be considered to determine whether or not the behavior is moral. Exceptionists are pessimistic, believing that undesirable consequences will likely occur even when rules are followed. An exceptionist would say that the Rite Aid executives did not follow laws of behavior, but to determine whether their behavior was ethical, a full examination of the consequences of the behavior would need to be conducted, because even when the rules are followed, there can be undesirable consequences.

A person's decision as to whether a particular behavior is "right" or "wrong" depends on his or her ideology. For clarification, consider the following retailing example: Is it morally right for a salesperson to lie to a customer? The situationist would say it depends on why the salesperson tells the lie. Perhaps the lie is that the customer looks nice in the outfit he chose when in reality the salesperson thinks it is unflattering. Because the salesperson does not want to hurt the customer's feelings, she tells him a lie.

The subjectivist would also examine the situation to determine what is right or wrong. The subjectivist would most likely believe that undesirable consequences would result from telling a lie. The absolutist would say that a universal moral rule is to tell the truth. People in this category would agree that telling the truth is the best course of action in all circumstances. Finally, the exceptionist would say that moral absolutes guide judgments but that consequences should be considered; if necessary, exceptions should be made to universal standards of conduct. Thus, if telling a lie were the best for all parties concerned, the exceptionist would agree that is the best course of action.

THE PROFIT-PRINCIPLE RELATIONSHIP

According to the marketing concept, companies should strive to satisfy customer wants and needs at a profit. Sometimes ethical conflicts arise because the retailer is under pressure from stockholders and other publics to show profits. Four perspectives clarify the relationship between profits and principles.[18] The interplay of profits and principles vary depending on the perspective a particular company employs.

win-win perspective A perspective on the relationship between profit and principles that assumes the more ethically a business operates, the higher its profits will be.

license to operate perspective A perspective on the relationship between profit and principles stating that firms must have a minimum value of principles required by society to obtain a license to operate.

acceptable profit perspective A perspective on the relationship between profit and principles that assumes companies want to maximize principles but are restricted because the market demands that profitability reach a certain level to ensure financial continuity.

integrated perspective A perspective of the relationship between profit and principles stating that firms strive for an optimal balance between profits and principles.

1. The **win-win perspective** assumes that the more ethically a business operates, the higher the profits for the business. Therefore, no conflict exists between ethics and profits. Instead, profits and principles reinforce each other. This perspective is the most ideal situation.
2. According to the **license to operate perspective,** a company maximizes profits under the condition that the level of principles adhered to by the company is enough for it to receive a "license" from society to operate. The license stands for the acceptance of a company's operations by all stakeholders (*i.e.*, customers, stockholders, government) who can impact the profitability of the company. This perspective recognizes that not all ethical behavior will increase competitive advantage, especially when others are operating unethically. In the license-to-operate perspective, firms strive to maximize profits as opposed to principles.
3. The **acceptable profit perspective** assumes that companies want to maximize principles but are restricted because the market demands that profitability reach a level required by the capital market to ensure financial continuity. In this perspective, firms strive to maximize principles as opposed to profits, but they are restricted by the need to generate a minimum level of profits to ensure the company survives.
4. The **integrated perspective** attaches an optimum intrinsic value to both profits and principles, and the company selects the optimal balance between the two. The optimal balance depends on the relative weights of profits and principles in company operations. This perspective is the most balanced of the four.

These divisions are not clear-cut, because changes in the environment may alter outlooks. But they provide a framework for viewing profit-principle conflicts.

CULTURE AND ETHICAL PERSPECTIVES

A country's culture can have a significant effect on ethical perspectives. More and more retailers are extending their trade areas through both the Internet and global expansion. Therefore, it is increasingly important for retailers to be aware that differences exist. In addition, a retailer must understand the international laws that may affect the company.

Although most companies have policies regarding integrity, relatively few have established practices regarding bribery and human rights violations encountered in the global marketplace.[19] In many countries, bribery is not illegal; thus, ethical questions arise very quickly when a U.S. firm conducts business in those countries. It can be argued that U.S. laws against bribery place U.S. companies at a competitive disadvantage when conducting business in countries where bribery is a common practice.

Retailers encounter difficulties when it is not clear which standards the company should follow: those of the home country or those of the country in which it conducts business. Thus the importance of understanding the laws and ethical codes of the country in which the retailer operates cannot be underestimated. Globalization is forcing countries to examine their laws and

GLOBAL RETAILING

The Foreign Corrupt Practices Act

On February 3, 1975, the chief executive officer of United Brands Company committed suicide. Two months later, the Securities and Exchange Commission discovered that the CEO had bribed the president of Honduras with $1.25 million. The investigation that followed revealed that more than 400 U.S. companies (117 from the *Fortune 500* list) had paid over $300 million in bribes or other illegal payments to foreign officials to gain business opportunities in foreign countries. As a result, the Foreign Corrupt Practices Act was enacted in 1977 to curtail bribery practices.

The act makes it illegal for a U.S. company to pay, or offer to pay, a foreign official to gain or maintain business in that country. American corporations claim the act makes it difficult, if not impossible, to compete internationally, especially because bribery is a widespread practice in many countries. In recent years, however, many other countries have recognized the legal and ethical issues surrounding bribery and have developed their own antibribery laws.

The Ethics Officer Association, headquartered in Belmont, Massachusetts, has developed a business conduct management system standard that it hopes to make a global standard under the International Organization for Standardization. A worldwide standard would help businesses and consumers alike evaluate individual companies and their ethical practices.

Sources: S. Thomas Moser, "Meeting the Challenge of the 'Corporate Watergate' Phenomenon," *The Internal Auditor,* April 1978, retrieved July 2002 from Proquest; Judith Scott, Debora Gilliard, and Richard Scott, "Eliminating Bribery as a Transnational Marketing Strategy," *International Journal of Commerce & Management,* 12, no. 1 (2002), pp. 1–17; Amy Zuckerman, "Managing Business Ethics in a World of Payola," *World Trade,* December 2001, pp. 38–39.

ethical codes of conduct; in the future there may be international standards, which will make ethical choices easier.

HOW TO RUN AN ETHICAL BUSINESS

The downfall of many U.S. executives in recent years has been called a "commercial Watergate."[20] Instead of enjoying the appreciation and respect typically experienced by CEOs, executives are increasingly being regarded with hostility and suspicion. There are several ways a retailer can run an ethical business. Table 14.1 contains suggestions from Ivy Sea Online (*www.ivysea.com*), a website devoted to leadership and communication.[21]

LAWS

To facilitate the flow of business while protecting consumers, many local, state, national, and international laws are created. The following sections describe laws that are specific to retailers. Prior to discussing the legal environment of retailing, we will look at some legal issues facing retailers. Keep in

TABLE 14.1

SUGGESTIONS FOR RUNNING AN ETHICAL BUSINESS

Examine the intention. Examine your reasons for implementing ethics policies. Are you implementing ethics policies because it's the "hot topic," or does management plan to make ethics a priority for the long term? Whose ethical standards will be applied in determining the policies? The rationale behind intentions will help to better communicate policies to employees.

Highlight the company's "legends" that personify the ethics. Celebrate the models of ethical conduct by sharing stories with employees and the public. Keep traditional or inspiring stories alive to motivate employees.

Make ethics a company "action." Every manager must "walk the talk" because employees watch managers' behavior and become confused if actions don't mirror words.

Provide parameters and examples. Provide employees with guidelines that support the company's standards of ethics, while understanding that some people see ethical behavior differently. Communicate these standards consistently to all employees.

Incorporate new ways of understanding ethics. It may be beneficial to hire a skilled facilitator to engage employees in discussions about ethics. If managers feel comfortable enough, they can conduct discussion sessions themselves, but it's important to respect participants' differences, beliefs, and insecurities about the subject.

Meld ethics with business. Integrate ethics in all aspects of the operation, including hiring new employees, pricing products, implementing standards, and choosing suppliers.

Tie ethics to individual and departmental goals. Incorporate support of the company's ethical standards in performance reviews. Make sure associates understand that they will be rated on ethical behavior and that they understand the consequences of unethical behavior.

Develop safe feedback mechanisms. Make sure employees feel safe in reporting unethical behavior. Some ways to ensure employees are comfortable include anonymous hotlines, suggestion boxes, designating an ethics officer, and confidential one-on-one discussions.

Use an advisor. Soliciting outside advice from an expert on how to best implement and communicate an ethics policy is a good tactic.

A word of advice: A good rule of thumb is: If your family or friends would think less of you if knowledge of an activity surfaced, you should not participate in such an activity.

Source: Ivy Sea Online, "Defining and Communicating Ethics in Your Business," by Jaime S. Walter, founder, Ivy Sea, Inc. San Francisco, CA (www.ivysea.com) and author, *Big Vision, Small Business;* copyright.

mind that many times laws and ethics overlap; although there are laws against theft, for example, ethical perspectives also play a role.

EMPLOYEE THEFT

According to the 2002 National Retail Security Survey, total inventory shrinkage cost U.S. retailers $32.3 billion in 2001 and $31.3 billion in 2002. In 2002, employee theft accounted for about 48 percent of inventory shrinkage, with the remainder coming from shoplifting (32 percent), administrative error (15 percent), and vendor fraud (5 percent). In comparison to 2001, employee theft

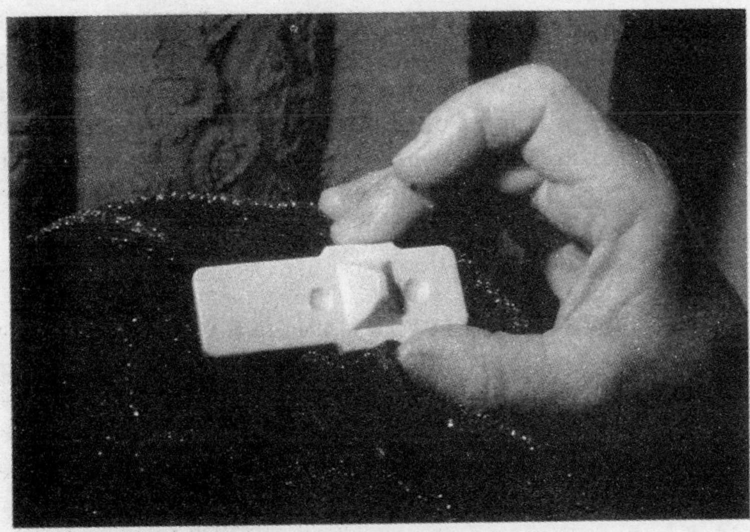

To protect against customer and employee theft, many retailers use theft prevention mechanisms such as the one shown here.

and shoplifting increased whereas administrative error and vendor fraud decreased.[22] At a cost of more than $15 billion, the amount of inventory shrinkage attributed to employee theft was the highest yet observed in the ten-year history of the National Retail Security Survey, replacing the high from the previous year. No other form of theft costs Americans more money than employee theft.[23]

The five retail categories reporting the highest amounts of employee theft were convenience stores, supermarket and grocery stores, men's apparel stores, office supply stores, and consumer electronics and appliances retailers. The categories of retailers reporting the lowest levels of employee theft were sporting goods stores, department stores, home centers, hardware/lumber/garden supply stores, and cards/gifts/novelty retailers.[24]

Employee theft can be extremely costly for retailers, but by taking precautions, retailers can minimize shrinkage and eliminate temptation for employees to behave unethically.

CUSTOMER THEFT

Although the majority of retail theft is by employees, customer shoplifting is also a big concern for retailers. It is estimated that the average family pays about $440 a year as a result of employee and customer theft.[25] Customer theft cost retailers about $10 billion in 2002. Retail categories reporting the highest amounts of shoplifting were drugstores, women's apparel, department stores, home/hardware/garden centers, and card/gifts/novelty stores. Those categories with the lowest incidence of customer theft were consumer electronics/appliances stores, supermarket/grocery stores, children's apparel stores, and office supplies/stationery stores.[26] Ways to reduce shrinkage due to customer theft include supervising the selling floor, making would-be shoplifters feel uneasy, and getting employees involved in the prevention process.[27]

SUPERVISE THE SELLING FLOOR. It is important that managers be on the sales floor as much as possible during the day. While walking the floor, managers should observe and respond to mismarked merchandise, incorrect prices on signs, unlocked security displays, merchandise concealed for later pickup, fitting room attendants off their posts, inattentive security guards, unpaid-for merchandise under counters, and suspicious activities by customers. Another effective method is to pay plainclothes security personnel to walk the selling floor.

GIVE SHOPLIFTERS AN UNEASY FEELING. An effective way to deter shoplifting is to make shoplifting difficult. Methods include the following:

- Train employees to maintain frequent eye contact with customers who insist on browsing on their own.
- Assign zones for staff coverage so that vulnerable areas are not left unattended.
- Instruct employees to give directions to people taking items into the fitting room.
- Use bright lighting, mirrors, video cameras, and anti-shoplifting signs to let customers know the retailer is serious about theft. Let potential shoplifters know that all offenders will be prosecuted.

GET EMPLOYEES INVOLVED IN THE THEFT PREVENTION PROCESS. Employees can be very effective in detecting and deterring theft. Given that retailers report more than $31 billion in losses yearly due to theft, it is important to get everyone involved in the theft prevention process. There are several ways to ensure employee involvement:

- Do not criticize employees who are overcautious; in fact, employees who report theft should be rewarded.
- Keep employees well informed about what is happening within the company. Informed employees feel like they are part of the company and will be more protective of the company's assets.
- Train employees in how to get assistance when a security crisis occurs.
- Install silent alarms and educate all employees in company policies and procedures in the event of a theft.

OTHER LOSS PREVENTION STRATEGIES

Loss prevention strategies reported in the 2002 National Retail Security Survey[28] are grouped into four categories: pre-employment integrity screening measures, employee awareness programs, asset control policies, and loss prevention systems.

PRE-EMPLOYMENT INTEGRITY SCREENING MEASURES. Retailers using these measures most often verify past employment history and check for prior criminal convictions. Other methods include drug screening, driving record checks, credit checks, multiple interviews, education verification, personal reference checks, and paper-and-pencil honesty checks. Different measures are undertaken depending on the level of personnel being considered, with greater scrutiny being applied to potential managerial employees than to employees lower in the organizational hierarchy.

EMPLOYEE AWARENESS PROGRAMS. The most common employee awareness programs involve discussions during new-hire orientation, bulletin board notices and posters, anonymous telephone hotlines, and presentations and lectures. Other programs include codes of conduct, training videos, newsletters, and honesty incentives.

ASSET CONTROL POLICIES. The most widely used retail loss prevention strategies are in the asset control policies category. These policies include refund controls, void controls, employee package checks, point-of-service (POS) exception-based reporting, trash removal controls, interstore transfer controls, POS bar coding/scanning, price change controls, unobserved exit door controls, inventory bar coding/scanning, and detailed merchandise receiving controls. The least used method was the use of electronically controlled access to cash-handling areas.

LOSS PREVENTION SYSTEMS. The most common programs in this category include burglar alarms and live, visible CCTV (closed-circuit television). Other actions include check approval database screening, hidden CCTV and armored car deposit pickups, cables/locks/chains, digital video recording systems, secured display fixtures, mystery/honesty shoppers, silent alarms, observation mirrors, plainclothes detectives, and merchandise alarms.

INTERNET FRAUD

Fraud committed over the Internet is an especially important issue for e-tailers because it is not covered under many of the rules and laws that apply to the typical brick-and-mortar retailer. According to the Department of Justice, **Internet fraud** refers to "any type of fraud scheme that uses one or more components of the Internet to present fraudulent solicitation to prospective victims, to conduct fraudulent transactions, or to transmit the proceeds of fraud to financial institutions or to others connected with the scheme."

Internet fraud The use of the Internet to present fraudulent solicitation to prospective victims, conduct fraudulent transactions, or transmit the proceeds of fraud to financial institutions or others connected with the scheme.

An example is customer credit card purchases over the Internet. Laws related to customer loss due to fraudulent use of credit cards for purchases at brick-and-mortar retailers or even through direct retailers, such as catalog retail outlets, do not apply to Internet transactions. E-tailers incur the cost of the loss of fraudulent credit card purchases because most credit card issuers and processors require the customer's signature; thus, the e-tailer is unprotected without this signature.[29] Investigating Internet fraud is difficult because victim and perpetrator may be located thousands of miles apart.[30]

The Federal Trade Commission and the Internet Fraud Watch report that auction and retail frauds are the most frequent online schemes. According to the Internet Fraud Complaint Center's (IFCC) *Annual Data Trends Report*,[31] 43 percent of fraud reported during 2001 came from auction fraud and 20 percent came from nondelivery of and nonpayment for merchandise. These types of schemes purport to offer high-value items likely to attract many consumers. The victims send money for the promised items, but either never get the items or receive counterfeit items instead of the promised goods. In May 2001, the IFCC brought criminal charges against nearly ninety individuals during its Operation Cyber Loss. The fraud schemes exposed by the initiative represented a total of 56,000 victims and losses of more than $117 million.[32] See Table 14.2 for a list of government and nongovernment websites that contain more information on general fraud and Internet fraud.

TABLE 14.2

WEBSITES CONTAINING INFORMATION ON FRAUD AND INTERNET FRAUD

Government Websites	
Commodity Futures Trading Commission	www.cftc.gov
FirstGov for Consumers	www.consumer.gov
Computer Crime and Intellectual Property Section, Criminal Division, U.S. Department of Justice	www.cybercrime.gov
Federal Bureau of Investigation	www.fbi.gov
Federal Trade Commission	www.ftc.gov
Internet Fraud Complaint Center	www.ifccfbi.gov
Securities and Exchange Commission	www.sec.gov
U.S. Customs Service	www.customs.ustreas.gov
U.S. Postal Inspection Service	www.usps.com
U.S. Secret Service	www.treas.gov/usss
U.S. Sentencing Commission	www.uscc.gov
Nongovernment Websites	
Better Business Bureau	www.bbb.org
BBBOnLine	www.bbbonline.org
Internet Fraud Council	www.internetfraud
Internet Fraud Watch	www.fraud.org
Internet ScamBusters	www.scambusters.org
National Association of Attorneys General	www.naag.org
National Association of Securities Dealers Regulation	www.nasdr.com
National Consumers League	www.natlconsumersleague.org
National Fraud Information Centers	www.fraud.org
North American Securities Administrators Association	www.nasaa.org

REGULATING BODIES

The Federal Trade Commission (FTC) is a regulatory agency of the U.S. government that enforces federal antitrust and consumer protection laws. The FTC protects consumers and businesses from acts or practices that are unfair or deceptive.

With regulatory powers similar to those of the FTC, the U.S. International Trade Commission (ITC) (*www.usitc.gov/webabout.htm*) provides trade expertise to both the legislative and executive branches of government; determines the impact of imports on U.S. industries; and directs actions against certain unfair trade practices, such as patent, trademark, and copyright infringement.

Other countries have regulatory agencies similar to the FTC and ITC. Examples include the Canadian Trade Commission, the Taiwan Fair Trade Commission, the French Trade Commission, and Peru's Export Promotion Commission. Many of the regulations imposed by local, state, federal, and international bodies aim to protect the consumer, give the consumer a broad range of choices, provide the consumer with reliable, timely information, and prevent unfair trade practices.

SPECIFIC LAWS THAT AFFECT RETAILERS

Authorities, societies, or custom establish laws. Retailers must abide by the laws imposed by various local, state, and federal authorities. Companies that run global operations must keep in mind that laws in effect in the United States may not apply in other countries. Conversely, other countries have laws that the United States may not have. When a company breaks established laws, it must pay the consequences for illegal activity. Consequences may include paying a fine, providing restitution to affected parties, publicly admitting to crimes, and in severe situations, jail time for the individual(s) who committed the crime. Frequently, the negative publicity generated by law breaking hurls a company into bankruptcy. The investment in a legal department is highly recommended for both national and international companies.

Retailing laws have the greatest effect on retail tactics (pricing, integrated marketing communications, customer service, etc.). However, laws that affect retailers also apply to other areas of the retail management flow chart. Let's take a closer look at laws and how they may affect various areas in the IRM flow chart.

trademark A firm's brand name, symbol, or design used to identify the company to other businesses and consumers as the source of a product.

servicemark A firm's brand name, symbol, or design used to identify the company to other businesses and consumers as the source of a service.

TRADEMARK REGULATIONS

All businesses must be aware of trademark laws. A **trademark** is a firm's brand name, symbol, or design that is used to identify the company to other businesses and consumers. Trademarks give a business the legal right to use a given design to identify its products. **Servicemarks** are the counterparts to trademarks for services.

The Lanham Trademark Act, enacted by Congress in 1946, protects the rights of trademark/servicemark owners. Under the Lanham Act, a company

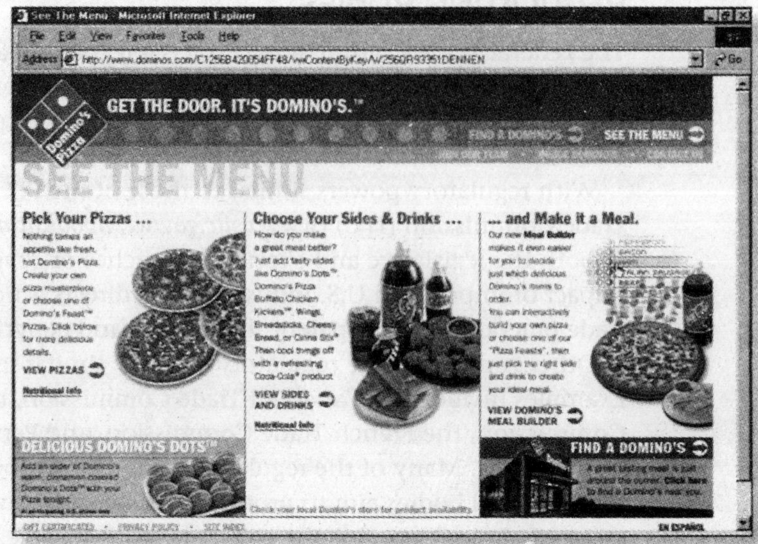

Domino Sugar sued Domino's Pizza for trademark infringement. Domino's Pizza won the case because the court ruled that most people would not confuse pizza with sugar. (Courtesy of Domino's Pizza and Domino Foods, Inc.)

can register its brand name or design with the U.S. Patent Office. A search is conducted to ensure that no other company is already using the mark. Eventually the application to register a trademark is either accepted or rejected. If it is accepted, the company is protected, under federal laws, against unauthorized use of the trademark. If it is declined, the company can file an appeal. There is no single organization that polices trademarks and servicemarks. If a company believes its trademark has been infringed on, it needs to follow up. The courts will decide if an infringement of trademark law has occurred.

In the 1960s, the company that owned Domino Sugar took Domino's Pizza to court over trademark infringement. Domino Sugar believed Domino's Pizza unfairly used its trademarked name "Domino's." While the case was in court, the owners of Domino's Pizza changed the name to

INTERNET IN ACTION

Internet Brand and Trademark Abuse on the Web

The International Chamber of Commerce reports that companies lose $25 billion to $30 billion a year to Internet brand and trademark abuse. According to the International Anti-Counterfeiting Coalition (IACC), about 25 percent of all branded goods sold online are counterfeit. When companies fail to pursue counterfeiters, the brand can be damaged.

One company that is fighting back is New Balance. New Balance places unique identifiers, or "fingerprints," on its products. These help the company determine whether a product is authentic. In addition, the company has increased its monitoring of Internet commerce. In so doing, it can determine whether counterfeits are being sold and pursue strategies to stop the practice.

Firms must have lawyers and investigators ready to respond within twenty-four hours when counterfeit activity is suspected because the goods are typically available only for a short period of time. New Balance even took out ads overseas to notify consumers about counterfeit merchandise and to let criminals know that New Balance is fighting brand erosion.

The Web attracts illegal activity for many reasons, including low barriers to entry. It is a low-cost sales and distribution channel, provides the ability to transact instantaneously, enables criminals to look legitimate, has a global reach, and makes it easy to steal metatags intended for legitimate sites. (Metatags are used to store information relevant to browsers and search engines.) Major types of illegal activity on the Web include fraud in online auctions, retail schemes, and business opportunities; identity theft; and online investment and credit card scams.

Sources: Lucy Farmer, "Online: Working the Web; Scams: The Net Is Great Medium for Unraveling Fraud and Fighting Scams," *The Guardian* (Manchester, UK), November 21, 2002, p. 4; Bruce D. Mandelblit, "Clicks & Crime: The Inside Story of Internet Fraud," *Security*, September 2001, pp. 31–32; Liz Evans, "Brand Fraud Grows Online," *Sporting Goods Business*, October 2001, p. 38.

Dominic's Pizza. The court ruled in favor of Domino's Pizza, arguing that a reasonable person would know the difference between sugar and pizza.

ANTITRUST LAWS

Many antitrust laws restrict unfair or unlawful partnerships between retailers. The *Sherman Antitrust Act*, passed in 1890, outlaws monopolies as well as contracts or other forms of conspiracy to restrain or limit free trade. For example,

TABLE 14.3

SECTIONS OF ANTITRUST LAWS

Section 1 of the Sherman Act outlaws "every contract, combination . . . , or conspiracy, in restraint of trade," but the Supreme Court decided long ago that the Sherman Act prohibits only those contracts or agreements that restrain trade unreasonably. What kinds of agreements are unreasonable is up to the courts.

Section 2 of the Sherman Act makes it unlawful for a company to "monopolize, or attempt to monopolize," trade or commerce. As that law has been interpreted, it is not necessarily illegal for a company to have a monopoly or to try to achieve a monopoly position. The law is violated only if the company tries to maintain or acquire a monopoly position through unreasonable methods. For the courts, a key factor in determining what is unreasonable is whether the practice has a legitimate business justification.

Section 5 of the Federal Trade Commission Act outlaws "unfair methods of competition" but does not define *unfair.* The Supreme Court has ruled that violations of the Sherman Act also are violations of Section 5, but Section 5 covers some practices that are beyond the scope of the Sherman Act. It is the FTC's job to enforce Section 5.

Section 7 of the Clayton Act prohibits mergers and acquisitions where the effect "may be substantially to lessen competition, or to tend to create a monopoly." Determining whether a merger or acquistion will have such an effect requires a thorough economic evaluation or market study.

Section 7A of the Clayton Act, called the **Hart-Scott-Rodino Act,** requires prior notification of large mergers to both the FTC and the Justice Department.

Source: Federal Trade Commission, retrieved July 2002 from www.ftc.gov/bc/compguide/antitrst.htm.

in 2002, J. Hilary Rockett, Jr., attempted to build a hotel in Salem, Massachusetts. Up to that point, no new hotel had been built in the city for seventy-five years. The Hawthorne Hotel, the only local competitor, made numerous attempts to impede construction on the project. In response, Rockett filed a $1.8 million suit charging the owners of the Hawthorne Hotel with holding a monopoly on the hotel industry in Salem and demonstrating anticompetitive conduct in violation of the Sherman Antitrust Act. The suit was settled out of court when the Hawthorne Hotel's owners agreed to withdraw opposition to the construction.[33,34]

The *Clayton Act,* passed in 1914, regulates price discrimination, tying contracts, exclusive dealing arrangements, and acquisition of stock of another company. Three revisions to the Clayton Act were made that affected trade. The first was the *Robinson-Patman Act,* passed in 1936, which regulates seller-induced price discrimination, buyer-induced price discrimination, and price discounts such as advertising allowances. The second was the *Celler-Kefauver Amendment,* passed in 1950, which regulates the acquisition of assets as well as stock of another company. The third was the *Hart-Scott-Rodino Antirust Improvement Act* (1976), which required large firms to prenotify the FTC of intentions to merge. Violation of these laws is a felony. Corporations may be charged up to $10 million for violations, and an individual breaking these laws may be jailed for up to three years and fined up to $350,000 per violation. Table 14.3 summarizes important sections of various antitrust laws.

HORIZONTAL AGREEMENTS

According to the FTC, agreements among parties in a competing relationship can raise antitrust suspicions. If agreements hurt competition, they are considered violations of federal law. **Horizontal agreements** are arrangements between a business and its competitors. Following are some of the more common horizontal agreements that retailers must avoid.

horizontal agreement A restrictive agreement between two competitors in the same market.

Agreements on price. Illegal agreements on price or price-related matters such as credit terms are potentially the most serious violations, because price often is the primary means of competition among retailers. Sometimes retailers appear to be in collusion because their prices are so similar, but to prove illegal activity, the FTC needs evidence of price fixing.

Agreements to restrict output. An agreement to restrict production or output is illegal because when the supply of a product or service is limited, its price usually goes up.

Boycotts. A group boycott is an agreement among competitors not to deal with another person or business. If the boycott is used to force another party to pay higher prices, it is illegal.

Market division. Agreements among competitors to divide sales territories or allocate customers are essentially agreements not to compete.

Agreements to restrict advertising. Restrictions on price advertising can be illegal if they deprive consumers of important information. Restrictions on nonprice advertising also may be illegal if evidence shows the restrictions have anticompetitive effects and lack reasonable business justification.

Codes of ethics. A professional code of ethics may be unlawful if it unreasonably restricts the methods by which professionals may compete.

VERTICAL AGREEMENTS

vertical agreement An agreement between at least two parties operating at different levels of the supply chain that relates to the conditions under which the parties may purchase, sell, or resell goods or services.

Vertical agreements are arrangements occurring in a buyer-seller relationship, such as between a retailer and a manufacturer or wholesaler. The following types of vertical agreements are illegal.

Resale price maintenance agreements. Illegal activity includes price fixing between a supplier and a dealer or between a manufacturer and a retailer. Such activity is illegal because it fixes the minimum resale price of a product, resulting in unfair competition. Although the laws are restrictive, a manufacturer has some latitude to adopt a policy regarding a desired level of resale prices and to deal only with retailers that independently decide to follow that policy. A manufacturer can also cease dealings with a retailer that breaches the manufacturer's resale price maintenance policy.

tie-in A practice in which a company tries to sell one product on the condition that the customer purchase a second product. (Also called a *tying agreement*.)

Tie-in sales. A **tie-in** (also called a *tying agreement*) is an arrangement in which a company tries to sell one product on the condition that the customer purchases a second product. In some cases, the customer does not want the second product or can buy it elsewhere at a lower price. Such a tie-in sale may prevent the consumer from shopping for the product at a competitor; thus, it can potentially harm competition and therefore is illegal.

CONSUMER PROTECTION ACTS

Before the 1900s, merchants followed the *caveat emptor* doctrine: "Let the buyer beware." In the early 1900s, Congress passed a series of laws designed to protect consumers from increasingly exploitive business practices. The slogan for consumers became *caveat vendor,* meaning "Let the seller beware." The Federal Food, Drug, and Cosmetic Act (passed in 1906 and amended in 1938 and 1997) protects consumers from adulteration of food and misbranding of food, drugs, cosmetics, and therapeutic devices.

In the 1960s and 1970s, as consumers gained more power relative to government and business, a series of laws were enacted that have greatly affected the way businesses interact with their customers. The following sections describe these laws.

FAIR PACKAGING AND LABELING ACT (1966). This law prevents deceptive product labeling and makes it easier for consumers to make product comparisons due to the required information on product labels.

TRUTH IN LENDING ACT (1968). This law requires creditors to disclose all costs and terms of credit in a clear manner. Although the disclosure process still confuses some consumers, if you read the terms carefully, you will see that credit agreements must contain information about interest rates.

FAIR CREDIT REPORTING ACT (1971). This act gives consumers the right to inspect their credit reports and to correct mistakes found in these reports. This act was amended in 1997 to require the major credit reporting agencies to include a toll-free telephone number at which customer service personnel are accessible to answer consumer questions. Under the amendment, consumer credit bureaus must take actions to investigate customer disputes within thirty days.

CONSUMER PRODUCT SAFETY ACT (1972). This act monitors and regulates product safety issues, safety guidelines, and banning and recalling of products.

FAIR CREDIT BILLING ACT (1975). This law was enacted to help consumers correct mistakes made on their billing statements.

MAGNUSON-MOSS WARRANTY ACT (1975). This act requires that warranties be written in easy-to-understand language.

EQUAL CREDIT OPPORTUNITY ACT (1975). This act makes it illegal to discriminate in any aspect of the credit transaction due to sex, marital status, race, national origin, religion, age, or receipt of public assistance.

CONSUMER PRODUCT SAFETY COMMISSION IMPROVEMENT ACT (1976). This act permits consumers to file civil suits against the Consumer Product Safety Commission.

FAIR DEBT COLLECTION PRACTICES ACT (1978). This act makes it illegal to harass people when attempting to collect payments. The act also prohibits lying or using unfair tactics to collect payments.

CORPORATE DISCLOSURE ACTS

Like all companies, retailers have an obligation to disclose relevant information to the consumer. In general, advertising must tell the truth and claims made about products and services must be substantiated. The FTC has determined that a particular practice is deceptive if it is likely to mislead consumers and affect their behavior or decisions about the product or service.

A practice is deemed unfair if the injury it causes (or is likely to cause) is substantial and not outweighed by other benefits or if it is not reasonably avoidable. Third parties, such as advertising agencies, Web designers, or direct marketers, may be held liable for making or disseminating deceptive representations if they participate in the preparation or distribution of such representations, especially if they knew in advance that the practice was deceptive and/or unfair.

ELECTRONIC FUND TRANSFER ACT (EFTA). This act requires businesses to adopt practices that protect information transferred electronically. Liability limits are also specified for losses caused by unauthorized transfers. Banks and other financial institutions were affected by this law in 1999 when the Gramm-Leach-Bliley Act (GLBA) amended the EFTA and made it necessary for automated teller machine (ATM) operators to disclose their service fees on or near the ATM. The amendment requires that disclosure of the fee be made before the transaction is completed so the consumer may cancel the transaction if she or he chooses not to pay the fee.[35]

FRANCHISE AND BUSINESS OPPORTUNITY RULE. This rule requires franchise and business opportunity sellers to give detailed disclosure information to help buyers make informed decisions. The disclosure documents should include names, addresses, and telephone numbers of at least ten previous purchasers who live closest to the inquirer, a fully audited financial statement of the seller, the background and experience of the business's key executives, the costs of starting and maintaining the business, and the responsibilities the potential purchaser and the seller will have to each other once the franchise is purchased. Several franchisers have websites containing this information. For example, Dunkin' Donuts™ has a special website for people interested in starting a franchise (*www.dunkin-baskin-togos.com/html/home.asp*). The website provides the steps to follow to obtain a franchise as well as information about the franchise.

TESTIMONIALS AND ENDORSEMENTS. These guides require that testimonials and endorsements reflect typical consumer experiences, unless

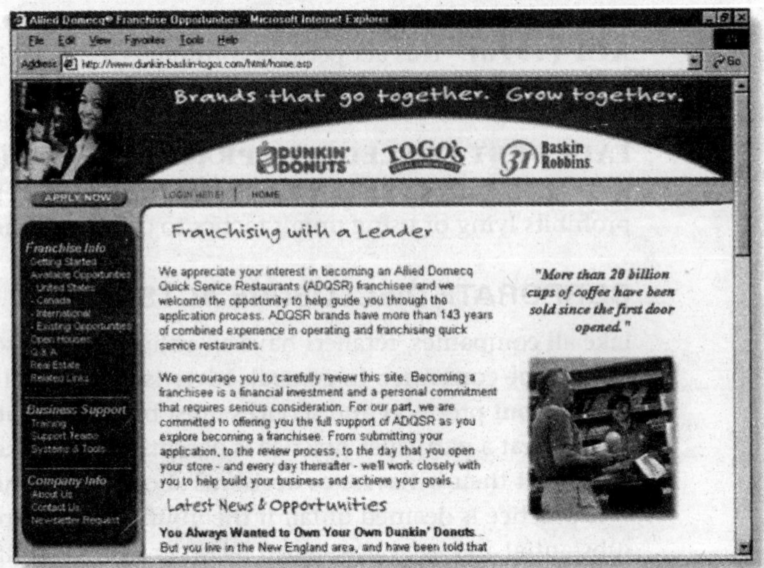

The franchise and business opportunity rule requires that franchisers give detailed information about their operations. Dunkin' Donuts™ and other franchisers use the Web as a source of information for potential investors. (Dunkin' Donuts trademark is owned by Allied Domcq Quick Service Restaurants and is used with permission.)

otherwise clearly and conspicuously stated. The statement has to be more than the typical "not all consumers will get the same results." Also, a testimonial or an endorsement cannot be made unless the advertiser can substantiate the claim and reveals any connections between the endorser and the company. For example, many actors providing testimonials must disclose whether they are getting paid for their testimonials.

WOOL AND TEXTILE PRODUCTS ACTS. These acts require companies to disclose country-of-origin information in all ads for textile and wool products. In addition, ads that say or imply anything about fiber content must disclose the generic fiber names in order of predominance by weight.

"MADE IN THE U.S.A." To be able to carry the label "Made in the U.S.A.," a product must be "all or virtually all made in the United States."

REGULATIONS SPECIFIC TO E-TAILING

Some laws and regulations apply more to e-tailers than to brick-and-mortar businesses. These are described in the following sections.

MAIL- OR TELEPHONE-ORDER MERCHANDISE RULE. This rule requires that e-tailers ship products as promised or within thirty days. If a business cannot ship when promised, it must notify the customer, who then has the right to cancel the order. The FTC frequently files suit against companies that are in violation of this rule. For example, the FTC filed a complaint against *Bargains & Deals Magazine* alleging that the company made misrepresentations over the Internet to sell merchandise and then either failed to deliver the products as promised or, in some cases, did not send the merchandise at all.[36]

CHILDREN'S ONLINE PRIVACY PROTECTION ACT (COPPA). This act makes it illegal to collect information from children under age thirteen without parental permission. Any company operating on the Internet that targets children must supply notice of its information collection practices, the type of information it collects, how it is used, parental permission prior to collection of personal information, and information on confidentiality of the information.[37]

GOVERNMENT RESPONSE TO VIOLATIONS OF LAWS

In July 2002, in response to the wave of ethical breaches by both retailers and e-tailers, President Bush signed a law designed to curtail corporate fraud. The Sarbanes-Oxley Act (also called the Business Fraud Bill) quadruples sentences for accounting fraud, imposes restrictions on accounting firms that do both consulting work and financial statement audits for the same corporation, requires company executives to personally vouch for the accuracy of their companies' reports, creates a new felony for securities fraud that carries a twenty-five-year prison term, places new restraints on corporate officers, and establishes a federal oversight board for the accounting industry. The new law is the greatest overhaul of corporate law since the aftermath of the 1929 stock market crash.[38,39]

As we have seen, there are many laws of which retailers must be aware. Smaller retailers typically monitor local, state, and national laws and determine which ones apply to them. Larger retailers typically have a legal department that handles all legal actions for and against the company.

SUMMARY

Many ethics, rules, and laws pertain to the operation of a retail business. The retailer must be aware of these laws and rules for every geographic area in which it competes. In addition to federal laws, the retailer must abide by regional and local rules and regulations that affect the business, as well as international laws if the retailer has global operations. Retailers engaged in interstate commerce come under the purview of federal laws. Retailers involved in intrastate commerce may also be subject to some federal laws and must answer to the state and locality where they do business.

Although the concepts of laws and ethics are related, they actually differ somewhat. Ethics involve concepts of what is right and wrong and are often based on moral and religious beliefs. Laws are rules established by society. Differences in ethical perspectives explain why different people can have differing views on whether an act is right or wrong. In retailing, ethical conflicts can arise from the conflict between profit and principles. Retailers are often under pressure to show profits, and this can cloud ethical judgments.

Employee and customer theft are the two biggest sources of inventory shrinkage. Retailers can reduce theft by implementing loss prevention strategies such as pre-employment screening, asset controls, supervision of the selling floor, and employing devices to deter theft. Internet fraud is a concern in e-tailing. Customers are especially concerned about the security of their online transactions.

There are several laws that affect retailing. Consequences for breaking these laws range from paying a fine to imprisonment. Retail laws have the greatest effect on retail tactics (pricing, integrated marketing communications, and customer service). Nonetheless, every area in the IRM flow chart has the potential to be affected by ethics and laws. The area where laws and ethics become most apparent is the situational analysis.

The ethical and legal environments have played, and will continue to play, an important role in the retail industry.

KEY TERMS

ethics (410)
law (410)
metaethics (410)
normative ethics (410)
applied ethics (410)
win-win perspective (414)
license to operate perspective (414)
acceptable profit perspective (414)
integrated perspective (414)
Internet fraud (419)
trademark (421)
servicemark (421)
horizontal agreement (425)
vertical agreement (425)
tie-in (425)

QUESTIONS FOR DISCUSSION

1. What is the difference between ethics and laws?
2. Explain the profit-principle relationship.
3. What are some ways to reduce the amount of employee theft in a retail outlet?
4. Why do you think there has been such a large increase in Internet fraud? What do you think can be done to reduce this fraud?
5. Explain the concept of a retail price maintenance agreement.
6. How do the laws that govern e-tailers differ from those governing brick-and-mortar retailers?
7. Why do you think horizontal agreements in retailing are restricted and sometimes illegal?
8. Do you believe the government should allow vertical agreements for businesses? Why or why not?

E-TAILING EXERCISE

There are many websites that discuss business and professional ethics. Choose three of the following sites to explore:

AccountAbility (*www.AccountAbility.org.uk*). AccountAbility is an organization that aims to promote social and ethical responsibility within the business community. It is composed of member organizations.

Applied Ethics Resources on the WWW (*www.ethics.ubc.ca/resources*). This site provides links to ethical resources in a variety of professions as well as links to business ethics and professional ethics sites.

Business for Social Responsibility (*www.bsr.org*). BSR is an organization composed of companies that wish to promote socially responsible business practices.

E-Center for Business Ethics (*e-businessethics.com*). This is a research center based at Colorado State University.

Ethical Trading Initiative (*www.ethicaltrade.org*). ETI is a nonprofit organization composed of companies, trade unions, and other organizations with the "aim of helping to make substantial improvements to the lives of poor working people around the world."

European Business Ethics Network (*www.eben.org*). EBEN is a nonprofit organization with the goal of promoting ethical business practices throughout Europe.

Institute for Global Ethics (*www.globalethics.org*). The Institute for Global Ethics is composed of educational institutions and research centers. The site contains publications, news items, and a fictional ethical dilemma.

International Business Ethics Institute (*www.business-ethics.org*). The IBEI is a nonprofit, educational organization that works to "foster global business practices that promote equitable economic development, resource sustainability and just forms of government."

International Society of Business, Economics, and Ethics (*www.synethos.org/ISBEE*). The ISBEE is "the first world-wide professional association to focus exclusively on the study of business, economics, and ethics."

Answer the following questions:

1. Do you think organizations that promote professional ethics are effective? Why or why not?
2. What should employees do when one of their colleagues or a company executive is being investigated for ethical violations?
3. Write your own code of ethics reflecting on what you expect from yourself in terms of ethical behavior.

Continuing Case 14.1

Sherwin-Williams Company: Facing Legal Issues

In late 2001, the attorney general for the state of Rhode Island, Sheldon Whitehouse, asked a judge to approve a plan that would allow the state to pursue a damage suit against many of the largest paint manufacturers and retailers. Whitehouse claimed that the companies were wrongfully selling lead-based paint. Sherwin-Williams was among those named as defendants in the case. Lawyers for Sherwin-Williams and other paint companies believed the state was placing blame at the wrong place and that the case, as stated by the attorney general, denied the paint companies their legal right to a fair trial.

The state of Rhode Island contends that 300,000 homes were contaminated by lead paint and 3,000 children had elevated levels of lead in their blood, with the number increasing each year. Lead has been found to cause developmental and learning problems in some children. According to the suit, 35,000 Rhode Island children have been poisoned by lead since 1993. Rhode Island is the first state to attempt to hold the paint industry responsible by claiming the paint created a public nuisance.

Sherwin-Williams argued that it was legal to sell the product and that lead paint is not harmful if properly maintained. In addition, Sherwin-Williams and the other defendants claimed that not all of the homes mentioned in the state's case had been identified. They pointed to a study by Brown University showing that only a limited number of homes were affected, not 300,000.

It was found later that two former attorneys general had worked with paint companies for years prior to the suit. In addition, state law in Rhode Island does not ban lead from housing; rather, it calls for lead-safe housing.

In May 2002, the judge decided to let the paint companies broaden their search for state records regarding the case, an action that the state had been opposing. The judge also ordered that the state allow the paint companies the right to interview as many state employees as they thought were relevant to the case as potential witnesses.

The case was tried, but the six-person jury failed to reach a unanimous verdict, and a mistrial was declared in November 2002. In January 2003, the case was sent to the Rhode Island superior court. It was also revealed in January 2002 that some of the 35,000 children diagnosed with lead poisoning were improperly diagnosed. At the time this book went to press, the case was waiting to be retried by the Rhode Island superior court. The outcome of the case is important not only because of potential monetary damages that Sherwin-Williams may incur, but also because the outcome could affect the company's reputation.

Questions

1. What do you think will be the outcome of this case?
2. Do you believe the state of Rhode Island is justified in pursuing this case? Why or why not?
3. Do you think the paint companies violated ethics or laws when selling the lead-based products prior to the 1970s?
4. If you were the public relations manager for Sherwin-Williams, how would you handle this situation?
5. If you were the judge, how would you rule in the case?

Sources: Peter B. Lord, "Paint Firms Allowed to Expand Records Search," *Providence Journal*, May 2, 2002, p. B3; Peter B. Lord, "Whitehouse Battles Paint Companies in Lead Case," *Providence Journal*, December 15, 2001, p. A3; Peter B. Lord, "Lead-Paint Defendants, Plaintiffs Seek Resolution," *Providence Journal*, January 22, 2003, p. B1; Amy Forliti, "Rhode Island to Begin Retrial of Lead Paint Industry in April," June 19, 2003, retrieved July 2003 from newsobserver.com.

Case 14.2

MCI and the Legal Environment

MCI (formerly known as WorldCom, Inc.) is the nation's second largest telecommunications firm, operating under the MCI brand. In July 2002, WorldCom filed Chapter 11 bankruptcy due in part to charges from the Securities and Exchange Commission (SEC) that it fraudulently counted $7.2 billion in costs as $7.2 billion in capital expenditures. Chapter 11 bankruptcy allows a company to continue business operations while it develops a plan for reorganization.

At the time of the bankruptcy, WorldCom employed about 60,000 people in 65 countries and served more than 20 million residential and business customers. MCI, the number two long-distance carrier in the United States, was one of the business units owned by WorldCom. WorldCom eventually entered a settlement with the SEC in which WorldCom neither admitted to nor denied the allegations but promised not to violate securities laws in the future. In 2003, WorldCom, Inc., in an effort to leave scandal behind, changed its name to MCI and moved its headquarters from Mississippi to Virginia. Prior to being called WorldCom, the company name was MCI WorldCom.

This isn't the first time WorldCom has come under scrutiny for suspicious business practices. In 2000, WorldCom agreed to pay a $3.5 million slamming fine. (Slamming is the practice of switching a consumer's long-distance carrier without his or her consent.) According to the Federal Trade Commission, there were 2,900 consumer complaints against the company (then known as MCI WorldCom). In April 2002, WorldCom agreed to pay $8.5 million to settle another slamming lawsuit brought by the state of California. Although these fines served as a wake-up call for other telecommunications companies, the practice of slamming has not stopped. Several other companies are currently under investigation for slamming, including WebNet Communications, Inc.; One Call Communications, Inc.; and Sprint Corporation.

On July 29, 2002, WorldCom announced the delisting of its securities from the NASDAQ. In response to claims by competitors that the company inappropriately handled access fees, MCI issued a press release dated July 28, 2003. In the press release, Michael D. Capellas, MCI chairman and chief executive officer, states: "We have a zero-tolerance policy, and if any wrongdoing is discovered, you can be certain that we will take appropriate action swiftly." As a result of WorldCom's offenses, as well as other corporate scandals, the Sarbanes-Oxley Act was enacted. This act holds CEOs and CFOs personally accountable for the integrity of their companies' financial reports.

Questions

1. List the stakeholders affected by WorldCom's actions. How are they affected?
2. Why would a company like MCI employ slamming practices or engage in financial statement fraud?
3. Do you think a CEO and other executives should be held personally liable for financial statement fraud? Why or why not?
4. Should the government get involved in corporate ethical matters? Why or why not?

Contributing author: Laurel Brown, team member, general accounting, D&B Shared Services.

Sources: Yochi J. Dreazen, " 'Slamming' Complaints to FCC Increase by 31%," *Wall Street Journal,* October 16, 2002, p. D2; "WorldCom, Inc. Announces Delisting by NASDAQ of Its Securities," company press release, July 29, 2002, retrieved December 2002 from www.mci.com; "FCC Action Nets Highest Slamming Payment Ever—MCI, WorldCom to Pay $3.5 Million," *FCC News,* June 6, 2000, retrieved December 2002 from www.fcc.gov; "FCC Proposes $1,200,000 Fine Against WebNet for Slamming Violations," *FCC News,* June 20, 2002, retrieved from www.fcc.gov; Rebecca Blumenstein, "WorldCom to Pay $3.5 Million 'Slamming' Fine," *Wall Street Journal,* June 7, 2000, p. A4; "MCI Responds to Competitors' Claims," press release dated July 28, 2003, retrieved July 2003 from mci.com.

Diversity and Trends in Retailing

Chapter 15

Progress is impossible without change; and those who cannot change their minds, cannot change anything.
George Bernard Shaw, Nobel laureate in literature, 1925

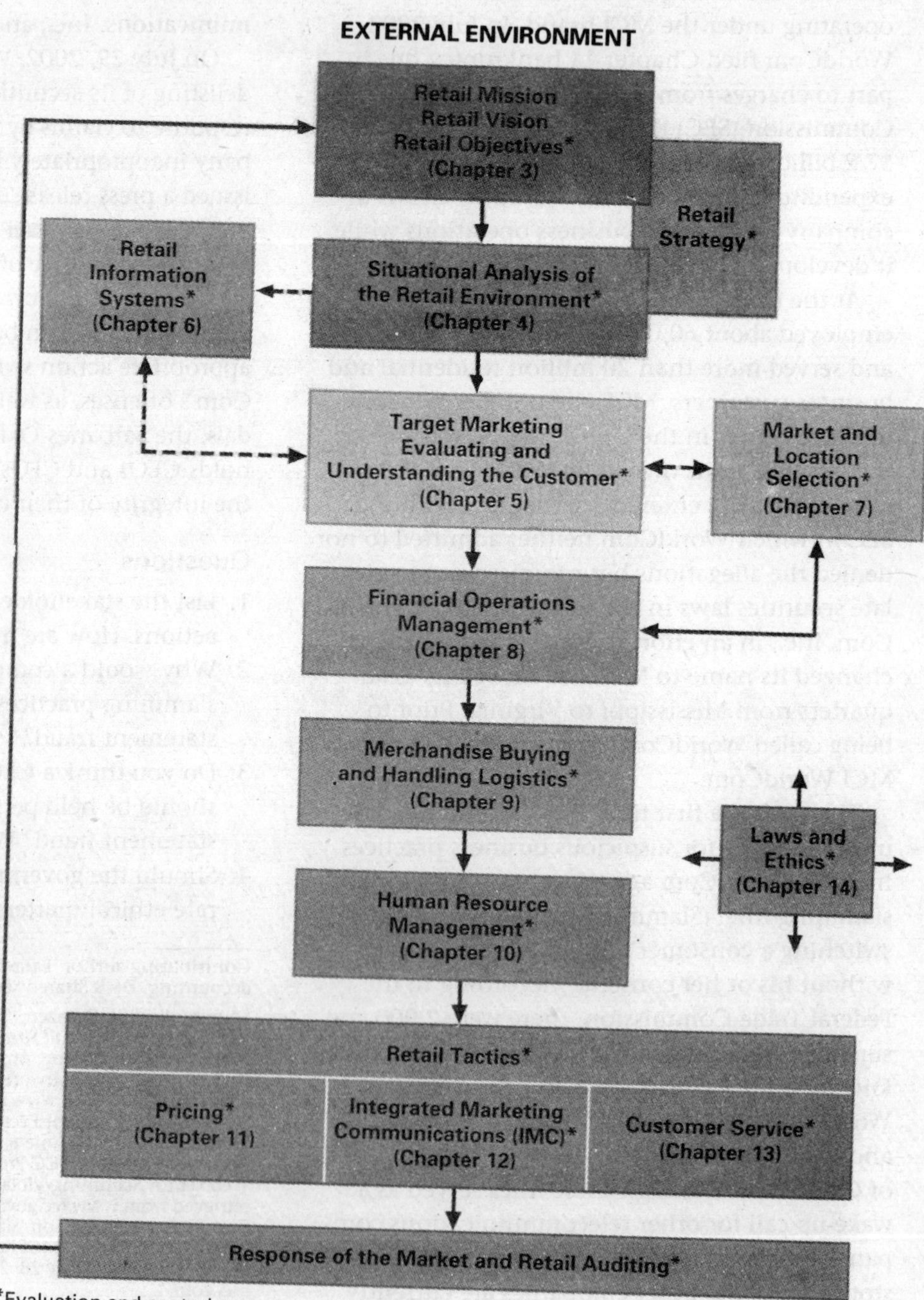

*Evaluation and control occurs at all these stages.

CHAPTER OBJECTIVES

After completing this chapter, you will be able to:

1. Explain the benefits of a diverse work force.
2. Outline current trends in retailing.
3. Describe some best practices in the retail environment.
4. Apply the integrated retail management flow chart to a hypothetical retail outlet.

Fannie Mae Ranked One of the Best Companies for Minorities

Fortune magazine publishes various lists on a yearly basis. In its ranking of the nation's fifty best companies for minorities, Fannie Mae, the leader in home financing in the United States, has ranked no lower than fourth place for the six years *Fortune* has been compiling the list. Most recently, Fannie Mae ranked number two.[1] In 2002, the company ranked number one.[2]

Many factors have contributed to Fannie Mae's success in this area. For example, the company incorporates diversity into its overall strategy. According to Franklin Raines, chairman and CEO, "Our diversity initiatives are underscored by a commitment to create a workforce that at all levels, including senior management, looks like America. It's a principle that permeates every aspect of how we do business."[3]

The company has also created a number of programs that serve as "best practices." Programs include a mandatory diversity training course for all employees, diversity training for its lender customers, hosting regular benchmarking sessions for other employers that want to strengthen their diversity efforts, creation of a Diversity Toolkit (available on the company's website, *www.fanniemae.com*), a corporate mentoring program, assistance for college education, and a diversity supplier program.[4] Fannie Mae serves as a role model for other companies that want to enhance their diversity management efforts.

INTRODUCTION

The first fourteen chapters of this book covered issues and systems involved in developing an effective IRM plan. This chapter highlights current and future issues that will both challenge and excite retailers in the twenty-first century. Each topic covered affects the situational analysis of the flow chart, as well as the retailer's strategies and tactics.

What should a retailer expect in these changing times? What innovations are on the horizon? Discussed in this chapter are the evolving U.S. demographics, which have altered the retail landscape. Trends in retailing are highlighted and best practices discussed. This chapter also provides an example of the development and execution of integrated retail management by a hypothetical retailer.

Many environmental issues influence the IRM program. A retailer's effective response to these issues will contribute to its success. One such issue is diversity in the retail environment.

DIVERSITY IN THE RETAIL WORK FORCE

diversity Differences among people, including but not limited to age, gender, ethnicity, race, and ability.

leveraging diversity The practice of seeking out different voices and viewing them as opportunities for added value.

equal employment opportunity (EEO) laws Laws that collectively prohibit discrimination on the basis of color, race, sex, religion, national origin, age, or physical disability.

affirmative action (AA) Programs that address conditions that systematically disadvantage individuals based on group identities such as gender or race.

Diversity is defined as differences among people. These differences include but are not limited to age, gender, ethnicity, race, and ability. **Leveraging diversity** occurs when different voices are sought out and viewed as opportunities for added value. Different perspectives and frames of reference have been proven to offer competitive advantages in teamwork, product quality, and work output.[5]

Numerous laws have been passed to foster diversity in the workplace. **Equal employment opportunity (EEO) laws** collectively prohibit discrimination on the basis of color, race, sex, religion, national origin, age, or physical disability. **Affirmative action (AA)** addresses conditions that systematically disadvantage individuals based on group identities such as gender or race.

Given the changing American ethnicity demographic, retailers need to pay increasing attention to the issue of diversity in the retail work force. Figure 15.1 gives a view of the projected growth of the four largest ethnic groups in the United States.

Based on U.S. Census Bureau counts, the following is the demographic breakdown of the United States: of the 288.4 million people, 196.8 million (68.2%) are white (non-Hispanic); 38.8 million (13.5%) are Hispanic; 35.3 million (12.2%) are Black or African American (non-Hispanic); 11.3 million (3.9%) are Asian (non-Hispanic); 2.2 million (.76%) are American Indian or Alaska Native (non-Hispanic); and .4 million (.14%) are Native Hawaiian and other Pacific Islander (non-Hispanic).[6] Because Hispanics can be of any race the breakdown includes the term *non-Hispanic,* to show that Hispanics have been taken out of the count for that category. As the United States moves toward a population with lower percentages of whites and higher percentages

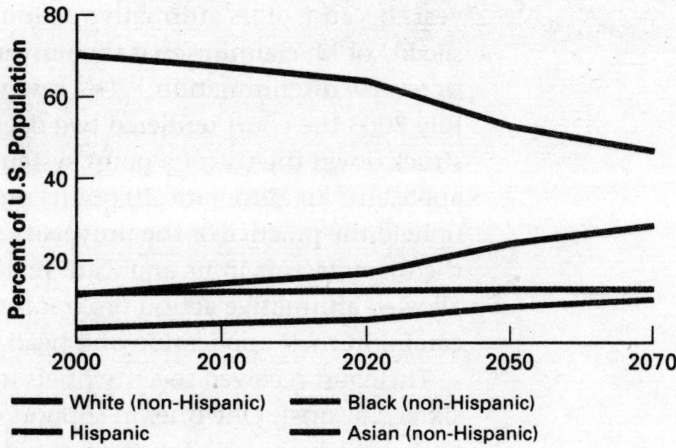

FIGURE 15.1 **Projected Growth of Selected U.S. Subcultures** Source: Compiled based on data from the U.S. Census Bureau, Population Division, retrieved July 2003 from www.census.gov.

of Hispanics, African Americans, and Asians, it becomes essential for businesses to manage diversity well.

In addition to ethnic and racial changes, the growth of the 50-plus age group is a trend that will change the retail landscape. In 2003, there were 78 million people in the 50-plus age group in the United States,[7] representing about 27 percent of the total population. Projections indicate that by 2015, 45 percent of the population will be in the 50-plus category. Retailers will have to pay attention to this group—because of its size, but also because it is wealthier than younger populations. Combined, people in the 50-plus category own about 75 percent of the country's financial assets and represent 50 percent of the discretionary spending power.[8]

Retailers will need to become competent at managing diversity, keep abreast of changes in the U.S. demographic profile, and determine how these changes will alter their strategy.[9]

AFFIRMATIVE ACTION

Although there were early economic incentives for a diverse work force, many companies chose not to have one. Consequently, the federal government passed the Civil Rights Act of 1964, which prohibited employment discrimination by companies with more than fifteen employees and established the Equal Employment Opportunity Commission (EEOC). In 1965, President Lyndon B. Johnson signed an executive order requesting all government contractors and subcontractors to take "affirmative action" to expand job opportunities for minorities.[10] Women were also included in a 1967 order. Under affirmative action, among equally qualified candidates, those from underrepresented groups may be favored over those from overrepresented groups.

Affirmative action has sparked much controversy over the years, with numerous lawsuits related to discrimination as well as reverse discrimination. The University of Michigan (U of M) has been in the spotlight for several years because of its affirmative action policies. In 1997, three white students sued U of M, claiming that the university's racial preference programs resulted in reverse discrimination.[11] The case went to the U.S. Supreme Court, and in July 2003 the court rendered two decisions. In the first decision, the court struck down the use of a point system that awarded minority undergraduate applicants an automatic 20 points on a 150-point scale. The second decision upheld the practice of the university's law school of considering race as one of the many factors in its applicant review process.[12] In essence, the ruling allowed affirmative action programs to continue as long as universities are careful in their application and head toward race-neutral alternatives.

The court received seventy briefs in support of affirmative action and sixteen against. One brief in support came from sixty-five *Fortune* 500 corporations, which argued that diverse student enrollments aid businesses in achieving a diverse workforce—a requirement to compete globally.[13]

Acceptance of the programs related to AA has depended on how the particular business presents the programs. A recent trend in the recruitment of members of underrepresented groups is to focus on the business case for diversity instead of the underrepresentation argument.

THE BUSINESS CASE FOR DIVERSITY. The business case for diversity centers on the premise that a company will be more profitable if it has a work force that mirrors the demographics of the environment. The U.S. Census Bureau estimates that 90 percent of total population growth from 1995 to 2050 will be among blacks, Hispanics, Asians and Pacific Islanders, and Native Americans.[14] A retailer's understanding of the implications of increased diversity in the work force (and in the customer base) will, hopefully, translate into increased sales.

Customers prefer to purchase products from people to whom they can relate. As an example, the impetus for change in a then *Fortune* Service 500

Changing demographics in the United States are leading to retailers hiring employees and having customers who are ethnically and racially diverse.

The Multicultural Food-service and Hospitality Alliance (MFHA) is an organization formed to promote diversity and deal with diversity issues in the food-service and hospitality industries.
(Courtesy of Multicultural Foodservice and Hospitality Alliance, © 2003.)

company resulted from listening to its customers' request for a more diverse personnel base. The company had sent out a team of salespeople to try to create a relationship with a potentially large client. When the team came back to the corporate office, one of the vice presidents got a call from the client, who asked why the office had not sent out a team of salespeople who "looked" like the client, or at least people to whom the client could relate. The vice president realized that the group he had sent was representative of the company rather than of the client and that the company lacked a broad, diverse personnel base from which to select its sales teams. This incident made the company realize that without a diverse work force it would lose sales; that realization led to a major thrust toward diversity.

In addition to improving a retailer's bottom line, diversity initiatives help the company avoid future corporate complications. A poll of *Fortune* 1000 executives about their diversity initiatives showed decreases in complaints and litigation as one of the top benefits of diversity programs.[15] Some retailers learned this lesson the hard way. For example, in the early 1990s, the Denny's restaurant chain was sued by a group of black customers for racial discrimination. The company eventually settled the lawsuit for about $54 million. The lawsuit forced Denny's Corporation (formerly Advantica Restaurant Group) to examine its treatment of customers and its hiring practices. Since then, Denny's has become a model for its diversity initiatives. Other companies, such as Texaco and Coca-Cola, have also settled lawsuits and have changed their hiring practices for the better.[16]

Organizations, generally serving companies within particular industries, have formed to promote diversity and deal with diversity issues. One such organization is the Multicultural Foodservice and Hospitality Alliance (MFHA; *www.mfha.net*).[17] Its goal is to be an educator, facilitator, and source of information on multiculturalism in its industry.

RECRUITMENT

Retailers should develop a personnel base that mirrors their current and potential target markets. Thus, for an international retailer, employees should mirror the populations of the countries where the retailer does business. A retailer conducting business in Asia, for example, will improve its chances for success if it employs Asians. For domestic companies, the retailer's personnel should mirror the basic U.S. or regional population base. For example, for a retailer located in a city with a large population of Hispanics, hiring employees with Hispanic backgrounds can be a competitive advantage.[18]

A common misunderstanding about diversity programs is that they are designed to benefit only women and "minorities." Diversity encompasses not only differences in gender, skin color, and ethnicity but also differences in religion, age, sexual orientation, and varying physical and mental abilities. The goal of diversity programs should be to offer a work environment that fosters growth and encourages each individual to thrive. Mary Jane Sinclair of Sinclair Consulting Inc. suggests that instead of just talking about "minorities," companies focus on an inclusive culture. An *inclusive culture* "welcomes what everyone can contribute."[19]

According to Sandy Kennedy, president of the International Mass Retail Association, "retail, in its simplest form, is about relationships. For retailers, the most important are the relationships with their customers and employees. Indeed, one of the most significant challenges faced by retail today may not be the drive for market share, but how to retain, attract, and develop human capital."[20] Retailers must examine their recruitment methods and benefits. A workplace offering benefits that appeal to a diverse group of people will attract more diverse employees. For example, a trend among companies is to offer domestic-partner and other family-friendly benefits. More than 2,500 employers provide domestic-partner benefits, including corporations, local governments, and 121 of the *Fortune* 500 companies.[21] Family-friendly policies include such programs as child care and elder care.

In summary, all employees and customers have different needs and wants. The goal of leveraging diversity should be based on this principle, and retailers need to develop methods of diversity management that adhere to it. Retailers must create a corporate culture that includes the development of a broad and diverse employee base. Diversity management should include programs that allow for continuous training of employees, support groups or mentoring programs that facilitate diversity, career development programs that focus on diversity issues, and promotional programs that include diverse ideas and populations.[22]

TRENDS IN RETAILING

There are many global trends that will affect the retail industry. The World Future Society reports that future trends focus on economic, environmental, and societal issues.[23] Just as demographics are changing the retailing environment, so are these three types of influences. A retailer should keep the following trends in mind when creating and maintaining the IRM flow chart.

ECONOMIC TRENDS

In terms of economic trends, improved manufacturing technology will continue to boost productivity and reduce the unit cost of goods. The labor market will remain tight, meaning retailers will need to be creative in their hiring methods. The growth of information industries is creating a knowedge-dependent, global society. A positive trend is that the "digital divide" is getting smaller as more and more minority populations own computers. This means that e-tailing will continue to grow as small businesses gain the ability to compete on an equal footing with large retailers.

ENVIRONMENTAL TRENDS

Trends concerning the environment center around new technology to lessen reliance on oil as a natural resource. Retailers of gas and oil may face consumer dissatisfaction as prices rise. Alternative energy sources will be explored to keep prices stable. People around the world are becoming increasingly concerned about environmental issues such as air pollution and recycling. This means that legislation addressing the environment may increase. Retailers may need to become more proactive in protecting the environment, turning their attention from the here-and-now to the future.

SOCIETAL TRENDS

Societal trends deal with two major issues: the growth of the world's population and the lengthening lifespans of people in developed countries. Implications for retailers include growth in the health care industry and a wealth of new products geared toward an increasingly older population. Costs of health

Many consumers are concerned with environmental issues such as pollution and recycling. To address these concerns, retailers may need to become more active in protecting the environment.

care are expected to rise and may create a crisis in health-care financing and services. As the senior population expands, there will be a need for doctors specializing in diseases of the elderly. The nursing shortage will become even more apparent by 2020, when many baby boomers will have retired. There is certainly an expansive market for retailers interested in capitalizing on the aging-population trend.

Another societal trend deals with gender. An estimated 57 percent of American college students are women.[24] As more educated women enter the work force and fill higher-level positions, an increase in child-care and other family care businesses is likely. There will be a greater need than ever before for services and businesses that can accommodate this trend.

THE CHANGING RETAIL ENVIRONMENT

Profound changes are taking place, and will continue to occur, in the retail industry.[25,26] It has been suggested that a comprehensive definition of retailing needs to be developed to help identify the changing retailing environment of the future: "Unless there is at least a modicum of agreement as to what constitutes retailing, its boundaries (*e.g.*, financial, industrial, behavioral) will remain amorphous and elusive."[27] Academic researchers Robert Peterson and Sridhar Balasubramanian contend that without an adequate definition of retailing for the twenty-first century, knowledge about retailing will evolve in a piecemeal, unorganized fashion.[28]

Although the future is difficult to predict, forthcoming trends in retailing will focus on demographics, geographic convenience, time convenience, increased food expenditures away from home, and rapid changes in information technology. In addition, retailers will find a convergence of electronic methods and traditional methods of retailing.

In terms of sales, the retail landscape is moving away from specialty stores and department stores toward discount retailing. Discount retailing will continue to grow in the United States, Europe, Japan, and other industrialized nations.[29] Even though travel declined after the September 2001 attack on the World Trade Center, airport retailing will continue to grow as passengers spend more time and money shopping in terminals.[30]

BEST PRACTICES IN RETAILING

Although there is a lack of definitive data on the future of retailing (some cannot even agree on a proper definition of *retailing*), many recent findings on best practices in retailing will have an impact on decision making in the management of a retail operation. Figure 15.2 provides a checklist of best practices for the retailing industry.

The H. R. Chally Group has also identified several best-practice areas used by world-class sales organizations.[31] These areas include customer-centric cultures; market segmentation; market adaptability; information technology; customer feedback and satisfaction; sales, service, and technical support systems;

- ❑ Operate effectively as Internet-based retailers (e-tailers).
- ❑ Create and ensure brand relevance with targeted customers.
- ❑ Leverage global scale and global best practices while understanding and responding to local needs.
- ❑ Maximize supply chain value through global sourcing.
- ❑ Leverage information systems and business processes for greatest effectiveness and synergies with suppliers.
- ❑ Identify the new frontier new market spaces.
- ❑ Develop clear strategy that drives behavior for every person in the organization.
- ❑ Operate distribution like a unique business unit.
- ❑ Deliver the right customer experience consistently; a consistent, well-designed customer experience shifts the basis of competition from product and price to total value.
- ❑ Excel in relatively few areas strategically selected to create a competitive advantage (and more effectively allocate organizational resources/capabilities).
- ❑ Utiltize business partnering.

FIGURE 15.2 **Checklist for Best Practices in the Retail Industry** Sources: "Global Retailing in the Connected Economy," *Chain Store Age,* December 1999; William N. Goff, "Borrow the Best: Eight Lessons for Field Managers from World-Class Giants," *The National Underwriter,* 105:12 (2001).

and selecting and developing sales and marketing personnel. Each of these areas has relevance for retailing.

CUSTOMER-CENTRIC CULTURES

customer-centric culture An active philosophy within a company that focuses on meeting the needs of individual consumers rather than those of the mass market.

Customer-centric cultures require the creation of a performance-driven culture that is focused on individual consumers rather than the mass market.[32] Activities aimed at shifting the focus to individual customers include the adoption of a relationship or partnership business model with shared rewards and risk management, redefining the selling role in terms of consulting with customers and solving their problems, becoming more proactive in consumer education (teaching customers about value chains and cost reduction strategies), and focusing on continuous-improvement processes.[33]

Retailers will continue to rely on customization to increase sales and gain customer loyalty. For example, Bath Junki, a franchise specialty shop in Richmond Heights, Missouri, allows customers to create their own lotions, soaps, and body washes by mixing and matching up to 160 different fragrances. In 2000, Nike, Inc. created the Nike iD website, which allows users to design their own athletic shoes. Lands' End also utilizes a technological customization approach. Customers can create online models that resemble themselves.

Customer-centric companies focus on the individual versus the mass market. The Ritz-Carlton chain of hotels has been praised for its customer-service and relationship-building practices.

They can then dress the models to determine how various items of clothing will look on them.[34] All of these initiatives demonstrate a true customer-centric culture.

MARKET SEGMENTATION

We explored the practice of market segmentation in Chapter 13, which focuses on customer service. Retail segmentation appears to be leaning toward the development of a system that creates segments based on how the customers prefer to buy their products.[35] Some customers prefer distance in the customer-retailer relationship; others want to develop longer-lasting relationships or obtain solutions to problems. It is important for retailers to recognize and nurture relationships when customers are receptive.

market adaptability Retailers' knowledge about environmental changes and their ability to react to these changes in a way that benefits both the retailer and the consumer.

MARKET ADAPTABILITY

Market adaptability refers to retailers' knowledge about environmental changes and their ability to react to these changes in a way that benefits both

INTERNET IN ACTION

Retail Sector Outperforms Others in Respect Survey of Online Companies

CustomerRespect.com, a division of International Ventures Research, conducted a study benchmarking attributes of customer respect that a company exhibits through its online site. The *Fortune* 100 corporate websites were examined to determine what attribute combinations resulted in the best online experiences for customers. The key areas defining customer respect were

- Privacy (respects customer privacy)
- Principles (values and respects customer data)
- Attitude ("body language" of site)
- Transparency (open and honest policies)
- Simplicity (customer-focused, usable site)
- Responsiveness (quick and thorough responses to inquiries)

The study found that when these attributes are not practiced, customers become frustrated. CustomerRespect.com developed a Customer Respect Index, a qualitative and quantitative measure of a customer's online experience when interacting with companies via the Internet. The firm's "Online Customer Respect Study" is the first report to bring objective measures and science to online interactions from the customer's perspective.

Of the twelve industries studied, the retail sector scored highest overall. Surveyed retailers included Wal-Mart, Home Depot, Kroger, Target, Albertson's, Kmart, Costco, Safeway, JCPenney, Walgreens, CVS, Lowe's, and Sears, Roebuck. The highest-ranked retailer was Costco (9.2), and the lowest was CVS (5.5). Retailers' average score was 7.8, whereas the overall average was 6.5. According to Donal Daly, CEO of CustomerRespect.com, companies should try to get a score of at least 8.5 to show they are truly meeting customer needs.

Sources: "Retail Sector Outperforms All Others in 2002 Online Customer Respect Study of *Fortune* 100 Web Sites," press release, November 5, 2002, retrieved December 2002 from www.customerrespect.com; "Retail Leads in Knowing How to Relate to Customers over the Web, Study Says," *Internet Retailer*, October 25, 2002 (www.internetretailer.com); Scarlet Pruitt, "Online Shoppers Get No Respect," *PCWorld*, October 28, 2002 (www.pcworld.com).

the retailer and the consumer. Critical components of adaptability include decentralizing decision making to more quickly adapt to consumer needs, streamlining processes, focusing on core competencies, implementing the free exchange of information, and developing reward systems based on responsiveness to customers.[36]

INFORMATION TECHNOLOGY

Information technology (IT) will continue to play a major role in developing competitive advantage in retailing. Best practices in the IT area include an emphasis on market and customer tracking, and leveraging IT to create and solidify retailer-customer relationships.[37]

The movement in IT in retailing is toward "rocket science retailing," described as a blend of employee intuition and the power of information technology.[38] Four critical areas in rocket science retailing are (1) demand forecasting, (2) supply chain speed, (3) inventory planning, and (4) data gathering and organization.[39] In addition, standardization of applications and integration of various IT systems are very important undertakings for retailers.[40]

U.S. Retail IT Spending Forecast, 2003–2007, a report by IDC, a global market intelligence and advisory firm, noted that IT spending in the retail industry is projected to increase. The increase is expected to reach $29.6 billion by 2007, which represents a five-year compound annual growth rate of 5.3 percent.[41]

In 2003, Keynote Systems, a Web performance monitoring company in San Mateo, California, introduced the Keynote Consumer E-Commerce Transaction Index, the retail industry's first Internet transaction performance benchmarking index.[42] The index offers retailers an improved method of evaluating Internet retail performance relative to direct competitors instead of a cross-section of general business sites. Powerhouse e-tailers such as Amazon, eBay, Barnes & Noble, Target, Wal-Mart, JCPenney, Sears, Nordstrom, Neiman Marcus, and L. L. Bean make up the index.

CUSTOMER FEEDBACK AND SATISFACTION

Customer feedback and satisfaction remain important areas of best practices. The use of feedback systems will increase the value of customer concerns and allow retailers to better understand their changing customer segments. To be effective, feedback must be systematic and timely.[43] Best practices include involving customers in the measurement processes and sharing customer feedback throughout the organization.[44]

SALES, SERVICE, AND TECHNICAL SUPPORT SYSTEMS

The benchmark for sales, service, and technical support systems is applying the tools of total quality management to enhance the customer's perception of quality with regard to his or her overall shopping or service experience.[45] According to the Chally Group, best practices include building specialized sales approaches for each target market, separating marketing functions from logistics functions, and streamlining flows in the sales cycle.[46] In addition, retailers must utilize new sales and support technologies. All retailing functions must be integrated and focused on understanding customers' sales and technical support needs.

SELECTING AND DEVELOPING SALES PERSONNEL

Selecting and developing sales personnel are vital to the retailer's success. The emphasis will be on the need to upgrade the competency, as well as the commitment, of sales personnel on a long-term basis. More and more companies are using multiple-channel systems, cross-functional teams, and global/strategic account managers. Because these trends require new-skills-based employees, retailers should consider shifting from a job-based model of retailing human resource management to a competency-based perspective.[47,48] According to Edward E. Lawler, "Instead of thinking of people as having a job with a particular set of activities that can be captured in a relatively permanent and fixed job description, it may be more appropriate and more effective to think of them as human resources that work for an organization."[49]

FIVE PILLARS OF RETAILING

In an article from the *Harvard Business Review,* Leonard Berry describes five important actions for retailers.[50] These actions, deemed pillars, sound simple but are often difficult to implement:

1. Solve your customers' problems.
2. Treat customers with respect.
3. Connect with your customers' emotions.
4. Set the fairest (not the lowest) price.
5. Save your customers' time.

Retailers should always keep these pillars in mind when conducting business. As the work force becomes more diverse and the retail environment continues to change, consumers' needs are rapidly changing. Retailers must prepare for the challenges ahead and pay particular attention to this evolving consumer. In addition to following the five pillars, a good grasp of consumer trends is essential for retailer success.

SIX FACES OF THE CHANGING CUSTOMER

In an editorial for the Center for Retailing Studies, two authors looked at trends within the retailing industry. By conducting an in-depth study of these trends, the authors were able to project what they believe will be the major trends for retailers, called the "six faces of the changing customer."[51] The following paragraphs briefly describe these trends.

1. Composite Nation Understanding the diverse base of consumers is increasingly important. Although diversity has always been a part of the environment, its magnitude continues to intensify. Culture, race, and ethnicity and the changing composition of the family are just a few aspects of diversity that the retailer must consider.

2. Cueless Customers As consumers become more complex and multidimensional, they can defy all familiar assumptions. Thus, there is a movement away from past methods of research to "gauge" the customer. Today's retailers need more advanced segmentation tools to help them understand the changes in their customer bases.

3. Consumer Power Shift Information is becoming increasingly available to consumers. The Internet has made comparison shopping easier. This information has empowered consumers to demand fairness in their transactions. In addition, consumers are placing more value on their time and thus are increasingly intolerant of retailers that do not respect their time. In general, consumers are more demanding and seek ways to control the shopping situation. As a result, consumers may become less store loyal and more willing to go elsewhere to shop when their demands are not met.

4. Stimulation and Sanctuary Because consumers have less time, they want to get the most out of the time they do have. In addition, consumers have developed a desire for more speed and excitement. On the other hand, consumers also want to be left alone *when* they choose to be left alone. In other words, consumers will want both greater stimulation and greater sanctuary. It is up to the retailer to satisfy those wants.

5. Amorphous Codes and Spaces Because of increasing diversity and the redefinition of households, consumers are creating new "codes" or norms from which to operate. Although some carryover from past norms exists, new norms are slowly replacing many older norms, paving the way for new values. Thus, consumers have new codes of conduct and create norms and behaviors from situation to situation as they reinvent themselves.

6. Communities Everywhere Consumers value communities more and more, although the faces of those communities are changing. Consumers will seek diverse and nontraditional communities from which to operate. There will be an increase in online communities as well as in neighborhood associations, self-help groups, church groups, and volunteer groups.

RETAILERS' RESPONSES TO THE CHANGING CUSTOMER

Retailers will need to alter their way of thinking to adjust to the changing customer. Recently, five new values have been suggested for retailers.[52]

1. Customer Respect as Central, Not Tangential, to Success Retailers must strive to show respect for their individual customers. They must demonstrate respect for individualism and personal differences such as ethnicity, sexual orientation, and differing abilities. Retailers that convey the appropriate level of respect will experience an increase in customer loyalty and sales.

2. Soul of the Customer, Not Superficial Understanding Retailers must get to know the *real* customer. The traditional segmentation categories will become useless if they are not changed to reflect a more genuine customer understanding. Thus, retailers must dig deep to learn who their customers are, so they can develop viable customer segments.

3. Customer Enthusiasm, Not Just Satisfaction Retailers will have to engage the customer to create a passion for the retail outlet. The old marketing concept will need to be modified from satisfying customers to "wowing" customers.

4. Customers Customize, Not Retailers Retailers will have to create infrastructures that allow their patrons to customize their retail shopping experiences. This will allow each customer to get the value he or she wants from the shopping experience.

5. Community Leadership, Not Participation Retailers need to be leaders in creating and interacting with the communities where they do business. They must be perceived as leaders in the community, not just members.

Blunders or Best Practices?

Online Grocers Benefit from Niche Retailing

Niche retailing is one of the trends emerging as a best practice. According to Don Schultz, professor of integrated marketing communications (IMC) at Northwestern University, niche retailers are specialists that, while offering limited selections, expand services and facilities.

One area where niche retailing may be an appropriate strategy is online grocery markets. The online grocery market appeals to a very small segment, namely convenience-oriented, upscale shoppers. Some online grocers target tourists, whereas others target consumers who don't own vehicles and are willing to pay a premium for delivery.

While the majority of direct-delivery companies have failed, competition in the online grocery industry is growing. Some large supermarket chains, such as Albertson's and Safeway, have developed their own online grocery delivery services. One trend is for an established brick-and-mortar grocer to acquire an ailing online grocer. For example, retail giant Royal Ahold acquired Peapod to save Peapod from bankruptcy. Many grocers across the United States and Canada have introduced Web-based delivery services that allow customers to place orders from their cellphones. Only time will tell if online grocery retailing will expand on a larger scale.

Sources: Don E. Schultz, "Another Turn of the Wheel," *Marketing Management,* March–April 2002, pp. 8–9; Lisa Biank Fasig, "Peapod Bringing Shop-at-Home Market to City," *Providence Journal,* October 24, 2002, p. E1; David Goll, "Safeway Looks Online to Pump up Q4 Sales," *East Bay Business Times,* October 25, 2002, p. 5; Gary L. Geissler, "Targeting Tourists: An Exploratory Study of a Proposed Online Grocery Delivery Service," *Journal of Vacation Marketing* (London), June 2002, pp. 277–286.

The future of retailing is truly exciting. Many changes will occur in retail institutions. There are indications that the face of retailing as we currently know it will not be around in the future. In addition, trends point toward a dramatic change in the typical retail customer. A key characteristic that separates successful businesses from failures is the capacity to respond to change. Companies that thrive in the face of a volatile environment are adaptive in their infrastructures, processes, and philosophy.[53] It is imperative that new retail owners and managers develop comprehensive and integrated plans to deal with these issues.

APPLICATION: THE IRM FLOW CHART

The IRM flow chart can provide retail managers with tools to create greater efficiency and competitiveness in the retail arena. Thus, the IRM flow chart provides a best-practice tool for current and aspiring retail managers. This section illustrates the use of the IRM flow chart for a new retail store for Z-Tech, Inc. (doing business as Z-Coil). The particular store in this application is fictitious, but we use information from a real-world company (Z-Tech) as a basis for the plan's development.

BACKGROUND

Dean, Don, and Denise (aka "the partners") are seeking to open a retail outlet. After assessing the market area, the partners have decided to sell pain-relief footwear and have chosen Z-Tech, Inc. as their supplier. To effectively compete in the marketplace, the partners have determined that the IRM flow chart would be the best planning tool to use. They have adapted and modified the flow chart to make sure it is a good fit for their operations.

RETAIL MISSION AND VISION

The first step is to ascertain that the supplier's (Z-Tech) and retail partners' mission and vision are synergistic. The partners have decided to use Z-Tech's "belief statement" as a launching point for their own mission and vision statement, because this statement will guide the overall development of an IRM plan for the shoe store.

The following information was abridged and modified from Z-Tech's belief statement, "Changing the Way the World Walks" (2000):

> We're not interested in being a different kind of Shoe Company. We are interested in helping people enjoy life on their feet: running, walking, working, or just standing around. . . . We're on a mission to change the way you walk.

Utilizing this initial mission and vision statement, the partners created their own:

> We're on a mission to change the way our customers walk. We believe in relieving our customers' foot pain; thus, we sell shoes for pain relief. It is our vision that all of our customers will experience more comfort and less pain with their Z-Coil shoes. At the same time, we are committed to providing business partners with a return on their investment.

SITUATIONAL ANALYSIS AND INTEGRATION OF A RETAIL INFORMATION SYSTEM

Because retailers operate in a world of constant change and increasingly available technology, the partners will utilize a retail information system (RIS) to facilitate the integration of all areas of retailing. After completing an external environmental analysis, the partners selected Jacksonville, Florida, as the physical site for the retail operation.

Jacksonville was chosen based on a number of criteria. First, there are currently no other Z-Coil dealers in the Jacksonville area. Second, a number of skilled laborers are available for hire. Third, the demographic profile of Florida, and of Jacksonville in particular, indicates a large elderly population. (See Figure 15.3 for regions of the United States with large elderly populations.) Specifically, the total adult population of Jacksonville is 1,102,643, almost 11 percent of whom are over age sixty-five. This is an ideal market, because the elderly population is a primary segment for the Z-Coil shoe. Six-

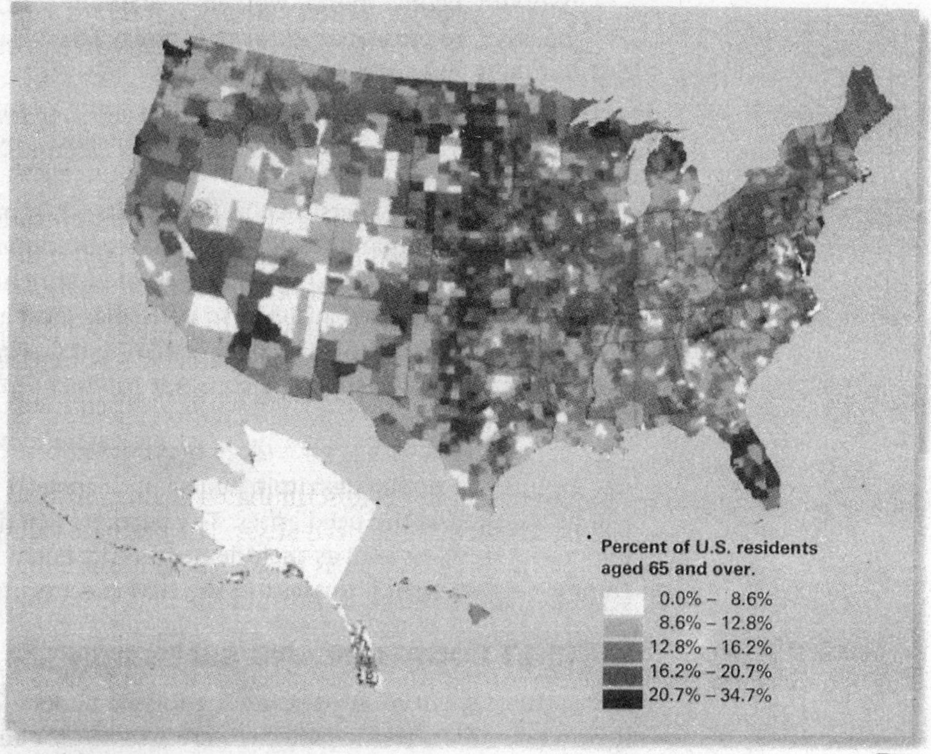

FIGURE 15.3 Percentage of U.S. Residents Age 65 or Older
Source: www.censusscope.org/us/map 65 plus.html.

teen percent of the adult population of Jacksonville is between ages forty-five and sixty-four. Income levels are steady, with more than 50 percent of the population having incomes exceeding $40,000 per year. In addition, 33 percent of the population enjoys walking for health, 20 percent plays golf, 14 percent enjoys running or jogging, and 40 percent engages in exercise and other physical fitness activities. The lifestyle of the Jacksonville population, therefore, makes this segment ideal for the new retail store.

An RIS will be used to store and disseminate information that is collected, such as demographic and location statistics, so the decision makers will have the data at their fingertips. The data will also guide the development of the retailer's tactical executions.

Based on the data, the partners have created a strategy for market development. Because the Z-Coil shoe is a relatively new product, the partners have the added task of more closely defining their target market(s). Utilizing the data from the RIS, the partners have defined their target market, described next.

TARGET MARKET

The partners decided to mirror Z-Coil's target market of people who spend excessive time on their feet. This market can be broken down into the target segments listed on the next page.

1. Working people (postal workers, restaurant staff, doctors, nurses, other health care providers, etc.)—ages thirty-five to seventy.
2. Runners and sport walkers—age 20+.
3. People with pain or discomfort (heel spurs, plantar fascia, diabetes, arthritis, foot pain, leg pain, back pain caused by the impact of running and/or walking)—all ages.
4. Health care providers such as podiatrists, chiropractors, other MDs, and insurance companies will be used to reach individuals who are under medical care or receiving some type of treatment for pain.
5. Current and retired athletes, in particular local athletes (including the Jacksonville Jaguars), will be targeted—both as customers, to help relieve their pain and as spokespersons, for product promotion, publicity, and public relations.

Age groups will not be discriminated against; instead these targeted groups will be adjusted as the need arises. The partners will develop a database of customers' interests, as well as their demographic, behavioristic, and psychographic characteristics, to assist in the IRM executions.

MARKET LOCATION AND SELECTION

The partners spent months searching for the perfect Jacksonville location for their retail outlet. Traffic patterns were assessed for automobiles, buses, foot traffic, and main traffic arteries. Based on this research, a freestanding site with plenty of parking was selected in a highly traveled part of Jacksonville. This also allows for additional walk-in traffic.

FINANCIAL OPERATIONS MANAGEMENT

Because the partners want to establish a new venture and develop their market, they need to generate enough funds to start up the retail outlet. Thus, the partners want to make sure that the variable and fixed costs of running the store will be met. Cash and credit are needed for the physical site and for racks and display units for the products. In addition, the partners want to have enough capital left over to create an effective and balanced integrated marketing communications plan. Although salaries are a concern, the partners are willing to take less money up front to generate sales and revenues.

The partners have developed a five-year plan that will assist them in forecasting sales and profits for these periods. In addition, the partners are planning to sell complementary items, such as T-shirts, socks, insoles, and additional orthotics, although the majority of the planned sales will come from the shoes themselves.

Because they lack enough capital to create an attractive sales floor, the partners plan to use credit for the first three years to have enough cash on hand to meet changes in the retail environment; thus, they will have a "buffer" for unplanned events.

The partners developed a breakeven point for their business. When they crunched the numbers, the breakeven point, in units, was 10,000 pairs of shoes per year. Thus, the partners used an averaging method and found they needed to sell 2,500 pairs of shoes per quarter. This figure will be integrated into the evaluation portion of the IRM plan (Response of the Market and Retail Auditing).

MERCHANDISE BUYING AND HANDLING

Because the partners will be exclusive dealers of the Z-Coil product, they will have one supplier, Z-Tech, for their main product. To supplement their revenue, the partners have decided to include ancillary products. They have found a company that specializes in promotional products such as T-shirts, socks, water bottles, and other items that the partners can use for promotion.

It was decided that all products will be stored at the physical retail location, thus reducing costs associated with storage. The disadvantage to this approach is that the actual selling space will have to be reduced to provide room for inventory. Inventory will be sold using the FIFO (first in, first out) method of inventory management.

The store will utilize point-of-sale (POS) terminals that allow for automatic reordering and replenishment of supplies. In addition, the POS will allow the partners to maintain control of their inventory levels and to generate financial statements at any point in time, thus integrating this function with the financial operations.

HUMAN RESOURCE MANAGEMENT

Due to the small size of the overall retail operation, two of the partners will be in charge of all retail activities. Denise will run the marketing portion of the business, and Don will serve as general manager. Dean is designated as the chief financial officer (CFO) and will be responsible for all financial matters pertaining to the partnership.

The partners estimate that in addition to Denise and Don, they will need four additional sales and service personnel. These employees will be paid on an hourly basis, and their main function will be to provide customer service and follow-up with customers. They will deal with each customer who comes into the retail outlet. Benefits will be offered to each employee based on the financial plan, but the employees will be responsible for paying for a portion of them. This amount will be deducted from their biweekly paychecks.

LAWS AND ETHICS

An attorney will be retained for legal guidance in terms of all laws applicable to the Z-Coil store. The state of Florida requires that at least one owner of products marketed as "pain relief" devices have certification. It was decided that Dean would undertake the certification process during the first year and the other partners would also certify during upcoming years.

The partners decided they need a diverse employee base. They themselves are a diverse group, including an African American male, a female, and an Hispanic male. They want to ensure this diversity in their employee selection as well, so that the employees are representative of their client base. This diversity will mirror the diverse customer base developed in the situational analysis.

Ethical business practices are of utmost importance to the partners, so they have designated Dean to be in charge of business ethics for the Z-Coil store. Checks and balances will be instituted to ensure mistakes are caught early and corrected. The store will follow the ethics of Z-Tech, Inc., the main supplier for the store.

RETAIL TACTICS

Retail tactics include pricing, integrated marketing communications (IMC), and customer services decisions. The following sections outline the tactical executions the partners are planning based on data from the situational analysis, financial plan, and product mix. Each area must be integrated with the others to generate as much awareness as possible of the store's targeted markets.

PRICING. For products other than the shoes themselves, the partners plan a 100 percent markup on the product's cost. The shoe prices will follow the suggested prices given by Z-Tech, Inc. for its complete line of products. By following the Z-Tech pricing schedule, the partners will be able to better estimate demand and revenue flows.

Each shoe product will be tracked at the current prices, and adjustments to the retail price will be made based on supply and demand for each unit. The store will carry a wide breadth and depth of Z-Coil shoes. In addition, allowances for the purchase of multiple products will be addressed at a later date. To create and maintain a high-quality product image, the prices of Z-Coil shoes will be above the industry average for similar products.

The partners foresee that there may be demand for the products from groups of individuals or organizations (*e.g.*, the Jacksonville athletic teams) and will provide prorated pricing and quantity discounts. The partners will also, when possible, use individuals from these organizations as spokespersons for the product or include testimonials from customers as part of the IMC program (discussed next).

INTEGRATED MARKETING COMMUNICATIONS (IMC). Because the market is geographically defined (that is, the primary geographic market is Jacksonville, Florida, and surrounding areas), local media vehicles will be used. At present, the partners plan to use local newspapers, local radio and television stations, and outdoor media such as billboards.

There will be a tie-in with customer testimonials for each piece of IMC offered to the potential market. Testimonials and spokespersons will be vehicles for educating the public about this unique product. Presentations at local activities, festivals, fairs, and sporting events will take place. Presentations to educational institutions will also be a featured execution. The partners are expecting that the unique look of the shoes will generate publicity, which could mean "free" media coverage.

To keep down costs for the IMC tactics, the partners plan to use cooperative advertising with Z-Tech, Inc. Z-Tech has produced a number of television advertisements that the store will use. The cost of the ads to the partners is zero; however, there will be an associated cost for media placement. In addition to the TV ads, the store will use Z-Tech–created print advertisements that feature the store's location, phone number, and website. As a natural element of IMC, the website will include hotlinks to podiatrists; feature stories about the Z-Coil shoe; Z-Tech's headquarters in Albuquerque, New Mexico; and any other sites that may be of interest to the store's customer base.

To develop a customer list for the RIS, the partners plan to create contests and sweepstakes. The contests will require that each entrant supply his or her name, address, phone number, and e-mail address to be eligible to win a free pair of Z-Coils or other promotional items. By generating these data, the partners will be able to expand their understanding of the Z-Coil store customer. This database will be used to generate e-tailing campaigns.

For the future, the partners are planning store expansions and an increase in the amount and types of products they carry. Each of these expansions will be supported with IMC promotions.

CUSTOMER SERVICE. The cornerstone for the success of Z-Tech, Inc. is outstanding customer service. The store will borrow these success techniques from the main supplier. Each employee will be required to attend a three-day training session at Z-Tech's headquarters to ensure they have the skills and abilities necessary to promote and sell the products.

In addition to the corporate training, Z-Coil store employees will be required to attend customer service training seminars offered by a national consulting group. This training focuses on customer satisfaction, but also includes different methods of selling. The Z-Coil store will utilize the consultative approach to selling.

Employees' performance with regard to customer service will be assessed by evaluating each individual's sales as well as communications received from customers. An evaluation questionnaire will be developed and placed in the box of every pair of shoes sold. In addition, a random telephone survey of customers will be made, inquiring about the treatment the customer received from the Z-Coil staff. This will also allow the store's employees to understand how well they are performing and how well accepted the product is. Any suggestions for product improvement will be forwarded to Z-Tech. Rewards will be given to high-performing employees. This process will be developed throughout the first year of operation and adapted as the retail outlet thrives.

RESPONSE OF THE MARKET AND RETAIL AUDITING

The partners understand that the only constant in the universe is change. Therefore, they will give a great deal of attention to end-of-year assessments of sales and service. In addition, there will be a quarterly assessment of sales both to identify high-volume selling times and to correct any problems that occurred during the operating quarter.

Each member of the organization will be reviewed twice a year. The first review will be informal. Team members will be informed of their strengths and weaknesses regarding sales and service of the products. The end-of-year review will be a formal process, with raises, job terminations, or promotions based on that review.

Each year the store will undergo a major retail audit. The audit will be both performed in-house and outsourced. The internal audit will show how the partners believe the organization is performing; the external audit will be used to verify or dispute the findings from the internal audit. One important reason for undertaking the retail audit is to make sure all the functions are clearly defined and all the elements are being effectively integrated.

The partners want to ensure that their plan is dynamic and flexible. They know that they need to be able to respond to changes in the retail environment and have developed an environmental scanning process that allows them to identify changes. When coupled with the IRM, the overall plan becomes exciting and adaptable, and will enable the partners to compete at a high level with other shoe retailers in their geographic market.

SUMMARY

As we move further into the twenty-first century, retailers will face many challenges and opportunities. This chapter discussed diversity and other trends in retailing. Many of the issues and trends in retailing focus on technological improvement. Emerging technologies allow for better customer segmentation and give retailers a more comprehensive knowledge of their markets. In addition, the technologies help retailers build relationships with their external customers as well as their internal customers (employees) and retail stakeholders.

The U.S. demographic base is changing. Thus, it is important for retailers to understand how to leverage diversity. In addition, changes in the economy, environment, and society are forcing retailers to look at their operations and how these trends will affect them.

Best practices in retailing help identify the actions of world-class organizations. Best practices include focusing on individual consumers versus the mass market, segmenting markets more effectively, adapting to market changes, and using information technology to improve operations. As customers become more informed, retailers must strive to treat them with respect and find new ways to connect with them.

The integrated retail management flow chart developed and presented throughout the text will propel retailers to develop new retail formats. As a dynamic tool, the IRM process allows retailers to make adjustments in their plans. By understanding the IRM plan and how to execute it, a retailer will be in a good position to compete in a saturated market that demands more and more new product and service offerings.

KEY TERMS

diversity (436)
leveraging diversity (436)
equal employment opportunity (EEO) laws (436)
affirmative action (436)
customer-centric culture (443)
market adaptability (444)

QUESTIONS FOR DISCUSSION

1. Why is it important for retailers to understand future trends in the retail industry?
2. List five trends that you think are occurring in the retail industry.
3. What role do you believe diversity will play in the next five years? Ten years?
4. Do you believe e-tailing will continue to grow? Why or why not?
5. If your future plans involve retailing, what type of retailer would you prefer to be, and why?
6. Do you agree with the IRM plan devised by the Z-Coil partners? What, if anything, would you change?

E-TAILING EXERCISE

Choose five retailers that have an online presence. Browse each site for indications that the company has a diversity program in place. Then answer the following questions:

1. What types of information concerning diversity programs were included on each retailer's site?
2. On a scale of 1 to 5, with 5 meaning "very strongly committed to diversity" and 1 meaning "not committed at all to diversity," rate each retailer on your perception of their commitment to diversity.
3. Does having online information about diversity programs increase the success of recruitment efforts? Why or why not?
4. What other attributes might differentiate retailers that have diversity program information on their websites from those that do not?

Continuing Case 15.1

Sherwin-Williams Company: Moving Forward

Sherwin-Williams is a $5 billion manufacturer and retailer of paint, coatings, and related products. It is one of the largest paint manufacturers and retailers in the world and the largest in the United States. Sherwin-Williams has more than 2,500 company-owned stores; recently, it hired IBM to develop the technology infrastructure for those stores. The company sells many different brands, not only within its own stores but also through other stores such as Wal-Mart, Kmart, and Home Depot. One of Sherwin-Williams's major strengths is its powerful assortment of brands.

To increase the value of its stock and future earnings, Sherwin-Williams initiated a stock repurchase in the late 1990s. The company faces competition from Valspar Corporation; RPM, Inc.; E. I. DuPont de Nemours & Company; Imperial Chemical Industries (ICI) PLC, the world's number one paint maker; and Akzo Nobel N.V., the world's largest paint and chemical manufacturer.

Sherwin-Williams wants to increase its U.S. market share of paint and coatings, and expand its global market presence and leadership. Currently, it is number one in the United States and number three worldwide.

Questions

1. Create an IRM plan for Sherwin-Williams's retail division.
2. After analyzing the data in the case and any other information you can gather, provide three strategies Sherwin-Williams can use to meet or exceed its growth goals.
3. Do you think Sherwin-Williams is ready to confront the changes forecasted for the retailing industry?
4. How do you think Sherwin-Williams can compete more effectively in the global marketplace?
5. Using secondary data, provide information that Sherwin-Williams's strategists can use for the company's various divisions. Do you think all divisions should concentrate on the same goals or have different goals?
6. What major challenges do you think Sherwin-Williams will face in the next year? The next decade?
7. Do you think any legal issues are associated with Sherwin-Williams's vertical integration structure? Why or why not?
8. Using your understanding of retailing and the retail industry, what changes would you make in Sherwin-Williams's channels of distribution? Do you think Sherwin-Williams competes against itself by selling to other paint retailers? Why or why not?

Sources: Investment Recommendation, The Sherwin-Williams Company, APMP Superior Fund, retrieved July 8, 2002 from www.sbea.mtu.edu/apmp/reports/sherwin.pdf; "Sherwin-Williams Chooses a Big Blue Shade of Linux," press release, IBM homepage, retrieved July 9, 2002 from www-916.ibm.com/press/prnews.nsf/jan; Brae Canlen, "HomeBase Seeks to Put 'Everything Under One Roof,'" *National Home Center News*, October 23, 2000, pp. 22–23.

Case 15.2

Office Depot Seeks to Diversify Its Pool of Workers

As the demographic picture of the United States changes, companies are realizing that diversity in their work force provides a competitive edge. One company, Office Depot, has altered its business plan to reflect the need for a diverse pool of workers. Following is Office Depot's mission and direction for diversity:

At Office Depot, we are committed to creating an inclusive environment where all people are valued and respected. Diversity is an important dimension of respect for the individual—one of our core values—and a key to our success in a global marketplace.

We take the following actions to achieve this policy:

- *Recruiting a work force that is reflective of the communities in which we do business.*
- *Providing a work environment based on honesty and mutual respect.*
- *Ensuring that all people-related decisions are made objectively, based on merit.*
- *Utilizing a base of diverse suppliers.*
- *Managers at all levels are accountable for implementing action plans to achieve these goals.*

This unwavering commitment to diversity enables us to be an employer of choice, serve the needs of all of our customers, and stand as valued corporate citizens in the communities in which we do business. It is an essential element of achieving our vision to be a compelling place to work, shop, and invest.

To implement its vision for diversity, Office Depot has forged partnerships with the National Minority Supplier Development Council and the Women's Business Enterprise National Council. Office Depot also began diversity training at its corporate headquarters and expects to implement the training throughout the chain by 2003. At the store level, Office Depot donates $1,000 to the National Urban League and $500 to a local organization that helps ensure that each Office Depot store focuses on the community.

Questions

1. Why should retailers focus on increasing diversity within their employee pool?
2. What are the positive and negative aspects of implementing a diversity program?
3. Why must diversity initiatives be incorporated into the company strategy?
4. Do you think diversity initiatives within corporations are a passing fad? Why or why not?

Sources: Chistopher Mele, "Diversity Has to Begin at the Top, Panelists Say," *The Journal News,* March 22, 2002, retrieved December 2002 from www.thejournalnews.com; "Office Depot Reverses Notion of 'One Size Fits All,' " *DSN Retailing Today,* May 20, 2002, p. 25; Office Depot homepage (www.officedepot.com), accessed December 2002. Diversity mission statement courtesy of Office Depot.

Indian Supplement

Teaching from Western textbooks, instructors are able to impart to students an excellent analytical framework for designing appropriate retailing strategies but there is a flip side too. There is a feeling of incompleteness of the subject matter, which appears pronounced when one realizes the vast difference between the Western and Indian contexts in terms of retailing.

This is where the 'Indian Supplement' written by Dr Mukesh Pandey, Associate Professor of Marketing at the FORE School of Management, New Delhi, along with his team of management students will add the Indian edge to the international edition of this book. Dr Pandey has been a Corporate Manager with MNCs and Indian companies and has been teaching Marketing for several years. He has written this Supplement after being seized of the need of Indian content be it cases for classroom discussions or Chapters for individual study.

The Supplement takes into cognizance the unchaining of Indian economy post-1990s, globalization of culture, choking up of distribution channels and aggressive retailing strategies of extremely customer-focused new entrants. The exercise is in conformance with Biztantra's mission to provide Indian students an opportunity to study from world-class textbooks fortified with an Indian dimension to bring in a closer-home feeling.

Indian Supplement

Part 5

Indian Organized Retailing: Eyeing the Future

Chapter

16

CHAPTER OBJECTIVES

1. To study the growth and spread of organized retailing in India vis-à-vis traditional retailing.
2. To deal with issues in organized retailing affecting the growth, spread and performance of organized retail outlets in India
3. To list the emerging retail and shopping trends among various segments of organized retailing in India.
4. To highlight immense employment opportunities in Indian retail sector.
5. To focus on high potential categories and interest among the Indian corporate houses.
6. To study the application of global concepts and suitable modifications to suit Indian business environment.

This chapter has been prepared by Dr. Mukesh Pandey, Associate Professor of Marketing at FORE School of Management, New Delhi. He did his PGDBM from IIM- Calcutta and B.Tech. from College of Technology, G.B.Pant University, Pantnagar, Uttranchal. Before joining academics, he worked with Electrolux Kelvinator Ltd., Polar International and Usha Fan Industries handling Branding, MIS, Sales and distribution functions. He was assisted by Amber Wajahat, his student at FORE (Class of 2005) in writing this chapter.

RETAIL – THE INDUSTRY

India has been called a nation of *dukandaars* (shopkeepers) due to the huge number of its retail enterprises, which totaled over 12 million in 2003. About 78 per cent of these are small family businesses utilizing only household labour, bulk of them too using less than three workers (Source: Report on Retailing in India, www.the-infoshop.com).

Retailers today will have to support the large retail infrastructure in terms of malls and superstores that are being created. The challenge for leading retailers shall therefore shift from diverting demand to creating demand. With all the modern stores offering convenience in terms of an assortment of products, ambience, service and innovative products, the paradigm shall shift from competing with the kirana stores to an in-house demand creation.

Even though India has well over 12 million retail outlets of all sizes and styles (or non-styles), the country sorely lacks anything that can resemble a retailing industry in the modern sense of the term. This presents international retailing specialists with a great opportunity.

UNORGANIZED SECTOR IN RETAIL

Retailing in India is thoroughly unorganized. There is no supply chain management perspective. According to a survey by AT Kearney, an overwhelming proportion of the Rs. 400,000 crore retail market is UNORGANIZED. In fact, only a Rs. 20,000 crore segment of the market is organized. About 96 per cent of the 5 million-plus outlets are smaller than 500 square feet in area. This means that India per capita retailing space is about 2 square feet (compared to 16 square feet in the United States). India's per capita retailing space is actually the lowest in the world (source: KSA Technopak (I) Pvt Ltd, the India operation of the US-based Kurt Salmon Associates).

ORGANIZED RETAILING IN INDIA

A tremendous opportunity exists in the Indian market and organized retail will prevail as in other parts of the world. Since, it's only a matter of time, this is the right time to invest and reap profits in around 5-7 years.

Organized retail is transforming the neighborhood grocery store (commonly known as kirana store); gone are the days of dust-coated, cluttered shelf-displays and actualization of buying power is now in the hands of the consumer. Modern retail in India, in the last decade has been characterized by a shift from traditional channels to new formats including department stores, hypermarkets, supermarkets and specialty stores across a range of categories. Modern retail formats with sprawling shopping centers, multi-storied malls offering shopping, entertainment and food all under one big, comfortable roof have mushroomed in metros and mini-metros. In the last few years modern retail has also established its presence in the second rung cities thus, exposing the residents of these cities to shopping options like they have never experienced before. It has been forecasted that the share of modern retail will increase from 2 per cent currently, to about 15-20 per cent over the next decade.

According to consultants KSA Technopak; the organized retailing is expected to be worth a whopping Rs 1,80,000-2,00,000 crore by 2010. It means that the organized retail pie will move up from the current 2 per cent (Rs 22,500 crore) to 10-12 per cent in another six years. High growth projections are being translated into frenetic activity on the ground. It is estimated that by 2007-08 over 300 malls spread across 50 million sq. ft. of retail space will come up. Over 600 malls with an area of 100 million sq. ft. will spring up on the Indian landscape by 2010.

(Source: *Big Boys Go Retail* by Swati Prasad, *Business Today,* Oct. 24 2004, Vol. 13 No. 21)

A consumer revolution is on its way as organized retail is uniquely positioned to take care of the convenience and aspirational needs of Indian consumers. Even as modern retailers garner share from traditional channels, there is a larger role that they would be required to play in boosting the overall consumption levels of the Indian economy. The retail arena is today is very different – the opportunities are incredible but exploiting them calls for being in the know. One has to be constantly on the move, keeping tabs on the shifting trends in the marketplace and maneuvering one's strategy to stay on top.

However retailers will have to strive hard to meet the tough expectations of today's super smart shoppers who instantly lap a good buy and dismiss a bad product. Today's consumers demand superior quality at an affordable price and they want it instantly. For retailers aiming to make a big sale, there is not much of a choice but to find ways to win customers over and keep them permanently happy, which is a. tough ask in a restrictive Indian business environment that too lacking infrastructure.

CHANGE ACCELERATORS

The following factors will be significant in driving growth in the retail sector:

- Consumer factors
  - Increase in income
  - Working women
  - Changes in lifestyle – demand for "global" trends.

- Supply side factors
  - ➢ Growing importance of retailing in political and economic agenda
  - ➢ Real estate reforms
  - ➢ Major restructuring of the manufacturing sector easing product supply constraints for efficient retailing.
  - ➢ Reduction in import duties-offering more global sourcing

SEGMENTS OF ORGANIZED RETAILING IN INDIA

Retail trade is represented by large segments of food, clothing, consumer durables and books & music. Other segments include jewellery, furniture and footwear.

- ❑ **Food and Groceries**. This segment is worth upwards of Rs 6,00,000 crore per annum. The biggest player in food retailing—FoodWorld—is no bigger than Rs 400 crore. The opportunity is huge for new entrants. The food and grocery segment accounts for 14 per cent of the market.

- ❑ **Clothing & Textiles.** Textiles are a Rs 85,000-crore business (including clothing, home furnishing, lingerie, sleepwear, etc.). The largest supplier—Madura Garments—is only around Rs 400 crore. Even Shoppers' Stop, which gets about 60 to 70 per cent of its turnover from textiles, is a Rs 404-crore company. In comparison, Japanese retail firm Aeon is $20-billion (Rs 92,000-crore) firm. For textile companies in India, the retail opportunity is one way of beating the dismantling of quota system in 2005.

- ❑ **Consumer Durables**. Retailing of consumer durables continues to be a fragmented market except in the south where organized retail has a strong foothold. Viveks and VGP are the large players here. While there are several single large stores in the metros, the chain stores are yet to make a significant impact. Vijay Sales and Akbarallys are the main players in Mumbai. A new trend has been sale of consumer durables through stores like Big Bazaar. Shoppers' Stop too has added consumer durables to its portfolio in certain outlets. Every city has several large one-store retailers who can be classified as organized due to the size of their business and the implementation of several management practices by these players.

- ❑ **Books & Music**. The books and music market saw several new entrants recently. Fountainhead in books and Planet M, Music World, Fast Forward and Groove in music are shaking up the market. Established stores like Crossword, taken over by Shoppers' Stop, Higginbotham's and Landmark are expanding rapidly. There has been an increasing focus on the retailing of books. Landmark, for instance, is credited to be the first ISO 9000 certified bookstore in the country.

In recent times, publishing majors have started to focus to a greater extent on the kids segment. Consequently, the segment is witnessing the advent of sophisticated packaging and they are also supplementing it with aggressive marketing efforts. With the establishment of malls and large department stores, many players are experimenting with setting up book and music corners in high traffic locations within these premises – like Planet M in several department stores and Crossword in Shoppers' Stop.

(Source: *Big Boys Go Retail* by Swati Prasad, *Business Today,* Oct. 24 2004, Vol. 13 No. 21)

Size of organized retail market-Indian bazaar (crore Rs.)

Category	Format	2001-02	2007	CAGR(%)
Food	Chain Stores	1500	6726	35
	Single large stores & others	300	746	20
	Sub-total	**1800**	**7473**	**33**
Clothing	Manufacturer Retailers	1350	2715	15
	Chain Stores	1450	3919	22
	Single large stores	2150	3789	12
	Sub-total	**4950**	**10423**	**16**
Consumer durables	Manufacturer Retailers	650	1307	15
	Chain Stores	450	1373	25
	Single large stores	550	1106	15
	Sub-total	**1650**	**3787**	**18**
Books & Music	Chain Stores	250	928	30
	Single large stores	200	498	20
	Sub-total	**450**	**1426**	**26**
Others	All formats	7150	14107	
Total organized retail		16000	37216	18

Source: ORG-Marg, *The Economic Times*

BIG PLAYERS ENTER THE RETAIL MARKET

Some of the India's biggest Corporations like ITC, Bombay Dyeing, Reliance and Godrcj arc climbing onto the organized retail bandwagon. They are setting up malls, hypermarkets, supermarkets, and specialty stores.

Table – The key players in Indian retail space and their future plans

PLAYER	PLANS
Tatas	After stabilizing operations of their Westside chain of lifestyle stores, the Tatas are launching a chain of hypermarkets called **Star India Bazaar**. Each hypermarket will be around 50,000 sq. ft., and the first will open in Ahmedabad in the next few months.

Reliance	Into telecom and broadband-driven retailing through their WebWorlds, 200 of them. Petroleum retail outlets—for which the Ambanis have licences for 5,849 outlets—could also have food and groceries stores, **WebWorlds and Java Green coffee shops.**
ITC	Embraced the rural retail model and plans to put up stores called Chaupal Sagars, each catering to 100 villages. The first Chaupal Sagar in Sehore (MP) is already operational. ITC plans to have 1,000 of such Chaupal Sagars, with 50 of them scheduled to be set up in the first year itself at **an investment of Rs 150 crore.**
HLL	In the retail space with its **Lakme Beauty Salons** and Ayush Therapy centers. Currently has 65 Lakme salons and 12 Ayush Therapy centers. Plans to expand to 100 Lakme salons and 30 Ayush Therapy centers in one year.
Hero Group	Creating a chain of 7-11 type of **convenience retail stores**, for which the Munjals will tie up with companies and banks. From the current level of 700-odd stores, the group plans to have 10,000 outlets spread across the country over the next three years.
Bharti	Foraying into **broadband retailing**, with scope to offer video conferencing, high-speed internet and virtual gaming.
Wadias **Singhanias, Godrej**	In various stages of evaluation of different models. Wadias will probably set up a chain of lifestyle stores, Raymond is evaluating various models including **hypermarkets**, and Godrej has embarked on an **environment-scanning process**.
RPG Group	One of the few conglomerates to venture relatively early into retail, the group is aggressively expanding its **beauty centres** (Health & Glow), **music stores** (Music World), and hypermarkets Food World and Giant (which could be renamed Spencer's). The largest organized retailer has envisaged an investment of **Rs 140 crore** over the next three years.
Ajay Piramal	Another early entrant, Piramal is expanding his **lifestyle stores** (with supermarkets), Piramyd, from three to 16 in three years, at a cost of Rs 320 crore

(*Big Boys Go Retail* by Swati Prasad, *Business Today,* Oct. 24 2004, Vol. 13 No. 21)

Current state of organized players in Indian retail industry

Retail Rush

Current State of Organized Players (Data for 2001-02)

Cities	No. of Stores	Turnover Rs.Cr	Total Area Sq.Ft	Sales Per Sq.Ft
Mumbai Based				
Shoppers' Stop	9	256	400,000	6,250
Crossword	13	35	45,000	7,807
Globus	3	57	70,000	7,000
Pantaloon	13	149	150,000	10,000
Westside	7	93	140,000	6,786
Piramyd	2	55	50,000	11,000
Benzer	1	29	15,000	18,667
KBN	1	22	20,000	10,950
Akbarallys	3	57	47,000	12,231
Nagani's	1	14	15,000	9,333
Sahakari Bhandar	15	51	37,500	13,333
Apna Bazar	75	126	112,500	11,111
FoodLand	1	7	3,000	20,000
Bombay Store	3	72	60,000	11,667
Premsons	2	32	31,000	10,000
Amarsons	2	22	22,000	10,000
Haiko Supermarket	1	12	12,000	10,000
Delhi Based				
Ebony+Wordworth	10	109	130,000	8,462
Big Jo's	1	9	18,000	4,444
Wills Sport	29	38	60,000	6,333
Sabka Bazaar	5	16	20,000	8,000
Chennai Based				
Nalli's	4	353	40,000	87500
Lifestyle	3	76	115,000	6,522
Subhiksha	112	201	125,000	16,000
Jainsons	17	57	85,000	6,588
FoodWorld	75	363	350,000	10,286
Naidu Hall	2	81	20,000	40,000
Hyderabad Based				
Meena Bazar Chain	4	61	25,000	24,000
Chermas	4	16	20,000	7,500
Chandana Bros	16	400	280,000	14,286
Trineta	19	28	15,000	18,667
Bangalore-Based				
Nilgiris	26	230	90,000	25,556
Kemps Fort	1	81	120,000	6,667
Others				
Giant	1	29	50,000	6,000
Big Bazaar	3	67	52,000	12,500
Dev's Supermarket	1	14	10,000	14,000
Adani Ravji	6	16	15,000	10,000

Note: Since most of the companies are not listed, the above data is estimate not actual. The figures have been arrived at after substantial field analysis and study of each format.

Source: Industry, Websites, Magazines & Companies

Reason for retail boom: Liberalization and economic growth have mainly driven a vast change in India. Till a few years ago Indian consumers were happy with one TV channel, few retail stores and only one footwear chain-Bata. The scenario in totally different as of today, with malls, lifestyle stores, and specialty stores coming up in a big way .In a short span of ten years, market scenario has changed dramatically. The person changing this change is we ourselves, as consumers.

CHANGING INDIAN MARKET STRUCTURE

Increase in the disposable income and rise in the middle class

Table: Changing Indian Market Structure

Classification	*Households Millions (% of Population)*					
(Annual HH Income)	*1995-96*		*2001-2002*		*2006-07*	
Very Rich (>INR 360,0001)	1.2	0.8%	2.6	1.5%	5.2	2.7%
Consuming Class (INR 80,001 - 360,0000)	32.5	20.1%	46.4%	25.9%	75.5	39.5%
Climbers (INR 40,001 - 80,000)	54.1	33.7%	74.4	41.9%	81.7	43.1%
Aspirants (INR 28,0001 - 40,000)	44.0	27.4%	33.1	18.8%	20.2	10.7%
Destitutes (<28,000)	33.0	20.5%	24.1	13.7%	16.5	8.7%

Source: National Council for Applied Economic Research (NCAER), Projects on Structure of Market released in 2001.

- Growth of the urban middle class which demands value for money, has led to a lot of changes on the retail front.
- There is a substantial increase in the number of youth who are beginning to earn early. According to NRS, there is a 20 per cent increase in the number of persons between the age of 15 to 19 who have started earning.
- This is largely due to the growth opportunities for urban youth in the business process outsourcing and software sector.
- The increase in the double income households has also led to change in the spending habits across the urban India.

Effect of lifestyle changes on buying behavior

The rise in the income level of Indian households shows a direct relationship with the increased spending habits.

Asset Acquisition Rate

Asset	1999	2001	Increase (%)
Own House	40,164	42,883	7
Receive FM	8,204	10,215	25
Colour TV	16,758	21,527	28
Cable & Television Households	22,348	27,216	22
Hi-fi CD	577	982	70
Motorcycle	4,465	5,441	22
Refrigerator-Frost Free	6,580	7,199	9
Microwave	251	358	43
Camera	5,044	5,810	15
Telephone - STD/ISD	3,437	4,488	31
Telephone - Local	7,681	10,343	35
Vacuum Cleaner	796	856	8
Air Conditioner	557	762	37
Water Purifier	1,082	1,466	35
Washing Machine Fully Automatic	1,175	1,627	38
Mobile	567	661	17
PC	380	1,089	187
Computer Printer	186	376	102
Fax Machine	72	78	8
Video Camera	81	172	112
No Servant	47,213	50,459	7

Source: NRS 2002 — Number of Households

From the above table, the following deductions can be made about the asset acquisition rate of urban Indian consumers:

- The acquisition of the assets is increasing fast with rising income levels.
- Lifestyle assets figure among the top buys by the consumers
- Although regular assets like scooters, radios have seen flat or negative growth rates, the second rung lifestyle assets like ovens, vacuum cleaners and air conditioners, which previously had negligible market potential are witnessing double digit growth rates.
- This depicts that urban households, with rising composition of both husband and wife working, are trying to improve their lifestyle thus relying on gadgets to reduce household work.
- The above study also reveals the fact that the number of urban households without a domestic help has risen by 7 per cent, thus increasing the demand for lifestyle products.

Priority List of Spending on various segments by Indian consumers

Year-on-Year Spending Across Segments

Segment	2000	2001
Grocery	47.8	48.0
Personal Care Items	7.5	7.1
Books & Music	7.8	6.7
Home Appliances	0.7	2.0
Home Textiles	1.0	1.5
Savings & Investments	6.1	6.4
Clothing	6.5	4.7
Consumer Durables/Electronics	4.8	5.5
Vacation	3.3	3.1
Eating out	7.9	8.8
Footwear	2.0	2.2
Movies/Theatres	2.7	2.6
Entertainment	3.0	3.0

(% of total wallet)

Source: KSA Consumer Outlook 2002

Taking a look at the table, the following deductions can be made about the spending habits of the Indian consumers:

- Buying food is the top priority of the Indian consumer and 48 per cent of their total income goes in buying food.
- Another factor that has gained prominence is eating out.
- Spending on consumer durables and electronics has shown increment.
- To sum up, all in all, food is at the top of purchase list for consumers.

Regional Preferences

The fast changing profile of Indian consumers is affecting their shopping patterns and practices. The differences between the spending habits of high end consumers who come in A category and B class category is narrowing down, however there is a need to look at other segmentation criteria, that is "regional segmentation. The retailers need to carefully analyze the money spending priorities of the consumers by the region of their living.

Across Borders

Money Spending Priorities By Region

West	North	South	East
Grocery Eating Out Books & Music Personal Care Savings	Grocery Personal Care Eating Out Books & Music Savings	Grocery Eating Out Apparel Books & Music Savings	Grocery Apparel Savings Personal Care Eating Out

Source: KSA Consumer Outlook 2002

- We can see that eating out ranks as number two for western and southern part of India as these regions have large number of restaurants and eating joints that are affordable and hygienic, and also because these regions have maximum number of working women.
- On the other hand North Indians are more fashion conscious, hence personal care is the second most important area of spending for them.
- People living in the eastern region like spending more of their income on apparel. It is primarily clothing that drives consumers in Kolkata.
- Consumers living in metros like Mumbai and Delhi spend more time and money buying and reading books and listening to music, this is simply due to the fact that most of the people spend about 2-3 hours each day while travelling.

FUTURE PROFILE OF INDIAN RETAIL

In India the trends are mainly in the following sectors. These sectors are:

Table - Key Sectors in Indian Retail

Food & Grocery	***Non Food***
Groceries FoodWorld Nilgiris Subhiksha Food Bazaar **Restaurants & Fast Food** McDonald's Pizza Hut Domino's Barista Coffee Day	**Apparel** Arrow, Lee, Benetton, Weekender, Wills Sport, Marks & Spencer, Mango, Provogue, etc. **Books & Music, Stationery** Crossword, Planet M, Archies, Music World **Electronics** Viveks, Vijay Sales, VGP **Departmenta Stores** Shoper's Shop, Westside, Globus, Pyramid, etc. **Furnishings** Zeba, Yamini, FabIndia **Beauty** Lakme, Shahnaz Herbals **Jewellery** Tanishq, Gili, Oyzterbay, Intergold **Watches** Titan, HMT, Omega, Fossil, etc. **Hypermakets** Big Bazaar, Giants, Sabka Bazar

I. Food and grocery

Opportunity: Rs. 6,00,000 crore

Big Players: RPG, Pantaloon, Nilgiris, Food Bazaar, Subhiksha, Foodworld.

Likely Big Players of Tomorrow: Reliance through its malls at fuel pumps, Tatas, Godrej

Over 53 per cent of the total consumer spending in India is in food and groceries. However, organized retail of food and groceries is estimated at less than Rs. 2,000 crore. The gestation period can be as short as nine months. According to KSA Technopak, a start-up investment of Rs. 50-60 crore is needed for a regional chain and over Rs. 250 crore for a national chain. Breakeven can happen within 5-7 years.

II. Lifestyle retailing

Opportunity: Rs. 150,000 crore

Big Players: Shoppers' Stop, Pantaloon, Piramyd, Westside, Lifestyle, Wills Sport, Lee, Levis, Weekender

Likely Big Players of Tomorrow: Raymond/Singhanias, Wadias

Clothing and textile retailing accounts for about 7 per cent of the total private consumption of Indian consumers, of which branded products account for around 20 per cent. This, along with fashion accessories like watches, perfumes, jewellery and cosmetics, make lifestyle retailing a fairly lucrative business. The name of the game, however, is to get the customer hooked to you through memberships and loyalty programs. Just the way Shoppers' Stop, Lifestyle and Westside are doing it.

III. Consumer durables

Opportunity: Rs. 50,000 crore

Big Players: Vivek Ltd., Vijay Sales

There are no national players in this business as of today. And some players like Viveks in the south, want to go national only after 2007, when it would have 100 stores in the three states of Tamil Nadu, Karnataka and Andhra Pradesh. The scope for such retailing is tremendous. KSA for instance estimates the market for new mobile handsets at around 26 million a year — a Rs 10,000 crore odd industry. Besides, categories like air-conditioners and microwaves are growing at over 15 per cent per annum. The return on investment in this business is 25 per cent per annum.

IV. Rural retail

Opportunity: Rs. 3,00,000 crore

Big Players: ITC

Likely Big Players of Tomorrow: ITC, M&M, DCM Shriram

ITC recently opened a rural mall / 'Chaupal Sagar' — near Sehore, Madhya Pradesh. Chaupal Sagar offers multiple services under one root at a tractor-able distance from the villager's house. It houses a soil testing laboratory, a farmer training centre, medical consultation and diagnostic facilities, a restaurant, a store selling quality products for both farm and household consumption and banking and insurance services. According to Y.C.Deveshwar, Chairman, ITC, 87 per cent of the villages in the country have population lower than 2000, and low per capita income coupled with poor connectivity makes the economic spending power of rural India extremely poor. Each Chaupal Sagar therefore caters to over a 100 villages. ITC's dream is to open 1,000 Chaupal Sagars, and around 50 of them will be coming up in the next one-year in Madhya Pradesh and Uttar Pradesh.

V. Broadband-driven retailing

Opportunity: Not Available

Big Players: Reliance Infocomm

Likely Big Players of Tomorrow: Reliance, Bharti

From offering video-conferencing, to high-speed Internet for gaming to computer classes, a broadband retail store offers a lot. Around 140 Reliance WebWorlds are already doing much of that. And with Reliance offering broadband for homes and offices very soon. WebWorlds can also double up as sales and service points for these services.

VI. Fuel-pump driven retailing

Opportunity: Rs. 10,000 crore

Big Players: Indian Oil, BP, and Hindustan Petroleum

Likely Big Players of Tomorrow: Reliance, Indian Oil, Bharat Petroleum, Hindustan Petroleum

The Reliance group promises to offer a whole new experience in petroleum retailing as it rolls out 5,849 fuel pumps over the next three to five years. We learn that not all of them would have food and grocery stores, or a WebWorld and a Java Green Coffee Shop. But some, like the one in suburbs and on highways, certainly would.

After all, it is Reliance Group Chairman Mukesh Ambani's resolve to "revolutionalize" petroleum retailing.

(Source: *Big Boys Go Retail* by Swati Prasad, *Business Today,* Oct. 24 2004, Vol. 13 No. 21)

CHALLENGES FACING THE RETAIL INDUSTRY

- **Unorganized sector:** The first challenge facing the organized retail industry in India is competition from the unorganized sector. Traditional retailing has established in India for some centuries. It is a low cost structure, mostly owner-operated, has negligible real estate and labor costs and little or no taxes to pay. Consumer familiarity that runs from generation to generation is one big advantage for the traditional retailing sector. In contrast, players in the organized sector have big expenses to meet, and yet have to keep prices low enough to be able to compete with the traditional sector. High costs for the organized sector arises from: higher labor costs, social security to employees, high quality real estate, much bigger premises, comfort facilities such as air-conditioning, back-up power supply, taxes etc. Organized retailing also has to cope with the middle class psychology that the bigger and brighter a sales outlet is, the more expensive it will be.
- **Human resources:** Availability of trained personnel and retaining the human resources is a major challenge that these retailers have to face. The bigwigs like Crossroads offer high compensation and create cohesive environment that makes employees proud to be a part of such retail chains.
- **Space and infrastructure:** To establish a retail shop/mall the real state and infrastructure are very important, the expenditure and availability on both the accounts do hinder the growth of the retail chain. The lack of secondary infrastructure also affects the logistics and supply chain management of retail companies.
- **Labor laws:** Existing labor laws in India forbid employment of staff on a contractual basis that makes it difficult to manage employee schedule, especially 365-day operation.

RECIPE FOR SUCCESS

Focus on the consumer: It is clear that consumers have changed and they are looking for something different. Understanding their evolving needs, aspirations and lifestyles is the underlying key to success for any retailer. The primary emphasis should be on access, experience and service and the secondary emphasis on product and price. There should be an effort to improve service by having better trained sales staff, better availability of products, and minor but important conveniences, e.g. delivery of goods either to the car or even home. Collaborative advertising and promotion can then round off this effort

Brand the store: Branding the store will increase volume and enhance customer loyalty. Branding is critical to maintaining competitive differentiation in an increasingly challenging retail environment. However, the brand needs to be clearly communicated to the customer.

Develop private label brand: Private labels act as margin generators, increasing sales volume by positioning the label as providing higher perceived value to consumers. In the long run, they also increase the retailers' bargaining power with national brand suppliers.

Private labels generate customer loyalty by providing exclusive products, which works towards differentiation strategy, much sought after by the retailers.

In terms of location some entrepreneurs should put efforts in creating custom-developed solutions for tapping the rural and semi-urban spending potential. Even in non-metro urban centers, there are very good opportunities in looking at starting or expanding operations. Some cities that should see greater organized retail action in the future would be Ludhiana, Chandigarh, Lucknow, Nagpur, Ahmedabad, Surat, Pune, Kochi, Thiruvananthapuram, Guwahati and Bhubaneshwar.

CONCLUSION

Lifestyles in India are changing and the concept of "value for money" is picking up. The retailers need to invest much more in capturing more specific market intelligence as well as almost real-time customer purchase behavior information. The retailers also need to make substantial investments in understanding/acquiring some advanced expertise in developing more accurate and scientific demand forecasting models. Re-engineering of product-sourcing philosophies - aligned more towards collaborative planning and replenishment should then be next on their agenda. The message, therefore, for the existing small and medium independent retailers is to closely examine what changes are taking place in their immediate vicinity, and analyze whether their current market offers a potential redevelopment of the area into a more modern multi-option destination. If it does, and most commercial areas in India do have this potential, it would be very useful to form a consortium of other such small retailers in that vicinity and take a pro-active approach to pool in resources and improve the overall infrastructure. The next effort should be to encourage retailers to make some investment in improving the interiors of their respective establishments to make shopping an enjoyable experience for the customer.

References

- *Big Boys Go Retail* by Swati Prasad, *Business Today,* Oct. 24 2004, Vol. 13 No. 21
- *Unlocking Opportunities in Retail* by Arvind Singhal, Marketmind column, *Business Standard*, Sept. 10, 2004
- *Retail Industry – Witnessing a Paradigm Shift* by Pradeep K.Singh, *Saket Industrial Digest*, Nov. 2002, Vol. 8, Issue 11
- Case Study Series on *Retailing Sector*, 2002 edited by Senthil Ganesan and published by The Institute of Chartered Financial Analysts of India (ICFAI), Hyderabad
- *Gentlemen, fasten your seatbelts* by M.Rajshekhar, In-depth column on Retail, *BusinessWorld*, Feb. 10-16 2004, Vol. 23 No. 38
- www.ksa-technopak.com

Coffee Retailing in India: Of Refreshing Tastes and Places

Chapter

17

CHAPTER OBJECTIVES

1. To focus on coffee retailing in India as a coffee drinking culture brews
2. To look at coffee production economics in India and the world
3. To study coffee consumption patterns, penetration of coffee drinking and consumer behavior in India setting the stage for the growth and spread of coffee retailers
4. To understand the demand-supply dynamics and distribution trends in coffee
5. To note the changes coming about in various countries
6. To look closely at the concept of Coffee Bars and critical success factors at play in the marketplace
7. To profile various key players in liquid coffee retailing through Coffee Bars

This chapter has been prepared by Dr. Mukesh Pandey, Associate Professor of Marketing at FORE School of Management, New Delhi. He did his PGDBM from IIM- Calcutta and B.Tech. from College of Technology, G.B.Pant University, Pantnagar, Uttranchal. Before joining academics, he worked with Electrolux Kelvinator Ltd., Polar International and Usha Fan Industries handling Branding, MIS, Sales and distribution functions.

INTRODUCTION

The revolution in coffee drinking has had its biggest boost through the opening of thousands of coffee parlors around the world. The growth in the café segment is underpinned by several factors including increasing demand for innovative, sophisticated products as well as growing demand for specialty cuisine and beverage outlets as opposed to broad-menu outlets.

Starbucks is the world's largest chain of cafes and operates over 4,000 outlets around the globe with an annual turnover in excess of $5 billion in the fiscal year 2003-04. Other major café chains include:

- ✓ Diedrich and Tully's in the US,
- ✓ Costa Coffee in the UK
- ✓ Doutours and Nestle chain of cafes in Japan
- ✓ Douve Egberts chain of coffee shops (Jacqmotte) in the Netherlands.

Poland is also strongly emerging as a coffee market with players such as Nestle, Tchibo and Stoney Point Java extending their presence to coffee outlets.

The key positioning platforms for these specialty outlets is a good quality product range coupled with an ambience that promotes relaxation and indulgence.

Even in India, the proliferation of coffee parlors /cafes has spawned a rapid growth of coffee drinking culture. For a largely tea-drinking nation, switching over to a cup of cappuccino or mocha at neighborhood coffee vend has never been more dramatic and satisfying than before. Coffee drinking is fast becoming a leisure accessory and a lifestyle statement. It has developed a distinctly sophisticated image over tea among most consumer sets, a factor driving investors to envisage national businesses in coffee retailing.

KEY DRIVING FACTORS

The café segment is poised to take off in India as there are significant shifts in income and demographic patterns leading to increased urbanization, higher disposable incomes and growing exposure to consumption trends in developed markets. Various studies reveal that the Indian consumer is upbeat on spending more time as well as more money on eating out (as already established in Chapter, *Retailing in India: Eyeing the Future*).

The Indian Coffee Board has estimated that by 2005, India would be home to about 5,000 coffee houses. With the boom in coffee shop business, this sunrise sector is expected to notch up to Rs 300 crore by the end of 2005. (Source: *Coffee Break* by Tulika Sen, pages 16-24, *Images Retail*, September 2002)

As the new places that serve coffee can casually price their cuppa starting at Rs 50 as compared to the modest Rs 7 at the erstwhile coffee joints, it has to be rather serious business going. Today, names like Barista, Café Coffee Day, Qwiky's etc. have become familiar names as they spread in different parts of the country and promote the growth of urban neighborhood culture. Though Nescafe remains by far the most iconic coffee brand of our time, the concurrent formats have begun to brand the coffee drinking experience along with the brew. It is not just the business of selling coffee but retailing an altogether novel experience.

COFFEE: FROM FARM TO PLATE

- ✓ After crude oil, coffee is the largest traded commodity in the world. Being an agricultural commodity it is exposed to vagaries of weather, which affects its prices. Brazil and Columbia are top two coffee producers in the world. Coffee is grown in over 50 countries and consumed in just about every country and employs more than 24 million people worldwide.
- ✓ Indian coffee is acknowledged as the finest mild coffee in the world because of having been gifted with rare climatic and soil conditions that are conducive to the growth of good quality coffee.
- ✓ The area under coffee in India is around 3.49 lakh hectares, with 3.23 lakh hectares in production. (*Business Line*, May 18 2004)
- ✓ In India, coffee cultivation is largely confined to the hilly regions of the three southern states of Karnataka, Tamil Nadu and Kerala.
- ✓ Karnataka accounts for 53 percent of the planted area (59 per cent planted to Arabica, 41 percent to Robusta). (There are two general broad categories of coffee, Robusta and Arabica. Robusta is grown on low lands and is used predominantly for the manufacture of instant coffee, due to its bitter flavor, dark color and low price. Robusta is a common coffee for North America.)
- ✓ Robusta is dominant in Kerala (which has 28 per cent of planted area) and Arabica in Tamil Nadu (which has 11 per cent of planted area).
- ✓ Most coffee holdings are small and about two-thirds of the area is farmed by smallholders with an average holding size of 1.4 hectares. Large landholders, with an average size of 38.4 hectares, farm 35 per cent of land and account for 40 per cent of output.
- ✓ Arabica coffee is grown at comparatively higher altitudes (1,000-1,500 metres) than Robusta (500-1,000 metres). Arabica areas obtain greater annual rainfall (1,600-2,500 mm) than Robusta areas (1,000-2,000 mm).

For world coffee market statistics and India's production, consumption and export of coffee, please see tables on the following pages. It is evident that India exports a large part of its production and quantity of coffee exported is on the rise. Domestic consumption of coffee in India is growing albeit slowly. The table on statewise production of coffee focuses on Karnataka, Kerala and Tamil Nadu along with non-traditional coffee producing states.

Table: World Coffee Market Statistics (in million 60-kg bags)

Calendar Year	1997	1998	1999	2000	2001	2002	2003
Production	103.8	97.5	108.4	113.3	117	110.7e	122.1e
Total use	108.9	103.1	110.3	116.5	114.7	114.3e	117.9e
Ending stocks	29.1	24.7	24.3	21.3	23.6	20.1e	24.3e
Ending stocks to use Ratio (%)	27	24	22	18	21	18e	21e

e=estimates Source: *Coffee Break* by Tulika Sen, pages 16-24, *Images Retail*, September 2002

Table: Indian Production, Consumption and Export of Coffee (lakh tonnes)

Years	Production	Export			Domestic Consumption
		Qty.	Value (Rs. crore)	Value (Million $)	
990-91	1.70	1.00	279	108	0.54
1996-97	2.05	1.81	1467	452	0.55
1997-98	2.28	1.79	1708	477	0.50
1998-99	2.65	2.12	1752	431	0.50
1999-00	2.92	2.45	1901	447	0.55
2000-01	3.01	2.47	1374	334	0.58
2001-02	3.06	2.13	1050	246	0.60
2002-03	2.80*	1.37#	694	158	-

*Estimated # 1.4.2002 to 13.1.2003 Source: Economic Survey of India - 2002-03

OTHER SUPPLY CHAIN ISSUES IN COFFEE MARKETING IN INDIA

- India produces both Arabica and Robusta in almost equal proportion though Robusta is showing comparatively higher growth in production.
- After 1999-2000 annual production of coffee in India averaged 4.82 million bags of 50 kgs. Indian coffee output has been rising since the mid-1990s (*Business Line*, May 18 2004).
- Coffee production is affected by a strong biennial cycle.
- Most small growers prefer to sell coffee in the form of dry cherry and parchment. Many private buyers who are active in the coffee-growing zones buy coffee directly from growers.
- Larger growers and estates sell coffee in green and graded form either directly to exporters or by private auction.
- The coffee is processed to the quality specification of the Coffee Board before it is exported or auctioned.
- Domestic distribution of coffee takes place through wholesale and retail roasters.

(Author S.Radhakrishnan, www.indiacoffee.org)

Table: State-wise Production (2002/03- POST MONSOON FORECAST)

State/District	2002/03- POST MONSOON FORECAST		
	Arabica	Robusta	Total
Karnataka			
Chikmagalur	43,850	31,125	74,975
Coorg *	23,950	68,625	92,575
Hassan	17,250	6,500	23,750
Sub total	85,050	106,250	191,300
Kerala			
Wyanad	75	54,050	54,125
Travancore	650	7,650	8,300
Nelliampathies	450	1,550	2,000
Sub total	1,175	63,250	64,425
Tamil Nadu			
Pulneys	6,475	275	6,750
Nilgiris	1,350	2,800	4,150
Shevroys (Salem)	2,900	0	2,900
Anamalais (Coimbatore)	1,500	450	1,950
Sub total	12,225	3,525	15,750
Non Traditional Areas			
Andhra Pradesh & Orissa	3,300	0	3,300
North Eastern Region	175	125	300
Sub Total	3,475	125	3,600
Non Conventional Areas	200	0	200
Grand Total (India)	102,125	173,150	275,275

Source: http://www.indiacoffee.org/coffee/indiaproduction.html

PLAYERS IN INSTANT AND R & G COFFEE

- The instant coffee segment is almost entirely branded and packaged. The absence of smaller players in this segment may be attributed to the high level of investments required in producing instant coffee. While Hindustan Lever Ltd (HLL) and Nestle are the major players in the instant chicory mix segment, Nestle dominates the pure instant coffee segment with its Nescafe brand.
- The Roast & Ground segment is dominated by numerous small, local brands. The branded category consists of HLL (Green Label) and Tata Coffee (Coorg), etc. in the packaged coffee segment.
- In terms of supply chain, there has been an emergence of a new breed of coffee players. As against packaged R&G coffee, the focus is now on promotion

of fresh R&G coffee. Players in the fresh R &G coffee segments are Amalgamated Bean Coffee Trading Company (ABCTC) with its chain of over 235 exclusive outlets (Coffee Points), Narasu (60 outlets) and Leo (35 outlets).

- Players such as ABCTC are promoting their chain of outlets – Coffee Points – as an exclusive R&G coffee chain with an attractive ambience and a range of over 20 blends. Such efforts are promoting the consumption of coffee, both among the traditional coffee-drinkers as well as the non-coffee consumers.

PROFILE OF COFFEE DRINKERS IN INDIA

The Coffee Board commissioned market research studies in 2001 and 2003 to understand the habits and practices with respect to coffee consumption; coffee consumption by location and form; share of coffee in the daily basket of beverages consumed, etc. The attitudes towards coffee, and drivers and barriers to coffee consumption were studied in 2001. The salient results of these studies are as follows:

- Coffee seems to be more a beverage of the upper Socio Economic Classes (SECs).
- The proportion of non-drinkers is the highest in the oldest age group of 55+ years.
- Amongst coffee consumers in the rural areas, a majority (43 per cent of all adults) is light drinkers, consuming 1-2 cups everyday.
- About a fifth of rural consumers consume coffee occasionally. The average number of cups of coffee consumed increases marginally from summer to winter.
- Visiting cafes is not a frequent habit.
- Of all respondents surveyed, about 12 per cent visit cafes and there is a greater tendency among the upper SECs to visit cafes. Of all the respondents, about 10 per cent have ever visited cafes, this proportion is higher among men and the younger age groups (15-34 years).
- Around 65 per cent of households buy instant coffee and only 18 per cent buy filter coffee. Among filter coffee drinking households, 49 per cent are branded coffee drinkers and 51 per cent are unbranded coffee drinkers. In the South, filter coffee is bought mostly from R&G outlets. Penetration (beverage consumed in the past 12 months) of coffee at 59 per cent is low compared to that of tea. Penetration of filter coffee is highest in South India. Penetration level was found to decrease from higher Socio Economic Class (SEC) to the lower Socio Economic Class.
- If coffee volumes have to compare favorably with that of tea, the base of coffee consumers needs to be increased. About 41 per cent of the respondents are non-drinkers of coffee. The potential for growth lies with occasional drinkers who constitute 40 per cent of the population. The potential is more in the north and the east zones. The proportion of non-drinkers of coffee increases from Socio Economic Class (SEC) A to C, while that of occasional and light drinkers

decreases. Coffee drinkers (71 per cent) buy packaged and branded coffee powder. Of those buying branded/ packaged coffee powder, 47 per cent buy instant coffee and 53 per cent, filter coffee. (Author: S.Radhakrishnan, www.indiacoffee.org)

COFFEE DRINKING IN INDIA: CHANGING EQUATIONS

- The demographic composition of coffee consumers has changed drastically since the establishment of India's first coffee house way back in 1780. The grubby intellectualism of the old coffee houses of Kolkata and Delhi no longer exists. Coffee cafes are more of popular hangouts for young Indians aged between 15-25 years.
- For a generation driven by appearances and with money to spend, coffee bars are a timely mean between five stars and Udipis. Today, at Food & Beverages (F & B) outlets in any five-star hotel, a cup of coffee would be priced somewhere near Rs. 95 excluding sales tax; a cold coffee somewhere near Rs. 125 sans sales tax.
- The friendly neighborhood coffee bars/parlors are the next best things to exorbitantly expensive coffee shops of hotels. The image and the ambience provided in a Barista, Café Coffee Day or Qwiky's outlet is equivalent to the high profile hotels' coffee shops.
- Traditionally a tea-drinking country, the average coffee consumption in India does not do justice to its global stature. The annual per capita tea consumption in India is around 620 grams while coffee consumption is just 52 grams. (*Coffee Break* by Tulika Sen, pages 16-24, *Images Retail*, September 2002)
- Coffee consumption in India has been largely concentrated in three southern states – Tamil Nadu, Karnataka and Andhra Pradesh.
- The total domestic market of about 52,000 tonnes means a per capita consumption of 4.5 grams (1 cup) per annum in the North and 240 grams (50 cups) in the South.(Source: *Branding the brew*, pages 43-45, *Retail Biz*, May 2003)

INDIAN CONSUMER BEHAVIOR

- Coffee at home is significantly different to coffee outside. It is interesting to observe that rating for coffee outside home is better than tea outside home, specifically in the north and the east. Restaurant coffee is rated better on quality in the West and South, particularly when compared with the East.
- Coffee from vending machines rated significantly more satisfactory in the North as compared to the East or the West. In the weak coffee markets defined as the markets in the North, East and West, the key barriers to coffee appear to be its bitter taste (East) and its inconsistent taste outside. High price of coffee

is also felt as a barrier in the South and the North. Attitude towards coffee available outside of home is least favourable in the East

- The knowledge levels on Coffee appear to be relatively weak in the North and East where consumers
  - do not know how to make filter coffee.
  - do not know what chicory is.
  - would make filter coffee if they knew how to make it well (East).
- Consumers in the North also believe that making filter coffee is time-consuming.
- While consumers in the North believe that instant coffee is convenient and tastes good the seasoned coffee consumer in the South believes that all instant coffee contains chicory and that filter coffee is the gold standard in coffee.
- Respondents in the North, followed by East, appear to be most positively inclined to consume more coffee at home if
  - the price was less.
  - they were reassured on health.
  - they could try new/ different recipes.
- Respondents in the North, followed by West, and East appear to be most positively inclined to consume more coffee outside if
  - the price was less.
  - consistently good coffee was more easily available outside.
  - they were reassured on health.

In the coffee strong markets comprising the four southern states, consumers believe that they would consume more coffee at home if their family and friends consumed coffee. In the East, there appears to be a certain level of eagerness to learn about making 'just right' coffee and, as seen earlier, they would make filter coffee if they knew how to make it well. (Author: S. Radhakrishnan, www.indiacoffee.org)

BURGEONING COFFEE MARKET

- Of the global coffee market, the soluble (instant) segment accounts for 40 per cent, while the Roast and Ground (R&G) segment, better known as the filter segment, accounts for the remaining 60 per cent (Source: *Branding the brew*, pages 43-45, *Retail Biz*, May 2003).
- In terms of volume, however, the R&G segment accounts for 84 per cent of the total market.
- Each segment (instant and R &G) can be further categorized into the pure and chicory mix segments. The emergence of the chicory mix segment can be attributed to price desirability of mix over pure coffee.

- World coffee consumption in calendar year 2003 was 11.7 million bags and 109.3 million bags (of 50 kgs) in 2002 (*Business Line*, May 18 2004).
- As for the demand, a growing paucity of time is translating into consumers increasingly seeking convenient product forms and delivery channels (vending machines).
- Furthermore, the consumer is constantly seeking specialty consumption experiences, which combine quality with a pleasing ambience, leading to an increasing demand for specialty food and beverage outlets in the country.
- In the US, for example, specialty coffee outlets for liquid coffee retailing increased from 500 units in 1991 to more than 12,000 in the year 2000. These numbers include 3,500 cafes, 2,700 coffee bars & kiosks, and 2,100 espresso carts. Starbucks, a leading chain, has been experiencing a compounded annual growth rate of over 30 per cent in the recent years (Source: *Branding the brew*, pages 43-45, *Retail Biz*, May 2003).
- The non-traditional coffee distribution channels comprising coffee bar chains, vending machines and specialty coffee powder shops are expected to reach a size of Rs 1,900 crore ($380 million) in India by 2005.(Source: *Branding the brew*, pages 43-45, *Retail Biz*, May 2003)

LIQUID COFFEE RETAIL IN INDIA

Of late, there has been a mushrooming of coffee pubs and cafes across regions, and across the country as a whole. Coffee chains like Barista, Qwiky's and Cafe Coffee Day (run by Amalgamated Bean Coffee Trading Co Ltd) have become hugely popular hangouts for Indian cities' young and trendy consumers. These cafes and pubs are not just places where people buy coffee; they also try to sell a certain lifestyle. The chains, with their glitzy interiors and designer furniture, are targeted at urban, upper-middle-class and rich Indians. Coffee served in these chains includes latte, mocha, cappuccino, espresso, friazzo and even the perennial old favorite, Madras filter coffee.

The market for vending products in India is opening up. With organized retailing coming in, consumers have started believing in brand names. Vending products through machines started not only for coffee and tea, but also for soft drinks, chocolate confectionery and magazines, amongst others. The total strength of vending machines in the country is approximately about 45,000 machines in 2003, which includes a large number of unbranded machines too. Cafe Coffee Day's vending machines have a special niche in the market compared to competitors because Cafe Coffee Day machines offer filter coffee unlike the instant coffee offered by competitors' brands. They have more than 5,000 machines in the market as of 2003. The company is focusing on the southern states of the country such as Tamil Nadu, Karnataka, Andhra Pradesh and Kerala, and the western region, starting with various markets in the state of Maharashtra. (www.euromonitor.com)

CONCEPT OF A COFFEE BAR

The concept of a Coffee Bar is European and the idea is to provide a place for having quality coffee with personalized selection assistance and an ambience where one can think, read, have dialogue, interact for personal, social and business needs. A Coffee Bar is a getaway from the daily grind where one can sit back, relax and surrender to the simple pleasures of coffee to enjoy the finest coffee experience. Thus a Coffee Bar provides not only stimulating coffee but also a fulfilling experience.

Smart marketers are building communities of loyal shoppers who value their brands not only for core benefits they give, but also for the experiences that surround searching, buying and consuming those products or services. Experience marketing in India is "the in thing" in a big way as today in the 21st century, customers are getting to see movies or just hang-out in a new breed of air-conditioned multiplexes with numerous screens within the same building and having food courts, entertainment zones, shopping arcades, not to mention, clean toilets and ample parking space. 'Coffee bars' have taken coffee values beyond just the drink by creating a real environment around coffee drinking that makes the beverage an experience.

The Coffee Bar enjoys a place of honor and is built very much on the same lines of a bar. The place provides an outlet to non-alcoholic drinking community, where one can visit with family, friends etc. It boasts of delivering the best tasting straight coffees like Espresso. Cappuccino, South India Coffee and other varieties such as Iced Coffees and Laced Coffees to satisfy the most demanding coffee lover, cup after cup.

Different varieties of coffee are brewed and blended using fresh coffee beans and served in lively coffee mugs of vivid colors. Coffee beans like Robusta and Arabica are displayed in transparent glass bottles. These beans are roasted to different stages for different flavors and kept ready. As and when required, these are grounded in small quantities and thus each cup of coffee is made to order. The coffee is brewed in a special brewing apparatus, which can make 2 to 4 cups at one time. It is brewed on slow heat on a burner. Generally, bars use the espresso method to brew each cup, which is a far superior method that administers the delicate pressure to extract the flavor and aromatic oils from each bean.

Most of the outlets are in the range of 1000-1500 sq. feet. The Coffee Bars feature professionally designed interior layout to maximize efficiency in production and delivery. It is operative right from the kitchen design to the computerized order entry system, to interior décor, appealing wall signage and custom-made neon window signs. A Coffee Bar is generally located near entertainment complexes, shopping centers and food joints.

The Coffee Bar manager should ideally have professional qualification in the area of catering, housekeeping and food science with specialization in coffee brewing and preparation. Special diet cookery course, hotel supervisory and management course and proficiency in computer use are added advantages.

KEY SUCCESS FACTORS

The Coffee Bar business is strongly driven by efficient logistics management and secondly by offering a price-performance proposition that allows it to become a part of the natural drink of the population. Starbucks is a case in point. Here are a few observations made by industry experts regarding successful running of Coffee Bar business in India:

- Menu design should cater to the Indian tastes. For example, a range of snacks and eatables may also be available at Coffee Bar.
- There should be continuous addition of new flavors to the menu.
- It has been observed that instead of giving discounted prices, it is more effective to just add value to the purchase by topping it with other things such as customer service.
- As business depends on repeat visits, the people may be encouraged to sit out and develop a rapport with bartenders.
- Quality and sourcing of raw materials is crucial.
- In a price sensitive market like that of India, real battle is fought over pricing.
- Ambience is the most important factor for successful running of a Coffee Bar.
- The Coffee Bar must make sure that customers obtain what they need quickly and little or no effort. Efficient service is a key success factor.
- The ability to produce and obtain large amounts of things rapidly. The calculability also ensures customers are served quickly.
- The manager should search for the means to exert increasing control over both employees and customers; the employees should have guides and handbooks to tell them exactly how to look and what to say. The customer is unobtrusively made aware how to go about ordering.
- There should be predictability about what you are going to get. Franchising plays on predictability to sell its products.

You only get one chance to make the first impression. Every customer who sits in the Coffee Bar evaluates service at the Bar on the basis of customer service provided by each and every individual employee they encounter. If the staff does a good job, the customer will tell others. To make the customers happy, one should try and improve:

- Illumination
- Noise discomforts
- Décor and color planning
- Temperature control factor
- Designing for customer's comfort
- The work area and working habits
- Personal assistance in flavor selection

PROFILES OF KEY PLAYERS

BARISTA

Barista traces its roots back to the old coffee houses in Italy- the hotbeds of poetry, love, music, writing, revolution, and of course, fine coffee. Drawing inspiration from them, Barista appears to have taken on the objective of transporting the magic of Italian coffee houses to various chosen Indian locations.

Barista, a chain of specialized Espresso bars, was established in February 2000 to recreate the ambience and experience of the typical Italian neighborhood Espresso Bars in India. Barista aims to provide a comfortable place for people to relax and unwind over a cup of coffee. Turner Morrison has a 60 per cent stake in Barista Coffee Company Ltd. with Tata Coffee holding 34 per cent and six per cent stake is held by the employees.

In just a few years. Barista has created a niche in not only the speciality coffee segment, but in the lives of millions of satisfied consumers across the country. At present, the Barista Coffee has 130 Espresso Bars and Espresso Corners in Delhi, Mumbai, Kolkata, Chennai, Bangalore, Hyderabad, Chandigarh, Panchkula, Goa, Pune, Ahmedabad, Lucknow, Kanpur, Shimla, Ludhiana, Baroda, Nagpur and Dehra Dun, etc. making it one of the largest retailers of speciality coffees in Asia. It also has presence in Sri Lanka and Dubai.

The ambience of the Barista Espresso Bars is a recreation of the Italian aura. Barista brings to Indians the concept of the neighborhood Espresso Bars that has originated from Italy and unlike the coffee bars in other countries, promotes an interactive, social bright environment in its bars.

Traditionally, coffee has always been associated with some core passions - primarily reading, music, art and culture. Barista along with Art Today sponsored the art exhibition of Jatin Das's latest water collection and serving exquisite coffee for the patrons to relish. Through its associations with Art Today, Barista reiterated the bond between coffee aficionados and art patrons.

To add to the informal ambience, Barista Coffee also provides stimulating and interactive games like pictionary and scrabble for the guests. Open sevens days a week, most Barista Espresso Bars begin brewing from 9 a.m. and are open till late night.

Barista places strong emphasis on the quality of coffee beans and the process of preparing, rich aromatic coffee. Barista's coffee comes in many interesting variations and flavors. The coffee at Barista is a blend of finest Arabica beans, grown on high altitudes and roasted with precision. The coffee is created with carefully hand picked mature cherries of the Arabica coffee plant. This 100% Arabica coffee is sourced from Tata Coffee's plantations in Karnataka. The coffees of Origin (Colombia Supremo, Cuba Caracolilo Crystal Mountain, Jamaica Blue Mountain and others) are sourced from their respective estates and roasted at Barista Coffee's captive roastery in Venice.

Using the best espresso machines of international standards, sourced from an Italian based company, La Cimbali, Barista captures the authentic flavors of espresso, in India. The bartenders, employed by Barista, are given special training in the art of making coffee, by Italian experts, in order to acquire the skills of creating the perfect blend.

From the traditional favorites: Cappuccino, Espresso Macchiato, Espresso Italiano, Caffe Mocha to a variety of Cold coffees, such as Brrista, frozen coffee and Iced Mocha, Barista serves an eclectic range of genuine espresso based beverages. Apart from the variety of delightful coffee, there is a range of tea, Italian styled chilled summer drinks called Granitas and a selection of sandwiches and desserts offered at the Espresso bars.

Barista believes that great coffee is 33% the blend, 33% the machine and 34% the hand, that makes the drink.

Capitalising on its brand name and seeking to drive home the brand; Barista launched the Barista Merchandise. Barista introduced an array of packaged merchandise to be taken home by regulars. The launch of Barista Merchandise is aimed at taking the Barista experience right into the homes of consumers. The introduction of lifestyle products by Barista is a step towards enhancing the coffee-drinking experience of consumers.

CAFÉ COFFEE DAY

Café Coffee Day is part of India's largest coffee conglomerate, Amalgamated Bean Coffee Trading Company Ltd. (ABCTCL), a Rs. 250 crore ISO 9002 certified company with a tradition of over 125 years of coffee growing and the first to roll out the 'coffee bar' concept in India with its first café in Bangalore. Café Coffee Day is the largest retail chain of cafes with 181 cafes across 46 cities in India.

Café Coffee Day serves the coffee it grows on its 5,000 acres of coffee estates and is India's only vertically integrated coffee company. ABCTCL has two curing works at Chikmagalur and Hassan curing over 70,000 tonnes of coffee per annum, the largest in the country. A well-equipped roasting plant caters to the specific requirements of the consumers. The process is carried out under the control of experienced personnel to meet highest quality standards. The most modern technology available is used to maintain consistency and roast the beans to the demanding specifications of the discerning coffee consumer.

Café Coffee Day is essentially a youth-oriented brand with majority of its customers falling in the 15-29 year age bracket. Its menu ranges from hot and cold coffees to several exotic international coffees, food items, desserts and pastries. In addition, exciting merchandise such as caps, T - shirts, mugs, badges etc are available at the cafés. The coffee is attractively priced between Rs. 16/- and Rs. 65/- while food items and desserts are priced between Rs. 15/- and Rs. 60/-.

The company participates in cross promotions with other lifestyle brands and regular events like art exhibitions and live music. This is mainly to popularise coffee drinking, to draw traffic to cafes and to make the cafes a happening place for regulars.

Cafe Coffee Day runs many types of cafes to address the various segments. Most of its cafes are stand-alone cafes but it also has corporate cafes which are located in the premises of large office campuses like Infosys. In office campuses subsidized rates are worked out with the administration departments in lieu of rentals.

It also has retail stores where it conducts business in the premises of retailers like Music World, Pune. Café Coffee Day also has cafes within food court where it shares seating between several non-competing food and beverage outlets.

QWIKY'S - BECAUSE THE WORLD CAN WAIT

It is an increasingly competitive world that we all find ourselves coping with from day to day. We seem to have grown accustomed to the marvels of technology that allow us to conduct almost instantaneous business and social communication with people around the globe. Amazingly, however, we might never have the opportunity to meet to share food and conversation with most of these impersonal contacts.. How have cities like San Francisco, Paris and Vienna guarded and retained the civil attitude and romantic air of the earlier time?

The concept for a neighborhood meeting place grew out of these musings of the founders of Qwiky's at Chimayo Chains. Qwiky's was conceived as 'a heaven where guests can sit back, relax, reconnect with neighbors and make new friends while enjoying specialty coffees and other simple pleasures of life in a friendly low-key environment'. 'Because the World Can Wait' became the consumer proposition for Qwiky's.

Qwiky's first coffee pub came up in Chennai in October 1999. Chimayo Chains has been developing the market in the Indian sub continent as a master franchisee for the region. At the same time, Qwiky's is also building its presence in the United States. The company is also in active negotiation to open in Indonesia, Singapore and other locations under franchising agreements with entrepreneurs who share its vision. In early 2003, the company expanded to Sri Lanka.

Qwiky's operates more than 20 outlets in India and is looking to expand rapidly. It has pioneered the Shop-in-Shop (SIS) gourmet coffee bar business. It has successfully developed coffee islands in large retail stores like Lifestyle, Musicworld and Piramyd Stores Qwiky's Coffee kiosks have also been started at Bharat Petroleum pumps.

Qwiky's SIS stores are managed by its team who provide Qwiky's coffee and service experience to businesses who want to provide their customers with world class coffee house experience. Customers in SIS stores can relax with an excellent cup of coffee and food offering as they take a break from shopping, or wait while their other family members shop.

A co-branding policy is also followed at Qwiky's. Various products are on display at different Qwiky's coffee bars. Some of these are Cadbury's, Hidesign and ITC-owned Expression cards. Company officials claim that a significant per cent of turnover has accrued from the sales of non-coffee items.

CRAZE-NOT JUST COFFEE

The Delhi-based Rs 300-crore Enkay Group of Companies has diverse interests in real estate, finance, tours & travels, restaurants and publishing. In 2002, the group diversified into the hospitality business with plans to tap the coffee retail chain market with a chain of coffee shops under the brand name of Craze.

A new company floated for the purpose is called Enkay Coffee Shop Pvt Ltd. Craze Coffee's existing five of the nine outlets in the National Capital Region are located in Gurgaon. Apart from Gurgaon, three of them are in Delhi and one in Noida.

The company believes if a customer is stepping out for coffee and is hungry at the same time, why not serve him a larger variety. Positioned as 'Craze...not just coffee', the coffee chain is being pitched as a fusion of the Coffee bar concept and continental, Italian and Mughlai food platter and therefore it does not directly compete with Barista or Qwiky's. The company, however, plans to attract footfalls into its outlets through its aggressive pricing strategy: all the fare is priced 25 to 30 per cent cheaper than Barista. The coffee machines have been imported from La Cimbali of Italy.

The company is looking to girdle new Gurgaon city with Craze outlets. It also hopes to target cities in Punjab, starting with Ludhiana, Amritsar and Chandigarh.

Competitive prices, conducive ambience and variety of eatables in the Craze Coffee outletss are being considered its strengths to be at the cutting edge of the market.

References

- *Branding the brew,* pages 43-45, *Retail Biz*, May 2003
- *Coffee Break* by Tulika Sen, pages 16-24, *Images Retail*, September 2002
- *Shortfall seen in global coffee output, Business Line*, May 18 2004
- http://www.retailyatra.com
- http://www.indiacoffee.org
- http://www.cafecoffeeday.com
- http://www.quikys.com
- http://www.euromonitor.com
- Detailed Prefeasibility Report on Franchise Coffee Bar prepared by SBP Consultants and Engineers Pvt. Ltd., New Delhi

INDIAN CASE 1

Food Retailing in India: Challenges & Opportunities

This case has been prepared by Dr. Mukesh Pandey, Associate Professor of Marketing at FORE School of Management, New Delhi. He holds a PGDBM from IIM- Calcutta and B.Tech. from College of Technology, G.B.Pant University, Pantnagar. Before joining academics, he worked with MNC's and Indian companies like Electrolux Kelvinator Ltd., Polar International Ltd. and Usha Fan Industries handling Branding, MIS, Sales and distribution functions.

ABSTRACT

Organized retailing is on the verge of a boom in India with a distinct visibility in food retailing, the focus of study here. Indian food buying behavior is changing in response to increasing proliferation of nuclear families, double-income households and working women, greater work pressure and increased commuting time. Food retailing is emerging as a high opportunity business area.

There are a large variety of retailers operating in the food retailing segment. Traditional types of retailers, who operate small single outlet businesses mainly using family labor, dominate this sector. Organized food retailing in India is among the least developed, and contributes just about 2 per cent of the total retailing in the country. However there are strong opportunities in food retail as a result of encouraging changes in consumer purchasing pattern, the availability of real estate and supply chain development.

The major formats being followed for organized food retailing in India are: Supermarket (e.g. Food World, Nilgiri's), Discount Store (e.g. Subhiksha), Fresh Product Outlets (outlets selling fruits and vegetables in value-added packing), Specialty Stores (narrow product line of an individual food processing firm e.g. Haldirams), and Convenience Store (relatively small store located near residential area).

Indian consumers are rapidly transforming, they are driven not only by income and socio-economic factors but also how they can buy time for a price. Consumer of today are witnessing a paradigm shift in every aspect of life they are now eating McDonald's burgers, driving luxury cars and shopping at malls. Nowadays they are not only shopping for money, they are giving equal importance to convenience as well saving time. According to a study done by KSA Technopak:

1. For the same amount of grocery shopping... consumers are spending 20 per cent less time.
2. For the same amount of eating out spends, consumers are spending about 50 per cent less time.
3. 51 per cent respondents said that saving time is more important than saving a few rupees.
4. 59 per cent respondents prefer to shop closest to their home/office.

India has seen rapid developments in several areas, most notably in incomes, demographic shifts to younger populations and reach and exposure to media and different cultures. Indians shell out up to 52 per cent of

their incomes on food. Food consumption has been rising at an average annual rate of about 10 per cent in nominal terms. However, the retailing of food and staples remained largely unchanged. Over 90 per cent of all produce is sold via the wet markets with organised business accounting for just 2 per cent of food and staples retailing.

India: Agricultural giant but processed food pygmy

Although Indian consumers are becoming more sophisticated with regard to the food they purchase, convenience packaged food products are affordable only to certain consumer groups. When it comes to packaged food products, consumers are price-sensitive, especially as the average Indian household does not consider most packaged food essential. Middle and upper-middle income segments are thus the major targets for value-added food products, such as pasta and frozen food. The majority of households still prefer fresh foodstuffs, which are readily available at affordable prices. Freshly prepared food is also overwhelmingly preferred and has achieved high sales through the huge number of eating establishments. The unorganized segment, in the form of cottage industries produces mostly unbranded and often unpackaged food products, which are sold alongside branded/packaged offerings in retail outlets for snacks, oils and fats. In fact, packaged food accounts for less than 5 per cent of total food value in the country.

Driving force-The New Indian Customer

The media burst, growing popularity of Internet has brought the Generation Y closer to all developed world economies. The young 15 to 30 years old are technology-savvy, discerning shoppers, believe in self gratification, have money, are spoilt for choice, look out for differentiation that adds 'fun' to the experience of consuming that product. The Table below captures the extent of change in socio-cultural aspect and attitude from 60s/70s.

The changes in the nation's social structure like improvement of the Indian economy, consumerism, urbanization, profusion of brands have been the main causal factor for the development of the modern formats. Indian food buying behavior is gradually changing in response to the changing social structure. The increasing

Three consumer types across 3 generations of India

Parameter	Traditionalist (60s/70s) Pre-liberalisation	Transient (80s/90s) Liberalisation	Millennium (2000s) Pre-liberalisation
Mindset	Security Conformity Family Obligation Discipline Risk-avoidance Moderation	Freedom Individuality Work Entitlement Self-indulgence Risk-taking Excesses	Meaning Personal style Personal pleasure Accountable Self-control Risk-management Balance
Motto	I want my children to be better off than mine.	I want to be better off than my parents.	I want to enjoy.
Accomplishment	What I've done for my family?.	What I have and own?	What I do?
Obsession	My country	Myself	My society
Purchase behaviour	Functionality Is it good for my family?	Statement Is it good for me?	Enjoyment Is it good for me and my society?
Key driver	Information	Enticement	Entertainment

Source: Madhukar Sabnavis, Indian Management, Volume 41, Issue 7, 2003

numbers of nuclear families, double-income households and working women, greater work-pressure and increased commuting time have put the consumers under constant time pressure. The other equally important factors in the changing Indian landscape are the increasing influence of children, gradual acceptance of frozen, semi-processed and processed foods by the Indian consumer, the growing influence of television in decision-making and improvement in literacy rates. The modern housewife has now started shopping for herself; in fact she appreciates and welcomes:

- A pleasant shopping environment;
- Convenience of one-stop shopping with wider
- Product portfolio at a single location;
- Speed and efficiency in processing;
- More information;
- Better quality and hygiene; and
- Discount too if possible.

The improved income and the increased purchasing power of a larger section of the Indian population makes the opening of outlets, which provide the whole bunch of these improved services a viable opportunity.

How does an Indian consumer spend?

In a developing country like India, a large chunk of consumer expenditure is on basic necessities, especially food related items (see Table). The share of food related items however is going down, which means with income growth, Indians, like consumers elsewhere, spent more on non-food items compared with food products. A recent study by KSA Technopak India Private Ltd has revealed that food and beverage (F&B) sector still gets the major chunk (as much as 52 per cent) of the total consumer spending in India followed by clothing and footwear, which gets 11 per cent. It was also revealed that although transportation expenses were not part of retailing, the transport sector gets 12 per cent (marginally higher than clothing and footwear) of consumers' coffers. Quite contrary to popular perception, the entertainment sector with a meager 3 per cent share is yet to catch up in India, unlike trends in other South Asian countries, the study mentioned. The other categories with increasing share in consumer spends are consumer durables and furniture (7 per cent), healthcare (2 per cent) and housing (9 per cent). Apart from the food segment, home improvement stores are the upcoming segment.

Sector wise Indian Consumer Expenditure

S.No.	Sector	Share of Customer spending in India
1	Food and beverage (F&B)	52 per cent
2	Cloth & footwear	11 per cent
3	Entertainment	3 per cent
4	Consumer durables and furniture	7 per cent
5	Healthcare	2 per cent
6	Housing	9 per cent
7	Others	16 per cent

Source: www.economictimes.indiatimes.com of March 6, 2004

What exactly is food retailing?

According to Mr. Raghu Pillai, the Managing Director of Food World, which is one of the leading organised food retailing chains in India, 'Organised Retailing presupposes a retailers' ability to manage or more importantly influence a set of supply chain variables in a commercially viable and sustainable way.'

Features of a modern retail store

- Efficient management of the supply chain to ensure the profitability of the entire chain,
- Large outlets with modern ambience and facilities,
- Wide product profile,
- Self service facilities etc.

Organised retailing aims at providing an ideal shopping experience for the consumer based on the advantages of large-scale purchases, consumer preference analysis, excellent ambience and choice of merchandise.

International Business Trends in food retailing

In many European countries, such as France, Denmark and Sweden, the share of the top three retailers is more than 50 per cent. Consolidation is leading to the emergence of mass merchandiser and discounter formats to the detriment of other retail formats like the supermarket. In the US, for instance, Wal-Mart, Kohl's and Target are showing impressive year-on-year growth whereas leading department stores are showing little or no growth. The share of private labels in the basket of key food retailers is also increasing, with in-house brands competing fiercely with well-established brands of leading FMCG companies. In the UK, for example, the share of private-label in sales of UK retailers rose from 22 per cent to 38 per cent between 1980 and 2000. In the same period, their share at German food retailers increased from 5 per cent to 21 per cent. This trend is likely to become more established, leading to higher gross margins and greater control by retailers of the quality and price of their merchandise.

Status of Organized retail industry internationally	
Country/Region	Organised retail sector as an approx. % of retail sales
USA	80 per cent
Western Europe	70 per cent
Brazil	40 per cent
Argentina	40 per cent
Korea	35 per cent
Taiwan	35 per cent
Malaysia	20 per cent
Thailand	20 per cent
China	20 per cent

In the international arena, retailing is done in a more organised and professional manner than it is done in India.

Genesis of retail chains in India

Emergence of retail chains was at first witnessed in the textiles sector with companies like Bombay Dyeing, Raymond, S. Kumar's and Grasim opening their own outlets. Titan then successfully created a retailing concept, by establishing its series of elegant showrooms. The later half of the nineties has been a witness to a fresh wave of entrants in the retailing business. The new chains have not been restricted to textiles and garment sellers but there have been entrants from various fields of commerce. Foodworld and Subhiksha

Profile of organized retailers In India					
Format	Brands	Group	No. of stores (approx.)	Estimated turnover (INR million)	Locations
Neighbourhood stores	Margin Free (Discounter)	Margin Free	215	5500	Kerala
	Safal	Mother Dairy	279	1000	Delhi
	Subhiksha (Discounter)	Subhiksha	112	1500	Tamil Nadu
	Radhe	Nirma	3	100	Gujarat
Supermarket	Foodworld	RPG	75	3600	Tamil Nadu, AP, Karnataka
	Nilgiri's	Nilgiri's	30	500	Tamil Nadu, Karnataka
	Sabka Bazaar	Sabka Bazaar	19	110	Delhi
	Haiko	Lakewood Mall Pvt. Ltd.	1	120	Mumbai
	Trinetra	Trinetra	19	400	AP
	Ravji's	Adani	5	150	Gujarat
	Shoprite	Shoprite, South Africa	Opening soon	—	Mumbai
Hypermarket	Giant (Discounter)	RPG	1	850	Hyderabad
	Big Bazaar	Pantaloons	5	1800	Delhi, Mumbai, Hyderabad, Kolkata, Bangalore
Cash & Carry	Metro	Metro	1	—	Bangalore
Mother Dairy	Mother Dairy	Opening soon	—	Bangalore	Daily Fresh
Source: *Retail Biz, February 2004*					

in food and Fast-Moving Consumer Goods; Musicworld and Musiccafe in music; Viveks and Vijay sales in the consumer durables etc were the beginners. Now the number of players and the variety of formats and product categories reflect variety.

Indian food retail industry

India is one of the largest producers of milk, fruits and vegetables in the world. Yet, the organised food retail business in the country is among the least developed and still contributes to only about 2 per cent of the total retailing in the country. There are a large variety of retailers operating in the food-retailing sector. This is not surprising considering the enormous size of the market for food. However, traditional types of retailers, who operate small single outlet businesses mainly using family labour, dominate this sector. In comparison, supermarkets account for a minuscule proportion of food sales. This is because of the strong competitive strengths that traditional retailers possess. These include low operating costs and overheads, low margins, proximity to customers, long opening hours, and additional services to customers (such as home delivery). The irony is not so difficult to comprehend if one looks at the Indian food chain. From the farm to the store, the links are too many and full of problems. A large chunk of fresh fruits and vegetables is lost due to lack of post-harvest handling, storage and processing facilities. Tonnes of grains are wasted due to improper handling and storage, pest infestation and poor logistics management. Intermediaries or 'middlemen' gobble up a large portion of the earnings, which should go to the farmer. Not only that, these middlemen cause delays, which in a business of perishable goods can be lethal. The result is a chain stuffed with inefficiencies. Nevertheless, supermarket sales expanded at a much higher rate than other retailers. This is because greater numbers of higher income Indians prefer to shop at supermarkets because of convenience, higher standards of hygiene and the attractive ambience. For organised retail of food to be successful, it is important to get rid of these inadequacies so that costs are pruned and, more important, the benefits of the gains are passed on to the consumer.

The move towards multi-category and multi-format outlets is diminishing the scope of existing retailers to differentiate on the basis of assortment or location alone. Differentiation on the basis of value for money and value-added services will, however, become increasingly important. Retailers across the world are experiencing a wave of consolidation that is being driven by the desire for economies of scale, saturation in domestic markets and the desire for access to new markets.

Growth opportunities

The Indian retail industry is no more nascent today. There has been a significant change in retail trading over the years, from small kiranawalas in the vicinity to big super markets; a transition is happening from the traditional retail sector to organized retailing. The unorganised sector still holds a dominant position in this industry. The organized segment holds just about 1.2 per cent of the current US$ 245 billion retail market, which is expected to reach about US $ 385 billion by the middle of this decade (Source: www.etretailbiz.com, Dec2002). Despite the retail store density in India with regard to population being the largest, it is estimated that over 90 per cent of the stores are less than 500 sq. ft in size. Industry estimates put the number of retail outlets at 12 million. This is clearly indicative of small-shop ownership crowding the unorganized segment of retailing. While this fragmented market structure does pose significant challenges for organized retailing, potential does exist if modern information and supply chain management systems are deployed to support the development of convenience shops that match customer expectations.

The size of the F&B and grocery segment is estimated to be $75,000 million and organised retailing currently stands at less than $400 million. As such the likely growth rate and opportunities in F&B and grocery segment sector are phenomenal; also there was no national chain so far and current formats were much smaller than ideal, near home convenience stores were also missing. As per the KSA Technopak study, the key challenges in this sector are: ability to build the scale quickly and merchandise and supply

According to a study (Source: (www.financial express.com) commissioned by Confederation of Indian Industry (CII), organized retailing, which includes shopping malls, departmental stores, specialty stores and discounters and is presently limited to metros and 'A' class cities, is likely to become a feature of semi-urban and rural areas where disposable income is increasing. This growth as per the study will be led by food, fast moving consumer goods (FMCG), durable and home improvement product categories, facilitated by organised retail formats. It is important to note that Indian domestic retail sector has 12 million outlets, which includes unorganized sector such as grocery stores and other traditional formats. Cooperatives have been present in India for several decades, spurred by the encouragement given by the Indian Government, which viewed the cooperative movement as an integral component of its erstwhile socialist policies. However, since the 1990s, there has been a reduction in government support for cooperatives. In 2002, there were about 35,000 outlets run by cooperatives (Source: Retailing in India, Euromonitor International, 2004).

The core categories and diversified formats of the world's leading food retailers		
Retailer	Assortment	Formats
Wal-Mart	Food, Clothing, Furniture & Furnishings, Auto Services, General Merchandise, Electrical, Financial Services, Appliances, etc.	Discount, Hypermarkets, Warehouse Clubs, Neighbourhood Stores, Convenience Stores
Tesco	Food, General Merchandise, Clothing, Home Products, Fuel, Automobiles, etc.	Supermarkets, Hypermarkets, Neighbourhood stores, Convenience Stores, Internet, Catalogue, Department Stores
Carrefour	Food, Clothing, General Merchandise, etc.	Hypermarkets, Convenience Stores, Supermarkets
Royal Ahold	Food, General Merchandise, Homeware	Supermarkets, Hypermarkets, Clubs, Internet,
Source: Rabobank International		

Various retail formats

The change in the social formats has led to the development of modern retail outlets, mainly in the southern parts of the country. Chennai, Bangalore and Hyderabad are developing as the hub of organised retail in India. The culture is spreading to the other parts of the country too, with the western and northern parts of the country too providing good opportunities currently. Different players are trying out different formats. A successful fully Indian or 'swadeshi' model in Indian retailing is yet to be developed. The models, which are highly successful in certain areas of the country, are able to achieve only moderate success in certain other areas. The major formats being followed for organised food retailing in India are:

Supermarket: Relatively larger-low cost, low margin, high volume, self service operation designed to serve total need for food, laundry, and household maintenance products. e.g.: Food World, Nilgiri's, Shoppers Stop.

- Discount Store: Standard merchandise sold at lower prices with lower margins and higher volumes. True discount stores regularly sell merchandise at lower prices and mostly national brands. e.g. Margin Free Markets, Subhiksha.
- Fresh Product outlets: Outlets selling fruits and vegetables in value-added packing. These outlets generally cater to the higher segment of the society. e.g. Namdhari and Safal.
- Specialty Stores: Narrow product line of an individual food-processing firm. e.g. Haldirams, MTR.
- Convenience Store: Relatively small store located near residential area, open long hours seven days a week, and carrying a limited line if high-turnover convenience products at slightly higher prices. e.g. Outlets near petrol pumps, cinema halls, etc.

Problems in food retailing in India

While food retailing is a high opportunity business area, it also has its own complexities viz.

1. Retailing is subject to plethora of laws and regulations at Central, State and Municipal/local level. For example restrictive zoning legislation limit availability of land for retail/ commercial purposes and restrictions on interstate movement of food grains deprive farmers from getting

remunerative prices. Restrictive labour laws, urban land ceiling regulations, restrictions on shop opening timings, requirements for shops to close once a week, lack of uniform tax structure and multiple layers of taxes are other factors impeding growth of supermarkets & retail food chains.

2. The demand pattern varies significantly from one location to another and the storage and transportation infrastructure are not sufficient enough to accommodate this.
3. At present the biggest bottlenecks are the lack of infrastructure and technical know how. Both these problems are primarily due to lack of capital and experience in food retailing. Because of these problems, majority of food retailers are still limited to a few cities or one particular region, even when they have significant experience in food retailing, like Nilgiri's and Food World.
4. Sales tax on various food items varies from state to state. Complexity is added by the fact that smaller retailers avoid paying taxes, as the sales are not recorded at the point of sale. This makes the product sold by organised retailers comparatively expensive.
5. There are also restrictions on the movements of goods due to multi-point patent system. The introduction of a uniform taxation policy and value-added-tax (VAT) in the near future should help overcome this barrier.

Some critical socio-economic issues that need to be researched

1. Does the marketing arrangement work to the exclusion of the small and marginal farmer or are there ways to include these vulnerable groups of farmers in the production process?
2. Do food chains improve the marketing efficiency of agricultural commodities and benefit both the farmer and the consumer?
3. Will regional specialization induced by food chains lead to unsustainable farming practices by adopting mono cropping etc?
4. What impact will it have on the farmers' incomes and sustainability in use of natural resources?
5. In a labor surplus economy like India where the retailing industry employs a considerable amount of labor, will the development of super markets chains lead to the displacement of labor due to the excessive mechanization?
6. Traditionally marketing employs a large number of women for the post harvest activities. Will the creation of food chains lead to the displacement of this important source of employment to women?
7. What are the bottlenecks that face the food super market chains in their entry and operations?
8. Are consumers benefited by the entry of food chains?

FDI in Indian Retail Industry

Though the Indian retail industry is still a "protected industry" from the standpoint of foreign direct investment (FDI), the government is expected to provide some flexibility on this front. Though FDI can help generate employment in this sector, it is likely to pose stiff competition for existing small businesses. There has been vigorous opposition to foreign direct investment (FDI) in retailing from small traders who fear that foreign retailing companies would take away their business, lead to the closure of many small trading businesses and result in considerable unemployment. Given the political clout of the small trading community, because of their enormous numbers, the government has barred FDI in retailing since 1997. Hence, at present, foreign retailers can only enter the retailing sector through franchising agreements.

Unlike the country's FDI investment objective of technology transfer and export promotion of the 1980s, today's infusion of capital - specifically in the retail segment - can bring to the table issues on size of investment, actual inflows and domestic company take-overs. Given the constraints, FDI should be viewed as a developmental resource that can help in restructuring the industry, which can fill up the resource and technology gaps in the retail segment. Experience elsewhere also shows that the entry of international retailers provides momentum for the growth of organised food retail. This is exemplified by the growth of food retailing in another Asian economy, China has followed a policy of gradually opening up permitted in purely retailing ventures, but this is a major impediment for international retailers wishing to invest in India.

To start retail operations in India, an International retailer requires the approval of the Foreign Investment Promotion Board (FIPB). While the FIPB has recently allowed foreign investment in duty-free shops at international airports, international retailers have largely been obliged to enter India either through the franchisee route or as Non-Resident Indians. Some examples in food categories are Marks & Spencer, Mango and Lifestyle. Nevertheless, foreign retailers are allowed to invest in the cash-and-carry format.

Paradigm shifts happening in the world of food retailing

Following transition, which is reflected by formats of leading food retailers, is collated as per Table on an earlier page.

1. Retailers are looking to capture a larger share of consumer spending by expanding their product portfolios.
2. Increasing pressure on financial performance is also prompting food retailers to look at high-margin categories, which include non-food products and services.
3. Retailers have also realised that they need to become multi-format if they are to expand their customer base and gain a competitive edge.

In line with international trends, the Indian market has already seen organised food retailers going multi-format and multi-category with an increasing focus on private labels. Consolidation is likely to be triggered by the entry of leading Indian Corporates and international retailers into the food-retail arena.

Entry of large Corporates in Indian food retailing

As per KSA Technopak, the organised retailing industry grew by 25 per cent to Rs 22,500 crore in 2003-04. Organised food retailing in India is on the verge of a boom with almost all the big corporate houses including Tatas, Reliance, ITC group, K Raheja Corp i.e. promoters of retail chain Shoppers' Stop, Lohias promoted Indo Rama, Mumbai based R K Hospitality, Kishor Biyani with his Food Bazaar, hypermarket store Giant, RPG group with its hypermarket 'Food World' and even multinationals such as Shoprite as well as Metro AG eyeing the sector aggressively. The Rs 4,000-crore Godrej group is also foraying into food retailing either by adopting the acquisition route or by setting up a Greenfield project, Godrej group was in talks (Source: Reeba Zachariah, July 26, 2004, www.rediff.com) for the acquisition of the South India-based retail chain, Trinetra. Offering a one-stop shopping experience within an air-conditioned and comfortable environment, these new retail stores are vying to capture the attention of urban households, who seek value added products away from the no-frills service and products offered by traditional food stores. More importantly, these up-market retail stores offer consumers a wider range of products, as well as premium goods not typically found in kirana-stores. The entry of so many professionally managed business houses will raise the standards of customer service, improve category management and make sourcing more efficient.

Private labeling

Given the commodity nature of many products like cereals, pulses, and staples, there is strong potential for private labeling and creating in-house brands. Private labels help retailers to increase gross margin as well as help in controlling merchandise, quality and price. Nilgiri's, one of the successful retailers in the country, retails about 40 per cent under its own label.

Food is the largest category in consumer's spending basket (about 52 to 53 per cent of the value of final private consumption) but Indian consumers are deprived of quality food products, variety and value-added services at the retail end largely because of the highly fragmented nature of food retailing. This share is significantly higher than in developed economies, where food and food products account for about 20 per cent of consumer spending. Organised food retailing industry in India, though in a stage of infancy (with share less than 1 per cent of food retail market) has the potential and great opportunity to bridge this gap. In India, the majority of food consumption is still at home. There are strong opportunities in food retail as a result of encouraging changes in consumer purchasing patterns, the availability of real estate and supply chain development.

Organised retail is sure to fulfill its potential in the Indian sub continent and to provide more and more opportunities to the Indian investors. The unfulfilled demand of the

Indian consumers for quality products at the right price and environment with the perfect service and ambience will fuel the growth of the Indian retail industry. Organised food retail is a win-win situation for end-customers and suppliers. The different service providers would also get a level playing field in such an environment. Change in the Governmental stance, however, would be of course required for realising the full potential of this vibrant sector.

As has already been seen in many non-food categories the organization on the demand side will fuel organization in the supply chain. The greatest challenges for the retailers are to reduce supply chain inefficiencies and develop infrastructure and technical expertise that will make their chosen business model viable. The retailer with the right location and investment in the supply chain will have the competitive edge. The entry of International retailers in the short to medium term will make the market competitive and will drive consolidation, mergers and acquisitions.

Questions

1. What changes does the future hold for food retailing in India in the light of sweeping changes transpiring in the processed foods industry?
2. Why do you think big corporate houses have jumped onto the food retailing bandwagon?
3. What kind of resistance do you expect from the traditional households to patronizing well-lit, elegant food retail stores and how will you overcome it as a food retailer?

McDonald's & Domino's: Supply Chain to enhance Customer Value

This case has been prepared by Dr. Mukesh Pandey, Associate Professor of Marketing at FORE School of Management, New Delhi. He holds a PGDBM from IIM- Calcutta and B.Tech. from College of Technology, G.B.Pant University, Pantnagar. Before joining academics, he worked with MNC's and Indian companies like Electrolux Kelvinator Ltd., Polar International Ltd. and Usha Fan Industries handling Branding, MIS, Sales and distribution functions. He was assisted in this research by Amber Wajahat, his student at FSM (Class of 2005).

ABSTRACT

The case study focuses on supply chains of McDonald's (a multinational fast food chain that started operations in India in 1996) and Domino's (it also entered India in 1996 developing more than 150 outlets covering over 20 major cities for Pizza delivery business) in the backdrop of rapidly changing food industry with a view to analyse as to how supply chain can provide a strategic competitive advantage. It critically analyses Domino's and McDonald's revamped supply chain operations in India, which have been designed to ensure fast deliveries at the lowest cost to the customer's without compromising on the quality. The case also illustrates how the low costs achieved can then be passed on to the customers in the form of lower prices and hence significant competitive advantage can be derived.

The case study highlights various suppliers for different ingredients to be used for food items being sold at the respective McDonald's and Domino's centers. Various aspects of supply chain management are brought out through descriptions of various suppliers and what they supply, logistics and quality control. A consistency in quality is achieved at all the centers through strategic and cost-effective procurement from different parts of India while keeping the costs low.

The case study provides two real-life examples of how supply chain management is a key function in marketing successfully. You maintain a consistent quality of the food products being sold while offering the customer a location-independent assurance of quality. Keeping the input costs under a tight leash also affords an opportunity to keep the prices attractive enough to make the customer keep coming back for more.

Supply Chain providing a strategic competitive advantage

Supply chain represents a value delivering system starting from raw material to final product carried to final buyers. Supply chain involves procuring the right inputs (raw materials components and capital equipments: converting them efficiently into finished products and dispatching them to the final destinations; an even broader perspective calls for studying how the company's suppliers themselves obtain their inputs. The supply chain perspective can thus help a company identify superior suppliers and distributors and help them improve productivity, which ultimately brings down the company's cost.

Supply chain management addresses the fundamental business problem of supplying product to meet demand in a uncertain world especially post 1990's where product life cycles are getting shorter and product variety is increasing thus making the task more complex. Outsourcing, globalization and business fragmentation thus make it imperative that the issue be tackled from the point of view of entire supply chain rather than the more limited view of an individual company. When the multi-company nature of the supply chain is combined with a process flow, it can be analyzed that supply chain management is not just about order-fulfillment; it must be a part and parcel of product design, introduction, promotion, fulfillment and recycling. Further more, to achieve its full impact, it must be embedded fully in business strategy and considered throughout the product life cycle.

The supply chain view sees markets as destination points and amounts to a linear view of the flow. A broader view sees a company at a center of a value network that includes its suppliers and it's suppliers' immediate customers and their end customers. The value network includes valued relations with others such as university

researchers, government approval agencies, and so on. A company needs to orchestrate these parties to enable it to deliver superior value to the target market. The company should first think the market and then design the supply chain backward from that point.

Facets of food industry

The food industry presents many facets, from the traditional labor intensive activities which includes slaughtering, preparing and preserving meat; milling grains and manufacturing bakery products; canning and preserving fish products, fruits and vegetables, manufacturing vegetables and animal oils and fats and animal feeds; and processing sugar, coffee, tea. In addition to this the food industry is increasingly engaged in the manufacturing higher stage processed products such as convenient and ready to eat frozen foods. The drink industry covers such activities such as distilling and blending spirits; and processing malt liquors, wine, soft drinks, mineral water, and fruit juice.

India is primarily considered to be an agrarian economy and today is one of the world's major producers of food grains. India has developed self-reliance in cereals, grains, and vegetables and fruits. This self sufficiency over a period of time turned out to have its own drawbacks like agricultural surpluses, wastages, reduction of rural jobs, lower pricing for growers etc. A pioneering study done by McKinsey for its 'FAIDA' report on food and grocery retailing estimated 'wastage' loss in the Indian food chain at over Rs 50,000 crore annually, almost all of it attributable to the archaic intermediary chain food has to go through to reach the end customer. This wastage in India is because of lack of proper infrastructure for storage and transportation under controlled conditions, which ranges from physical damage and vermin infestation to improper temperature, humidity and airflow. It's a double whammy, so that while the customer ends up paying more, the original producer, in many cases the Indian farmer, gets paid much less than what he would have got in a modern retail environment.

The entire processed food industry can broadly be classified into the following sub sectors:

- Grain processing
- Fruit and vegetable processing
- Fish processing
- Milk processing
- Meat and poultry processing
- Packaged and convenience foods
- Alcoholic beverages and soft drink

Sweeping changes happening in Indian Food Industry

The Indian food processing industry is witnessing a lot of activity in the ready to cook, ready to eat and snack foods as well as beverages and nutraceutical foods. With changing food habits and market dynamics, the scope of processed food has graduated from bakery, milk products and confectionery to ready-to-eat products like cooking pastes and packed agro products. Growing urbanization coupled with improvement in overall education levels and infrastructure is providing a strong impetus to the Indian food processing industry With food processors like Britannia, Godrej, GCMMF (Amul), Parle, Tasty Bite eatables, MTR Foods, Nestle, Dabur, Cadbury's, ITC Foods, Satnam Overseas, Enkay Texofood, Mother Dairy, ADF Foods and many other dishing out newer and newer products to meet the demand of Indian palate, the ready-to-eat foods business is reported to have reached a turnover of around Rs. 70 crore (Year 2003). Ready-to-eat foods have now become a strong option in Home-meal-replacement segment along with conventional fast food joints and take-away/ carry-home outlets.

India, which is an agrarian economy, is considered major granary of the world and has developed self-reliance in cereals, grains, and vegetables and fruits. This self sufficiency over a period of time turned out to have its own drawbacks like agricultural surpluses, wastages, reduction of rural jobs, lower pricing for growers etc. This clearly indicates that there is immense potential to fight out the evils associated with an excessive food scenario and its alleged drawbacks. As per CII-McKinsey report on India's food, agro products and food processing sector titled FAIDA, agro products and food processing sector in India has a turnover of approximately Rs. 25,00,000 million out of which value added food products comprise Rs. 8,00,000 million.

Logistics management practices

The integration of the economies of the world has forced the companies to look for the minimum cost locations as a means of satisfying increased demand. Studies reveal that total logistics cost constitute nearly 10 per cent of India's GDP, of which nearly 40 per cent is due to transportation alone. In today's competitive environment, companies all over the world are shifting their attention towards understanding and implementing extended supply chain management that integrates product, process and information flows within and across organizational boundaries. Rapid developments in information technology are forcing companies to look for and implement continuous improvements in their supply chain models. Infrastructure in India is considered to be very poor compared to other developed and developing countries.

Agricultural raw materials sourcing is a key factor for controlling production costs as well as for ensuring quality of food products, the social, sensorial or food safety aspects. Thus, it is important that reliable sources of raw materials are ensured at the qualities and quantities needed and at competitive conditions. A link with farming and farmers therefore is needed but the form of this link depends on overall business conditions, the availability of the raw materials, their characteristics and the company's needs (qualities and quantities). Thus, food-marketing companies buy raw materials through the trade as primary processed materials or directly from farmers, in the process securing long-term business objectives by building long-term collaboration with suppliers, the farmers, traders and primary processors. Keeping this in mind we decided to analyse the logistics management practices of Domino's and McDonald's.

Domino's entered India in 1996 through a franchise agreement with Delhi based industrial Vam Bhartiya Corp. In late 1999, Indocean Chase, the private equity fund bought a 25 per cent stake in Domino's operations from the Bhartia's, who held Domino's franchise in India. Indocean Chase then advised Domino's to go beyond its 16 outlets in Delhi to exploit the potential in the pizza delivery business. By 2002, Domino's had around 150 outlets covering over 20 major cities in India.

Domino's USP of home delivery in 30 minutes

When Domino's entered Indian market, the concept of home delivery was still in its nascent stages . It existed only in some major cities and was restricted to delivery by the friendly neighborhood fast food outlets. Eating out at "branded" restaurants was more common . To penetrate the Indian market, Domino's introduced an integrated home delivery system from a network of company outlets within 30 minutes of the order . This home delivery proposition worked its way into the Indian mindsets as it offered compensation of Rs 30 on the price tag if there was a delay in delivery , thus for the first four years Domino's concentrated on "Delivery Strategy".

Initial Supply Chain model of Domino's

Initially, Domino's had a simple mode comprising of three self-contained commissaries in New Delhi, Mumbai, Bangalore which bought their own wheat, tomatoes and other ingredients, processed them and then delivered them in refrigerated trucks to each outlet.

However, with increasing volumes due to rapid expansion across India of Domino's, the existing Supply Chain model of Domino's had to be revamped. It was necessary for Domino's to rethink its supply chain operation, as it was the biggest area of costs. However, there was one favourable business situation and that was that almost 75 per cent of Domino's customer's ordered either from office or home; as a result, it did not have to lease large plots of land in prime locations to attract traffic.

Domino's revamped Logistics Model-2000

Domino's felt the need to revamp its supply chain operations primarily because it wanted to open a large number of new outlets to increase the volume of its operations. Another reason was the company's realization that an efficient and improved supply chain would help it significantly to reduce costs. Further cost effective supply chain offered many opportunities for flexible pricing making the product affordable to large number of customers. In early 2000, Domino's came out with its own unique logistics model revamping it's entire supply chain operations, from sourcing raw materials to shipping them from processing at central location to delivering it to the customer's plate. This model had the following features:

1. **Cost effective procurement:** It began at the point Domino's purchased wheat for making the pizza dough. Domino's first decided the procurement for its key raw materials: wheat, baby

corn, tomatoes and spices. However, regular ingredients like onions were sourced and processed locally by the commissaries. For instance, wheat was procured from Jalandhar (Punjab) wholesale markets as it offered an excellent quality-value proposition. Based on the agricultural map of India, Domino's looked at the best product at the lowest cost. Thus, tomatoes would come from Bhubaneshwar, spices from the South, baby corn from Nepal (where it is 40 per cent cheaper than in India) and vegetables from Sri-Lanka. Domino's refrigerated trucks got the wheat commissary in Delhi. Commissary processed the wheat and prepared the pizza dough. The pizza dough and other item prepared in the Commissary's were then sent to the retail outlets by refrigerated trucks. The temperature was fixed based on the distance between the retail outlets and the commissaries.

This new model offered opportunities for achieving not only the cheapest procurement rate but also provided substantial economies of scale vis-à-vis the old model wherein each commissary purchased its own raw materials within its area of operation and thus was not getting the benefits of cheapest rates available. Earlier Domino's used to sell its products only from its in house outlets but in the new model it started supplying the products to outlets to co-operate offices, railway stations, cinema halls etc. This move increased the company's reach and improved its profits. The benefits derived from the Domino's revamped supply chain were easily seen; in April 2000 Domino's announced a cut in Pizza prices to Rs. 49. This was a clear cut progress towards price flexibility in the market.

2. **Converting logistics problems into business opportunities:** This can be best understood through this real life example. To get to Jalandhar, the trucks had to pass Chandigarh, which because of its cosmopolitan population, was a potential market; therefore Domino's opened a outlet there as the cost of entry was low because there was no additional cost incurred on transportation of products.

3. **Excellent fleet management for optimum resource utilization:** Domino's opened an outlet in every potential market, which fell in route between the commissary in Delhi and Jalandhar, its prime-sourcing base. The same logic was extendable to large market (especially in the tourist season) Shimla that is just a three-hour drive from Chandigarh. On their way back to Delhi, the trucks could pick up cheese from Karnal, a small town on the Chandigarh - Delhi highway and transport it to its commissaries across the country. Similarly, Domino's India planned to extend its operations in Nepal, Sri-Lanka and Dhaka. The company plans to commissary in Sri-Lanka. Earlier if Domino's had to open a new outlet, the commissary in Delhi would have to process the raw material and send it to the outlet and the truck would return empty. With the revamped supply chain Domino's was able to leverage its fleet much better. The logistics model adopted by Domino's offered some obvious benefits including lower transportation cost, cheaper procurement and economies of scale. Domino's has already cut out the duplication in procurement and processing of raw materials across each of the three commissaries.

4. **Understanding Agro-climatic zones-crop specialization practices:** Domino's identified specialty crops in each region and then entrusted the commissary in that region to process that specialty crop. For instance, the commissary for the Eastern region in Kolkata was responsible for buying tomatoes, processing them and then sending them to all commissaries. Similarly the Northern commissaries had to deliver Pizza bases.

5. **Developing the cold-chain logistics:** Once the new model was formalized, Domino's used 25

Domino's: Outsourcing the ingredients

Ingredient	Source from
Wheat	Jalandhar (Punjab)
Cheese	Karnal, Haryana
Tomatoes	Bhubaneshwar, Orissa
Spice	South India
Baby corn	Nepal
Exotic Vegetables	Sri-Lanka
Pepperoni	Australia
Jalapeno	Spain

Source: Business World June 2000

Refrigerated trucks to transport its raw material. Refrigerated trucks were also used to transport product for other companies in the same route. For instance, if an operator in Kochi (Kerala) needed to transport specialty cheese, he could use Domino's fleet to transport his product. The reason for this is simple: not too many people have refrigerated trucks in the country. And Domino's can offer them quality service because it will give them the same standards what they use for themselves. Company sources said that in queries from clients for such working for Domino's were confident that the logistic profit center has the potential to bring in Rs. 10 billion by 2006. However they said that profit center would not be allowed to impede the growth of Pizza business, Domino's core operation. Only those deliveries that do not delay or de-route the truck would be considered.

McDonald's supply chain

For a common man, who may not know the complexities of a supply chain model, it is difficult to fathom how a burger gets served in McDonald's so fast and in the most hygienic packing with consistency in quality and at such cheap prices (just Rs. 40/- for two burgers.). This all has become possible as the traditional three golden mantras of retailing success i.e. location, location, location has been augmented by three more ingredients i.e. supply chain, supply chain, supply chain by McDonald's. McDonald's, through its unique cold chain, has been able to both cut down on its operational wastage, as well as maintain the freshness and nutritional value of raw and processed food products. This has involved procurement, warehousing, transportation and retailing of perishable food products, all under controlled temperatures. An in-depth analysis shows that a super efficient supply chain is what lies behind this global food chain's ability to deliver high customer value at purse friendly prices.

McDonald's-Starting early to ensure product compliance

From farm to factory to fast food in a customer's tray, the well-oiled supply chain of McDonald's has taken several years to build. Although McDonald's made it's entry around the same time as fellow American food giant Kentucky Fried Chicken but eight years later, Kentucky is still a non-starter in India whereas McDonald's has gone places. For McDonald's, foray in India goes back quite a time as it's supply chain work began almost four years before it started its operations in India in 1996. McDonald's not only identifying farmers for each of its ingredients but also hand-held them to churn out products as per company's specifications. For example iceberg lettuce, peas etc. need to be of certain weight and dimension lest they protrude through the patty and get burnt.

McDonald's has one of the best logistics model in India, which follows an extremely systematic procedure outlined as follows:

1. **Quality Assurance:** To maintain consistency and quality of it's products, McDonald's ships all the raw materials viz. Lettuce, patties, et al to a cold storage close to the main market.
2. **Demand based delivery:** Based on a daily demand schedule that is prepared a day in advance, the required amount of raw material is transported to individual outlets.
3. **Centralized warehousing:** In India, McDonald's selected Mumbai based Radhakrishna Food Land Pvt. Ltd (RFPL) as a distribution agent, which acts as a hub for all its vendors. The iceberg lettuce from Ooty, the mutton patties from Hyderabad or the sesame seed buns from Punjab are all brought to RFPL's distribution center (cold storage) in its refrigerated vans. RFPL then stores the products in controlled conditions in Mumbai and New Delhi, and supplies it to McDonald's outlet on a daily basis.
4. **Cold chain maintenance:** The semi-finished raw material is then transported at a particular temperature to ensure freshness and adequate moisture content in the food. This temperature is maintained inside the chamber of specially made trucks throughout the journey and drivers are instructed specifically not to switch off the chilling system to save electricity even in the case of the traffic jam.

Vital links in McDonald's cold chain

In India, all suppliers have to adhere to Indian government regulations on food, health and hygiene. Over and above the McDonald's suppliers have to continuously maintain company recognized standards. As the ingredients move from farms to processing plants to restaurant, McDonald's quality inspection programme (QIP) carries out quality checks at over twenty different points in the cold chain system thus enabling the company to cut down on operational wastage.

Focus on prevention than detection through HACCP: McDonald's systematic approach to food safety through Hazard-Analysis-Critical-Control-Point (HACCP) emphasizes prevention at supplier's facility and restaurants rather than detection through inspection of illness or presence of microbiological data. Based on HACCP guidelines, control points and critical control points for all McDonald's major food processing plants and restaurants in India are identified and limits are established for those followed by monitoring, recording and correcting any deviations. HACCP verification is done twice in a year and certified.

Relationship between McDonald's and its suppliers

To ensure that its relationship with its chain of Indian suppliers is mutually beneficial McDonald's gave its suppliers the opportunity to expand their business and have access to the latest food technology, exposure to advance agricultural practices and ability to grow or to export. There are many cases of local suppliers operating out of the small town who have benefited from their association with McDonald's India.

Some of the suppliers who have benefited immensely due to their relationship with McDonald's India are:

1. Trikaya agriculture-Supplier of iceberg lettuce

Exposure to better agricultural management practices and sharing of advanced agricultural technology by McDonald's has made Trikaya Agriculture extremely conscious of delivering its products with utmost care and quality. Initially lettuce could only be grown during the winter months but with McDonald's expertise in the area of agriculture, Trikaya Farms in Talegaon, Maharashtra, is now able to grow this crop all the year round. McDonald's has provided assistance in the selection of high quality seeds, exposed the farms to advanced drip-irrigation technology, and helped develop a refrigerated transportation system allowing a small agri-business in Maharashtra to provide fresh, high-quality lettuce to McDonald's urban restaurant locations thousands of kilometers away. Trikaya has implemented advance agricultural practices to successfully grow specialty crops like iceberg lettuce, special herbs and many oriental vegetables. Their farm infrastructure features:

- A specialized nursery with a team of agricultural experts.
- Drip and sprinkler irrigation in raised farm beds with fertilizer mixing plant.
- Post harvest facilities at Trikaya include a cold chain consisting of a pre-cooling room to remove field heat, a large cold room and a refrigerated van for transportation where the temperature and the relative humidity of the crop is maintained between 1° C and 4° C and 95 per cent respectively. Vegetables are moved into the pre-cooling room within half an hour of harvesting. The pre-cooling room ensures rapid vacuum cooling to 2° C within 90 minutes. The pack house, pre-cooling and cold room are located at the farms itself, ensuring no delay between harvesting, pre-cooling, packaging and cold storage.
- Refrigerated trucks for transportation.

With this cold chain infrastructure in place, Trikaya Agriculture plans to export this high value product to other international markets, especially to McDonald's Middle East and Asia Pacific operations. McDonald's expertise in packaging, handling and long-distance transportation has helped Trikaya to do trial shipments to the Gulf successfully. In addition to export, McDonald's assistance has enabled Trikaya Agriculture to supply this crop to a number of star-rated hotels, clubs, flight kitchens and offshore catering companies all over India.

2. Vista Processed Foods Private Limited-Supplier of chicken and vegetable range of products

Having struck a joint venture with OSI Industries Inc, USA and McDonald's India Private Limited the organisation called Vista Processed Foods Private Limited produces a range of frozen chicken and vegetable foods. Their world class infrastructure at their plant at Taloja in Maharashtra has:

- Separate processing lines for chicken and vegetable foods.

- Capability to produce frozen foods at temperature as low as -35 degree Celsius to retain total freshness.
- International standards, procedure and support services.

With continued assistance from its international partners, Vista has installed hi-tech equipment for both the chicken and vegetable processing lines, which reflect the latest food processing technology (de-boning, blending, forming, coating, frying and freezing). For the vegetable range, the latest vegetable mixers and blenders are in operation. Also, keeping cultural sensitivities in mind, both processing lines are absolutely segregated and utmost care is taken to ensure that the vegetable products do not mix with the non-vegetarian products.

Now, at Vista, a very wide range of frozen and nutritious chicken and vegetable products is available. Ongoing R&D, both locally and in the parent companies, work towards innovation in taste, nutritional value and convenience. These products, besides being supplied to McDonald's, are also offered to institutions like star-rated hotels, hospitals, project sites, caterers, corporate canteens, schools and colleges, restaurants, food service establishments and coffee shops.

3. Dynamix Dairy-Supplier of cheese

Dynamix Dairy, which is situated in Baramati district of Maharashtra, has brought immense benefits to farmers by setting up a network of milk collection centers equipped with bulk coolers. This easy accessibility has enabled farmers to augment their income by finding a new market for surplus milk. Dynamix Dairy has also made efforts to see that the bulk cooling centres are located in a way that farmers do not have to travel more than an hour from their farms to reach the collection centre thus drastically reducing the time from milking to refrigeration, which is critical, especially since the lack of proper refrigeration can greatly impact the quality of milk. On receipt, the milk is immediately stored in the bulk coolers at the collection centres, to prevent growth of bacteria in the milk and preserve its freshness - thus, maintaining the 'cold chain'. The factory has:

- Fully automatic international standard processing facility.
- Capability to convert milk into cheese, butter/ghee, skimmed milk powder, lactose, casein and humanized baby food.
- Stringent quality control and continuous R&D.

4. Amrit Food-Supplier of long life UHT Milk and milk products for frozen desserts

McDonald's-Outsourcing Base	
Ingredient	**Supplier**
Cheese	Dynamix Dairy Industries, Pune
Dehydrated onions	Jain Foods, Jalgaon
Iceberg Lettuce	Trikaya Agriculture, Pune
	Mina Agritech, New Delhi
	Ooty Farms and Orchids, Ooty
Chicken Patty	Vista Foods, Taloja
Vegetable Patty, Veg Nuggets, Pineapple Pie, Apple Pie	Kirten Foods, Taloja
Chicken Dress	River Dale, Talegaon
Buns	Cremica Industries, Phillaur
Egg less Mayonnaise	Quaker Cremica Pvt. Ltd., Phillaur,Punjab
Sesame Seeds	Ghaziabad
Fish Fillet Patties	Amalgam Foods Ltd., Kochi
Vegetable For Patties	Finns Frozen Foods, Nasik
	Jain Foods, Jalgaon
Mutton and Mutton Patties	Al-Kabeer,Hyderabad

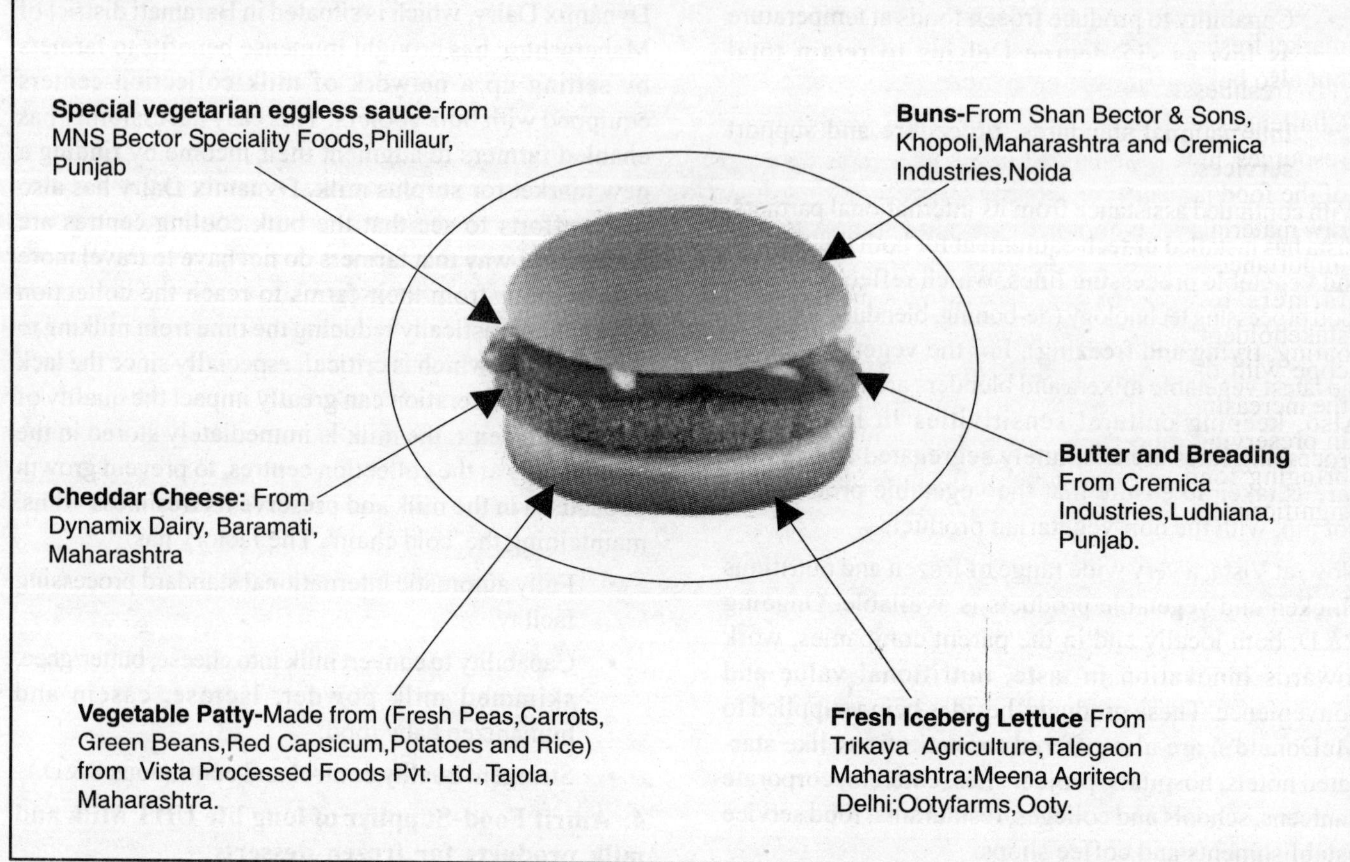

Amrit Food, an ISO-9000 Company, which manufactures widely popular brands-Gagan milk and Nandan ghee at its factory in Ghaziabad, Uttar Pradesh has:

- State of the art fully automatic machinery requiring no human contact with product, for total hygiene.
- Installed capacity of 6000 liters/hr for producing homogenized UHT (ultra high temperature) processed milk and milk products.
- Strict quality control supported by a fully equipped quality control laboratory.

5. Radhakrishna Foodland-Distribution centers for Delhi and Mumbai

An integral part of the Radhakrishna Group, Foodland specializes in handling large volumes, providing the entire range of services including procurement, quality inspection, storage, inventory management, deliveries, data collection, recording and reporting. McDonald's local supply networks through Radhakrishna Foodland, which operates distribution centres (DCs) for McDonald's restaurants in Mumbai and Delhi. The DCs have focused all their resources to meet McDonald's expectation of 'Cold, Clean, and On-Time Delivery' and plays a very vital role in maintaining the integrity of the products throughout the entire 'cold chain'. Ranging from liquid products coming from Punjab to lettuce from Pune, the DC receives items from different parts of the country. These items are stored in rooms with different temperature zones and are finally dispatched to the McDonald's restaurants on the basis of their requirements. Its salient strengths are:

- A one-stop shop for all distribution management services.
- Dry and cold storage facility to store and transport perishable products at temperature up to -22 degree Celsius.
- Effective process control for minimum distribution cost.

All the suppliers of McDonald's share the company's commitment and education to satisfying customers by supplying them the highest quality products. To ensure this, they work cohesively so that the final product reaches the customer consistently taking every care to guard against any interruption in the cold chain, which can break the link and have a detrimental effect on the quality of the product. Also, more products reaching the market fresher and quicker not only benefit the economy but also help the farmer earn more.

Challenges such as the increasing food needs, limited resources, high post harvest losses as well as the needs of the food industry for reliable sources of agricultural raw materials are common to the whole industry and of importance to all stakeholders of the food chain, from farmers to consumers. Common efforts of all stakeholders of the food chain are therefore needed to cope with the current and future challenges to cover the increasing food needs. The role of the food industry in preserving food quality, in reducing food losses, in bringing food to the places of need is increasing in significance.

Questions

1. What are the key changes which have made supply chain management a critical function to succeed in present day business world?
2. How does an efficient supply chain lead to strategic competitive advantage? Answer this question keeping the case of McDonald's in mind.
3. Write a short note on how Domino's revamped its supply chain model in the wake of its extended spread in Indian cities.

INDIAN CASE 3

Large Format Rural Retail Stores: Mera Gaon, Mera Desh

This case has been prepared by Dr. Mukesh Pandey, Associate Professor of Marketing at FORE School of Management, New Delhi. He holds a PGDBM from IIM- Calcutta and B.Tech. from College of Technology, G.B.Pant University, Pantnagar. Before joining academics, he worked with MNC's and Indian companies like Electrolux Kelvinator Ltd., Polar International Ltd. and Usha Fan Industries handling Branding, MIS, Sales and distribution functions.

ABSTRACT

This case study analyses how India can overcome tradition and poverty to create opportunities for retailers thus impacting the whole rural economy. Despite talks of tempting market, big opportunity, large masses to be tapped, success in rural India has eluded several Corporates. It will be interesting to study how rising incomes, media explosion, trade liberalization, sophisticated manufacturing techniques, high quality-low cost products proposition are enticing a larger portion of the population. Most importantly, can India Inc have an ingenious gameplan and really make it big in rural markets?

Tobacco and hospitality major ITC recently took the lead in rural retailing by soft-launching its first rural hypermarket 'Chaupal Sagar' at Sehore in Madhya Pradesh. This case study details the operation of Chaupal Sagar as to how this project has been planned as second layer of ITC's e-Choupal agribusiness model. When a farmer brings his soya bean produce to ITC godowns on a tractor he brings his family along. After he has sold his produce his family visits the hypermarket which provides his family a ready source of daily necessities, agri-inputs and consumer durables along with swings and video games. The goods bought can be lugged back on the tractor. Footfalls to this one-stop destination for farmers are generated during the lean season through organizing activities and events including melas.

ITC has derived the concept of Chaupal Sagar from the traditional *haat* system only difference being its permanent nature. It is a typical urban mall sans the usual razzmatazz and sells at cheaper rates compared to traditional stores elsewhere. The consumer proposition, 'mera gaon mera desh' (my village is my country) aptly sums up the spirit behind Chaupal Sagar.

"Retailing is the pivotal part of delivering value to the consumers. Moment of Truth is spelt at the end of every retailing business."

Y.C.Deveshwar, Chairman, ITC Ltd, Kolkata at Retail India 2004 meet organized by CII.

"Ordinary people are buying what the rich can afford,"

Kishore Biyani, CEO-Pantaloon and Food Bazaar in a panel moderated by Harvard Business School professor Ananth Raman as reported by Julia Hanna, Associate editor of the Harvard Business School Bulletin, April 19, 2004.

"The urban-rural divide gap is melting."

Rajesh Jejurikar, Executive V.P.-Marketing at Mahindra & Mahindra

As a country of enormous economic and social contrasts, India offers a complex marketing arena and demands high specificity in the assessment of its market opportunities for various classes of goods. India's complexity goes beyond sheer numbers: its one-billion

people inhabit four climatic zones-from the temperate north to the tropical south, from the parched west to the inundated east; speak one or more of at least 15 official languages, follow several religious and personal beliefs, differ enormously in their food habits and social customs, and live *together* under varying states of human development, from the highly affluent to the utterly destitute. Besides internal contrasts, India is culturally different from several other markets including Asian markets for historical and social reasons. Consumer goods marketers find India a very unique market that may defy replication of strategies used successfully in other emerging markets, and must be dealt with on its own terms. In the experience of many transnational companies, dealing with India is like dealing with several small markets, at the same time…

Young India

Compared with several advanced countries, where the overall population is aging, India is a very young nation, with more than 70 per cent of its population below the age of 40, and more than 47 per cent below the age of 20. This age distribution is of significance to various consumer product marketers, and explains the boom in all Indian cities in consumption of impulse products and leisure-related expenditure in general, since the onset of liberalization. The projected increase in the economically active population of young Indians holds the key to India's prosperity and its economic potential over the next twenty years, and is expected to unlock a new wave of consumer demand provided the current trend of economic liberalization continues and generates continued investment and trade opportunities in the economy.

Geographical Dispersion of Market Potential

There is considerable variance in economic prosperity levels among various Indian states, linked to the overall wealth creation from agriculture, trade and industrial development. Accordingly, there are affluent and poor districts in most states, classified according to their market potential. At a national level, India has 500 active districts (excluding Jammu and Kashmir), of which the top 150 districts (Class A) account for 78 per cent, while the next 150 (Class B) account for 15 per cent of the national market potential for a wide category of goods. The remaining 200 districts (Class C), which have 40 per cent of the geographical share, are backward and account for only 7 per cent of India's market potential. The spread of affluent and non-affluent districts is uniform in all the four regions. However, the Eastern, Northeastern and Central regions of India have the largest share of backward districts.

These villages and small towns of India, which were once inconsequential dots on maps, are now getting the attention of global marketing giants and media planners. Thanks to globalization, economic liberalization, IT revolution, Indian diaspora, improving infrastructure, advent of commercial and market–oriented farming, use of modern agricultural technology, manufactured inputs like fertilizers, pesticides, high yielding varieties of seeds, middle class rural India is emerging as a growth engine for Indian economy.

NCAER Rural Survey

According to the NCAER, there are five classes of consumer households, ranging from the destitute to the

Age distribution of Indian population (Millions)

Year	Kids	Children	Adolescents	Young Adults	Mid Aged	Aged	Total
	0-4 years	5-14 years	15-19 years	20-34 years	35-54 years	55 & above	
1996	119.5	233.2	90.7	224	178.1	88.7	934.2
2001	108.5	239.1	109.0	246.8	207.3	101.7	1012.4
2006	113.5	221.2	122.4	279.1	239.2	118.7	1094.1

highly affluent, which differ considerably in their consumption behaviour and ownership patterns across various categories of goods. These classes exist in urban as well as rural households both, and consumption trends may differ significantly between similar income households in urban and rural areas.

India's rural areas also have a high incidence of weekly floating and assembly markets besides seasonal markets linked to special occasions, festivals, and harvest seasons, etc. Given the lower quality of infrastructure (all weather roads, telecommunications density, organised banking and finance and credit systems) in rural markets, cost-effective marketing and distribution of goods in rural areas is a continuing challenge in India. The growth of the rural market is considered very important to the overall growth in all essential and basic consumer goods.

Reasons for Rural-Urban Disparity in Retailing

The main reasons why rural India is not getting the kind of retailing urban India gets are lack of economic power and connectivity among the rural producers, markets and consumers. Since 72 per cent of India lives in villages and agriculture being the main source of income, and due to various uncertainties rural people save more and invest less thus caught in a vicious circle.

An idea, according to Mr. Y.C.Deveshwar, Chairman, ITC Ltd to overcome this could be:

- Building retail services to increase productivity and income of the rural population and also providing them with risk and insurance claim facilities.
- On reaching surplus productivity, helping individual farmers with the alternate uses of land.
- To cluster number of goods and services, lay infrastructure and make return on it.
- Bringing extension services to the farmers.

India-The brighter side of life

The Indian economy, which registered growth of 8.2 per cent in FY2003 as a result of nearly 15 years of reforms, is now one of the world's fastest growing economies. This high growth is likely to be sustained over the next three years, unless there are major shocks.

The gold rush in retailing seems to be shifting to the villages. More big-ticket companies, including tobacco-to-hospitality major ITC, petroleum marketers BPCL and HPCL, and the DCM Shriram group, are making a beeline to set up elaborate shopping plazas in the villages to tap the purchasing power of the rural folk.

The creation of infrastructure like rural roads, IT initiatives and corporate India's rural focus have started throwing up jobs in non-urban areas and thus got a huge potential for temporary or contract staffing in secondary locations mainly in sectors like FMCG, banking and insurance and telecom. Companies involved in agri-inputs and fertilizers need temporary employees, as the nature of business is very seasonal. There is lots of action in rural areas with NGOs, educational bodies and hard-core Corporates doing their bit to create infrastructure, both tangible and intangible. There are efforts at providing urban infrastructure in rural areas. Projects like IIT-developed SARI, which aim to provide internet access via 1,000 connections in 350 villages in Madurai, go a long way in creating rural IT infrastructure. IT infrastructure in rural areas will bring low-end, data entry kind of outsourcing jobs in the future to the village level. On the corporate side, Hindustan Lever's Project Shakti has 540 exclusive sales promoters in four states and the self help group-driven model is proposed to be extended to other areas. According to industry sources, other FMCG majors like Dabur and P&G are also upping their ante on rural penetration. ITC plans to cover one lakh villages through its e-choupal network by 2010. ITC e-choupal, an online initiative, gives information of crops to farmers,and is present in over 4,000 village clusters as on Oct, 2004 (*J.Padampriya, http://economictimes.indiatimes.com of 8th Oct 2004)*

Rural Retailing Ventures in India

- ITC has already taken the lead by soft-launching its first rural hypermarket 'Choupal Sagar,' at Sehore in Madhya Pradesh.
- DCM Shriram Consolidated Ltd (DSCL) is planning to tap the opportunity, with plans to open up 30 stores in rural areas of north India over the next two years.
- Not to be left behind, the local sugar cooperatives in rural Maharashtra have opened comparatively smaller supermarkets on their own. These markets stock goods at cheaper prices than those available in the local kirana shops.
- HPCL's venture, called 'Apna Pump', consists of de-scaled petrol pumps situated away from the highways and run by rural entrepreneurs.

- Petroleum major BPCL has also kicked off its rural retail foray with its "Hariyali Kissan Bazaar" store at Shahjehanpur in Uttar Pradesh. BPCL plans to extend the Bazaar, which stocks a host of items ranging from pesticides to farm equipment currently, to include large format retail stores stocking grocery and other everyday items. (*Source: Anil Sasi ,www.thehindubusinessline.com, New Delhi Sept. 24, 2004)*

Chaupal Sagar- ITC's rural retailing initiative

Shopping malls are unlikely to remain a purely urban phenomenon for long. ITC soft-launched its first rural hypermarket called Chaupal Sagar, spread on 8 acres of land with a shopping area of 7,000 square feet at Rafiqganj village of Sehore in Madhya Pradesh in late rainy season of 2004 recording an initial response of about 700-800 footfalls on weekdays and soaring to 1,000 on weekends with conversion levels of 35 per cent. ITC now plans to open about 50 such stores, spread across rural Madhya Pradesh and Uttar Pradesh by end 2005 investing in the range of Rs 2-4 crore for each such store; ultimately taking the figure to 1000 malls based on successful results and acquired experience.

Let us attempt a simple concept explanation of Chaupal Sagar's business model:

- ITC has derived this concept from the traditional *haat* system only difference being the permanent nature of Chaupal Sagar.
- Assumption: Farmers who will come to ITC godowns to sell their produce and with cash in hand would visit the mall nearby.
- By setting up the mall next to the warehouse, it is possible to monetize the footfalls from farmers. The mall will store things of daily needs from soaps/oil/grocery/clothes/pumps/agri-inputs etc and appear like a urban Delhi mall but without the razzmatazz and will sell at cheaper rates compared to traditional stores elsewhere.

Chaupal Sagar: 'Second layer' of ITC's e-Choupal agri-business model

- ITC management calls the initiative as 'second layer' of its agri-business model viz. e-Choupal.
- While the first layer provided the farmers necessary information about weather and prices, the hypermarket initiative is aimed at providing them another platform to sell their produce and purchase necessary farm and household goods under the same roof.
- Chaupal Sagar is the logical culmination of the e-Choupal scheme launched by ITC. Prosperity in Bhopal region has been rising for the past ten years - ever since farmers began switching to soya bean cultivation. Thanks to the information revolution catalysed by the choupals, farmers are beginning to hold their stocks, knowing that there is an advantage in selling later. It helps that most of them grow soya, which is very inexpensive to store. In that sense, what ITC is doing with this warehouse is similar to what it did with its kiosks. In the first phase, having wired up the hinterland, it began using the network to enable a two-way flow of products and services to the rural economy. Working through the sanchalaks, ITC first pushed its own products, like salt, into the hinterland, and then invited others like Parachute and Philips to ride on this distribution chain.

Catching the farmer when he has the money and the mood

- What had started four years ago as an experiment to use IT tools to enable farmers find the best price for their produce has now metamorphosed into this shopping idea.
- The scenario ITC foresees is something like this: Post-harvest, the farmer, with his family, drives into Chaupal Sagar in a tractor trolley laden with the grain he proposes to sell. He parks the tractor on the digital weighing bridge close to the entry point. His grain weighed, he drives on to the godown where the produce is unloaded and he gets his money.
- Meanwhile, his kids can enjoy the swings and video games and his wife may be going around the shopping mall mentally drawing up a shopping list.

- Cash in hand, the farmer family can then make its purchases and drive back by evening, with the tractor laden with the goodies. If they like, they can have a bite in the cafeteria. And the farmer may even carry fertilizers and pesticides for the next crop and get his tractor fuelled at the diesel pump.
- ITC realised the importance of capitalizing on the farmers' good mood, who having got money would spend it anyway and who also have an empty vehicle with which they can lug the stuff back.

Features and facilities at ITC malls

Creating a one-stop destination for farmers, the very sharply thought-out ITC rural store has opted for self service, stocking its merchandise on shelves lining the neat aisles. It stocks and sells everything that a rural consumer may ask for-sarees to kurta-pyjamas to shirts (in the range of Rs 99-500), footwear, cigarettes, soaps, biscuits, namkeens, watches, detergent, toothpaste, oil, spices, other groceries, electronic durable from fans, TVs, microwaves, refrigerators, washing machines, DVD players, pressure cookers, room heaters, watches, sewing machines, grinders, educational supplies, plastic household items, cosmetics and other accessories, farm consumption products like seeds, fertilizers, other agri-inputs, pumps, generators and even tractors, motorcycles and scooters. ITC has launched its own rural range of clothing and shoes too—trousers at Rs 166 a pair tailored for the village folk. According to ITC, fast moving consumer goods and white goods manufacturers are keen to tap the fast prospering rural markets.

Other proposed facilities include:

- A fuel pump for which ITC has tied-up with BPCL
- A cafeteria
- A primary healthcare facility to be serviced by a private healthcare service provider. Here, farmers can consult a doctor who will be available on the premises.
- Veterinary doctors and artificial insemination banks
- Display of large agricultural machinery like threshers and implements.
- Banking facilities and Automated teller machines. ITC is in talks with various financial sector entities in this regard.
- Soil-testing laboratory
- Entertainment area with video games and swings
- An insurance company office
- A training centre for farmers on improved, modern farm techniques.
- Restaurants, public facilities and parking space.

ITC will charge a fee for the services and items sold at the mall limiting its role to creation of infrastructure such as space, computers, building, etc. By offering a slew of other goodies and the above mentioned value add-on facilities, the company is also trying to ensure that farmers keep coming to Chaupal Sagar even at times other than harvest thus hoping to capture the rural folks' out-of-village shopping desire.

Trading Operations at Chaupal Sagar

- ITC is planning to set up 40 rural shopping centres in those states where it has a presence through its e-choupals and IT hubs.
- The trading operations will be on the lines of e-choupals.
- E-choupal is an internet knowledge provider to the farmers started by ITC. Each choupal is made up of 5 villages; 25-30 choupals make way for one Choupal Sagar. The first Choupal Sagar was set up in Madhya Pradesh. The sanchalak of the Choupal Sagar provides services, knowledge to the farmers and sells his produce on behalf of them. This further induces in converting village population into economic organization. Thus, it provides disintegrated, customized and appropriate information to the farmers enabling them to increase productivity leading to increased income and spending capacity. E-choupal also aims at giving the farmers a larger share of consumer spend by giving them multiple choices both on the market and supply side.
- The supermarkets are coming up at ITC's 'hubs', where farmers can come to sell their produce. The hubs are a part of ITC's e-choupal project, wherein farmers can come and log on to the Internet and check the pricing and sell their commodities. During the peak season, a hub sees traffic of about 200 tractors per day on an average, as farmers come to sell their crops at the hubs.
- Samyojaks, who are basically traders, will operate the shopping malls and ITC will place all household

items, commodities there and will create facility for providing online information on commodity rates and weather.

- ITC is offering a very compelling proposition to the companies whose brands it sells, most of whom are national players like Marico, LG, Philips, Eveready, ITC's apparels, TVS bikes and Eicher tractors.
- To solve age-old problem of reach and setting up viable distribution channels in rural India, Eicher Tractors evolved a rental model and gave about 50 tractors to the sanchalaks, who in turn leased them out to farmers, thus generating awareness; Now, lots of companies like Philips, TVS and Eicher plan to use the mall to showcase their entire range. On its part, ITC is accepting stocks on a consignment basis.
- To attract footfalls during the lean season, ITC plans to organise various activities and events including melas. Also, the hubs are strategically located to attract suburban crowds as well.

ITC: Solving one of the biggest bugbears facing Indian rural marketers

Companies like Philips Lighting, riding on its own distribution network, have reached all Indian villages with a population of 20,000, but could not go any deeper. Trouble is that if a marketer has to go deeper into the country, beyond the 20,000-population villages, he would have to hire a van that would blow a hole in his economics, a conundrum that all rural marketers are familiar with.

Philips can now tie-up with ITC, which is anyway looking for other companies to ride on its chain. Today, Philips dealers in the 20,000-population villages' supply to ITC, which in turn sends a van to all its sanchalaks once every 15 days, dropping off their orders. This has enabled Philips to cover 50-60 per cent in these areas, which was only 20 per cent two years ago. On their part, the sanchalaks either sell the goods directly, or, more often, sell them to the village's shopkeepers.

Philips only distributes its 60W and 100W bulbs through the sanchalaks; it is hard to get the more costly products like energy-saving bulbs, placed in the village shops as they are too costly and block up too much of the village kiranas' working capital. However, Philips plans to use the mall to showcase its entire range. At the same time, the basic products will continue to go to the village as bulbs are bought only when the previous one fails, and thus, need to be sold through the village.

Consumer's reaction: An enigma to decode

The rural malls will throw up a lot of valuable, real-life data about the rural consumer, thus allowing the rural customer to test a lot of assumptions and myths, like:

- How hard is it, to change villagers' buying habits? For the first six months Choupal Sagar began offering tractors on rent, there was no offtake. Slowly, some people used them, word of mouth got generated, and rentals picked up gradually.
- It is important to gauge the rural consumer's buying patterns. Is it true what people say about the rural consumer i.e. the men do all the shopping and that the women aren't allowed to go out? How does one then explain groups of village women who descend on the store and spread out across the shop examining the soaps, hair oil, face creams, tooth powder, cooking utensils, refrigerators, plastic-ware and so on.
- The proof of success of these farmer-run centres of ITC will be in the volume of sales. In the metros many malls are doing slack business with more window-shoppers than buyers. It will be interesting to study whether the rural populace be any different?

It is important that marketers don't try to copy any Western model blindly rather adopt a flexible model that captures the value chain and allows the organization to evolve with the customer. It's possible to adapt successful U.S. strategies but India would need a sustainable competitive advantage to survive.

Questions

1. Discuss how can the concept of ITC's Chaupal Sagar be replicated in other parts of India. What are the key success factors?
2. What are the distinguishing characteristics of organized rural retailing in India as brought to light by Chaupal Sagar?
3. Chaupal Sagar represents just a tip of the iceberg for rural marketing in India. Comment.
4. What could be the issues in having the right manpower in running a rural mall?

INDIAN CASES 4-11 (CASELETS ON INDIA'S LEADING RETAILERS)

ABSTRACT

Indian cases from 4 to 11 are eight mini-cases chosen to represent various issues in organized retailing as they relate to different sectors and formats. **Case 4, FoodWorld: A Study in Organized Food Retailing** focuses on organized food retailing as practiced by this India's largest and fastest growing supermarket chain. The mini-case brings out how FoodWorld successfully took recourse to backward integration to keep a tight leash on prices.

Currently Pantaloon brand and Food Bazaar (the company's other retail brand) are looked after by Pantaloon Retail. **Case 5, Pantaloon Fashions: Switching to a Young and Trendy Image** traces the makeover of Pantaloon brands and how the fashion garments are driven high up on the style graph to stay in tune with changing preferences of the youth. **Case 6, Shoppers' Stop: Grappling with Attrition of its Frontline Staff** spotlights on how its stores tackled the tendency towards attrition among the frontline staff. Merely according recognition was not enough; Shoppers'Stop took into account the employees' need to grow.

Case 7, Tanishq: Adding Glitter to Indian Jewellery Retailing captures how a manufacturer realizes that selling jewellery is a retail-intensive business and the real value addition and competitive challenge is to establish itself at the front-end. **Case 8, Crossword Bookstores: Booklovers' Paradise** is a study in book retailing.

Case 9, Planet M: A Strong Brand Experience brings out how this new 'planet' moved into consumer's cosmos and went from strength to strength in music retailing. **Case 10, Titan Watches : Retail is the Watchword** relates the story of how a watchmaking company injected excitement into the hitherto staid activity like buying a wristwatch. **Case 11, Archies: Keeping in Step with the Times** is the story of a greeting cards retailer as to how it has been adapting incessantly to the changing times since 1987.

CASE 4

FoodWorld : A Study in Organized Food Retailing

The role of large format organized retail has been largely accepted in clothing and lifestyle markets but in the foods and grocery, the situation is in a flux..A successful organized retail format will have to make an effort to integrate the food chain closer to farm gate levels.

Many organized players which emerged in the late 1990s have established themselves quite firmly in the local markets, have yet to make an impact on a national level. Subhiksha is largely in Chennai and has just started spreading in Tamil Nadu whereas Margin Free operates in Kerala. FoodWorld, one of the more successful super market chains in India (RPG Group) has tried to move across beyond a state. It has 50 stores in Tamil Nadu and about 67 outside. Rather than just offering lower prices it has also striven to offer an appealing ambience.

The success of an organized food retailer depends on how best it can leverage its scale to bring down merchandise costs, increase stock turns and get better credit terms from its vendors. The supermarket chain, FoodWorld has focused on backward integration.

FoodWorld was started in Chennai in May 1996. FoodWorld has stressed on supply chain for its stores. For basic foods, it sources close to the producer and for processed foods, it sources close to the processor. The objective behind the exercise is to save as much as 15 per cent in supply chain costs. The supply chain is quite different from what it was a few years ago. FoodWorld has gone for disintermediation to such an extent that it is almost at the source. It aggregates volumes at the village level and has also taken recourse to contract farming.

This case is intended to be used as a basis for class discussion rather than as an illustration of either effective or ineffective handling of the situation. Reprinted by permission of the author.

Nearly 300 farmers in Ooty and Bangalore areas supply fruits and vegetables to FoodWorld. It services them with technology, harvesting techniques and transport. The farmers offer best quality produce; FoodWorld makes sure they store it well and also guarantees that it will offtake the produce at competitive prices. In due course FoodWorld has forged long term relationship with farmers. The farmers have realized that the inputs from FoodWorld help them to improve yields and they can sell excess production profitably.

FoodWorld realised savings up to Rs 3 crore in 2001 by better procurement, trucking, storage and in general time and material loss. Having pruned losses at farm level, the next phase is to set up value addition centers. There are plans to underwrite the production of farmers and processors up to 70 such SKUs that are sold in the retail outlets. A grading center is in the planning stage which will sort out the right goods at the farm level itself and hence reduce unnecessary tonnage costs. Grading can also enable FoodWorld to pay the right price.

In staples, FoodWorld has been depending on the millers. It buys rice centrally but gets it processed at several millers and also buys from reverse auctions on the Internet. It purchases nearly 2,000 tons of rice a month. For various products, FoodWorld makes farmers deliver to the central warehouse from where it redistributes to its stores to step up efficiency.

While disintermediation helps in slashing costs, FoodWorld is looking to have many stores to get a catchment area of customers. It has to segment its customers and appeal to them who will buy more and thereby raise volumes for FoodWorld from the same number of stores.

Private labels are another means to cut costs. Today the company has 75 SKUs in private label which cover products like jams, pickles, staples, rice, atta and so on. Private labels allow for better control, faster coordination and more direct relationships. A retailer has to be adequate with numbers, scale and reach versus the well-entrenched national brands. It is not easy to reduce costs on a national level although at city or suburbs level, reduction in prices of staples or low-involvement goods can be targeted.

CASE 5

Pantaloon Fashions: Switching to a Young and Trendy Image

The company started in 1987 under the name of Menz Wear (P) Ltd. and was converted into a Public Limited Company with the name Menz Wear Ltd. in 1991. The name was changed to Pantaloon Fashions (India) Ltd. in the same year. The company began with the manufacture and marketing of quality Ready-made Garments for men including trousers, shirts, denims, blazers and sleep suits. The company's products have been marketed under the brand names Pantaloon and Bare Necessities. The retailing activity started with a network of exclusive retail shops and 'Pantaloon Connections' in the major metropolitan cities in the country.

Currently Pantaloons brand and Food Bazaar (the company's other retail brand) are looked after by Rs 650-crore Pantaloon Retail. Some of the Pantaloons brand outlets are in the process of a complete makeover. To begin with, the exercise is being undertaken for 20 Pantaloon outlets.

When the first Pantaloo store opened in Kolkata in 1997, its proposition was clear: to appeal to the consumers as India's family store. The store appealed to middle-class shoppers. Pantaloon garments were serviceable and offered value for money.

As a retail chain has to keep in step with the times, plans are afoot to establish the Pantaloon stores and its brands high up on the style graph. The objective is to project that Pantaloons is all about fashion. The repositioning started in 2003 when the communication and merchandise mix changed, with a focus on fabric ranges and fashion lines. A new range of garments in stylish linen and "crush" fabrics was introduced and communicated through a new print media campaign.

The advertisements marked a change from the earlier campaign that showed families. Now the visual featured trendy young men and women wearing the latest fashions. The latest campaign in April 2004 reflected the similar approach. The focus has shifted to accentuate the variety of merchandise lines while the message is that Pantaloons stocks the latest designs and fashions.

The emphasis on fashion is also evident in the changing store layouts. The Pantaloons stores no longer stack garments on the shelves, they are on display on hangers, like they are in boutiques. The furniture has been imported from Italy to give the stores a contemporary look.

There is more in store for the makeover initiative. Virtually everything from the store identity to branding and even the Pantaloon store name will change. The reason behind Pantaloon stores going for an image upscaling, according to retail consultants, is that Pantaloon wants to distance itself from Big Bazaar, its discount store launched in 2002. Big Bazaar offers value shopping for the home, from electronics and furnishings to staples and apparel. Pantaloons could no longer have remained the family departmental store and needed to upgrade its image further to stand out.

Another reason being forwarded is that the profile of the Indian shopper is changing. Students are no longer empty pocket window shoppers, with an increasing number opting for part-time jobs at fast-food outlets and call centers, they have the disposable income to buy what they like. Population trends have also changed. At present, roughly 54 per cent of the Indian population is below 25 years and 70 per cent is below 35 years. Young women shoppers are spending more at malls. Most of that spend is on apparel (apparel is the most important category for departmental stores, contributing to as much as 70 to 75 per cent of revenues).

As all stores stock the same national brands there is little scope for differentiation. With the relatively limited choice among national brands for women, they are more enthusiastic about trying out private labels. Pantaloon offers 19 in-house labels; some of them launched in 2002-03. Most target youth and children. To bring in more attitude and glamour to its in-house offering, Pantaloon has become the sole licensee for international youth brands like UMM and has launched another youth brand Rig, as well as children's-wear labels such as Popeye and Olive Oil. A new club and lounge wear brand called Leone is also being added to the repertoire.

Pantaloon's increased emphasis on private labels its captive manufacturing facilities. Currently, only 10 to 15 per cent of the manufacturing for private labels-70 per cent men's wear and 30 per cent women's wear-is done at the company's Tarapur plant. This will shortly increase to 70 per cent. This will include a few contract manufacturers for some styles or embellishments that need different skills. The rest 30 per cent will largely comprise the licensed brands. The plant is being revamped and capacity is being increased from 2000 pieces to 8,000 pieces a day. Structured fashion forecasting has been integrated with the manufacturing process. This has been done to react to style and fabric trends more quickly, always a strongpoint for a fashion apparel manufacturer.

Vertical integration is being counted upon to help reduce the time-to-market of new collections. Although margins in private apparel labels can be up to 50 per cent higher than in national labels, there is immense pressure to sell stocks to allow the next range to come in faster. That is because fashion clothing needs to change according to trends, which change every one to two months. If stocks languish on the shelves, the company has to undersell, thus losing on margins.

The challenge lies in fashion forecasting and faster time-to-market. Presently it takes Pantaloon about two months to bring an outfit from the design stage to the store shelves. That is double the ideal time to get a range in the market. The company plans to reduce the time-to-market to 30 days which is better than the Indian average.

The makeover will be a selective phenomenon. Some of the older stores will continue to retain the family store ambience. Meanwhile Pantaloons is eyeing new stores at multiplexes and malls in a bid to tap into a younger customer base.

Print media campaigns are supported by on-ground promotions especially for the newer and younger brands. For instance, for the launch of the UMM label, Pantaloon organized music shows at pubs and discotheques. Customers who bought UMM clothes got invited to the events, where the DJ was dressed in UMM apparel, to drive home the brand's connection with contemporary music. Similarly for outdoorsy clothing brand Rig,

Pantaloon plans to offer shoppers free or discounted weekend adventure packages. (Adapted from *Cashing in on Fashion* by Gouri Shukla, *The Strategist, Business Standard,* July 6, 2004)

CASE 6

Shoppers' Stop : Grappling with Attrition of its Frontline Staff

A young workforce as the frontline staff at the 14 Shoppers' Stop stores became a liability for the Rs 404-crore retail chain arriving on the Indian scene in 1993. The company had stressed on young graduates as frontline employees for the customers who came to buy mostly apparel or accessories preferred to talk to a younger set of customer care associates, since they were perceived to be in sync with fashion trends.

In 2002 the attrition rate among the frontline employees at Shoppers' Stop had touched 70 per cent. Called Customer Care Associates (CCAs), the high attrition rate was a cause of alarm as these young CCAs accounted for close to 90 per cent of the chain's 1,800 employees. If the departure of the young salesforce continued, there would be an altogether new set of frontline employees every 1.5 years. As the management invested up to 52 hours in training a CCA, the training cost was also bound to escalate with high attrition.

The attrition was attributed to something being wrong with Shoppers Stop's selection procedure. It focused on people who were ready to work on a low salary. As soon as these employees got the required experience in addition to the recognition of having worked with a large retailer like Shoppers' Stop, they started fishing for a better job.

As Shoppers' Stop is among the first of organized retailers in the country. Its frontline staff also tend to be heavily poached. The CCAs have ready access to any competitor or a headhunter who could freely visit a Shoppers' store and try to lure them away.

With the retail sector booming, the opportunities for frontline staff are tremendous. Apart from large format retail chains there has also been a rise in other retail ventures like coffee chain. Many CCAs, who may not be above-average, were being offered managerial positions in other retail outlets. The proliferation of call centers meant that CCAs with good communication skills could join them. Shoppers' Stop was not in a position to match the salaries offered by call centers.

When the company extended its customer satisfaction survey (conducted by the research agency IMRB since 2000) to measure employee satisfaction, the exigency of doing something about checking attrition came to the fore. Only five out of the 14 stores had an above-average employee satisfaction index (ESI).

The research also brought out that customer commitment and loyalty was directly linked to employee loyalty. For instance, in the five Shoppers' Stop stores with higher-than-average employee loyalty , customers with loyalty cards spent 28 per cent more. These stores also had more customer footfalls. It was also found that 15 per cent of the customer base contributed to 50 per cent of the turnover.

The research discovered that salary was only the fourth in priority for most CCAs. For Shoppers' Stop employees, the dominant issues in order of importance were as follows:

- **A congenial working climate**
- **Growth opportunity**
- **Healthy supervisor-CCA relationship**
- **Salary**

Thrust on training

Since for a CCA, his or her first link with the organization was his or her floor supervisor, the research suggested that quality of supervisor would affect employee loyalty. In 2003, the retail chain held 40 workshops over 52 days to coach its 110 floor supervisors on soft and hard skills. Each supervisor attended 200 hours of advanced courses ranging from management techniques and leadership training to personal counseling skills and detailed product knowledge.

The training was aimed at making supervisors stronger in areas like giving performance feedback to CCAs, coaching skills, etc. In the past, performance reviews conducted by the supervisors used to be more of a compromise. In performance reviews, CCAs rated themselves on the highest score and supervisors did not know how to give them a lower rating. The training sessions helped supervisors evaluate against set criteria and taught them the art of offering negative feedback in a positive manner.

For its new employees, Shoppers' Stop began to have a 21-day induction training session that included seven days in the classroom, followed by a buddy training system for 14 days. During the fortnight, the new recruit worked with CCAs who were certified to be buddies. This also helped the new recruit find a friend in the system and establish a sense of bonding with the workplace.

Fostering loyalty

Further the management followed the existing system with an introduction program for its CCAs. After 60 days of a group of CCAs joining the company they were asked to participate in a talent contest, Parichay. Parents of the performers were invited to be judges at the event. In Re-tale, the in-house newsletter, family members of the employees were invited to write articles on their relationship with the store. All this built Shoppers' Stop's bonding with the employees' families and acted as deterrent to the frontline staff contemplating quitting.

The newsletter provided employees with an open forum to interact with the management. It also targeted at providing recognition to high performing CCAs with a view to foster loyalty. It recognized CCAs who were praised by customers for going beyond the call of duty. These CCAs were also given prizes like gift vouchers.

The management also instituted a group reward program. Called Jo Jita Wohi Sikander (winners are champions). CCAs in each store were rated on the counts of product knowledge, operational skills and customer feedback. Individual CCAs and supervisors who score highly on these parameters are designated as champions. The leading store receives a cash reward that is divided among the team members.

Favorable employment climate

As recognition alone would not suffice, Shoppers' Stop took into account the employees' need to grow. First, the chain introduced several non-monetary rewards. For example, any employee willing to do a professional course could get his entire tuition fee reimbursed by the company. Also, the employee could participate in a certification program of the UK-based retail institute City and Guilds where high performers are awarded certificates. In 2003, 13 CCAs from Shoppers'Stop were awarded certificates.

The chain has begun to fill 65 per cent of the vacancies through internal promotions. In 2003, of the 400 CCAs who applied for the supervisory post, 30 were shortlisted for six months of training on development inputs and assessment. Finally 13 of them became supervisors.

The upshot of all the conscious steps has been that the rate of attrition is down to 36 per cent from a peak of 70 per cent in 2002. (Adapted from *Shoppers' HaRDsell: How retail chain Shoppers' Stop tackled attrition of its front-line staff* by Prasad Sangameshwaran. The Strategist, *Business Standard,* Sept. 7, 2004)

CASE 7

Tanishq: Adding Glitter to Indian Jewellery Retailing

Titan entered the jewellery business in 1995, primarily as a manufacturer, with retailing as a distribution channel. But the company soon realized that selling jewellery was actually a more retail-intensive business, and that the real value addition and competitive challenge was to establish itself at the front end.

Today Tanishq is the only national jeweller in India with an unmatched consumer reach through 62 exclusive boutiques in 47 cities and an annual turnover of Rs 389 crore (2003). Tanishq has showrooms in cities from Srinagar to Tirunelveli, and is successful in small towns too. The showrooms are company owned as well franchisees.

The locations are chosen on the basis of geographical spread and the shopping dynamics of a particular metro. The primary promotional medium for Tanishq is its boutiques, which explains the emphasis on store design and layout. Its stores demonstrate design leadership and differentiation. The challenge is to provide excitement around the collections in its outlets.

For the launch of Diva, Tanishq's pearl and diamond collection, the flagship store on Dickenson Road in Bangalore had two huge cutouts of models displaying the designs. Inside the stores, jewellery is artistically displayed in floor- and wall-mounted showcases, and highlighted through lighting. The entire ambience is one of opulence. Tanishq is today perceived as a design leader in jewellery; as a distinct, fashionable brand which defines trends in jewellery; as a retail brand which offers an elegant, clearly differentiated shopping experience which is quite unique in this category.

In India, gold buying is still to mark special occasions like festivals, anniversaries and auspicious days like akshaya tritiya. So, whether it is Varalakshmi Puja in Andhra Pradesh, Durga Puja in Bengal, Onam in Kerala or Karva Chauth in the north, the company celebrates it with its customers in the right cultural spirit.

Tanishq's jewellery business is said to be on firm ground. The reasons: first-mover advantage; a scalable national model in organized retailing; and an increasing contribution to Titan's revenues.

The Rs 40,000-crore jewellery business with about 3.5 lakh players in India is fragmented and ruled by traditional local players. The share of the organized sector in this just Rs 1,000 crore (about 2.5 per cent). For Tanishq to be able to break the stranglehold, it had to find a way to connect with the need for finely crafted jewellery at affordable prices. Previously, Tanishq was positioned as an international jewellery brand for the Indian elite. This meant it catered to a niche market; the masses were ignored. Moreover, its Italian designs in 18-carat, mostly studded jewellery did not go down well with the traditional Indian woman, as she was used to 22-carat jewellery.

Given this reality, design was back in focus at Tanishq - but with a difference. Abandoning its westernized look from the past, Tanishq chose to work on a fusion of contemporary and traditional Indian motifs. Tanishq's primary customer is the young Indian woman, who has a modern, contemporary outlook towards life but is still firmly rooted in her traditional Indian values. Tanishq Aria was the first line to be launched with the new concept. It gave a fresh perspective to the traditional seven stone setting. It was a great success. Then, came another success, Diva, which combined the brilliance of diamonds with the soft luminosity of pearls.

The introduction of 22-carat plain jewellery was the first step in getting Tanishq where it is today. The range was strikingly different from the standard fare available in the market, yet it was traditional. The 'lightweight' collection looked heavy, but felt light, just under 25 gm. This met the working woman's growing need for great-looking and beautiful jewellery that was affordable and extremely comfortable to wear.

The production process was made more flexible. New Japanese manufacturing machines were introduced at Tanishq's Hosur plant. The emphasis turned to customer demands across all segments and surveys were conducted to shape business strategies.

Tanishq focuses on a relevant consumer need. When it develops strategies for any marketing programme the core philosophy is to link it with a particular consumer need, felt or otherwise, and then bring it to light in the most evocative way possible. Collection G and Tanishq Solo are examples of this doctrine.

Surveys showed work-wear jewellery to be a dilemma for the working woman. Tanishq's Collection G 9 to 5 range, with its modern, innovative designs, marked the first-ever collection custom-made to suit their requirements. Unique finishes and different textures, as well as a contemporary touch gave a distinctive look to the jewellery crafted in pure 22-carat gold. Moreover, it also addressed the homemaker's need for everyday-wear jewellery. The entry points for the collection was just Rs 595, with more than 90 unique designs, including earring-pendant sets, neckwear, bangles, bracelets, chains and rings. The concept took the market by storm.

Likewise, solitaires were a woman's dream. But solitaires were perceived to be the sole preserve of the upper middle class.. Tanishq debunked the myth and launched an exclusive brand of solitaire diamonds - 'Solo', priced at Rs 7,500 and upwards.

Customer acquisition meant employing innovative marketing initiatives. Like some players in the apparel industry, it decided to launch an innovative collection in every quarter of the year to encourage customers to frequent the stores. The path-breaking 'impure to pure exchange' enabled customers to exchange impure gold for 22-carat gold.

During the offer period, customers could go to the Tanishq showroom and get a free gold purity check done on a 'Karatmeter' (an internationally acclaimed device for purity checking). Even if they find their jewellery to be less than 22c (which has more than 19 carats of pure gold), they could exchange it for Tanishq's certified jewellery.

The response was tremendous. Most of Tanishq's strategy revolved around breaking the bond of customers with their jeweller - by building on the weakness of the jeweller and on its strengths. Which explains why Tanishq is now synonymous with trust and purity, and is perceived as a leader in jewellery design in India.

In the highly fragmented sector there were unethical practices and - surprisingly, for such high-value products - no branding. Branding provides reassurance and builds a relationship. There was no attempt to differentiate on any other factor but price. Research showed that woman perceived jewellery as their only personal possession. India being the world's second largest gold jewellery market after the United States, the potential for Tanishq was good.

Tanishq worked hard on a two-pronged brand-building strategy: cultivate trust by educating customers on the unethical practices in the business, and use innovative methods to change the perception of jewellery as a high-priced purchase. The big challenge was to get consumers to visit the stores. Tanishq stressed on changing the attitudes of customers from blind trust to informed trust.

As for the competition the branded players (*Gili, Carbon, Oyzterbay, Sparkle*) taken together are but a quarter of Tanishq's size. Also, there are the traditional jewellers such as TBZ and Popley.

Today Tanishq has successfully democratized luxury and fashion in jewellery and by making the best of designs accessible to a wide segment of Indian women. In 2002 more than 1 million Indian women shopped at Tanishq, a fact that's testimony to the brand's broad appeal, and an indicator of its success in enabling consumers to access higher levels of quality without compromising on the Tata Group's traditional values. Someday all jewellery will be sold in this manner, it is believed.

CASE 8

Crossword Bookstores: Booklovers' Paradise

In India, shopping for books has always been thought of as a book-lover's hobby. The traditional bookstores, with their serious, and intimidating atmosphere, and limited browsing facility have discouraged all but serious booklovers. Though without a 'Members Only' signboard, they seem to dissuade people from visiting them, thus creating a high-brow impression of bookstores.

Crossword, positioned as a lifestyle bookstore, has been able to change this by designing large, spacious, well laid out stores, with bright cheerful interiors that encourage people to stay and browse. Simple innovations such as methodical classifications, clear signage, a dedicated enquiry /orders desk, electronic POS and inventory control systems and attractive displays make looking for books a much more pleasurable experience. A welcoming café, reading tables and chairs and toilets within the store, (some of the innovations pioneered by Crossword in India) help to ensure that customers are able to browse in comfort for several hours without having to leave.

Crossword, with twenty-one stores, both company owned and franchised, across Mumbai, Ahmedabad, Pune, Vadodara, Chennai, and Hyderabad as on March 2002 is India's fastest growing chain of bookstores, and the only national one. Over 2.4 million customers visit Crossword stores every year. As a retailer trying out smaller versions of its stores, Crossword is experimenting with Crossword Corner, to increase reach and business from its stores. Crossword's promoters are Shopper's Stop Limited - India's leading department store chain (promoted by K Raheja Corp.) and ICICI Venture, part of India's leading financial services group.

While we do crossword puzzles for fun, they are also a learning experience. The name Crossword was therefore chosen to reflect the dual fun and learning experience of a visit to Crossword. The name embodies the vision of Crossword as a place and space for people who seek information, knowledge or just the pleasure of reading.

Crossword also addresses a wider audience than existing stores with its unique product mix. There is of course, the widest range of books for the young and old alike, along with magazines, CD-ROMs, music, stationery and toys. With its large children's section and its focus on making the store a friendly, safe, fun-filled place, Crossword attracts many families who normally don't think of visiting bookstores. Services like Dial-a-book, Fax-a-book and Email-a-book enable customers to shop from their homes; and when they come to the store, the unobtrusively helpful staff assists them in finding the right book, the right CD or the right gift for the right occasion. Loyal customers are rewarded through the Crossword Book Rewards Program with points, discounts, promotional offers and more. 'Words', a monthly newsletter with over 50 reviews of new books, news about in store events and bestseller lists, is currently mailed free to over 20,000 customers.

Crossword aims to be a point of cultural and social interaction where authors and poets hold court, where children are regaled, where people gravitate to be informed, to be entertained, even enlightened. There are regular readings, discussions and debates on varied subjects from literature and art to child sexual abuse, war and peace, business and management, travel, parenting and health. Among the numerous writers who have visited the store are Arundhati Roy, Vikram Chandra, Vikram Seth, Kiran Nagarkar, Andrew Motion, Michele Roberts, Shashi Tharoor, Shobha De, Charles Handy, Patricia Seybold, and Jack Canfield. Promotional events include pictionary contests, quizzes, slide shows and the annual affair with Santa and his elves.

Crossword launched the Crossword Book Award in 1998 to recognise and reward the best of Indian writing. There was one cash prize of Rs 200,000 in 1998 for the best original work of fiction in English by an Indian author, and it was won by Allan Sealy for The *Everest Hotel*. In 1999 it added a new category: Indian Language Fiction Translation into English and also increased the cash prize to Rs.300,000 for each category. The 1999 prize for the best work in English Fiction went to Vikram Seth for *An Equal Music* and the prize for the best work in the Indian Language Fiction Translation category was won by the author M. Mukundan and the translator Gita Krishnankutty, for *On the Banks of the Mayyazhi*. The 2000 prize for the best work in English Fiction went to Jamyang Norbu for *The Mandala of Sherlock Holmes* and the prize for the best work in the Indian Language Fiction Translation category was won by the author Bama and the translator Lakshmi Holmstrom, for *Karukku*.

Since its inception in 15th October 1992, Crossword has received wide recognition for its achievements; articles on retailing in India invariably feature Crossword. It has been featured in Advertising Age International, USA, as one of the Marketing Superstars for 1994. The Bookseller, UK, has also described it as 'being on the cutting edge of retailing' in India.

(Source : http://www.crosswordbookstores.com)

CASE 9

Planet M: A Strong Brand Experience

On 15 August 1999, a new planet moved into the consumer's cosmos. It inevitably spawned a number of lookalikes. Some worked, most didn't. But Planet M - 'the music store of the universe' - went from strength to strength.

What started with a 10,000-sq-ft store at the Times of India Group's eponymous building in downtown Mumbai - still its largest property - has spread to 77 outlets (as on October 2004). Of its 77 outlets, 34 are exclusive outlets and 43 are shop-in-shops - what Planet M calls 'Satelites'. It has established a lead over other wannabes in this segment that would not be easy to bridge.

Unlike the cosmos, it did not come about in an instant. It has taken years of dogged pursuit and crafty planning. The management reposed faith in the burgeoning retail trade and found obvious synergies with the Group's extant outfits in the domain of entertainment.

In the late nineties, the Times Group was a vast media conglomerate, but lacked a youthful dimension. Planet M was an ideal solution.

Entertainment packages - with celebrities and brands - earns the support of the Times Group and it makes sense to serve that to a music and entertainment-driven youth. But Planet M initially chose not to emphasize its connection with the Old Lady of Boribunder. Now that a brand identity has been forged through other means, the parentage is being brought to the fore. A visible association with the conglomerate that had a dignified, aged image may have worked adversely then. Today, the brand is strong enough to sustain its perception.

What's this perception? The brand had to be young, hip, happening, futuristic and a place where the young would like to hang out. That explains metal floors, guitars on the ceiling, funky graphics and the overall 'spaceship feeling'...

A large part of the success recipe derives from the fact that Times Retail, retailing arm of the Times Group has always had a finger on the pulse of the complex urbanite - a creature continuously evolving. That has been reflected in its openness with formats, merchandising and brand communications along with its clear view of consumer behavior.

Like most retailers today, Planet M is looking at offering shoppertainment - a whole shopping experience. This excitement will continue and percolate. Entertainment retail as a category is doing well, though India has a long way to go. In terms of products, it is just developing, though music has seen a lot more consolidation and movement towards organized retail since 2000.

This view of the consumer's purse would help explain the Barista coffee bars at some Planet M's or the company's willingness to be a part of larger retail spaces. It would also explain the phenomenon that about 35 per cent of sales came from the non-music section. Products on offer apart from cassettes and CDs included DVDs, video CDs, multimedia, books and stationery and accessories..

In the beginning, there was only one function of merchandising - ordering. Also, the supply chain hadn't been streamlined and the stock cover would vary between 4 months' worth to more than a year's. Planet M now insists on having three months' average plus 15 days' worth. Macro-ordering takes place twice a month. And this system is customized as per the production cycle of the music company supplying the stock. The result: Stockouts are a thing of the past.

After FM radio, it's now the turn of online download formats to challenge the brick-and-mortar set-ups. For once, the retail chains are not ruffled, and are quite ready to take up the challenge. Indians may still be a long way from embracing the download format but there are indications that youngsters would be more willing to do so. MusicWorld is ready to host a site at short notice should the need arise. The inputs for the site, musicworld4u.com, are being fed on a continuous basis. Once downloading becomes big, Planet M also is set to promote it. It appears both formats will co-exist in the future. Deriving on the strength of the group's portal, Planet M also has a significant online presence.

One of the challenges would be to create a viable pricing model for online music. The online format will take off without the pricing model but then the pirates will exploit the situation.

The ultimate test of relevance, though, is the product mix. The buying pattern is unique for each store. Over 60 per cent of the orders come from the catalogue. Though the balance between the three broad categories of chartbusters, new releases and catalogue is driven by demand, Planet M tries to associate in a special manner with certain categories - jazz and Indian classical are two prominent ones. Hence there are lecture-cum-demonstration sessions on these topics and associations with events like the Jazz Yatra. There is clear business sense in this too as the aficionados of these music genres tend to be high-value customers and may also purchase in a typically lean season. Planet M has a customer CRM format with about one lakh members on its rolls.

But several of these measures may be replicable, it is brand experience that sets Planet M apart from the rest.

CASE 10

Titan Watches: Retail is the Watchword

Launched in 1987, Titan is credited with transforming the face of India's watch industry. By offering consumers quality products that blended classy designs with superior technology, Titan became a byword for success stories. Outstanding service, a wide variety of models, and effective marketing have helped Titan consolidate its early gains, to the point where the company is a force to be reckoned with beyond Indian shores.

Understanding the Indian consumer's psyche has been vital to Titan reaching its current position of strength. The company today has a model for every price segment and every market, urban and rural, regional and international. Within the Titan mother brand are Nebula, which comes draped in 18-carat gold; the exclusive Insignia; PSI, for those turned on by technology; and Raga, which has been designed exclusively for women.

Titan's focus has always been on India. Research reveals some interesting facts and figures about this heterogeneous market. The Indian market is estimated at 25 million watches a year, with 50 per cent being sold by the organized sector. Titan is the runaway market leader, with domestic sales of 6 million watches a year. There are 190 million watch-owning Indians; between them they own about 210 million watches. Urban India accounts for 120 million of these watches and 90 million are on rural wrists.

More men than women own watches in India, and more working women than housewives own watches.

It is the rural segment within this diverse market that Titan is now looking to tap. The key to success is getting into the rural market on a larger scale. The company's Sonata range is targeted at rural customers, and is part of a strategy where the alignment of price and reliability are crucial. The range costs between Rs 495 and Rs 1,200, has showrooms exclusively for it, and is sold mainly in small-town India.

Fast Track is a different kettle of fish. This range is broadly aimed at young Indians looking for watches that are fashionable and stylish. Then there's Dash, a range that Titan launched for children. Introduced in early 2000, Dash is priced low, but it hasn't sold too well. The company plans to change that with enhanced advertising and a different marketing strategy.

Titan's retail operations are a mix of company-owned and franchisee outlets, with the idea being to ensure a dominant presence in all market areas through different kinds of stores, and to assure the availability of every Titan product. Titan's products are sold in over 1800 cities in India through 7,000 outlets. Of these, 150 are exclusive World of Titan stores and another 136 are TimeZone outlets, a chain of multi-brand outlets with a significant Titan presence (as in May 2003). Titan has concentrated on customer perspective, and has engineered the entire chain to suit different customers.

Earlier there was no attempt in the retailing sector to entice customers to buy a watch. Titan has tried to bring the brand to the customer in an appropriate setting. The company does this through its 'World of Titan' showrooms.

The Indian customers have become more sophisticated and are looking for an engaging retail experience which encourages them to browse leisurely, without much interference from the salespersons. And, this trend cuts across metros and other urban towns as well.

Titan Industries' new retail strategy focuses on consumer convenience and the shopping experience. New looks, an international shopping aura and ultimate customer convenience are the latest buzzwords at Titan Industries. The company is looking at retailing as a strategic investment for the brand.

Titan is focusing on attracting the impulse buyer. With watches becoming a fashion statement and buyers wanting to own more than one watch, the watch buying habit in India has become more impulse driven instead of the earlier trend of `considered buying'. A casual browser who walks into the showroom without an intention of buying could well like something and decide to buy, apart from the person who comes to a watch showroom with an intention of buying a watch.

From being a mere 'functional' store, Titan retail stores are now graduating to the 'hot, hip and happening' look with a distinct touch to the design aspect with apt use of steel, wood, colors, graphics and style.

The new layout encourages casual browsing. At many of the stores Titan has done away with the counter system and has taken its product display to the walls, so that the customer has enough space for himself and can browse comfortably. All the displays are at eye level, and Titan has also used a lot of vibrant colors and interesting graphics to attract more footfalls.

Titan has come up with the new design strategy by studying international and domestic stores across different product categories within the retailing industry. It has also made considerable investments in piloting, prototyping, counter designs, lighting, and so on, so that it can offer a great retail experience to Titan consumers.

Unlike most international watch brands which have opted for shop-in-shop retail formats and prefer to be present in large format retail stores such as Shoppers' Stop or LifeStyle, to generate more footfalls, Titan claims that a bulk of its volumes come from its standalone stores.

The franchisee is a critical cog in Titan's retail matrix. The company organizes various programs for franchisees, their managers and customer relationship officers. These include training workshops and seminars on market trends, visual merchandising, store operations and maintenance, and customer service initiatives.

The real challenge in retailing is managing the franchisee network through processes and systems that ensure a superior brand experience for every customer. Franchisee relationship management is important because of increasing competition, not only from the watch business but also from other businesses in the retail industry. The market is opening up and the franchisee is, after all, looking for what is most profitable.

Besides the franchisees and its own showrooms, Titan sells its products through other outlets as well. Among them are the Time Zone stores, which stock all the leading brands, and the Value Mart outlets, which operate in Bangalore and Chennai and sell surplus-to-export watches at a discount.

For its many customers Titan has Tata Signet, a 1,36,000-member club that looks to build relationships through rewards, regular discounts and special offers. Customers can also count on a service-center network that's 550-strong and spread over 30-odd cities and towns across the country. The service centers have been deliberately kept apart from Titan's showrooms.

Titan's blueprint for the future includes making watches for international heavyweights such as YSL, Christian Dior and Gucci. There is huge potential at the designer end of the market. The marketing investment is lower because the brand is doing the marketing for you. Interestingly, the company has also begun to merchandise a range of accessories such as card holders, wallets, bags, scarves, cell phone holders, etc.

CASE 11

Archies: Keeping in Step with the Times

Archies is in the business of manufacturing and selling greeting cards and other social expression products like gifts, posters etc. The company is presently market leader in social expression industry with more than 50 per cent market share. The company has also set up a music division and has been expanding the range of products sold at its outlets.

The social expression industry in India is still in the nascent stage with per unit consumption being quite low as compared to European countries and US. The per capita consumption of greeting cards is 40 in the US and 50 in the UK, while in India the figure is just 0.5, which means great growth potential. The greeting card industry in India is estimated at Rs 20 billion with 50 per cent in the organized sector and balance in the unorganized sector. Archies has exploited the opportunity well and has introduced greeting cards for all major Indian traditional festivals such as Holi, Rakhi, etc besides the usual Birthday, Anniversary, New Year, Valentine's Day cards, etc. With the spread of western culture, increasing urbanization and improving standard of living the industry has got a good fillip.

Presently there are 4-5 major players in the organized sector having their presence across the country; other players in the organized sector are regional or local players. The two leading players in the organized segment of the greeting cards industry are Archies and Vintage (Hallmark). Other players are Wilson, Vakil, Meena and Ambassador. Smaller unorganized players in the market compete on the price front. Vintage is the most significant competitor at the national level and operates through a chain of franchise outlets similar to Archies. There are also a few social and non- profit organizations like CRY and HelpAge, etc.

Archies' greatest strength is its retail reach. At present, the company's products are available in 480 exclusive Archies Galleries and 2,000 retail outlets in 180 cities (as on March 2004). Archies is also present in Bahrain, UAE, Sri Lanka, Nepal and Bangladesh through franchisees. In a major company-owned retailing drive, Archies is looking at adding 50 stores by 2006 to the existing network of 35 exclusive company-managed stores, which account for around 23 per cent of overall Archies retailing revenues.

Before one starts looking at Archies as a success story in the retailing of greeting cards, it would be in order to provide a chronology of its growth, and facts and figures. Archies Greetings & Gifts was promoted by Mr. Anil Moolchandani and Mr. Jagdish Moolchandani in 1979 as a partnership firm. In the year 1995, the company was converted into a public limited company and in November 2002, the company was renamed Archies Limited. The company manufactures a wide range of greeting cards and stationery items. It has tie-ups with American Greetings Corporation U.S.A. and Gibson Greetings Inc. for sourcing designs and artwork. Over the years, Archies diversified into trading of gift items and perfumes through its outlets. In 2003-04, the company discontinued its less profitable perfumes business. In the same year, Archies recorded a turnover of Rs. 668 million, of which greeting cards constituted 51 per cent, gift items 32 per cent, and stationery products and others 16 per cent. The company earned a net profit of Rs. 53 million in 2003-04.

In the coming years, the company wants to emerge as a retailing enterprise rather than just a greeting card maker. Archies is betting on the gifting segment to grow the overall revenues. Malls have been identified as a critical driver for gift-related consumption.

Anil Moolchandani, Managing Director, Archies Gifts & Greetings, hails from a business family originally engaged in the business of sarees. His sharp acumen, keen sense of observation and ability to predict future trends helped him grow the business tremendously from a small beginning.

Discontented with his family business, Moolchandani started the business of songbooks-the lyric books of English songs-as a hobby. These were sold through mail orders at that time. Then Moolchandani started making posters which were also distributed through mail order. Subsequently, they started getting queries from retailers that they (the retailers) wanted to resell them so the wholesale network was started. There was some positive feedback about the demand for cards, so they went on to greeting cards also. After that, Moolchandani started opening exclusive stores because cards had limited appeal at the time.

The business was started in 1979 and the first store set up in 1987. Archies then made its own model suitable for Indian conditions. It created a branded franchise. Now the scenario has changed in India and everybody talks about franchising. But Archies was the first to take up franchising. It then went in for tie-ups so as to get a greater range to support these stores because these were exclusive stores. Earlier the cards were sold in shoeboxes in bookstores or stationery stores. Archies provides a comfort level and an ambience to the customer who shops for greeting cards. Generally a customer goes to a store to buy, say, `X' card, and he starts picking up many other things.

Archies has an exclusive arrangement with the world's largest publicly owned company - American Greetings. It reproduces their designs in India keeping in mind the Indian environment. There are a couple of other tie-ups to increase the range. Archies pays 5 per cent royalty on the designs it chooses from the principals. In certain cases, Archies buys at one fixed price and then reproduces it.

Once Archies started franchising it realized that 50 per cent of sales came from the gift items. Earlier, these franchisee outlets used to source these gift items themselves because Archies was not producing them. In 1996 Archies launched a gift division to source and make exclusive gifts. The company sees the gift line as having great potential for the future. Archies outsources gifts from its partners who manufacture for its outlets.

Archies does not perceive a threat from the e-greetings business as the penetration of computers is low in India. In the future the company sees it growing and is strengthening its presence in that media too.

The company has aggressive plans for online sales of its products. A subsidiary Archies Online.com was set up in May 2000 and has launched its website www.archiesonline.com that it plans to use for selling its products. The main proposition of the site is third party gifting. In the face of the growing usage of Internet and Short Messaging Service (SMS), Archies has launched a paid e-card in the form of Multi Media Service (MMS).

Appendix

Careers in Retailing

INTRODUCTION

After reading this text and learning about the various retail functions and the evolving retail environment, you should have a pretty good idea about whether or not a job in retailing is for you. As discussed in Chapter 1, a wide variety of retail positions are available, all requiring different or overlapping skill sets. To arm yourself with the tools for success in retailing, you will need to get a running start on the job-hunting process.

Before you delve into the specifics of your search, take a step back and think about the retail employer. What will this employer look for in you as a candidate for a retail position? Most retailers will emphasize that the following areas are the most important:

1. *Communication skills.* Communication skills are the most important skills for employees. Communication skills include the ability to (a) express oneself in an accurate, clear, and appropriate manner; (b) communicate well in writing (*i.e.,* with no typographical, grammatical, or syntactical errors in any pre-interview correspondence such as cover letters, e-mails, résumés, or letters of inquiry); and (c) carry on a professional discussion in a comfortable manner beyond the interview setting (*i.e.,* at lunch or dinner, or between or after interviews).
2. *Co-curricular activities.* A retail employer often looks for a candidate who is involved in many activities, either in the community or in the college setting. Examples of co-curricular activities include holding a leadership position (*e.g.,* president, vice president, captain, chairperson); being actively involved in an on-campus club or organization (*e.g.,* Marketing Club, American Advertising Federation, Accounting or Finance Club, International Business Students Club) or a community organization; or holding membership in an honorary or professional organization (*e.g.,* Alpha Kappa Psi professional business fraternity, Pi Omega Pi, Phi Delta Kappa).
3. *Nonrelated work experience.* Retailers often look for an applicant who is or has been a supervisor (but not in his or her area of academic endeavor), who currently or in the near past has worked at least part time, and who

demonstrates, either in the interview or in other correspondence, a strong work ethic.

4. *Related work experience.* Related work experience includes a work-related position, such as supervisor or retail sales clerk, or an internship in a work-related area. Prior experience is not always crucial, but it is often a bonus.
5. *Career goals.* Because the employer will invest time and money in a new employee, it is important that the employer assess early on the applicant's defined career goals. The applicant needs to communicate these goals to the employer.
6. *Knowledge of the company and industry.* The applicant must have a good working knowledge of the potential retail employer, the positions of employment within the firm, and a general knowledge of the retail industry. A good knowledge base will enhance the applicant's appeal in the interview setting and help the applicant demonstrate communication skills and career goals.
7. *Personal appearance.* Because retail professionals come into contact with many different publics, their appearance is very important. An applicant must be well groomed. Attention should be paid to one's attire (clothing should fit appropriately, neither too tight nor too baggy). The applicant should wear a conservative hairstyle, neaten or remove facial hair, and avoid excessive cosmetics and jewelry (including body piercings). Even if the work environment is business casual or completely casual, the applicant should err on the side of conservatism and enter the interview looking as professional as possible.
8. *References.* The applicant should have job references from individuals who know him or her. References can come from employers, professors, or personal friends. These references can take the form of a verbal recommendation (face to face or over the phone) or a written recommendation. The list of people the interviewer may contact can be provided verbally or in writing (a sheet attached to the résumé or listed in the body of the résumé). The applicant should always contact references to gain their permission before submitting their names to a prospective employer.
9. *Scholastic record.* The last important factor in securing employment is the applicant's scholastic record. The applicant should emphasize his or her major if the degree is in retailing or retail management. If relevant, the applicant should point out a high overall grade point average (3.5 or above where A = 4.0) or a high grade point average in the specific major (for retailing or marketing, 3.5 or higher). The applicant should also highlight any academic honors (*e.g.*, graduating with honors, dean's list, president's list).

By possessing or at least understanding these important attributes and accomplishments individuals who desire to work in the retail industry will be equipped not only for the job search but for success on the job as well.

THE JOB SEARCH PROCESS

College students spend four or more years preparing themselves to enter the professional work force. Upon graduation it is time to search for that perfect job. The employment search should be treated as a full-time job; that is, you should spend about forty hours a week researching and hunting for positions that are potential matches for your skills. Prior to starting a full-scale search, you should set the parameters that are important to you. For example, if you want to work in a specific geographical area, you should limit the initial search to that geographical area.

At times you may need to modify the parameters. For instance, if you want to work for a specific retailer, first make sure the retailer has a presence in your chosen geographic location. If the retailer is not in the desired area, you'll need to either eliminate that retailer from your list of potential employers or readjust the geographic parameter.

KNOW YOUR OPTIONS

Now that you know what skills employers are looking for, you can turn your attention to the retail position. Ask yourself, "What retail position do I desire? Do I want to be on front stage selling directly to the consumer, behind the scenes purchasing merchandise for retail outlets, or in the financial or human resources area of the retail operation?" Numerous options are available when pursuing a career in retailing (see Figure A.1).

START YOUR SEARCH

Once you have a relatively clear idea of what path you want to take, you are ready to begin searching for available positions. Remember to keep your options open and feel free to explore more than one type of retailing position at a time. The Internet has made the job search process much easier. Websites such as monster.com and CareerBuilder.com allow you to search for jobs based on your own criteria.

In addition, your college placement or career services office will assist in your job search and provide lists of open positions. Often the career services office will schedule interviews with on-campus recruiters.

Other good resources include trade publications, newspaper help-wanted sections, and trade associations. Additional online resources include a website for government jobs (*www.federaljobsearch.com*), America's Employers (*www.americasemployers.com*), the NationJob Network (*www.nationjob.com*), and HotJobs.com (*www.hotjobs.com*). The Houghton Mifflin website (*www.college.hmco.com/business/students*) is an excellent resource for your job search. It offers many useful links to other websites that will assist you in the process.

MAKING CONTACT WITH RETAIL EMPLOYERS

When contacting potential employers, it is customary to send a résumé and cover letter. A résumé is a summary of your education, job qualifications, and

Accountant Responsibilities include auditing, recording, and summarizing transactional information.

***

Advertising Specialist Works with outside advertising agencies to develop communication methods and promotional strategies.

***

Buyer (Assistant Buyer or Senior Buyer) Responsibilities include acquisition of merchandise, controlling sales, forecasting profits, and optimizing the product mix. Opportunity to specialize in specific product lines (such as women s sportswear). Also works with suppliers through product acquisition, negotiation, and evaluation. May be asked to assist in development of point-of-purchase displays, in conjunction with corporate merchandisers.

***

Catalog Manager Responsibilities include managing the operations for the catalog, including merchandise acquisition and customer fulfillment.

***

Commercial Artist/Visual Director Duties include creating the illustration of advertisements and handling the package design. May also be asked to communicate divisional merchandising directives to stores and to partner with the Merchandise Team Manager in organizing and executing selling-floor fixture/merchandise moves.

Collections and Credit Specialist Assists with the develoment of credit terms, types of credit accepted, credit eligibility, and collections of delinquent accounts.

***

Department Manager/Assistant Manager Responsibilities include ensuring that displays are effective and illustrate the retailer s mission. Must train, lead, control, and evaluate departmental sales staff. Also assists buyers in merchandising purchase decisions.

***

District Manager Responsible for maximizing sales volume and profits for assigned stores through effective management; development of field and store staff; and execution of company programs, policies, and procedures.

***

Line Manager Works with other line managers. Responsible for either the hard lines or the soft lines of the store, to provide leadership on all sales-floor processes, ensuring that merchandising and floor events conform to high standards of quality. Plans and directs all sales events for maximum profits, sales, guest service, team spirit, and team development.

***

Merchandise Manager Assists buyers and departmental managers with merchandise buying to ensure that all departments are offering an integrated product mix. Works closely with a team of associates to ensure accuracy and timeliness of the markdown process. May be asked to act as a liason between buyers and store managers.

***

Operations Manager Ensures that all store operations are running smoothly and profitably by inspecting, marking, and distributing merchandise.

***

Personnel Manager Recruits and helps retain employees. Performs various training functions and outlines benefits and compensation for employees. Must provide all human resource needs and engage in personnel forecasting.

***

Store Manager Oversees all operations of a specific store. Develops creative plans to increase store sales and decrease losses. Provides training and development for Assistant Store Manager and Associates. Ensures consistency of store presentation with company standards. Maintains communication with district/regional management to stay abreast of company initiatives.

***

Miscellaneous Positions Positions available for e-tail managers, warehouser/warehouse specialists, salespersons, site location specialists, or merchandise analysts.

FIGURE A.1 Help Wanted: Retail Positions

employment background. The cover letter serves as an introduction to potential employers. A well-written cover letter will make the reader want to review your résumé. Using the AIDA (*a*ttention, *i*nterest, *d*esire, *a*ction) approach from advertising, the combined cover letter and résumé should attract enough *attention* and *interest* to make the employer *desire* you as an employee. Then (usually) the employer will take *action* and call you for an interview.

Because most employers will ask for references, you should provide a separate sheet listing at least three references with full contact information. As stated earlier, make sure your references have given you permission to use their names.

Before sending out the cover letter and résumé, have at least three people review the documents. You most certainly will not be called for an interview if these documents contain errors.

THE INTERVIEW

Employers will call in top candidates for an interview. It is at the interview that the employer determines whether or not the candidate is a good fit for the organization. It is also the time when the applicant determines whether the organization is a good fit for him or her. It is customary that candidates go through several interviews before being offered a job. A best practice is to engage in a "practice" interview prior to the first real interview.

The interview can be compared to a sales presentation where the applicant is the product and the salesperson rolled into one. Interviewers look for a polished presentation. Both verbal and nonverbal communication play a part in forming impressions. Desired qualities include good communication skills, a positive attitude, confidence, self-awareness, and motivation. Simply having these qualities is not enough, however. You must *communicate* these qualities to the interviewers.

Prior to the interview, learn as much as you can about the organization through sources such as the company's annual report, newspaper articles, the company's website, and company brochures. Interviewers often test a candidate's knowledge about the company to check whether she or he conducted the appropriate research.

As discussed earlier, physical appearance is very important during an interview because grooming and clothing send messages to the employer about the candidate's professionalism. Dress conservatively; your outfit should be clean and pressed, and of a dark, solid color. As the saying goes, you won't get a second chance to make a good first impression.

After the interview, send the interviewer a thank-you note within two days, even if you think you will not get the offer. The note serves three purposes: to express appreciation for the interviewer's time, to express continued interest in the position, and to bring your name to the forefront of his or her memory. Of course, you will need the interviewer's name, title, and address. Therefore, a good habit is to collect a business card from everyone who interviews you. At a minimum, send a thank-you via e-mail.

THE OFFER OR REJECTION

In today's tough retail market, one job opening will attract a large number of applicants. Be optimistic, but be prepared for this competitive market. Hang in there and stay determined. If your job search is not proving fruitful after a few months, do not be afraid to redefine your search criteria or goals. Sometimes broadening or altering search criteria can steer you in helpful directions.

If all goes well and you are offered a position, be sure to ask questions about the terms of your employment. Best of luck to you in this exciting endeavor!

Appendix B

A Comprehensive Case Study of Z-Tech., Inc., dba Z-Coil

INTRODUCTION

Alvaro Gallegos has always been an entrepreneur. He grew up in New Mexico, and after serving in the U.S. Air Force as a fighter pilot, he began a career in retailing. He has owned and operated many retail businesses, including a department store in Española, New Mexico. During this period, he developed a penchant for long-distance running and continues to run many miles every day. This passion for running led him to develop a side interest in running shoes that became a retail opportunity.

HISTORY

Alvaro Gallegos, founder of Z-Tech and currently CEO and president.

While jogging in Santa Fe one morning, Gallegos became aware that the hard earth and his own energy were colliding in his sneakers. "How can I get rid of this problem?" he thought. Finally, after seven years of designing and testing shoe products, Alvaro answered his question by inventing an unusual running shoe. Today these running shoes adorn the feet of New Mexico's governor; many entertainers, including Shirley MacLaine and George Jones; marathon runners; workers who stand for long periods of time; and people with back, foot, or knee problems. In January 1996, Gallegos established Z-Tech, Inc., to take advantage of this expanding market. The innovative Z-Coil shoe line has been the major product for Z-Tech since the company's inception.

In 2001, the year the company completed an initial, limited stock offering, Z-Coil shoes were said to be cushioning the feet of more than 15,000 loyal customers. Within two years, the company had expanded its Albuquerque, New Mexico, headquarters by buying new properties, including 4,000 square feet of new warehouse space and a new 1,000-square-foot retail showroom, to handle customers' steadily increasing demand. The company plans to expand its manufacturing operations, now located in South Korea, and is looking at China and Mexico as possibilities.

In addition to expanding its warehouse, manufacturing, and retail showrooms, Z-Tech has altered its executive board. The company added veteran chief financial officer Tom Clausen, a CPA and former CFO for numerous multi-million-dollar operations in the Southwest. While CFO of Allied Bancshares, Clausen oversaw the firm's growth from $250 million to $10 billion in assets, using a strategy of steady internal growth. Clausen was also involved in Allied Bancshares' initial and subsequent public offerings, SEC filings, and listings on the over-the-counter market and on NASDAQ, as well as providing communications to investors and industry analysts. His track record shows he is a shrewd and intuitive CFO.

THE PRODUCT

Z-Coil shoes are pain relief shoes with a patented spring suspension system that provides enhanced built-in orthotic cushioning (200 percent more than other shoes). Z-Coil shoes offer relief from foot pain caused by such ailments as heel spurs and plantar fascia, as well as arthritis and back pain. With a special metal spring beneath the heel, Z-Coil shoes may appear awkward or strange looking. A test conducted at the U.S. Department of Energy's Los Alamos National Laboratory (LANL) concluded that Z-Coil shoes reduce skeletal shock by 50 percent. LANL evaluators also estimated that the energy return levels of the shoes fall somewhere in the range of 40 to 50 percent. Z-Coil shoes are available in two types: spring visible or spring invisible.

The bizarre appearance of Z-Coil shoes (when the spring is visible) gives the company a significant advantage for its word-of-mouth integrated marketing communications (IMC). The corresponding marketing drawback of the spring-

Z-Coil shoes are designed with a patented spring technology to help reduce skeletal pain and absorb impact.

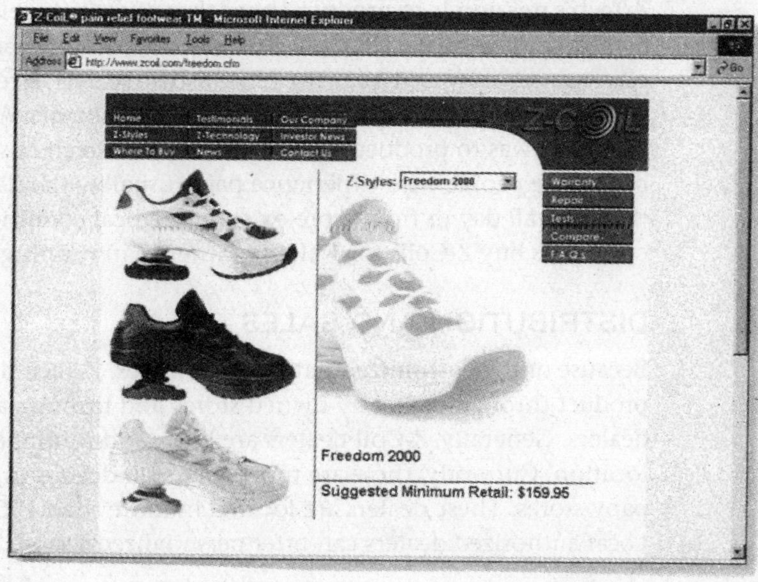

invisible (spring is enclosed) product is that it does not draw the attention of potential customers the way the visible-spring product does. Z-Tech sees this as a lost opportunity for product recognition within its market.

THE FOOTWEAR INDUSTRY

The general footwear industry in the United States is relatively mature. Competition is fierce, especially in the sports shoe segment. Nike, Reebok, Adidas, Puma, and others are trying to maintain or increase market share. The U.S. footwear market reached approximately $40 billion in 2002, representing an increase of only 1.3 percent over the previous year, spurred by the sales of sports shoes. Sales in the footwear market are expected to reach about $44.4 billion by 2004. The average price paid for a pair of shoes in 2001 was $38.36. Forty-four percent of total sales go to low-end retailers, whereas mid-range retailers and athletic shoe retailers account for about 30 percent. The market continues to grow at a moderate pace, but this can be attributed to higher unit prices for products rather than more units being sold.

Nike is number one in the footwear market, with a 12 percent market share. It is estimated that one out of four American adults purchases athletic footwear, with casual sneakers being the most popular.

Compared to Nike's target market, consisting of teens who base their purchase decisions primarily on fashion and trends, Z-Tech's target is composed of buyers age thirty-five and older who buy shoes reported to protect against physical problems and deterioration associated with repetitive-exercise trauma.

MARKETING STRATEGY

Z-Tech's mission is to produce shoes that effectively relieve foot and leg discomfort and reduce back pain. By reducing pain, the product enhances the earnings capacity and quality of life of the wearer. In recent years, Z-Tech has worked to refine and focus its message to consumers. Although the original intention was to produce shoes for runners, Z-Tech has found that some of its buyers are people who experience pain (usually job related) from being on their feet all day or from a pre-existing medical condition. Today 25 percent of customers buy Z-Coils for walking rather than running.

DISTRIBUTION AND SALES

Because of the customized nature of its shoes, Z-Tech decided to distribute the product through company-owned stores and through a network of authorized dealers. Generally, Z-Coil dealers are brick-and-mortar and can retail from any location. Currently, there are more than 160 dealers in addition to the company stores. These dealers are located in more than 100 cities worldwide. Local authorized dealers can offer personalized service to customers, helping them choose appropriate product models. This reduces unnecessary product returns. Prior to moving to this system of distribution, Z-Tech had found that in nonpersonal retail environments (such as catalogs and e-tailing), it had a much higher incidence of product returns.

From July 2001 to June 2002, total sales of Z-Coil shoes increased 270 percent. This growth was attributed to the increase in authorized dealers and a new dealer training program that was developed and implemented in 2002. Wholesale sales represent 75 percent of sales, and retail sales account for about 25 percent of all total sales. Prior to 2002, retail sales represented about 35 percent of total sales.

ADVERTISING AND PROMOTION

National footwear consumer advertising exceeds $400 million annually. It is estimated that Nike accounts for about 40 percent of total consumer footwear advertising expenditures, with Adidas-Solomon a close second. In contrast, Z-Tech spends around $30,000 total for advertising and IMC. In light of this, Z-Tech relies heavily on word-of-mouth communications within its publics. These communications are driven by the unique aesthetics of the exposed-coil shoes. For the enclosed-spring shoes, Z-Tech's marketing department is considering new advertising strategies.

Z-Tech has indicated that it will not invest significantly on advertising until specific needs arise. The company has remarked that it is years away from any national IMC campaign. For the near future, or until a need arises, Z-Tech will likely use focused IMC tactics because of its unique market of people with foot, leg, and back pain, as well as those working in jobs that require them to

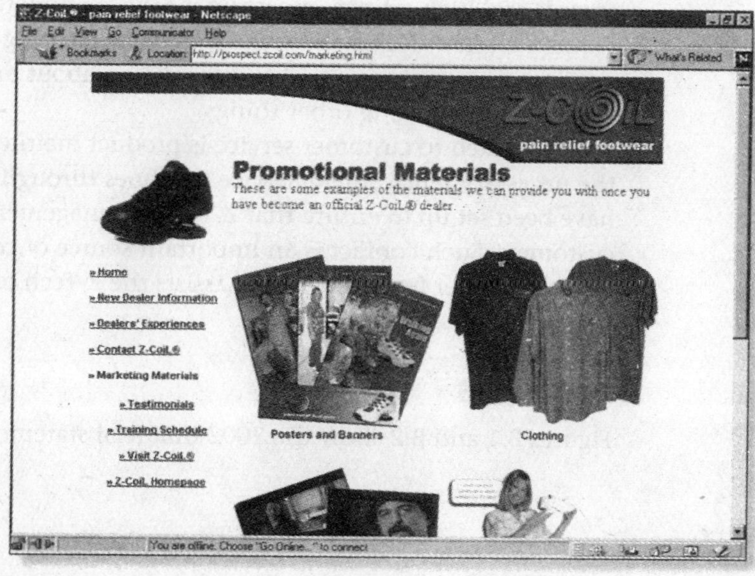

Shown here is the homepage for Z-Tech. The site is used by the company to disseminate investor and consumer information.

be on their feet for a large portion of their day (factory workers, food servers, doctors, nurses, etc.).

Z-Tech supports the local advertising efforts of its distributors. It has developed new sales brochures, banners, posters, and other promotional and educational materials to enhance product recognition and service capabilities for its dealers. Recently, the company completed its first thirty-second spot television commercial, which each retail dealer can customize.

Z-Tech also promotes its products through an associated line of T-shirts, denim shirts, caps, pens, and other promotional items that are sold in the main retail stores and by some dealers. In addition, Z-Tech promotes its shoes at well-attended public events, such as the Olympic torch relays. In January 2002, several Olympians passed the Olympic torch wearing Z-Coils.

A final promotion was launched during the third stock offering. Every investor who invested $250 or more received a coupon good for one free pair of shoes. Those who invested $500 were given gift certificates for three pairs of shoes. Z-Tech used the investor information as part of the database-marketing program currently being developed.

Andres Gallegos, Z-Tech's executive vice president, believes the company's best IMC channel is "people who buy our stock and also wear our shoes."

CUSTOMER SERVICE

At Z-Tech, the customer is king or queen. All company employees are required to respond to customer inquiries and problems as soon as they are received, in addition to fulfilling the specific requirements of their jobs. Also, more than one-half of Z-Tech's staff is specifically responsible for customer service. Because Z-Tech sometimes sells it product through dealers, it has the additional task of ensuring that the dealers also make the customer their number one priority. Z-Tech takes care to select authorized dealers that have proven records and high ratings in customer service etiquette. The company also requires all new dealers to attend a two-day training session at corporate headquarters. The seminars provide information about products and customer service strategies, among other things.

Also related to customer service is product maintenance. Z-Tech provides all the necessary replacement service for shoes through its dealers. Showrooms have been set up to ensure that Z-Tech's management has direct contact with customers. Such contact is an important source of company research through quick customer feedback, which assists the Z-Tech team in research and development efforts.

FINANCES

Figures B.1 and B.2 show the 2002 financial statements for Z-Tech, Inc.

Z-Tech, Inc.
Balance Sheet
As of June 30, 2002 and 2001

	2002	2001
Assets		
Current Assets:		
Cash	$2,245,850	$2,229,934
Accounts receivable, less allowance for doubtful accounts ($32,628 in 2002 and $19,163 in 2001)	232,046	78,759
Inventory	990,606	164,548
Advances to officers	135,766	212,143
Other current assets	8,166	5,595
Total Current Assets	$3,612,434	$2,580,979
Property and equipment	540,246	172,146
Other assets	43,105	16,148
	$4,195,785	$2,769,543
Liabilities and Stockholders Equity		
Current Liabilities:		
Current portion of long-term debt	$10,208	
Accounts payable	45,849	29,897
Accrued expenses	69,486	33,534
Accrued common stock promotional costs	392,466	326,530
Total Current Liabilities	$508,009	$389,961
Long-term debt	238,463	
Stockholder s Equity:		
Common stock, no par value, 60,000,000 shares authorized; issued and outstanding: 28,480,894 shares in 2002 and 27,093,108 shares in 2001.	5,494,391	4,357,241
Accumulated Deficit	(2,045,078)	(1,977,659)
Total Stockholders Equity	$4,195,785	$2,769,543

FIGURE B.1 **Z-Tech, Inc.: Balance Sheet** (Sources: Z-Tech internal company reports; personal interview with Andres Gallegos, executive vice president, Z-Tech, Inc.; Z-Tech, Inc. annual reports for the years 2000–2002.)

Z-Tech, Inc. Income Statement For the Years Ended June 30, 2002 and 2001	2002	2001
Gross Sales	$2,794,283	$774,183
Less: Sales returns and allowances	123,105	3,309
Net Sales	2,671,178	740,874
Cost of sales	1,200,625	306,917
Gross Profit	1,470,553	433,957
Operating expenses	1,600,237	869,276
Loss From Operations	(129,684)	(435,319)
Other income	62,265	23,918
Net Loss	$(67,419)	$(411,401)

FIGURE B.2 **Z-Tech, Inc.: Income Statement** (Sources: Z-Tech internal company reports; personal interview with Andres Gallegos, executive vice president, Z-Tech, Inc.; Z-Tech, Inc. annual reports for the years 2000–2002.)

CASE PROJECT

Develop an integrated retail management flow chart for Z-Tech, Inc. Pay particular attention to the company's retailing operations rather than its manufacturing and distribution activities. Use any outside resources that are applicable to the case. Be sure to relate the chapter concepts to the flow chart. The following outline will assist you in your analysis:

- Retail mission/vision
- Retail objectives
- Situational analysis of the retail environment
- Retail information systems
- Retail strategy
- Target marketing
- Market and location selection
- Financial operations management
- Merchandise buying and handling/logistics
- Human resource management
- Retail tactics: pricing, integrated marketing communications, and customer service
- Response of the market and retail auditing
- Evaluation and control

QUESTIONS FOR DISCUSSION

(For more information, visit Z-Tech's website at *www.zcoil.com.*)

1. Do you think Z-Tech should develop an e-tailing system? Why or why not?
2. Calculate the value of (a) Z-Tech's customers and (b) its stockholders.
3. What type of information should Z-Tech collect and insert into its retail information system?

4. Do you think Z-Tech's mission is on target? If not, how would you change it?
5. Identify some new markets for Z-Tech to explore.
6. Assess the financial strengths, weaknesses, opportunities, and threats for Z-Tech.
7. Who do you think are Z-Tech's major competitors? Why?
8. Classify Z-Tech using the NAICS system (see Chapter 4).
9. Do you believe Z-Tech has accurately defined its customer base? Would you include other groups? If so, what groups?
10. Assess the levels of price for Z-Tech. If you were in charge of pricing, what changes would you make to this tactical area?
11. Do you think Z-Tech is on target with its IMC? What, if anything, would you change given its financial constraints?
12. Do you believe Z-Tech provides good customer service? What does the company do that you like? What would you change?
13. What laws do you believe are applicable to Z-Tech? Do you see a problem with product liability? Explain your answer.
14. What trends do you think will affect the company within the next two years? Five years? Ten years?

Notes

Chapter 1
The World of Retailing

1. Toys "R" Us website at "About Toys 'R' Us," at www.204.toysrus.com/corporate-info/tru/tru_about_toysrus.cfm, September 2002.

2. Kelly Barbieri, "Toys 'R' Us Becomes Big Wheel in Times Square," *Amusement Business,* April 29, 2002, p. 10.

3. Toys "R" Us website at "About Times Square," at www.204.toysrus.com/corporate-info/timesquare/timesquare_main_content.cfm, September 2002.

4. *The American Heritage College Dictionary,* 4th ed. (Boston: Houghton Mifflin, 2002), p. 1186.

5. William M. Pride and O. C. Ferrell, *Marketing,* 12th ed. (Boston: Houghton Mifflin, 2003), p. 352.

6. Ibid., p. 375.

7. Christian Millman, "Stores Still Sell in Downturn," *The Morning Call,* July 22, 2001, pp. D1, D4.

8. Thelma Snuggs, "Retailing: The Quest to Keep up with Market Forces," *Black Collegian,* 23:2 (February 2003), pp. 68–74.

9. Bob Egelko, "Sex Discrimination Cited at Wal-Mart: Women Accuse Wal-Mart/Lawyers Seek OK for Class Action Suit," *San Francisco Chronicle,* April 29, 2003, p. B1.

10. Charles W. L. Hill and Gareth R. Jones, *Strategic Management: An Integrated Approach,* 5th ed. (Boston: Houghton Mifflin, 2003), p. 86.

11. James R. Ogden, "Retailing and Consumer Behavior," Chapter 2 in *Marketing's Powerful Weapon: Point of Purchase Advertising* (Washington, DC: POPAI, 2001).

12. Gary P. Schneider, *New Perspectives on E-Commerce* (Boston: Course Technology, a division of Thomson Learning, 2002), p. 1.04.

13. Debra Sparks, "Who Will Survive the Internet Wars?" *Business Week,* December 27, 1999, p. 98.

14. Jon Swartz, "Dot-com Decline Sees No End Soon," *USA Today,* June 7, 2002.

Chapter 2
Customer Value, Services, and Retailing Technologies

1. Leslie Kaufman, "William T. Dillard, Founder of a Retail Chain, Dies at 87," *New York Times,* February 9, 2002, p. A17.

2. Dillard's homepage, retrieved September 2002 from www.dillards.com.

3. Hoover's Company Capsule, "Dillard's Inc.," retrieved September 2002 from www.hoovers.com.

4. Kaufman, "William T. Dillard."

5. William M. Pride and O. C. Ferrell, *Marketing,* 12th ed. (Boston: Houghton Mifflin, 2003), p. 11.

6. *The American Heritage College Dictionary,* 4th ed. (Boston: Houghton Mifflin, 2002), p. 1514.

7. Earl Naumann, *Customer Value Toolkit* (Cincinnati: Thompson Executive Press, 1995), pp. 17, 163.

8. R. B. Tucker, *Win the Value Revolution* (Franklin Lakes, NJ: Career Press, 1995).

9. Michael J. Dorsch and Les Carlson, "A Transaction Approach to Understanding and Managing Customer Equity," *Journal of Business Research,* 35 (1996), pp. 253–264.

10. Pride and Ferrell, *Marketing,* p. 299.

11. David A. Aaker, *Managing Brand Equity: Capitalizing on the Value of a Brand Name* (New York: The Free Press, 1991), pp. 16–17.

12. U.S. Department of Labor, Bureau of Labor Statistics, "Industry at a Glance," retrieved November 27, 2002, from www.bls.gov/iag/iag.services.htm.

13. U.S. Department of Labor, Bureau of Labor Statistics, "Services," retrieved December 2002 from www.bls.gov.

14. Ibid.

15. G. Lynn Shostack, "Breaking Free from Product Marketing," *Journal of Marketing,* 41 (April 1977), pp. 73–80.

16. Earl W. Sasser, Paul R. Olsen, and Daryl D. Wyckoff, *Management of Service Operations: Text, Cases, and Readings* (Boston: Allyn and Bacon, 1978).

17. Christopher H. Lovelock, *Services Marketing,* 3d ed. (Upper Saddle River, NJ: Prentice Hall, 1996).

18. Leonard L. Berry, "Services Marketing Is Different," *Business,* May–June 1980.

19. Mary Jo Bitner, "Servicescapes: The Impact of Physical Surroundings on Customers and Employees," *Journal of Marketing,* April 1992, pp. 57–71.

20. Earl Naumann, *Creating Customer Value: The Path to Sustainable Competitive Advantage* (Cincinnati: Thompson Executive Press, 1995), pp. 17, 163.

21. Frederick R. Reichheld, "Learning from Customer Defections," *Harvard Business Review,* March–April 1996, p. 57.

22. Lois Geller, "Customer Retention Begins with the Basics," *Direct Marketing,* September 1997, pp. 58–62.

23. Dataquest Technologies, "E-commerce: An Overview," 2001, retrieved July 2002 from www.dqindia.com.

24. J. Weiss, "10 Questions About E-commerce," August 31, 1999, retrieved July 2002 from www.builder.cnet.com/webbuilding/pages/Business/Ecommerce20/ss01.html.

25. Clifford Anthony, "JCPenney Workers Still Follow Founding Philosophy," *Knight Ridder Tribune Business News,* May 12, 2002.

26. "Corporate Social Responsibility: The WBCSD's Journey," World Business Council for Sustainable Development, p. 23, retrieved September 2002 from www.wbcsd.org.

27. Citibank press release, "Citigroup Foundation Awards $1 Million to Habitat for Humanity to Support Nationwide Employee Volunteer Program,"

retrieved July 2002 from www.sriworld.com.

28. Cy's Work Clothes press release, "Supplier of Work Clothing and Lab and Shop Wear to Schools Announces Low Price Programs to Stretch Budgets," retrieved July 2002 from www.sriworld.com.

29. Stop & Shop Supermarkets press release, "23 Massachusetts Retailers Join Forces to Support 9/11 Families," June 27, 2002, retrieved July 2002 from www.sriworld.com.

Chapter 3

An Overview of the Retail Planning and Management Process

1. "About Wal-Mart: Neighborhood Market," retrieved June 2003 from www.walmartstores.com.

2. Thomas Lee, "Wal-Mart CEO Is Optimistic About Retail Future: Lee Scott Says Lower Gas Prices and Fewer Scandals Will Help," *St. Louis Post–Dispatch*, April 17, 2003, p. C3.

3. Debbie Howell, "Supermarket Concept Set to Take Off," *DSN Retailing Today*, 41, no. 11 (2002), pp. 109–110.

4. William J. Morin, "Silent Sabotage: Mending the Crisis in Corporate Values," *Management Review*, 84 (July 1995), p. 10.

5. Ibid.

6. Francis J. Aguilar, *Scanning the Business Environment* (New York: Macmillan, 1967).

7. Fred Nickols, "Three Forms of Strategy: Corporate, Competitive and Strategy in General," retrieved June 2003 from Distance Consulting at http://home.att.net/~nickols/personal.html.

8. Henry Mintzberg, *Mintzberg on Management: Inside Our Strange World of Organizations* (New York: The Free Press, 1989), p. 30.

9. Steven P. Schnaars, *Marketing Strategy: A Customer-Driven Approach* (New York: The Free Press, 1991), p. 27.

10. Michael Porter, *Competitive Strategy* (New York: The Free Press, 1980).

11. K. H. Hammonds, "Michael Porter's Big Ideas," *Fast Company*, March 2001, pp. 150, 152–154, 156.

12. "7-Eleven and Ingenico Implement Chainwide Electronic Payment System," *PR Newswire*, New York, April 9, 2003.

13. Nielsen Media Research homepage, retrieved June 2003 from www.nielsenmedia.com.

14. *What It's All About 2001* (Oak Brook, IL: Council of Logistics Management, 2000).

15. Council of Logistics Management homepage, "About Us," retrieved June 2003 from www.clm1.org.

16. William H. Pride and O. C. Ferrell, *Marketing*, 12th ed., (Boston: Houghton Mifflin, 2003).

17. *International Law Dictionary and Directory*, retrieved June 2003 from http://august1.com/pubs/dict/l.htm.

18. James Fieser, "Ethics," *The Internet Encyclopedia of Philosophy* (2001), retrieved June 2003 from http://www.utm.edu/research/iep/e/ethics.htm.

Chapter 4

The Retail Environment: A Situational and Competitive Analysis

1. Sneakerpimp.com homepage, retrieved June 2003 from www.sneakerpimp.com.

2. Maureen Takcik, "Fancy Footwork: How Young Dealers of Rare Sneakers Challenge Nike—Using the Web, Mr. Eways, 16, Subverts a Giant's Control of Its Marketing Strategy—Air Jordans for $700 a Pair," *Wall Street Journal*, August 20, 2002 (Eastern edition), p. A1.

3. Original source is J. Jeffrey Inman and Russell S. Winer, "Where the Rubber Meets the Road: A Model of In-Store Consumer Decision Making," working paper (report no. 98-122, The Marketing Science Institute, October 1998), p. 5. As cited by James R. Ogden, "Retailing and Consumer Behavior," in *Marketing's Powerful Weapon: Point-of-Purchase Advertising*, ed. Robert Liljenwall and James Maskulka (Washington, DC: Point-of-Purchase Advertising International, 2001).

4. "Bye, SICs! NAICS Is the New Industry Nomenclature," *Purchasing Magazine*, March 12, 1998.

5. North American Industry Classification System, retrieved June 2003 from www.naics.com.

6. 1997 Economic Census, Retail Trade, "Establishment and Firm Size," U.S. Census Bureau, issued October 2000.

7. James R. Lowry, "The Fight for Survival by Independent Retailers," *USA Today*, July 2000, pp. 22–25.

8. Ibid.

9. Kenneth E. Stone, *Competing with the Retail Giants* (New York: John Wiley & Sons, 1995).

10. Jeffrey S. Conant and J. Chris White, "Marketing Program Planning, Process Benefits, and Store Performance: An Initial Study Among Small Retail Firms," *Journal of Retailing*, 74, Winter 1999, pp. 525–541.

11. J. C. Penney 2002 annual report.

12. Lowry, pp. 22–25.

13. Carpet One website, www.carpetone.com, retrieved June 2003.

14. "Unadjusted and Adjusted Estimates of Monthly Retail and Food Services Sales by Kinds of Business: 2002," U.S. Census Bureau, *Service Sector Statistics*, retrieved online at www.census.gov.

15. Walter K. Levy, "Are Department Stores Doomed?" *Discount Merchandiser*, 31, May 1991, p. 56.

16. James T. Madore and Christian Murray, "A Very Wary Holiday: Many Hit the Stores, But Few Buy Without Heavy Discounts," *Newsday*, December 24, 2002, p. A5.

17. Frank Green, "A New Bag: Once-Loyal Department Store Shoppers Turn to Discounters for Better Prices and Specialty Stores for Serve and Selection," *The San Diego Union–Tribune*, October 27, 2002, p. H1.

18. Triversity Top 100 Retailers (2001), www.stores.org, retrieved June 2003.

19. Kathleen Parrish, "Discount Retailers Know It's All About Finding a Niche: Chains' Successes Lie in Offering Quality Service Alongside Low Prices: Wal-Mart and Target Rule," *The Morning Call*, March 9, 2002, p. C10.

20. "The Great American Spice Company Enters Electronic Commerce Arena," press release (third quarter 1998) obtained from TEK Interactive Group, Inc. at www.tekinteractive.com.

21. George S. Dahlman and Steven T. Denault, "The Blurring Food Retail Channels," Report by U.S. Bancorp Piper Jaffray Equity Research, January 2002, p. 5.

22. "FMI's State of Food Retailing 2003: Despite Challenges, Many Food Retailers Post Strong Sales Growth Figures: Companies Compete for Value, Convenience, Ethnic and Aging Consumers," press release from Food Marketing Institute, Washington, DC (June 6, 2003).

23. Food Marketing Institute home page at www.fmi.org; retrieved June 2003.

24. "Language of the Food Industry: Glossary of Supermarket Terms," retrieved June 2003 from Food Marketing Institute at www.fmi.org.

25. "Facts and Figures," retrieved June 2003 from Food Marketing Institute at www.fmi.org.

26. "Supermarket Facts, Industry Overview 2002," retrieved June 2003 from Food Marketing Institute at www.fmi.org.

27. "Key Facts Grocery Store Sales," prepared by FMI Information Service, retrieved May 2003 from Food Marketing Institute at www.fmi.org.

28. "Language of the Food Industry: Glossary of Supermarket Terms," retrieved June 2003 from Food Marketing Institute at www.fmi.org.

29. "Wegmans Food Markets, Inc.: An Overview," retrieved September 2002 from www.wegmans.com.

30. "About Meijer," retrieved September 2002 from www.meijer.com.

31. Dahlman and Denault, p. 19.

32. Ibid.

33. Ibid.

34. Ibid.

35. "What Is Aldi?" retrieved January 2003 from www.aldifoods.com.

36. U.S. Census Bureau, retrieved January 2003 from landview.census/gov/epcd/ec97sic/def/G531.TXT.

37. "What Is Direct Marketing?" Direct Marketing Association, retrieved June 2003 from www.the-dma.org.

38. "E-commerce: An Overview," Dataquest Technologies, 2001; available at www.dqindia.com.

39. "New NAM Poll Shows That Despite Tech Advances, Most Manufacturers Still Not Using E-Commerce," National Association of Manufacturers press release, February 22, 2000; available at www.nam.org/News/Releases/Feb00/pr0222.html.

40. J. Buskin, "Tales from the Front: Firsthand Look at Buying Online," *Wall Street Journal;* available at www.interactive.wsj.com.

Chapter 5
Evaluation and Identification of Retail Customers

1. "Nextel Communications Tops Business Week's 'Info Tech 100' List: Dell Computer, Samsung Electronics, Nokia, IBM and Hewlett-Packard Also Included," *PR Newswire*, New York, June 12, 2003.

2. John Pletz, "Dell Takes over Top Spot in Home PC Sales," *Knight Ridder Tribune Business News*, March 6, 2002, p. 1.

3. Lewis Lazare, "Lew's Review—Latest Dell Ad a Dud Without the Dude," *Chicago Sun Times*, July 22, 2002, p. 51.

4. Erik Rhey, "Dell's Detour: 'Dude you're getting a white box' doesn't have the same ring as Dell's well-known slogan, but the company has announced that it will sell unbranded PCs known as 'white boxes' through small-business dealers," *PC Magazine*, October 15, 2002.

5. Laura Italiano, Jamie Schram, and Bill Hoffmann, "Dell Dude Nabbed in Lower East," retrieved March 5, 2003, from www.nypost.com/news/regionalnews/68896.htm.

6. Theresa Howard, "Dude! You've Been Replaced; Dell Tries Interns to Pick Up Where Steven Left Off," *USA Today*, March 10, 2003, p. B4.

7. Roland T. Rust, Valerie A. Zeithaml, and Katherine N. Lemon, *Driving Customer Equity: How Lifetime Customer Value Is Reshaping Corporate Strategy* (New York: The Free Press, 2000).

8. Yoram Wind, "Issues and Advances in Segmentation Research," *Journal of Marketing Research*, 25 (August 1978), pp. 317–337.

9. Turan Senguder, "An Evaluation of Consumer and Business Segmentation Approaches," *Journal of American Academy of Business*, 2 (March 2003), pp. 618–624.

10. Frederick W. Winter, "Market Segmentation: A Tactical Approach," *Business Horizons* (January/February, 1984), pp. 57–63.

11. Barry Janoff, "Targeting All Ages" (supplement: "66th Annual Report of the Grocery Industry"), *Progressive Grocer*, April 1999, pp. 37–46.

12. "The Generation Game: America's Mosaic of Age Groupings Remains a Handy—If Often Fuzzy—Map to Who We Are," *Austin American Statesman*, April 1, 2001, p. H1.

13. Rebecca Gardyn, "Whitewashed," *American Demographics*, 25 (February 2003), pp. 14–15.

14. "The Generation Game," p. H1.

15. Danny Hakim, "Talk About Generation Gaps. This One's 38 Million Strong," *New York Times*, November 10, 2002, p. 4.

16. "Baby Boomers Meet Their Match," *Knight Ridder Tribune News Service*, January 14, 2003, p. 1.

17. "Guide to Recent U.S. 'Generations,'" Department of Translation Studies, University of Tempere, retrieved June 2003 from www.uta.fi/FAST/US7REF/genguide.html.

18. Levi Strauss & Company, "Dockers," retrieved January 2003 from www.levistrauss.com/brands/dockers.htm.

19. Michael J. Weiss, "Great Expectations," *American Demographics*, 25 (May 2003), pp. 26–35.

20. Shannon L. Hatfield, "Understanding the Four Generations to Enhance Workplace Management," *AFP Exchange*, 22 (July/August 2002), pp. 72–75.

21. Ed Lovern, "New Kids on the Block," *Modern Healthcare*, 31 (January 29, 2001), pp. 28–32.

22. Milton M. Gordon, *Assimilation in American Life* (New York: Oxford University Press, 1964).

23. Elizabeth M. Grieco and Rachel C. Cassidy, *Overview of Race and Hispanic Origin*, C2KBR/01-1 (Washington, DC: U.S. Census Bureau, 2001).

24. "Census 2000 Shows America's Diversity," press release from the U.S. Department of Commerce, March 12, 2001.

25. "Hispanic Population Reaches All-Time High of 38.8 Million," press release from the U.S. Department of Commerce, June 18, 2003.

26. Tom Maguire, "Ethnics Outspend in Areas," *American Demographics* (December 1998).

27. Alison Stein Wellner, "Diversity in America," supplement to *American Demographics* (November 2002), pp. S1–S20.

28. Alison Stein Wellner, "The Money in the Middle," *American Demographics,* 22 (April 2000), pp. 56–64.

29. Debra Goldman, "Paradox of Pleasure," *American Demographics,* 21 (May 1999), pp. 50–53

30. "The Middle to Upper-Middle Class," *American Demographics,* 24 (December 2002/January 2003), pp. 38–39.

31. "The Upper Echelon," *American Demographics,* 24 (December 2002/January 2003), pp. 44–45.

32. Martha Farnsworth Riche, "Psychographics for the 1990s," *American Demographics* (July 1989), pp. 24–31, 53.

33. Peter Francese, "Top Trends for 2003," *American Demographics,* 24 (December 2002/January 2003), pp. 48–51.

34. Jacob Jacoby, "Consumer Psychology: An Octennium," in *Annual Review of Psychology,* ed. Paul Mussen and Mark Rosenweig (Palo Alto, CA: Annual Reviews, vol. 27, 1976), p. 332.

35. Abraham H. Maslow, *Motivation and Personality,* 2d ed. (New York: Harper and Row, 1970).

36. Hans Baumgartner, "Toward a Personology of the Consumer," *Journal of Consumer Research,* 29 (September 2002), pp. 286–292.

37. Leon Festinger, *A Theory of Cognitive Dissonance* (Evanston, IL: Row, Peterson, 1957).

38. Original source is J. Jeffrey Inman and Russell S. Winer, "Where the Rubber Meets the Road: A Model of In-Store Consumer Decision Making," working paper (report no. 98-122, The Marketing Science Institute, October 1998). As cited by James R. Ogden, "Retailing and Consumer Behavior" in *Marketing's Powerful Weapon: Point-of-Purchase Advertising,* ed. Robert Liljenwall and James Maskulka (Washington, DC: Point-of-Purchase Advertising International, 2001).

39. Ibid.

Chapter 6

Retail Information Systems and Research

1. Kim Zimmermann, "Many Franchisees, One Infrastructure," *Retail Information News.com,* June 2002, retrieved July 2002 from www.risnews.com.

2. Midas press release, "Midas Acquired Provider of Automotive Aftermarket Software," January 4, 2001, retrieved July 2002 from www.midasinc.com/news.html.

3. A. B. Blankenship, George E. Breen, and Alan Dutka, *The State of the Art Marketing Research,* 2d ed. (Lincolnwood, IL: NTC Business Books, 1998), p. 15.

4. "Albertsons Standardizes Its Product Information with Trigo Technologies Software . . . ," *PR Newswire,* May 19, 2003.

5. "Yankee Candle Smells Sweet Success with Kronos," *Business Wire,* June 9, 2003.

6. Usama Fayyad, "Optimizing Customer Insight," *Intelligence Enterprise,* 6 (May 13, 2003), pp. 22–26.

7. "What's So Groundbreaking About Merchandise Optimization?" *PR Newswire,* June 10, 2003.

8. Uniform Commercial Council website, retrieved June 2003 from www.uccouncil.org.

9. Mark Frey, "Is Bar Code Quality the Weak Link in Your Supply Chain?" January 1, 2003. Article retrieved June 2003 from www.uc-council.org.

10. "QRS Retail Intelligence Services Targets Improved Pricing Integrity," *PR Newswire,* June 10, 2003.

11. Al Garton, "Become 2005 Sunrise-Compliant Now and Avoid Supply Chain Disruptions," press release from the Uniform Code Council, June 13, 2003.

12. John Teresko, "Winning with Wireless," *Industry Week,* 252 (June 2003), pp. 60–66.

13. "What Is Radio Frequency Identification (RFID)?" Webpage from the Association for Automatic Identification and Data Capture Technologies, retrieved June 2003 from www.aimglobal.org.

14. Leslie Langnau, "Keeping Shelves Stocked at Retail Show," *Material Handling Management,* 57 (August 2002), p. 15.

15. "Introducing AutoID, Inc." press release from the Uniform Code Council, Inc., May 21, 2003.

16. John Teresko, pp. 60–66.

17. Shonda Novak, "The Age of Self-Checkout: Retailers Are Buying into the Idea of Letting Customers Ring up Their Own Purchases," *Austin American Statesman,* June 8, 2003, p. K1.

18. Sandra Guy, "Retailers Turning to High Tech," *Chicago Sun,* June 10, 2003, p. 55.

19. Shonda Novak, p. K1.

20. Jeff Miller, "Healing Retail's Pain," *Mass High Tech,* 21 (May 26, 2003), p. 1.

21. "New Management Team Sets Bold Course at Retail Technologies International," press release, March 31, 2003.

22. "Best Buy to Expand Use of MicroStrategy Enterprise-Wide," press release, April 28, 2003.

23. Gilbert A. Churchill and Dawn Iacobucci, *Marketing Research Methodological Foundations,* 8th ed. (Orlando: Harcourt College Publishers, 2002), p. 6.

24. Ranjit Kumar, *Research Methodology* (Thousand Oaks, CA: Sage Publications, 1999).

25. Usama Fayyad, pp. 22–26.

26. Brian M. Gomme, "Free Search Engine Tips," retrieved June 2003 from www.freesearchenginetips.com.

Chapter 7

Selecting the Appropriate Market and Location

1. "Avon History," retrieved June 2003 from www.avoncompany.com.

2. "Avon Info," retrieved October 2002 from www.avoncompany.com.

3. Carolyn Edy, "Avon Malling," *American Demographics,* April 1999, pp. 38–40.

4. Ibid.

5. William H. Pride and O. C. Ferrell, *Marketing,* 12th ed. (Boston: Houghton

Mifflin), p. 169. Copyright © 2003 by Houghton Mifflin Company. Reprinted with permission.

6. "OMB Designates 49 New Metropolitan Statistical Areas," press release (June 6, 2003) from the Office of Management and Budget.

7. James R. Ogden, *Developing a Creative and Innovative Integrated Marketing Communication Plan: A Working Model* (Upper Saddle River, NJ: Prentice-Hall, 1998).

8. "What Is a DMA?" retrieved June 2003 from www.nielsenmediaresearch.com.

9. "Standards for Defining Metropolitan and Micropolitan Statistical Areas," Office of Management and Budget, *Federal Register*, 65, no. 249 (December 27, 2000), pp. 82228–82238.

10. "OMB Designates 49 New Metropolitan Statistical Areas."

11. Gregory Karp, "Lehigh Valley, Warren County Reunited as a Metro Area," *Morning Call*, June 22, 2003, p. A1.

12. *International Marketing Data & Statistics* (London: Euromonitor Publications, 1996), Table 1201.

13. Peter D. Bennett, ed., *Dictionary of Marketing Terms*, 2d ed. (Chicago: American Marketing Association, 1995), p. 287.

14. Tom Feltenstein, "McDonald's Father Knew Best: Think 'Small'; Win over the Neighborhood and Earn Big Profits," *Nation's Restaurant News*, 37 (February 3, 2003), p. 22.

15. Albert P. Barnett and Ason A. Okoruwa, "Application of Geographic Information Systems in Site Selection and Location Analysis," *The Appraisal Journal*, 61, no. 2 (1993), p. 245.

16. Chris Alewine, "Looking for Customers?" *Chain Store Age*, 78 (September 2002), p. 142.

17. Example from DSS company, retrieved June 2003 from www.dsslink.com.

18. Randy Southerland, "The Science of Site Selection," *National Real Estate Investor*, 44 (October 2002), p. 90.

19. "Slashing E-commerce Fraud through Geotechnology," *Electronic Commerce News*, 7 (August 19, 2002), p. 1.

20. John Henry, "Engineers Finding More Uses for GIS," *Arkansas Business*, 19 (September 23, 2002), p. 1.

21. Robert W. Buckner, *Site Selection: New Advances in Methods and Technology* (New York: Lebhar-Friedman Books, 1998).

22. William J. Reilly, *Method for the Study of Retail Relationships*, Research Monograph Number 4 (Austin, TX: University of Texas Press, Bulletin Number 2944, 1929).

23. Richard L. Nelson, *The Selection of Retail Locations* (New York: F. W. Dodge, 1958).

24. David L. Huff, "Defining and Estimating a Trade Area," *Journal of Marketing*, 28 (1964), pp. 34–38.

25. Bernard LaLonde, "The Logistics of Retail Location," in *American Marketing Proceedings*, ed. William D. Stevens (Chicago: American Marketing Association, 1961).

26. G. L. Drummey, "Traditional Methods of Sales Forecasting," in *Store Location and Store Assessment Research*, ed. R. L. Davies and D. S. Rogers (New York: John Wiley & Sons, 1984), pp. 279–299.

27. Bill Levine, "The Store Stands Alone," *Chain Store Age*, April 1998, pp. 107–108.

28. "Fun Facts," retrieved June 2003 from www.mallofamerica.com.

29. Dave Bodamer, "Top Strips Vie for Neighborhood Centers," *Shopping Centers Today*, July 2002, pp. 1, 61, 62.

30. "Lifestyle Centers—A Defining Moment," *ICSC Research Quarterly* (Winter 2001–2002), retrieved July 2002 from www.ICSC.org.

31. Chern Yeh Kwok, "Lifestyle Mall Centers Mix Upscale Retail, Convenience," *The Detroit News.com*, November 20, 2001, retrieved July 2002 from www.detnews.com/2001/business/0111/20/b04-347928.htm.

32. Dean Starkman, "This New Mall Concept Has Great Curb Appeal," *Wall Street Journal Online*, August 2001, retrieved June 2003 from homes.wsj.com/propertyreport/propertyreport/20010801-starkman.html.

33. Edmund Mander, "Lifestyle Centers Elude Classification," *ICSC Industry News*, August 2001, retrieved July 2003 from www.icsc.org.

34. Merrie S. Frankel, "Outlet Centers Come of Age Overseas," September/October 2002, retrieved June 2003 from www.nareit.com.

35. "Who's Buying at Factory Outlets?" *Businessline*, June 5, 2003.

36. The Mills Corporation 2002 Annual Report.

37. "The Mills Corporation," Hoover's Online, company capsule, retrieved June 2003 from www.hoovers.com.

38. "Baltimore-Washington Airport Seeks Developer to Broaden Retail Choices," *Knight Ridder Tribune Business News*, June 24, 2003.

39. Ibid.

Chapter 8
Financial Aspects of Operations Management

1. "Kmart Ends Arrangement with Grocery Supplier," *New York Times*, February 4, 2002 (East Coast edition), p. C4.

2. Susan Chandler, "Kmart Files for Chapter 11; Expects to Emerge in 2003; Experts Say up to 500 More Stores May Close," *Chicago Tribune*, January 23, 2002, p. 1.

3. Donna De Marco, "Kmart Comes out of Bankruptcy, But Will It Survive?" *Washington Times*, May 5, 2003, p. C12.

4. Marc J. Epstein and Moses L. Pava, "How Useful Is the Statement of Cash Flows?" *Management Accounting*, 74 (1992), p. 52.

5. Donna De Marco, p. C12.

6. Andrew Bary, "Back to Life," *Barron's*, 83 (June 9, 2003), pp. 21–24.

7. Charles W. L. Hill and Gareth R. Jones, *Strategic Management: An Integrated Approach* (Boston: Houghton Mifflin, 2004), pp. 6–8.

8. Larry P. Bailey and Raymond R. Poteau, "Accounting Rule Making—A Two Headed Monster?" *The CPA Journal*, 64 (June 1994), p. 28.

9. Joseph T. Wells, "So That's Why It's Called a Pyramid Scheme," JOURNAL OF ACCOUNTANCY ONLINE (Oct. 2000). Copyright © 2000 from the JOURNAL OF ACCOUNTANCY by the American Institute of Certified Public Accountants, Inc. Opinions of the authors are their own and do not

necessarily reflect policies of the AICPA. Reprinted with permission.

10. Ibid.

11. U.S. Customs Service website (www.customs.ustreas.gov/about/welcome.htm), accessed July 2003.

12. A. Ivanovic and P. H. Collin, *Dictionary of Marketing,* 2d ed. (Middlesex, England: Peter Collin Publishing, 1996), p. 132.

13. Jennifer Baljko, "Apple Employs Third-Party Tools to Improve Planning Process," *EBN,* November 11, 2002, p. 25.

14. Jennifer Caplan, "Your Supply Chain Has a Weak Link," May 21, 2003, retrieved July 2003 from www.CFO.com.

15. James Frederick, "2003 Annual Report: Walgreens-Industry Leader Forges Ahead," *Drug Store News,* 25 (April 28, 2003), pp. 71, 130.

Chapter 9
Merchandise Buying and Handling

1. Maria Elena Salinas, "Latinization of U.S. a Reality," *Seattle Post–Intelligencer,* July 1, 2003, p. B5.

2. "Kmart Marketing: Urban/Ethnic Strategy Remains Pillar of Competitive Advantage," *DSN Retailing Today,* March 5, 2001, pp. 44–46.

3. Ibid.

4. Anne D'Innocenzio, "U.S. Retailers Hope to Woo Hispanics; Thalia Clothing, Spanish Videos Line Shelves," *Chicago Tribune* (final edition), May 20, 2003, p. 5.

5. Doris Hajewski, "Kmart Still Needs to Find Reason to Exist, Experts Say," *Knight Ridder Tribune Business News,* June 23, 2003.

6. Anne D'Innocenzio, "Retailers Pursue the Expanding Hispanic Market," *Columbian,* Vancouver, Washington, May 18, 2003, p. E3.

7. Marshall L. Fisher, Ananth Raman, and Anna Sheen McClelland, "Rocket Science Retailing Is Almost Here: Are You Ready?" *Harvard Business Review,* July–August 2000, pp. 115–124.

8. David Flaum, "Pazo Fits Trend at Saddle Creek," *The Commercial Appeal,* Memphis, Tennessee, March 13, 2003, p. C1.

9. Debra Hazel, "More Chic, Less Chico's," *Shopping Centers Today,* June 2003, pp. 31–32.

10. Russell Shor, "Control Inventory to Control Costs," *National Jeweler,* 97 (March 16, 2003), p. 18.

11. Verlyn D. Richards and Eugene J. Laughlin, "A Cash Conversion Cycle Approach to Liquidity Analysis," *Financial Management,* 9 (Spring 1980), pp. 32–38.

12. Jane M. Cote and Claire K. Latham, "The Merchandising Ratio: A Comprehensive Measure of Working Capital Strategy," *Issues in Accounting Education,* 14 (May 1999), pp. 255–267.

13. Phil Weiss, "Warner-Lambert vs. Pfizer, Plus an Explanation of the Cash Conversion Cycle," November 2, 1999, retrieved July 2002 from The Motley Fool at www.fool.com.

14. *The Entrepreneur's Guidebook Series* (Patsula Media, 2001), retrieved July 2002 from pdf file from www.smallbusinesstown.com.

15. John Cravenho, "Revenue Chain Excellence—Using Speed as the Best Practice," *Business Credit,* September 2002, pp. 20–21.

16. Susan Salisbury, "Nemo Spawns Clown Fish Craze," *Palm Beach Post,* West Palm Beach, Florida, June 11, 2003, 1A.

17. Stephanie Thompson, "Retailers Thwart Food-Price Hikes," *Advertising Age,* 74 (May 5, 2003), p. 3.

18. Debbie Howell, "JCPenney Making Shifts in Structure to Boost Quality," *Discount Store News,* 39 (February 7, 2000), pp. 6, 74.

19. Laura Heller, "12 Hot Issues Facing Mass Retailing—8: Brands—Private and Proprietary Drive Differentiation," *DSN Retailing Today,* 41 (May 20, 2002), p. 39.

20. "Managing the Trading-Partner Link Is the Key to Success," *Chain Store Age,* 79 (June 2003), pp. 2A–11A.

21. "Buyers Launch 7 Major Initiatives to Reduce Inventory," *Supplier Selection & Management Report,* 3 (April 2003), p. 1.

22. Robin Fields and Melinda Fulmer, "Markets' Shelf Fees Put Squeeze on Small Firms," *Los Angeles Times,* January 29, 2000.

23. Ibid.

24. Linda S. Beltran, "Reverse Logistics: Current Trends and Practices in the Commercial World," *Logistics Spectrum,* 36 (July–September 2002), pp. 4–8.

25. Council of Logistics Management homepage, "About Us," accessed July 2003 from www.clm1.org.

26. Victor H. Pooler and David J. Pooler, *Purchasing and Supply Management: Creating the Vision* (New York: Chapman & Hall, division of International Thomson Publishing, 1997), pp. 26–27.

27. Martha C. Cooper, Douglas M. Lambert, and Janus D. Pagh, "Supply Chain Management: More Than a New Name for Logistics," *International Journal of Logistics Management,* 8, no. 1 (1997), pp. 1–5.

28. Margaret Webb Pressler, "Why the Long Wait for Furniture? Logistical Snags Are in the Industry's Fabric," *Washington Post,* Washington, DC, June 30, 2002, p. H4.

29. Alexandra Eyle, "Family Business Now a Regional Giant," *Business Journal—Central New York,* Syracuse, April 13, 2001, p. 4.

30. *What It's All About 2001* (Oak Brook, IL: Council of Logistics Management, 2000).

Chapter 10
Human Resource Management

1. "FleetBoston Financial Company Profile," retrieved October 2002 from www.fleet.com.

2. Elisabeth Goodridge, "The Best Way to Find the Best People," *InformationWeek,* March 25, 2002, retrieved July 2003 from InformationWeek.com.

3. Ibid.

4. Sandy Kennedy, "The Three R's," *Chain Store Age,* 79 (February 2003), p. 24.

5. Raymond A. Noe, John R. Hollenbeck, Barry Gerhart, and Patrick M. Wright, *Human Resource Management: Gaining a Competitive Advantage* (New York: McGraw-Hill Higher Education, 2003), p. 5.

6. Kennedy, p. 24.

7. "Top HRIS Challenges," *HR Focus,* October 2002, pp. S1, S3.

8. Bureau of Labor Statistics, *Occupational Outlook Handbook* (2002–2003), retrieved July 2002 from www.bls.gov/oco/home.htm.

9. Paul Mazur, *Principles of Organization Applied to Modern Retailing* (New York: Harper & Brothers, 1927).

10. A. E. Barber, *Recruiting Employees* (Thousand Oaks, CA: Sage Publishing, 1998).

11. Sanjib Chowdhury, Megan Endres, and Thomas W. Lanis, "Preparing Students for Success in Team Work Environments: The Importance of Building Confidence," *Journal of Managerial Issues* 14 (Fall 2002), pp. 346–359.

12. K. Helliker, "Sold on the Job: Retailing Chains Offer a Lot of Opportunity, Young Managers Find," *Wall Street Journal*, p. A1.

13. Rohit Deshpande and Frederick E. Webster, "Organizational Culture and Marketing: Defining the Research Agenda," *Journal of Marketing* (January 1989), pp. 3–15.

14. Terrence Deal and Allen Kennedy, *Corporate Cultures—The Rites and Rituals of Corporate Life*, (New York: Addison-Wesley, 1982).

15. John Lewison, "From Fired to Hired," *Journal of Accountancy*, 193 (June 2002), pp. 43–50.

16. William J. Holstein, "Making a Career Leap, Sore Muscles and All," *New York Times* (East Coast, late edition), December 22, 2002, section 3, page 5.

17. Lewison, pp. 43–50.

18. Susie Oh, "Outplacement Firms Reap Reward from an Unstable Economy," *Daily Herald*, Arlington Heights, Illinois, January 12, 2003, p. 3.

Chapter 11
Pricing in Retailing

1. Sora Song, "The Shrink Rap," *Time*, New York, 161 (June 2, 2003), p. 81.

2. Lyrysa Smith, "The Incredible Shrinking Products: Consumers Cry Foul at 'Weight Out' Pricing," *Times Union* (Albany, NY), July 21, 2003, p. C1.

3. John Curran, "Ice Cream Makers Are Quietly Downsizing Packaging," *The Morning Call* (Allentown, PA), November 19, 2002, retrieved from www.mcall.com.

4. David Leonhardt, "Cereal-Box Killers Are on the Loose," *Business Week*, October 12, 1998, pp. 72–77.

5. Byung-Do Kim, Kannan Srinivasan, and R. T. Wilcox, "Identifying Price Sensitive Consumers: The Relative Merits of Demographic vs. Purchase Pattern Information," *Journal of Retailing*, 75 (Summer 1999), pp. 173–193.

6. Raymond P. Fisk and Stephen J. Grove, "Applications of Impression Management and the Drama Metaphor in Marketing: An Introduction," *European Journal of Marketing*, 30 (1996), pp. 6–12.

7. "Price Doesn't Count for Everything in Retail," *Home Textiles Today*, 23 (May 27, 2002), p. 6.

8. Daniel Akst, "Seniors Treated Better Than Nerds," *Los Angeles Times*, October 22, 1991, p. 1.

9. Ellen Joan Pollock, "Law," *Wall Street Journal*, October 15, 1991, p. B1.

10. Francine Schwadel, "The 'Sale' Is Fading as a Retailing Tactic: In Pricing Shift, 'Everyday Lows' Replace Specials," *Wall Street Journal* (Eastern edition), March 1, 1989, p. 1.

11. S. J. Diamond, "Sears' Biggest Problem May Be Its Service," *Los Angeles Times*, February 8, 1991, p. 1.

12. Lisa Holton, "As All Else Fails, Here Come Sales Incentive Blizzard Starts," *Chicago Sun-Times*, November 9, 1990, p. 45.

13. Gene Koprowski, "The Price Is Right," *American Demographics*, September 1995, pp. 56–61.

14. David Segal, "Overcharged Music Buyers Stuck with the Bill," *Washington Post*, May 13, 2000, p. C1.

15. K. N. Rajendran and Gerard J. Tellis, "Contextual and Temporal Components of Reference Price," *Journal of Marketing*, 58 (January 1994), pp. 22–34.

16. Kent B. Monroe, "Buyers' Subjective Perceptions of Price," *Journal of Marketing Research*, 10 (February 1973), pp. 70–80.

17. Koprowski, pp. 56–61.

18. Mary J. Cronin, "Business Secrets of the Billion-Dollar Website," *Fortune*, February 2, 1998, p. 142.

19. J. E. Palmieri, "Department Store Discounting Hits 76%," *DNR*, September 23, 2002, p. 4.

20. Koprowski, pp. 56-61.

21. Michael Frick, "The Missing P," *Lottery Insights*, July 2002, pp. 10–12.

22. Greg Saitz, "Why We Pay What We Pay," *Newhouse News Service*, June 10, 2003, p. 1.

Chapter 12
Developing an Effective Integrated Marketing Communications (IMC) Mix

1. Cara B. Dipasquale, "How to Play the Game—Seeking Truth for 'Holy Grail' of Marketing," *Advertising Age*, January 28, 2002, p. 24.

2. Jim Kirk and Thom Khanje, "Cutting-Edge Decision: No More Tags on T-shirts," *Chicago Tribune*, (North Sports Final Edition), October 17, 2002, p. 1.

3. Laura Burrows, "Hanes Retires Annoying T-Shirt Tag and Introduces New Tagless T-Shirt," Hanes Company press release, October 16, 2002, retrieved March 2002 from www.hanes.com.

4. Nancy Dillon, "ABC Super Bowl Ad Winner," *New York Daily News*, January 13, 2003, p. 29.

5. Jim Kirk, "Hanes, PepsiCo Like Mike for Super Bowl Ads," *Chicago Tribune*, Business Section, p. 3.

6. Lisa Lenoir, "Locker Room," *Chicago Sun Times*, January 28, 2003, p. 40.

7. Don E. Schultz, "Foreign Countries Getting IMC Concept Right," *Marketing News*, 35 (August 27, 2001), p. 9.

8. Don E. Schultz, "Integrate Marketing Communications: Maybe Definition Is in the Point of View," *Marketing News*, 27 (January 18, 1993), p. 17.

9. "Office Depot Launches First Hispanic Television and Radio Campaign in Support of 'Back to School' Initiatives," *Business Wire*, July 14, 2003.

10. James R. Ogden, *Developing a Creative and Innovative Integrated Marketing Communication Plan: A Working Model* (Upper Saddle River, NJ: Prentice Hall, 1998).

11. Laura Clark Geist, "GM's First Branded Store Takes Off at Detroit Airport," *Automotive News*, 77 (September 16, 2002), p. 4.

12. David Aaker, *Building Strong Brands* (New York: The Free Press, 1995).

13. Monique Reece Myron and Pamela Larson Truax, "Product's Positioning Vital to Getting Noticed," *Denver Business Journal,* November 11, 1996, retrieved July 2003 from www.bizjournals.com.

14. George S. Low and Jakki J. Mohr, "Setting Advertising and Promotion Budgets in Multi-Brand Companies," *Journal of Advertising Research,* 39 (January/February 1999), pp. 67–79.

15. Terence A. Shimp, *Advertising Promotion: Supplemental Aspects of Integrated Marketing Communication,* 5th ed. (Fort Worth, TX: Dryden Press, 2000).

16. Lisa Fortini Campbell, *Hitting the Sweet Spot* (Chicago: The Copy Workshop, 2001), p. 15.

17. Ogden, *Developing a Creative and Innovative Integrated Marketing Communication Plan.*

18. Anthony Birritteri, "Monitoring the Success of Advertising," *New Jersey Business,* 48 (November 1, 2002), p. 20.

19. Jenny Strasburg, "Mass Campaign May Spell Success for Madonna, Gap," *Deseret News* (Salt Lake City, UT), July 20, 2003, p. E9.

20. "Four-Year Research Study Concludes: Sales Promotion Benefit to Consumers and Businesses," *PR Newswire,* June 11, 2002.

21. Ibid.

22. Jim Kirk, "Disney, Hallmark Break the Ice as Co-Marketers," *Chicago Tribune,* January 19, 2001, p. 3.

23. Robert Liljenwall and James Maskulka, eds., *Marketing's Powerful Weapon: Point-of-Purchase Advertising* (Washington DC: Point-of-Purchase Advertising International, 2001).

24. Bob Stone, *Successful Direct Marketing Methods,* 4th ed. (Lincolnwood, IL: NTC Business Books, 1989), p. 2.

25. Jill Lerner, "Retailers Turn to Loyalty Deals to Stem Defections," *Boston Business Journal,* January 6, 2003, retrieved July 2003 from www.boston.bizjournals.com.

26. Philip Lesly, "Report and Recommendations: Task Force on Stature and Role of Public Relations," *Public Relations Journal,* March 1981, p. 32.

27. Mark Weiner, "A Forward Look at Public Relations," *Public Relations Strategist,* 8 (Spring 2002), pp. 32–35.

28. Richard L. Brandt, "Internet Kamikazes: Interview with CNET's Halsey Minor," from *Perspectives: Marketing on the Internet,* A. Cemal Ekin, ed. (St. Paul: Coursewise Publishing, Inc., 1997), pp. 16–21.

29. Thomas L. Harris, *Value-Added Public Relations* (Chicago: NTC Business Books, 1998), p. 10.

30. Ibid.

31. Lisa Biank Fasig, "Harry Carries—The Magic of Marketing Has Lots to Do with Harry Potter's Success," *Providence Journal* (Rhode Island), June 21, 2003, p. A1.

32. Mark Weiner, "A Forward Look at Public Relations," p. 33.

33. Mark Brown, "In Retailers' Eyes, Eagles Are Dirty Birds," *Rocky Mountain News* (Denver, CO), June 14, 2003, p. D9.

Chapter 13
Customer Service in Retailing

1. "Our Company Mission Statement," retrieved December 2002 from www.menswearhouse.com.

2. "Men's Wearhouse Acquires Trademark," company press release, November 18, 2002, retrieved December 2002 from www.menswearhouse.com.

3. "The Men's Wearhouse, Inc.," retrieved December 2002 from Hoover's Online, www.hoovers.com.

4. Victor D. Infante, "Optimas 2001—Managing Changes: Men's Wearhouse: Tailored for Any Change That Retail Brings," *Workforce,* 80 (March 2001), pp. 48–49.

5. Peter R. Dickson, "Person-Situation: Segmentation's Missing Link," *Journal of Marketing,* Fall 1982, p. 59.

6. Peter Glen, *It's Not My Department! How to Get the Service You Want, Exactly the Way You Want It* (New York: William Morrow and Company, 1990), pp. 11–19.

7. "Find Out What They Like and How They Like It" (1935). Words by Andy Razaf; music by "Fats" Waller.

8. "Sisters Face Ban at Filene's Basement Because of Too Many Returns, Complaints," *St. Louis Post–Dispatch,* July 20, 2003, p. E8.

9. "Many Unhappy Returns: Sisters Banned in Boston," *Chicago Tribune,* July 15, 2003, p. 36.

10. Marty Racine, "Five-Finger Discount: 23 Million Americans Shoplift Each Year for Reasons Not Always Financial," *Houston Chronicle,* November 8, 2002, p. 1.

11. Andrew M. Carlo, "Lowe's Dilutes Inhalants Policy," *Home Channel News,* June 2, 2003, p. 3.

12. "Man Charged with Attack on Ride Attendant," *Morning Call* (Allentown, PA), July 12, 2002, p. B3.

13. Melissa G. Hartman, "Separate the Vital Few from the Trivial Many," *Quality Progress,* September 2001, p. 120.

14. Ibid.

15. A. Parasuraman, Valerie Zeithaml, and Leonard L. Berry, "A Conceptual Model of Service Quality and Its Implications for Future Research," *Journal of Marketing,* 49 (Fall 1985), pp. 41–50.

16. Valerie Zeithaml, A. Parasuraman, and Leonard L. Berry, *Delivering Quality Service: Balancing Customer Perceptions and Expectations* (New York: The Free Press, 1990), pp. 15–33.

17. Art Weinstein and William C. Johnson, *Designing and Delivering Superior Customer Value: Concepts, Cases and Applications* (Boca Raton, FL: St. Lucie Press, 1999), pp. 70–77.

18. A. Parasuraman, Valerie Zeithaml, and Leonard L. Berry, "SERVQUAL: A Multiple-Item Scale for Measuring Consumer Perceptions of Service Quality," *Journal of Retailing,* Spring 1988, pp. 12–40.

19. Ibid.

20. Lillian Vernon, "Make Someone Happy—Your Customer," *Inc.,* July 1998, retrieved July 2003 from inc.com.

21. Ellen Neuborne, "It's the Service, Stupid: E-tailers May Be Missing Their Biggest Chance to Snare—and Keep—Customers," *Business Week,* April 3, 2000, p. EB18.

22. "What Seniors Want in Restaurant Dining," *USA Today,* May 2003, p. 7.

23. "'C' Rating for Web Sites," *Chain Store Age,* 79 (February 2003), p. 51.

24. Maura K. Ammenheuser, "Fitted to a 'T,'" *Shopping Centers Today,* June 2003, pp. 29–30.

25. Elaine Yetzer, "Upscale Hotels Tailor Amenities Specifically for Men, Women," *Hotel and Motel Management,* 215 (October 16, 2000), pp. 58–59.

26. Ellen Neuborne, "It's the Service, Stupid," p. EB18.

27. Robert C. Ford, Cherrill P. Heaton, and Stephen W. Brown, "Delivering Excellent Service: Lessons from the Best Firms," *California Management Review,* 44 (Fall 2001), pp. 39–56.

28. David A. Aaker, *Managing Brand Equity* (New York: The Free Press, 1991), p. 51.

29. Mark McMaster, "Incentive-Powered Marketing," *Potentials,* 35 (November 2002), p. 30.

30. Ibid.

31. Melody Badgett, Whitney Connor, and Jennifer McKinley, "Customer Satisfaction, Do You Know the Score?" Report #G510-1675-00, IBM Institute for Business Value, IBM Corporation, 2002.

32. Srini S. Srinivasan, Rolph Anderson, and Kishore Ponnavolu, "Customer Loyalty in E-commerce: An Exploration of Its Antecedents and Consequences," *Journal of Retailing,* 78 (Spring 2002), pp. 41–50.

33. Ibid.

34. Rashi Glazer, "Marketing in an Information-Intensive Environment: Strategic Implications of Knowledge as an Asset," *Journal of Marketing,* 55 (October 1991), pp. 1–19.

35. Joseph B. Pine II, Bart Victor, and Andrew C. Boynton, *Mass Customization: The New Frontier in Business Competition* (Boston: Harvard Business School Press, 1993).

36. Eric Norlin, "In CRM, Size Matters and Smaller Is Better," *Inc.,* May 2001, retrieved July 2003 from inc.com.

37. Don Peppers and Martha Rogers, *The One to One Future: Building Relationships One Customer at a Time* (New York: Doubleday, 1993), p. 15.

38. Susan Greco, "The Road to One to One Marketing," *Inc.,* 17, no. 14 (1995), p. 56.

39. Eric Yoder, "A 'Sharp' Role Model," *1to1 Magazine,* November–December 2001, p. 33.

40. "Successful CRM Takes More Than 7 Habits," *1to1 Magazine,* July–August 2002, p. 11.

41. Ibid.

42. Linda S. Pettijohn and Charles E. Pettijohn, "Retail Sales Training: Practices and Prescriptions," *Journal of Sales Marketing,* 8 (1994), pp. 17–26.

43. "Focus on the Core Customer," *Chain Store Age,* 79 (May 2003), pp. 52–56.

Chapter 14
Laws and Ethics

1. Rite Aid homepage at www.riteaid.com, accessed December 2002.

2. David Voreacos, "U.S. Denies Ethics Violations in Rite Aid Probe," *Los Angeles Times,* October 15, 2002, p. C6.

3. Al Lewis, "Trust Takes a Holiday," *Denver Post,* June 30, 2002, p. K1.

4. "Ex-Executive of Rite Aid Assisted Prosecutors in Building Fraud Case; Retailing: Timothy Noonan Agreed to Record Sessions with Former Chief Executive and Chief Counsel, Defendants Seek to Have Tapes Banned," *Los Angeles Times,* September 11, 2002, p. C3.

5. Tom Dochat, "One Former Rite Aid Executive Pleads Guilty, Another Waits," *Knight Ridder Tribune Business News,* June 27, 2003, retrieved July 2003 from Proquest database.

6. Kurt Eichenwald, "Enron's Management, Ethics Blasted in Report," *New York Times,* posted February 3, 2002, retrieved June 2002 from www.dfw.com.

7. Patrick Dorton, "Statement of Arthur Andersen, LLP," press release, June 15, 2002, retrieved June 2002 from www.arthurandersen.com.

8. Floyd Norris, "Warning to Banks That Aided Corporate Fraud," *International Herald Tribune,* Paris, July 30, 2003, p. 14.

9. Robin Fields, "Florists Hope for a Law to Nip Copycats in the Bud; Retail: State Measure Seeks to Ban Telemarketers That Advertise Under Local Phone Numbers or Names Without Disclosing an Address," *Los Angeles Times,* September 11, 1999, retrieved June 2002 from Proquest database.

10. Joseph B. Cahill, "Here's the Pitch: How Kirby Persuades Uncertain Consumer to Buy $1,500 Vacuum—The Door-to-Door Hard Sell Brings Profits, Criticism, to Berkshire Hathaway—'Pushiest People I Ever Saw,'" *Wall Street Journal,* October 4, 1999, retrieved June 2002 from Proquest database.

11. Ken Jorgensen, "Gunmaker Tells Sellers: Obey Law; Smith & Wesson Dealers Must Sign Ethics Code," *Cincinnati Post,* October 26, 1999, p. 31.

12. Alan Cowell, "Controversy over Diamonds Made into Virtue by De Beers," *New York Times,* August 22, 2000, retrieved June 2002 from Proquest database.

13. Alex Berenson, "Ex-Tyco Chief, a Big Risk Taker, Now Confronts the Legal System," *New York Times,* June 10, 2002, retrieved June 2002 from Proquest database.

14. James Fieser, "Ethics," *Internet Encyclopedia of Philosophy,* 2001, retrieved July 2002 from www.utm.edu/research/iep/e/ethics.htm.

15. International Law Dictionary and Directory, retrieved July 2002 from www.august1.com/pubs/dict/l.htm.

16. Fieser, "Ethics."

17. Donelson R. Forsyth, "A Taxonomy of Ethical Ideologies," *Journal of Personality and Social Psychology,* 39:1 (1980), pp. 175–184.

18. Johan J. Graafland, "Profits and Principles: Four Perspectives," *Journal of Business Ethics,* 35 (February 2002), pp. 293–305.

19. Asgary Nader and Mark C. Mitschow, "Toward a Model for International Business Ethics," *Journal of Business Ethics,* 36 (March 2002), pp. 239–246.

20. John A. Challenger, "Where Have All the Good CEOs Gone?—Corporate America May Face Shortage of Experienced Leaders After Commercial 'Watergate'—Independent Boards Are Drawn More into Governance, Management," *Asian Wall Street Journal,* June 26, 2002, retrieved July 2002 from Proquest database.

21. Ivy Sea Online, "Defining and Communicating Ethics in Your Business," retrieved June 2002 from www.ivysea.com.

22. Richard C. Hollinger and Jason L. Davis, *2002 National Retail Security Survey,* Security Research Project, University of Florida, 2003.

23. Richard C. Hollinger and Jason L. Davis, *2001 National Retail Security Survey* (final report), Security Research Project, University of Florida, 2002.

24. Ibid.

25. Stephen Pounds, "Employee Thefts Exceed Shoplifting Losses, University of Florida Study Finds," *Knight Ridder Tribune Business News,* December 30, 2002, retrieved July 2003 from Proquest database.

26. Richard C. Hollinger and Jason L. Davis, *2001 National Retail Security Survey* (final report).

27. ADT Security Services, Inc., "Retail Tips," retrieved February 2002 from www.adt.com.

28. Richard C. Hollinger and Jason L. Davis, *2001 National Retail Security Survey* (final report).

29. Greg Sandoval, "E-tailers—Defenseless Against Fraud?" *ZDNet News,* October 5, 2001, retrieved July 19, 2002, from www.zdnet.com.

30. "New Report Shows What Internet Scams Cost Americans Most," press release, U.S. Department of Justice, Federal Bureau of Investigation, April 9, 2002.

31. *IFCC 2001 Internet Fraud Report,* report prepared by the National White Collar Crime Center and the Federal Bureau of Investigation, January 1, 2002–December 31, 2001.

32. "New Report Shows What Internet Scams Cost Americans Most."

33. Steven Rosenberg, "Hotel to Be Built; First in 75 Years," *Boston Globe,* October 13, 2002, p. 8.

34. Steven Rosenberg, "Salem Hotel Gets Go-Ahead; Hawthorne Owners Drop Opposition," *Boston Globe,* October 13, 2002, p. 3.

35. Stacey Saunders, "The Rising Role of ATMs in Alaska," *Alaska Business Monthly,* 19 (January 1, 2003), p. 30.

36. "US FTC: Bargains & Deals Magazine Charged with Internet Fraud: Company Allegedly Misrepresented Products, Did Not Deliver Merchandise to Consumers," *M2 Presswire,* October 17, 2001, p. 1.

37. Joel J. Davis, "Marketing to Children Online: A Manager's Guide to the Children's Online Privacy Protection Act," *S.A.M. Advanced Management Journal,* 67 (Autumn 2002), pp. 11–21.

38. Jennifer Loven, "Bush Enacts Law Cracking Down on Corporate and Accounting Fraud," Associated Press, July 31, 2002, retrieved August 2002 from www.yahoo.com.

39. Jennifer Loven, "Bush to Sign Legislation Designed to Combat Corporate Fraud," Associated Press, July 30, 2002, retrieved August 2002 from www.yahoo.com.

Chapter 15
Diversity and Trends in Retailing

1. "Fortune Announces Sixth Annual List of Best Companies for Minorities," *Business Wire,* June 23, 2003, retrieved July 2003 from Proquest database.

2. Jonathan Hickman, "America's 50 Best Companies for Minorities," *Fortune,* 146 (July 8, 2002), pp. 110–117.

3. "Fannie Mae Ranks First on *Fortune*'s List of the 50 Best Companies for Minorities," company press release, June 27, 2002, retrieved December 2002 from www.fanniemae.com.

4. "Diversity Programs," retrieved December 2002 from www.fanniemae.com.

5. "EEO-AA—Leveraging Diversity—Inclusion: They're Not All the Same!" Kaleel Jamison Consulting Group, Inc., 1997.

6. "Hispanic Population Reaches All-Time High of 38.8 Million, New Census Bureau Estimates Show," press release dated June 18, 2003 from the U.S. Census Bureau, retrieved July 2003 from www.census.gov.

7. Michael J. Weiss, "Great Expectations," *American Demographics,* 25 (May 2003), pp. 27–35.

8. Ken Dychtwald, "The Age Wave Is Coming," *Public Management,* 85 (July 2003), pp. 6–10.

9. Sales & Marketing Management, *2001 Survey of Buying Power and Media Markets* (New York: Bill Communication, September 2001), p. 7.

10. Abigail Klingbeil, "History of Diversity in Business Tied to Economics, Laws," *Journal News,* March 22, 2002, retrieved February 2003 from www.thejournalnews.com.

11. "Supreme Court Upholds University of Michigan Affirmative Action," *Jet,* 104 (July 7, 2003), pp. 4–5.

12. Dana Wilkie, "Racial Preferences Upheld," *San Diego Union–Tribune,* June 24, 2003, p. A1.

13. Mark Walsh, "Court Deluged with Advice on Michigan Case," *Education Week,* April 2, 2003, p. 31.

14. Julie Moran Alterio, "Does Diversity = Dollars?" *Journal News,* March 29, 2002, retrieved February 2003 from www.thejournalnews.com.

15. Ibid.

16. Karen Jacobs, "More Companies Seek Diversity as Internal Bias Suits Increase," *Houston Chronicle,* February 10, 2002, p. 2.

17. Dina Berta, "Mixing It Up: Diversity Good for Business, Confab Finds," *Nation's Restaurant News,* August 26, 2002, pp. 1, 103.

18. Sondra Thiederman, "Why Diversity Counts: The Business Case," retrieved February 2003 from www.monster.com.

19. Ellen Alcorn, "Good-Bye M Word," retrieved February 2003 from www.monster.com.

20. Sandy Kennedy, "The Three R's," *Chain Store Age,* February 2003, p. 24.

21. Alexis M. Herman, "Domestic Partner and Family-Friendly Benefits," retrieved February 2003 from www.monster.com.

22. Parshotam Dass, "Strategies for Managing Human Resource Diversity: From Resistance to Learning," *Academy of Management Executive,* May 1999, pp. 68–69.

23. Marvin J. Cetron and Owen Davies, "Trends Shaping the Future: The Economic, Societal, and Environmental Trends," *The Futurist,* 37 (January–February 2003), p. 27.

24. Sarah P. Rousey and Michelle A. Morganosky, "Retail Format Change in U.S. Markets," *International Journal of Retail & Distribution Management,* 24 (1996).

25. Cetron and Davies, "Trends Shaping the Future."

26. Stacy L. Wood, "Future Fantasies: A Social Change Perspective of Retailing in the 21st Century," *Journal of Retailing,* 78 (2002), pp. 77–83.

27. Robert A. Peterson and Sridhar Balasubramanian, "Retailing in the 21st Century: Reflections and Prologue to Research," *Journal of Retailing,* 78 (2002), p. 10.

28. Ibid., pp. 9–16.

29. Cetron and Davies, "Trends Shaping the Future."

30. Cherie Jacobs, "Airport Retail Industry Is Booming," *Knight Ridder Tribune Business News,* January 20, 2003, retrieved May 2003 from Proquest database.

31. H. R. Chally Group, *The Customer-Selected World Class Sales Excellence Research Report* (Dayton, Ohio), 1998.

32. Jagdish N. Sheth, Rajendra S. Sisodia, and Arun Sharma, "The Antecedents and Consequences of Customer-Centric Marketing," *Academy of Marketing Science,* Winter 2002, pp. 55–66.

33. H. R. Chally Group, *The Customer-Selected World Class Sales Excellence Research Report.*

34. Thomas Lee, "Customization Counteracts Dull Retail Industry," Knight Ridder Tribune News Service, May 1, 2003, retrieved May 2003 from Proquest database.

35. Thomas W. Leigh and Greg W. Marshall, "Research Priorities in Sales Strategy and Performance," *Journal of Personal Selling and Sales Management,* Spring 2001, pp. 83–93.

36. H. R. Chally Group, *The Customer-Selected World Class Sales Excellence Research Report.*

37. Ibid.

38. Marshall L. Fisher, Ananth Raman, and Anna Sheen McClelland, "Rocket Science Retailing Is Almost Here: Are You Ready?" *Harvard Business Review,* July–August, 2000, pp. 115–124.

39. Ibid.

40. "Lawson Retail Advisors Identify Improving Profitability, Accurate Analysis, and Inventory Management as Critical Issues," *Business Wire,* April 14, 2003, retrieved July 2003 from Proquest database.

41. "U.S. Retail IT Spending to Resume Growth in 2003 and Beyond, IDC Says," *PR Newswire,* March 24, 2003.

42. "Keynote Announces Retail Industry's First Web Transaction Index," *Business Wire,* May 5, 2003, retrieved July 2003 from Proquest database.

43. H. R. Chally Group, *The Customer-Selected World Class Sales Excellence Research Report.*

44. Leigh and Marshall, "Research Priorities in Sales Strategy and Performance."

45. Ibid.

46. H. R. Chally Group, *The Customer-Selected World Class Sales Excellence Research Report.*

47. Edward E. Lawler III, "From Job-Based to Competency-Based Organizations," *Journal of Organizational Behavior,* January 1994, pp. 3–15.

48. Tiger Li and Roger J. Calantone, "The Impact of Market Knowledge Competence on New Product Advantage: Conceptualization," *Journal of Marketing,* 62 (October 1998), pp. 13–29.

49. Lawler, "From Job-Based to Competency-Based Organizations," p. 3.

50. Leonard L. Berry, "The Old Pillars of New Retailing," *Harvard Business Review,* 79 (April 2001), pp. 131–137. Reprinted by permission.

51. Jay A. Scansaroli and David M. Szymanski, "Who's Minding the Future?" Center for Retailing Studies, Texas A&M University, *Retailing Issues Letter,* January 2002, pp. 1–8.

52. Ibid.

53. "The New Business Imperative: The Capacity to Respond," *Chief Executive,* May 2003, retrieved July 2003 from Proquest database.

Glossary

acceptable profit perspective A perspective on the relationship between profit and principles that assumes companies want to maximize principles but are restricted because the market demands that profitability reach a certain level to ensure financial continuity. (14)

accounts receivable (A/R) turnover in days A measurement of the number of days, on average, it takes to convert accounts receivable into cash. (8)

acid-test ratio (quick ratio) Quick assets divided by current liabilities. (8)

activity ratios Ratios used to determine how well a firm manages current assets, pays off current liabilities, and uses assets to generate sales. (8)

additional markup An increase in the retail price of a product in addition to what has already been added as a markup. (11)

advertising A form of either mass communication or direct-to-consumer communication that is nonpersonal and is paid for by an identifiable sponsor to inform or persuade members of a particular audience. (12)

advertising allowance A price concession given by a manufacturer of a product to a retailer to defray the retailer's costs associated with advertising the product. (10)

affirmative action Programs that address conditions that systematically disadvantage individuals based on group identities such as gender or race. (15)

airport mall A community shopping center located in an airport. (7)

allowance A discount offered to retailers that agree to participate in the vendor's marketing efforts. (9)

all-you-can-afford method A method of budgeting in which the retailer allots all the money it can manage to bear toward the IMC functions. (12)

applied ethics The study of ethics that involves analyzing specific instances of ethical dilemmas. (14)

assets Anything of value that a retailer owns. (8)

assortment (depth) The number of SKUs (brands, colors, and sizes) that the retailer stocks within each product line carried. (9)

assurance A component of quality that addresses a customer's satisfaction with the retailer or its products and services. (13)

atmospherics The attempt to create an overall positive atmosphere in a retail outlet. (12)

balance sheet A financial statement that itemizes the retailer's assets, liabilities, and net worth as of a specific point in time. (8)

basic stock method An inventory planning tool that allows the retailer to include a few more items *(basic stock)* than were forecasted in an order for a given period of time. BOM stock (at retail) = Planned sales (monthly) + Basic stock. (9)

behavioristics The subdivision of a retailer's current or potential markets based on buying responses, product usage patterns, product loyalty, or store loyalty. (5)

best-guess method A method of budgeting in which the retailer makes a subjective guess at how much to allocate to IMC. (12)

bottom-up approach A method of budgeting in which each retail department supplies data. The budgets are passed up to the next levels of management until all budgets reach an individual who is responsible for the budgeting process. (8)

brand associations Attributes or personality that the owners of a brand wish to convey to their current or potential customers. (2)

brand equity The consumer's perceived level of quality for the retailer's product lines. (2)

breakeven point (BEP) The level of activity at which income from sales (total revenue) equals total costs. (11)

breakeven pricing A pricing method in which pricing is based on the breakeven point for a given product. (11)

brick-and-click A retailer that offers products both at a physical location and online via the Internet. (4)

brick-and-mortar store A traditional retail outlet that sells out of a physical location. (4)

business franchising A situation characterized by a great deal of interaction between franchisee and franchiser; the franchisor agrees to support all of the business functions while listening to the needs and wants of its franchisees. (4)

business sales Sales from one business organization to another business organization; also called *business to business* or *B2B*. (1)

buyer The employee whose basic responsibility is to make purchases. (9)

buyer's remorse (cognitive dissonance) A consumer's doubt associated with a purchase. (5)

cannibalization A situation in which a company introduces a product that takes away sales from an existing product. (11)

carrying costs The costs of storing and maintaining inventory. (8)

cash conversion cycle (CCC) A measure of how many days it takes to turn purchases of inventory into cash. (9)
cash discount A discount offered to retailers to encourage them to pay early or pay with cash. (9)
cash flow from financing activities Cash received or disbursed from activities dealing with a company's own debt and capital instruments. (8)
cash flow from investing activities Cash received or disbursed from extending or collecting loans and acquiring or disposing of investments or long-term assets. (8)
cash flow from operating activities Cash received or disbursed from all of the activities involved in a company's operations. (8)
cash flow objective A type of pricing objective in which the retailer attempts to generate money quickly. (11)
category killer Sometimes known as a *power retailer* or *category specialist,* a discount specialty store that offers a deep assortment of merchandise. (4)
central business district (CBD) An unplanned shopping site in the downtown area of any city. (7)
centralized organizational structure An organizational structure in which decisions are made from one central location, often termed "headquarters" or the "home office." (10)
chain store A retailer that operates multiple (more than one) retail stores. (4)
channel captain The company or person that plays the biggest role in the supply chain. (9)
channel of distribution A network that includes all members of a team of businesses and organizations that help direct the flow of goods and services from the producer to the end user, or ultimate consumer. (1)
closeout retailer A type of retailer that sells broad assortments of merchandise purchased at closeout prices. (4)
combination store A retail format in which food items are combined with nonfood items to create a one-stop shopping experience. (4)
commercial merchandise Articles for sale, samples used for soliciting orders, or goods that are not considered personal effects. (8)
commodity Something useful that can be traded; can refer to physical objects or services. (1)
common size financial statement A financial statement in which common size ratios are used to compare financial statements of different-size companies. For balance sheet items, ratios are typically expressed as a percentage of total assets. For income statement items, ratios are expressed as a percentage of total revenue. (8)
community shopping center A retail center typically between 100,000 and 400,000 square feet in size. Tenants often include smaller stores, branch department stores, and a large discount store. (7)
company analysis An analysis that includes data on sales and profit figures, company mission/vision, company's risk or conservative orientation, corporate resources, level of aggressiveness, market share, sales trends, etc. (4)
comparative financial statement A financial statement that reflects more than one year of financial information, to show changes over time. The information is typically presented in a side-by-side, columnar format. (8)
competition-oriented pricing Pricing of products based on the industry leader's prices. (11)
compulsiveness The degree of openness shoppers have to impulse purchases. (5)
consignment selling A method in which the retailer sells goods for the supplier and receives a commission on sales instead of taking title to the merchandise. (11)
consumer behavior The study of how customers buy products. (5)
consumer cooperative A retail establishment owned and operated by a group of consumers. (4)
consumer market approach A method in which a retailer generates data about prices based on controlled store experimentation. (11)
continuity One of the attributes of media objectives, indicating a stable level of IMC activity. (12)
controllable variables Those areas of the retail operation that can be effectively controlled and changed by retail managers. (3)
convenience store A small retailer that caters to a neighborhood and carries a very limited assortment of products. (4)
conventional supermarket A self-service food store that generates annual sales of at least $2 million. (4)
corporate social responsibility (CSR) The commitment of business to contribute to sustainable economic development, working with employees, their families, the local community, and society at large to improve their quality of life. (2)
cost complement Total value at cost divided by total value at retail. (8)
cost of goods sold (COGS) The amount a retailer pays for its merchandise. (8)
cost-oriented pricing A pricing method in which a fixed percentage is added to the cost of products; also called *cost-plus pricing.* (11)
creative platform The creative strategy of a selected IMC tactic; includes the promise, creative objectives, and reasons the customer should buy; also called *copy platform* or *creative strategy.* (12)
cumulative discount A discount that runs for an entire purchase period and allows the retailer to order several times until the agreed-on discount level is reached. (9)
current assets Cash and other items that can be converted to cash quickly. (8)

current liabilities Financial obligations that must be paid back within the upcoming year. (8)
current ratio Current assets divided by current liabilities. (8)
customer-centric culture An active philosophy within a company that focuses on meeting the needs of individual consumers rather than those of the mass market. (15)
customer equity The value of the complete set of resources, tangible and intangible, that customers invest in a firm. (2)
customer response management (CRM) The management of databases that assist retail managers in identifying trends and responding to customer characteristics. (13)
customer services The additional practices, both tangible and intangible, that an organization provides in addition to its core product or service. (3, 13)
customer spotting An observational technique in which the retailer utilizes various types of already-acquired data to try to ascertain where customers are located. (7)
cybermall (virtual mall) A "mall" whose "tenants" are usually brought together online or through a catalog or newspaper ads. (7)

data News, facts, and figures that have not been organized in any manner. (6)
deal proneness The shopper's propensity to purchase products that are on sale or where some type of "deal" for the product is offered. (5)
debt-to-equity ratio Total liabilities divided by total owner's equity. (8)
decentralized organizational structure An organizational structure in which decisions are made at the local level, such as at individual stores. (10)
demand-oriented pricing Pricing of products based on consumer demand. (11)
demographics Statistics about any given population base. (5)
department store A large retailer that carries a wide breadth and depth of products and is organized into departments. (4)
designated market area (DMA) A designation developed by A. C. Nielsen to describe a particular geographic area that serves a specific market. (7)
direct marketing An interactive system of marketing that uses one or more advertising media to generate a measurable response or transaction at any location. (4, 12)
direct selling A type of sales interaction that involves personal contact—via telephone, at the consumer's home, or at an out-of-home location such as the consumer's office, and so on. (4)
discount store A type of department store that offers limited customer services and has merchandise priced below that at department stores. (4)
display type and location The exact in-store locations of products and the type of display used to sell the products. (5)
diversity Differences among people, including but not limited to age, gender, ethnicity, race, and ability. (15)
divertive competitors Retailers that compete by selling the same type of merchandise or services; they do not necessarily specialize in that merchandise. (4)
divisional chart An organizational chart based on the divisions or business units within an organization. (10)
downsizing The planned elimination of a group of employees in order to increase organizational performance. (10)

e-commerce The conduct of selling, buying, logistics, or other organization management activities via the Web. (1)
economic order quantity (EOQ) A calculation of how much merchandise to reorder. (6, 9)
economies of scale Achieving lower costs per unit through higher-quantity purchases. (4)
efficiency The productivity of a store's selling space. (12)
efficiency ratios Ratios that provide evidence of how effectively management is running the business. (8)
80/20 rule *See* **Pareto principle.**
electronic data interchange (EDI) A technology that allows retailers to conduct business with vendors electronically. (6, 9)
empathy A component of quality that promotes understanding of the customer's needs. (13)
encryption system A system that codes data so that the data can be understood only by the intended user. (2)
environmental analysis A study of the various market environments prior to deciding on a target area and a target customer group. (7)
environmental scanning A systematic process whereby the retailer acquires and uses information to assist in the management and planning of future actions. (3)
equal employment opportunity (EEO) laws Laws that collectively prohibit discrimination on the basis of color, race, gender, religion, national origin, age, or physical disability. (15)
equity The marketing and financial value that the customer provides for the retailer. (2)
e-tailing A form of retailing utilizing the Internet, the World Wide Web (WWW), and other electronic forms of commerce to take the place of or supplement a physical retail location. (1)
ethics Concepts of right and wrong behavior. (3, 14)
ethnic group Any group defined by race, religion, national origin, or some combination of these categories. (5)

evaluation An area of management that involves assessing an employee's performance in relation to goals and objectives designated for that employee's position. (10)

everyday low pricing (EDLP) A retailing strategy that emphasizes consistently lower-priced merchandise. (4)

executive summary An abstract of an entire paper. (6)

executive training programs (ETP) Training available to the company's managers or executives. (10)

exit interview An interview conducted when an employee leaves an organization, for the purpose of determining the reasons behind the departure. (10)

extended marketing concept The concept of exceeding customer wants and needs at a profit. (2)

external secondary data Sources of data and information that are external to the firm. (6)

extrinsic motivation The desire to achieve something that comes from outside the individual (money, acknowledgment, etc.). (10)

facilitators External individuals or groups that help the retailer make a sale. (1)

feature proneness The tendency of shoppers to use or not use coupons or other promotional items in their shopping decisions. (5)

FIFO (first in, first out) An inventory costing method that assumes older merchandise is sold before newer stock is sold. (8)

flea market A retail format in which many vendors sell used as well as new and distressed merchandise. (4)

follow-the-leader budgeting A method of budgeting in which the retailer generates estimates of competitors' IMC budgets from outside sources and attempts to match the industry leader's budget. (12)

franchise A contractual agreement between a franchisor and a franchisee that allows the franchisee to operate a retail establishment using the name and (usually) the franchisor's operating methods. (4)

franchisee The owner of a retail establishment who has a contract with the franchisor to use the franchise's name and (usually) methods of operation. (4)

franchisor A business that grants the franchisee the privilege to use the franchisor's name and (usually) operating practices. (4)

frequency The number of times a target audience is exposed to an advertising message over a particular time period. (12)

functional chart An organizational chart based on the company's functional activities. (10)

general merchandise retailer A retailer involved in the sale of general, nonfood items. (4)

generational marketing The study of age groups and how they behave in the consumer market. (5)

geodemographics The combination of geographics and demographics, used to describe the customer more clearly. (5)

geographic information system (GIS) A computer-based tool for integrating and analyzing spatial data from multiple sources. (7)

geographics Analysis that helps the retailer find out where customers are physically located. (5)

geolocation Technology that uses Web geography to determine where an online buyer is located. (7)

gross margin The total cost of goods sold subtracted from net sales. (1, 11)

gross margin return on inventory (GMROI) A calculation of how much investment is being returned for each type of merchandise purchased. (9)

gross profit The difference between the retailer's net sales and the cost of goods sold. (8)

gross rating points (GRPs) An advertising measurement taken by multiplying reach by frequency. (12)

group training A type of training offered to groups of employees with similar training needs. (10)

horizontal agreement A restrictive agreement between two competitors in the same market. (14)

horizontal analysis An analysis that uses comparative financial statements for two consecutive years. (8)

human resource information system (HRIS) A method for systematically gathering, analyzing, storing, and utilizing information and data related to personnel management. (10)

human resource management (HRM) Policies, practices, and systems that influence employees' behavior, attitudes, and performance. (10)

human resource recruitment The process of identifying and attracting the best potential employees to an organization. (10)

human resources A function that ensures that a company has the right mix of skilled people to perform its value creation activities effectively. (1)

hypermarket A large retailer that carries many types of products in addition to foods; originated in Europe. (4)

image advertising A type of advertising that attempts to enhance the retailer's image. (10)

IMC mix All the communications activities undertaken in an integrated marketing communications approach, including personal selling, advertising, public relations, direct marketing, sales promotions, and cybermarketing. (12)

impulse buying The purchase of products and services by consumers that was not planned in advance. (4)

income taxes Federal and state income taxes on net income before income taxes. (8)

independent retailer A type of retailer that operates a single establishment. (4)

index of retail saturation (IRS) A formula used to assess the saturation levels of various trading areas. (7)

individual training A trial-and-error approach to training in which employees take responsibility for training themselves. (10)

industrial market approach An approach in which the retailer sells its products to other businesses in addition to the final consumer. Prices for products or services may be different for business customers than for nonbusiness customers. (11)

information A meaningful body of facts organized around some specific topic. (6)

initial markup The price set on a product less the cost of the merchandise. (11)

initial markup percentage The initial markup expressed in percentage form. (11)

integrated marketing communications (IMC) A customer-focused philosophy in which all communications a company delivers are integrated and consistent with corporate strategies; also called *marketing communication* or *MARCOM.* (1, 12)

integrated perspective A perspective of the relationship between profit and principles stating that firms strive for an optimal balance between profits and principles. (14)

integrated retail management (IRM) flow chart A chart that provides a framework to guide retail decision making. (1)

integration The condition wherein all parts of the retail organization have the information necessary to carry out their functions and the strategic philosophies are incorporated consistently throughout the plan. (1)

internal search A process in which the consumer looks inwardly or internally for product or service information. (5)

internal secondary data Sources of data and information that are internal to the firm. (6)

Internet fraud The use of the Internet to present fraudulent solicitation to prospective victims, conduct fraudulent transactions, or transmit the proceeds of fraud to financial institutions or others connected with the scheme. (14)

intertype competitors Different types of retailers that compete by selling the same lines of products and compete for the same household dollars. (4)

intratype competitors Retailers that compete for the same customer bases or households. (4)

intrinsic motivation The desire to achieve something that comes from within the individual (happiness, satisfaction, etc.). (10)

inventory turnover A measure of how many times a store sells its average investment in inventory during a year. (9)

inventory (I/V) turnover in days A measurement of the number of days, on average, from the time a retailer receives inventory to the time the inventory is sold to the customer. (8)

job (position) A general category used by managers to assign responsibility of task performance to members of a retail organization. (10)

job description An explanation of the tasks involved in the performance of a given position in an organization. (10)

just-in-time (JIT) inventory A process in which a supplier delivers products to a retailer right before they are needed, thus saving the retailer storage costs. (9)

just noticeable difference (JND) The price at which consumers believe they are paying more or less than the norm or reference price. (11)

law A rule established by authority, society, or custom. (3, 14)

leader pricing A type of promotional pricing in which products are priced below the usual markup, near cost, or below cost; also called *loss leader pricing.* (11)

leased department A department in a large retail store in which space is "leased" or rented to an outside vendor that in turn operates under the larger retailer store's policies. (4)

leveraging diversity The practice of seeking out different voices and viewing them as opportunities for added value. (15)

liabilities Financial obligations owed by a retailer. (8)

license to operate perspective A perspective on the relationship between profit and principles stating that firms must have a minimum value of principles required by society to obtain a license to operate. (14)

life cycle pricing Price planning based on the stage of the product (or store) life cycle that the product (or store) has reached. (11)

lifestyle center A planned shopping center targeted to upper-income shoppers. Typically outdoors with a "Main Street" ambience, tenants that sell nonessential items, higher building and landscaping costs than those of other retail developments, and parking in front of the stores. (7)

LIFO (last in, first out) An inventory costing method that assumes newer merchandise is sold before older stock is sold. (8)

limited-line store (box store) No frills food and merchandise discounters that offer a small selection of products. (4)

liquidity ratios Ratios that reflect management's control of current assets and current liabilities. (8)

list price The price given in the vendor's price list. (9)

logistics (logistics management) Every action taken to ensure that products and services get from the point of origin to the final customer. (1, 3, 9)

long-term assets Property, equipment, and other fixed assets used to operate a business. (8)

long-term liabilities Financial obligations due in more than a year's time. (8)

macro retail environment The external environments that affect retailers. (1)

maintained markup The amount of markup the retailer attempts to sustain for a particular product or product grouping. Calculation: Net sales − COGS. (11)

maintained markup percentage The maintained markup expressed in percentage form. (11)

markdown A decrease in the initial retail price, typically expressed as a dollar amount or a percentage. (11)

market adaptability Retailers' knowledge about environmental changes and their ability to react to these changes in a way that benefits both the retailer and the consumer. (15)

marketing concept The philosophy that an organization should try to satisfy customers' needs through a coordinated set of activities that also allows the organization to achieve its goals. (2)

marketing intermediary (middleman) A business that links producers to other middlemen or to ultimate consumers through contractual arrangements or through the purchase and reselling of products. (1)

marketing research Research conducted to identify and define marketing opportunities and problems; generate, refine, and evaluate marketing actions; monitor marketing performance; and improve understanding of marketing as a process. (6)

market penetration objective A type of pricing objective in which product prices are initially set low to attract large numbers of buyers. The resulting increase in sales volume offsets the lower introductory price. (11)

market research The process of data collection, organization, analysis, and dissemination of data relating to a particular area. (6)

market share The proportion of sales of a particular product (or brand) to the total sales of that product (or brand) in a given area. (11)

market share objective A type of pricing objective in which the retailer adjusts price levels based on competitors' changes in price, with the goal of gaining market share. (11)

markup The dollar amount added to the cost of a product to determine its final price. (11)

marquee A large exterior sign that includes the retailer's name. (12)

mass marketing approach An approach in which the retailer utilizes one unique marketing mix to try to capture the market. (3)

megamall A mall that is often several times larger than a regional center; also known as a *superregional center.* (7)

mentoring A type of training in which an experienced employee is assigned to train and act as a role model for a new employee. (10)

merchandise Products or services a retailer currently offers, or plans to offer, for sale. (8)

merchandise buying and handling The physical purchase of products and services and how those products and services are brought to the retail outlet, handled, and finally placed ready for sale. (3, 9)

merchandise mix The combination of merchandise variety, assortment, depth, quality, and price points. (9)

merchandising Activities involved in organizing the display of products and services. (8)

metaethics The study of the origin of ethical concepts and theories. (14)

metropolitan standard area (MSA) A government designation of an area within the United States that has a minimum of 50,000 permanent residents. (7)

mission statement A statement that explains why the firm is in business, what it does, and what it stands for. (3)

modified breakeven pricing A pricing method wherein the retailer estimates the market demand for a product and then applies it to the breakeven point. (11)

monopolistic competition A market in which there is a limited amount of competition from other retailers for consumer dollars. (4)

monopoly A market in which there is only one seller selling a specific good or service. (4)

motivation A basic drive of all humans; in business, it is usually associated with the need to create personal or job satisfaction. (10)

multichannel retailer A retailer that uses more than one means of distribution for products and services. (6, 7)

name equity The value of the organization's name. (2)

need Something the consumer perceives as required for his or her well-being. (5)

neighborhood business district (NBD) An unplanned shopping site that provides shopping for a neighborhood rather than a larger trading area. (7)

neighborhood center A planned shopping district with a smaller anchor store. (7)

net income after taxes The difference between net income before taxes and income taxes. (8)

net income before taxes (NIBT) The difference between net income from operations and the net effect of other income (expenses). (8)

net income from operations Gross profit minus operating expenses. (8)

net sales All gross sales a retailer earns during a specified period of time, minus sales discounts given to customers to promote sales and minus returns and allowances given to customers for returned items or defective products. (8)

net worth (owner's equity) Assets minus liabilities; represents the net value of a retail business on a cost basis. (8)

nonprobability sampling Sampling in which no member of the population has an equal and known chance of being selected for the research study. (6)

non-store-based retailer A retailer that has no physical location but sells via cyberspace, catalogs, vending machines, or other nontraditional places of business, such as a home. (4, 7)

normative ethics The study of ethics using criteria to determine whether certain behavior is right or wrong. (14)

North American Industrial Classification System (NAICS) A business coding system that will replace the SIC system. NAICS provides better accuracy and improved comparability with other countries. (4)

notes to the financial statements The section that provides supplemental information about the balance sheet, income statement, and statement of cash flows. (8)

objective-and-task method A method of budgeting in which the retailer specifies the role IMC will play and the outcomes desired in the overall operation. (12)

odd/even pricing The practice of using prices that end in either an odd or even number. (11)

off-price retailer A retailer that sells brand-name merchandise, which may include overruns or distressed merchandise, at 40 to 50 percent below traditional retailers. (4)

oligopoly A market characterized by similar products and very few sellers. (4)

1:1 marketing Using customer response management techniques to personalize products and services. (13)

open-to-buy The amount the buyer has left to spend for a given time period, typically a month. Each time a purchase is made, the open-to-buy amount decreases. (9)

operating expenses The normal costs associated with doing business, not including the cost of the merchandise for sale. (8)

operations management A planning function dealing with the implementation of store policies, tactics, and procedures. (3, 8)

order lead time The span of time required to fulfill an order. (9)

organizational chart A graphical display that delineates who is responsible for the various areas of the firm. (10)

organizational culture The pattern of shared values and beliefs that helps employees understand how their organization functions and provides guidelines for behavior on the job. (10)

other income (expenses) Income and expense items such as interest income, dividend income, interest expense, and gains or losses on disposal of assets. (8)

outlet center A type of community center that brings together retail establishments for manufacturers and retailers of consumer goods. These centers increase drawing power by providing deep discounts on brand-name products. (7)

outplacement A process in which a business hires experts to offer support, personal assessments, and job-search skills training to employees that are being downsized. (10)

outsourcing The practice of hiring an individual, a group, or an organization outside the company to perform certain work. (6)

overstored A situation in which too many stores (or too much selling space) are devoted to a product or product line. (7)

Pareto principle (80/20 rule) A guideline stating that 20 percent of a business's customers account for about 80 percent of its sales. (5, 13)

percentage-of-profit method A method of budgeting in which the retailer determines a basic percentage amount to be used for IMC based on overall profits. (12)

percentage-of-sales method A method of budgeting in which the retailer allots a basic percentage amount for the store and, in some cases, for each of the store's brands or products (or product lines). (12)

percentage variation method An inventory planning tool in which the beginning-of-month planned inventory during any period (typically a month) differs from planned average monthly stock by half of that month's variation from average monthly sales. BOM stock (at retail) = Average stock for the sales period (at retail) × ½ [1 + (Planned monthly sales/Average monthly sales)]. (9)

periodic inventory system A cost accounting system in which sales are recorded as they occur but inventory is not updated. (8)

perpetual inventory system A cost accounting system that shows the level of inventory on hand at all times. (8)

personal selling Selling to a customer by face-to-face communication. (12)

planning The establishment of objectives, policies, and procedures to carry out goals. (3)

point of indifference The distance at which the choice between two shopping destinations is equal. (7)

point-of-purchase communications A type of sales promotion that includes in-store materials such as posters and displays designed to influence consumer purchases; also called *point-of-purchase advertising.* (12)

point-of-sale (POS) terminal A terminal or computer workstation designed to collect information from sales of products and services. (6, 9)

power center A type of community center that includes at least one category killer with a mix of smaller stores. (7)

prestige pricing The practice of selling products at high prices to build a reputation for quality. (11)

price elastic A term referring to consumers who are sensitive to changes in price. (11)

price elasticity of demand A measurement of the responsiveness of quantity demanded to a change in price, with all other factors held constant; also called *price elasticity.* (11)

price gouging A tactic wherein a retailer takes advantage of high demand and limited supply to raise the price of a good or service beyond customary amounts. (11)

price inelastic A term referring to consumers who are relatively insensitive to price changes. (11)

price leveling Also called *customary pricing,* the practice of setting prices on products and services such that prices remain stable for a defined period of time. Products are generally priced above, below, or at market prices. (11)

price points The range of prices for a particular merchandise line. (9, 11)

price stability policy A practice in which the retailer attempts to create a one-price policy for individual products. (11)

price variability The practice of varying the price of merchandise or services based on established criteria. (11)

pricing flexibility The range of prices consumers are willing to pay for a particular product or service. (11)

pricing policies General rules or guidelines for price development based on company strategies. (11)

primary data Data that are gathered for a specific purpose and have not yet been published. (3, 6)

probability sampling Sampling in which each and every member of the population has an equal and known chance of being chosen for the sample. (6)

product/brand chart An organizational chart based on the products or brands an organization carries. (10)

product franchising A situation in which the franchisee agrees to sell the franchisor's products or services. (4)

product history and analysis An analysis that addresses the question "What do customers want and/or need?" (4)

product line A group of related products that satisfy a class of need, serve a particular market, have similar methods of distribution, or fall within a specific range of prices. (1, 9)

product quality objective A type of pricing objective that focuses on recouping costs associated with retail research and development or to develop a desired product image. (11)

profit objective A type of pricing objective in which the retailer attempts to meet or exceed projected profit levels. (11)

programmed learning A structured, formal training process that allows the employee to study material pertaining to the retailer's operation and then respond to questions about the material studied. (10)

promotional pricing The practice of coordinating pricing with the promotion variable of IMC. (11)

psychographics Lifestyle analysis data used to determine "what consumers do" over specified time periods. (5)

psychological pricing A method of pricing in which the retailer takes into account consumers' perceptions and beliefs. (11)

public relations (PR) The efforts of an organization to win the cooperation of various publics. (12)

publicity A subfunction of public relations in which the organization attempts to attract attention through various media. (12)

purchase discount Reduction in the payment amount a vendor is willing to accept to satisfy the amount due if the payment is made earlier. (8)

purchase involvement The consumer's involvement in the overall shopping experience. (5)

pure competition A market in which there are many different buyers and sellers. (4)

QSP Categorization of customer value by quality, service, and/or price. (2)

quantity discount A discount offered to retailers that purchase in large quantities. (9)

race A group of individuals sharing common genetic traits that determine physical characteristics. (5)

radio frequency identification (RFID) Wireless technology that uses radio waves to read product information. (6)

ratio analysis The computation of several financial ratios derived from the financial statements. (8)

reach The percentage of a target audience that is exposed to an advertising message at least one time during an advertising campaign. (12)

reference pricing A concept of what the price of a product should be based on the consumer's frame of reference. (11)

regional center A retail site that provides general merchandise and is typically enclosed with parking surrounding the center. (7)

regional chart An organizational chart based on geographic designations. (10)

relationship marketing A type of marketing that focuses on building long-lasting relationships with customers. (2)

reliability A component of quality that addresses the dependability of the retailer or its products and services. (13)

responsiveness A component of quality that tells the customer the retailer is willing to provide high levels of prompt customer service. (13)

retail To sell goods and services in small quantities directly to consumers. (1)

retail accounting system (RAS) A method for systematically gathering, analyzing, storing, and utilizing financial information and data. (8)

retailer A company or an organization that purchases products from individuals or companies with the intent to resell those goods and services to the ultimate, or final, consumer. (1)

retail information system (RIS) A system in which data are gathered and stored, turned into useful information, and disseminated to employees and managers to assist in making retail decisions. (3, 6)

retail (corporate) objectives Goals that are for a medium-length term and provide measurable statements. (3)

retail saturation The point at which consumers' needs are just being met with the existing retail facilities. (7)

retail-sponsored cooperative A type of retail organization in which several retailers have banded together to create an organization that helps to overcome many of the problems associated with running a small retail operation. (4)

retail strategy A plan that provides the retail decision maker with a framework for current and future actions and dictates how objectives will be achieved. (3)

retail technology Any tool that helps retailers succeed in carrying out strategy. (2)

return-on-assets ratio Net income plus interest income, net of its tax effect, divided by average total assets. (8)

return-on-equity ratio Net income available to owners divided by average owner's equity (net worth). (8)

return on investment (ROI) objective A type of pricing objective in which the retailer attempts to meet or exceed stated return on investment figures. (11)

return-on-sales ratio Net income divided by sales. (8)

reverse logistics The development of policies and procedures for the return of merchandise purchased by customers to a store or to a vendor or manufacturer. (9)

safety stock Extra merchandise carried to keep a retailer from running out of a product. (8, 9)

sales promotion A short-term activity that enhances or supports other IMC variables. (12)

sampling The process of choosing a subset of the population of interest to collect problem-specific data. (6)

sampling frame A list of all population members from which a sample will be drawn. (6)

scaling technique A method used to measure attitudes, knowledge, opinions, or perceptions on a given topic or issue. (6)

seamless Functioning as one cohesive unit, with no "seams," or vulnerabilities, in the strategy that may weaken the company. (1)

seasonal discount A discount given to retailers for making purchases out of season. (9)

secondary business district (SBD) An unplanned shopping site (smaller than a CBD) that is located around the major transportation intersections of cities. A typical SBD has at least one department store or variety store, coupled with a number of smaller stores. (7)

secondary data Published data that have already been collected for some other purpose. (3, 6)

segmentation The process of breaking up the target market into more controllable subgroups. (3)

segmented approach An approach in which the retailer breaks up the mass market into submarkets (called segments) and then develops a unique marketing mix for each segment. (3)

self-checkout system A format in which shoppers scan, bag, and pay for their own purchases. (6)

servicemark A firm's brand name, symbol, or design used to identify the company to other businesses and consumers as the source of a service. (14)

servicescape All the variables of the service operation that are visible to consumers, including facilities, personnel, equipment, and the service's customers. (2)

services retailing A type of retailing in which the "product" being sold is actually a service; the customer derives value from the "service product" that is provided. (2)

skimming objective A type of pricing objective in which the price for a newly introduced product is set high. After competitors enter the market, the price is adjusted downward. (11)

slotting allowance An allowance given to retailers to get the vendor's products and/or services on the shelves or in choice locations in the retailer's stores. (9)

special-event pricing A type of promotional pricing in which advertised sales, typically coinciding with a major holiday or event, are used to generate store traffic. (11)

specialty store A store that carries a limited number of products within one or a few lines of goods and services. (4)

Standard Industrial Classification (SIC) A government classification system that uses numbers or codes to identify business types. (4)

statement of cash flows A financial statement showing cash receipts and cash payments during a given period. (8)

status quo objective A type of pricing objective in which the retailer attempts to maintain the current situation. (11)

stockkeeping unit (SKU) The smallest unit of measure used to inventory products. (9)

stock-to-sales method An inventory planning tool in which the amount of inventory planned for the beginning of the month is a ratio of stock to sales. BOM stock = Stock-to-sales ratio × Planned sales. (9)

stock-to-sales ratio A formula used to calculate beginning-of-month stock in the stock-to-sales method. Stock-to-sales ratio = Value of stock/Actual sales. (8, 9)

store-based retailer A retailer that has one or more permanent, fixed physical location(s). (7)

strategic clarity The commitment to achieve an in-depth understanding of the retailer's strengths and weaknesses, including the strengths and weaknesses of its integrated retail management plan and marketing program. (4)

strategic thinking Utilization of the retail mission statement, the vision statement, the environmental scanning results, and the situational analysis to understand the environmental forces that affect a retail business. (3)

strategy Planning that provides the total directional thrust of the retail plan. (1)

strip (or string) shopping district An unplanned shopping site with stores that are visible from the road and arranged in a strip. (7)

super center A retailer that is a combination of a superstore and a discount store. (4)

superstore A food-based retailer that is larger than a traditional supermarket and carries expanded service deli, bakery, seafood, and nonfood sections. (4)

supervision An area of management in which managers direct employees in various tasks and monitor employees' productivity. (10)

supply chain The group of vendors and trading partners, including the retailer, that a retail business uses to create and stock supplies for the company. (9)

supply chain management The coordination of a retailer's vendors and trading partners for the purpose of improving the long-term performance of the individual companies and the supply chain as a whole. (3, 9)

survival objective A type of pricing objective in which the retailer increases price levels to meet sales expenses. (11)

tactical executions The day-to-day operational activities that implement the strategic plan; also known as tactics. (1, 3, 11)

tangibility A component of quality that involves the physical characteristics of the retail store. (13)

target market All of those individuals toward whom the retailer plans to aim its marketing efforts. (3, 7)

task A duty to be performed in a given job. (10)

task analysis A technique used to facilitate the listing of tasks. (10)

termination The legal dismissal of an employee. (10)

tie-in A practice in which a company tries to sell one product on the condition that the customer purchase a second product; also called a *tying agreement.* (14)

top-down approach A method of budgeting in which members of upper management prepare budgets and pass them down to departments to follow. (8)

total assets Current assets plus long-term assets. (8)

total liabilities Current liabilities plus long-term liabilities. (8)

trade discount An offer by a vendor to reduce the price of merchandise if the retailer provides the vendor with a service in return for the discount. (9)

trademark A firm's brand name, symbol, or design used to identify the company to other businesses and consumers as the source of a product. (14)

trademark franchising A situation in which the franchisee acquires the franchisor's identity and utilizes the trademarks developed by the franchisor. (4)

trading area A geographical area containing the customers of a particular firm or group of firms for specific goods or services. (7)

trip type A classification to determine why a particular shopping trip was initiated. (5)

typical customer profile A description of a retailer's most frequent customers. (3)

ultimate consumers Families, individuals, and/or households that plan to consume the products or services themselves. (1)

uncontrollable variables Those areas of the retail operation that cannot be controlled by retail managers. (3)

understored A situation in which a trading area has too few stores (or too little selling space). (7)

unitary elasticity A situation in which the percentage change in price equals the percentage change in quantity demanded. (11)

Universal Product Code (U.P.C.) A bar code found on many consumer packaged goods that stores all pertinent product information. (6)

unplanned shopping site A site that develops when two or more retailers move into the same area or in close proximity to each other. These sites are a function of evolution; they are not planned but develop over time. (7)

usage rate Average sales per day of a specific product in units. (9)

value An amount, as of goods, services, or money, considered to be a fair and suitable equivalent for something else; monetary worth of something; relative worth, utility, or importance. (2)

variety (breadth) The number of different lines of product a retailer stocks. (9)

vending machine A nonstore retailing format in which consumers purchase products through a machine. (4)

vendor-managed inventory (VMI) A technology that allows a vendor to track sales of its products through its various retail outlets using scanner data. (9)

vertical agreement An agreement, between at least two parties, operating at different levels of the supply chain, that relates to the conditions under which the parties may purchase, sell, or resell goods or services. (14)

vertical analysis An analysis that concentrates on the relationships among items within the same set of financial statements. (8)

vision statement A statement that focuses on the firm's future goals. (3)

visual merchandising An attempt to inspire customers to purchase through the use of design techniques that enhance the overall buying experience. (12)

want A learned need. (5)

warehouse club A warehouse store that charges a membership fee to consumers or businesses who buy from the store. (4)

warehouse store A retailer that offers a limited assortment of goods and services, both food and merchandise, to both end users and small to midsize businesses. (4)

weeks' supply method An inventory planning tool in which beginning-of-month inventory equals several weeks' expected sales. BOM (at retail) planned inventory = Average weekly sales (estimated) × Number of weeks to be stocked. (9)

wholesaler An individual or organization that facilitates and expedites exchanges that are primarily wholesale transactions. (1)

wholesale-sponsored cooperative An organization that is developed, owned, and run by a group of wholesalers. (4)

win-win perspective A perspective on the relationship between profit and principles that assumes the more ethically a business operates, the higher its profits will be. (14)

Name Index

Subject Index

Photo/Ad/Cartoon Credits

Mall photo in part openers: © Getty Images.
Photo in Part 1 opener: © David Young-Wolff/Getty Images.
Photo in Part 2 opener: © Ron Chapple/Getty Images.
Photo in Part 3 opener: © Ryan McVay/Getty Images.
Photo in Part 4 opener: © Rob Lewine/Corbis Images.

p. 9, Reprinted by permission of American Express and Ogilvy & Mather; p. 11, © Geri Engberg/The Image Works; p. 22, © Pascal Le Segretain/Getty Images; p. 26, Reprinted by permission of The Sherwin-Williams Company; p. 33, Reprinted by permission of Saks Fifth Avenue; p. 34, Reprinted by permission of Hallmark Cards, Inc. and Leo Burnett Worldwide; p. 37, Reprinted by permission of FTD, Inc.; p. 50; © Tom Matsui/Getty Images; p. 61, © Randy Glasbergen; p. 66, © Mark Gibson/Index Stock Photography; p. 68, © Rhoda Sidney/The Image Works; p. 76, Reprinted by permission of Neiman Marcus; p. 76, Reprinted by permission of Target Corporation; p. 91, © Kunio Owaki/Corbis Stock Market; p. 93, Reprinted y permission of Wal-Mart Corporation; p. 95, © Spencer Grant/PhotoEdit; p. 103, Reprinted by permission of PETsMART, Inc.; p. 105, © Spencer Grant/PhotoEdit; p. 124, Reprinted by permission of Levi Strauss & Co.; p. 133, BLOCKBUSTER name, design, and related marks are trademarks of Blockbuster, Inc. © 2003 Blockbuster, Inc. All rights reserved. P. 137, © AP Wide World Photos/Anat Givon; p. 139, © Don Mason/Corbis Stock Market; p. 153, © David Young-Wolff/PhotoEdit; p. 158–159, © Quick Test/Heakin. Reprinted by permission; p. 168, © Jason Love; p. 182, © Franz Peter Tschauner/Agence France Presse/Corbis Images; p. 184, © David Young-Wolff/PhotoEdit; p.188, Reprinted by permission of Lillian Vernon Corporation; p. 197, © Ralph Krubner/Index Stock Photography; p. 199, © Jeff Greenberg/PhotoEdit; p. 212, Reprinted by permission of Target Corporation; p. 241, © Mark Richards/PhotoEdit; p. 243, Advertisement of *Harry Potter and the Order of the Phoenix,* by J. K. Rowling. Copyright © 2003 by Scholastic, Inc. Used by permission; p. 254, © Tomas del Amo/Index Stock Photography; p. 262, Reprinted by permission of Home Depot, Inc.; p. 263, © Fujifotos/The Image Works; p. 268, © 2003 Lands' End, Inc. Used with permission; p. 271, Spencer Grant/PhotoEdit; p. 300, Reprinted by permission of Careerbuilder.com; p. 303, © Michael Newman/PhotoEdit; p. 304 Reprinted by permission of Best Buy Co., Inc.; p. 308, © Jon Feingersh/Corbis Stock Market; p. 333, Reprinted by permission of Wal-Mart Corporation; p. 336, © Bill Aron/PhotoEdit; p. 337, Reprinted by permission of Mercedes-Benz USA and Darran Rees, photographer; p. 346, © AP/Wide World Photos/Merced Sun-Start/Marci Stenberg; p. 362, © Kohl's Illinois, Inc.; p. 365, Susan Van Etten/PhotoEdit; p. 374, © Monika Graff/The Image Works; p. 375, © Mark Richards/PhotoEdit; p. 388, © Adam Smith/Getty Images; p. 390, © Bruce Ando/Index Stock Photography; p. 394, © Lands' End, Inc. Used with permission; p. 400, © Bill Bachman,/PhotoEdit; p. 409, Reprinted by permission of The Diamond Trading Company and J. Walter Thompson Co.; p. 417, © Spencer Grant/PhotoEdit; p. 423, Reprinted by permission of New Balance and Leon Steele, photographer; p. 438, © Michael Keller/Corbis Stock Market; p. 441, © Tony Freeman/PhotoEdit; p. 441, Reprinted by permission of The Ritz-Carlton Hotel Company. L.L.C.; p. 466, Photo courtesy of Z-Coil® Footwear, Inc.